The Complete Guide to Managing Your Money

The
Complete Guide to
Managing
Your Money

Your Finances
in Changing Times

Using Your Money
Wisely

Debt-Free
Living

by Larry Burkett

Inspirational Press . New York

First Inspirational Press edition published in 1996.

Inspirational Press
A division of Budget Book Service, Inc.
386 Park Avenue South
New York, NY 10016

Inspirational Press is a registered trademark of Budget Book Service, Inc.

Published by arrangement with Moody Press

Library of Congress Catalog Number: LC# 95-81659

ISBN: 0-88486-132-5

Printed in the United States of America

Contents

I

YOUR
FINANCES
IN CHANGING TIMES

To
My wife, Judy
My sons, Allen, Danny, and Todd,
and
My daughter, Kimberly

Also to my dear Christian friends who helped make this book a reality through their prayers and financial assistance. Charles and Edna Bearden, Greg Brezina, Bill Buck, Sid Cook, Victor Diffee, Bob Field, Hal Hayes, John Haynes, Reid Hughes, Thelma Kerr, Bob Lahr, Dave McGill, Frank McGowan, Vickie Shanahan, and all of the other brothers and sisters in Christ whom I forgot to mention but love dearly.

Contents

Foreword

THIS STUDY ON Christian finances deals with one of the most important subjects that can occupy the Christian mind today.

Jesus had much to say about money. In fact, more than about almost any other subject. It is apparent as I speak to and counsel with many thousands across our country and throughout the world that economics play a major role in the affairs of men and nations. Countries are born and others die because of money or the lack of it. Wars are fought over wealth and ownership of resources.

And yet, few Christians seem to understand the devastation generated through the misuse of money. There are those who have accepted God's financial plan as their own and stand out like giants among their brothers. But more common is the Christian who withholds this area of his life from God and struggles within the world's financial system. The same frustrations, worries, and anxieties that characterize the nonbeliever are common to many, perhaps most, Christians.

Without a large scale return to God's plan for making, spending, and sharing wealth, I fear the same disaster that has overtaken the nonbelieving world will befall Christians. Outside of God's will we have no immunity to Satan's schemes. Yet we leave ourselves vulnerable to his blows in the realm of finances.

I personally believe that the worldwide economic system is in imminent danger. In the coming changes, *everyone* will be forced to make tremendous financial adjustments. Christians will no longer be able to ride the fence between God and the world. Sunday morning Christianity will no longer be acceptable. Although God will provide for those who adhere to His plans, the temptations of the world and the pressures of compromise will lead many Christians to violate God's ordained way—to their own detriment and ultimate regret.

Our Lord commands His own to "seek first His (God's) Kingdom and His righteousness," to "lay up . . . treasures in heaven" rather than on earth. Most

Christians have failed to do this and, accordingly, have missed the blessing of God while amassing their fortunes.

I believe God's patience is running out, just as it did in the days of Noah. No longer will He allow us to choose a middle-of-the-road existence. Those Christians who seek God will adopt His principles of finance. Those who fail to do so will suffer His chastisement as never before. God will withdraw resources from the poor stewards, as related in Matthew 25, and give it to the good stewards.

No one is immune to financial temptations and difficulties. That is why I endorse this study for every committed Christian seeking God's wisdom. These principles have been verified as only God's Spirit can do: through the changed lives of Christians who have applied them. Countless hundreds of dedicated, sincere Christians who have found themselves victims of Satan's trap have achieved financial freedom through the application of God's plan outlined in this book.

It is God's financial plan that is presented in this study, and I find great diligence has been applied in referencing God's Word to every concept discussed. For this reason this book is a must reading for every Christian who seeks a life of maximum fulfillment for our Lord.

> BILL BRIGHT
> President and founder
> Campus Crusade for Christ

Introduction

THE PURPOSE OF this study is to help clarify God's perspective on finances. For too long we have allowed others to influence what we think, feel, and believe about money. It seems that we have lost the point of reference in understanding why we have money and what we are to do with it. Throughout this book, we will focus on what God says about handling money.

In the past, this area of study has been largely ignored by both Christian organizations and individuals. Many false conceptions have been introduced about money and Christianity. People hear, "Money is the root of all evil," and believe it comes from Scripture. It does not. Many people believe that poverty is inherently spiritual or that there is something innately sinful about having money. Neither is true. Those attitudes come from men, not God.

Christians have become victims of one of the most devious plots Satan ever created—the concept that money belongs to us and not to God. Indeed, everything that we own belongs to God—including money—and He will use it to direct our lives.

As we go through this study, we will examine hundreds of Scriptures dealing with money. It is easy to determine the importance money plays in God's plan by the abundance of Scripture that relates to it—more than seven hundred verses directly refer to its use.

Many of those references commonly are misinterpreted to assume some spiritual principle not directly related to money. That is not totally in error because often God's Word does contain more than a single lesson. But you should always address the *simplest* meaning *first*. When God speaks about *money*, He means *money*. When He speaks about multiplying assets, He means multiplying financial assets. When He talks about the evils of co-signing, He really means co-signing.

The Search for Answers

In Christian circles, almost everything that is heard relating to money deals with giving and sharing and why God says to do so. Obviously sharing is a part of God's plan for our lives. But that is not where God starts; He wants our spiritual commitment first. Once that commitment is made, God wants to direct how we make, spend, save, invest, and share the money He supplies.

In this book we are going to deal with the following questions—from *God*'s perspective.

—How should your money be earned?
—How does your money affect attitudes?
—How does money affect your family?
—Is it proper to save money, or should you give it away?
—Is it proper for a Christian to have insurance?
—Is it better to own a home or rent?
—Can a Christian be wealthy, or is it better to be poor?

Application

The emphasis throughout this study is on *application* rather than information.

I sincerely believe that once Christians have been educated in God's plan for their finances, they will find a freedom they never have known before.

For those engaged in making money—as virtually all are—more than 80 percent of the waking day is spent thinking about how to make, save, and spend it. Money is such an important subject that nearly two-thirds of Christ's parables deal with the use and handling of it. That alone should tell us the importance of understanding God's plan for finances.

Content

In the course of this study, we will cover many controversial areas; some you will agree with, others you may not. But God's principles of finance are no longer on trial; they have held true over the years. They are not dependent on the economy or how much money we do or do not have. God's principles depend simply on obedience to His will and turning those areas over to Him.

We will discuss some modern financial devices such as insurance, leverage, and investments, as well as different types of credit and how they are used. Some areas will require an interpretation, but that interpretation will be based on a scriptural point of reference wherever used. You are encouraged to study those Scriptures and verify for yourself the principles to which they are applied.

This book is meant to be a complete reference guide on Christian finances, containing important concepts upon which to build a financial program. Those principles should become as familiar to you as your own name. Every time you are faced with a financial decision, they should tell you whether you are handling money God's way.

The Economy

Throughout our society, particularly in secular business circles, discussions center around the economy and the prospect of future collapse. Most economists believe that although there will be some temporary ups and downs, on the whole our economy is suffering from an incurable malady. We are going to address that malady, how you can understand it, and how you can be a part of the solution rather than the problem.

Many signs predict an economic disaster—the severity of which has been assessed from a depression, which is a prolonged economic slowdown, to a collapse, which is an absolute halt in our economy. It is difficult to tell how much of either view is true but, as we review our economy, each area will be explored.

One fact is clear: we are facing dire financial and social crises. Data from every segment of society support this, and it is clear that Christians living outside God's plan are going to suffer needlessly.

Part One

THE ECONOMY

1
How Economies Begin

TIMES ARE CHANGING rapidly. Long established economic principles are dissolving, and new economic theories are born every day. The old "classical" economists are shaking their heads as they discover they no longer know what is happening. They realize the "traditional" techniques of restoring the economy no longer work. The ideas behind cost-push and price demand no longer hold true because we see that prices can rise while production falls off. Employment declines in one segment of the economy while wages rise in another. Why? What can we expect in the future?

Attitudes and Actions

Too often we react to events around us without understanding what is *really* happening and why. Overreaction is the norm, and in nearly any crisis the sequence of events is predictable—alarm, temporary panic, then apathy and disinterest.

We tend to look at the future with anxiety and worry. God says that worry is a sin. What is worry? Taking on a responsibility that belongs to someone else.

Unlike the majority of the population (who are not attuned to God's financial plan), we don't have to worry about circumstances. God has revealed in His Word what has happened and will happen. Parts of the Bible are history, parts are current events, and portions of it are prophecy. Through His Word God tells us what to expect in this economy and how to respond.

I did say *respond* as opposed to *react*. When we respond to something, we bring in the information, check it against known values, and act accordingly. When we react to something, we bring it in, amplify whatever we receive, and put it back out. That is *not* what God wants for us.

As we look at the economy today and where it may be headed tomorrow, we need to view it from God's perspective. The most important part of that perspective is the imminent return of Christ. When we hear that Christ may return during our time, we say that we believe it. But when God's plan is beginning to be unveiled to us, many refuse to accept it. Seemingly, we react as the early Christians did in Acts 12.

Peter had just been imprisoned and was to be executed. The Christians who traveled with him had retreated to his house to pray. They stayed that entire evening, praying that God would release Peter unharmed.

Then God performed a miracle and Peter walked out of prison a free man. He went to where the small group was praying and knocked on the gate.

A young girl answered and swung open the gate. There stood Peter. Shocked at the sight of him, she rushed back to the group saying, "Come quickly, Peter stands at the gate!" And what did they do? They chided her. "No, Peter can't be here," they said. "We're praying for him in prison."

Nevertheless, there he stood. They had prayed for a miracle. God had granted their prayer, and yet they didn't have enough faith to believe it.

Sometimes we are the same way. We *say* that we believe the Second Coming is near, but when we see the imminent signs, including the changing pulse of the economy, we refuse to accept it.

The Economy

Isolating the economy from any other event, a prudent observer would say that we have a problem. Notice that the United States economy and most of the world's economy is very unstable.

The value of the U.S. dollar is shrinking on the world market. Consequently, most other countries that have depended on our stability in the past are pushed to virtual bankruptcy. The economic balance has shifted to the Mideast cartel where little money is actually necessary. What does all this mean? Where are we headed?

Obviously, inflation is growing. In recent years it has increased at an alarming rate, whereas real production has dropped off. Major industries are pursuing a self-preservation attitude—some of them to the brink of disaster. Prices continue to soar while real production declines. Thus a new term has been coined, "inflationary recession" (prices increase while output declines).

Inflationary recession is not unique in the world economy, but it is unique in the United States. For years we touted our fiscal controls in the belief that it couldn't happen here. It was believed inflation could be halted simply by reducing the money supply, and recession could be controlled by the opposite technique. This is no longer credible. If we enter an inflationary period and begin to control the money supply, the economy immediately slips into a recession. Then, in order to get out, it is necessary to flood the market with additional money which, in turn, fans the fires of inflation even further.

Economic Trend

These events should alarm economic decision makers, because they verify that the highly publicized controls no longer work. The trend toward economic collapse—runaway inflation followed by major depression—seems irreversible.

Lack of fiscal discipline and sound management is partly responsible for the trend. These inadequacies reflect an economic system created by popularity. Politicians who make decisions based on what is popular rather than what is financially sound have virtually bankrupted us.

It is hard to visualize the kind of political climate necessary to reverse this trend.

Rather than working on a feasible solution to our problems, government officials quibble about which group should get the most handouts. They grant price supports to one group, unemployment benefits to another, and gratuities to many people who are undeserving. They provide grants to New England ski resorts because of insufficient snow one year, then support beaches in the South because of too much rain. They pay people not to grow products in a time of shortage, apply price supports to foods when they begin to drop, and then complain of runaway inflation on these same products.

The Federal Reserve System cuts off credit to industries that are profitable, protesting that they should become self-sufficient without credit, when for forty years the system promoted the use of nothing but credit. Nor is the "average" American guiltless either. Most families today live on the brink of disaster. The excessive use of personal and business credit has weakened the already shaky family structure. All of these factors contribute to an almost uncontrollable economy.

Understanding the Economy of Today

In order to understand *where* our economy is, it is necessary to understand *what* an economy is. Let's go back to an earlier time and see how an economy comes into existence.

For simplicity's sake, let's look into a community where people were basically barterers. Residents of the community include Dan Dairyman, who raised cows; Frank Farmington, who raised corn, wheat, and barley; and Blake Smith, who manufactured horseshoes and nails.

Dan Dairyman decided he would like to build a barn for his cows. He had lots of timber on his property. He was able to cut down his trees and store his timber until it was cured and ready to use, but he was tired of using wooden pegs to put up his buildings—it was so much trouble to drill holes, pound pegs, and sand them down. Then he had an idea.

He thought, *Boy! I'll bet I could build a great barn if I used nails, instead of wooden pegs!* So he went to see Blake Smith and said, "Blake, if you'll make me up a large sack of nails, I'll trade you this cow. How about it?"

Blake said, "It's a deal, Dan."

After he got the nails, Dan used them to build his barn and was so pleased he decided to get some more to repair his house. He went back to Blake Smith and asked if he would trade for some more nails.

"Sure, Dan. I'll make you some more nails but, for now, one cow is all I can use. Sorry!"

Dan was disappointed at the blacksmith's refusal. He went to his neighbor, Frank Farmington, and told him about the problem.

"I understand your dilemma, Dan. Let me swap you some corn for the cow. Then you can trade the corn for some of Blake Smith's nails," Frank Farmington told his friend.

Dan now took the corn he had swapped the cow for and approached the blacksmith again.

"Now we have got a deal, Dan! I can really use some corn. I'll have your nails ready right away," said the blacksmith.

Dan Dairyman happily repaired his house and began to promote the virtues of using nails to all his friends. And soon other people began going to Blake Smith to trade their products for nails.

Blake was doing a thriving business. Soon it struck him that he wouldn't have to make horseshoes anymore because the nail business was so good. So he began to "specialize" and manufacture only nails.

As more and more people used nails, the blacksmith developed a flourishing business. Everybody wanted nails to trade for other items. Nails became what we call "money." Money, in any system, must satisfy three basic functions: It must have *value*, it must be *storable*, and it must be *divisible*. Blake Smith's nails satisfied every one of these aspects and so they were used as money.

Blake had been in business several months when Frank Farmington placed a large order for nails. He came by to pick them up one afternoon and asked, "Blake, you got my hundred bags of nails made up?"

"Yep, I've got them right here," replied Blake.

"Good!" Frank said. "Now here's what I want you to do. Hold on to my nails, and write me out a piece of paper saying you have them and they belong to me. Okay?"

"Sure Frank!" the blacksmith replied.

When Blake Smith wrote on a piece of paper that he had one hundred bags of nails that belonged to Frank Farmington, he had created a new medium of exchange—*paper money*. This paper money had to satisfy the same basic functions that our original money does to be called *money*, and it did. Nothing new was created by this paper. It merely represented the nails in storage.

The distribution of paper money, rather than nails, continued as more and more people discovered that it was easier to carry pieces of paper than nails.

Blake began to notice that most of the nails he was making for his customers remained in his warehouse. Although they belonged to somebody else, he always had surplus nails. He began to think, *Why should I let these nails sit idle? No sense in making more nails when all these are just sitting here.*

Then one day Fred Farmer needed some nails but didn't have the money to pay for them and had nothing to swap until his crops came in, so Blake loaned him some nails to be repaid later. But this time, instead of making new nails, he had Fred sign a piece of paper and loaned him some nails already stored in his warehouse.

What had Blake Smith become? A banker. He stored money (nails) for some and loaned it to others. Blake had created a new kind of money—*credit*. Now credit seemed like a good thing. Without even knowing it, others were able to use this credit to build houses and barns. Blake's business prospered through his use of *credit*—other people's money.

Unfortunately, to keep his business growing, the blacksmith was forced to expand, using more and more credit. Then one day a depositor came to collect a large order of nails that Blake was supposed to be storing for him.

Marvin Messenger said, "Blake, I've got an order here for 500 bags of nails, and I need them right now!"

"Uh, just a minute Marv . . . I've just got 250 bags in stock, and I'll make up the rest by tomorrow. Okay?" Blake asked hesitantly.

A red-faced Marvin shouted, "Whaddayamean? This paper says, 'On demand,' not 'tomorrow.'" He stomped out and immediately called a meeting of the other men who had nails stored. A discussion revealed that one had 1,000 bags coming, another 500, another 350, and so on. It was obvious something was wrong!

They all rushed to Blake Smith and demanded their nails.

What happened? The blacksmith went bankrupt (or "nailrupt" if you will). Why? Credit was his downfall. When his "depositors" lost confidence in him, Blake was finished as a banker. He just loaned too many nails that belonged to others.

Blake Smith and the Federal Reserve have a lot in common. Blake went from producing nails to letters of deposit, to lending based on average balances in his "nail bank," to "nailruptcy." In reality, the Federal Reserve, created by an act of Congress in 1913, has the ability to do the same thing.

The Fed, as it is called, has the ability to create money (credit) out of thin air by purchasing government debt (Treasury bills or bonds), thus expanding the money supply. This system works reasonably well as long as most people trust the system and don't demand too much of their money back at one time. If they do, the same thing that happened to Blake's nail deposit system would happen to our banking system. On any given day there is never enough ready cash in the banking system to cover deposits. The system succeeds or fails, based on trust—not cash.

In the early stages of our nation many people, including Benjamin Franklin, warned against allowing a central banking authority, such as the Federal Reserve, to acquire too much control over our currency (paper money). Without a controlling element (such as gold or silver) to back the currency, there is always the risk that the money supply will be hyperinflated, and the whole banking system will collapse.

You see, although credit looks like money, it isn't. Credit is storable and divisible, but it lacks one essential element—*value*. Credit costs nothing to create.

As we will see later, this same difficulty has occurred in real economics as well. Governments, playing the role of world bankers, have issued credit until few people realistically believe they can repay their debts.

2

The United States Economy

WE WILL BEGIN our discussion of the U.S. economy in the period prior to World War I. During this time, money used was equal to the value of the products being purchased. The dollar (our paper money) was backed by gold or silver (our equivalent of Blake's nails) and was accepted throughout the world without reservation because of great supplies of both. There is nothing inherently valuable in gold and silver except that they are relatively scarce and have been accepted as standards of exchange for thousands of years. A broad generalization of the pre-World War I American economy would be stability.

For every increase in the money supply, something of value was created to back it up. Thus, as the money supply increased, there was an offsetting increase in the product supply.

As the nation approached the 1920s, few businesses relied on credit, but individuals began to use credit to speculate in the stock market. The industrial boom was underway and companies were flourishing. It was thought prosperity was assured. Money had value and companies were able to expand without real concern for future inflation. But disaster loomed when, through speculation, confidence in the stock market faded.

Depression—Speculation

It was speculation, not expansion, that sparked the Great Depression. Expansion was proper as long as it was based on sound value; it was when individuals began to borrow money to speculate in stocks, and businesses used this borrowed money to expand, that disaster occurred. When caught in the squeeze, neither were able to pay their bills.

By the late 1920s the stock market had inflated completely out of proportion. It was being used as a vehicle for get-rich-quick speculation, rather than long-term growth.

During the pre-Depression era, the banking industry, in spite of the Federal Reserve System controls, was generally unregulated. Just as in Blake's nail bank few, if any, real controls were enforced. Banks made speculative loans backed by little or no security. They used *credit* to expand, just as Blake had.

Then in 1929 the collapse came. First the stock market collapsed, followed by large-scale loan defaults and almost total economic devastation. Shortly thereafter, banks that were thought stable and had been so for decades, collapsed. Unable to recover their deposits, individuals lost their life savings, and companies lost most of their operating capital. Businesses that were heavily credit-oriented were forced out of existence.

The New Deal

Each new wave of panic created more worldwide unemployment as the situation worsened. Then, in the 1930s, the New Deal brought stiff government controls and more people on welfare or on the government's payroll.

The government first attempted to fund the increase in money by confiscating private stocks of gold and reissuing paper money. When that was exhausted, the Treasury began printing fiat money for the first time (known in monetary circles as "funny money"). This new credit expanded the money supply but without restoring something with sound value. During this period the national debt was established.

During the 1940s and World War II, the great national debt was firmly entrenched. Additional capital was created to fund the war effort, while products were consumed by the billions of tons.

Consumer Credit

In the 1950s the onslaught of consumer credit and the reconstruction of Europe by the United States began. Hundreds of billions of dollars were spent in rebuilding the war-torn countries in Europe and Asia.

The consumer credit boom generated trillions of dollars in new money. The post-World War II housing boom in the United States provided millions of houses on credit, and banking channels again expanded drastically. More supports were instituted by the government with more taxes being extracted to pay for welfare, Social Security, and government employment.

Paper Prosperity

The 1960s were thought to be years of endless prosperity. Few people thought that the boom would actually disappear. Europe began to adopt the credit system the United States had triggered, and individual credit cards, personal credit, and business debt grew astronomically. As the money supply grew faster, the product supply struggled to keep up. Production showed signs of difficulties and began to level off, rather than climb, while the debt continued to accelerate.

Then, in the 1970s reality appeared. Worldwide, we began to suffer pollution because of the rapid industrialization that came about in the 1940s, 50s, and 60s. For the first time, shortages in basic commodities were apparent. Inflation, sparked by this rapid expansion of the money supply, became a critical statistic. More subsidies became necessary, with almost every major industry in the United States receiving government aid. Consequently, more new money was created to fund the subsidies. Foreign governments began to lack confidence in American currency and seek other security in international trade.

Current Situation

The dollar is no longer the standard for exchange throughout the world, and larger amounts of American currency are necessary due to this lack of confidence. Where will it end? It is difficult to assess the exact changes, but with some reasoning, I believe it is possible to determine the *direction* we are going.

The Inflation Spiral

Technological changes in the United States occur at a mindboggling rate. New products are introduced every day. But though production is high, so is inflation. As the situation worsens, new theories develop and the government generates ideas to control recession—and then fight inflation. Unfortunately, all of these ideas are treating *symptoms*, and none are treating *problems*.

If the economy is in an inflationary spiral, the controls choke off the money supply (primarily credit) in an attempt to stop the increases. This stifles those segments of the economy that are dependent on credit, as most are. The economy then plunges into a recessionary period, and it takes greater quantities of money to reverse that trend. Each time the economy inflates, it generates higher prices. Each time it deflates, it picks up higher unemployment. What does the future hold for us economically? We will explore this in the next chapter.

3
The Cashless System

THE IMPORTANT QUESTIONS are: What can we expect in the future? and, What kind of decisions can we make based on those expectations? To answer those questions, it is necessary to make some assumptions and observations.

Future Economic Trends

I believe we are going to see ever-intensifying recessionary and inflationary spirals. During the inflationary periods, Americans will experience higher prices. These prices will be caused by more money being created and disbursed into the market, with fewer products being produced to offset this new money. Government controls will expand, causing increased subsidies with fewer people contributing. Combined with the higher prices will be higher taxes.

During the recessions, more individuals will become unemployed as basic industries contract. Many of these people will be added to the government payrolls in an effort to appease those being hurt by the system. I believe we will develop what might be termed "shear economy." In a shear economy, one segment will boom while another will suffer. Workers in the boom industries will be able to demand higher wages, while those in a lagging industry will be laid off. The unemployed will then demand compensation from the government, which will step in with subsidies, welfare, and job supports, thus creating the need for more money to be put back into the system.

It is easy to envision shortages in industries involving fuel, food, and shelter. As other nations, such as oil countries, demand higher levels of affluence for their people, we must begin to relinquish some of our affluence to compensate.

In this situation, more people will depend on the government for the answers—perhaps even a national hysteria in which the government is expected to make virtually every decision.

Pressure groups will chastise government leaders whenever they make wrong decisions. Consequently officials will become less prone to make *any* decisions but, when forced to act, they will be more likely just to treat the symptom to pacify the people, whatever the cost. During the recessions, they will spend all the money necessary to reverse the cycle. In inflationary spirals, leaders will try to appease the people by giving them something "for nothing." The attitude will be to deal with whatever happens to exist at that time. It will become almost a necessity for the government to have total control of the money supply through some form of nationalization of the banking interests.

Will we ever have another Great Depression or collapse? I don't know. But I do know that we are evolving into a new system, perhaps precipitated by a collapse. No matter what happens, we will have another "New Deal"— one that people will ask for because of devastating problems (high prices, high unemployment, money almost worthless because of inflation, and the prospect of a crime epidemic).

The New System

I believe that ultimately we can look for a new, *cashless* system. If the present system collapsed and we had high prices even in the midst of that collapse, people would become hysterical and even riot, stealing what they wanted. The government would be forced to establish some kind of control, which could best be done by temporarily stopping the flow of money and then totally reorganizing the monetary system. It would have to be virtually dictatorial under government control so that the new economic system could operate on a cashless or credit card system.

I believe that initially each individual will be issued a number of digits (or units) for the amount of money held in the bank and proportional to earnings. A master credit card will be used to make most or all purchases. Eventually, as the system progresses, there will be no money, only a credit card per individual. The card will be checked through the electronic cash register at the store and also against a central computer to determine allocation of credit so that no one will be able to borrow beyond his or her ability to repay; nor will anyone be able to accumulate excessive amounts of money. It is conceivable that each individual will have a definite accumulation limit so that no large surpluses will exist. Profits may be allowed in business, but they will be contained within the maximums that the government prescribes.

Additionally, crime can be drastically reduced through this system, since crime prevention will become one of the major goals of the government. As the economy continues to slip, the cashless system will be an important tool in the battle against criminals. Money thefts will become a thing of the past because there will be *no* money. It will be fruitless to rob banks because they will only store computer tapes. It will make no sense to kidnap someone, because the criminal could only have his account credited. Retail store thefts will be reduced to product losses only. Thus, two major problems could he solved at one time—crime reduced and a common medium of exchange established throughout the world. I believe that whatever system is enacted, it will have to be worldwide, thereby creating a common medium of exchange.

The Flaw in the System

The only factor left to deal with is the credit card itself. Because credit cards could be destroyed, lost, counterfeited, or forged, the credit card black market would soon become a major problem. A functional and workable system to eliminate the credit card would be to indelibly imprint on each individual a number equivalent to his credit card number that could not be forged or altered. Perhaps a magnetic ink number tattooed just under the skin. The number could be detected by an electronic scanner and verified against the central computer at any time.

Is a Cashless System Possible?

This cashless system may seem farfetched to those unacquainted with monetary trends, but even a cursory investigation clearly establishes that systems similar to the one presented here are now being tested throughout the United States and Europe in contemplation of a totally "cashless" banking system. Virtually no one in major banking circles will deny either the necessity of such a system or its future certainty. In fact, the World Bank has already begun work on a massive computer system that will be used to catalog and categorize every individual in the world.

How does this relate to Christian finances? This is the kind of system that *must* exist prior to the last days. It must be a system so subtle that people will ask for it and, unless they are aware, even the "elect" may be deceived.

Part Two

GOD'S PRINCIPLES
OF FINANCE

4

What Is Wealth?

SINCE CREATION, MAN has suffered from his own greed and inability to obey God. In the Garden of Eden, Adam and Eve disobeyed God and were cast out to earn their own way. In Genesis 3:19 God says, "By the sweat of your face you shall eat bread." Until Christ returns, man will be concerned with acquiring and managing possessions.

Most individual tension, family friction, strife, anger, and frustration are caused directly or indirectly by money. But for Christians seeking God's best, He has established basic principles for the management of possessions. Just as Christians cannot experience the fullness of the Holy Spirit until they surrender ownership of their lives to Christ, so too they cannot experience peace in the area of finances until they have surrendered total control of this area to God and accepted their position as stewards.

A steward is one who manages another's resources. Each of us is a manager, *not an owner*. God is the owner, and we are to manage according to *His* plan. All of the promises God has made regarding His blessings in this area are predicated on the principle that we relinquish ownership. If we refuse to do this we can never experience God's plan for our finances. As a consequence, our lives will be characterized constantly by turmoil and anxiety in the area of money.

Wealth—Attitude—God

What is wealth or money? What is the proper attitude toward wealth? How is God's will expressed in the area of finances?

I recall a story written by the chief accountant for one of the wealthiest men who ever lived—John D. Rockefeller, Sr. Someone asked the accountant, "How much did John D. leave? We know he was an immensely wealthy man." And the accountant answered, "Everything." God would have us remember that we all leave *everything*.

The book of Ecclesiastes deals with stewardship and a principle that Solomon found valid—regardless of his station in life, man accumulates nothing. For each person's wealth and possessions amount to *nothing* upon his death. As we look into the New Testament, we see that God admonishes us not to "lay up for yourselves treasure upon earth . . . but lay up for yourselves treasures in heaven" (Matthew 6:19-20).

What Is Wealth?

Past civilizations show that wealth has often been based on the number of cattle or camels owned, land possessed, oil owned, and many other material possessions. In the early economy of the United States, wealth was related to how much land one owned. Later, wealth related to resources such as gold or silver or other natural elements in the earth. Then during the Industrial Revolution it related to how much one had accumulated in worldly goods—namely money.

In today's economy, wealth is still related to money, but position is also a measure of wealth. Professional men such as doctors, attorneys, dentists, and others are thought to be "wealthy" because of their income-earning potential.

For example a doctor coming right out of residency is capable of borrowing great amounts of money to go into business without any collateral other than his education. What is his credit based on? His potential productivity. Therefore, even the talents and the abilities that we have are part of our wealth, as is our credit or borrowing ability.

Creation and Uses of Wealth

According to our attitude, wealth can be creative—it can be used to spread God's Word, build hospitals and churches, feed the poor, or take care of orphans. Or it can be wasted—spent on frivolous activities, lavish living, gambling, or other foolish activity. Wealth also can be corruptive—used to purchase influence, bribes, illegal businesses, or guns and bombs.

For the Christian, wealth is that which God entrusts to each of us. From the world's perspective, the creation of wealth evolves around many things, including self-will—how much self-control and will power one has to devote to earning money.

As we will see later, that is not God's perspective because, in every instance, individuals who spend their lives in the pursuit of money end up frustrated and miserable. They never really understand *why* they have money, and as they get close to death they realize how futile the attaining of wealth was.

There is a lot of *worldly folklore* surrounding *wealth*. Some of it states:

1. *It takes breaks to get ahead.* Whoever gets the best breaks or has the most influence is "the one who gets ahead."

2. *It takes money to make money.* In other words, the rich get richer.
3. *You can't be too honest and get ahead today.* Why? You must be willing to shade the truth. If you're extremely honest with people, then you will not be able to deal with the world system.

None of these are God's principles. They are nonsense put out by those who seek to rationalize their behavior. The creation of wealth is both a gift and a talent. For some, acquiring wealth is easier than it is for others. But it is possible for anyone who is willing to sacrifice and to achieve by setting and reaching goals.

I'm not suggesting that this is good because, as we will see in God's plan, it's *attitude,* not *aptitude,* that He honors. The gaining of wealth as an end in itself is a very poor investment of a life. *First*, it requires a great deal of time—to the virtual exclusion of everything else including family, friends, hobbies, and relaxation.

Second, there is no correlation between wealth and happiness. That is an important key! Many Christians are inwardly disturbed by the prosperity of some non-Christians. Yet we should recognize that Satan is the prince of this world, and it would be an extremely poor recruiting practice if he recruited only the impoverished.

But there is a great different between God and Satan in our finances. "It is the blessing of the *Lord* that makes rich, and He adds *no sorrow to it*" (Proverbs 10:22). This establishes the foundation for the remainder of our study—*how to have wealth without worry* (wealth being our money, our family, our creative abilities—*everything* we have acquired since we arrived and everything we must leave when we go).

Thus we should remember that money is *temporary*. The importance of money to God is that for this small sliver of time in which we are living He wants to use it to help determine our usefulness to Him throughout eternity. Our commitment to God's Word on this earth is proportional to our use of money.

Second Peter 3:11 says, "Since all these things are to be destroyed in this way, what sort of people ought you to be in holy conduct and godliness."

Attitude About Wealth

What, then, is the correct attitude for us to have toward wealth? To seek *God*'s purpose for what is supplied to us.

It is important for the Christian to trust God in *every* circumstance. If we believe that God really loves us and will give us only that amount of money that we can handle without worry, we can have perfect peace in finances. But not until we have committed our *entire* resource to Him.

It becomes clear that money is a training ground for God to develop (and for us to discover) our trustworthiness. "If therefore you have not been faithful in the use of unrighteous mammon, who will entrust the true riches to you?" (Luke 16:11).

Why do Christians have difficulty trusting God in this area? We really don't believe that He will only do the *best* for us. So we have the tendency to want to withhold a part of what we have. But until we have experienced freedom in the area of money, we will *never* experience God's total plan for our lives.

Folklore

In order to dispel some of the religious folklore that exists concerning money, let's look at each myth and then consider what attitude God wants us to have.

1. Folklore suggests that *poverty is next to spirituality. Wrong!* There is no inherent virtue in poverty. There are dishonest poor just as there are dishonest rich. Look through Scripture. God never impoverished anyone *because* of spirituality. Even in Job's case, God allowed his wealth to be removed as a testimony to Him. When Job stood true to God, He returned Job's wealth twofold. God never once relates spirituality to poverty. Therefore, there is no way Christians can attain spirituality by impoverishing themselves or their families.

God condemns the *misuse* or the *preoccupation* with money, *not* the money itself. In Scripture, God lists the production of money as a spiritual gift. Romans 12:5–8 describes the gift of giving. Obviously, if there is a gift of giving, there must be a gift of gathering, as it is impossible to give otherwise. In every scriptural reference, God promises that as we give, so it will be given back to us.

2. *Money brings happiness* is another myth. There is no relationship between money and happiness. "Instruct those who are rich in this present world not to be conceited or to fix their hope on the uncertainty of riches, but on God, who richly supplies us with all things to enjoy" (1 Timothy 6:17). If riches could bring happiness, then the wealthy of the earth ought to be the most content. Instead, we find many frustrated wealthy people. They have anxieties over what they are going to do with their money, how they are going to leave it to their children, and what effect it will have. And few children are appreciative of the large amounts of wealth their families leave them. Most, having grown up in affluence, see the devastating effect that an excess of money used unwisely can have on a family.

3. *To be wealthy is a sin.* That is false too. Having money is *not* a sin. As a matter of fact, many times when God finds someone with the proper *attitude*, He blesses them with great riches. When God bestowed riches on Abraham, it was not His intention to corrupt the nation of Israel. And when Solomon prayed for wisdom to be able to manage the people of Israel, God responded by granting him wisdom *and* great wealth. Psalm 8:6 says, "Thou dost make him to rule over the works of Thy hands." This is God's stewardship to us over *everything* on earth.

4. *Money is the root of all evil.* Many people believe this misquote comes from Scripture. They say, "I don't know exactly where, but the Bible says that money is the root of all evil." That is *not* what the Bible says at all. Paul points out in 1 Timothy 6:10, "For the *love* of money is a root of all sorts of evil, and some by longing for it have wandered away from the faith, and pierced themselves with many a pang." This is God's perspective; the *love* of money is the root of all sorts of evil.

Christ relates this attitude to the rich young ruler. He came before Jesus and asked Him, "'Good Teacher what shall I do to inherit eternal life?' and Jesus said to him, 'Why do you call Me good? No one is good except God alone. You know the commandments, "Do not commit adultery, Do not murder, Do not steal, Do not bear false witness, Honor your father and mother."'" And he said, 'All these things I have kept from my youth.' And when Jesus heard this, He said to him, 'One thing you still lack; sell all that you possess, and distribute it to the poor, and you shall have treasure in heaven; and come, follow Me'" (Luke 18:18–22).

That young man turned sadly and went away, for he was very rich. And Christ said, "How hard it is for those who are wealthy to enter the kingdom of God!" (Luke 18:24). Why? Christ knew that *inside* this man loved his money. He had kept all the external commandments, but he could not keep that internal *attitude* straight. Because of this, Christ asked him to sell what he had and follow Him. He refused to do so; yet, in death, he surrendered what in life he could not.

Attitude is always God's concern. Christ's statement dealing with the rich young ruler was based on that man's attitude, his motivation, and the purpose behind his money.

How Is God's Will Expressed in Finances?

The key to realizing God's will in the area of finances is a proper understanding of stewardship. Unfortunately, this term has been so misused that today most people think of stewardship only in terms of Christian fund-raising activities. As defined earlier, a steward is one who manages another's property. We are merely stewards of God's property while we are on this earth, and God can choose to entrust us with as much or as little as He desires. But in no case do we ever actually take *ownership.* When we try to do so we are depending either on what Satan can supply or what we can achieve through our own self-will.

Once we accept our role as a steward and manage God's resources according to His direction, God will entrust more and more to us. But why would He entrust property to those He knows will hoard it and to those who feel they are owners?

God will not force His will on us. A verse that relates specifically to God's attitude is Proverbs 28:26, "He who trusts in his own heart is a fool, but he who walks wisely will be delivered." God is looking over the entire earth for men who have the proper attitude toward money and who will use it according to His direction and not according to their own interests.

Every parable that Christ left us about money tells us many things about the attitude He desires for us. The parable of the talents is rich in wisdom (Matthew 25:14–30, summarized).

The master was going on a trip, and he called in three of his servants, telling them, "I'm taking a long trip and entrusting to you money to use on my behalf." To the first he gave five talents, to the second he gave two talents, and to the third he gave one, each according to his own ability. (Note that he didn't give each the *same;* he gave them according to the physical, worldly ability that they possessed.)

Immediately, upon the master's leaving, the first took the five talents, invested them, and promptly earned five more. The second, who had the two talents, took them out and invested them and promptly earned two more. But the one to whom one talent had been entrusted, knowing that his master was a harsh man, wrapped it in a handkerchief and buried it in the ground.

Later the master returned and called for his three servants. He spoke to the first saying, "How did you fare?" The first said, "I've done well, Master; I've taken your five and gotten five more talents with them." His master then replied, "Well done; you were good and faithful with the few things I put you in charge of, and you have entered into my great joy."

Then the one who had the two came up and said, "Master, you gave me two, and I've gained two more with them." The master said, "Very good. You are faithful also. I'll put you in charge of many things."

And the one who had received the one talent came to the master and told him, "Master, I knew you to be a hard man, reaping where you did not sow and gathering where you scattered not seed. I was afraid and I went away and hid your talent in the ground. Here, I'll return it to you." But his master told him, "You are a wicked and lazy slave. You knew that I would reap where I did not sow and gather when I scattered no seed. You should have put my money in the bank and at least earned interest on it." He told those around him, "Take the talent from the one who has invested poorly and give it to the one who had five. Because to every one who has shall more be given, and he shall have abundance. But from the one who does not have, even what he does have will be taken away, and cast him out into the darkness."

This parable is *prophetic* in nature. It is given in Matthew 25, a chapter that deals with the Second Coming of Christ. It reveals many things.

1. God will entrust to us that which is within our own ability and not beyond it.
2. God is the owner and has the right to recover what He has given us to manage.

3. God thoroughly disapproves of slothfulness on our part and expects multiplication of the assets He leaves us, not just maintenance. That multiplication is to be achieved according to *ability*.

God expects those who have the ability to invest, but He also expects the return of what is given. This involves *wisdom* in finances—another key to understanding God's plan.

God's Wisdom in Money

How can we seek God's wisdom in Christian finances? God says that if we pray anything in His will, believing, it shall be given to us. But God's will and His ways are not always coincidental with ours. So when we turn our finances over to God, we must also be willing to accept His direction.

Too often we strike out on our own without any clear direction, sometimes borrowing money to do His work. We forget God says He will not frustrate His work for the lack of money.

There is nothing wrong with asking God's direction. But it is wrong to go our own way, then expect Him to bail us out. Christians who do this regularly have not accepted that God's wisdom is superior to theirs.

How God Works Through Our Finances

1. *God will use money to strengthen our trust in Him*. It is often through money that God can clearly and objectively show us that He *is* God and in control of everything. Matthew 6:32-33: "For all these things the Gentiles eagerly seek; for your heavenly Father knows that you need all these things. But seek first His kingdom and His righteousness; and all these things shall be added to you." This principle establishes that God will use money to strengthen our trust if we will just accept our positions as stewards and turn it over to Him.

2. *God will use money to develop our trustworthiness*. This principle is important because our lives revolve around the making, spending, saving, and other uses of money. Luke 16:11 states: "If therefore you have not been faithful in the use of unrighteous mammon, who will entrust the true riches to you?"

3. *God will use money to prove His love*. Many Christians remain outside God's will because they are afraid to yield their lives and their resources to Him. Matthew 7:11 has the answer: "If you then, being evil, know how to give good gifts to your children, how much more shall your Father who is in heaven give what is good to those who ask Him!" By this Scripture, we can see God assumes the responsibility of providing the basic necessities for everyone trusting Him.

4. *God will use money to demonstrate His power over this world*. Too

often we forget that we worship the creator of the universe. We think of God in human terms and relate to Him as we relate to a human. It is important that we understand God's power and His resources.

Let's say that one day you are in your home and a man knocks on the door. When you answer, he says, "I've decided I'm going to give you $1,000 in two weeks." He then leaves you his card and shuts the door. You think, "How strange that was," but the first thing you do is start checking him out. You want to find out what his bank balance is and how much money he is worth. You begin to talk to people around you who might know something about him.

You discover that he is a multi-billionaire and that he has given thousands of dollars to other people. Knowing this, your confidence in him grows. But still, you don't have any real trust in him because he has not given *you* any money. However, in two weeks he delivers $1,000. Your trust in him grows more. But, even while you are rejoicing in your good fortune, you still have some questions. Then, in another two weeks, he returns and says, "Sir, I've decided to give you $10,000 in two more weeks." You already know that he is a multi-billionaire so you know that he has the resources. Then, in talking to other people, you discover that, sure enough, he has given away tens of thousands of dollars as well. This time, you discover something else: He never lies under any circumstances. When he says that he's going to do something, he always does it. In fact, he has put his money into trust and the trust will pay out simply on his word.

In two weeks, he delivers $10,000. Now your trust really grows. Over the next few months he continues to give you more and more money; each time your trust in him grows.

Then he comes to you, after having departed for awhile, and says, "In three months, I will give you $100,000." Well, by this time you have absolute confidence in him. You know exactly how he operates. You know that he has the funds and that he has put them in a trust; and once he says it, it will be done. You also know that he has given hundreds of thousands of dollars to other people as well. And so, with full confidence, you can actually spend that money, knowing that he's going to deliver exactly what he said.

Trust in God is similar. When God promises us things, He promises them through His Word. And the Bible has in it everything God will ever do for us. As we read it, we begin to understand that God indeed is the owner of everything. He is a *multi-zillionaire*, He is a *multi-universaire,* and when He *says* He can supply things, He can. In talking to others, we find that what God promises in Scripture He delivers.

He then begins to give—small things at first, because we are only capable of trusting Him for small things. But as He gives us small things, our confidence begins to grow; and the more our confidence in Him grows, the more He is able to supply. Thus God can use money to demonstrate His power to us. "For the Scripture says, 'Whoever believes in Him will not be disappointed.' For there is no distinction between Jew and Greek; for the same

Lord is Lord of all, abounding in riches for all who call upon Him" (Romans 10:11–12).

5. *God will use money to unite Christians through many shared blessings.* "He who gathered much did not have too much, and he who gathered little had no lack" (2 Corinthians 8:15). God will use the abundance of one Christian to supply the needs of another. Later He may reverse the relationship, as described in 2 Corinthians 8:14: "At this present time your abundance being a supply for their want, that their abundance also may become a supply for your want, that there may be equality." It is important, as we face times of economic chaos, that Christians accept the principle that a surplus of money in our lives, indeed everything that we have, is there for a purpose.

For example, God sent Joseph into Egypt specifically to supply the needs of Israel. Had Joseph refused his position of stewardship, God simply would have assigned it to someone else.

6. *God uses money to provide direction for our lives.* There is probably no way God can direct our lives faster than through the abundance or lack of money. Too often we believe God will direct our lives only through an abundance of money, and we keep probing to see where He supplies it. However, through the lack of money, God will steer us down His path just as quickly. "And let us not lose heart in doing good, for in due time we shall reap if we do not grow weary" (Galatians 6:9). We don't give up just because we face some difficulty. God will ultimately supply the direction we are seeking, and one of the primary ways He gives insight into His will is by providing or withholding money. A Christian seeking God's will must be certain that he has first relinquished control of his life, including his finances, and is truly seeking God's direction.

7. *God can use money to satisfy the needs of others.* Christians who hoard money and never plan for their financial lives cannot experience this area of fulfillment. Often I hear Christians say, "How can I give! I only have enough to barely meet my needs now." If we have never learned to give, God can never give back. God cannot be in control as long as we believe we are the owners.

Attitudes of Self-control

Now, let's look at some guides that will clearly define when God is *not* in control; understanding that is just as important as understanding when He *is* in control.

1. *God will never use money in our lives to worry us.* If a Christian is worried, frustrated, and upset about money, God is *not* in control. God said that wealth without worry is His plan for our lives. "For this reason I say to you, do not be anxious for your life, as to what you shall eat, or what you shall drink; nor for your body, as to what you shall put on. Is not life more than food, and the body than clothing?" (Matthew 6:25). If we are operating

within His plan, God promises to supply food, clothing, and shelter—the *needs* of life. Believing that, we can concentrate on other things, using the ability God has given us to accomplish the plan He has for our lives.

2. *God will never use money in our lives to corrupt us.* Naturally, God would not use money to corrupt us. But many Christians have fallen into Satan's trap and are being corrupted. They fail to realize that *God cannot be in control when they are becoming corrupted.* "For the Lord knows the ways of the righteous, but the way of the wicked will perish" (Psalm 1:6). A Christian whose financial life is characterized by greed, ego, deceit, or any of the many other worldly snares is not God's ally.

3. *God will never use money in our lives to build our egos.* Frequently, Christians are trapped by financial ego. Most people cater to the wealthy in our country (Christians included). Read through the book of James. It makes very clear the admonition not to fawn over the wealthy.

In Christ we are all financially equal. The things of this world will quickly pass away. Death will remove all wealth from us. And, when we as Christians meet again, there are going to be many surprises. Those who will have the crowns of heaven and are placed in charge of the cities of God will not be those using money to build egos. "And let the rich man glory in his humiliation, because like flowering grass he will pass away. For the sun rises with a scorching wind, and withers the grass; and its flower falls off, and the beauty of its appearance is destroyed; so too the rich man in the midst of his pursuits will fade away" (James 1:10–11).

4. *God will not allow Christians to hoard money.* There is a distinct difference between saving and hoarding. Solomon said (in paraphrase), "Lord, I ask but two things from You: first, help me to never tell a lie; second, give to me neither riches nor poverty because in my poverty, I might steal, and in my riches I might become content without You." The wealthy have a great responsibility to understand why God gave them money and to avoid hoarding.

I believe that as the economy crumbles it will not be possible to hoard. Those who have been storing up wealth in contemplation of things unknown, retirement, or the better life, will be greatly disappointed when it is all consumed like so much chaff and fodder.

A Christian *cannot* be within God's will and hoard money. "For he sees that even wise men die; the stupid and the senseless alike perish, and leave their wealth to others. Their inner thought is, that their houses are forever, and their dwelling places to all generations; they have called their lands after their own names" (Psalm 49:10–11). That is an important spiritual lesson.

Those who hoard large sums of money to leave to their children or for "security" are fooling themselves. It cannot be done. It is important that Christians understand and believe that. Scripture speaks very strongly about true values: "I advise you to buy from Me gold refined by fire, that you may become rich, and white garments, that you may clothe yourself, and that the shame of your nakedness may not be revealed, and eyesalve to anoint your eyes, that you may see" (Revelation 3:18).

Hoarding can evolve into a trap. It is possible to see others in need and ignore them rather than abandon a hoarding plan. Unfortunately, those trapped by hoarding can rationalize their behavior with arguments that contradict God's Word.

5. *God will not use money to allow us to satisfy our every whim and desire.* It is important that we begin to adjust to lifestyles compatible with a Christian commitment. That means something less than lavishness. God does not want us to live in poverty; we have discovered that there is nothing inherently spiritual in poverty. Neither is there any sin in wealth. However, God does not desire for a Christian to live in worldly lavishness while His work needs money and other Christians go without food and clothing. So, while we can live well—and in this country we live very well—it is important that there be a difference in our commitment as compared to that of the nonbeliever.

What kind of commitment is it to be? It must be one for *you* personally, brought on by a conviction of the Holy Spirit. But you must ask yourself, "Is there a difference between my lifestyle and the nonbeliever's?" If not, you need to seek God's direction. First Timothy 6:6-8 says, "But godliness actually is a means of great gain, when accompanied by contentment. For we have brought nothing into the world, so we cannot take anything out of it either. And if we have food and covering, with these we shall be content."

God does not supply money to satisfy our every whim and desire. His promise is to meet our needs and provide an abundance so that we can help other people. It is when we accept this principle that God will multiply our abundance as well.

Application

To achieve God's best, we must *apply* what He says. Information without application leads to frustration. A Christian who is not experiencing the peace and fulfillment in financial matters that the Bible promises is in bondage. In the next section, we are going to discuss exactly that—financial bondage from God's perspective.

5

What Is Financial Bondage?

WHAT IS FINANCIAL bondage? As we look in Scripture, it becomes obvious that excessive debts meant exactly that—bondage. If a man who owed could not repay his obligations, then the lender had the right to imprison him until he could pay up every cent. The lender then owned everything that had once belonged to the debtor—his wife, his family, all of his possessions.

Physical Bondage

The biblical perspective of bondage is expressed in Matthew 5:25–26: "Make friends quickly with your opponent at law while you are with him on the way; in order that your opponent may not deliver you to the judge, and the judge to the officer, and you be thrown into prison. Truly I say to you, you shall not come out of there, until you have paid up the last cent." In the Bible, financial bondage means physical bondage.

Such harsh treatment was meted out because failure to repay a debt was equated with dishonesty. Dishonesty was judged so strictly that usually when a thief was caught, his hand was cut off as a punishment for his crime A man who failed to repay an obligation was thrown into prison for the rest of his life and sold as a slave. Why? A man's word was his mark of honor. When one gave his word, he was expected to keep it. Anyone who failed to do so could no longer be trusted. Today, society has become too sophisticated to incarcerate someone simply because of debts. Unfortunately, a new punishment has supplanted the old one.

Mental Bondage

Physical bondage has been replaced by *mental bondage*. Every year, thousands of families are destroyed because of financial bondage. Thousands, perhaps millions, of people encumber themselves with debts beyond their ability to repay. Christians become involved in the world system just as non-Christians do and begin to purchase on impulse. Credit cards have supplied the means of buying on impulse, allowing everyone to encumber themselves far beyond their ability to repay.

Danger of Borrowing

Why are Christians trapped by this system? Because they have violated one or more scriptural principles that God laid down, particularly those relating to financial bondage. It is important that a Christian understand God's attitude about *debt*. Proverbs 22:7 says, "The rich rules over the poor, and the borrower becomes the lender's slave." God says that when you borrow, you become a *servant* of the lender; the lender is established as an *authority* over the borrower. This should clearly define God's attitude about borrowing from secular sources to do His work. After all, how many Christian organizations would like to be the servant of a secular banking or financial institution?

Christians can get into financial bondage in either of two ways.

Credit Bondage

The most common type of bondage is excessive use of credit. Many individuals today think the credit card companies will not allow them to borrow beyond their ability to repay, but such is *not* the case. The average credit card company in the United States will allow people to borrow 250 percent more than they can conceivably repay.

Delinquent accounts are generally regulated by statutes favoring the creditor, meaning that *delinquent debts* fall under a different set of rules. Those rules allow the creditors to charge more interest for debts in delinquency than they can for accounts that are current.

Debt

The scriptural definition of a debt is the inability to meet agreed-upon obligations. When a person buys something on credit, that is not necessarily a debt, it is a contract. But, when the terms of that contract are violated, scriptural debt occurs.

The fact that someone is in debt is the result of an earlier *attitude*—that of not understanding or obeying God's principles. "And He said to them, 'Beware, and be on your guard against every form of greed; for not even when one has an abundance does his life consist of his possessions'" (Luke 12:15). When a Christian continues to borrow without the means to repay, his or her attitude falls into the category of deceit and greed. This mindset will surely separate any Christian from God's will.

Many Christians today are shackled by excessive debts, and misuse of finances has ruined their spiritual lives. They are no longer able to minister to people as God directs; they feel encumbered and have a timidity in speaking about Christ. They are also defeated in their homes, harassed by their spouses, and frustrated or intimidated by creditors constantly bearing down on them.

Proverbs 21:17 says, "He who loves pleasure will become a poorman: he who loves wine and oil will not become rich." One who is never willing to sacrifice, never willing to deny impulses, but constantly seeking to indulge whimsical desires, will always be in bondage and frustrated. Until a Christian has brought his or her debts under control according to God's plan, no peace will *ever* be realized. Remember, God is concerned with *attitude*; He will begin to work in a Christian's finances, regardless of past actions, as soon as the attitude is correct.

No Allowance for Avoiding Creditors

There may be legal remedies to avoid creditors, such as bankruptcy, but there are no scriptural remedies. "The wicked borrows and does not pay back, but the righteous is gracious and gives" (Psalm 37:21).

In worldly terms, this principle will not seem logical. Many times even Christians begin to doubt God, often saying, "How will I live if they take everything?"

Thus we begin to seek "logical" ways to shelter possessions from legitimate creditors. But as Christians we cannot do that. We must accept the fact that God is in control and that He understands our needs and promises to provide them.

Attitude is the key, for it is attitude that brings into play a source of supernatural power. God says, "If you ask Me anything in My name, I will do it" (John 14:14). So we must accept God's plan of recovery when in financial bondage.

God's Promise

If we really trust God with everything we have, He will satisfy all of our needs as He promised. "For all these things the nations of the world eagerly seek; but your Father knows that you need these things. But seek for His kingdom, and these things shall be added to you" (Luke 12:30–31).

One of the greatest scriptural references to attitude can be found in the story of Abraham. God asked Abraham to sacrifice his most important possession—his son Isaac. Born of his old age, Abraham truly loved his son, and, although Abraham was a wealthy man by worldly standards, nothing meant as much to him as Isaac.

But God asked Abraham to take his son up to the mountains and sacrifice him unto the Lord. He asked Abraham as He asks us, to sacrifice everything for His name's sake. Abraham could have argued with God concerning the logic of sacrificing Isaac, but he did not. Abraham knew that if God had given him a son in his old age, surely God could recover him from death.

So he packed up the mules, his servants, and Isaac, and set out for the mountain. Laying his son upon the altar, Abraham raised the knife.

It was at that point that God stopped him, saying, "Abraham, I know that you are a true man and you have withheld nothing. Because you withheld nothing, I'll make your seed as abundant as the sand upon the shore. And I'll bless you beyond every nation on earth" (Genesis 22:16-17, paraphrased).

As a result of Abraham's obedience, God entrusted to him stewardship of His kingdom on this earth. For not only did Abraham love and trust God, but he bowed his will to God's judgment. Christians must accept this concept of total stewardship, because when they transfer assets to avoid creditors, when they file bankruptcy to avoid creditors, or when they deal deceitfully with creditors, God's channel for help is blocked.

Bondage Through Wealth

Financial bondage can also exist through an *abundance* of money. Some Christians have been supplied a surplus of money and have misused or begun to hoard it. Those who use their money totally for self-satisfaction or to hoard it for that elusive "rainy day" are just as financially bound in God's eyes as those in debt.

The accumulation of wealth and material pleasures of life can be an obsession that will destroy a Christian's health, fragment family unity, promote separation from friends, and block God's will. Everything and everybody can become objects to be used on the ladder to success. Those shackled by these wrong attitudes are always striving for the goal of money. Job 31:24-28 says: "If I have put my confidence in gold, and called fine gold my trust; if I have gloated because my wealth was great, and because my hand had secured so much; if I have looked at the sun when it shone, or the moon going in splendor, and my heart became secretly enticed, and my hand threw a kiss from my mouth, that too would have been an iniquity calling for judgment, for I would have denied God above."

As discussed earlier, it is important for Christians to understand this truth. Many Christians have taken the very resource that God provided for their peace and comfort and transformed it into something full of pain and sorrow. There is nothing inherently evil in money itself—only in the preoccupation with and the misuse of it.

Symptoms of Bondage

It is important to be able to recognize and detect these *symptoms* of financial bondage:

1. Overdue Bills.

Christians are in financial bondage when they experience anxiety produced from overdue bills. In counseling, I find that as many as 80 percent of Christian families today either suffer from overspending or have suffered from it in the past. That is partly because most families have no plan for their finances and continue to borrow beyond their ability to repay.

If a Christian is shackled in this area, it is virtually impossible to be an effective witness for Jesus Christ. Frustration created in the home life will be reflected in the spiritual life. Proverbs 27:12 says, "A prudent man sees evil and hides himself, the naive proceed and pay the penalty." God is saying that a man who plans well will foresee dangers and avoid them, but the foolish man will rush in, do whatever is convenient, and end up paying the penalty later.

2. Investment Worries.

Worrying over investments, savings, money, or assets also causes financial bondage and interferes with the Christian's spiritual life. As many Christians begin to accumulate material goods (or worry about not accumulating them), worry is carried over to every aspect of their lives. They never enjoy their families because of concern over investments or the lack of investments. This worry follows them home, to church, even to bed. They go to bed with money on their minds and wake up to the same thoughts.

If these investments generate worry, a Christian can be absolutely sure that he or she is not within God's will. "No one can serve two masters; for either he will hate the one and love the other, or he will hold to one and despise the other. You cannot serve God and mammon. For this reason I say to you, do not be anxious for your life, as to what you shall eat, or what you shall drink; nor for your body, as to what you shall put on. Is not life more than food, and the body than clothing?" (Matthew 6:24–25).

3. "Get-Rich-Quick" Attitude.

This attitude is characterized by attempts to make money quickly with very little applied effort. An investment is a "get-rich-quick" program if an individual must assume excessive debt, borrow the money to invest, or deal deceitfully with people.

Proverbs says that a man who wants to get rich fast will quickly fail. "A faithful man will abound with blessings, but he who makes haste to be rich will not go unpunished" (Proverbs 28:20). Money that may have taken years of effort to accumulate can be lost in days in a get-rich-quick program.

Not only is that get-rich-quick attitude prevalent in investments, but it also surfaces in the home when a family borrows to get everything desired rather than saving for the items. It's important to assess exactly what your *motives* are for financial involvement.

4. No Gainful Employment.

Financial bondage also exists when there is no desire for gainful employment. Paul said in 2 Thessalonians 3:10, "For even when we were with you, we used to give you this order: if anyone will not work, neither let him eat."

Unfortunately, we have lost this point of reference in society today. The government has assumed responsibility to support those deserving and non-deserving. This must also be assessed in every Christian's life. For many people who desire "to start at the top" never get started at all. Each of us must have a real desire to work if we are to accomplish what God put us on this earth to do.

We should ask ourselves, when approached for assistance, "Am I asked to supply others' needs, wants, or desires? Does this individual really have an internal commitment to work?" It is possible to keep someone from God's perfect plan for them by satisfying their requests.

Paul is a good example of the kind of attitude we should have. He worked throughout his Christian life. But Paul found through his travels there were many Christians who had no real desire to work. They relied on the brethren to take care of them. Paul admonished those people, particularly those in the church at Thessalonica, and he reminded those who did work that it was not their responsibility to support those who did not. "Now we command you, brethren, in the name of our Lord Jesus Christ, that you keep aloof from every brother who leads an unruly life and not according to the tradition which you received from us" (2 Thessalonians 3:6).

5. Deceitfulness.

A Christian is in financial bondage if he is dishonest in financial matters.

Each Christian must assess his or her own life. Have you dealt honestly and openly with everyone? In the worldly way, that will not seem logical many times. For instance, someone selling insurance or investments can easily shade the truth (rather than telling the whole truth, tell only *part* of the truth). That deceit will financially bind a Christian, removing peace and contentment.

Christian families must make a similar assessment. Bondage can occur, for instance, if a couple purchases an appliance on credit, knowing that they are already behind in their average monthly obligations. They are dealing deceitfully with the supplier.

Luke 16:10 relates God's attitude toward deceit: "He who is faithful in a very little thing is faithful also in much; and he who is unrighteous in a very little thing is unrighteous also in much." If we are not faithful in small things, we are *not* going to be faithful in large things. The amount is not important.

6. Greediness.

Financial bondage will also result from greed, which is reflected when someone always wants the best or always wants more. Someone who is never able to put others first, never able to accept a necessary loss, or is always looking at what others have suffers from greed. A Christian who cannot put his or her own *wants* aside to satisfy the *needs* of others suffers from greed. "For this you know with certainty, that no immoral or impure person or covetous man, who is an idolater, has an inheritance in the kingdom of Christ and God" (Ephesians 5:5). What is an idolater? One who puts material possessions before God. We are often guilty of establishing other idols before God.

The rich ruler in Luke 18 suffered from this malady. He had put an idol, his money, before God, and he could not give up that idol, even to follow Christ.

7. Covetousness.

Financial bondage exists if the Christian looks at what others have and desires it. We might call that "keeping up with the Joneses."

I often hear young married couples' discussions about their start on the road to indebtedness. They simply followed the example of other people who borrowed to get the things they wanted—furniture, new cars, televisions, and such.

It's too bad they can't look *inside* the Joneses' house. They need to see the strife when the paycheck comes in and there's never enough to satisfy all the creditors. Or the anxiety that takes place when a notice comes from a collection agency taking them to court. Or the despair of a housewife when a creditor calls at 10 A.M. asking for money.

Covetousness should not characterize the Christian. Set your goals and standards based on God's conviction—not on what others possess. *Peace and contentment* are worth anything. I am positive that virtually any couple in bondage would willingly go back to zero with no assets and no liabilities if they could.

8. Family Needs Unmet.

You are in financial bondage if, because of your past buying habits, your family's needs cannot be met. The reasons for unmet needs can be many: you may refuse gainful employment; be shackled with debts to the point that creditors take necessary family funds; or your standard of living may allow "luxuries" to deprive your family of "needs." This is not as uncommon as one might think—many Christians live far beyond their means and sacrifice basic necessities such as medical or dental care as a result.

The "symptoms" of financial bondage are almost inexhaustible but are all related to a common attitude—*irresponsibility*. There is a definite difference between a Christian who is financially bound because of irresponsibility and one who cannot meet family needs because of circumstances such as medical bills, injury, illness, or other unforeseeable events. In those instances, it is the responsibility of other Christians to help satisfy the family needs.

The financial bondage discussed here concerns those who are lacking because of past bad habits and those who will not meet the needs of their families. Paul said in 1 Timothy 5:8, "But if anyone does not provide for his own, and especially for those of his household, he has denied the faith, and is worse than an unbeliever." No Christian can achieve God's will until the attitude that caused this bondage is changed.

9. Unmet Christian Needs.

Unfortunately, this is the norm in today's society. But it is the responsibility of each Christian to supply the *needs* of others who *cannot* do so for themselves.

James 2:15–16 states, "If a brother or sister is without clothing and in need of daily food, and one of you says to them, 'Go in peace, be warmed and be filled,' and yet you do not give them what is necessary for their body, what use is that?"

Harry Truman once said of the presidency, "The buck stops here." The same is true for each Christian. If we see a brother or a sister in need, and we close our hearts to that person, what kind of love is that? Of course, God will not lay *every* need on *every* Christian's heart, but He will lay on our hearts specific needs that we are to meet. And if we pass them by, He must simply seek out someone else to share in the blessing.

10. Overcommitment to Work.

A life that is devoted to business pursuits, to the exclusion of all else, is a life of bondage. Not only are many Christians worried and frustrated about investments, but their lives are dominated by work. Everywhere they go their work follows them and every discussion is centered on their business. But God's plan for work is to *excel,* not *exceed.*

11. Money Entanglements.

God says we are in financial bondage when our money entanglements reduce our Christian effectiveness. Entanglements differ from overcommitment to work in that they stem from a mishandling of finances, perhaps even deceitfully. We say we have "too many irons in the fire."

People trapped by entanglements are so stretched out that they have to continually apply "Band-Aids" to their financial ventures. Those entanglements become so complex that continual manipulation is required to keep the whole mess from collapsing. Often someone in this situation has dealt with so many people unfairly that he or she can no longer be an effective witness for Christ and, many times, has involved other friends in the ventures.

Remember the parable of the sower? Some of the seed fell among the thorns, and those thorns were the pressures and riches of life. As they grew up they choked out God's Word. A Christian can understand God's Word and be willing to obey it, but the pressures and riches of life can choke out God's Word so that the Christian can no longer respond.

12. Financial Unfairness.

God says we are in financial bondage if we deal unfairly with others. We promote our own interests to the detriment of others. A classic example is the Christian who discovers someone in need and pressures the needy person to accept a poor offer, or even worse, forces him or her to borrow.

This tactic is often used in dealing with recent widows or applying pressure sales tactics through church-related contacts. Widows are besieged by "Christian" wolves who attempt to sell them things they don't need or encourage them to make investments under duress when they are very vulnerable

Many people use religious contacts as a means to solicit business— approaching others at church and applying pressure because of Christian involvement. Christians (particularly young couples) often overbuy life insurance or similar services from an older individual who is usually a church leader. Pressure is applied on the basis of church involvement rather than the value of what is offered.

But God warns those caught up in this attitude, "He who increases his wealth by interest and usury, gathers it for him who is gracious to the poor" (Proverbs 28:8).

Such an individual is never able to deny material desires but satisfies every whim.

God promises to satisfy every *need* that we have, not every *desire*. To continually satisfy every desire moves us outside of God's will. A self-indulger can be identified by one or more of the following signs.

—Purchasing without regard for utility.
—Living a lifestyle characterized by lavishness.
—Consistently trading cars and appliances for new models.
—Having closets full of clothes that are seldom or never used.
—Spending money frivolously on any "sale" item.

13. *Lack of Commitment to God's Work.*

A Christian is in financial bondage if there is no financial commitment to God's work. This principle is basic to Christian financial management. "Honor the Lord from your wealth, and from the first of all your produce; so your barns will be filled with plenty, and your vats will overflow with new wine" (Proverbs 3:9-10). It is only by honoring the Lord from the first part of our incomes that God can take control. We are stewards; God is the *owner.* The tithes that we give to God are a *testimony* of His ownership. The Christian who fails to give a minimum testimony to God never acknowledges that He is the owner.

14. *Financial Superiority.*

This attitude often occurs in those who are blessed with abundance. But Scripture holds to a different perspective. Someone who has wealth should think of it not as an honor or a right but a *responsibility.* There should be no financial superiority within the Body of Christ. According to God's plan, those who have much should share it with those who have little. But most Christians and Christian organizations cater to wealthy individuals, and many wealthy Christians demand special attention.

God's plan for the last days allows no provision for the financially superior. When in need, everyone is equal, and in the last days no amount of wealth will yield protection. But Christians who understand God's Word and have planned accordingly will have plenty.

15. *Financial Resentment.*

The converse of superiority is resentment because of God's provision—thinking God has not given us what we deserve or desire. Not only do we covet what others have but also, basically, we are resentful toward God for our station in life. I believe it is a very dangerous thing for us to ask God to give us what we deserve. He might do it!

Assess any feelings of resentment in relation to need rather than desire. We live better than 98 percent of the rest of the population on earth.

It is easy to adjust to large homes, two cars, automatic washers and dryers, refrigerators, and air conditioners and then to resent the "things" that other people have. Why? Have we become no different than the infidel? Are we no different from the Jews who resented God's provision? In our time of plenty, many want to adjust to lavishness.

Do you believe that everything works together to accomplish God's will for your life? Consider John 6:27: "Do not work for the food which perishes, but for the food which endures to eternal life, which the Son of Man shall give to you, for on Him the Father, even God, has set His seal." Be fearful of resentful feelings lest you begin to resent even God.

Summary

Financial bondage can exist not only from a lack of money or by overspending, but also from an abundance of money or misunderstanding why God gave it to us.

Continuing to adjust the spending level to exceed our income level will result in financial bondage; borrowing is the most common way into bondage. Every Christian must understand God's attitude about debts. He discusses little about *what* we buy with borrowed money but describes in depth the requirement to repay.

Common sense should tell us not to borrow for depreciating assets. They are usually worth less than the amount owed and may well fall into what God calls "surety." Surety is putting yourself up as a guarantor for material assets. But the economy determines whether a particular item is depreciating or appreciating.

There is a range of possible responses a Christian could have regarding borrowing within God's will.

The one end of the range is expressed in Romans 13:8, "Owe nothing to anyone except to love one another; for he who loves his neighbor has fulfilled the law." At this end of the range, God describes borrowing in terms of *owing no man.* I know personally that there is no greater sense of freedom than to owe no man a financial obligation.

The other end of the range is found in Psalm 37:21, "The wicked borrows and does not pay back, but the righteous is gracious and gives." God accepts nothing less than repayment of every obligation. God requires every Christian to operate somewhere between those two points.

6

God's Plan for Financial Freedom

What Is Freedom?

A CHRISTIAN MUST be able to recognize financial bondage, but also know how to achieve freedom. Financial freedom manifests itself in every aspect of the Christian's life—relief from worry and tension about overdue bills, a clear conscience before God and before others, and the absolute assurance that God is in control.

That is not to say that a Christian's life will be totally void of any financial difficulties. Often God will allow the consequences of earlier actions to reinforce a lesson; God does not promise to remove every difficulty. But no matter what the circumstances, God promises peace.

When God manages our finances, we need not worry. *He* is the master of the universe. It is *His* wisdom that we are seeking. We are still human beings and subject to mistakes, for even when we understand God's principles, it is possible to step out of His will. But as soon as we admit the error and let God resume control, we are back under His guidance.

Once a Christian truly accepts and experiences financial freedom, there will never be a desire to stay outside of God's will.

In our society, there are some who have found financial freedom, but I have never met a non-Christian who had true freedom from worry, anxiety, tension, harassment, or bitterness about money. Once someone experiences and *lives* financial freedom (meaning freedom from the bondage of debts, freedom from oppression of others, freedom from envy and covetousness or greed, and freedom from resentfulness), that person stands out like a beacon at sea.

Steps to Financial Freedom

How can we achieve financial freedom? What must we do according to God's plan?

1. Transfer Ownership.

A Christian must transfer ownership of *every* possession to God. That means money, time, family, material possession, education, even earning potential for the future. This is *essential* to experience the Spirit-filled life in the area of finances (Psalm 8:6).

There is absolutely no substitute for this step. If you believe you are the *owner* of even a single possession, then the events affecting that possession are going to affect your attitude. God will not force His will on you. You must *first* surrender your will to Him.

If, however, you make a total transfer of everything to God, *He* will demonstrate His ability. It is important to understand and accept God's conditions for His control (Deuteronomy 5:32–33). God will keep His promise to provide every need you have through physical, material, and spiritual means, according to His perfect plan.

It is simple to say, "I make total transfer of everything to God," but not so simple to do. At first, we may experience some difficulty in consistently seeking God's will in the area of material things because we are so accustomed to self-management and control. But financial freedom comes from knowing God is in control.

What a great relief it is to turn our burdens over to *Him*. Then, if something happens to the car, you can say, "Father, I gave this car to You; I've maintained it to the best of my ability, but I don't own it. It belongs to You, so do with it whatever You would like." Then look for the blessing God has in store as a result of this attitude.

A friend once shared an experience he had after transferring everything to God. Only a few months earlier he had had the air conditioning system in his house repaired. Then, one day in summer, the air conditioner quit again. He began to wonder, "Well, Lord, why did You have this happen? Do You want another $500 put into that air conditioning system? I just can't believe that's Your will, but if so, I submit to it." Then he said the Lord convicted him, saying, "What were you going to do with the $500?"

Again he puzzled, "Well, Lord, if it is Your will that I spend the money on that air conditioning system, I'll do it. But if it's not Your will, then I'll put that money into whatever You decide."

The Lord did have another plan. A brief check showed there was nothing wrong with his air conditioning system—it cost nothing to return it to operation. He then found the purpose for that $500 God had entrusted to him. He had no anxiety, no frustration, no worry associated with the incident because he had transferred total ownership to God. And God, in turn, was simply showing him that He had a specific use for that money.

2. Freedom from Debt.

A Christian must get out of debt altogether. Again, let me define a scriptural *debt*. Debt exists when any of the following conditions are true.

—Payment is past due for money, goods, or services that are owed to other people.

—The total value of unsecured liabilities exceeds total assets. In other words, if you had to cash out at any time, there would be a negative balance on your account.

—Anxiety is produced over financial responsibility, and the family's basic needs are not being met because of past or present buying practices.

Steps to Getting and Staying Current

1. Written Plan.

A written plan is an absolute *necessity* for the Christian in financial bondage. (It would benefit everyone else, too.)

Use a written plan of all expenditures and their order of importance. The order of importance is crucial because it will help us differentiate between needs, wants, and desires. Let's examine those differences.

—*Needs.* These are necessary purchases such as food, clothing, home, medical coverage, and others.

—*Wants.* Wants involve choices about the quality of goods to be used. Dress clothes versus work clothes, steak versus hamburger, a new car versus a used car, and so on.

—*Desires.* Desires are choices according to God's plan, which can be made only out of surplus funds after all other obligations have been met.

The difference between needs, wants, and desires can be illustrated as follows. We can see in our society that most people need an automobile. That *need* can be satisfied by a used Volkswagen. The *want* can be satisfied by a larger car such as an Oldsmobile And the *desire* may only be satisfied by a brand new Cadillac.

A parallel would be in the food we eat. The protein requirement of food can be satisfied by selecting good quality vegetables or hamburger. The want may be steak, and the desire may be satisfied only by eating out every night.

Each of us must assess those levels according to God's plan for *our* lives. For instance, if you are in financial bondage and are not able to keep your family's needs met and bills paid, you must assess whether a television set is a need, a want, or a desire. You must also assess entertainment or vacations accordingly. Those who are in debt have no prerogative but to meet their needs and then satisfy the needs of their creditors according to God's plan. Always analyze every expenditure in terms of those categories.

2. Living Essentials.

A Christian in debt must stop any expenditure that is not absolutely essential for living (Proverbs 21:17). Look for services around the home that can be done without outside cost. Also begin to develop some home skills. By utilizing individual skills, you can begin to cut down on some of the non-essential expenditures.

Learn to substitute for items of lower depreciation. For example, when purchasing appliances, select those with fewer frills; the basic components of most appliances are the same. Keep an automobile even though you may be bored with it.

Learn to conserve. Begin to eliminate expenditures that are not *essential*, remembering that many expenditures are assumed to be essential only because society says so. Fifty years ago almost all the labor supplied in the home was through family members—not paid professionals. Christians in bondage *must* begin to assess what things they can do for themselves. Once a Christian has begun to do those things, whether in debt or not, it will become fun and will help stabilize family life.

3. Think Before Buying.

A Christian who is in debt (and even those who are not) should *think* before every purchase (Proverbs 24:3). Every purchase should be evaluated as follows.

- —Is it a necessity? Have I assessed whether it is a need, a want, or a desire?
- —Does the purchase reflect my Christian ethics? (For example, *Playboy* magazine does not reflect Christian ethics.) Should I continue to take magazines, encyclopedias, or book and record subscriptions while I owe others?
- —Is this the very best possible buy I can get or am I purchasing only because I have this credit card?
- —Is it a highly depreciative item? Am I buying something that will devaluate quickly? (Swimming pools, boats, sports cars all fall into this category.)
- —Does it require costly upkeep? (There are many items that fall within this category—swimming pools, home entertainment centers, recreational vehicles.)

4. Discontinue Credit Buying.

A Christian in debt should also begin buying only on a cash basis. Often someone in debt, with an asset that can be converted into cash, will ask, "Would it be better to sell this asset and pay off the debts?" That's a normal mistake to make, but it only treats the symptom rather than the problem.

I remember a couple who was in dire financial bondage from credit card debts. They owed more than $20,000 and paid in excess of $4,000 a year in interest alone. In our planning it seemed reasonable for them to sell their home and apply the money to their debts, which would have paid them off. They did so, but less than a year later they were back in again with about $6,000 in credit card debts and no home.

What happened? I had treated a symptom rather than the problem. The problem was an attitude dealing with credit cards. I had their assurance that they would not use the credit cards; but without working out a plan for them to discontinue the use of those cards, they fell right back into the same trap again. As soon as they needed something and lacked the cash to purchase it, out came the card.

The principle in this: If you are in debt from the misuse of credit, stop— *totally stop*—using it. One of the best things to do with credit cards when in debt is to preheat the oven to 400 degrees and put them in it. Then mail the cards back to their respective companies and ask them to mail you no more. Include in your letter the plan for paying that credit card debt, and then commit yourself to buying solely on a cash basis.

Once good habits have been developed and the bondage from the misuse of credit cards has been broken, then evaluate the feasibility of converting assets to pay off the debts. In that way you won't simply be treating the symptom. Once you have overextended your finances, it is necessary to sacrifice some of the wants and desires in life to get current; otherwise, you will continue to borrow and only get deeper into bondage.

5. Avoid Leverage.

When in debt, avoid using "leverage." Leverage is the ability to control a large asset with a relatively small mount of invested capital.

For example, if you bought a piece of property that cost $10,000 and required $1,000 down, that represents a nine-to-one lever. You have invested 10 percent of your money and borrowed 90 percent.

Borrowing money to invest is not a scriptural principle, because the repayment of the bank loan is dependent on the investment making a profit. But if a profit is not made and the investor can't make the payments, he or she loses the investment and still owes the bank. The result? Financial bondage.

Let me clarify a point on the use of leverage. Let's say the 10 percent downpayment is made out of your own money, and the value of the property secures the other 90 percent. If payment could not be met, you would simply return the property and lose the 10 percent. That is not a *debt*, it is a contract.

Understand that although leverage itself does not violate a scriptural principle, it can fall into the category of a get-rich-quick scheme if used excessively.

6. Practice Saving.

A Christian should practice saving money on a regular basis. This *includes* those who are in debt. Even if it is only $5 a month, develop a discipline of saving.

This does not mean to save money at the expense of creditors. But one of the best habits a young couple can develop is saving a small amount on a regular basis.

Everyone living above the poverty level has the *capability* to save money, but many fail to do so because they believe the amount they can save is so small that it's meaningless. Others believe God frowns upon a Christian saving anything. Neither of those reasons is scriptural. "There is precious treasure and oil in the dwelling of the wise, but a foolish man swallows it up" (Proverbs 21:20).

7. Establish the Tithe.

Every Christian should establish the tithe as the *minimum* testimony to God's ownership. As mentioned earlier, how can we say we have given total ownership to God when we have never given testimony to that fact?

It is through sharing that we bring His power in finances into focus. In every case, God wants us to give the *first* part to Him, but He also wants us to pay our creditors. That requires establishing a plan and probably making sacrifices of wants and desires until all debts are current.

You cannot sacrifice God's part—that is not your prerogative as a Christian. So what is the key? If sacrifice is necessary, and it almost always is, do not sacrifice God's or your creditor's share. Choose a portion of your own expenditures to sacrifice.

8. Accept God's Provision.

To obtain financial peace, recognize and accept that God's provision is used to direct our lives.

Finding God's Plan

How can we actually *apply* those principles and find the level of living God has planned for our lives? We can begin putting those attitudes into practice in the following areas.

1. Extra Income.

Often when a family cannot pay its bills, the first thought is, "More money will help." Perhaps the husband takes a second job or the wife goes to work Before either step is taken, Christians should assess whether they are living outside God's will for their finances. Is the real problem a lack of money or a wrong attitude toward spending?

Seek the possibility of extra income *only* after correcting buying habits. Quite often, when analyzed on paper, a working mother does not contribute any more actual income. In many cases it costs *more* money, considering the costs of child care, travel, and clothing. But the greatest sacrifice is the loss of family guidance from the mother. I believe there is no provision in God's Word for a mother with children to work if she must sacrifice her children's welfare. If there are no children at home, or the children are in school during the day, it should be an individual family decision. But it is necessary to first assess whether you are rationalizing that you cannot live within God's provision.

2. Asking God First.

Before making any purchase, regardless of the amount, give God the opportunity to provide that item first. Many times we forego blessings God has in store for us because, being impulse buyers, we purchase without giving God the opportunity to show us His will. God will often manifest Himself by providing our needs from a totally unexpected source.

One of the greatest joys a Christian can experience is God's faithfulness. Psalm 37:7 says, "Rest in the Lord and wait patiently for Him." Give God an opportunity to provide before you go out and purchase.

The following are some things a Christian should do before every purchase that is outside his or her normal budget.

—*Pray about purchases.* Absolutely no purchase is too large or too small to pray about. How can you know God's will if you never ask Him?
—*Seek family counsel.* Bring the entire family into the petition before God and allow them to share in the blessing of God answering prayer.
—*Seek God's will.* Learn to discern God's will in requests. God is not under any obligation to grant our every wish since often we ask for things that hurt us. It is God's wisdom that we are seeking; not ours.

3. A Clear Conscience.

A Christian must have a clear conscience regarding past business practices and personal dealings. If you will remember, earlier we discussed dealing unfairly with others through greed or ego. Freedom from those may well require restitution as well as a changed attitude.

Proverbs 28:13 says, "He who conceals his transgressions will not prosper, but he who confesses and forsakes them will find compassion." The New Testament reaffirms this in Matthew 5:24, "Leave your offering there before the altar, and go your way; first be reconciled to your brother, and then come and present your offering."

God is saying, "Don't give anything to the Lord as long as you have transgressed against your brother and you are not willing to make it right."

I recall a friend who, before he became a Christian, had wronged an individual financially. God convicted him about that and indicated that he should go and make restitution. He contacted the individual, confessed what had been done, and offered to make it right. The person refused to forgive and refused to take any money.

For a while it hurt my friend's ego and pride—until he realized that it was not for the offended person that he had confessed, but for himself. It was not for the loss that restitution was offered, but for his relationship with God. God had forgiven him, and he had done exactly what God had asked. Nothing further was required.

4. Put Others First.

A Christian seeking financial freedom must always be willing to put other people *first*. That does not imply that you have to be a doormat for others; it simply means that you don't profit at the disadvantage of someone else. The key, again, lies in *attitude*.

To avoid financial superiority a Christian must apply the attitude God shows us in His Word: "Do nothing from selfishness or empty conceit, but with humility of mind let each of you regard one another as more important than himself; do not merely look out for your own personal interests, but also for the interests of others" (Philippians 2:3-4).

5. Limit Time Involvement.

A Christian must also limit time devoted to business affairs when family involvement suffers. Many Christians are trapped in this cycle of overcommitment to business or money pursuits.

Money is not always the prime motive for that overcommitment. Often it is ego, escape, or simply habit that drives a person to such excess. Many people overcommit out of pure habit, not ever questioning what they are doing, why they are earning money, or why God put them on this earth.

Psalm 127:2 says, "It is vain for you to rise up early, to retire late, to eat the bread of painful labors; for He gives to His beloved even in his sleep."

It's important to remember that God's priorities for us are clear. The *first* priority in your life is developing your personal relationship with Jesus Christ. You must understand who God is to be able to trust Him, to be able to ask Him for answers and to expect to get them. Understanding God comes from the following.

  —*Reading His Word*. When situations arise, decisions can be made according to biblical principles.
  —*Praying*. Prayer is communication with God. How else can you discern God's perfect will for your life?
  —*Sharing your relationship with Christ with others*. That does not mean a "forced" witness, either.

The *second* priority of your commitment is to your family, including teaching them from God's Word.

Such training requires a commitment to the family unit—and that means a specific time commitment, too. Christ deserves the best part of our day. If you study best in the morning, get up early and give time to the Lord. Sacrifice if necessary. If you find that your family time can take place best between eight and nine in the evening, commit that time to God. Turn off the television, have the children do their homework early, and begin to study the Bible together. It is important for the whole family to understand God and pray together. Pray for others in need, too. And have your children become aware that Christians, as intercessors, can pray for others and expect God to answer.

The *third* priority in your life should be church activities, social groups, work, and all the hobbies that you might have.

You need to assess whether you really allow God to have first place in your life. An assessment can be made by keeping a twenty-four hour calendar for about one week. Write down, on an hourly basis, each activity of each day. Observe how much time you give to God, how much time to your family, how much time to work, and how much time to pleasure.

I don't mean to imply that God expects us to set aside eight hours each day for Him. But how much time do you give to God? Is it five or ten minutes a day, or even less? How much time is devoted to television or newspapers that might be given to God? When you find a balance in your life, God will make the time spent more profitable. I believe that the majority of Christians could, if they planned their schedules properly, trim their average day substantially and accomplish the same amount of work or perhaps more. But seek a balance. If business involvement requires that you sacrifice God's work or your family, it is *not* according to His plan.

6. Avoid Indulgence.

Every Christian, to achieve financial freedom, must avoid the indulgences of life.

The range in which God's will can be found is between Luke 9:23 when Christ said, "If anyone wishes to come after Me, let him deny himself, and take up his cross daily, and follow Me" and John 6:27, "Do not work for the food which perishes, but for the food which endures to eternal life, which the Son of Man shall give to you, for on Him the Father, even God, has set His seal."

Does your lifestyle fit within that range? Are you willing to trust God and deny yourself some indulgences? As you do, He will supply even more. Unfortunately, most of us are self-indulgers, rarely passing up a want or desire, much less a need. But, in light of the needs around us, it is important that Christians assess their standards of living. Most of us can reduce our expenditures substantially without a real reduction in living standard.

7. Christian Counseling.

It is important to seek *good* Christian counseling whenever in doubt. "Without consultation, plans are frustrated, but with many counselors they succeed" (Proverbs 15:22). God admonishes us to seek counsel and not to rely solely on our own resources. In financial planning, many Christians become frustrated because they lack the necessary knowledge and then give up. God has supplied others with the ability to help in the area of finances. Seek them out.

The very first counselor to seek is your *spouse*. Many times God will provide the answer right within your home. Husbands should not avoid their wives' financial counsel, for many times I have found the wives' suggestions useful and enlightened. Husbands and wives can frequently work out financial problems that would frustrate either of them separately.

Don't avoid your children's counsel either. Let them know your problems. Allow them to know and understand why you must adjust your standard of living. Inform them that skating, boating, or other recreation may not fit into the new budget, and help them adjust to the necessary changes. Don't simply dictate to them; begin to communicate with them.

Let your need for counsel be made known to other Christians. Too many times we set up the facade that we have no problems. How can others help unless they are aware? Sometimes we act like hypocrites—we don't mind helping others, but we don't want to ask for help. We don't mind counseling someone who has a problem, but we don't want others to know when we have problems. It is not necessary to broadcast every problem throughout the Christian community, but at least allow others the opportunity to exercise their ministry.

If necessary, seek professional financial counseling. I would advise counseling *only* from a Christian source. Often good, sound financial counseling can come from a non-Christian source, but many of your goals will not be understood by the non-Christian.

We can see that God clearly outlines *when* a Christian is in financial bondage, as well as the steps that lead out. Begin to put those principles into practice and share them with other Christians.

7

How to Plan a Financial Program

PLANNING IS AN essential element for any financial program, but it is particularly important for Christians. Too often Christians argue whether or not they should plan *at all*. Those who argue no planning is necessary misunderstand what God says about finances. They argue that God does not expect us to plan but to rely on Him for everything. Other Christians say we should plan every second of our lives. Accordingly, they create plans so inflexible that they are no longer responsive to God's leading. That is wrong, too. The answer lies somewhere in between.

God is an orderly provider and expects us to be exactly the same. The physical world we live in is not chaotic but is orderly and well planned. The universe stays in its path because God ordered it so. Atoms stay together because God so ordered them.

Finances are just another aspect of the Christian's life that God wants to manage. If we are stewards and God is the owner, then it is *His* wisdom that we must seek. Therefore, we must go to God's Word for our plans.

Changed Attitude

First we must develop a changed attitude. But you must do more than just make an initial *attempt* at creating a plan. You must first generate a plan according to God's conviction and then *utilize* it—apply God's principles to your life.

If you make plans that are inflexible, they will only hinder God's work because you won't be able to live with them. Develop plans that guide your financial life but also provide for some recreation and personal enjoyment as well.

Flexibility

Do not make plans that are totally dependent on financial increases. God's wisdom can be manifested through a reduction, if necessary, to redirect our lives. Naturally, we would all be happy only to get involved in profitable ventures. But sometimes God's will is accomplished by a loss rather than a gain.

Paul says in Philippians 4:12–13, "I know how to get along with humble means, and I also know how to live in prosperity; in any and every circumstance I have learned the secret of being filled and going hungry, both of having abundance and suffering need. I can do all things through Him who strengthens me." We should have that same perspective in planning.

Guidelines

1. Learn to practice *patience* and moderation in every financial decision.
2. Have a *positive* decision attitude.
3. Never get involved in financial decisions that require instant action, but allow God to take His course. The difference between a profit and a loss may well be the attitude with which we approach financial investments.
4. Avoid any *get-rich-quick* schemes, no matter how tempting.
5. Maintain your plans as long as you have peace about them; they're the plans for your life.
6. Do *not* be inflexible, but don't change your plans just because somebody tells you something different.

The majority of businesses that fail do so because they are undermanaged or undercapitalized. They have inadequate planning. It is futile to operate a business without a cash flow plan (income versus expenses) to allocate resources for paying bills. How could anyone maintain a business without knowing where the capital was coming from?

God has exactly the same plan for a Christian's home, but unfortunately most of us ignore it. How can anyone manage a home without coordinating income and expenses?

Very important attitudes are necessary to develop a sound, basic financial plan for the family. That plan falls into two areas—short-range goals and long-range goals.

Short-Range Plans and Goals

Short-range plans are those that are happening *today,* and they require our attention today. Short-range plans are basically day-by-day occurrences.

For example, a housewife must have a short-range plan for buying groceries. That will include how much she buys, how often she buys, and the type of groceries necessary. If she does no planning at all, she has to rush down to the store to buy more groceries before every meal. Likewise, there must be some plan for paying bills. Otherwise, when the paycheck comes, it seems like a windfall. The natural reaction is to spend all the money and ignore the bills that are not due immediately. Later there is no money to meet the obligations. Obviously, that is not an adequate plan.

In business, short-range plans include such things as what raw materials need to be ordered to manufacture the products for sale. If a business did no planning at all, every day the assembly line would have to shut down while they rushed out to purchase necessary materials. Obviously that is not practical, so businesses make *goals* and develop plans to accomplish them.

Who Needs Goals?

Thus, as we have observed, *everyone* has short-range plans or goals. Some are carefully considered, others are more haphazard. If your short-range goal is to make money, you should review it because it is *not* a Christian objective. Having money as a goal means that you are really depending on yourself and not on God. As we discovered earlier, the mere ability to make money does not enrich you spiritually (Proverbs 2:4-5). But to do something God has directed you to do will enrich you spiritually and financially. Every Christian who has ever had money as a goal can testify that it does not satisfy. What are short-range goals from God's perspective? How can we develop plans to accomplish them?

Written Plans

A written plan provides a visible and objective standard to work toward. It is all right to have a mental goal as well, but a written plan will better help you to measure your progress. It allows you to refer to the original objective and stay on track. It is also important to periodically update it to reflect new insights.

An example of a written plan inside the family is the budget. A budget has many functions. It will show where you are financially, how much you are currently spending, and how much you can spend according to your current income.

Very few, if any, families with financial difficulties have a written plan Consequently, their financial lives are in chaos. They have little idea how much they owe or where the money goes. Predictably, at the end of a month the reaction is, "I don't know where all the money goes; I know it doesn't cost us that much to live." That's why a written plan is so essential for the family.

Short-Range Goals

1. Excellence.

God wants us, as Christians, to *excel* at whatever we do to the best of our ability. Too often Christians rationalize that it is somehow in God's plan

64 **YOUR FINANCES IN CHANGING TIMES**

to be second best. Thus they always hang back, never really achieving their potential for fear others will think them egotistical.

We *can* excel at whatever we do without egotism. Paul excelled without being egotistical; Simon Peter excelled, though he remained a humble man. Each knew his source of power, each knew what God had asked him to do, and each would accept nothing less than excellence. We also should expect excellence as part of our short-range goals.

First Peter 4:11 says, "Whoever speaks, let him speak, as it were, the utterances of God; whoever serves, let him do so as by the strength which God supplies; so that in all things God may be glorified through Jesus Christ." We are to use our abilities to God's glory.

It is equally important that wives and mothers excel at what they do. Usually the mother becomes the "habit" teacher in the home; her attitudes are generally reflected by her children. If she excels at what she does and keeps the home well organized, she can be a great asset to home financial planning.

2. Limit Credit.

As previously mentioned, a part of short-range planning should be to limit or curtail the use of credit. If you are looking for God's best plan, adopt a cash-only basis as much as possible.

Often Christians say, "It isn't possible in our society today; we must have credit cards." That is absolutely false. Many Christian families I know personally live on a non-credit basis and have done so for several years (usually with the exception of a home mortgage). Admittedly, it does take more planning, and it is necessary to establish check cashing privileges at most stores, but it *can* be done. The result will be a great sense of freedom and relief when there are no debts.

That does not mean that a Christian *cannot* use credit cards. As long as the accounts are current there is no violation of scriptural principles, but many Christians abuse the privilege of credit and *must* relinquish the use of credit cards. Most others *should* to avoid overspending.

3. Set Your Own Goals.

Establish your goals in relation to what God asks you to do, not what your neighbor asks you to do.

It is easy to get caught up in the frenzy of someone else's schemes. We see others apparently doing well and get talked into joining many half-baked ideas.

Unfortunately, many people who like their profession or business feel frustrated because somebody else is making more money in some speculative venture. Consequently they get involved in a program they know little or nothing about. The usual result is a costly financial education. There are limitless ways to lose money; one of the very best is through bad advice coupled with a little envy.

4. *Work to Honor God.*

Every Christian should stop to assess the following.

—Does my business always exemplify the Christian life?
—Will every one of my actions, day after day, be a witness to Christ?
—Can I do my work and honor God?
—Does the company I work for deal ethically with others?
—Am I helping others to violate principles that I believe?
—Am I really providing a service or simply satisfying my own ambitions?

Those are questions that every Christian *must* deal with if his or her work is to honor God. For instance, I believe the insurance trade can be a great service for families. But so often it is promoted on the basis of profit for the salesperson rather than the needs of the client. Frequently individuals are sold too little insurance at too high a price or too much insurance altogether. Few salespeople provide the *quality* and *quantity* of insurance that fits the exact needs of the buyer. Certainly it takes more time and effort but, in the end, not only will the salesperson prosper, but the buyer will be a representative to whom many more people will be referred.

Galatians 6:9, "And let us not lose heart in doing good, for in due time we shall reap if we do not grow weary."

5. *Establish a Sharing Plan.*

One of the first goals a Christian family should establish is to tithe the first part of their income This step is sometimes the most difficult, but it is also the most rewarding. Why? Because it is a material testimony to a spiritual commitment.

Long-Range Planning

In *addition* to short-range planning, a Christian needs to assess long-range goals. Any financial plan for Christians should be in harmony with prayer-guided, long-range goals.

—What are you here to achieve?
—How are you going to accomplish God's plan?
—If God blesses you with an abundance of money, what will you do with it?
—What kind of a plan do you have for such an eventuality?

Too many Christians go through their entire lives without establishing any prayerful goals for the use of their wealth. Many get trapped into a dog-matic, day-by-day routine. They have minimal short-range goals and almost no long-range goals. Understandably, many find themselves after forty or fifty years of work with an accumulation of wealth and in a quandary about where it should go. Others find themselves surrounded with problems and financial difficulties without any prearranged plan of action. Christians should visualize their long-range financial objectives.

Not every Christian will be wealthy, nor should everyone be wealthy. But everyone, wealthy or otherwise, has a responsibility to plan well, to have good, sound objectives, and to operate according to God's principles.

A Christian should establish long-range goals *only after* much personal and family prayer. The following biblical principles should be the cornerstone of all such goals.

Accept the Necessity to Plan

First, recognize the *need* to do long-range planning. Just as in your short-range plans, your long-range plans should be written. Often, by writing down what you hope to accomplish, God will provide an insight into His plan.

Your long-range goals should reflect your personal financial objectives, a plan for the surplus, and an after-death plan.

Long-Range Goals

1. Set a Maximum Goal.

You should have a goal of how much you want to accumulate—*maximum,* not *minimum.* Think in terms of storing for provision rather than storing for protection.

Christians who have minimum financial objectives have not really assessed what's happening to this economy. It is possible that God has asked some Christians to store up for the future needs of others, but the issue again relates to attitude. Is your attitude one of hoarding or sharing?

When God sent Joseph to Egypt, did he hoard the food that he put aside or did he store it for the time when it would be needed? Those who are not sharing in good times certainly will not do so in difficult times.

Once a maximum goal is established, peer approval will cease to be important, and the truth of Proverbs 11:28 will be more apparent: "He who trusts in his riches will fall, but the righteous will flourish like the green leaf." Those who fail to acknowledge that have already been identified by the Lord. Ezekiel 7:19 states: "They shall fling their silver into the streets, and their gold shall become an abhorrent thing; their silver and their gold shall not be able to deliver them in the day of the wrath of the Lord. They cannot satisfy their appetite, nor can they fill their stomachs, for their iniquity has become an occasion of stumbling."

2. Surplus Plan.

You should have a long-range plan for the surplus God supplies. How much should you return to the Lord's work? How much should you supply to your family? How much should you invest? Should you provide everything your children ask for? (Many times, as a rationalization for an overcommitment to work, we will purchase *things* for our children instead of spending time with them.)

Each Christian must assess for himself God's plan for the surplus. However, God does provide some clear guidelines for doing this.

First Corinthians 3:12–13 states, "Now if any man builds upon the foundation with gold, silver, precious stones, wood, hay, straw, each man's work will become evident; for the day will show it, because it is to be revealed with fire; and the fire itself will test the quality of each man's work." What is this work that God refers to? Revelation 2:19 has the answer, "I know your deeds, and your love and faith and service and perseverance, and that your deeds of late are greater than at first." Will God be able to say to you when He returns, "Well done, My good and faithful servant"?

Establish a surplus plan while the opportunity and the capability exist. *Do not* count on future events to support God's work. If you have money stored and God lays a need on you, give right then. It may even be necessary to disregard some tax advantages. Many people retain investments to take maximum advantage of the tax law. I don't disagree with the "logic" of that; I'd rather have God as my partner in a venture than the government.

3. *Obey God's Principles.*

In formulating your long-range plans, pay specific attention to God's principles.

Honesty. Never allow yourself to be trapped into anything that is unethical, immoral, or dishonest, no matter how inviting it seems. Proverbs 16:8 says, "Better is a little with righteousness than great income with injustice." It is important that we observe honesty in all of our plans. There aren't any small lies; there are just lies. There aren't any small thefts; there are just thefts.

Employee Welfare. Christian employers have an absolute responsibility to *care* for their employees. A part of your long-range planning in your business involves the welfare of your employees. If you expect a fair day's work, pay a fair day's wage.

A part of company profits belongs not only to management, but also to the employees. God has a personal management plan in Scripture that will revolutionize a business. But too often Christian employers are more intent on making money than providing for the welfare of employees. First Timothy 5:18 says, "For the Scripture says, 'You shall not muzzle the ox while he is threshing,' and 'The laborer is worthy of his wages'" Christian employers not only have additional authority but additional responsibility as well.

Concern for Others. Often opportunities will arise to take unfair advantage of others. You must precondition your attitude to avoid any temptation. "Do not rob the poor because he is poor, or crush the afflicted at the gate; for the Lord will plead their case, and take the life of those who rob them" (Proverbs 22:22–23).

Obey the Law. God demands obedience to the law in your long-range plans. I speak here specifically of tax laws. There are two terms used to describe tax planning. One is *tax avoidance,* taking all the legal remedies available under the law, while another is *tax evasion,* taking all the legal remedies plus some not allowed within the boundaries of the law. The lines between the two are very narrow and easily crossed.

In counseling, I find many Christians rationalize their violation of the tax laws. People who would not think of robbing a bank justify stealing from the government. I object to the highly lopsided tax structure of our system, but to illegally avoid the debt due is stealing. It is easy to rationalize because the government is a large, inflexible institution. But it is still stealing.

Proverbs 15:27 states, "He who profits illicitly troubles his own house, but he who hates bribes will live." Take maximum advantage of every tax law in existence—charitable giving, tax sheltering, depreciation, expenses, and any other step—but be careful not to cross the line and become involved in tax evasion and theft.

4. A Long-Range Family Plan.

A family living plan. Every Christian must establish a long-range family plan. What do you want for your family? Have you ever brought your family together to pray about *how* God wants you to live?

God cares about the house you live in, the car you drive, where you work, whether your wife should work, your children's college, and even the food you eat. Have you ever prayed over those things? If you have not, how can you expect to determine exactly what God's will is for your family?

Can you ever store *enough to* protect your family? I don't believe so. The best you can do is short-term provision. God has a better plan for every Christian that seeks His wisdom. Then God says, "Be not anxious," that does *not* mean to be unconcerned or imprudent. There is a distinct difference between concern or preparedness and worry. Later we will discuss how you can plan for your family using God's principles.

Establish priorities. Your long-range goals should focus on financial priorities. Remember how we defined the priorities of needs, wants, and desires? Needs are basic living requirements, wants are to improve our standard of living, and desires are the luxuries of affluence.

Establish those priorities with your family, particularly children. Help them understand the difference between a need, a want, and a desire. When your child approaches you with a request, discuss whether it is a need, a want, or a desire.

If it is a need, it should be supplied. That includes medical attention, dental work, food, clothing, or shelter—all within limits.

But if it is a want or a desire, you should establish the fact that if the child wants it badly enough, it should be earned. When your children learn that they must earn some of their wants and desires, a quick adjustment is made.

Comic books are weighed against good books, or a cheap toy against something more costly—such as a bike or an electronic game or wristwatch.

Be consistent and fair, but firm. Just as God will not grant us whims that work to our detriment, so you must hold the same position with your children.

Have a family sharing plan. Why should God trust you with a surplus? Does your family manage money well? Do your children understand the proper attitudes about material possessions? What plans do the other members of your family have for the money they earn? Are they willing to tithe openly and willingly without you pressuring them? Bring them into the decision and pray as a family.

Have an estate plan. Do you have a plan for how much to leave your family after your death? One based on provision, not *protection?* I hope by now you realize you cannot *protect* your family. Those who store up great amounts of life insurance seeking after-death protection for their families are fooling themselves. We attempt to build great walled cities around our families because we believe it is necessary to protect them against everything. But there is a better way. God's plan will revolutionize our concept of protection. In a later section we will examine the practical *amount* for an estate or inheritance plan.

Have a contingency plan. Christians must establish contingency plans in the event they accumulate wealth faster than anticipated. Scripture is clear on this point; God's surplus is to be shared. In Proverbs 11:24–25 we find, "There is one who scatters, yet increases all the more, and there is one who withholds what is justly due, but it results only in want. The generous man will be prosperous, and he who waters will himself be watered." *That* is God's plan for Christians, but unless one has a predetermined plan for those increases, expenses will be adjusted to offset any additional increases. Consequently, there will never be a surplus to share.

8

Why Accumulate Wealth?

EARLIER WE REVIEWED the biblical definition of wealth, recognizing that it related not only to our money, but also to our homes, families, abilities, intelligence, educations—*everything* we have. We also discovered that God's perspective of our wealth is always centered on our *attitudes.*

Keeping that in mind, why do people accumulate wealth? Accumulation means more than just storing away; it also refers to making, using, spending, and sharing wealth.

As discussed previously, money can be used for the comfort and convenience of our families. It can be used to provide the needs of others. It can be used to spread the gospel. Or it can be used for destructive purposes (such as buying bombs or guns).

Attitude will determine its uses, so it is vital to discover what attitudes God wants us to have. Why does He allow us to accumulate wealth? What are the limits of our accumulation? Can we define what God's will is so that we can have the peace He promises?

Money, if misused, as in the case of the rich young ruler (Matthew 19:16–30), can be an object of devotion and idolatry. Love of money has separated families and shattered friendships. Countless marriages have split up over the love of, or the misuse of, money. Christians, therefore, must assess *why* they accumulate money in light of God's principles.

Ministry of Money?

Many Christians have the ability to accumulate large amounts of wealth. Virtually everyone in America has the potential of accumulating a surplus. What we consider to be a *minimum* standard of living is significantly above that experienced in most other parts of the world. It is not unheard of for someone living on a small fixed income to accumulate tens of thousands of dollars through scrimping and sacrificing. With that potential, it becomes vital that God's attitude about accumulating money becomes a part of our personalities.

God will provide a ministry in money for Christians attuned to His plan. But it is a ministry of sharing, not of selfishness. Christians who reclaim ownership of their finances step right out of God's will. Others, who share as God commands, receive the blessings of the Lord and the great harvest promised in Scripture. Once a Christian accepts money as a *ministry,* a whole new area of God's will opens up.

In 2 Corinthians 9:8, we are told, "And God is able to make all grace abound to you, that always having all sufficiency in everything, you may have an abundance for every good deed." What are the absolute promises given here?

1. God will make all *grace* abound in each one of us.
2. We will always have *sufficiency* for our needs.
3. We will have an *abundance* for other good deeds.

If you have the ability to make money, as a Christian you *must* have the desire to share. If you are making money and not sharing it, you can be certain you are *not* within God's will and probably that money is being supplied from another source.

It's important to realize some more religious folklore comes to the fore in this area: to give money is gracious, but to make it is a sin. *Wrong!* God said giving is a gift. If giving money is a gift from God, making it must also be a gift from Him. Christians should accept the principle that there is nothing wrong with making money, provided they do so *within* God's plan.

Do not violate the principles that God established. Remember the symptoms: sacrifice of friends, family, health, and personal relationship with Jesus Christ to the pursuit of wealth; attitudes characterized by bitterness, anxiety, frustration, or worry. Exactly the same principles apply for those who have not learned to live within the provision God has supplied.

Why Do People Accumulate Wealth?

Keep in mind the *range* of God's will in Scripture. By understanding the limits of God's plan you can evaluate your own position.

1. Others Advise It.

Many people get into investments, businesses, or other ventures simply because someone else advises them to do so. They don't have any clear personal plans or goals. Most have neither short-range nor long-range plans. If God supplied them an abundance, they would not really have a plan for sharing, re-investing, or saving. They simply commit their resources to some program because somebody else thinks it is a good idea. Usually they have little or no knowledge about the use of their money and react to investment fluctuations with anxiety or alarm. What is the proper attitude?

In Proverbs 15:22, God states, "Without consultation, plans are frustrated, but with many counselors they succeed." Proverbs 18:15 says, "The mind of the prudent acquires knowledge." Paraphrased, this says, "It is the wise one who seeks many counselors." Christians are advised by God to seek many counselors on everything; with too few counselors, plans go astray.

But, in Ephesians 4:14 Paul expresses the other end of the range: "As a result, we are no longer to be children, tossed here and there by waves, and carried about by every wind of doctrine, by the trickery of men, by craftiness in deceitful scheming."

Therefore, according to God's plan, we are to seek counsel, especially in money management. But we must weigh everything against His Word. *Listen* to new ideas, but seek *God's* direction before taking action. Also, seek the counsel of your spouse; many times God supplies the necessary wisdom within your own home.

Make the following assessments for all advice. First, is it within God's plan at all? Then, is it compatible with your plans? Don't get involved in an investment simply because somebody has a new idea. Do so only because you believe it enhances your ministry and your family life and you feel a clear sense of peace about it.

2. Envy of Others.

Many people accumulate money simply because they envy other people. They fall into the trap of "keeping up with the Joneses."

They could easily identify with a character by the name of *Ernie Envy*. Ernie is a "secret service Christian" (nobody can tell from his activities if he is or isn't a Christian). Ernie maintains a "follow-the-leader" attitude. He moved into a large home because his friend Bill got a new job. Then, because his neighbors had new cars, Ernie bought one too.

By the time Ernie recognized he was in deep water and sinking, a new challenge appeared. One of his closest friends was selling a new franchise product and really making a "killing." Ernie heard how easy it was. All you had to do was sell two or three of your friends the same idea and you could "get rich quick."

Ernie had never sold anything in his life and this sounded a little fishy, but his basic envy and greed overcame any internal hesitation. So he borrowed the money to buy into the franchise.

Several months later Ernie lost most of his franchise fee and several friends when the whole scheme fell apart. Now, Ernie is ashamed to even talk about Christ because of his personal lifestyle.

We are not to envy those who are storing up riches. Unfortunately, it is easy to fall into this trap. We begin to envy others and allow our lifestyles to be dictated by those around us.

Advertising promotes this attitude as acceptable, but God does not. "And He said to them, 'Beware, and be on your guard against every form of greed;

for not even when one has an abundance does his life consist of his possessions'" (Luke 12:15).

3. Game of It.

This is the plan that ensnares Christians and non-Christians. Many people accumulate money as a game; they match themselves against others relentlessly. The world system heavily promotes this concept. We elevate the *winners* regardless of how they played the *game*. The only problem is that the game quickly overwhelms the players. Participants get so wrapped up in the contest that they sacrifice family, friends, or health to keep winning.

Walter Winner portrays their lifestyle. Walter started his "gaming" career early in life. He was the kid in high school who knew *all* the rules. He also tested most of them to see how much he could get away with. Walter never could keep any real friends because he always got involved in conflicts with them, particularly when they disagreed with him. Walter made it through college and into a profession, but his work quickly bored him since it was no fun competing against himself.

So Walter began to diversify into investments and business. And he did well, cutting every corner possible and using every friend available. Soon Walter was well known as an investor and a "wheeler-dealer." Although he wouldn't purposely cheat anyone, he seemed to always come out on the high side.

He gave to his church, but not in relation to what he received. He felt it was dumb to give more than you could write off in taxes. Besides, if he gave away the investments that were losers, he could get the same tax deduction. Walter also failed to use any of his surplus, either for his family or for others. After all, almost all of the money was needed to expand his investment portfolio.

The purpose of a game is to entertain, and non-Christians entertain themselves in the area of money. God does not provide this alternative for the Christian. Those who get involved with the game of making money are soon overcome by their own pastimes. They quickly lose sight of why they have money. They also lose sight of their families because they are so involved with the game that *everybody* becomes a pawn.

As we discussed earlier, one of the best ways to avoid this trap is through a long-range plan for surplus. Commit a *large* portion of each investment to the Lord's work. The results are predictable; there will be a change in your attitude and perhaps even in the supply. Doing so will transfer your ability from serving self to serving God.

4. Self-esteem.

Those who accumulate money for self-esteem do so that others might envy them. This is a worldly motive, yet it characterizes many Christians.

Those who suffer under this motive use their money in an attempt to buy esteem even from their own families. They want people to cater to them, to elevate them, and to always yield to their way. Such people never share with anyone except to *promote themselves*. They do nothing anonymously; when they give, they do it in sight of other people And they expect esteem in return.

This attitude characterizes *Sam Superior* and his wife *Sally Society*. Sam tries to convince everyone that he came up the hard way. He points out that he never had a new sports car in high school. He worked his way through college on the polo team and then started at the bottom in business as a junior vice president in his father's factory.

Sam and Sally go to church every Sunday (except for an occasional Sunday golf game), where Sam is the chief elder. They have several pews named after them and have pledged to the building program. Neither is sure exactly how to become a Christian, but they assume it must be by osmosis. Their names always appear in the society pages in connection with charitable benefits.

Sam thinks life has been pretty good to him, except he can't understand why his daughter ran away and his youngest son dropped out of school to be a "roadie" with a rockband.

He's sure Sally was right in telling him to get rid of that young preacher who talked about knowing God personally. And he agrees with her that the church has enough problems without inviting a bunch of strangers to visit, as that preacher kept suggesting.

A Christian cannot accumulate for self-esteem within God's plan. Esteem and importance will fade as quickly as the money. Are you working for the esteem of men or the rewards of God?

5. *The Love of Money.*

Those who *love* money wouldn't part with it for anything—not even for esteem. Their lives are characterized by hoarding and abasement. They may have accumulated thousands, tens of thousands, or even millions, but the loss of even a few dollars is traumatic. They become embittered, nervous, frustrated, and angry when others invade their financial domain. This is a form of idol worship, just as surely as worshiping pagan images of clay or metal.

That attitude characterizes *Greg Greed*. Greg has hoarded money for years. It is difficult to say exactly when it began, probably in childhood. Everybody knows and dislikes Greg; many fear him. It is said that Greg would cheat his brother if there were a profit in it.

Unfortunately, Greg doesn't see himself that way. He believes those are all shrewd business deals. After all, everybody has to look out for himself. Greg's life is one big emotional roller coaster. If his business and investments are doing well, he is happy around the home and office. But if his investments drop even a little bit, he is mean, irritable, and even hostile.

Greg's total downfall is due when a real economic reversal occurs. Then he will be a statistic in the paper—either a mental breakdown or a suicide.

Unfortunately, many Christians cling to every material possession they can. Trapped by the love of money, they would let their families do without rather than part with their most precious possessions. We are reminded in

1 Timothy 6:10, "For the love of money is a root of all sorts of evil, and some by longing for it have wandered away from the faith, and pierced themselves with many a pang." In Hebrews 13:5 we are told, "Let your character be free from the love of money, being content with what you have; for He Himself has said, 'I will never desert you, nor will I ever forsake you.'"

The love of money separates us from God. What foolishness it is for a Christian to fall into this trap. "For what is a man profited if he gains the whole world, and loses or forfeits himself?" (Luke 9:25).

6. Protection.

People accumulate money for protection. On the surface this sounds proper; certainly we need to protect ourselves, don't we?

Obviously, if we don't know what is going to happen in the future, we should protect against future events. That kind of logic causes Christians to accumulate large amounts of money for *protection*. But, if we look below the surface, it is apparent that they don't really trust God enough to *believe* that He can supply their needs. So they begin to stash it away.

Those pursuing protection don't really love money, nor are they accumulating money for esteem. They are just nervous and anxious over what *might* happen in the future.

At first, the goal is a few hundred dollars, just to tide them over. Then, the attitude adjusts quickly and that few hundred becomes a few thousand. Allowed to continue unabated, the attitude will grow and there never will be enough money.

The desire for protection is also displayed through obtaining large amounts of life insurance, disability insurance, liability insurance, or massive amounts of any assets. Understand, none of those are bad within themselves; it is only through misuse that they become corruptive.

Willie Worrier is our example of this attitude. Willie began his retirement savings program the first week he started working. By the time he met the right girl and settled down, he had a tidy nest egg. But he couldn't use any of it because, after all, he had bigger responsibilities then.

Willie had a good job with an above-average income, but he never could get far enough "ahead" to share much. He believed in God, but he didn't believe in the tithe. After all, doesn't the Bible say someplace, "God helps those who help themselves"?

Willie carried plenty of insurance. He had disability, liability, casualty, health, life, and insurance-policy insurance. After working most of his life, squirreling every extra penny away, Willie was approaching his lifelong ambition—*retirement.* Then, through a catastrophe, almost all of Willie's funds were lost, gone in almost no time. Willie became nearly neurotic, crying and bemoaning the fact that *God* had let this happen to him.

Willie could be any Christian in our generation, storing for that elusive "rainy day," passing by the *only* investment program with a written guarantee—God's. I don't mean to say that Christians shouldn't save. They should! God may also convict some to "store," but He will do so only to committed Christians who have the correct attitudes about sharing.

Anxiety over the future traps many Christians into *protection*. Having stepped out of God's will, they are no longer trusting in Him but in worldly things. When those worldly things collapse, their faith collapses. God says to *provide* for the family, but those who seek *protection* are blind.

7. A Spiritual Gift.

There is only *one* reason that God supplies a *surplus* of wealth to a Christian—so that he will have enough to provide for the needs of others. Because *true* wealth comes with the gift of giving. God promises His blessings to all who freely give and promises His curse on those who hoard, steal, covet, or idolize.

Paul defines the reason for having wealth as meeting the needs of the saints. The gift of giving is defined as the foundation for a life of selfless devotion to others. "You will be enriched in everything for all liberality, which through us is producing thanksgiving to God" (2 Corinthians 9:11).

Being a wealthy Christian establishes a greater responsibility than being a poor Christian. Being rich or being poor is a matter of providence in God's will, and He will give us only that which we are capable of handling. But the duties and responsibilities of wealth are very heavy because of the temptations. You can step outside of God's plan simply by *attitude*.

Wealthy Christians need only to adjust their lifestyles to lavishness and indulgence to totally buffer God's direction. The poor Christian usually has a clear-cut decision of honesty versus dishonesty.

Proverbs 30:8-9 says, "Feed me with the food that is my portion, lest I be full and deny Thee and say, 'Who is the Lord?'" Becoming content without God in our abundance is a much more subtle sin than stealing. We just slip outside of God's will and never realize it until calamity hits.

The Christian's responsibility is awesome and sobering. God, in His eternal plan, has decided to use *us* to supply His work. One day we must all stand before God and give an account of what we have done with *His* resources.

Why does God provide an accumulation of wealth? So His people can exercise *the spiritual gift of giving.*

9
How Much Is Enough?

NOW THAT WE'VE studied why Christians are to accumulate wealth, let's examine God's Word to determine the range we are to observe. How can you tell when your finances are in balance? When are you accumulating too much? When have you stepped over the range of provision and begun to protect rather than provide? How much should you leave your children? How much should you invest or hold for retirement?

Current Provision

Christians should be concerned with providing for their families. But how much is enough? Of course, there is no magic formula that can be uniformly applied to every family. There are several variables that need to be considered, such as the ages of the family members, the size of the family, educational needs, personal aspirations, and where the family lives.

But other factors should be taken into consideration in making decisions about future provision.

—God's plan for your life
—Present spending level
—Future income potential
—Dependability of present income
—Potential vocational changes

There are many individual factors to consider. However, there are certain basic decisions that can be made.

—You should adjust your lifestyle until it fits the plan God has for your life.
—A minimum savings plan for purchases should be started.
—A minimum expenses buffer should be established.
—Future education plans should be made.

Just as protection is wrong, so is too little or no provision. Neglect occurs when we have the capability of supplying our family's needs but fail to do so.

If circumstances change so that we are no longer able to live within a reasonable budget, God will provide for our needs beyond any doubt. But we have the requirement from God to be prudent.

What are the requirements for us as Christians to provide for our families? Let's look at a parable in Proverbs 6:6–11. "Go to the ant, O sluggard, observe her ways and be wise, which, having no chief, officer or ruler, prepares her food in the summer, and gathers her provision in the harvest. How long will you lie down, O sluggard? When will you arise from your sleep? 'A little sleep, a little slumber, a little folding of the hands to rest'—and your poverty will come in like a vagabond, and your need like an armed man."

God uses this parable to tell us that if we are slack and do not earn our way poverty will come upon us and our families. This same admonition to work is found in 1 Timothy 5:8. We *must* provide for our families, lest we be considered worse than an unbeliever. But ants *never* hoard; they store only that which they can eventually use.

The other end of the range is expressed by these verses: "For all these things the nations of the world eagerly seek; but your Father knows that you need these things. But seek for His Kingdom, and these things shall be added to you" (Luke 12:30–31). Do you recognize the importance of this principle? While God expects us to provide for our families and allows no attitudes of laziness, He also supplies every one of our needs. And He will *never* allow us to lack for anything when we follow His principles.

Investment Reserves

How much is enough for investment reserves? Obviously, if a part of God's plan for your life is to invest money, you must determine just how much that should be. But how do you know when you have gone beyond investment reserves into that area of hoarding?

It all revolves around your *attitude*. First, ask yourself: Why am I investing? What kind of a plan do I have for the surplus?

As an investor, you must retain some funds out of each investment to make additional investments. But, too often, Christians believe that setting aside those funds comes first, and they take the bulk of the proceeds from one investment and put it into another one. This is an easily rationalized action, usually with an eye on the tax advantages and sometimes with the plan of multiplying God's portion.

Neither case is scriptural, however. God is capable of using His money in His ministry *today*. After every economic downturn there are many disappointed Christian investors. They keep the Lord's money for years, planning to give it to Him, but never take the opportunity to share in His work. Then one day it is all gone, consumed as chaff and fodder.

Few Christians have the proper perspective on investments. On one side stand those who believe Christians should not be involved at all. On the other side stand those who are indistinguishable from the world.

I believe one aspect of God's will in this area is found in the previously discussed parable of the stewards in Luke 19:12-24. Let's review the parable from another viewpoint in relation to making investments. Beginning in verse 20 where the nobleman confronts the third servant: "And the other came, saying, 'Master, behold your mina, which I kept put away in a handkerchief; for I was afraid of you, because you are an exacting man; you take up what you did not lay down, and reap what you did not sow.' He said to him, 'By your own words I will judge you, you worthless slave. Did you know that I am an exacting man, taking up what I did not lay down, and reaping what I did not sow? Then why did you not put the money in the bank, and having come, I would have collected it with interest?' And he said to the bystanders, 'Take the mina away from him, and give it to the one who has the ten minas.'"

We can learn many things from the parable of the talents.

—God is the *owner*, and He only gives us what He wishes us to handle.
—He gives to us according to our *abilities*.
—As we prove to be more trustworthy, He entrusts much more to us.
—He takes from those who are untrustworthy and gives to the faithful.
—God expects multiplication, not just maintenance. We are worthless servants if we withhold the bounty of our efforts.

In fact, God gives the *requirement* to invest. (So God has nothing against investments in a Christian's life at all.) But also, understand the servants' attitudes. They knew they weren't the *owners*. Even the worthless one recognized that, and he returned to the nobleman what was his. Two recognized their duty to use their abilities; the third refused. Thus, if God gives us the requirement to invest and multiply, He will supply only what we are capable of handling. As we show our faithfulness, He will give us even more. Our responsibility is to return it to His work.

I believe the other end of the range is expressed in 2 Corinthians 9:10-11. "Now He who supplies seed to the sower and bread for food, will supply and multiply your need for sowing and increase the harvest of your righteousness; you will be enriched in everything for all liberality, which through us is producing thanksgiving to God."

God is the perfect partner in any investment program. It is *He* who supplies all the seed to be planted. We plant it, He multiplies it. What could be simpler? And so any investment program ought to be based around multiplying assets that God supplies and returning the bulk of the crop. The seeds that we retain then bring in a greater harvest the next time.

Every Christian should remember, no matter how fertile the soil is, it remains barren without rain from God. Also, it is foolish to plow, till, and fertilize the soil and never put in any seeds, for then you can anticipate a large crop of tares and weeds.

Retirement-Savings

Retirement provision is something that confuses many Christians. As previously noted, we have developed a mania about retirement savings and the necessity for storing large amounts of assets. Many people think they need to retire and spend much more than they did during working years. That is not true. Once you set a pattern for living, it will not change substantially after retirement, except in most cases to go down. If you have learned to adjust your standard of living during your income years, then retirement will be a comfortable adjustment. The Christian who hoards money to be used for retirement is being deceived.

Who can best provide for your retirement years, God or man? Begin to assess right now how much you will really need later. How many clothes can you buy and how many trips can you take? How much food can you eat? Reassess your *need* for retirement and take a portion of that which you don't consider *necessary* and give it to the Lord's ministry today. God will not let a Christian with the right attitude suffer.

Where does a retirement (or savings) program fit into God's plan? "There is precious treasure and oil in the dwelling of the wise, but a foolish man swallows it up" (Proverbs 21:20). God declares that we *should* have something for the future. That may include saving for purchases or, ultimately, retirement.

But it is important that Christians get their priorities straight. There is nothing wrong with retirement, but there is something wrong with hoarding, whatever its guise.

Our whole concept of retirement is nonsense. We have been conditioned to believe that people lose their usefulness when they are sixty or sixty-five years old. But many of the apostles did their greatest work after the time we would have considered them to be "old men." When Paul admonished Timothy not to let anybody mock him because of his youth, Timothy was older than forty at the time. So at what point should we retire? If you have a good, full life and enjoy what you do, you will be useful throughout your entire life, not just in the early years. There is nothing wrong with saving in moderation for retirement. But, there is something wrong with storing unnecessarily, believing that is the *only* way to provide for later years.

The other end of the range of God's will can be found in Luke 12:16–20. "And He told them a parable saying 'The land of a certain rich man was very productive. And he began reasoning to himself, saying, "What shall I do, since I have no place to store my crops?" And he said, "This is what I will do: I will tear down my barns and build larger ones, and there I will store all my grain and my goods. And I will say to my soul, 'Soul, you have many goods laid up for many years to come; take your ease, eat, drink and be merry.'" But God said to him, "You fool! This very night your soul is required of you; and now who will own what you have prepared?"'"

Can you see God's attitude through this parable? The man was rich, but God did not condemn him for his wealth. His downfall came when his income *increased*. Knowing he didn't have enough room in his barns, what did he decide to do? *Hoard!* Build larger barns to store his crops and then—contentment without God. Rather than seeking God's plan for the surplus, he decided to store it away. That is not the plan God has in mind for Christians.

There is nothing wrong with retirement planning. But there is something wrong with living for retirement. There is nothing wrong with saving either, except when the motive is *protection* against the world.

Reassess your attitudes as a Christian. Are you really worried that if you don't store now you will have to do without later? Do you *believe* that God is capable of supplying in your old age, or is your faith a myth?

Inheritance

If I had to identify the area of Christian finances that is least understood, it would be inheritance. Not only do many people wreck their lives by hoarding, but they also wreck the lives of their children and grandchildren with an abundant inheritance. The result of giving large amounts of money to those who are untrained in its use can be seen in the parable of the Prodigal Son, Luke 15:11-24.

At least the father in this parable had enough sense to give his son the inheritance while he was living. He then had the opportunity to provide his son with counseling. Even so, the result of the inheritance was trouble for the recipient.

Large amounts of money given to children will usually be squandered to their disservice, and large amounts of money stored up for children in trust can be used to buffer them from God's will. Is that your wish? Allow your children the joy of earning their own way. That doesn't mean to impoverish them; provide for your family, but *do not* buffer them with great hoards of money.

God's will concerning inheritances is partly expressed in Ecclesiastes 6:3. "If a man fathers a hundred children and lives many years, however many they be, but his soul is not satisfied with good things, and he does not even have a proper burial, then I say, 'Better the miscarriage than he.'" This parable denotes the necessity of leaving the family *some* provision. God said that as godly men we leave our children's children an inheritance, but that inheritance is *spiritual*.

The other aspect of God's will can be found in Psalm 37:25-26. "I have been young, and now I am old; yet I have not seen the righteous forsaken, or his descendants begging bread. All day long he is gracious and lends; and his descendants are a blessing."

It becomes obvious that the same promises *God* makes about lifetime provision extend from generation to generation. *Provide* for your family within reason. Trust God for their protection. God promises He will not let your offspring be forsaken.

Summary

Listed below are the pertinent points from God's Word dealing with *why people accumulate wealth* and *how much is enough*.

1. *Because others advise it.* A Christian should *listen* to the advice of others but should seek God's wisdom before acting. (Proverbs 15:22; 18:15; and Ephesians 4:14.)

2. *For the envy of others.* This is not within God's plan for the Christian. (Psalm 73:2-3 and Luke 12:15.)

3. *Because it is a game* to *them.* (Psalm 17:13-14 and Proverbs 13:22.)

4. *For self-esteem.* (1 Timothy 6:17 and Revelation 3:17.)

5. *For the love of money.* Again, this is outside God's plan. (Hebrews 13:5 and 1 Timothy 6:10.)

6. *For protection.* God shows us that we cannot protect ourselves outside of His mercy. (Psalm 50:14-15.)

7. *Because it is their spiritual gift.* (2 Corinthians 9:11 and 1 Timothy 6:17.)

How much is enough provision? God asks us to *provide* for our families but not to *protect* them.

1. How much should one provide? Current *provision* for the family. (Proverbs 6:6-11 and Luke 12:30-31.)

2. Should a Christian invest? God not only allows it, but actually directs it for some. (Luke 19:20-26 and 2 Corinthians 9:10-11.)

3. What about retirement or savings? God admonishes some savings, but allows no hoarding. (Proverbs 21:20 and Luke 12:16-20.)

4. Should we leave an inheritance to our children? Yes, God requires that we provide for our children, even after death, if possible. But for those who cannot, He will never let our children suffer. (Ecclesiastes 6:3 and Psalm 37:25.)

As we look at why people should accumulate wealth, it becomes apparent that *attitude* is foremost in God's plan. But how much can we store and still be within God's plan? In His Word it says, "Give me neither poverty nor riches; feed me with the food that is my portion, lest I be full and deny Thee and say, 'Who is the Lord?'" (Proverbs 30:8-9).

10
Sharing—God's Way

So FAR WE have reviewed many aspects of God's Word, from an overview of the economy to financial planning. We are now ready to examine sharing—from God's perspective.

This subject is intertwined in every other area of finances. Sharing is important, but a Christian should realize it is only one aspect of God's plan.

God's freedom cannot be experienced in the area of finances unless one:

—acknowledges God's ownership over everything and accepts the role of a steward,
—surrenders the first part back to God,
—seeks the reason that God supplies him a surplus above his own basic needs.

We need to dispel some religious folklore that has developed about sharing. Christians stand on both sides of the tithing issue. On one side are the legalists who say that unless one tithes, he cannot join the "Christian club." Tithing is sometimes elevated to the exclusion of virtually everything else. The theory is that tithing assures spirituality. But that is not the case. Examine what Christ said about some self-righteous men during His time. The Pharisees tithed down to even the last mint leaf in the garden, but they left other things undone—such as justice and mercy (Matthew 23:23).

On the other side of this issue stand those who believe the tithe is a legalism meant only for the Jew. Therefore, they never establish any goals for tithing or sharing. They give, but on a hit-and-miss basis. They also are wrong. It is necessary to understand *God*'s attitude in this area.

In many instances Christ clarified certain principles and amplified them for us. Others, He said, were relinquished for a higher authority. For example, it is no longer necessary to make blood sacrifices because Christ said He came to shed His blood as the ultimate sacrifice. We are no longer slaves to the law because Christ's death pardoned us. But as Paul said, the law didn't make him sin, it *convicted* him of his sin. When God gave the law of tithing, the law didn't *make* the Jews tithe, it showed them where they fell short of what God expected. For a Christian seeking God's will, those principles point the way to peace, happiness, and prosperity.

There are many Scriptures dealing with sharing from what God supplies to us. We will look at a few of those to determine God's attitude about the tithe and its applicability today.

How much is the tithe? Is it applicable to the Christian? Why did the Jews tithe? Why is money so important to God that He commands a testimony from it? The answers are important, lest we fall trap to the folklore around us. As you read this section, open your mind to the Holy Spirit. Assess what you read on the basis of what *God* says, without any preconceived bias.

The Tithe

God's Word describes the tithe as a *testimony* to God's ownership. It was through the *tithe* that Abraham acknowledged God's ownership. Thus, God was able to direct and prosper him (Genesis 14:20).

If the tithe is a legalism, why did Abraham tithe a tenth of all his spoils back to God? After all, *Abraham had no law.* The written law didn't come until Moses.

Abraham did so because he loved God and was convicted that the tithe belonged to Him. Abraham was a true steward, able to surrender everything, including his most prized possession—Isaac. When God convicted Abraham of the necessity to surrender a tithe, he understood its significance and did so willingly.

The amount of the tithe is not important to God; He owns *everything*. The amount is important to *us*. The tithe, given as a testimony, reaps a great harvest because it is the seed we plant in God's garden. God is able to take our tithe and multiply it.

Christians often discuss whether one should tithe the gross or the net. I believe that depends on whether you want God to bless your gross or your net. If we are legalistic with God, we can expect the same reward as the Pharisees. If we're loving and generous toward God, God will be loving and generous with us.

Given as a testimony, God promises to prosper it. But God is under absolutely no requirement to return what is given to Him. "Who has first given to Him that it might be paid back to him again?" (Romans 11:35). Uniquely, God promises that if we give out of a true and loving heart, He will return it multiplied.

The Old Testament reveals a clear understanding of what the tithe was then and is today. Malachi deals with many admonitions about tithing and the blessings of doing so. "Will a man rob God? Yet you are robbing Me! But you say, 'How have we robbed Thee?' In tithes and offerings. You are cursed with a curse, for you are robbing Me, the whole nation of you! 'Bring the whole tithe into the storehouse, so that there may be food in My house, and test Me now in this,' says the Lord of hosts, 'if I will not open for you the windows of heaven, and pour out for you a blessing until it overflows'" (Malachi 3:8–10).

Those words from God are a promise of blessing *and* a warning. God is saying, "Trust Me, bring to Me the full measure of your tithes and offerings that I may open the storehouse for you and give it back. But do not withhold from Me that which I ask."

The amount is not important to God. Paul pointed out in 2 Corinthians 9:7 that we shouldn't force anyone to give grudgingly, because it's a willing giver that God loves. Give what you believe God has committed *you* to give.

I personally began giving 10 percent as a young Christian because I believe that is a *minimum* testimony. And God has repeatedly blessed that commitment. I have never seen a Christian give out of love and obedience to God without receiving a blessing.

Deuteronomy 14:23 says, "And you shall eat in the presence of the Lord your God, at the place where He chooses to establish His name, the tithe of your grain, your new wine, your oil, and the first-born of your herd and your flock, in order that you may learn to fear the Lord your God always."

Why did God establish the tithe? In order *that we may always learn to fear the Lord our God.* Is this applicable today? Review what God's Word says: "The fear of the Lord is the beginning of wisdom" (Proverbs 9:10).

If we are looking for ways to be wise with our finances, we must seek that wisdom from God. One of the ways God said to do it is through tithing.

Sharing Out of Obedience

Many of the decisions we make in our Christian lives—perhaps even most—do not make sense to the world. Therefore, we make them because of a commitment to God's Word—in other words, out of obedience. We must predetermine that if God defines a course of action in Scripture, we will follow it.

I say this in relation to sharing out of obedience or duty. If we share out of obedience, we do so because God's Word says we are to help others. This attitude begins when we accept the needs of others as our own.

Attitudes play an important part in sharing with others. Have you ever given to someone resentfully? I have, and almost immediately realized I had given up more than money. Remember, when you give to meet the needs of others, you give to God.

God *does not* need the money. He is allowing us to share in His work. Anyone that gives willingly receives a blessing that comes only with true love. God will honor your *attitude* more than the amount.

When God places the needs of others on your heart and you supply those needs, that is obedience. Perhaps it is the need of a Christian organization you are involved with, or perhaps the victims of a natural disaster. You may well be giving to a group that you don't even know, simply out of obedience to God. God will bless the use of your resources for His work.

Get Involved

Be certain that you are not using a gift of money to avoid a larger responsibility. It may be that God desires your physical involvement as well. In other words, don't just give your money, give of yourself.

I know a Christian who helps to care for the poor in a major city. By caring, he not only gives money, but also gives of himself by establishing thrift shops for the poor in the downtown ghetto areas. Those shops supply clothing, furniture, food, and other necessities to the poor at prices they can afford. Although his time is limited, like everyone else's, he does that out of obedience to God and love for others.

He says often when he contacts other Christians to help, the vast majority would rather give a little money to God's work than to get personally involved.

I'd like to emphasize that sharing from obedience differs from the tithe. The tithe is given in recognition of God's ownership (hence, a testimony), whereas obedience is sharing with others who are in need out of a conviction that they should not do without.

One aspect of God's will can be found in Matthew 25:45: "Then He will answer them, saying, 'Truly I say to you, to the extent that you did not do it to one of the least of these, you did not do it to Me.'" Christ is saying that when He returns He will test the sincerity of our words by the commitment of our resources. This is our duty and obedience—to help those in need because of love for Jesus Christ.

The other end of the standard is expressed in Matthew 10:42: "And whoever in the name of a disciple gives to one of these little ones even a cup of cold water to drink, truly I say to you he shall not lose his reward." It does not cost much to share water with others. What is Christ saying? *What* you give is not important—not the amount or the value—only the *attitude* with which it is given.

Sharing from Abundance

This is a very difficult area for most of us. In our abundance, the normal tendency is to feel secure and become less involved. As shown before, dangers of abundance are much more subtle than those of poverty.

What is abundance and how can a Christian recognize and acknowledge God's direction? Remember when we were discussing financial planning and living on a budget? The budget helped to establish a surplus and a *plan* for the surplus. The surplus is our abundance. It is easy to fall trap to feelings of contentment, slipping away from God in our abundance. Many do so because they fear having to share with others. To share from this surplus requires great love; it really means a greater love for God than for money.

Giving out of love makes sharing our abundance possible. Scripture defines at least two levels of love. One is *phileo* and another is *agape*.

Phileo is a brotherly love. It is based on mutual compatibility or the sharing of common interests. In other words, it is primarily a love of emotion. When love is given, it is returned; but when one withholds love, no love is returned. *Agape* allows one to give love regardless of the response. What the other person does will not really affect me if I am in true *agape* with God.

Therefore, when we give out of abundance, we cannot give *phileo,* expecting that God will return it. We must give out of *agape,* simply because we love God and expect no reward. To share out of abundance means you have much and want to share with others who need much. Although God has no obligation to return what is given, He wants to do so. Once you have shared out of your abundance, you will find that you cannot outgive God. The more you give, the more He multiplies.

One aspect of God's will can be found in 1 John 3:17-18, "But whoever has the world's goods, and beholds his brother in need and closes his heart against him, how does the love of God abide in him? Little children, let us not love with word or with tongue, but in deed and truth." Also look into James 2:14-16, "What use is it, my brethren, if a man says he has faith, but he has no works? Can that faith save him? If a brother or sister is without clothing and in need of daily food, and one of you says to them, 'Go in peace, be warmed and be filled,' and yet you do not give them what is necessary for their body, what use is that?"

The other end of God's will can be seen in 2 Corinthians 8:11-12, "But now finish doing it also; that just as there was the readiness to desire it, so there may be also the completion of it by your ability. For if the readiness is present, it is acceptable according to what a man has, not according to what he does not have." When you give, give out of what you have. Don't worry about what somebody else has to give, or what they are not giving. Give out of the abundance that God has supplied you.

Sharing from Sacrifice

Sacrificial giving with a right attitude is possible *only* for those Christians submitted to God. In the United States, giving sacrificially is almost unknown. Worldly attitudes have clouded our thinking and dulled our sensitivity to others.

As I said before, God will not allow His work to tarry for lack of funds; He will simply redistribute the necessary funds to Christians who have the correct attitudes—primarily those who are seeking His will and are willing to sacrifice their luxuries for the needs of others.

The use of our money is a very objective measure of our commitment to Jesus Christ and to His work. Christians who bypass God's work because they refuse even a slight discomfort have missed the mark.

When God suggests sacrifice, He does not necessarily mean sacrificing needs. It may mean abandoning some wants and desires. Perhaps it requires giving up bowling, golfing, or eating out. It may mean foregoing new cars, boats, swimming pools, or a larger home.

Sacrificial giving is possible for those who have a little as well as those who have much. All Christians can give sacrificially. The best way to begin is by giving up some small part of your plenty for others who have little.

The first generation church set the example for us. They brought their possessions together, pooled them, and sold them so that no one would be without. There will come a time in the last generation when that will be a necessity of life. Sharing common ownership by Christians will be the way to survive. We see that pattern in 2 Corinthians 8:15, "As it is written, 'He who gathered much did not have too much, and he who gathered little had no lack.'"

Today, unfortunately, that concept has been virtually lost. But it is still a viable part of God's plan for the last days. The more Christians accept the necessity for personal sacrifice, the easier the transition will be.

One reference of God's will concerning sacrifice is found in Luke 3:11, "And he would answer and say to them, 'Let the man who has two tunics share with him who has none; and let him who has food do likewise.'" Christ considered this a *minimum* sacrifice for those who wished to follow Him—to give, not out of our needs, but from our wants and desires.

His promise for those making sacrifices can be found in Mark 10:29. "Jesus said, 'Truly I say to you, there is no one who has left house or bothers or sisters or mother or father or children or farms, for My sake and for the gospel's sake, but that he shall receive a hundred times as much now in the present age, houses and brothers and sisters and mothers and children and farms, along with persecutions; and in the age to come, eternal life.'"

Christ gave us another reference point when He was standing in the Temple, observing the Jews as they came by giving their gifts to the treasury. "And He looked up and saw the rich putting their gifts into the treasury. And He saw a certain poor widow putting in two small copper coins. And He said, 'Truly I say to you, this poor widow put in more than all of them; for they all out of their surplus put into the offering; but she out of her poverty put in all that she had to live on'" (Luke 21:1-4).

It is interesting how sacrifice works. Christ said that she put in *more* than all the rest and yet it was only two small copper coins. This widow wasn't giving to impress others. Obviously the Temple didn't need her pennies, for it was plated with gold and brass, within and without. Nor did she give from her abundance. She gave all that she had because she loved God and obviously felt a bigger need than that of food. She felt the *need* to sacrifice for God.

Sacrifice is an essential attitude for every Christian to adopt. Begin to sacrifice a small portion from your wants or desires for the needs of others. Ask God to lay their needs on your heart. Strive to reflect a difference outside that is equivalent to the commitment inside.

Summary

I hope that by now you have the perspective of what sharing means from the Scriptures.

The minimum testimony for any Christian is the *tithe*. A Christian who has never surrendered the tithe to God has never established God's ownership.

We can also share out of *duty* or *obedience* to His Word. Christians must be willing to act out of obedience, not because we understand it, but because it is God's wisdom that we are seeking. To do this requires that we both understand and accept God's Word.

The third step is to share from our *abundance*. It first requires that we establish an abundance by adjusting our standard of living. But once we establish a surplus, it is necessary to *share* rather than store the excess.

Fourth, we can share out of sacrifice. Beginning with some of our wants and desires, we work into a pattern of living that characterizes the life of Christ. If we, who are so mightily blessed, are not willing to sacrifice any of our desires for others, God will simply reallocate the supply to those who are.

11
Who Deserves Help?

THERE ARE SOME important questions all Christians should ask. With whom does God direct us to share? Who is deserving and why? Should we share only with other Christians, or do we have an admonition from God to help non-Christians as well? What about our families? Should we support our churches and contribute our entire tithes to them?

As previously stated, it is important in giving that we assess the difference between the needs, wants, and desires of others. God has directed us to satisfy the *needs* of others. Whether or not one satisfies the wants or desires of others is an individual decision. This assessment should be made of every individual and organization that asks for assistance.

Family Needs

God requires that we provide for our families. "But if any one does not provide for his own, and especially for those of his household, he has denied the faith, and is worse than an unbeliever" (1 Timothy 5:8).

This provision for the family goes beyond just the husband, wife, and children. It includes others in the family—mother, father, grandparents, right on down the line. "If any woman who is a believer has dependent widows, let her assist them, and let not the church be burdened, so that it may assist those who are widows indeed" (1 Timothy 5:16). Paul's admonition tells us to support the members of our family. Thus, they will not be a burden on the church (or the government).

Here again, we have seared our consciences, turning those responsibilities over to the government. The government is not adequate to accomplish this task, and government officials neither understand the problems nor have the resources to provide adequately. God wants Christians to provide for their families. What kind of a witness will we be to the non-Christian community if the members of our own families go without? Christians must awaken to this responsibility.

Ministering Brethren

Unfortunately we have also slighted the ministering brethren. It is somehow believed that those in full-time Christian service should live on less than those in the secular world. Why shouldn't a pastor have a comfortable salary? Why shouldn't an evangelist, for instance, live as well as someone who is in business? Do we believe that God's worker is not worthy of an adequate wage?

Review what God says in 1 Corinthians 9:9, "For it is written in the Law of Moses, 'You shall not muzzle the ox while he is threshing.' God is not concerned about oxen, is He?" And in 1 Corinthians 9:14, "So also the Lord directed those who proclaim the gospel to get their living from the gospel." And in 3 John 6-7, "And they bear witness to your love before the church; and you will do well to send them on their way in a manner worthy of God. For they went out for the sake of the Name, accepting nothing from the Gentiles." Those references tell us:

1. The requirement of every Christian is to supply the needs of those ministering God's Word.
2. We are to send them out in a way worthy of God, *not second class.* I believe a good principle to observe is to pay a pastor as much as the average member of his congregation. If he feels he is overpaid, let it be his responsibility to distribute the surplus.
3. Christians are admonished by God to accept nothing from nonbelievers but to receive their support from the believers. That admonition must hold equally true of the church; the church should not borrow money from a non-Christian source. Christian organizations should fund their work within the Body of Christ, as John said, "Accepting nothing from the Gentiles" (3 John 6-7). How can those needs be met unless Christians accept this responsibility to supply the ministering brethren?

Christian Community

Care for the Christian community. "Honor widows who are widows indeed" (1 Timothy 5:3). The directive Paul gave for "widows indeed" concerns those who have no family to support them. Therefore, the burden of support is placed on the church; and the *church* is to supply their needs.

How many churches really do that today? How many congregations in the United States have, as a regular part of their budget, money to supply the needs of Christians in their church who cannot make their own way? That applies to those who are temporarily out of work, to the injured or disabled, and to the elderly.

I believe it is an abomination before God to see widows in the Christian community depending on welfare for support. If they are qualified and have established themselves accordingly, it is a direct requirement from God to the church to care for them.

Here is also the key to where our tithe goes. In God's plan, the church is to administer the tithe and distribute it to the needs of the body. Unfortunately, not all churches adhere to this plan. I believe that if a church observes God's plan, both teaching His Word and administering His money, then all of the tithe should be placed in its care. However, if the church ignores its physical responsibilities, then Christians must follow their own convictions. Under no circumstances can the qualified needy be ignored. Christ gave this admonition to the Pharisees in Matthew 15:5-6: "But you say, 'Whoever shall say to his father or mother, "Anything of mine you might have been helped by has been given to God," he is not to honor his father or his mother.' And thus you invalidated the word of God for the sake of your tradition."

As long as you receive teaching from the church you must provide the needs of its workers. If the church does not understand God's plan, you should work diligently to help them do so. If you find a closed attitude in this area, I would recommend changing to a place of worship compatible with your commitment where you can entrust God's wealth.

Non-Christian Community

We are also *directed* to share with the non-Christian community. When God talks specifically about the "believer," the "elect" or the "Body of Christ," He is referring to Christians. Other Scriptures that deal with sharing but do not refer directly to the Body of Christ are intended to include the non-Christian community.

I have found that the majority of Scripture deals with supplying the needs of the non-Christian community. Perhaps ten times as many references pertain to sharing with non-believers as opposed to only Christians. It is obvious that God set up absolute standards.

1. We are not to accept resources from non-Christians.
2. We are to be witnesses to them through our readiness to share.

Matthew 5:42 states, "Give to him who asks of you, and do not turn away from him who wants to borrow from you." Matthew 10:42: "And whoever in the name of a disciple gives to one of these little ones even a cup of cold water to drink, truly I say to you he shall not lose his reward." Neither of those Scriptures, as well as more than fifty others, deals only with Christians. They deal with the community at large, both believers and nonbelievers.

We are to be witnesses to non-Christians through our material resources, demonstrating that Christ, not money, is ruling our lives. Commitment in

Christianity is often related to whether one is more committed to money than the needs of others. Upon this principle Christ based much of His teaching, such as in Luke 12:33, "Sell your possessions and give to charity; make yourselves purses which do not wear out, an unfailing treasure in heaven, where no thief comes near, nor moth destroys."

Ask God to relieve you of the burden of worry and anxiety and frustration surrounding money. Ask Him to place on your heart only those people that you are able to help. *Believe* that God is going to give you the ability, as well as the responsibility, to do so. Commit yourself to becoming a Christian witness in this area of giving.

Evaluate the Recipient

Christians should be very sensitive, not only concerning whom they assist, but how the money is used.

What about the myriad of individuals and organizations who approach us? How can you assess whether they are doing God's work?

God has established the requirements for us. The standards are clear for individuals—assess whether they are willing and able to work. Also, are they asking for needs, or wants, or desires? Get personally involved with the people you help, if possible. Share God's principles of finance with them. Help them establish a budget and live by it. Find out *how* they are living. Would they spend the money you might give them for alcohol? Are they wasting their present income in foolishness? If so, you have no requirement to support them. In fact, by doing so you may well be interfering in God's plan for them.

Christian organizations should be assessed likewise. Not only does God provide opportunities for giving to the needs of the saints but also to invest tithes, offerings, and sacrifices into His work. Unfortunately, today Christians are besieged by charitable requests from every side. Many are deserving, but some are poorly managed, unfruitful, and even dishonest. Seek God's wisdom *before* giving. Get literature from them that thoroughly describes the organization and its doctrine. Talk to others who have invested. Require references if you have never heard of the group before. Let the organization know *why* you are questioning them. Be discerning; be a good steward of God's resources. The following is a minimum check list.

1. Is the organization communicating the true message of Jesus Christ? If they are not, do not get involved with them. This refers to organizations that come in the name of Christ. There are other charitable organizations that do great work through secular channels.
2. Are people responding to the organization positively? Are lives being changed as a result of their input?
3. Is the organization seeking and accomplishing goals? If so, they should be able to explain their goals to you.

4. Are the lives of those in leadership positions consistent with the scriptural principles that God outlines for Christian organizations?
5. Is the organization multiplying itself, or is it dying out? (This is not always an absolute standard because you may find new leadership in an organization that is seeking to expand previous boundaries.) Ask around and be discerning. Pay a visit to them personally, particularly if the decision involves a large amount of money.
6. Is there a standard of excellence along with a freedom from lavishness and waste? How much do they spend raising money? If you find an organization spending half or more of its finances in order to raise more money, I would question their effectiveness. Can you invest elsewhere and get better return for God's money?
7. Check them out with other Christian organizations. Tell them you are looking for an *honest* answer.

Share willingly according to God's plan, but be discerning and cautious as a steward. Accept nothing less than excellence for the Lord's money.

12
Financial Breathing

IN THIS SECTION I will amplify some of the previously stated concepts, particularly those that will help you understand how to make financial decisions by God's plan. The principles presented are practical and applicable and can be traced back to one or more of the scriptural concepts that have been given previously.

Looking back on my Christian growth, I recall one of the most important concepts I learned was that of spiritual breathing. This concept is taken from 1 John 1:9: "If we confess our sins, He is faithful and righteous to forgive us our sins and to cleanse us from all unrighteousness." A sequence of spiritual events occurs.

—God convicts us of our sins.
—We acknowledge them and ask forgiveness.
—God cleanses us and forgives our transgressions.

Remember, God will convict us and Satan will condemn us. Once our sins are cleansed and restitution made (if God so declares), He no longer remembers them.

What a great relief it was for me to understand that because for the first few months after accepting Christ, I tried to make myself into the kind of Christian I thought God wanted me to be. After struggling unsuccessfully, I found myself totally inadequate. No matter how hard I tried, I could not overcome my past. I had few victories over the burdens that kept me shackled.

I shared my frustration with a Christian friend, and his reply was, "Really makes you feel inferior, doesn't it?" To which I answered, "Amen!" Then he said, "Someone who struggles, trying to evolve into a Christian, quickly develops an inferiority complex. But it's not all that complex; we really are inferior."

None of us is adequate to make ourselves into the kind of Christian God wants us to be. Why? Because God cannot tolerate sin. And all of us have sinned. We sinned before we came to God, and we will sin as Christians.

The concept of spiritual breathing tells us to exhale the bad air and inhale the good air.

All that was required was to confess my sin, exhaling the bad air, and appropriate the fullness of the Holy Spirit, inhaling the good air. What a change it made in my life! There was a freedom that I had never experienced before. It gave me the ability to put the things of the past in the past and to start afresh with God from that point.

Be careful not to adulterate the concept of spiritual breathing. Forgiveness does not provide us with a license to sin and expect forgiveness, because if there is no *changed attitude,* there can be *no* forgiveness. But when there is a changed attitude, God says He will forgive us. As I thought about this in relation to finances, I realized that Christians can appropriate the forgiveness God promises in the area of finances too.

I'd like to share how you, as a Christian, can *breathe financially.*

1. Acknowledge God's Ownership Daily.

Be certain that every day the affairs and decisions of that day are surrendered to God. Since problems are day-by-day occurrences, our acknowledgment of God's authority and His forgiveness should be daily as well. Each day must begin with a clean heart, meaning that we have no unconfessed sin in our lives.

What are the essential elements in making sound financial decisions? Adequate knowledge and the wisdom to apply it. "The fear of the Lord is the beginning of knowledge; fools despise wisdom and instruction" (Proverbs 1:7). Thus it is vital in financial breathing to recognize that it is God's knowledge and wisdom you are seeking.

To do so you *must* surrender *every* decision to God. "So you will find favor and good repute in the sight of God and man. Trust in the Lord with all your heart, and do not lean on your own understanding. In all your ways acknowledge Him, and He will make your paths straight" (Proverbs 3:4-6).

Then apply the discipline taught in Luke 9:23, "If anyone wishes to come after Me, let him deny himself, and take up his cross *daily,* and follow Me."

2. Accept God's Direction.

Once you have surrendered control of your finances to God, accept His judgment. Do not precondition your response by expecting only *increases.*

Paul said he had learned to abase and to abound but in all things to give thanks. So after you have surrendered decision making to God, accept His wisdom.

God may be using the adversities you face as a testimony for other people or to reinforce a lesson. I have often heard, and found it to be true in my own life, that during times of trial we grow the most. God says that it is through fire that silver is purified.

Don't seek escape from difficulties, seek peace during them. "Be anxious for nothing, but in everything by prayer and supplication with thanksgiving

let your requests be made known to God" (Philippians 4:6). In every decision trust that God guides your direction. Verify your decisions by checking
against the Lord's Word, confirming them in prayer and accepting His answer.

There is one final step in accepting God's decisions found in 1 Thessalonians 5:18: "In everything give thanks; for this is God's will for you in Christ
Jesus." When you ask God for a decision and He answers, thank Him, whether
or not it is the answer you were seeking.

I once counseled a couple having financial difficulties. Their income was
not sufficient to meet their wants, and they had drifted into financial bondage.

In reviewing the circumstances with the husband, I found that he was
not really satisfied in his work. It seems his company was not dealing fairly
with him because of his Christian commitment. That hindered his witness in
dealing with customers. I asked him if he was committed to seeking God's
wisdom rather than man's. He replied, "Yes, I am." I then asked if he was
willing to surrender the decision on his employment back to God and let Him
decide the next step. After we prayed about it, he reaffirmed his commitment
to God's will no matter what it was.

He prayed for two things: That God would provide a definite direction
concerning his work and would relieve him of his debt. God worked specifically on both.

First, he was convicted to confront his employers concerning their attitude about his religious beliefs. They declared they no longer had a place for
him in their company and dismissed him. Upon termination, they surrendered
the money that was due him in a savings plan. That money was sufficient to
pay off all his debts.

Although it was not the method we might have chosen, he thanked God
for the answer. Indeed God's answer was *very* specific, for he was removed
from a position that was not honoring to God and his debts were cleared at
the same time.

More Christians should learn to accept God's wisdom when they ask for
it. God loves us deeply, and He will never give us less than the very best.

3. Establish the Tithe.

As previously defined, give God the *first* part of your income as a testimony of His ownership. "Give, and it will be given to you; good measure,
pressed down, shaken together, running over, they will pour into your lap.
For by your standard of measure it will be measured to you in return" (Luke
6:38). This is an essential step in financial breathing. Not only do we surrender our decisions to God and accept His leading, but then we surrender back
to God a minimum testimony of His ownership.

The tithe is a *spiritual* investment and cannot be evaluated on the basis
of profit and loss. Too many Christians look at tithing in worldly terms. But
God is the only business manager who can make 90 percent go farther than
100 percent.

4. *Sacrifice.*

As previously discussed, the concept of sacrifice is not very popular with most Christians or Christian organizations. Most of us like to discuss this area in glowing generalities rather than specifics. It's all right for the pastor to mention sacrifice in terms of missionaries or full-time Christians, but when he talks about giving up golf or a new car for God's work, suddenly he is a radical.

Many Christians have been asked to sacrifice their lives, while others sacrifice the needs of everyday life to deliver God's Word. But for most of us, sacrificing amounts only to delaying or eliminating a few desires.

Those who have truly surrendered their finances to God have also experienced His faithfulness. "And everyone who has left houses or brothers or sisters or father or mother or children or farms for My name's sake, shall receive many times as much, and shall inherit eternal life" (Matthew 19:29).

God provides many opportunities to invest in the lives of others in need. A Christian friend once told me of such an opportunity. Bob lived in a middle-class suburb and for several months the neighbor in back had been the source of much conflict. Though both were professing Christians, neither was willing to admit he could possibly be wrong.

They argued about fences, dogs, trash cans, and many other things, to the point they no longer had communication. To cap off the whole issue, his neighbor moved some chicken coops housing about a dozen chickens into his backyard. At this point the cold war got hot. Bob said he just knew that his neighbor got those chickens to irritate him. Every time he went into his backyard and heard or saw those chickens, he grew more irritated.

Bob got nastier with his neighbor until, finally, his own Christian witness deteriorated to nothing. In the depths of despair, he was convicted that he was wrong and should make it right with his brother. Going to his neighbor's house, he knocked at the door. As his neighbor answered, Bob told him, "I'm sorry that I've been so obnoxious; it's my fault and I ask your forgiveness." Immediately accepting the apology, his neighbor thanked him and asked him in.

As they began to talk, it became apparent why the Lord had been convicting Bob. Several months before, this neighbor and his wife had been in an automobile accident. His wife had been injured and was still disabled. He had had several fractured vertebrae and was unable to work. Being self-employed, he drew no income at all. For several months they lived off their savings, but with the doctors' bills and living expenses, their finances had been totally depleted. He had moved the chickens into his backyard to have food to eat. Bob said he broke down and cried and asked his neighbor to forgive him for being so callous.

As a result, a bond of friendship grew in which one Christian was able to help meet the needs of another. Bob also said it was a great blessing to no longer see those chickens in the backyard!

This is just another case of being aware and sensitive to the needs of others. It is amazing, when you allow yourself to be sensitive, how painless a personal sacrifice becomes. Without personal contact this sensitivity becomes more remote and less apparent.

Thus if you want to give God control of your finances, you must:

1. Daily surrender to God every financial decision, no matter how large or how small.

2. Accept God's wisdom for every decision.

3. Give the minimum testimony to God of His ownership.

4. Willingly seek to share with other people, even if it requires a sacrifice to do so.

13
Principles of Financial Decision Making

HOW CAN A Christian make financial decisions according to God's plan? By understanding His directives. Every decision requires a thorough understanding of God's attitudes, and that understanding comes as a result of reading God's Word and communicating with Him.

One who never prays, or never listens while praying, cannot hear God speak through prayer; just as one who never reads God's Word cannot hear God speak through Scripture. If a Christian never asks God's direction on an investment or a financial decision, he will never get an answer.

These principles for financial decisions summarize how God would have us manage money.

1. Avoid Speculation.

Every Christian should seek God's increase and make no provision for speculative schemes. Many times enticing programs are not only unethical but border on being illegal. Included in those are pyramid franchising systems, multi-level marketing systems, unregistered stock offers, and scores of other questionable ventures.

Assess *every* "opportunity" in relation to your own commitment to Christ. *Do not* let others make your financial decisions for you. We are not to be as children, influenced by somebody's new idea. Make *your* decisions in light of your goals; evaluate whether a venture is necessary.

Often in speculative schemes you will lose your witness, your credibility, and your money. So *avoid* them.

Money that may take years to save can be lost in an instant. Even worse is the compromise of a Christian who has talked others into the same trap.

Precondition your attitudes to avoid speculative "opportunities." The temptation of easy money and the emotionalism of its sponsors will sorely test your commitment. But Satan doesn't have to attack in a "spiritual" area if he gets a foothold in your finances, because that will soon affect you spiritually.

2. Keep Your Finances Current.

The second principle of financial decision making is to always manage your finances on a current basis. In other words, make no provision in your financial planning to borrow money beyond your ability to repay, even for one day. Many Christians have become involved in investment programs they could not afford and borrowed money to invest where repayment was dependent on a future event. To do so is to flirt with financial disaster.

If what you buy jeopardizes your future financial freedom, forget it. Impulse buying, either for investment or consumption, is disastrous. When you evaluate a purchase, investment, or otherwise, consider the obligation in light of *known incomes.*

Certainly that is a conservative attitude, but that philosophy is directed toward long-range peace, not short-range profit. "For which one of you, when he wants to build a tower, does not first sit down and calculate the cost, to see if he has enough to complete it? Otherwise, when he has laid a foundation, and is not able to finish, all who observe it begin to ridicule him, saying, 'This man began to build and was not able to finish'" (Luke 14.28–30). Plan for tomorrow by prudence today; make your plans in light of present circumstances, not on some future event.

Maintain the principle of staying debt free; make *every* decision on the basis of whether it may ultimately result in bondage.

3. Consider Your Witness.

Consider every decision on the basis of its effect on the work and reputation of Christ. Do not put God into a financial corner and place Him in the role of a "bailer"; I suspect God does not like to sit in the back of a leaky boat and continually have to bail us out. We are told in 1 Corinthians 10:31, "Whether, then, you eat or drink or whatever you do, do all to the glory of God."

To launch out on feelings, even in doing God's work, and then to depend on God to bail you out is *not* according to His plan. Christians in full-time ministry should accept this as one of the basic financial decisions for doing God's work. If one must borrow outside of God's people in order to do His work, beware! That is not according to His plan. "The rich rules over the poor, and the borrower becomes the lender's slave" (Proverbs 22:7).

God *will not* frustrate His work for lack of money, neither will He place a Christian organization in servitude to a secular institution.

This same principle applies to dealing unethically with others. As stated earlier, there are *no* small lies or small thefts. There are only liars and thieves.

If you deal unfairly or unethically with someone, then it is *your* witness that will suffer. Establish that no matter the circumstance you will tell the *whole truth* to the best of your ability. There is no simple way to accomplish that for, frequently, just when you are most vulnerable, an "opportunity" will arise. If you stumble, make restitution and admit your error. God will honor your commitment.

4. *Give to the Needs of Others.*

Avoid lending to another person in need where *giving* is possible. Why? If someone in need approaches you for a loan, you are much better off to give. The witness and fellowship that provides will last while the temporary gratitude of a loan quickly fades.

I recall reading an article in which the question was asked: "What is a distant relative?" The answer: "It is a close relative you loan money to." Unfortunately, the same thing is often true with Christians. What is a distant Christian friend? It is a close Christian friend to whom you loaned money.

If someone approaches you for financial help in acquiring wants or desires, then you should question whether to supply them at all. But if they are in need and on your heart, you have a responsibility from God to supply that need.

5. *Never Co-sign.*

Co-signing means to pledge your assets against the debts of someone else. Scripture specifically forbids this whenever it speaks of "surety" or "striking of hands." There are many references to this in Proverbs.

It is interesting to note that Solomon, king and ruler of Israel, wrote much about not co-signing. It seems obvious that time after time lenders came before him collecting co-signed debts, taking every possession from those who co-signed. He noted how ridiculous that was, saying, "Friend, they'll not only take your house, they'll take your bed with it."

This concept goes beyond personal co-signing. It also applied to business co-signing. If you work for a company and consistently co-sign notes (with the possible exception of a privately held business), you are also violating this principle.

"My son, if you have become surety for your neighbor, have given a pledge for a stranger, if you have been snared with the words of your mouth, have been caught with the words of your mouth, do this then, my son, and deliver yourself; since you have come into the hand of your neighbor, go, humble yourself, and importune your neighbor" (Proverbs 6:1–3).

Of all the areas of Scripture, this would seem to be one of the most explicit. Yet, we continually violate this principle and rationalize it with human logic. Ask any banker what type of loans he considers the most likely to default and practically everyone will say co-signed notes. Not only is co-signing a violation of the principle of surety but, by doing so, the co-signer may be interfering with God's plan for someone else.

6. *Avoid Indulgence.*

Discern the difference between needs, wants, and desires in every purchase. That applies not only to purchases of material goods, but investments as well. Before you invest, discern *why* you are investing. Is it to help you fulfill a need? Is it to help you further God's work? Or is it to satisfy a hungry ego? What will you do with the money if God multiplies it?

If you believe the purchase is within God's will, you will have peace. But if you assess that the purchase is a desire or a whim, stop to recheck God's principles. Many Christians are frustrated because they cannot distinguish between luxuries and necessities. Consequently, they seek fulfillment through the same channels as non-Christians and then wonder why they have a fruitless Christian walk.

I believe God wants us to live comfortably. But He does not want us to live *lavishly.*

At a time when our resources could be used to promote God's work throughout the world, we should evaluate every financial motive. "Do not love the world, nor the things in the world. If anyone loves the world, the love of the Father is not in him. For all that is in the world, the lust of the flesh and the lust of the eyes and the boastful pride of life, is not from the Father, but is from the world" (1 John 2:15-16).

7. *Prepare for Decreases.*

Being prepared for unexpected decreases in funds is a vital part of keeping current. When you make a financial decision, consider what would happen if you have even a small decrease in funds.

This is especially important when the wife works and expenses are incurred, based on two incomes. What if you are forced to reduce your income? Are you prepared to adjust as necessary to live within your means? What if God asks you to do something in His work that requires a reduced income? To the Christian who is totally trusting in Christ, the quality of life is independent of the circumstances, as Paul states in Philippians 4:12-13: "I know how to get along with humble means, and I also know how to live in prosperity; in any and every circumstance I have learned the secret of being filled and going hungry, both of having abundance and suffering need. I can do all things through Him who strengthens me."

Do not operate at the upper limit of your income, but make your financial decisions considering you may need to reduce your level of living. The ability to thank God in every circumstance demonstrates full dependence and trust in Him.

8. *If You Don't Have Peace, Don't Buy.*

Often we are not responsive enough to God's Word or to His presence to hear Him except through that inner turmoil known as a *lack of peace.* As a last resort, God will use this to provide direction. Accordingly, *if you do not have peace, do not get involved.* If a quick decision is required, do not get involved. Take the time to think and to pray about it; perhaps God has an alternative provision for you.

Many times I have made decisions on the spur of the moment. There are very few of those decisions that I have not later regretted. Determine that you *will not* make a decision under pressure. You may miss a few "good deals," but you will miss a great many bad ones also. "It is the blessing of the Lord that makes rich, and He adds no sorrow to it" (Proverbs 10:22).

Become sensitive to God's inner guidance; He will *always* provide direction if you are seeking it. Even when we fail to see the right path clearly in God's Word or fail to hear it in prayer, God will place an unrest inside that will keep us out of financial bondage.

Summary

Principles of Financial Breathing
1. Acknowledge God's ownership daily (Proverbs 3:4-6).
2. Accept God's direction (1 Thessalonians 5:18).
3. Establish the tithe (Luke 6:38).
4. Seek self-sacrifice (Luke 3:11).

Principles of Financial Decision Making
1. Avoid speculation (Proverbs 28:22).
2. Keep your finances current (Luke 14:28-30).
3. Consider your witness (1 Corinthians 10:31).
4. Give to the needs of others (2 Corinthians 9:13).
5. Never co-sign (Proverbs 6:1-3).
6. Avoid indulgences (1 Timothy 6:8).
7. Prepare for decreases (Philippians 4:12-13).
8. Seek God's peace (Proverbs 10:22).

This concludes our study of God's financial principles. I would like to challenge you to pray concerning how God would have you specifically change your lifestyle as a result of the concepts you have learned.

Part Three

USING GOD'S PLAN

14

Practical Applications

A FRIEND ONCE told me that information without application leads to frustration. To help avoid that common problem, in this section you will find ideas to help you apply God's principles of finance.

Each area should be carefully and prayerfully considered and then acted upon. Some specifics, such as a family budget, may seem rudimentary, but unless the basic areas are under control, the more complex ones cannot be.

Family Financial Planning

Family Communication Goals.

Communication is vital to family financial planning. To enhance that communication, some questions are listed for both husband and wife. I suggest that each of you do them separately. Write down every answer as if your spouse were asking the question. Then, during a time when you won't be interrupted, evaluate these together. Begin your evaluation by praying about your time together, opening your hearts to the Holy Spirit.

The questions are intended to enrich the discussions of mature, communicating Christian couples. They are not intended to become an additional source of friction for couples totally void of communication. Use them as tools of love, not ammunition for war.

A. PERSONAL GOALS

To be answered as if your (husband) (wife) were asking:

1. What are your personal goals in life?

2. What personal goals have you set for this coming year?

3. How can I help you achieve your goals?

4. What can I do to help or improve our financial situation?

5. Do you feel there is a proper balance between my outside activity and my time at home?

6. Would you like me to do more things around the house such as cleaning and decorating?

7. In regard to my activities outside the home, what would you consider as priorities?

8. Do you feel I need to improve in any area, such as my appearance, manners, attitudes?

B. MARRIAGE GOALS

1. Do you believe our marriage is maturing and we are coming closer together?

2. Do you feel we clearly communicate?

3. Do you feel that I am sensitive to your personal needs?

4. What would you like me to say or do the next time you seem to be angry with me or you are not speaking to me?

5. The next time you are late in getting ready to go some place, what would you like me to say or do?

6. What would you like me to say or do the next time you seem to be getting impatient with something or someone?

7. What would you like me to say or do if you begin to criticize someone?

8. Do you feel I need to improve in getting ready on time or getting to meetings on time?

9. Do you feel we should go out together more often?

10. Do I make cutting remarks about you or criticize you in front of other people?

11. What should I do in public to encourage you?

12. Do I respond to your suggestions and ideas as if I had already thought of them instead of thanking you and encouraging you to contribute more?

13. Do I tell you enough about what I do every day?

14. What little acts of love do I do for you?

15. What most often causes you to get angry with me?

16. Do I convey my admiration and respect often enough?

17. Do we "play act" a happy marriage in front of other people?

18. What do you think 1 Corinthians 7:3-7 means?

19. Do you feel we need to see a marriage counselor?

20. What are the responsibilities of a "help-mate"?

21. Do we give each other the same attention we did before we had children?

C. FAMILY GOALS

1. What are our family goals?

2. Are we achieving our family goals?

3. a. (Wife) What can I do to help you fulfill your responsibilities as spiritual leader of our family?

   b. (Husband) How can I better fulfill my responsibilities as spiritual leader?

4. Do you feel we are meeting the spiritual needs of our family?

5. What kinds of family devotions should we have?

6. List the responsibilities stated for the husband and wife in the following passages:

   1 Peter 3:1-2 _____

   Colossians 3:18-19 _____

   1 Timothy 2:11-15 _____

   1 Corinthians 11:3 _____

   Ephesians 5:17-33 _____

7. Do you feel we have a consistent prayer life together?

8. Do you feel we are adequately involved in our local church?

9. Do you feel we are meeting the physical needs of our family?

10. Should we improve our eating habits?

11. Should we get more exercise?

12. Do we make good use of our time? For example, do we watch too much TV? Should we have more hobbies? Read more?

13. How and when shall we discipline our children? What do you think is the biblical viewpoint of discipline?

14. On a sheet of paper, list the responsibilities of parents and their children in the following passages:
    Colossians 3:20-21 _____
    Hebrews 12:5-11 _____
    Proverbs 3:11-12 _____

15. What kind of instruction and training should we be giving our children in the home?

D. FINANCIAL GOALS

1. Do you think I handle money properly?

2. How could I better manage our money?

3. Do you think I am:
   Too frugal? _____
   Too extravagant? _____
   About right? _____
   Why? _____

4. Do you think I accept financial responsibilities well?

5. Do you think we communicate financial goals well?

6. What is your immediate financial goal?

7. What is your primary goal for this year?

8. What is your plan for our children's education?

   _____

9. What is your retirement goal?

   _____

10. What do you think about tithing?

    Is tithing necessary? _____

    How much? _____

    Where should it go? _____

11. How do you feel about *giving* in general?

    _____

12. Do you like the way we live?

    _____

13. What changes would you like to see?

    _____

The Family Budget.

Why is a budget necessary?

—To help those who are not living within their means to do so.

—To help those with a potential surplus to fix their level of expenses.

—To help establish a reasonable level of living for those who want to do so.

The initial tendency is to create an unrealistic budget, one that makes no provision for variables like clothes, dentists, doctors, or entertainment. To do so will only frustrate your efforts, cause your budget to fail and cause you and your spouse to lose confidence in budgeting.

The next tendency is to create a budget—and then stop! There is no magic in a budget; it is only a written expression of what you must do to be a good steward. Action is required to make it work, and you may need to make sacrifices to live within your budget.

Two budgets are actually necessary. The first determines your present status. The second determines your goals (a budget based on spendable income). If you are really serious about being the best steward possible, then a budget is necessary. But no amount of intention is effective without action.

Steps to Making a Budget.

In making and using a budget, there are several logical steps, each requiring individual effort. A sample form for budgeting is shown in Figure 1 (page 126). Use this form to guide your budget preparation.

Step 1—*List Expenditures in the Home on a Monthly Basis.*

Fixed Expenses include:
—Tithe
—Federal income taxes (if taxes are deducted, ignore this item)

—State income taxes (if taxes are deducted, ignore this item)
—Federal Social Security taxes (if taxes are deducted, ignore this item)
—Housing expense (payment/rent)
—Residence taxes
—Residence insurance
—Other

Variable Expenses include:
—Food
—Outstanding debts
—Utilities
—Insurance (life, health, auto)
—Entertainment, recreation
—Clothing allowance
—Medical, dental
—Savings
—Miscellaneous

   NOTE: In order to accurately determine variable expenses, it is sug-
          gested that both husband and wife keep an expense diary for
          thirty days. List *every* expenditure, even small purchases.

Step 2—*List Available Income per Month.*

   NOTE: If you operate on a non-fixed monthly income, use a yearly
          average divided into months.

—Salary
—Rents
—Notes
—Interest
—Dividends
—Income tax refund
—Other

Step 3—*Compare Income Versus Expenses.*

If total income exceeds total expenses, you only have to implement a
method of budget control in your home. If, however, expenses exceed income
(or more stringent controls in spending are desired), additional steps are necessary. In that case, you need an analysis of each budget area to reduce
expenses. These areas are outlined below.

Budget Problems Analysis

   A. *Bookkeeping Errors*—In order to maintain an orderly budget, it is necessary to keep records. This includes both the previously established home
budget and adequate bank records. Many people fail to exercise any control

over checking accounts and seldom or never balance their records. It is *impossible* to balance a home budget without balancing your checking account. Go to your bank account manager and ask for help if you cannot balance your records. The following are some helpful hints for this area.

1. Use a ledger type checkbook (as opposed to a stub type).
2. List all check numbers before writing the *first* check.
3. Record *every* check in the ledger immediately, in detail.
4. Appoint one person to keep the ledger and checkbook.
5. Balance the ledger *every* month.

B. *Hidden Debts*—These include bills that may not come due on a monthly basis. Nevertheless your budget must provide for reduction of those items; failure to do so will only frustrate your efforts to be a good steward. Some debts of this type might include the following.

1. Books, magazines
2. Audio and video cassettes, compact discs
3. Retail outlet stores' credit
4. Family, friends
5. Doctor, dentist
6. Taxes
7. Yearly insurance premiums

C. *Impulse Items*—As mentioned in an earlier section, impulse buying is common to most of us. Unfortunately, credit cards have provided the means to buy beyond the means to repay (to the sacrifice of other needs).

A list of impulse purchases can range from homes, cars, and expensive trips to tools and entertainment items. The value is not the issue; its necessity is. Consider every purchase in light of your budgeted items and avoid buying anything on impulse. The following are some hints to reduce impulse buying.

1. Use a delayed-purchase plan. (Buy nothing that is outside your budget unless you wait for thirty days.)
2. During those thirty days, determine to find at least two items similar to the one you want to purchase to compare prices.
3. Allow only one new purchase at a time that is not part of your planned budget.
4. *Never* use credit cards for impulse purchases.
5. Stay out of the stores.

D. *Gifts*—These items can jeopardize a budget quickly. It is unfortunate that in our society we tend to place more emphasis on the gift than the giver, and too many times busy parents substitute expensive gifts for personal involvement with their children. Begin to seek alternatives for costly gifts—both within the family and with friends. Regardless of your financial status, determine to bring this area under control. The following are some hints.

1. Keep an event calendar during the year and plan ahead.
2. Initiate some *family* crafts and *make* the gifts you need. For example: wall plaques, knickknacks, purses, or string art. Not only do these make good gifts, but they reflect effort and love.
3. Draw family names for selected gifts rather than each family member giving to everyone.
4. Do not buy gifts on credit.
5. Help your children *earn* money for gifts.
6. Send cards on special birthdays and anniversaries.

Budget Busters

"Budget busters" are the large potential problem areas that can ruin a budget. Failure to control even one of these problems can result in financial disaster. This area is evaluated by *typical* budget percentages for a $12,000 to $30,000 income. Naturally, these percentages are not absolute and will vary with income and geographical location. The percentages listed total 100 percent. Remember, if your expenditures exceed the percentage allowed in one area, you must reduce another.

A. *Housing* (38 percent of net income).

Typically, this is one of the largest home budget problems. Many families buy a home they can't afford, motivated by peer pressure or some other pressure. It is *not* necessary for everyone to *own* a home. The decision to buy or rent should be based on needs and financial ability rather than internal or external pressure. The following are some hints to observe.

1. Purchase a home only if the total payments (mortgage, taxes, insurance and utilities) do not exceed 38 percent of your net income
2. Do not finance a second mortgage for the down payment.
3. Consider the monthly upkeep of a home. This usually averages 10 percent of the monthly payment.
4. Consider the tax deduction for interest paid as a reduction in monthly payment.
5. If trading, consider whether you *need* to do so.
6. Secure at least three insurance estimates. Normally, this type of insurance can best be satisfied with a comprehensive package (homeowners, renters policy, etc.). Use of the deductible feature will substantially reduce premiums.

B. *Food* (12 percent of net income).

Many families buy too much food. Others buy too little. Typically, the average American family buys the wrong type of food. The reduction of a family's food bill requires quantity and quality planning.

One of the best ways to plan food purchases is to decide on your daily menu *first*. Once you have established what your family is to eat, then select the various ingredients. Few homemakers take the time and effort to actually write out daily menus, but once the habit is developed, its benefits are obvious. Grocery shopping ceases to be a hunt-and-find weekly expedition; it becomes another step in financial planning. The following are some hints for grocery shopping.

1. Always use a *written* list of needs.
2. Try to conserve gas by buying food for a longer time period and in larger quantities.
3. Avoid buying when hungry (especially if you're a "sugarholic").
4. Use a calculator, if possible, to total purchases.
5. Reduce or eliminate paper products—paper plates, cups, napkins. (Use cloth napkins.)
6. Evaluate where to purchase sundry items such as shampoo, mouthwash, toothpaste. (These are normally somewhat cheaper at chain drug store sales.)
7. Avoid processed and sugar-coated cereals. (These are expensive and have little nutritional value.)
8. Avoid prepared foods, such as frozen dinners, pot pies, cakes, cookies. (You are paying for expensive labor that you can provide.)
9. Determine good meat cuts that are available from roasts or shoulders and have the butcher cut these for you. (Buying steaks by the package on sale is fairly inexpensive also.)
10. Try generic or house brand canned products. (They are normally cheaper and just as nutritious.)
11. Avoid products in a cyclical price hike. Substitute or eliminate.
12. Shop for advertised specials. (These are usually posted in the store window.)
13. Use manufacturer's coupons (cents-off on an item or items) only if you were going to buy the item anyway and it is cheaper than another brand would be without the coupon.
14. When possible, purchase food in bulk quantities from large discount stores; the per-item cost is cheaper. Do not buy from convenience stores except in case of emergency.
15. Avoid buying *non-grocery* items in a grocery supermarket, except on sale. (These are normally "high markup" items.)
16. For baby food, use normal foods processed through a blender.
17. *Leave the children at home* to avoid unnecessary pressure.
18. Check *every* item as it is being "rung up" at the store and again when you get home.
19. Consider canning fresh vegetables whenever possible. Make bulk purchases with other families at farmers' markets and such. (NOTE: Buy canning supplies during off seasons.)

C. *Automobiles* (15 percent of net income).

The advertising media refer to us as "consumers" but that's not always the best description. I believe that P. T. Barnum had a more apt word—suckers. Often we are unwise in our decision making when it comes to our machines—especially cars.

Many families will buy new cars they cannot afford and trade them long before their utility is depleted. Those who buy a new car, keep it for less than four years, and then trade it for a new model have wasted the maximum amount of money. Some people, such as salespeople that drive a great deal, need new cars frequently; most of us do not. We trade cars because we *want* to—not because we *have* to. Many factors enter here such as ego, esteem, maturity, etc. But few Christians seek God's will for the purchase of cars and so they suffer later because of the financial strains placed on home finances. The following are budget hints for buying automobiles.

1. Evaluate your reason for trading. Are you simply "tired" of your present car? (When you get that "car bug," the old machine will appear to be falling apart.)
2. Can your present car be repaired without great expense? How many miles are left in it?
3. Do you *really* need a brand new car, or will a used one do? (Unless the purchase is for business use, the new car may be unnecessary.)
4. What does your budget say about a new car?
5. Do you still owe on your present car? (If you do and you finance the new car, you are paying the maximum interest rate again.)
6. Pay cash if possible. Otherwise obtain your own loan outside the car dealership and bargain as if on a cash basis. (Consider buying on a "no-trade-in" basis and selling your old car privately.)
7. If it is a used car, talk to the previous owner *before* you buy. (Most people will tell you honestly about their cars if you ask.)
8. Bargain for a short-term 100 percent guarantee on a used car. (Avoid any percentage contract—you will lose.)
9. Do not be pressured by sales tactics. Set your own price and type of car desired and be willing to lose the "good deals" that require quick decisions.
10. Be willing to accept minor difficulties on a used car to secure substantial price reductions. (Be sure you anticipate those repairs.)
11. If buying a new car, avoid purchasing a new model when they first come out. (Buy year-end close-outs or demonstrators.)
12. A cheaper model with the same options as the luxury model will provide *substantial* savings (just a little less prestige).
13. Avoid the use of credit life insurance. It is expensive and unnecessary if you have an adequate insurance program.

/ / /

14. Avoid new car leases except where extremely high mileage is required and a substantial tax saving is offered as well.

Maintaining cars.

1. Learn to perform the routine maintenance: oil change, lubrication, tune-up. (The purchase of approximately $25 worth of tools will return at least $100 per year in service costs and repair bills.)
2. Repair minor conditions yourself and do them immediately. Do not let "little" problems pile up or you will be tempted to trade cars.
3. Purchase oil, grease, spark plugs, points, and the like from a wholesale distributor. Use best grades only and try to combine purchases with two or more friends for best buys.
4. Use a *written* maintenance chart for every car and attend to routine maintenance diligently. *Regular* maintenance will extend the life of a car.
5. Look into purchasing "take-off" tires from dealers who service fleet cars and cars owned by government agencies. First-line radial tires are available that provide more mileage than most second-line new tires.
6. Check your car's gasoline rating and use the cheapest gasoline recommended.
7. Get insurance estimates from at least three major insurance companies before purchasing. As stated in a previous section, evaluate as follows:
   —Select adequate liability coverage.
   —Consider collision and comprehensive coverage.
   (NOTE: Can you afford to have your car repaired if you have an accident in which you are at fault?)
   —The need for medical benefits.
   —Use at least $100 deductibles with above.

D. *Debts* (5 percent of net income).

It would be great if most budgets included 5 percent debts or less. Unfortunately, the norm in American families is far in excess of this amount. As previously discussed, credit cards, bank loans, and installment credit have made it possible for families to go deeply into debt. What things can you do once this situation exists?

—Destroy *all* of your credit cards as a first step.
—Establish a payment schedule that includes all creditors.
—Contact all creditors, honestly relate your problems, and arrange an equitable repayment plan.
—Buy on a cash basis and sacrifice your wants and desires until you are *current.*

E. *Insurance* (5 percent of net income, assuming you have some employee's insurance).

It is unfortunate to see so many families misled in this area. Few people understand how much is needed or what kind is necessary. Who would be foolish enough to buy a Rolls Royce when he or she could only afford a Chevrolet? Yet many purchase high-cost insurance even though their needs dictate otherwise.

Insurance should be used as supplementary *provision* for the family, not protection or profit. An insurance plan is not designed for saving money or for retirement. Ask anyone who assumed it was; the ultimate result was disillusionment and disappointment.

Do not allow someone else to decide what and how much you need. Select insurance based on God's plan for *your* life.

In our society, insurance *can* be used as an inexpensive vehicle to provide future family income and thus release funds today for family use and the Lord's work. In excess, this same insurance can put a family in debt, steal the Lord's money, and transfer dependence to the world.

One of your best insurance assets is to have a trustworthy agent in charge of your program. A good insurance agent is usually one who can select from several different companies to provide you with the best possible buy and who will create a brief, uncomplicated plan to analyze your exact needs.

Christians must learn to be prudent and creative in the area of insurance just as in any other purchase. A prudent application of insurance can help avoid calamitous financial debt by *reasonable* purchases.

1. *Adequate life insurance.* Considering the low cost of death provision, a Christian should evaluate life insurance, especially when there are minor children involved. Proper provision for the family involves carrying sufficient insurance to remove the burden from others if possible. That *does not* mean that God dies with you and, therefore, every contingency must be covered.

The discussion often arises about term insurance versus permanent or "whole life" insurance. Generally, unless insurance premiums can be tax deductible, term insurance is far less costly. The principle to observe is to purchase insurance for *provision*, not *investment*. Insurance cash reserves typically yield less than interest-bearing accounts. Therefore, purchase what is required at the least cost.

Term insurance is now available that extends to sixty-five or seventy years of age and will probably be extended further, but as age advances, the need for insurance normally diminishes. If whole life policies are in existence, a thorough analysis should be made by a qualified insurance agent to determine whether the policies should remain in force or be converted. Particular attention should be given to at least borrowing the cash reserve of the policy and reinvesting in a secure, higher interest program.

2. *Major medical insurance.* Except for the chronically ill with pre-

existing coverage, hospitalization insurance is generally a poor expenditure. (The exception to this would be "group" insurance policies. These normally provide inexpensive, broad-range medical coverage.) However, major medical insurance that will pay most costs involved in serious illnesses is relatively inexpensive. For example, for a family of five insurance paying 80 percent of medical expenses costs less than $800 per year.

F. *Recreation/Entertainment* (5 percent of net income).

We are a recreation-oriented country. That is not necessarily bad if put in the proper perspective. But those who are in debt cannot use their creditor's money to entertain themselves. The normal tendency is to escape problems, if only for a short while—even if the problems then become more acute. Christians must resist that urge and control recreation and entertainment expenses while in debt.

What a terrible witness it is for a Christian who is already in financial bondage to indulge himself at the expense of others. God knows we need rest and relaxation, and He will often provide it from unexpected sources once our *attitude* is correct. Every believer, whether in debt or not, should seek to reduce entertainment expenses. That can usually be done without sacrificing quality family time. The following are some recreation hints.

1. Plan vacations during "off seasons" if possible.
2. Consider a camping vacation to avoid motel and food expenses. (Christian friends can pool the expenses of camping items.)
3. Select vacation areas in your general locale.
4. Consider swapping residences with a Christian family in another locale to provide an inexpensive vacation.
5. Play family games in place of paid entertainment (like some of those unused games received at Christmas).
6. Consider two or more families taking vacation trips together to reduce expense and increase fellowship.
7. If flying, use the least expensive coach fare (i.e., late night or early morning usually saves 10–20 percent).

G. *Clothing* (5 percent of net income).

Many families in debt sacrifice this area in their budget because of excesses in other areas. And yet, with prudent planning and buying, your family can be clothed neatly without great expense. This requires *effort* on your part in terms of the following.

—Saving enough money to buy without using credit.
—Educating family members on care of clothing.
—Applying discipline with children to enforce these habits.
—Developing skills in making and mending clothing.

Learn to be utilizers of your resources rather than consumers. How many families have closets full of clothes they no longer wear because they are "out of style"?

Many families with large surplus incomes spend excessively in the area of clothes. Assess whether it really matters that you have all of the latest styles. Do your purchases reflect good utility rather than ego? Do you buy clothes to satisfy a need or a desire? The following are some budget hints.

1. Make as many of the children's clothes as time will allow. (Average savings of 50–60 percent.)
2. Make a *written* list of clothing needs and purchase during the "off" season as much as possible.
3. Select outfits that can be mixed and used in multiple combinations rather than as a single set.
4. Frequent the discount outlets that carry unmarked "name brand" goods.
5. Frequent authentic factory outlet stores for close-out values of top quality.
6. Select home washable fabrics in new clothes.
7. Use coin-operated dry cleaning machines instead of commercial cleaners.
8. Practice early repair for damaged clothing. Learn to utilize all clothing fully (especially children's wear).

H. *Medical-dental expenses* (5 percent of net income).

Anticipate these expenses in your budget and set aside funds regularly; failure to do so will wreck your plans and lead to indebtedness. Do not sacrifice family health due to lack of planning, but at the same time, do not use doctors excessively. Proper prevention is much cheaper than correction. You can avoid many dental bills by teaching children to eat the right foods and clean their teeth properly. Your dentist will supply all the information you need on this subject. Many doctor bills can be avoided in the same way. Take proper care of your body through diet, rest, and exercise, and it will respond with good health. Abuse your body and you must ultimately pay through illnesses and malfunctions. This is not to say that all illnesses or problems are caused by neglect, but a great many are.

Do not hesitate to question doctors and dentists in advance about costs. Also, educate yourself enough to discern when you are getting good value for your money. Most ethical professionals will not take offense at your questions. If they do, that may be a hint to change services.

Shop around for prescriptions. You will be amazed to discover the wide variance in prices from one store to the next. Ask about generic drugs. These are usually much less expensive and are just as effective.

1. *Savings* (5 percent of net income).

It is important that some savings be established in the budget. Otherwise, the use of credit becomes a lifelong necessity and debt, a way of life. Your savings will allow you to purchase items for cash and shop for the best buys, irrespective of the store. The following are some savings hints.

1. Use a company payroll withdrawal, if possible. This removes the money before you receive it.
2. Use an automatic bank withdrawal from your checking account.
3. Write your savings account a check just as if it were a creditor.
4. When an existing debt is paid off, reallocate that money to savings.

J. *Miscellaneous* (5 percent of net income).

This can include a myriad of items. Some of the expenses occur monthly, whereas others occur on an as-needed basis (such as appliances).

One of the most important factors in home expenses is *you*. If you can perform routine maintenance and repair, considerable expenses can be avoided. Many people rationalize not doing those things on the basis that their time is too valuable. That is nonsense. If every hour of the day is tied up in the pursuit of money as previously defined, then you're in bondage. A part of care and maintenance around the home relates to family life, particularly the training of children. When they see Mom and Dad willing to do some physical labor to help around the home, they will learn good habits. But if you refuse to get involved, why should they? Where will they ever learn the skills of self-sufficiency?

Some men avoid working on home projects because they say they lack the necessary skills. Well, those skills are *learned,* not *gifted.* There are many good books that detail every area of home maintenance. In the future many of those skills will be necessities rather than choices. The following are some budget hints.

1. *Reducing household appliance costs.*
    a. *Maintaining existing units.*
    —Review service manuals for ordinary maintenance care and perform as often as required.
    —Keep a *written* maintenance chart on or near the unit.
    —Purchase a shop manual from manufacturer. (Most major manufacturers will sell this upon written request.)
    —Use the unit within suggested standards. (Example: Do not overload washers and dryers.)
    —If an out-of-warranty unit breaks down, use the fix-it guide to determine the problem and repair it if possible. *Before* calling outside service, seek free counsel from Christian friends (often someone you know is a fix-it type).
    —Before discarding the old unit for a new one, consider an overhaul of the existing machine

    b. *Purchasing appliances.*
    —Use a consumer buying guide to determine the best manufacturer.
    —Select a unit based on functional use and not on dials and gadgets. (Deluxe models cost more but do not perform better and usually require more maintenance.)

—Shop around and compare prices on the leading products. (Keep a written record of findings.)

—Look for volume dealers who carry name brand products under their own labels.

—Purchase the item on a cash basis without a trade-in (the seller will discount for cash without trade).

—Avoid dealer service contracts. They are sometimes expensive and often frustrating. (If the product warranty is not sufficient, look for another brand.)

—Insist on *free* delivery and installation. (Dealer may resist, but probably will agree.)

—Look for similar used units in the newspaper or shopper's guide.

2. *Reducing furniture costs.*

—Consult a consumer buying index for best purchase value.

—Consider repairing and rebuilding used furniture of good quality. (Many good fix-it guides explain how to refinish and reupholster furniture.)

—Consult local shopper's guide for good quality buys.

—Shop local garage sales.

—Shop for discontinued furniture lines.

3. *Reducing "fixed" budget items.*
   a. *Saving on the telephone bill.*

—Evaluate the need for more than one telephone (how many calls received at night, convenience versus cost).

—Use a standard telephone in place of a special model.

—Use a three-minute egg timer for long-distance calls. (Be willing to schedule only three-minute calls to your family.)

—Call long distance during reduced-rate hours whenever possible.

—Limit the number of calls by strict agreement.

—Keep a *written* long distance phone log (date, time, duration) next to each telephone.

—Write letters instead of calling frequently. (Letters show more real consideration sometimes.)

   b. *Keeping the cost of electricity down.*

—With air conditioning or heating, check attic insulation, windows for air leaks, system filters (clean regularly), doors for air leaks, and excessive glass exposure.

—Attic insulation of at least 6" depth will save 10 percent in heating and air conditioning costs.

—Keep thermostats set at moderate comfort (68–70 degrees in winter; 74–78 degrees in summer).

—Delay using heating or air conditioning units until obvious discomfort is noticed.

—Lower system use when the house is vacant for eight hours or more.

—Use blankets instead of furnace for nighttime comfort.

—Close all vents in unused rooms and most of upstairs vents in two-story dwellings.

—Turn off unused lights; reduce bulb wattage in areas used only for "effect" lighting.

—Purchase 130 volt light bulbs. (They will last five times longer—normally available at electric company outlet stores.) Coordinate baths to conserve hot water. (Approximately 10 percent of hot water in the tank is used to heat the lines to bathrooms. Heat those lines as seldom as possible.)

—Insulate all exposed hot water lines.

—Optimize use of dishwasher, clothes washer, and dryer. (Fill them to capacity—but not over.)

—Stop dishwasher before drying cycle periodically. (Dishes dry normally from heat of previous wash cycle.)

—Use the cooking oven only for large food items. Coordinate baking to utilize the heated oven.

c. *Reducing home care costs.*

—Purchase a home sprayer for lawn spraying and pest control. It costs $25 but will save $200 to $300 over a three-year period.

—Reduce substantially your use of fertilizers and hybrid seed. Practice organic cultivation of grass and shrubs (i.e., use natural fertilizer from dairies or chicken farms).

—Use rental steam cleaner for carpets. For the average home that will cost $20 as opposed to $125 to $150 for professional carpet service.

—Use water-base, flat enamel paint in high-traffic areas. (It is washable and durable and easy to apply. Always use a high quality product.)

4. *Lowering costs in general areas of budgeting.*

—Shop for bank services where checking accounts are without cost. Even if you must bank by mail, the slight inconvenience will save per year.

—All pets cost money. Limit your pets to those you *really* care for and the family enjoys.

—Try reducing periodical subscriptions (newspapers, magazines, books, records). Before subscribing, purchase them at a store to evaluate how useful they are to you. Once you determine to subscribe to a periodical, longer contracts (two to three years) provide a substantial saving.

5. *Deciding whether to borrow in order to buy.*

—Avoid borrowing for highly depreciable or consumable items (pleasure cars, appliances, furniture, vacations, food). If you purchase those items for cash you will always be in a better bargaining position.

—Borrowing for household items such as appliances can bind you financially. You may find it difficult to escape the borrowing trap because of payments on the existing loans.

—Interest on credit card loans may exceed 50 percent* per year (due to interest compounded on delinquent payments).

—Installment loans may exceed 12 percent* per year and carry substantial prepayment penalties.

—Collateralized personal loans are generally the least costly method of financing.

—Credit life insurance on loans may cost two to three times as much as the equivalent amount in term life insurance.

Summary

At this point, you have the necessary tools to establish your own budget. Only one additional ingredient is necessary—desire. No budget will implement itself; it requires effort and good family *communication*.

Living on a budget is not only prudent, but it can be fun. As you have successes in various areas, share them with others. Challenge your children as well. Establish budget goals for them and rewards for achievement.

The following is a summarized list of the financial principles applicable to home financial planning. Study these and apply them. Then share God's blessings with others around you.

1. *Principles dealing with home finances.*
    a. Use a written plan.
    b. Provide for the Lord's work first.
    c. Excel at your tasks.
    d. Limit credit.
    e. Think before buying.
        —Is it necessary?
        —Does it reflect your Christian ethic?
        —Is it the best buy?
        —Is it an impulse item?
        —Does it add to or detract from the family?
        —Is it a highly depreciable item?
        —Does it require costly upkeep?
    f. Practice saving money regularly.
    g. Set your own goals—with your family.
    h. Get out of debt.
    i. Limit business involvement.

*Usually determined by state law.

j. Avoid indulgences, lavishness.

k. Seek good Christian counsel.

l. Stick to your plans.

2. *Purpose of a budget.*
   a. To define income versus expense.
   b. To detect problem areas.
   c. To provide a written plan.
   d. To aid in follow-up.
   e. To schedule money in and out of the home.

3. *What a budget will do.*
   a. Help you visualize your goals.
   b. Provide a written point of reference for husband and wife.
   c. Help family communications.
   d. Provide a written reminder.
   e. Reflect your habits.

4. *What a budget will not do.*
   a. Solve your immediate problems.
   b. Make you *use* it.
   c. Take the place of action.

5. *Learn how to:*
   a. Calculate actual expenses.
      —Use a thirty-day expense diary (notebook).
      —Use a checking account ledger.
      —Use a creditor ledger showing each debt due.
   b. Make out a family budget.
      —Define actual expenditures (present budget).
      —Define proposed expenditures (future budget).
      —Calculate income.
      —Calculate fixed expenses.
      —Calculate variable expenses.
   c. Use a budget.
      —Post it in the open.
      —Set an achievable goal.
      —Keep it up-to-date.
      —Establish a set time and day to review it.

NOTE: A workbook series on Christian finances is available for those who would like to study and/or teach these principles. Please contact Moody Press or your local Christian bookstore and ask for *How to Manage Your Money.* It is also available in computer software, complete with a User's Guide.

Figure 1—Monthly Income and Expenses

GROSS INCOME PER MONTH _____

- Salary _____
- Interest _____
- Dividends _____
- Other _____

LESS:

1. Tithe _____

2. Tax (Est. - Incl. Fed., State, FICA) _____

NET SPENDABLE INCOME _____

3. Housing _____
   - Mortgage (rent) _____
   - Insurance _____
   - Taxes _____
   - Electricity _____
   - Gas _____
   - Water _____
   - Sanitation _____
   - Telephone _____
   - Maintenance _____
   - Other _____

4. Food _____

5. Automobile(s) _____
   - Payments _____
   - Gas & Oil _____
   - Insurance _____
   - License/Taxes _____
   - Maint./Repair/Replace _____

6. Insurance _____
   - Life _____
   - Medical _____
   - Other _____

7. Debts _____
   - Credit Card _____
   - Loans & Notes _____
   - Other _____

8. Enter. & Recreation _____
   - Eating Out _____
   - Baby Sitters _____
   - Activities/Trips _____
   - Vacation _____
   - Other _____

9. Clothing _____

10. Savings _____

11. Medical Expenses _____
    - Doctor _____
    - Dentist _____
    - Drugs _____
    - Other _____

12. Miscellaneous _____
    - Toiletry, cosmetics _____
    - Beauty, barber _____
    - Laundry, cleaning _____
    - Allowances, lunches _____
    - Subscriptions _____
    - Gifts (incl. Christmas) _____
    - Cash _____
    - Other _____

13. School/Child Care _____
    - Tuition _____
    - Materials _____
    - Transportation _____
    - Day Care _____

14. Investments _____

15. Unallocated Surplus Income[1] _____

TOTAL EXPENSES _____

INCOME VS. EXPENSES
- Net Spendable Income _____
- Less Expenses _____

[1]This category is used when surplus income is received. This would be kept in the checking account to be used within a few weeks; otherwise, it should be transferred to an allocated category.

Figure 2—Insurance Needs

1. Present income per year $_____
2. Life insurance premium
   per year   (_____)
3. Savings per year   (_____)
4. Investments per year   (_____)
5. Estimated living costs
   for husband per year   (_____)
6. Other deductions
   per year   (_____)
7. Total   (_____)
8. Income required per year $_____
   (subtract step 7 from
   step 1)
9. Company retirement,
   Social Security, etc.
   supplied upon
   husband's death   _____
10. Investment income,
    other   _____
11. Wife's, children's income   _____
12. Total (Steps 8-11)   (_____)
13. Income provision
    needed per year $_____
    (Subtract step 12 from step 7)

NOTE 1—Multiply line 13 by 18. This equals approximate insurance necessary to continue present standard of living with no asset reduction.

NOTE 2—Add allowance for college or business to this amount.

NOTE 3—Total amount needed will vary if provision is anticipated for a *fixed* number of years only.

> Example: $100,00 insurance needed to generate a $10,000 per year income.
> Income earning rate estimate = 6 percent.
> At the end of a ten-year period, approximately $43,000 of insurance remains.

II

USING YOUR MONEY WISELY

My wife, Judy, and I dedicate this book
to the supporters of Christian Financial Concepts,
who make this work possible.

Contents

Dear Christian friends,

Finances are an integral part of daily living today and can affect us either positively or negatively. Through His Word, God gave us specific guidelines to direct our lives so that we can enjoy the blessings He promises us. There are more than sixteen hundred verses in the Bible that deal directly with financial situations. Only love is discussed more often than money in the New Testament, which says something about the importance of finances.

Using Your Money Wisely presents the financial principles found in the Bible and applies them to daily life in the home, business, and church. These simple principles will forever change the way you think about finances. I pray they will be used as a guide for making financial decisions in accordance with God's Word.

Because of Christ,
Larry Burkett

Part One

ATTITUDE

1

Fear of the Future

MANY OF THE decisions that God's people make on a day-by-day basis are motivated not by trust in God but rather by fear of the future. That is most often true with financial decisions. For example, many people stay with jobs they fear changing. That is particularly true with those who are forty and older. Society has convinced us to large degree that those over forty are past their prime. That is nonsense and runs totally contrary to God's intention.

Fear of the future causes Christian families to scrimp and sacrifice for retirement. Often the total focus of the earlier years is toward the eventful day when "we can relax and really enjoy ourselves." Unfortunately, the same fear that necessitated the hoarding for the latter years then forces further sacrifices "just in case."

I don't mean to imply that some planning is not God's will; obviously it is. But when a Christian looks inside and finds primary attitudes of fear and worry, bondage has occurred.

"Would a Man Rob God?"

Many families literally rob God and their families because of that underlying fear. They start a savings or insurance plan initially with an eye toward family provision but then more contingencies must be provided for. Finally there are so many contingencies that no amount of protection is adequate, and fear pervades all decisions about money. Some are willing to give a tithe from regular income, but any invasion of their surplus prompts resentment and alarm.

The net result of this life-style is bitterness, conflict within the family, and growing separation from God.

My heartfelt concern for this spiritual illness is that it is increasing among dedicated believers and is being rationalized as good planning for the future. That is an absolute lie. Any action that is not done from faith is done from sin (Romans 14:23). The growing mania for buffering ourselves against any pos-

sible future event is straight from the deceiver. When our sand castle of affluence comes tumbling down—and it will—our faith had better be founded in
the person of Jesus Christ and not in material security (Matthew 7:24-27).

Faith Conquers Fear

The opposite of fear is faith. Therefore, when dealing with fear, one must
first understand faith. In Hebrews, faith is described as things that we hope
for and things that we do not presently have. Therefore, if we have no needs,
we have no need of faith.

It is God's plan that we have some needs in order that we may develop
faith in Him. It is vital that we view these future needs as opportunities to
exercise and develop our faith.

In Hebrews 11:6 we are told that God is "a rewarder of those who seek
Him." Each Christian must decide, "Do I really believe that?" No Christian
can truly serve God and live in fear. Christ says that it is a black-and-white
choice: either you choose to serve God or you choose to serve money
(Matthew 6:24).

Can You Really Trust God?

We live in a materialistic generation. Priorities are established based on
desires, not needs. That is not limited to unbelievers. When we see how much
confidence other Christians place in money, including those in the pastor-
ate, it's easy to lose sight of the mark. Problems seem to erode our faith when
it seems that some who truly trust God suffer financially and physically. Finally,
we yield to the impulse and get caught up in the mad rush to protect against
the future. We are guilty of attempting to counsel God rather than accepting
His counsel.

We will never know with certainty why God allows problems to come
into the lives of some godly people. But we can look back upon the lives of
the apostles and see that God allowed them to suffer for their maturity and
His glory.

Have you ever asked God for something and when it didn't happen you
thought God had failed you? Isn't it strange that we usually expect God's
answer to be a "yes" rather than a "no"? There are many reasons why God
would not respond the way we desire:

1. We ask with the wrong motives (James 4:3).
2. It is the wrong time according to God's plan (Luke 11:3-10).
3. It is contrary to God's greater plan (Acts 21:13-14).
4. We are here to serve God, not for God to serve us (Job 41:11).

How To Trust God

1. *Find God's direction for YOUR life.* Most of the frustrations experienced by Christians come as the result of patterning their lives after someone else's. Even the most devout believer can drift off of God's path by trying to match assets with another. Remember that God's successes are not graded by accumulated savings.

Accept God's provision as His plan for your life, and find contentment in the source rather than the supply (1 Timothy 6:7-8).

2. *Make a conscious act of trusting God.* The method of doing that will vary from family to family. For one, it will mean actually withdrawing some of their stored resource and sharing it as God directs them. For another, it means taking the step of faith to leave that fruitless job. For another it may mean being content without that new, bigger home. The ways to practice putting our faith into motion are as different as God's plan for each of us. I would challenge you to find a way to express your faith through a material commitment.

3. *Develop a long-range viewpoint.* Since God rarely works on the same timetable that we do, it is important that we learn what patience is—waiting. Just because you don't understand what is going on in your life, don't begin to doubt God's direction. I don't think that Joseph really understood God's long-range plan as he sat in the Egyptian jail. He did understand what God expected of him each day and was faithful to do what God asked him. "Therefore do not be anxious for tomorrow; for tomorrow will care for itself. Each day has enough trouble of its own" (Matthew 6:34).

4. *Pray diligently.* It has been said that prayer is God's secret weapon. It's time we let the secret out and begin to exercise the most powerful tool that God has given us. Prayer is the key to unlocking God's blessings and power. It is the most neglected part of most Christians' lives. Faith is not possible outside of prayer, and with prayer all things are possible. "Pray without ceasing; in everything give thanks; for this is God's will for you in Christ Jesus" (1 Thessalonians 5:17-18).

2
Brokenness—God's Best

PERHAPS NO PRINCIPLE in God's Word is less understood than that of brokenness. Brokenness does not mean being broke financially. It is a condition in which God allows circumstances to control our lives to the point that we must depend totally upon God.

It would seem that the greater God's plan for a person, the greater the brokenness. The life of the apostle Paul reflects both great power and great brokenness. Yet Paul never considered his personal circumstances punishment. He consistently asserted that his sufferings were a direct result of service to Christ. "For just as the sufferings of Christ are ours in abundance, so also our comfort is abundant through Christ" (2 Corinthians 1 :5).

The Purpose of Brokenness

In God's wisdom He realizes what it takes to keep us attuned to His direction. He then allows problems to occur that will break our will and keep us dependent upon Him. Once a Christian makes a total surrender of that old self to God, then (and only then) God can begin to use him. Since "self" continues to surface, God must allow testing to continue in order to "kill" the old self.

Many times we pray, "God, mold me into a vessel You can use," and then when God's work begins, we want to run.

James 1:2–3 says, "Consider it all joy, my brethren, when you encounter various trials, knowing that the testing of your faith produces endurance." If you want the perfecting of your faith, it comes by way of testing.

The Evidence of Service

The principle of brokenness is easier to teach than to live. The teaching is very clear in the lives of those whom God has chosen to use throughout the Bible. The greater the service to God, the greater the potential for ego and self-centeredness. Thus, the greater the necessity for maintaining a "God first" spirit. Brokenness is an apt term for those being molded into Christ's image.

Clearly the purpose of brokenness is to make a Christian totally dependent on God and separate from this world. "And in all this, they are surprised that you do not run with them into the same excess of dissipation, and they malign you; but they shall give account to Him who is ready to judge the living and dead" (1 Peter 4:4-5).

How Is Brokenness Accomplished?

Since finances is one of the most often discussed topics in the New Testament, it would seem obvious that God would use that area to test our obedience to Him. In our society we have a value rating system that is based upon material worth. That is just as true within Christianity as it is in the unbelieving world. Fortunately, God's value system is based on spiritual worth and is measured by our willingness to accept *His* direction.

The conflict between materialism and Christianity is addressed directly by the Lord in Matthew 6:24, "No one can serve two masters; for either he will hate the one and love the other, or he will hold to one and despise the other. You cannot serve God and mammon."

Many Christians have had their egos shattered by financial setbacks. Some respond by panicking to the point that they abandon their Christian principles and cheat and lie to protect their security. Others fall back in defeat and lose their trust in God. Some live a life of fear, and as a result they lose their witness. Others accept God's authority over their lives and use this as an opportunity to trust God more fully and to demonstrate to others that they serve God. As was said of Job, "Through all this Job did not sin nor did he blame God" (Job 1:22).

Until a Christian is broken to the point of *total* dependence on God, he is not really useful in God's plan. "But whatever things were gain to me, those things I have counted as loss for the sake of Christ" (Philippians 3:7).

Ego: God's Enemy

Few Christians are willing to share an experience with brokenness. So often we equate problems with sin and illogically conclude that those who have problems are being punished by God. If that's so, then Paul was the worst sinner in the history of Christianity. He was flogged five times, beaten, stoned, shipwrecked, imprisoned, and deserted. And yet he said that he was in God's will and was comforted by God. "Therefore we do not lose heart, but though our outer man is decaying, yet our inner man is being renewed day by day" (2 Corinthians 4:16).

God desires to break our ego and pride—*not* our spirit. Indeed, in the spirit we should grow stronger under affliction. The purpose is to strip us of all self-gratification. "But he who boasts, let him boast in the Lord. For not he who commends himself is approved, but whom the Lord commends" (2 Corinthians 10:17–18). A man can accomplish a great deal in his own strength and ability, but the lasting effect is minimal.

Run or Relax?

Our first reaction to the pressures that accompany brokenness is to run. It's simply easier to withdraw and feel sorry for ourselves than it is to stand against the enemy. No one can question Elijah's courage or commitment to God. He regularly risked his life to deliver God's messages. And yet right after he had called down God's fire from heaven and had destroyed the prophets of Baal, he ran when Jezebel threatened him. In 1 Kings 19:4, he is found under a juniper tree asking God to let him die; instead, God comforts him, feeds him, and tells him to relax and rest. Later, when Elijah was refreshed, God sent him back into the battle.

There are times in all of our lives when we feel defeated and would like to simply get away from it all. If that happens to those between forty and fifty years of age, we usually label it a mid-life crisis. In reality such crises come at every stage of life. It's just that at mid-life they are amplified by doubts about the future.

Paul must have had some real doubts about the difficulties he faced throughout his service to the Lord. But the overwhelming characteristic we see in Paul's letters is the ability to relax and enjoy life regardless of his external circumstances. Paul was truly a broken man but not a defeated one. "For the sorrow that is according to the will of God produces a repentance without regret, leading to salvation; but the sorrow of the world produces death" (2 Corinthians 7:10).

The Lesson of Brokenness

Brokenness, whether it is financial, physical, emotional, or all three, has at its center the purpose of teaching us to trust in God. Paul knew that his tribulations were the result of constantly stepping on Satan's toes. They were neither pleasant nor enjoyable to Paul, but he knew they were necessary in order to build the courage of others. "Therefore I ask you not to lose heart at my tribulations on your behalf, for they are your glory" (Ephesians 3:13).

Financial Brokenness

God is in control. If we are serving Him, then nothing can befall us except that He allows it. It will rarely seem beneficial at the time, but if we believe God's Word, then we must believe He will ultimately receive the glory. "And we know that God causes all things to work together for good to those who love God, to those who are called according to His purpose" (Romans 8:28).

An important aspect of God's work in our lives is to teach God's people to love and care about each other. When Christians are suffering from a financial disaster, the last thing they need is an accusation.

In fact, they need help. So the testing of our faith through brokenness extends over to the testing of the faith of others through compassion. No message in God's Word is clearer than that of John's on this subject: "But whoever has the world's goods, and beholds his brother in need and closes his heart against him, how does the love of God abide in him? Little children, let us not love with word or with tongue, but in deed and truth" (1 John 3:17-18).

We are admonished to love with deeds. That is a prerequisite to having God answer our requests (1 John 3:22-24).

If you're going through a period of trials and testing, don't get discouraged. Share your struggle honestly with those around you, and get the prayer support and other support that God has already provided. Remember that God does not want to break you spiritually. He desires that you and I conform to His Son's image. To do that we must have our ego and pride broken.

3
Being Content

ONE OF THE great mysteries of Christianity is contentment. At least one must presume it is a mystery because so few people have found it. Actually, contentment is an attitude.

Extremes

There are many people who seemingly have little or no regard for material possessions. They accept poverty as a normal living condition, and their major concern is which doorway to sleep in. Are they living a life of contentment? Hardly so, because that description aptly fits the winos found in the Bowery of New York. In contrast are the affluent who have the best our society has to offer at their disposal. Their homes are the community showplaces, their summer cottages are more like small hotels, and their automobiles cost more than most families' houses. Does their abundance guarantee contentment? Considering the amount of alcohol and tranquilizers many of them consume, it's hard to imagine that this group is any more content than the previous one.

Balance

If money can't buy it and poverty doesn't provide it, what is contentment? Contentment, contrary to popular opinion, is *not* being satisfied where you are. It is knowing God's plan for your life, having the conviction to live it, and believing that God's peace is greater than the world's problems.

But often we get so involved in the day-to-day activities of earning a living and raising a family that we forget our real purpose: to serve God. Consequently, the trivial problems such as buying a new car or attaining a higher position begin to crowd our conscious mind, and God's plan becomes an abstract goal rather than our focus. "And others are the ones on whom seed was sown among the thorns; these are the ones who have heard the word, and the worries of the world, and the deceitfulness of riches, and the desires for other things enter in and choke the word, and it becomes unfruitful" (Mark 4:18-19).

Social Goals

Christians get trapped into a discontent life by adopting worldly goals. These goals always boil down to: more, bigger, best. Scripture defines that as indulgence, greed, and pride. Often a successful man comes to the Lord out of desperation when he realizes that his whole life is characterized by fear and anxiety, and the accumulation of assets has not alleviated the fear. For a while after accepting Christ as Savior, there is a peace and a real desire to commit everything to God. Unfortunately, since most other Christians are living "natural" lives, the tendency is to fall back into the same old routine, only now rationalizing that it is "serving the Lord." The evidence to the contrary is a lack of peace, a lack of spiritual growth, and a growing doubt about God. Satan's ploy is to use the riches of the world to keep people away from God's salvation. If that fails he simply uses it to steer them away from God's path.

Regression

In our society it is not normal to step down. Once a certain level of income or spending has been attained, it is considered a sign of failure to step down. Even in the face of certain disaster, the image must be maintained. Families that suffer a job loss will continue to maintain their style of living through debt rather than risk the stigma of failure. Others who have felt God's leading to reduce their living style fail to respond because of social status pressure.

Is the concept of conservation and moderation really a loser's attitude? Not according to biblical standards. Contentment cannot be achieved without personal discipline. "No servant can serve two masters; for either he will hate the one, and love the other, or else he will hold to one, and despise the other. You cannot serve God and mammon. Now the Pharisees, who were lovers of money, were listening to all these things, and they were scoffing at Him" (Luke 16:13-14). "And He said to them, 'Beware, and be on your guard against every form of greed; for not even when one has an abundance does his life consist of his possessions'" (Luke 12:15).

The Danger of Abundance

The majority of warnings in Christ's messages were to the wealthy, not the poor. In poverty, the issue is usually black and white—honesty or dishonesty. In affluence, it is much more subtle. In America I believe nearly everyone would be graded as wealthy by any biblical standard. Our anxieties and worries are not related to the *lack* of things but rather to the *loss* of things. Many, if not most, Christians inwardly fear they might lose the material goods they have acquired. Therefore, they compromise God's best for their lives to hang on to the very way of life that brought so much worry and turmoil before they met the Lord. This does not necessarily mean surrendering the assets. It means being willing to.

God's Plan for Contentment

Although many Scriptures teach about the dangers of material riches, God's Word does not teach that poverty is the alternative. God wants us to understand that money is a tool to use in accomplishing His plan through us. If we are to find true contentment we must establish some basic guidelines.

1. *Establish a reasonable standard of living*. Having a surplus does not mean that it's there for us to use as we want. "So is the man who lays up treasure for himself, and is not rich toward God" (Luke 12:21). It is important to develop a life-style based on conviction—not circumstances. "Since all these things are to be destroyed in this way, what sort of people ought you to be in holy conduct and godliness" (2 Peter 3:11).

Since there is no universal plan suitable for everyone, this must be a standard established among husband, wife, and God. Obviously, God will assign Christians at every economic tier. If God's plan for you is at the upper tier, there will be a purpose for the abundance and a ministry through it. Just having an abundance is not a sign of God's blessings. Satan can easily duplicate any worldly riches. God's riches are without sorrow and are for bringing others to salvation. A disciplined life-style with an abundance is a greater witness than the abundance could ever be.

2. *Establish a habit of giving*. Above the tithe God wants Christians to be involved with the needs of others. "And the King will answer and say to them, 'Truly I say to you, to the extent that you did it to one of these brothers of Mine, even the least of them, you did it to Me'" (Matthew 25:40). There is no better way to appreciate what we have than to observe those who truly have needs. Every Christian should be directly involved with the needs of another. There are many Christian organizations that act as a funnel for such funds. If you can't be personally involved, this is the best alternative. With millions of people literally starving in the world today, the rewards are saved lives as well as souls. "At this present time your abundance being a supply for their want, that their abundance also may become a supply for your want, that there may be equality; as it is written, 'He who gathered much did not have too much, and he who gathered little had no lack'" (2 Corinthians 8:14–15).

3. *Establish priorities*. Many Christians are discontented—not because they aren't doing well but because others are doing better. "Let your character be free from the love of money, being content with what you have; for He

Himself has said, 'I will never desert you, nor will I ever forsake you'" (Hebrews 13:5). Too often we let the urgent things take priority over the important things. Virtually every get-rich-quick scheme is directed at those who have not established firm priorities. They imply that more money is the way to glorify God and that it is a sign of failure not to have every desire met.

That is the same attitude that Paul admonished in 1 Corinthians 4:7–21. Paul's priorities were established according to God's plan for his life, and that didn't happen to include the accumulation of money. If spiritual and family priorities were considerd before financial desires, few Christians would get involved with "free time" money schemes. Most of the free time is actually robbed from the Lord and the family.

4. *Develop a thankful attitude.* It is remarkable that in America we could ever think that God has failed us materially. That attitude is possible only when we allow Satan to convince us to compare ourselves to others. "But you have bitter jealousy and selfish ambition in your heart, do not be arrogant and so lie against the truth. This wisdom is not that which comes down from above, but is earthly, natural, demonic" (James 3:14-15).

The primary defense against this attitude is praise to God. Satan uses lavishness and waste to create discontent and selfish ambition. Why else would a man drive himself to acquire more than he needs or can logically use and in the process destroy his health, family, and usefulness to God? Thankfulness is a state of mind, not an accumulation of assets. Until a Chistian can truly thank God for what he has and be willing to accept that as God's provision for his life, contentment will never be possible.

5. *Reject a fearful spirit.* Another tool of Satan is the question, "What if?" Dedicated Christians get trapped into hoarding because they fear the "What if?" of retirement, disability, unemployment, economic collapse, and so on. Obviously, God wants us to consider these things and even plan for them— within reason. But when fear dictates to the point that giving to God's work is hindered, foolish risks are assumed, and worry becomes the norm rather than the exception—contentment is impossible. A Christian must consciously reject the attitude of fear. It may be necessary to face the fear to claim God's victory. If the fear is a lack of surplus, it may be necessary to live without it in order to conquer it.

6. *Seek God's will for you.* "More than that, I count all things to be loss in view of the surpassing value of knowing Christ Jesus my Lord, for whom I have suffered the loss of all things, and count them but rubbish in order that I may gain Christ" (Philippians 3:8).

7. *Stand up to the fear.* "I can do all things through Him who strengthens me" (Philippians 4:13).

8. *Trust God's promise.* "And the peace of God, which surpasses all comprehension, shall guard your hearts and your minds in Christ Jesus" (Philippians 4:7).

4

Love Your Enemies

RECENTLY A CLOSE friend whom I will call Bill called to discuss a difficult situation he was facing. Several months before, Bill had released a key employee because of his belligerent attitude. Now that employee was going into competition with him with one of his clients.

Obviously, it was his right to start a new business, except that to do so he had to sub-contract his business to Bill until he could get his equipment functioning. Also, the ex-employee was calling on Bill's customers and casually dropping degrading remarks about his former employer.

The questions Bill asked were honest and difficult ones: How far do I go as a Christian in aiding my competitors? Is it really my responsibility to carry him with my business until he develops his and competes for my customers? And, Should I tell my customers what is going on to combat the innuendoes of the ex-employee?

Beware of Feelings

Generally, our initial impression is a purely emotional one, and unless we are controlled primarily by God's Word, that first impression is rarely the correct one. In fact, I have discovered that many initial impressions run opposite to God's direction. Therefore, we must turn to His Word.

Biblical Balance

The Scriptures present an interesting perspective of strength and compassion when dealing with enemies (I stretch that term to include deceitful competitors). The account of David's confrontation with Nabal is given in 1 Samuel 25. It seems that in spite of David's noble gesture to protect Nabal's property, when David needed help Nabal refused even to acknowledge him. That obvious affront infuriated David.

In anger David decided to take matters into his own hands and destroy Nabal. God used Abigail, Nabal's wife, to stop David from taking vengeance.

In the face of godly counsel, David cooled off and withdrew. His withdrawal could well have been interpreted as weakness by others—even his own men. However, the result was that God executed judgment in His own time. Thus, the use of restraint was more effective than the use of strength.

What Is Strength?

Even a cursory review of Scripture reveals that strength does not always mean the exercise of power. More often it means the relinquishing of personal rights to God. That may also mean relinquishing the "right" to retribution or revenge.

The opposite of strength is cowardice. Those who flee from any confrontation display cowardice. What is the difference then? Whether or not God receives honor from the action.

A person who allows others to cheat and abuse him because he is fearful of any conflict is a coward. Cowardice is generally motivated by self-preservation, not compassion. The classic example of that is found in Numbers 13 and 14 where God's people refuse to occupy their Promised Land because of the giants living there. Were they demonstrating compassion for their enemies? Hardly so—they were clearly self-motivated.

Strength, then, is the proper use of power to accomplish God's assigned task.

Hate the Enemy?

In our society, it appears acceptable to conform to the Old Testament law of "an eye for an eye." In truth, such retribution was always limited to an action of the community—the government. Its purpose was to maintain order by punishment.

A Christian must decide early in his spiritual life that surrendering to God necessitates giving up some personal rights, one of which is retaliation. "You have heard that it was said, 'You shall love your neighbor, and hate your enemy.' But I say to you, love your enemies, and pray for those who persecute you" (Matthew 5:43-44).

Aid the Enemy?

Loving your enemies is different from aiding them. Christ loved the Pharisees as He loved everyone, but He certainly did not help them. To the contrary, He opposed them often and warned His disciples to stay away from them (Matthew 16:6). They represented a counterforce that was anti-Christian.

That is not meant to imply that all competitors fall into the same classification as the Pharisees. But when a competitor purposely sets himself against your and God's interests, he certainly cannot be classified as a friend.

God would have us love competitors both prayerfully and spiritually, but that does not mean aiding them. There can be occasions when God directs us to aid a competitor, but only because it provides a witness for Him.

Love Your Enemies

Even a survey of this subject would be incomplete without discussing Proverbs 25:21. "If your enemy is hungry, give him food to eat; and if he is thirsty, give him water to drink." Paul makes reference to that proverb in Romans 12. The context in which it is used dispels any idea that a Christian has a right to revenge.

A common misconception is that you must hand your enemy a cup of water while he beats upon your head. Clearly that is not so. Rather, we are to forgive our enemy and acknowledge his needs as we would a friend's.

Summary

A Christian is instructed to love his enemies (I stretched this principle to include business competitors). However, we are not asked to aid an enemy in our defeat. The only motivation for doing so would be a personal revelation from the Lord that He was using us to accomplish a greater work.

God instructs a believer to forgive an offense, not to seek revenge. Before taking any action, a Christian must evaluate the motivation.

In the situation that generated this study, a Christian businessman was faced with a decision about aiding his competitors. What was the conclusion? He decided not to do so. He requested that they take their business elsewhere or do it themselves. The motivation was not to punish them but to be the best possible steward of God's business. He determined that he had a greater responsibility to his stockholders and employees than to his competitors.

To be as fair as possible, he gave them adequate notice so that they could transfer their business. He did not inform his customers of any of the events but left the matter in the Lord's hands.

5

Suffering for Christ vs. Living Like a King

SOME TIME AGO, I had the opportunity to view the misapplication of a scriptural principle in the lives of two people. The first was a believer working in a full-time Christian ministry. Along with his commitment to serve others, he had dedicated himself and his family to a life of virtual poverty. He sincerely felt that in order to serve Christ, one had to relinquish all ownership of worldly goods and look poor. He decided to sell his family's home, most of their furniture, and the majority of their other possessions.

Scriptural Club

His scriptural justification was based on Luke 9:3: "And He said to them, 'Take nothing for your journey, neither a staff, nor a bag, nor bread, nor money; and do not even have two tunics apiece.'"

Christ was teaching His disciples a simple truth: trust God—He is sufficient. There is no doubt that each of us needs to act in accordance with this principle. All through Scripture, God teaches that words without corresponding actions mean absolutely nothing. In a generation in which most people live by fear, God expects His people to live by faith.

This passage leaves no doubt that Christ directed His disciples to take no provisions with them. They were to live by faith; those to whom they were ministering would supply their needs. There is also no doubt that Christ has since directed many others to do the same thing. Most notable among them was George Mueller. However, one thing that identifies those who are chosen by God from those who impose such hardships on themselves is an attitude of peace and joy.

That was certainly not so with the individual I met. He was egotistical about his commitment and openly critical of other Christians who were living "carnal, worldly" lives. He was on the verge of bitterness and had rebellion in his home. His wife was resentful about the abrupt change in their lifestyle. She said his response to every material request by her or the children was, "God doesn't want us to have that." The more we discussed these inconsistencies with what he was doing, the more he rationalized them as sufferings for the Lord. I pointed out that another group had felt the same way

Legalisms

The Pharisees of Christ's day did what they thought were great things for God, and most of the things they did were even the right things. They prayed, they fasted, they tithed. Christ never challenged their actions—He challenged their motives. "But woe to you Pharisees! For you pay tithe of mint and rue and every kind of garden herb, and yet disregard justice and the love of God; but these are the things you should have done without neglecting the others" (Luke 11:42).

They were so blinded by their own self-righteousness they couldn't see God's true promises. He confronted them with this truth in Matthew 12:7. "But if you had known what this means, 'I desire compassion, and not a sacrifice,' you would not have condemned the innocent." Some were prideful in their poverty, while others required the best of everything. But in God's eyes they suffered from a common malady: ego.

Balance

It's interesting that Bible-believing Christians will sometimes focus on a single Scripture to justify their actions while ignoring other references contrary to their personal "revelation." That is not to discredit a believer's uniqueness from the world. God calls each of us to a radical life-style—total commitment to Him—but rarely does the Lord call one of His to voluntary poverty. And He never singles out an individual to such a life-style without other verifications of this calling. The least of these verifications will be love, compassion, and acceptance that God doesn't call everyone to sacrifice similarly.

That truth is evidenced in Scripture when Peter proclaims to Christ that he is ready to go to prison and die for his faith. Christ responded by telling him that he would deny his faith three times before morning. Then He reminded His disciples of the time earlier when they had been instructed to go out taking along no provisions, only this time He gave them new instructions. "And He said to them, 'When I sent you out without purse and bag and sandals, you did not lack anything, did you?' And they said, 'No, nothing.' And He said to them, 'But now, let him who has a purse take it along, likewise also a bag, and let him who has no sword sell his robe and buy one'" (Luke 22:35-36).

The possession or absence of material things is not an issue with serving Christ—the attitude about them is.

It is important for us not to assume the role of God's advisor in the area of sacrifice. God knows what each of us is called to do, and He equips us to do it. In the case of this Christian, the evidence was conclusive that a lot more prayer would be needed before he could make a decision to "suffer" for Christ in this way.

Living Like a King

Shortly after the "poverty syndrome" situation, I came in contact with another Christian who was also in full-time Christian work. But he presented the opposite and far more popular extreme. "I'm a child of the King," he said, "and I'm going to live like it." To emphasize his point, he told me about his $40,000 car, his son's private school, the new house, pool, and so on. With a little prompting, he told me how God had directed him into a home sales company with a pyramid marketing system, and how he was one of its leading new distributors. It was a great opportunity to help others in a more practical way, he said. I soon learned from his comments that he was prospecting for additional people to "help."

He went on to declare that God really wants to bless His people, and unless a Christian is materially successful, God isn't blessing him.

Selfishness

The theology of selfishness is an easy one to promote because most of us were raised with it, and today it virtually dominates our society. It's the philosophy called "get all you can out of life today, live with all the gusto you can get."

That is certainly not a new philosophy. Solomon described it very well in the book of Ecclesiastes. "I said to myself, 'Come now, I will test you with pleasure. So enjoy yourself.' And behold, it too was futility" (Ecclesiates 2:1).

It is important to discern the difference between the pride of wealth and the wealth itself. Christ never condemned the wealth—it belongs to God. He condemned the wealthy-minded of this world. God has made many people wealthy both spiritually and materially, but wealth was never a sign of God's blessing (1 Corinthians 4:9, 11). Overwhelmingly, those selected by God to manage a large surplus to feed His sheep manifest humility, not pride.

A Separated Life

One of the evidences of Christianity is that we desire to keep and obey God's statutes and commandments (1 John 3:22) and do what is pleasing to Him. We are called lights and God's people. Nowhere does God say that to follow Him we are to live like a king. In fact, He says that the tug of this world and its pleasures will be the greatest threat to our walk with Him. "Do not love the world, nor the things in the world. If anyone loves the world, the love of the Father is not in him" (1 John 2:15).

Certainly, it is initially easy to attract people to Christianity by a show of wealth, but the evidence in the world around tells us that the effect in changed lives is very temporary. A Christian whose witness is based on a supply of material things will quickly find that people are interested only if God will promise to do the same thing for them. If He won't or doesn't, then they look elsewhere. Give them a little truth about what Christ really expects in the way of commitment, and most would say, "It's not for me." "Sell your possessions and give to charity; make yourselves purses which do not wear out, an unfailing treasure in heaven, where no thief comes near, nor moth destroys. For where your treasure is, there will your heart be also" (Luke 12:33-34).

A Balanced Life

It's clear that neither a voluntary rejection of all wealth nor a display of material success is part of a balanced Christian walk. Obviously, God will have Christians at each end of the material spectrum. It is God's right to determine how we are to be used. "On the contrary, who are you, O man, who answers back to God? The thing molded will not say to the molder, 'Why did you make me like this,' will it?" (Romans 9:20).

There is little danger that the imbalance of self-enforced sacrifice will catch on in our society. Sacrifice to most of us means driving a standard shift car without air conditioning. However, there is a growing emphasis in Christianity toward a materialistic life-style. That is reflected in a de-emphasis on caring for the needs of others. Once that attitude catches on within our churches, the priorities shift from caring for the poor, invalid, and elderly to building bigger and better buildings.

Obviously, we need buildings in which to minister adequately, but we don't need palaces. The danger of affluence has been a real threat in every generation of Christians, but today it's becoming an epidemic.

Most Christians are familiar with the parable of the rich farmer in Luke 12:16-20, but it's also necessary to remember the preceding passage. "And He said to them, 'Beware, and be on your guard against every form of greed; for not even when one has an abundance does his life consist of his possessions'" (Luke 12:15).

Without a surplus, little could be done in God's work, so obviously some Christians must have an abundance. God allows us to use part of that abundance for ourselves and our families. That amount will vary according to God's unique plan for each of us. But when our attitudes become controlled by our possessions rather than by God's Word, we're no longer useful to God. "Now He was also saying to the disciples, 'There was a certain rich man who had a steward, and this steward was reported to him as squandering his possessions. And he called him and said to him, "What is this I hear about you? Give an account of your stewardship, for you can no longer be steward"'" (Luke 16:1-2).

That warning is one that each Christian should consider well. What a shame it is to be deceived by Satan into trading an eternity of riches for a few shiny trinkets. "And He said to them, 'You are those who justify yourselves in the sight of men, but God knows your hearts; for that which is highly esteemed among men is detestable in the sight of God'" (Luke 16:15).

6

Being Excellent in a Mediocre World

"DO YOU SEE a man skilled in his work? He will stand before kings; he will not stand before obscure men" (Proverbs 22:29).

I guess that's why there aren't very many kings left; there are very few skilled men to stand before them.

We live in a society where average is exceptional, and slothful is normal. The trend today is to seek the path of least resistance, and when the going gets difficult, give up. In school, when the total grades are averaged together, it's called "grading on the curve." In our society, we Christians have allowed our standards to be graded on the curve of the world.

We are no longer "the lights in a world of darkness," particularly where excellence is concerned. We are not noted as the best in any area, including business, education, and work—or even in the area of faith. We have lowered our standards to those of the average around us. More Christians depend upon the government than upon God. Why? Because we have found it easier to adjust to mediocrity than to the source of excellence—God's Word.

Therefore, it is vital that we walk according to God's Word. "Trust in the Lord with all your heart, and do not lean on your own understanding. In all your ways acknowledge Him, and He will make your paths straight" (Proverbs 3:5-6). To do so there are some basic attitudes to reassess.

First, recognize that the world has not conformed to God's standards; we have conformed to Satan's.

Second, recognize that God's standards are not always pleasant because they require discipline. In the long run, discipline yields greater freedom because it frees us to serve God even more. God's boundaries are not there to test or punish us. They are established because God made us and knows what truly gives us peace. In order to establish God's excellence, we must recognize the fallacy of the world's standards.

IOU vs. You-Owe-Me

The common attitude today is "somebody owes me something." Many Americans think that a lifetime job with good pay and a guaranteed retirement plan at sixty-five comes with being born; promotion is just a matter of time; forty hours a week is the maximum endurance for any worker; the last hour of each day is there to make the transition to home easier; a ten-minute coffee break should take at least half-an-hour; a half-hour lunch should take at least an hour-and-a-half; and an equal share of company profits belongs to the workers.

Honestly consider whether Christian employees act as if they believe differently from the you-owe-me attitude found in industry today. What does God require? "Whatever you do, do your work heartily, as for the Lord rather than for men" (Colossians 3:23).

God's principles demand that no matter what others are doing, we serve Him through every action we take.

Our Rights

The banner of nearly everyone in our society today is "we demand our rights." Exactly what are our rights as Christians? The rights of servants.

Being a servant is not a particularly appealing image to most Christians, but that is precisely what we are called to be. Perhaps one of the most common reasons many Christians are not useful to God is because of a proud, defiant attitude toward an employer, husband, or other person. But that attitude has its roots in a rebellious spirit toward God. When a person with a rebellious spirit is confronted with the principle of self-sacrifice from God's Word, the truth will become evident. "Do nothing from selfishness or empty conceit, but with humility of mind let each of you regard one another as more important than himself" (Philippians 2:3).

Why Do More Than Necessary?

There is an old saying, "If you want someone to do a good job, find a busy man." The precept is that a man who is not busy probably doesn't want to be. Obviously, that's not always true, but in the long run, I have found a great deal of truth in it. Many people do no more than is necessary to meet the minimum standards set for them. They will continually belittle others who work to capacity and will demand more and more protection for their position. Solomon described them well. "Poor is he who works with a negligent hand, but the hand of the diligent makes rich" (Proverbs 10:4).

Goal Setting

To avoid the trap of "curve grading" each of us must establish some minimum, godly goals. It means that we cannot be content to "get by." That does not justify swinging to the opposite extreme and exhibiting a perfectionist attitude or abandoning God and family in the pursuit of success. It means balance. Excellence is *not* extreme; it should be normal.

A wife and mother must become so skilled at homemaking that she is noted by others for her excellence. What a great opportunity for witness when the secular world comes to a Christian woman for counsel on how to live on a budget or how to economize in the home. "An excellent wife, who can find? For her worth is far above jewels" (Proverbs 31:10).

A husband and father must have standards that do not get eroded by slothfulness. It is important that the image a child perceives of his father is not of one who sits in front of a TV demanding silence from everybody. Many men who are excellent at work seem to feel that the same standard is not applicable to the home.

An employee must be willing to go far beyond the minimum demands to retain a job. That means adopting a steward's attitude about everything he does. If the job is sweeping the floors, it should be done with such thoroughness and excellence that it would be known even to the president of the company.

Summary

Obviously, we could go on and on reviewing the positives of excellence and negatives of mediocrity. It should be sufficient to say that God established excellence as our norm. "Whether, then, you eat or drink or whatever you do, do all to the glory of God" (1 Corinthians 10:31). To accept less is dishonoring to God and demoralizing to us. The result will be a loss of credibility in the eyes of others—especially the slothful—and the chastening of the Lord.

7

Finances and Your
Relationship with God

Without A DOUBT, there is a great need in Christianity to get back to the basics of God's Word. That is true whether we're talking about salvation, sanctification, service, or finances.

In reality, we have only one purpose for anything we do in this lifetime—to glorify God. If our day-to-day lives don't reflect that service, then we're not serving God.

There is a great deal of false service by many who profess to serve God but actually want God to serve them. They will give, but they always expect to be repaid. They will help the needy, but it's to keep God from allowing some tragedy to befall them. The list could go on and on and would eventually touch every one of us. Why? Because I believe so few really understand the function that finances play in our spiritual lives.

The financial principles given throughout God's Word are not there to see if we're strong enough to live by them—they're given because God knows that they are the *best* for us. God's principles of finances are not an arbitrary set of rules by which to govern us—they are a loving Father's wisdom to those who will listen and trust Him.

We have built an affluent society based upon a sand foundation of future debt. All that we have is in danger of being wiped out by any financial crisis, even a relatively minor one. Not so with those who observe and obey God's financial wisdom. God's financial wisdom builds to last, not to impress others.

Why Did Christ Teach on Finances?

It surprises many Christians to learn that approximately two-thirds of the parables that Christ used in teaching deal specifically with finances. The reason for that is very simple—He chose a topic with which everyone could identify. A parable is a form of teaching in which a well-known topic is used to explain a relatively unknown topic. Christ was describing a spiritual kingdom that is actually more real than this material kingdom. But in order to relate to worldly people, He had to use a worldly example—money.

Christ never said money or material things were problems. He said that they were *symptoms* of the real problems. He constantly warned us to guard our hearts against greed, covetousness, ego, and pride, because those are the tools that Satan uses to control and manipulate this world. Christ warned us a great deal more about materialism than He did any other sin. "And He said to them, 'Beware, and be on your guard against every form of greed; for not even when one has an abundance does his life consist of his possessions'" (Luke 12:15). In fact, in the parable about salvation in Matthew 13:18-23, "the deceitfulness of riches" is given as a cause for unfruitfulness.

Satan has taken the very riches provided by God to enhance our lives and bring others to salvation and has diverted them for his use. Today, even Christians evaluate others on the basis of how much they have and how successful they are in worldly terms. The poor are thought to be losers—less spiritual than the winners.

Is It Wrong to Be Rich?

Rich is a very subjective term, but here it's used in context with having enough money to meet all of your reasonable needs and still have funds left over. Clearly, God's Word teaches that many of His people will fit into that category. They will not only be able to meet their needs, but they will also be able to help others who have needs.

Obviously, in God's economy, He must either provide a material surplus to some Christians to meet the needs of others, or He must provide manna from heaven. God's plan is clearly stated in 2 Corinthians 8:14-15—that our abundance at the present time will meet the needs of others, and later their abundance will meet our needs—a good alternative to welfare within the church.

Christ warned those who are rich to always be on their guard (Luke 12:15-21). There is a great temptation to trust in the security that a surplus can provide. The greater the surplus, the greater the temptation. That's why those who are rich (most of American Christianity) must guard their hearts and minds with the principles from God's Word.

Finances: Our Spiritual Barometer

A definition of *faith,* according to Hebrews 11, is trusting God *totally.* It means trusting God for things you cannot see or manipulate into happening. Most of us truly desire to be able to exercise this faith. But the world around us tells us to do just the opposite. If you don't have the money for what you need, borrow to get it.

God's Word tells us to learn to be content and dedicate ourselves to serving God. In Hebrews 12:1 we are told, "Let us also lay aside every encumbrance, and the sin which so easily entangles us, and let us run with endurance the race that is set before us."

Instead, we encumber ourselves by following the worldly advice that says bigger and more are better. Just about the time most of our children are grown and leaving home, we can afford a big home and more cars, so we expand our life-styles rather than simplify them.

One of the surest signs of worldly values in Christianity is the love of money. That is manifested in fear of the future. This fear dominates the attitudes of most believers today. The evidence of that is the mania over guaranteed incomes and retirement plans. Neither of these is necessarily wrong in itself. Obviously, most Christians would like a steady income to provide for their family's needs, and that's not unscriptural, except when they compromise God's Word for fear of losing their tenure in an education job or when they fear speaking out against obvious sin.

Retirement planning so dominates the thinking of Christians who have sizable incomes that they overkill in this area enormously. The fear of doing without in the future causes many Christians to rob God's work of the very funds He has provided. These monies are tucked away in retirement accounts for twenty to forty years. God's Word does *not* prohibit but rather encourages saving for the future, including retirement (Proverbs 6:6–11; 21:20), but the example of the rich fool, given by the Lord in Luke 12:16–20, should be a clear direction that God's balance is "when in doubt—give; don't hoard."

The Greatest Need

The greatest need in our generation is for God's undiluted Word to be taught clearly. The next greatest need is for Christians who will demonstrate that it works. In Romans 10:14, we are told that for the unsaved to believe, someone must tell them about Jesus. The book of James tells us that we are the walking, talking evidence before the unsaved world that God's Word is true. As I think about our witness before the unsaved, it would appear to be evident that in our most visible area, finances, we don't have much of a witness.

In great part, that is because Christians just haven't been taught what God's Word says. A few examples from the Word should clearly point this out.

Borrowing. We are told to borrow very modestly and cautiously, always repaying what is owed (Psalm 37:21; Proverbs 3:27–28).

Lending. Christians are to lend to one another without interest and are not to engage in lawsuits to recover losses (Deuteronomy 23:19–20; 1 Corinthians 6:1–7).

Sharing. Christians should provide for every legitimate need within their own fellowships. That would include funds for illnesses, unemployment, and old age (2 Corinthians 8:14–15).

What Should We Do?

It would be negligent to conclude this study of ways finances reflect our faith without pointing out some simple steps to start applying God's wisdom.

First, study the available materials on God's principles for managing finances. You could glean all of the principles out of the Bible yourself—many Christians have. However, an organized study can reduce the time involved and give additional insights from others who have applied the principles.

Second, apply godly discipline to your life-style. It's clear that God doesn't demand the same life-style for any two families. Each of us is to witness to those whom God has placed around us. So there will be Christians at every level of income and society. But God's Word makes it *very* clear that lavishness and waste are worldly, not godly, values. Each Christian family must look at their spending habits, and particularly their waste, and give an account for their stewardship to God.

Third, teach your children God's principles. The toll that worldly financial values place on young families today is enormous. More than one-half of their marriages will fail because of unnecessary financial pressures. The vast majority of these problems could be avoided and marriages salvaged if families were taught early how to anticipate and avoid such problems. When a young couple is required to develop a budget prior to marriage, and then another couple works with them and monitors the budget for the first year, the financial problems are reduced dramatically. Christian parents should never let their children leave home without equipping them with the fundamental knowledge of finances that they will need to survive in a materialistically insane society.

Fourth, teach your neighbors. There are now several hundred Christian couples who regularly teach courses on God's principles of finances and basic budgeting in homes and churches around the country. Those who feared they would meet with indifference or disinterest found themselves swamped with requests for counseling and advice. Millions of people are hurting and don't know where to go for help. They will respond, not only to the financial advice, but also to the gospel message that always must go with it.

8

How to Be a Success

ADS IN MANY national magazines promise to reveal the secrets of being a success today. Naturally, the ads are obscure enough that they don't reveal these "secrets" unless you respond. But the implication is clear enough—success today is related to money, power, and position.

It's really not much different today from how it has always been. We look first at someone's material accumulation to determine if he is successful. The admiration of society is carried one step further because even those who earn their wealth by deceit, extortion, or pornography are elevated to a platform of success today. That seems odd even in worldly terms because the evidence doesn't support the idea that material accumulation is the same as success.

A successful person is one who accomplishes goals and is able to enjoy the fruits of them. Most of those we call successful today are frustrated and miserable people with terrible family lives. Many "successful" people terminate their own lives because they have nothing to live for. Sometimes the worst thing that can happen to those without Christ is for them to accomplish their goals, because they turn out to be so worthless.

The Christian's View of Success

Obviously, Christians don't fall into the same traps set by Satan, do they? We have our guard up so thoroughly that we recognize the dangers: if you spend too much time building security, the family grows up without proper guidance; when material priorities are substituted for spiritual priorities, children are spoiled by things and, thus, have an indifferent attitude; and so on and so on.

Unfortunately, Christians do fall into these traps. Why? Because the lies are so convincing that we believe they have to be true. From the outside, big homes, new cars, and private schools seem great. However, what had to be surrendered in the pursuit of them may have been greater—family relationships and the like. Remarkably, God's Word says that the things aren't the problem at all.

In fact, God promises His people the things that the unbeliever has: "For all these things the Gentiles eagerly seek; for your heavenly Father knows that you need all these things. But seek first His kingdom and His righteousness; and all these things shall be added to you" (Matthew 6:32–33). It is the desire that causes the grief, not the material possessions.

Poverty syndrome. Since the world puts so much store in material success, many Christians have naturally concluded that the opposite extreme is God's way, and Christians should be poor. Or if they aren't poor, at least they ought to look that way. Satan is tricky. Those that he can't trap into his plan, he tries to drive through and out the other side. He perverts one of God's blessings so that God's people will be careful to avoid it. Poverty is a reality in Scripture, but it certainly is not a promise. God said there would always be poor in the land, but He never said they would be His people. When God chose someone to live on limited resources, it was either to teach that person a lesson or to use him as an example.

The norm taught in God's Word is either enough or an abundance for those who believe and follow (Psalm 37:25; Proverbs 3:18;10:3;13:22; Matthew 13:12; Mark 11:24; Luke 6:38). Many Christians believe that giving up something makes them spiritual. Although they may not believe they "earned" their salvation, they now believe that by self-sacrifice they must earn God's acceptance.

Paul laid this deception to rest once and for all in his letter to the Corinthians. "And if I give all my possessions to feed the poor, and if I deliver my body to be burned, but do not have love, it profits me nothing" (1 Corinthians 13:3). God is not looking for martyrs but for believers (literally, "doers").

Riches syndrome. Many Christians have concluded that since poverty isn't normal, then riches must be. They, therefore, have assumed that God must make them wealthy to protect His image. Most then set about in a totally secular way to accumulate what is supposed to be a Christian testimony.

If God doesn't provide according to their preconceived plan, they rationalize that the end justifies the means and help Him out. So what if they don't have a personal prayer or study life? After all, just think what a witness God will get from their success. And even though their children don't get much parental direction, they do get the best possible advantages.

Others try to manipulate God to work for them. They give, but usually to get. They continually demand more and the best, while fervently trying to convince others that this is normal. Rarely, if ever, do they stop to consider God's plan for fear that it won't coincide with their concept of prosperity. "On the contrary, who are you, O man, who answers back to God? The thing molded will not say to the molder, 'Why did you make me like this,' will it?" (Romans 9:20).

There is a great danger in seeing God only from worldly eyes. Then all riches and all blessings are measured in terms of what God can do for us, rather than what we can do for God. "But a natural man does not accept the things of the Spirit of God; for they are foolishness to him, and he cannot understand them, because they are spiritually appraised" (1 Corinthians 2:14).

God's plan may not always provide the best or the most but always enough. To be a spiritual success, a Christian must be willing to relinquish all rights and accept God's plan. Of necessity, God will place believers at every tier in society to minister to those around them. "So then it does not depend on the man who wills or the man who runs, but on God who has mercy" (Romans 9:16).

God's View of Success

A look into God's Word quickly reveals that material blessings were given because God loved His people, not because they deserved them. They were withdrawn from those who used them foolishly and transferred to a more faithful steward. "You ask and do not receive, because you ask with wrong motives, so that you may spend it on your pleasures" (James 4:3).

To be a success from a biblical perspective, some prerequisites must be met

1. *Surrender.* Every successful servant of the Lord who was entrusted with material and spiritual rewards first demonstrated an acceptance of God's lordship. The list extends throughout the Scripture: Abraham, Noah, Nehemiah, David, and Paul. Even Solomon, who later strayed because of material riches, first demonstrated a surrender to God's authority.

2. *Obedience.* Those who are truly blessed by God have demonstrated a willingness to use their material resources for God. Literally, the more they let God, the more God is able to glorify Himself through them. An unwavering dedication to God's way is the mark of a true steward. "Because of the proof given by this ministry they will glorify God for your obedience to your confession of the gospel of Christ, and for the liberality of your contribution to them and to all" (2 Corinthians 9:13).

3. *Persistency.* One attribute of a successful person is persistency in the face of problems. God wants Christians who don't give up easily. Too often today Christians who live by the "open door" doctrine give up whenever an obstacle is encountered. If all the doors were to be open and waiting, there would not be so many Scriptures directing us to knock (Luke 11:10; 18:5). If God's people give up easily when faced with difficulties, the world will consider us losers. Nothing and nobody can shake a true believer from doing God's will once it is understood. The evidence of that can be observed in the lives of every servant who was ever used by God (Esther 4:16; Nehemiah 6:11; Acts 21:13).

Recognizing God's Will

It seems evident that many Christians fall prey to worldly success motivation. They have a lot of drive and ambition but fail to recognize God's will for them and thus fall dupe to the world's will. Often they spend too much time asking someone else about God's will for their lives when it is *God* they should be asking. Ask anyone who is truly living God's plan for his life how he found it, and usually he will say, "God just revealed it to me." Many times others helped to point him in the right direction, but usually just as many tried to talk him out of God's will. God will reveal His plan to those who seek Him diligently. "Trust in the Lord with all your heart, and do not lean on your own understanding. In all your ways acknowledge Him, and He will make your paths straight" (Proverbs 3:5-6).

The difficulty is that, although Christians may sense God's will, if it doesn't agree with what they had in mind, particularly in regard to income and ego, they may rationalize themselves out of it. For a while there is a feeling of loss, but with time it passes. The next time the direction is not quite so strong, and it's easier to ignore. Eventually, God's call just fades away, and the thorns choke out any further direction. "And the one on whom seed was sown among the thorns, this is the man who hears the word, and the worry of the world, and the deceitfulness of riches choke the word, and it becomes unfruitful" (Matthew 13:22).

Once a Christian examines his life and discovers that the fruitfulness is gone—regardless of the income—it is certain that God's will has been bypassed, and another master has become Lord. "No one can serve two masters; for either he will hate the one and love the other, or he will hold to one and despise the other. You cannot serve God and mammon" (Matthew 6:24).

There are no quick, simple solutions to resolving this condition. Only earnest, honest prayer and petition will restore that sensitivity to the Holy Spirit's guidance.

9

How to Handle a Surplus

A CHRISTIAN BUSINESSMAN asked a very pertinent question: "I have a surplus of money each year. What am I to do with it: give it away, invest it, put it into a retirement plan, or what?" On the surface, the Scriptures would seem to be confusing on this issue. One proverb says a wise man has a surplus in his home, while a fool has bare cupboards. However, another says that a poor man has God's blessings, and a rich man is a fool. Even the parables of Christ would appear somewhat confusing. In one parable He rebuked a rich fool who built larger barns to store his surplus, and in another he rebuked the man who failed to invest a large surplus wisely.

There is one absolute that helps to answer confusing questions: God's Word is always right and is never in conflict. God is always dealing with heart attitudes. We would call them motives. In each situation the motives must be analyzed. For one person, a surplus of money represents a trust from God that can be used for current and future needs. For another, it represents a trap of Satan to lead him out of God's path. The certainty is that Scripture warns that there is a greater danger in having a surplus than in having a need. "And Jesus looked at him and said, 'How hard it is for those who are wealthy to enter the kingdom of God! For it is easier for a camel to go through the eye of a needle, than for a rich man to enter the kingdom of God'" (Luke 18:24–25).

For those Christians with a surplus of money provided by God to meet future needs, good stewardship of that surplus requires that some or all of it must be invested. It is a fact that God has provided a great surplus to many Christians today.

Creating a Surplus

The first investment can be found in Genesis 3:23. Adam was cast out of the garden and told to cultivate the soil for his food. To do so he had to risk seeds that could have been eaten; thus, he became an investor. Every farmer understands the principle of investing. Each year he is faced with a choice of eating all the seeds, selling all the seeds, or retaining some to replant. It would be a very short-sighted farmer who would either eat or sell his entire harvest. A wise farmer not only holds back some seed for replanting, but also sorts out some of the best seed to insure a greater harvest. By doing so he exercises self-discipline to achieve greater prosperity.

Contrary to what many people believe, God is not against prosperity. The Scriptures give evidence that prosperity is one of God's blessings to those who love and obey Him (2 Chronicles 16:9; Psalm 37:4; Proverbs 8:21). The attitudes that God dislikes are greed, covetousness, and pride. Investing for selfish reasons breeds these attitudes.

Justification for "Investing"

The scriptural justification for investing is to multiply current assets to meet future needs. "And the one who had received the five talents came up and brought five more talents, saying, 'Master, you entrusted five talents to me; see, I have gained five more talents'" (Matthew 25:20). A talent, as described here, would be worth nearly $400,000 in our economy today. So it was not an insignificant sum of money that the Lord was discussing. It required investing a sizeable surplus of money.

Many Christians firmly believe that there is no scriptural justification for investing while others have a lack. That simply is not true. The justification for anyone's investing is that he has given what God asked him to give. He has met the *reasonable* needs of his family, and he still has a surplus.

Prerequisites for Investing

The number one prerequisite for investing is attitude. Why are you investing, and how will the surplus be used? If a Christian wants God to entrust greater riches to him, he must be found faithful in the smaller amount first. "He who is faithful in a very little thing is faithful also in much; and he who is unrighteous in a very little thing is unrighteous also in much. If therefore you have not been faithful in the use of unrighteous mammon, who will entrust the true riches to you?" (Luke 16:10-11).

To protect against the infectious diseases of greed and pride, the best weapon is a specific plan for returning the excess to God's kingdom. I find that once a commitment has been made to a disciplined life-style, regardless of the available income, the dangers of greed and self-indulgence are significantly reduced. The term used throughout Paul's writings is contentment. "But godliness actually is a means of great gain, when accompanied by contentment" (1 Timothy 6:6).

Scriptural Motive for Investing

There are several scriptural motives for investing.

To further God's work. Some Christians have received a gift of giving (Romans 12:8). To them the multiplication of material worth is an extension of their basic ministry within the Body of Christ. Even to those who do not have a gift of giving, investments are a way to preserve and multiply a surplus that has been provided for a later time. In Acts 4:34, the believers sold their assets and surrendered the proceeds to meet the needs of other believers. God blesses some with an earlier surplus to be used at a later date.

Family responsibility. We are admonished to provide for those within our own households (1 Timothy 5:8). That provision was never limited to the life span of a father. It extended to providing for—not protecting—the family even after the father's death.

Future needs. If parents believe God wants their children to go to college, is it more spiritual to expect the government to educate them than to store for the eventual need? The parable of the ant in Proverbs 6:6 says to "observe her ways and be wise." One of her ways is to plan ahead by storing. In an inflationary economy, even storing requires investing to maintain value.

Worldly Motives for Investing

There are also several worldly motives for investing. Unfortunately, these represent the most common motives of investors, both Christian and non-Christian, because Satan has so thoroughly dominated our attitudes about money.

Greed. The continual desire to have more and demand only the best. "But those who want to get rich fall into temptation and a snare and many foolish and harmful desires which plunge men into ruin and destruction" (1 Timothy 6:9).

Pride. The desire to be elevated because of material achievements. "Instruct those who are rich in this present world not to be conceited or to fix their hope on the uncertainty of riches, but on God, who richly supplies us with all things to enjoy" (1 Timothy 6:17).

Ignorance. Following the counsel of other misguided people because of a lack of discernment. "Leave the presence of a fool, or you will not discern words of knowledge" (Proverbs 14:7).

Envy. The desire to achieve based on observation of other people's success. "For I was envious of the arrogant, as I saw the prosperity of the wicked" (Psalm 73:3).

The bottom line is: worldly motives reflect worldly values. The result is anxiety, frustration, and eventually a deadening of spiritual values. Thus, as our Lord says, "No servant can serve two masters; for either he will hate the one and love the other, or else he will hold to one, and despise the other. You cannot serve God and mammon" (Luke 16:13).

How Much to Invest?

Once a Christian has accepted the purpose of investing to serve God better, the crucial decision is: how much to invest? Obviously, there is no absolute answer. It is an individual decision made by a Christian after much prayer. With earnest prayer the decision is difficult—without it, impossible. There are some initial choices to be made that will greatly simplify the decision about how much to invest.

1. *Give to God's work.* Give until you know that all the needs God has placed on your heart are satisfied. Don't be misled by thinking that means there will be no more needs in the world. There will always be needs, but God doesn't place every need on every heart. Giving, like spiritual discernment, is a matter of growth and practice. One suggestion is, "when in doubt, give." It is better to be wrong and give too much than to ignore God's direction and give too little. The spirit is never dampened by being too sensitive, only by developing calluses. "Therefore openly before the churches show them the proof of your love and of our reason for boasting about you" (2 Corinthians 8:24).

2. *Control personal spending.* Settle on a level of family needs that is God's plan for you. Too much spending by a family can rob surplus funds as surely as bad investments. Each Christian family must decide on the level God has planned for them and stick to it in spite of available surpluses. Remember that balance is essential. Too much spending breeds indulgence; too little is self-punishment. "And whatever we ask we receive from Him, because we keep His commandments and do the things that are pleasing in His sight" (1 John 3:22).

3. *Develop a written plan.* Have a plan for the use of your potential surpluses. One interesting characteristic about humans is that we can rationalize nearly anything including reinvesting God's portion or saving it for Him. Therefore, it is important to settle on a plan for distributing the profits from investments before they arrive. Decide what portion is to be reinvested. Clearly, the greatest danger is to continually reinvest the profits and rationalize it because of tax planning, lack of discernable needs, or a fear of the future. Do your planning before the money becomes available. One good way to do that is to give away a large percentage of the investment before it appreciates. "Because of the proof given by this ministry they will glorify God for your obedience to your confession of the gospel of Christ, and for the liberality of your contribution to them and to all" (2 Corinthians 9:13).

10
How to
Prosper from Problems

DISCOURAGEMENT IS ONLY one of many symptoms associated with problems. During today's economy we counsel a great many Christians who are discouraged over their problems. Many are discouraged to the point of suicide. Satan knows where we're vulnerable, and in America it's usually in our self-esteem about material things.

Discouragement abounds today because of unemployment or under-employment. When everyone is poor, it seems that most people can adjust to that. But when someone has lost a job and most of his friends still have theirs, it's hard to handle. High debt loads and creditor pressures simply add to the feelings of inadequacy and failure.

Causes of Discouragement

In a land of plenty like ours, even those who are poor are better off than the majority of the world. So why do we feel despair and discouragement? Because we have adjusted our expectations and made them relative to every-one else around us. It's the same symptom that causes despair in a multi-millionaire whose assets have shrunk to a few hundred thousand.

Contentment

Most of us suffer from unrealistic expectations of what God promised us. And as Christians we sometimes fear that our problems will make others think of us as less spiritual. We have actually come full circle from those Christians of the first and second century who believed that problems were evidence of spiritual depth. Actually, neither extreme is scripturally correct, but the case for Christians undergoing problems is more scriptural. "Consider it all joy, my brethren, when you encounter various trials" (James 1:2).

But the trials that James is addressing are a consequence of serving God uncompromisingly. Most of our current problems are the result of violating biblical principles, particularly those relating to money.

Certainly the most common cause of discouragement has finances at its roots. We grade people by their finances in America today, and it's no different within Christianity. We put subtle pressures on each other to achieve success as a testimony to the Lord. Therefore, the failure to do so must represent spiritual failure.

When Paul wrote in 1 Timothy 5:8 that a Christian is to provide, he didn't realize how much provision it would take for us. Therefore, when a man can't provide as much as those around him, discouragement sets in. That reaches its peak around Christmas. With all the giving and receiving during the holidays, those who are unable to participate often feel despair and even guilt. In fact, the incidence of suicide increases significantly during this period.

Christian Concern

Perhaps the number one cause of discouragement for Christians with problems is lack of support on the part of other Christians. Children are often cruel to someone who is different, and I sometimes wonder if Christians have reverted back to their childhood. What most people with problems don't need is for someone to point them out or "counsel" them on the "sin" in their lives that is causing the problems. That is not to imply that those who are sinning should not be confronted—they should be—but blatant sin is rarely the case. The majority of people who are discouraged already recognize that they have erred—if they have—and have more than adequately condemned themselves. What they usually need is support and love. "A friend loves at all times, and a brother is born for adversity" (Proverbs 17:17).

The lack of loyalty to Christians undergoing problems is not new. All through Paul's letters there is evidence that his problems caused others to doubt his calling and to avoid him. "At my first defense no one supported me, but all deserted me; may it not be counted against them" (2 Timothy 4:16).

Looking further back in time, the record of Job's friends stands as a testimony to disloyalty. "For the despairing man there should be kindness from his friend; lest he forsake the fear of the Almighty" (Job 6:14).

Unreasonable Expectations

As stated before, unreasonable expectations often create discouragement. The pastor obviously should be a Christian of very high character (Titus 1), but where in that description does it imply that he is perfect? Unfortunately, according to many Christians' opinions, pastors shouldn't have problems. So those who have trouble communicating with their wives or managing to live on half of what others live on often fall victim to discouragement. It would shock many Christians to find out that even their pastors doubt God from time to time and that their problems get so overwhelming they may suffer depression. "For we do not want you to be unaware, brethren, of our affliction which came to us in Asia, that we were burdened excessively, beyond our strength, so that we despaired even of life" (2 Corinthians 1:8).

Another area than can discourage Christians is spiritual expectations about children. That often means that if Mom and Dad have missionary zeal, the kids must too. I believe that nothing exposes our egos like our children. Even the most humble Christian is quick to brag about an achievement by his child, particularly if it's something in the Lord's work. It's as though we want to validate our commitment through our children. If we are elevated spiritually by the achievements of our children, then we are also demoralized by their failures—only more so.

It's probably time that we, as Christians, realize that God doesn't have grandchildren or stepchildren. Everyone decides individually to follow or not to follow the Lord. That does not mean that we shouldn't lead our children, correct them, or encourage them, but we must recognize their right to choose, just as we did. We must also support and encourage those who have children who learn by failure. It would be great if all children were as smart as most parents and could learn without any personal difficulties, just as we did—right? A good way to start this change is to share a few failures you have had with your own children and allow others to observe that Christians haven't totally arrived—we're still on the way.

I experienced such an event when one of my sons came home from college to ask me to help him clear up his checking account. It seems that he had about eight checks overdrawn and some seventy dollars in over-draft charges. Well, needless to say, I was discouraged. The only thing worse for a Christian financial counselor would be for his own account to be overdrawn (that happened one summer when I forgot to make a deposit). God used my son's problem to help me realize that just because I teach financial discipline doesn't mean that my children understand it. It gave me an opportunity to share why these principles are in God's Word. "Like apples of gold in settings of silver is a word spoken in right circumstances" (Proverbs 25:11).

Perhaps the most consistent area of discouragement for most people is financial failure. Not only are our egos involved with our ability to provide, but our security is also threatened. Quite often the demonstration of a Christian's stewardship is not how much he gives but how he reacts when there is not much to give. With many, if not most Christians, their faith at any given time seems proportional to their material resources. Not for all, obviously. Some Christians find that in the midst of their most difficult times their faith grows and matures, which is exactly what James says it will do if we abide in Christ.

God's Word teaches that it is impossible for a Christian to divide loyalties. We will serve but one God. "No one can serve two masters; for either he will hate the one and love the other, or he will hold to one and despise the other. You cannot serve God and mammon" (Matthew 6:24).

The greatest threat to our service to God is being sidetracked into a preoccupation about success. Therefore, God will allow financial crises to come into many of our lives to give us the opportunity to decide whom we *really* serve.

We signed a contract with God when we made Christ Lord over our lives and gave God the right to do whatever is necessary to keep us on His path. "When you make a vow to God, do not be late in paying it, for He takes no delight in fools. Pay what you vow!" (Ecclesiastes 5:4).

So rather than immediately seeking to escape a financial difficulty, first determine what faults can be corrected by turning to God in your time of need.

How to Defeat Discouragement

There is an old cliché that summarizes this area, "Keep on keeping on." You must decide what you believe and trust God regardless of the outside circumstances. Also, your response to any situation should be determined *in advance.* If anyone, Christian or otherwise, waits until a problem occurs to decide how he'll handle it, he will be controlled by the events, not God's Word. God gave us many examples of people who faced difficult situations. Some collapsed into despair and self-pity, while others grew stronger. Those who grew stronger could be categorized, as James said, as "doers" of the Word, not merely "hearers" who delude themselves.

Examples of doers would be Abraham, Nehemiah, Daniel, and Paul. It's pretty clear that they weren't perfect, but they were obedient. In their times of difficulty they did not panic or get depressed. They turned to the Lord. Some of them weren't rescued immediately, and some even died. But remember this—so did everyone else. If all we're looking for is what we can have in this world, then we're only slightly better off than the lost. God wants to bless us with peace in this life and eternal rewards in the next.

11

How Deceit Destroys

As I was reading a familiar passage in Matthew 13, I had to stop and reflect on what the Lord says in verse 22: that the deceitfulness of riches chokes out God's Word. As I pondered over that, I wondered, "Are the riches deceitful, or are they just a simple tool used in deception?" Obviously, the answer is that material possessions are not problems themselves; they are the reflection of problems. Deceit is an external, visible expression of inner spiritual flaws. It just happens that virtually every reference to deceit in God's Word is exemplified in materialism.

With believers, the most devastating loss associated with deceit is the dulling of our spiritual awareness. Guilt associated with a known deception will cause the Christian to withdraw from God's presence. Once withdrawn, subsequent deceptions become easier, and less conviction is felt. Often the pretense of spirituality remains (church, conferences, Bible studies, and so on), but the sensitivity and fellowship are gone. The believer no longer feels "worthy" and feels like he has failed God. If such an attitude is allowed to continue until a facade can be perfected, the result can easily be a life of defeat and frustration.

I have found that no one is immune to the temptation to deceive, particularly when money is concerned. Some people establish their responses prior to the situation and are able to resist, not on the basis of their own strength but on God's.

I can recall clearly that as an unsaved businessman, the temptation to deceive was a constantly nagging problem. Quite often it was not a desire to lie, but rather to just simply omit a few pertinent facts about a product to a potential buyer. After all, I would tell myself, what they don't know won't hurt them. Sometimes that old cliché is right, and sometimes it's wrong, but invariably I found the one that got hurt was me. I felt guilt and not just a little loss of honor each time I misled someone. After becoming a Christian, I just naturally assumed such weaknesses would never tempt me again, especially as I became more familiar with God's Word.

Allow me to share a personal observation here: the one way to fail is to deceive yourself into believing you're too strong to fail. Many times in our lives there are situations in which an undetected compromise to God's way could be made and in fact is made. Fortunately, God knew we wouldn't be perfect and made allowances for our weaknesses by a principle called confession. Those who practice this often find that confession is more difficult than honesty would have been originally, but it is absolutely necessary to restore fellowship with God. "He who conceals his transgressions will not prosper, but he who confesses and forsakes them will find compassion" (Proverbs 28:13). When confession is so painful, total honesty looks a whole lot more attractive the next time.

Deception Destroys Trust

"The perverse in heart are an abomination to the Lord, but the blameless are His delight" (Proverbs 11:20). The Christian walk is not an academic exercise in Scripture memorization—it's a way of life. The purpose of God's Word is to give us guidelines for making decisions in spite of our normal reactions. God wants us to be able to trust Him regardless of the circumstances around us. It is the physical evidence that we believe in a life greater than we now have and in the One who has ultimate authority over everything. Deception is not a problem. It is a testimony that we don't really believe God owns everything and has already considered the consequences. That is true whether we're taking a loss on a car, paying income taxes, or overcharging a travel expense.

Deception Leads to Hypocrisy

"A scoffer does not love one who reproves him, he will not go to the wise" (Proverbs 15:12). There is nothing more personally devastating to a believer than looking spiritual and living defeat. The immediate consequence is the loss of esteem in the eyes of family and close friends. Children are rarely attracted to a weak, watered down version of Christianity that says one thing and does another. If they see Mom and Dad put on their "church" faces on Sunday, they will believe that's what Christianity is all about.

Deception Leads to a Critical Spirit

"Put away from you a deceitful mouth, and put devious lips far from you" (Proverbs 4:24). When a believer is living a life-style that is contrary to God's way, the step from hypocrisy to a critical spirit is a short one. It is the desire to cut others down to his level that brings about the critical or judgmental attitude. Every small flaw in others will be amplified and expounded upon in an effort to justify the flaws in his own attitudes. Instead of accomplishing the desired result of hiding the deceptive spirit, usually the opposite occurs, and others who would not normally notice are even more aware.

The Effect on Children

"Train up a child in the way he should go, even when he is old he will not depart from it" (Proverbs 22:6). It is amazing how slowly children learn good habits and how quickly they pick up bad ones. The reason would seem to be that bad habits are more common and are in fact more enticing than good ones.

Children can easily be taught to deceive by parents. Young children want to please their parents, and if parents get very angry when they hear the truth, then a natural alternative would be to tell them a lie. Some parents would rather hear a lie, because they don't want to have to deal with a difficult situation. If childhood deceptions are allowed and reinforced by seeing Mom or Dad deceive, it can easily become a lifetime attitude. Perhaps more than anyone else, the father affects the attitudes of his offspring. He is the leader in the home, and as such is the authority.

If the children are made to fear being totally honest or are encouraged to develop pride in their parents, the result will often be deception. An attitude in the home that people do make mistakes, and as such need to be able to confess to each other, will go a long way in helping children to be honest rather than having to hide their initial lie by more lies.

Correcting Deception

Be accountable. "Without consultation, plans are frustrated, but with many counselors they succeed" (Proverbs 15:22). All Christians need to be accountable to others, so that when we stray off the path, someone else will correct us. Unfortunately, many Christians are accountable to no one because they don't have to be. That is particularly true of whose who are materially successful, because they isolate themselves behind a wall of ego and pride.

The best accountability comes within the home, especially between husband and wife. With rare exception, one spouse is acutely aware of the other's strengths and weaknesses. If they have an open and honest relationship, one will detect the other's deceptions quickly. Correcting must be done gently and in love, or the result will be bitterness. Always remember that the purpose is to restore a loved one to the right relationship with God, not to accuse him.

Children will participate wholeheartedly in the detection and correction process. (Mine never fail to detect when I exceed the posted speed limit.) In addition to family, every Christian should become accountable to one or more other Christians who care enough to admonish and correct. Sometimes it's painful for both parties, but it is absolutely necessary for spiritual growth.

Quick confession. "He who conceals his transgressions will not prosper, but he who confesses and forsakes them will find compassion" (Proverbs 28:13). Whenever you detect a deception in your own life, large or small, stop what you're doing and confess it immediately. That means not only to God, but to the others who are involved as well. There are many rationalizations for not doing this but really only one reason: pride. You must resolve yourself to confess before the situation presents itself, or it will be impossible. You can't always assume that the others involved will understand or accept an apology, either. It is not necessary for them alone; it is also for you.

Restitution. "If therefore you are presenting your offering at the altar, and there remember that your brother has something against you, leave your offering there before the altar, and go your way; first be reconciled to your brother, and then come and present your offering" (Matthew 5:23-24).

That means that if you must suffer a financial loss to correct an earlier deception, then do what is necessary. The most important relationship is between you and God, and after all, everything belongs to Him anyway. If you have established an absolute standard that you will retain no personal benefit as a result of deception, it will precondition your response to any temptation. That is particularly true if you adopt the same restitution that Zaccheus did and repay 400 percent (Luke 19:8). It then becomes economically unprofitable to deceive; you know that ultimately even more must be repaid.

12

How "Things" Demand Attention

THE AFFLUENCE OF the American way of life is a mixed blessing. On the positive side, our prosperity has made life much easier and has freed a great deal of money to spread God's Word. But on the negative side, prosperity requires a great deal of our time and attention. In fact, the urgency of our materialistic life-styles becomes a tyranny that demands most of our energies. It would seem that the labor cycle since the industrial revolution is reversing itself. Industrialization provided a higher standard of living with a shorter work week. In the early 1900s, it took every family member working sixty hours per week just to make ends meet. By the mid-twentieth century, the average work week was forty-eight hours, and in most families the husband was the primary wage earner. Now, in over 70 percent of American families two incomes are again necessary to support the family's life-style.

Concern About the Future

The American dream only a couple of decades ago was a good job, a comfortable home, and a nice car. Today, it has become guaranteed employment, retirement plans, a home, two cars, a summer cottage, and college educations for all the kids. The possession of "things" has become the scorecard to determine "success." The pressure to provide the luxuries that have now become commonplace causes many Christian families to encumber themselves with debts that eventually destroy their marriages. It's not surprising that many couples look back on their early years of marriage as the best, even though materially they were the leanest. Their lives were usually focused on the day-to-day events, and before the use of mass media advertising, most of us didn't even know what we were missing. It seems clear that the Lord would have all of us focus more on today and less on the uncertainty of the future. "Therefore do not be anxious for tomorrow; for tomorrow will take care of itself. Each day has enough trouble of its own" (Matthew 6:34).

Making Life Easier

The initial purpose of material things is to make our lives easier and more comfortable. But it's amazing how complicated they can become. A family wants to spend a relaxing vacation in the mountains or at the beach, so they buy a summer cottage in that area. Then they find they must spend most of their free time keeping it repaired or protecting it from vandals. Often the experience is so bad they end up loathing the very thing they thought would make life easier. Many times Christians get trapped into operating by the world's wisdom rather than God's.

The world says, "Whatever you see and desire, acquire." God's Word says, "But seek for His kingdom, and these things shall be added to you" (Luke 12:31).

The Real Purpose of Things

A survey of the scriptural warnings about riches and their dangers might suggest that we should avoid all luxuries. That simply is not true. God does not prohibit us from enjoying the benefits of this world (after all, they are His). Rather, we are admonished not to get entangled in them to the point that we are no longer able to fulfill our primary purpose—to serve God. "No soldier in active service entangles himself in the affairs of everyday life, so that he may please the one who enlisted him as a soldier" (2 Timothy 2:4). Unfortunately, today that is exactly where most Christians are. Individual ownership is a biblical principle, but carried to the extreme it becomes greed.

The real purpose of our resources is to free us to do more for Christ, not less. When the pursuit of things becomes our focus in life, there can be no doubt about whom we serve. "No one can serve two masters; for either he will hate the one and love the other, or he will hold to one and despise the other. You cannot serve God and mammon" (Matthew 6:24). It is more than just becoming enmeshed in this world. The real danger is that we will lose our first love and our only source of peace. "Do not love the world, nor the things in the world. If anyone loves the world, the love of the Father is not in him" (1 John 2:15).

Consistently, God's Word teaches that focusing on material things is the greatest danger we face. What makes it seem so normal today is that virtually everyone in America is doing it. Our great abundance has not made us more content; it has made us less content.

The Five Dangers of Things

1. *Adjusting to a life of indulgence as normal.* It is amazing that in less than fifty years we have grown to accept guaranteed salaries, insurance for every contingency, retirement benefits, and two-car families as normal. When

the economy couldn't supply those things quickly enough we simply mort-
gaged our future generations to pay for them. That selfishness is short-lived,
because eventually we borrow more than can ever be repaid. But the real
reason this debt-funded economy always fails is because it violates basic biblical principles. "A faithful man will abound with blessings, but he who makes
haste to be rich will not go unpunished" (Proverbs 28:20).

2. *Focusing on worldly success.* For people who have committed themselves to an eternity with God, it's amazing how worldly our value system
has become. We give positions of authority in our churches and organizations
most often on the basis of material success rather than spiritual maturity.
Obviously, many Christians are materially and spiritually mature, but when
we esteem people on the basis of material success, we begin to equate riches
with spirituality. Thus, those who are not materially successful are deemed
less spiritual. To be assured that God does not hold to the same value system, observe the apostles. "To this present hour we are both hungry and
thirsty, and are poorly clothed, and are roughly treated, and are homeless"
(1 Corinthians 4:11).

3. *Dulling God's direction.* Nothing prohibits Christians from obeying
God more than the tug of material comforts. Once we have adjusted to a life-
style that includes many comforts, it is very difficult to surrender them to serve
God. Obviously, God doesn't call everyone to leave his vocation and go into
what is traditionally called "Christian work." God can and does use Christians
everywhere. But in order to be used by God in any capacity, a Christian must
be willing to serve God no matter what the costs. "More than that, I count all
things to be loss in view of the surpassing value of knowing Christ Jesus my
Lord, for whom I have suffered the loss of all things, and count them but rubbish in order that I may gain Christ" (Philippians 3:8).

Whenever someone asked Christ about what would be expected of him
as a follower, He always tested their willingness to surrender everything for
God's sake. Without that attitude, we can't even be trusted with material riches
because we would spend them on our own indulgences or build larger barns
to store them in.

But God's Word says, "And without faith it is impossible to please Him,
for he who comes to God must believe that He is, and that He is a rewarder
of those who seek Him" (Hebrews 11:6).

We must believe that God wants to bless us, and until God individually
convicts someone that His plan is otherwise, we are not to accept failure.
Tribulation brings about proven character. Don't withdraw because of fail-
ure. Learn from it. Perseverance is a characteristic lacking in Christianity today.
Some Christians who fail get defeated and feel like God has abandoned them.
Some despair to the point of depression or suicide.

4. *Adopting an attitude of superiority.* You would think that knowing
everything belongs to God would make even the wealthiest among us humble.
But it's sad what a little bit of material success will do to our ego and pride.

Very few Christians can really handle success well. Some of the most devoted men of God have been sorely tested when they became known well enough to be a celebrity. Those who have been given responsibility in this life must be very careful to exercise it with great caution, lest they give up their eternal rewards for some temporary ones. "Do nothing from selfishness or empty conceit, but with humility of mind let each of you regard one another as more important than himself" (Philippians 2:3).

5. *Indifference toward the needs of others.* A real danger of material affluence is that we begin to think everybody has it. But that's simply not true. The vast majority of people in this world go to bed hungry and wake up hungry. They love their children as much as we do ours, and every day they die a little bit more because they cannot provide even the little food it takes to keep them alive. Let me assure you that most of them aren't lazy or evil—they are poor. They are the ones that Christ describes in Matthew 25:45: "Then He will answer them, saying, 'Truly I say to you, to the extent that you did not do it to one of the least of these, you did not do it to Me.'"

Most often our indifference is passive. It isn't that Christians don't care; we do. It's just that we don't personally know any really poor people, and we're wary of the give-away plans of many ministries. But let me assure you, there are many really poor people and legitimate ministries who care for them, one on one. Giving to feed the poor and homeless is a command, not a request. This area would seem to be the biggest lack of Christianity today and is a direct result of our great affluence. It's unfortunate that those in need are the most sensitive to the needs of others.

Establish a Balance

There must always be a balance in the area of material "things." God does not have an identical plan for any of us, and what one family spends is different from another. The common measure for all of us is to reach that balance between using material things and being controlled by them. To do this, a Christian must establish that he serves Christ first and all other considerations come after that. That means that all of our actions should be heavily weighted to Christ's service first. Our giving should reflect this commitment, and a tithe should not be our goal but rather our minimum. Each increase in our income should increase our outreach before it does our life-styles, and we should be known primarily for our commitment to God's work rather than our display of material things.

13
Dealing with Pride

ONCE A CHRISTIAN is trapped by his pride, he is no service to God. Without a change and a commitment to accountability, he will not be aware of his attitude of pride.

God will give us plenty of opportunity to recognize and correct the attitude of pride. The difficulty most times is admitting that we actually have a problem. Recently, God gave me the opportunity to assess myself about pride. I was working on some important material, and a deadline was approaching when I received a phone call from a widow I was counseling. I was a little irritated because she had been in several times previously with relatively trivial problems. She asked if she could come in right away because she had a crisis in her budget—her checking account didn't balance. I explained that I really didn't have any time available and suggested another counselor we had trained. A short time later I received a call from a businessman who wanted to bring by a celebrity who was in town working on a movie. I knew it was a rare opportunity, and I said yes.

As soon as I hung up the phone the words of James came ringing in my ears. "But if you show partiality, you are committing sin and are convicted by the law as transgressors" (James 2:9).

I found myself trapped by the most devious snare that Satan lays: pride. I also found that God's correction system is very painful sometimes. I had to call the businessman back and tell him I couldn't meet with them until later and call my counselee back and ask her forgiveness. By the way, the celebrity never did come in. He was too miffed by being put off.

Pride is so deceptive because it's so normal today. Christians are told to achieve and be the best so they can be an effective witness. Then somewhere along the way the goal of achieving takes a higher priority than the witnessing. By the time most Christians should have the greatest witness they become boastful and indulgent. They believe it's better to live their witness, so they surround themselves with enough indulgence to prove that God really blesses the faithful. He does, but not for the purpose of building our egos. "Because you say, 'I am rich, and have become wealthy, and have need of nothing,' and you do not know that you are wretched and miserable and poor and blind and naked" (Revelation 3:17).

Symptoms of Pride

In order to cure a disease, we must first be able to recognize its symptoms. They are the visible, outside indicators. Although we may not always recognize them in ourselves, others will. So it becomes vital for us to stay open to criticism, particularly from those who are spiritually discerning. Those most consistent in discerning our faults are usually our spouses. God has placed them in our lives as a balance, and they will help to offset our extremes if we will listen. That works both ways because we are also their balance. But more often than not it is the husband who refuses to take counsel from his wife. Why? Pride.

Be a Leader

"For who regards you as superior? And what do you have that you did not receive? But if you did receive it, why do you boast as if you had not received it?" (1 Corinthians 4:7).

Nothing points more clearly to a pride problem than an aloof leader. When Christians find that they only want to associate with the "right" people and look down at others because they're less educated, less intelligent, or less successful, then they are no longer useful to God's work. A businessman who looks down at his employees and other contacts will not be a witness on the job. He will have to go outside his company environment in order to share his faith. If you are in authority, it is important that you care as much about the least significant person in the company as you do the most important.

It is easy to be nice to those who can benefit you, but Christ said that anyone would do that. He said to give to those who can never repay you and you will be rewarded. "For if you love those who love you, what reward have you? Do not even the tax gatherers do the same? And if you greet your brothers only, what do you do more than others? Do not even the Gentiles do the same? Therefore you are to be perfect, as your heavenly Father is perfect" (Matthew 5:46-48).

That requires an attitude change on our part. We must actually demonstrate that no one person is more or less important than another. One might have the ability to make money, and another to teach, or write, or pray. But which is more important from God's perspective?

One businessman I know has made a concerted effort to step out of his executive mold and serve others first. He directed his efforts toward getting to know his lowest level employees. When he did, he found they had many financial problems he had long since forgotten even existed. The net result was that he substantially increased most of their wages. One employee had tremendous medical bills for a child with cancer. He paid the majority of the bills himself and raised the rest through friends. Initially, not one of the employees was a Christian, but today, over half are. Two have even left for full-time service. You can't grade that kind of commitment financially, but on an eternal scale it's a ten-plus. "Do nothing from selfishness or empty conceit, but with humility of mind let each of you regard one another as more important than himself" (Philippians 2:3).

Selfishness

It is easy to rationalize an indulgent life-style in a society where most people indulge themselves. In order to get the right balance, we must go back to God's Word. Obviously, it is not necessary to live poorly to serve the Lord. The only people who think poverty is spiritual are those who haven't tried it. But just as certainly, it is clear from God's Word that affluence presents the greatest threat to our walk with the Lord. "For where your treasure is, there will your heart be also" (Matthew 6:21).

It is a rare individual who can actually handle much wealth and keep his priorities straight. One wealthy man rationalized his need for a $2 million airplane because he had to wait two hours in an airport one day. It is easy to gratify every whim or indulgence simply because we can afford to. Today the cliché is, "Live like the King's kids." But I don't see anything in Christ's teachings that directs us to do so. I truly believe that poverty is not God's norm, but neither is lavishness. "But those who want to get rich fall into temptation and a snare and many foolish and harmful desires which plunge men into ruin and destruction" (1 Timothy 6:9).

A Christian must learn self-discipline in money to be able to teach others. Our affluence has distorted our priorities. While we go to sleep disturbed over whether or not to buy a big screen TV, over half the world's kids go to bed hungry and cold. Communism is taking over the world with its false promises, but Christianity isn't even making promises anymore. Many of the world's governments care more for human needs than the church does. Obviously, we can't give away all of our goods, but we've stopped even giving a fair share.

Everything starts with a first step, and that first step is to get involved with the needs of others. That will help focus more clearly on what your actual needs are. One businessman determined to help where he could. He and several other businessmen started buying run-down houses, repairing them, and making them available to the elderly at whatever they could afford. Several times they pooled their funds and purchased a small home outright for elderly widows. The homes were usually inner city houses that could be purchased and repaired for $20,000 or less. With twenty businessmen involved, the expense was not prohibitive.

Accountability

If you have a problem with pride, it's doubtful that anyone will point it out to you. Most of those with whom you have daily contact are people who won't say anything (at least to you), and besides, many people who are egotistical enough to show their pride are too proud to accept counsel from another. Once a Christian is trapped by his pride, he is not of service to God.

How do you break out of the pride trap? First, vow to serve God and God's people, and then make yourself accountable to others. Too often Christian leaders, including ministry heads, are not accountable to anyone. Consequently, they have little or no feedback from those who can recognize the symptoms associated with pride.

First and foremost, a husband and wife must be accountable to each other. Major decisions should be discussed together and opinions and insights exchanged. If a wife has the liberty to be honest, she will usually detect and expose her husband's pride, and vice versa.

Second, a Christian businessman should be accountable to a peer or someone he respects who is strong enough to be totally honest. Those I know who practice accountability find they must meet regularly and learn each other's basic flaws. They must both be studying God's Word and be seeking to truly serve God, or it won't work. The rules I use for those I have helped get started are: (1) The criticism must be honest and based on God's Word. (2) The person pointing out the problem must suggest a way to change the attitude and must testify how the change helped in his own life.

14
Assuming God's Will

HAVE YOU EVER witnessed a Christian who was obviously doing something rather dumb but rationalizing it to all dissenters by saying, "God told me to do it?" For most of us, that's a hard argument to overcome because by merely challenging it you feel as though you're doubting God. Later, when the whole thing falls apart, most Christians wish they had had the courage to speak up.

Why won't we speak up when we see another Christian who is obviously wrong? Because most of us are timid about applying biblical truth to a real-life situation and challenging anything contrary to God's Word. Sometimes the person in question is a notable Christian in the community. Let me assure you of this: no one has a perfect insight into God's will. The soundest, most mature believers can and do make mistakes about God's will. Usually, when confronted by either a loving but firm challenge from another Christian or the resulting problems, they will change direction.

Apparently, such was the case when Paul opposed Peter at Antioch. "But when Cephas came to Antioch, I opposed him to his face, because he stood condemned" (Galatians 2:11).

Paul knew the truth, and Peter's actions didn't conform to the truth, so he confronted the leader of the Christian church. Judging from the fact that Paul never mentions that incident again, Peter changed direction.

However, some Christians simply refuse to believe they could be wrong and cloak themselves in spirituality by saying, "I know God wants me to do this." Those who consistently do that confirm an old cliché, "Often wrong, but never in doubt."

Open Door Philosophy

Many Christians make decisions on major issues based on what is called the "open door" philosophy. In other words, God would never let anyone do something wrong and therefore, if the door is open, I should go through it. I often think of this as the "open mine shaft" philosophy because a lot of Christians stumble down open shafts thinking God wouldn't let them fail. Clearly, God has given us the authority to do dumb things. A brief review of those whom God chose to use, beginning with Adam, will attest to that. There is ample direction in God's Word to avert most errors. Unfortunately, too often Christians feel like God is dealing with them in a new and unique dispensation, especially where money is concerned.

I know of a Christian businessman who was involved in deception and rationalized it. It seems his business had failed when the economy dipped and interest rates didn't. Excessive debt load wiped out his capital and ultimately forced him out of business. His first personal revelation was that God told him to go bankrupt. That was confirmed by a Christian lawyer on a television program who said that bankruptcy was a modern-day form of "the year of remission" (Deuteronomy 15:1). Unfortunately, he forgot to mention that debt remission was always an option of the lender, not the borrower. God demands repayment of debt (Psalm 37:21), so the businessman filed bankruptcy, with the stated intent of repaying the debts later.

Since he needed a large amount of money to get started again, he approached several other Christians he had met while in business and got them to invest in a new venture, without any mention of the previous bankruptcy. Being rather persuasive, he raised enough capital to open a new office and hire some people. He then applied for and received a sizable government new-business loan. This he believed had to be from God because his previous bankruptcy didn't show up in the loan check. Further confirmation came when a major supplier shipped him tens of thousands of dollars worth of inventory on a 120 days' payment basis. He said God must have blinded them to let him get started again.

During that time, several Christians in his church felt his actions were contrary to good Christian conduct, and one even approached him about it. The reply was always the same, "God wants me to do this. I'm believing Him for a great success, and I won't listen to any negative talk." The success of such ventures won't be measured in dollars and cents. Even if such a venture succeeds, it's a failure according to God's Word. God does not work through guile and unspoken deceit. "He who walks in integrity walks securely, but he who perverts his ways will be found out" (Proverbs 10:9).

In this particular case, the unspoken deceit resulted in a fraud conviction and prison sentence. He had to default on the government loan when the business failed.

Confirmed by Success

It's worth repeating that material success does not necessarily constitute God's endorsement of our actions. That applies to businesses and ministries alike. Every decision we make should meet two criteria. First, it must be compatible with God's written Word. Some decisions are objective enough to be eliminated on the basis of direct contradiction to God's Word.

For instance, a short time ago, a friend told me that he received a notice from a Christian organization saying they would accept a gift of $100 or more through the month of January and receipt the donor in the previous year—a great tax planning help. I counseled my friend to contact the head of that organization and inform him that their proposed action was illegal. He did so and was told that this procedure was used every year and had proved to be very successful. The ministry head said he was sure it was legal as God wouldn't bless something illegal. A few calls to the I.R.S. absolutely confirmed its illegality. Unraveling the mess created over the last several years will probably destroy the effectiveness of that group. No, God won't bless something illegal, but He will let us do it and suffer the consequences.

Second, each decision must be compatible with our personal convictions. Paul wrote, "The faith which you have, have as your own conviction before God. Happy is he who does not condemn himself in what he approves" (Romans 14:22).

The Christian life is not just a set of rules that can be obeyed to the letter and thus satisfy our commitment. We are held to an even higher standard that requires constant input from the Holy Spirit to keep our direction straight. It means that we are accountable if we defile our conscience by doing something we feel is wrong. That feeling must be based on a firm conviction from God. How do you know? You just *know*. I usually know by a lack of inner peace.

A businessman called recently with such a doubt. He said he had a strong conviction from the Lord to get involved with helping unemployed people in his community. To do so he had provided jobs for three of them in his plant and had involved them in various community service projects. Then his accountant discovered that their employment qualified his business for the government "jobs" program and an associated grant. The grant provided more funds than their actual salaries and would have allowed him to hire more unemployed. But he had a lack of peace about accepting the grant—in stark contrast to the original peace he had felt about the work program. The grant was legal, and the funds could be put to good use; but for him it was wrong.

After much prayer and a great deal of searching, he found his answer in 1 Chronicles 21:24; "But King David said to Ornan, 'No, but I will surely buy it for the full price; for I will not take what is yours for the Lord, or offer a burnt offering which costs me nothing.'"

The project was to be God's project, not the government's. As a result of his stand, several other businessmen have joined with him in providing more jobs. Certainly, with the government involved the project might be bigger, but God's best is not always manifested in "bigness."

Failing Gracefully

There are many Christians who are "graceful failures." They don't demand anything of God and, in fact, expect nothing. Usually, they get what they expect—nothing. Just because manipulating God's Word for self-benefit is wrong, that doesn't mean that we shouldn't ask and expect. Many Christians accept failure as "God's will" when it is not at all. Scripture says that God wants to bless us and wants us to ask of Him. It's why we ask that's important. "You ask and do not receive, because you ask with wrong motives, so that you may spend it on your pleasures" (James 4:3). We have God's authority to ask and expect to receive when the motives are correct.

But God's Word says, "And without faith it is impossible to please Him, for he who comes to God must believe that He is, and that He is a rewarder of those who seek Him" (Hebrews 11:6).

We must believe that God wants to bless us, and until God individually convicts someone that His plan is otherwise, we are not to accept failure. Tribulation brings about proven character. Don't withdraw because of failure. Learn from it. Perseverance is a characteristic much lacking in Christianity today. Some Christians who fail get defeated and feel like God has abandoned them. Some despair to the point of depression or suicide.

Those who believe you should accept failure as a "no" from God or as some kind of punishment need to reread Christ's parables in Luke 11:5–13 and Luke 18:1–8. One of God's principles is persistence in the face of discouragement. Anyone would do God's will if God would prove Himself first. But do we trust God or just say we do?

Balance

Even with the best discernment it's possible, and even probable, that we will do things that are out of God's will. Paul said that now we see dimly, as through a mirror, and therefore our spiritual vision will be imperfect. The key is not to let pride get in the way and say, "Well, it's just God's will." That imbalance is usually a rationalization for slothfulness or an inner doubt about God. Our attitude should be to thank God for showing us what doesn't work and get back to the task of discovering what does.

On the other side, a sure way to step out of God's path is to compromise His Word or His will for us and justify it by the obvious "success" it brings. Satan is quite willing and able to "bless" any plan that serves his purpose rather than God's. Only by staying in God's Word and seeking strong godly counsel can you avoid these traps. If you find yourself outside of God's will and are experiencing a lack of peace, you must be willing to abandon everything and seek God's path again. "Brethren, I do not regard myself as having laid hold of it yet; but one thing I do: forgetting what lies behind and reaching forward to what lies ahead" (Philippians 3:13).

15

Christian Commitment— What Is It?

IF MOST CHRISTIANS in the West were as dedicated to Christian activities, such as Bible study, prayer, and evangelism, as they are to sports, we would truly have a spiritual revival today. As Christ taught, Christians are always confronted with a conflict between God's way and the world's attractions.

This came to mind some time back when I received a call from a pastor asking if we could change the date of a seminar that had been scheduled for over a year. When I asked why, he said that at a recent deacons' meeting it was noted that the seminar was being held on the same weekend as the traditional college football game. Unfortunately, he said, several of the church leaders had "conflicts" that weekend.

One pastor of a large dynamic church confided that he had come under severe criticism for allowing the Sunday morning services to go beyond twelve o'clock when the local professional football team had home games. Obviously, it is not sports, recreation, or other activities that are the problems. It is a lack of vital, dynamic commitments to God's way. The other things are merely outside indicators of an inside condition.

The non-Christian world will try to test our commitment to see if it's real. If it's not, they will reject our message as just another philosophy. Quite often, the testing ground will be on the job or in our own neighborhood. Many Christians have lost their witness because they weren't really "doers of the Word." "But prove yourselves doers of the word, and not merely hearers who delude themselves" (James 1:22).

Commitment to Self

There are many dedicated Christians who are willing to accept God's direction at any moment and surrender their jobs, home, and comforts to accomplish their assigned tasks. However, they do not represent a majority within the Christian community. We have a standard for Christian service that requires very little of us. It yields a sizeable body of believers who never really mature. It would seem in God's discipleship plan that some adversity and self-denial are necessary ingredients for spiritual maturity. "Consider it all joy, my brethren, when you encounter various trials, knowing that the testing of your faith produces endurance. And let endurance have its perfect result, that you may be perfect and complete, lacking in nothing" (James 1:2–4).

One has to wonder what Bible it is that some Christians claim promises them perfect health, unlimited success, and permanent residence at the location of their choice. Certainly, it's not the same one that says, "Whoever does not carry his own cross and come after Me cannot be My disciple" (Luke 14:27).

A commitment to the lordship of Christ means that we must be willing to go where God determines we can best be utilized. Paul describes us as soldiers in God's army, and we are admonished not to get so caught up in the everyday affairs of this life that we take ourselves out of the battle.

Priorities: God, Family, Work

Most Christians know that in God's priority system He must come first, family second, and work, recreation, and so on should assume lower priorities. However, it is possible to confuse this priority system and step out of God's will. Putting God first means the active, daily process of knowing and being known by God. It starts with a thorough understanding of God's handbook for life, the Bible. It requires a heartfelt desire to please God and a willingness to accept God's authority over us.

Many times in the pursuit of this first priority, conflicts will arise in the lower priorities. For instance, what happens when a husband's call to serve God requires relocating, which causes family conflicts? Usually, it's a conflict because of family ties to a particular area. It seems that through the years, those who were willing to be used by God have faced the same conflicts but have determined that the first priority lasts for eternity—all others cease at death.

Christ's Required Commitment

A review of Christ's ministry on earth demonstrates pretty clearly that He was seeking those who would commit everything to the service of God's kingdom. Even as He walked and taught, many people were attracted to Him because of the miracles He was performing. Each time someone asked Him if they could join His disciples, He directed them to lay aside their own desires and follow Him unreservedly. "But Jesus said to him, 'No one, after putting his hand to the plow, and looking back, is fit for the kingdom of God'" (Luke 9:62).

With few exceptions, they turned back to whatever they had been doing before; the price was simply too high for them.

The lesson for Christians today should be overwhelmingly clear: All of those who are too busy for Christ will regret it. All that truly matters then is what we can do for the kingdom of God. The things we accumulate are not important. They are tools for us to use in accomplishing God's work. Some will need a great resource and some only a little. God owns it all, anyway. Christ said we must make a choice about our commitment and there are only two choices. "No servant can serve two masters; for either he will hate the one, and love the other, or else he will hold to one, and despise the other. You cannot serve God and mammon" (Luke 16:13).

Committing Our Time, Talent, and Treasures

Sometimes it is easier to commit money than it is to commit our time and talent. Consistently, I find that a stewardship commitment involves all three. Perhaps the simplest truth about commitment ever written can be found in Matthew 6:21, "For where your treasure is, there will your heart be also." You can determine a great deal about a Christian's spiritual commitment by what he treasures.

Treasures. The way a Christian uses money is the clearest outside indicator of what the inside commitment is really like. The passage in Matthew 6:21 is a spiritual truth being reflected in a material way. "For where your treasure is, there will your heart be also." The opposite is also true that where your heart is, your treasure will follow.

In reality, it is the sowing and reaping principle taught by Paul in 2 Corinthians 9:6. "Now this I say, he who sows sparingly shall also reap sparingly; and he who sows bountifully shall also reap bountifully." The commitment of material resources to God's work is a proof that the spiritual seeds sown found good soil and matured.

Talent. Many Christians waste the intellect and abilities God has given by dedicating their entire lives to the pursuit of material success. There is obviously nothing wrong with success, as long as it is a by-product of a fruitful life dedicated to God's service. But it's time we realize that a sizeable portion of our talent must be utilized in serving Him too.

Time. I suspect that not many Christians would want to stand before the Lord today and give an account of their daily activities. For instance, if we look at our available day (less sleeping time, eating time, bathing, and so on) as equal to 100 percent, what percentage is spent in the first priority, seeking God? Most surveys show that less than two percent of the average Christian's day is spent in personal Bible study and prayer.

Serving the Master

The commitment of our treasures goes far beyond just giving money to the Lord's work. It encompasses our motives about earning a living. Many times a commitment will break down when it requires a sacrifice that may include a career change. Some time ago, I met a Christian who was an executive with a national hotel chain. He was faced with just such a decision. The company he worked for had made a decision to include a pornographic cable system in their rooms. After speaking as loudly as he could against it, he determined that he, as a Christian, could no longer be associated with them. At almost sixty years of age, he knew his decision was clearly one of deciding which master he must serve. Today, he is a successful real estate salesman who seeks to put the Lord first in everything. "But seek for His kingdom, and these things shall be added to you" (Luke 12:31).

The decision of choosing which master to follow is one that each of us must make every day. Are we willing to weigh every decision against God's Word and follow the narrow path God requires?

16

Is Gambling Wrong?

AT FIRST GLANCE, most Christians would respond to the question, "Is gambling wrong?" with a hearty yes. But is gambling *spiritually* wrong? It would appear that the apostles gambled, according to Luke's historical record in Acts 1:26, when they drew lots to determine who was to replace Judas Iscariot. Quite correctly you might say, "But they didn't risk money." The issue, though, is not what the risk or reward was, but rather the action itself. But we'll leave that discussion until later.

Does the fact that the secular world has greatly abused a concept like gambling necessarily make the activity wrong? If so, then we must expand our list to include sex, money, education, and so on. All of these areas have been greatly abused by our secular society. Indeed, today the list might include nearly every human activity. No, we're on shaky ground, spiritually, to exclude an activity on the basis of misuse in our society.

Perhaps we could approach gambling from the perspective of the harm it causes. After all, it attracts a very greedy element of society and robs families of needed resources. But couldn't we say the same thing about credit? We know it robs many more families of needed resources than does gambling, and it has long been associated with organized crime. Even a cursory review of God's Word reveals that all harmful practices aren't eliminated or prohibited—they are controlled. Again, the classic example from Scripture is debt. Even though a man could lose his freedom and family through debt, the practice was discouraged but allowed in both the Old and the New Testaments.

Why Gamble?

Before reviewing the principle of gambling, let's take a look at why most people gamble. Many people gamble because they have needs that cannot be met through earned income. They barely make ends meet, and gambling represents their opportunity to acquire material comforts. In the past, these were the people who played the two-dollar window at the race track. Today, they play the lotteries that many states now offer to attract more funds for the public coffers.

Another group gambles just for the fun of it. They say it doesn't matter if they win or lose. But let them start winning, and you find out that's not so. These are the social gamblers, and they represent most of the people found at Las Vegas or Atlantic City. They go on vacation with a set amount of money. Once it's gone, they pack up and go home, often living conservative lives that require disciplined budgeting.

One last group gambles compulsively. Gambling, to them, is a disease that wrecks their finances, families, and careers. The compulsive gamblers will lie, steal, cheat, and use virtually everyone around them. A game of chance to them is what alcohol is to the alcoholic. Often, they are successful professionals with promising careers. One compulsive gambler I counseled maintained a successful career for several years while flying to Las Vegas twice a month without his wife's even knowing about it. His dual life ended when he owed over $200,000 in gambling debts to underworld lenders and had embezzled over $100,000 from trust funds in his care.

At first glance, each of these types of gamblers would appear to have different motives for gambling, but, in reality, they all suffer from the same basic problem—materialism. The one who gambles when in need is looking for the "big hit" just like the social gambler or the compulsive gambler.

James described the symptom very well in James 4:1. "What is the source of quarrels and conflicts among you? Is not the source your pleasures that wage war in your members?"

What Is Gambling?

In order to evaluate gambling scripturally, we must first determine what it is. If it's labor, then it has scriptural value. "In all labor there is profit, but mere talk leads only to poverty" (Proverbs 14:23).

Well, gambling may be labor for a pit boss in Vegas, but for the gamblers, it's a scheme to escape labor, at least in most instances. Gambling is perhaps the ultimate in get-rich-quick schemes. It satisfies every element of get-rich-quick: (1) The participants are encouraged to risk money they usually can't afford to lose. (2) They know little or nothing about what they are doing. (3) They're forced to make hasty decisions. (4) The whole idea is to operate on the "greater sucker" theory. In other words, when you dump money into the slot machine, you believe there was a greater sucker who risked his money and then quit just before the big jackpot.

Any get-rich-quick scheme is developed to entrap the weak and especially the poor. After all, what does a wealthy man need with a get-rich-quick scheme? Gambling is an almost irresistible enticement to someone who desires to meet the wants and desires of his family but finds that he cannot. That's why the state lotteries are so popular. We don't have to wonder about the state of our society when governments resort to enticing their citizens to gamble to raise funds. "Even so, every good tree bears good fruit; but the bad tree bears bad fruit" (Matthew 7:17).

Is Gambling a Sin?

Gambling, in the strictest sense, is as much a sin as having a false weight in your bag. To entice someone to gain money at the certain loss of another violates virtually every principle taught by Christ. It breeds and promotes selfishness, greed, and covetousness. "For many walk, of whom I often told you, and now tell you even weeping, that they are enemies of the cross of Christ, whose end is destruction, whose god is their appetite, and whose glory is in their shame, who set their minds on earthly things" (Philippians 3:18-19).

A sin, according to God's Word, means missing the mark. Regardless of how socially acceptable the practice of gambling has become, it is still preying upon the weaknesses of others. It does *not* help to expand the gospel and, therefore, is a sin to a follower of Jesus Christ. "So that you may walk in a manner worthy of the Lord, to please Him in all respects, bearing fruit in every good work and increasing in the knowledge of God" (Colossians 1:10).

To preempt the question about this conclusion's being legalism rather than a principle, you need only do a survey of Paul's letters. We are first told, as believers, to live by a standard higher than the world's (Romans 12:2). Also, we are told to do nothing that would give cause for offense or that might discredit our ministry (2 Corinthians 6:3). Even if a Christian believes that he is free to gamble, the truth is it will cause others to stumble. We are clearly directed in 1 Corinthians 8:13 to avoid anything that would cause a weaker brother to stumble.

Compulsive Gambling

Many people are compulsive gamblers. A compulsive gambler is as addicted to risk taking as a dope addict is to drugs. He will bet on virtually anything and will rob his kid's piggy bank if necessary. Every church has at least one compulsive gambler, and some churches have several. All too often, they are supported out of a church benevolence fund without the benevolence group's even knowing about the gambling. The way to overcome this is to *require* counseling for any benevolence fund recipient and *absolutely* require that both husband and wife attend.

Having counseled several gamblers, I have found several common characteristics to look for. First, there is an unusually high debt load with little or no logical explanation for it. Second, there will be a history of borrowing from virtually every friend and family member. Third, you will find a vehement denial of anything to do with gambling. It is often in response to a direct question about gambling that the spouse will usually reveal the truth. A com-

pulsive gambler may hide his secret from the outside world but not from a
spouse.

Any gambler needs love and acceptance, but it must be accompanied by
accountability. He needs to be held accountable to pay his debts, tell the truth,
and stay away from *all* gambling. If God's people don't hold to this same standard, it's rather hard to give good counsel to a compulsive gambler.

Satan's Lie

In our society, sin is being spread under the guise of innocence. In the
case of gambling, we are being fed the lie that legalized gambling doesn't
promote crime and will lower taxes when, in fact, the evidence shows just
the opposite. Gambling promotes other vices that attract the criminal element.
That results in higher, not lower, taxes.

Many Christians are guilty of supporting lotteries, bingo, and racing all
under the assumption that gambling doesn't really hurt anyone. That's exactly
what Satan would have us believe. We pass our value system along to those
around us—first, to our own families, then to our friends and neighbors.

If our value system is no better than the world's, then truly we have been
conformed to the image of this world. "Whether, then, you eat or drink or
whatever you do, do all to the glory of God. Give no offense either to Jews or
to Greeks or to the church of God; just as I also please all men in all things,
not seeking my own profit, but the profit of the many, that they may be saved"
(1 Corinthians 10:31-33).

17
Christian Compromise

FEW CHRISTIANS WOULD willfully violate the Ten Commandments. Most appear to be basically moral. But what about inward doubts, temptations, and failures—are these sin?

The actual violations of many of God's commandments involve attitudes more than actions: lustful thoughts, anger, and pride. These attitudes develop over a period of time and are very difficult to guard against. Most of us simply find ourselves doing them without realizing how or when they started. It is apparent from God's Word that He also recognizes that and has provided an objective means for us to measure our internal attitudes. That measure is how we respond to the smaller temptations involving money (Luke 16:10). Knowing and using this truth can be a key to becoming a truly Spirit-controlled Christian.

God's Absolutes

God's *minimum* acceptable attitudes basically boil down to two: to love God totally and to love others as ourselves (Matthew 22:37–39). Christ said that loving God more than anything else was a prerequisite to receiving God's best. "But seek for His kingdom, and these things shall be added to you" (Luke 12:31). John repeated this command as a condition for expecting answers from God. "And whatever we ask we receive from Him, because we keep His commandments and do the things that are pleasing to His sight" (1 John 3:22).

That explains in great part why so few people are willing and able to totally trust God for material needs. It is not that they don't desire to obey and trust God—they just are not willing to stand without compromise, regardless of the situation.

Temptations to Compromise

Compared to overt sins, compromises don't seem so bad. If God was merely an accountant weighing good against bad, and one person against another, there would be no problem. However, God deals in absolutes, not comparisons, and each individual is totally responsible and accountable for his actions regardless of what others do. Compromises of God's Word are simply outside material symptoms of inside spiritual problems. Quite often in financial situations, the urge to compromise is evident. It may be the tendency to cheat on income taxes or to take bankruptcy in the face of overwhelming debts. It may be a white lie to sell a product or a padded expense account. The Lord said that the desire for money would lead to the worship of money and the violation of the first commandment. "No one can serve two masters; for either he will hate the one and love the other, or he will hold to one and despise the other. You cannot serve God and mammon" (Matthew 6:24).

The accumulation of money is a major deterrent to a humble spirit. The tendency is to desire to be served rather than to serve: "It is not so among you, but whoever wishes to be first among you shall be your slave" (Matthew 20:26-27).

Obviously, money is *not* the problem, it is only the symptom. Many temptations associated with materialism are so common today that most Christians accept them as a normal way of life. Fear of the future is so great in our society that millions of Christians have been persuaded to squirrel away literally billions of dollars without any real plans for its future use, even though it requires a direct compromise to God's instructions. "But seek first His kingdom and His righteousness; and all these things shall be added to you. Therefore do not be anxious for tomorrow; for tomorrow will care for itself. Each day has enough trouble of its own" (Matthew 6:33-34).

Greed has become such an accepted attitude that most major advertisements for luxury products are built around it. Many committed believers are convinced (often by other believers) that it is God's absolute responsibility to make them wealthy and successful. Just to help Him out (in case God neglects His responsibility), they are willing to borrow large amounts of money to invest in get-rich-quick schemes, abandon their families to provide the "good life" for them, rob God of His tithes and offerings, and rationalize all of it as serving Him.

God does have a plan for success. Although it is unique for each individual, it is common in the following ways: (1) God never provides success at the expense of serving Him first. "But those who want to get rich fall into temptation and a snare and many foolish and harmful desires which plunge men into ruin and destruction" (1 Timothy 6:9). (2) God never provides success at the expense of our peace. "Peace I leave with you; My peace I give to you; not as the world gives, do I give to you. Let not your heart be troubled, nor let it be fearful" (John 14:27). (3) God never provides success at the expense of the family. "It is vain for you to rise up early, to retire late, to eat the bread of painful labors; for He gives to His beloved even in His sleep" (Psalm 127:2).

Gos's Way: Optional or Mandatory?

It seems abundantly clear from God's Word that those who accept Christ as their Lord are to live by a much higher standard than the rest of the world, not because Christians are to be pious or super-spiritual but simply because they are to be normal. It is God's way that is normal and the world's way that is abnormal. Christians are to be lights to lead others to God in a dark world. What we say is not enough. God requires that we show and tell. "That you may prove yourselves to be blameless and innocent, children of God above reproach in the midst of a crooked and perverse generation, among whom you appear as lights in the world" (Philippians 2:15).

As Christians, we learn a great deal about discipline and dedication from the secular world. It is interesting that those in the secular business world are almost always more punctual and reliable in their work than Christians are in serving God. Usually, Christians apply a degree of excellence and dedication to their business careers that is woefully lacking in their walk with the Lord.

The secular business world practices what is called "preconditioned response." For instance, the airlines have found that it is not feasible to wait until an inflight emergency occurs to acquaint the pilot with emergency procedures. Therefore, they attempt to precondition his response. The techniques for responding to every kind of emergency are practiced again and again. Obviously, some pilots won't ever be faced with such emergences, and most won't be faced with more than one or two. But having the knowledge makes them more relaxed and confident and better pilots.

Many Christians have been duped into believing that no emergencies will ever occur in their lives, and even if they do, they can handle them by instinct. Thus they are ill-prepared and out of condition to handle problems and temptations. When faced with a potentially compromising situation, they lack the basic tools to make the choice God's way.

Even a cursory scan of Scripture will reveal that the truly successful servants of the Lord made decisions on the preconditioned belief that God's way wasn't just the best way—it was the *only* way. The consequences of not obeying God were so dreadful that any earthly consequences were considered trivial. The worldly consequences of making decisions God's way might be less income, no sale, the loss of a job, or overpayment of taxes. However, the consequences of compromising God's way are:

- Lack of peace (James 4:4)
- Cooling toward God (James 4:17)
- Critical spirit (James 3:16)
- Uselessness to God (Titus 1:16)

Just as Nehemiah did (Nehemiah 6:11) when he refused to compromise God's way even to save his own life, a Christian must precondition all responses to temptations and problems on the basis of what God says, *not* what is normal and acceptable. God promises that He will prosper us and protect us so that He may receive the glory (Psalm 50:14–15). It also makes life a whole lot simpler when facing decisions that many face every day about suing, borrowing, lending, co-signing, bankruptcy, and paying taxes.

God's Word challenges us to look beyond the temporary rewards of being a conformist to the eternal rewards of being a "light." "More than that, I count all things to be loss in view of the surpassing value of knowing Christ Jesus my Lord, for whom I have suffered the loss of all things, and count them but rubbish in order that I may gain Christ" (Philippians 3:8).

Part Two

CHURCH
AND SHARING

18
Financial Needs of Divorcees

THERE IS PERHAPS no more emotionally charged area of Christianity today than that of divorce. Approximately one-half of all current marriages fail in the first six years of marriage, including couples who profess to be Christians. Failed marriages within the church leave us with a great many divorcees. But recent statistics also indicate that a great many divorcees become Christians and, thus, find their way into a local church. It is estimated that if the trend continues into the twenty-first century, a typical local church would be made up of from 40 to 60 percent divorced members. At least half of these would be single, divorced parents—primarily women.

The Issue of Divorce

To teach that God condones divorce is to make God's Word conditional. In other words, if you keep your word, God will keep His. If that's so, then we're all in big trouble. I count on God being faithful and never changing, no matter what anyone else might do. If I have vowed to remain with my wife for life, then that vow is unconditional. If it's conditional, then it's not a vow— it's an option. "It is better that you should not vow than that you should vow and not pay" (Ecclesiastes 5:5).

Needs of Single Parents

Because of limited space, I would like to focus on the largest and most needy group of single parents—divorced mothers. Obviously, there are divorced men raising families and divorced singles with no families. They have the same emotional and spiritual needs as divorced women who are raising families. But few people understand the financial needs of these mothers.

The estimated average income for a North American family of three (husband, wife, and one child) is about $22,000 a year. The minimum need level is about $16,000 a year, and the official poverty level is about $13,000. For a typical divorcee with one child, her income is about $11,000, including Aid to Dependent Children. Her life-style is one of surviving from check to check, hoping that nothing breaks down, because there's no money to fix it. She will typically spend 30 percent of her net take home pay on child care (usually inadequate). Her housing is usually a small apartment that takes 40 percent of her pay. The 30 percent that is left over has to cover food, clothing, transportation, medical, dental, and so on. It just won't stretch far enough. If she has more than one child and is over thirty, her problems of finding a job are compounded.

Of course, we can take the position that she's reaping what she sowed, but so far that hasn't done much to reverse the trend, so I would discount that as being God's attitude. I have counseled enough divorced parents to know that quite often the divorce was not their option.

A young woman I'll call Sherri is a typical case. Her ex-husband was a chronic gambler who divorced her for another woman and left her with $6,000 in credit card bills because her name was on the accounts also. She lives in a small apartment with two children, owns a seven-year-old car, and makes about five dollars an hour as a steno-typist. She is a Christian and attends a major denominational church. When she appealed to the benevolence committee for help, they sent her to the state welfare department for assistance. Her financial needs are at least $300 a month more than she makes, with no foreseeable end to this need over the next several years. She desperately desires fellowship for herself and her children but no longer fits into a family unit. She feels like an outcast and feels betrayed by a church where she has tithed regularly for several years. Sherri's financial needs fit into a typical pattern for young divorcees with children:

1. *Child care.* She has a four-year-old son and an eight-year-old son. The four-year-old is in a day care center (at a monthly cost of $250). The eight-year-old is home by himself for about two hours a day after school. He wanted to play Little League baseball, but his mother couldn't arrange transportation.

2. *Repairs.* Her seven-year-old car has need of brakes, tires, and a tune-up. Even a minor repair of $100 strips her of any surplus funds for two to three months. Appliances are simply left broken for the lack of any mechanical skill to fix them and no budgeted funds available.

3. *Male influence.* She is particularly concerned that her two boys are growing up without a good role model for becoming young men. Her ex-husband lives out of state and refuses to take the children for even a short period.

4. *Low income.* She knows that she is basically peaked out on her job as a steno-typist and would like to go to school for computer training. She lacks the funds for child care or school. The credit card company is threatening to attach Sherri's wages for $100 a month. That would literally destroy her ability to provide for her family.

What Can We Do?

We could choose from any of nearly twenty references to helping those within the Body of Christ. By doing so, we're not condoning divorce or raising the divorced to some "official status"—we're merely following Christ's example of showing our love, rather than just talking about it. Consider Christianity from Sherri's eyes when she is told that the church can't meet her needs, but the government can. She knows that by accepting government aid she must also accept government supervision over her children. Yet it must seem inconsistent to Sherri that the very same church is in the midst of an expensive program to build a youth center to attract young people and their families to the church.

That is not to imply that a building program itself is wrong—but that we are guilty of having the form without the substance of Christianity. I wonder when we will wake up and recognize that more programs and buildings don't attract the lost to God. The lost are attracted by the love and dedication that they see. If a program can attract them to the church, then a bigger program can attract them away again. "But whoever has the world's goods, and beholds his brother in need and closes his heart against him, how does the love of God abide in him? Little children, let us not love with word or with tongue, but in deed and truth" (1 John 3:17–18).

There are several programs that any fellowship can start to minister to the singles within their midst.

1. *Helps program.* "Beloved, let us love one another, for love is from God" (1 John 4:7a). Any church can organize a program to help single women in the area of repair and maintenance of machines. For example, several churches can organize a joint effort to assist single women in repairing their cars. I'm aware of several churches that have done this. One Saturday (usually every other month), the men of these churches who have any mechanical ability meet in one of the church parking lots. The single women who have need for minor repairs on their cars can bring them to be fixed or serviced for only the cost of parts, or nothing at all.

Obviously, there must be controls and supervision, but that is normally done by a trained layman. The work is scheduled through a church counselor, and to participate, a woman must be actively attending church and counseling. Other churches also have appliance repair centers where single women can drop off appliances for repair without cost. Some churches even offer volunteer repair crews for work on homes, such as painting, roofing, and yard work.

2. *Counseling.* Churches with "helps" programs should always operate under the guidance of a singles' counseling center. The purpose is to work at restoring the family unit if possible and to share Christ with those who are lost. The singles who are involved with the helps programs should be discipled

and encouraged to work in other service for the church, such as babysitting, visitation, and health care.

This counseling center *must* be under the guidance and supervision of the church leadership, and all rules for singles' counseling should be observed. This is especially true of men counseling singled or divorced women.

3. *Child care centers.* Even if an individual church cannot afford to operate a child care center, certainly several churches (or businesses) working together could. There are several churches now doing this as a ministry— not a business. These centers are provided as an outreach to single parents in the church and are operated on a donation basis. The purpose is not to just babysit children, but to nurture them in the Lord. If you really want to reach single parents for the Lord, start ministering to them through their children. They will respond. Helping in a child care center can be an excellent ministry for mothers within the church who have child care and educational training skills but need to be with their own children during the day. "By this is My Father glorified, that you bear much fruit, and so prove to be My disciples" (John 15:8).

4. *Clothes closets.* Within every church there are both needs and surpluses. God's Word indicates that they will nearly always offset one another. The difficulty is in getting those with a surplus together with those who have needs. A "clothes closet" is a way to do this. This is a common location in the church that is used to hold goods that one family no longer needs, until that need surfaces in another family.

19

Is Welfare Scriptural?

THE BIBLE'S STAND on welfare is very clear: we are to help those in need. There may be a disagreement about how much help is necessary and who should receive it, but there should be no disagreement on the necessity to feed, clothe, and shelter the poor. Yet the church is no longer the prime mover in meeting the needs of the poor—the government is. And there can be no doubt that government welfare has helped produce a society where many families live in permanent poverty. Because of that, many Christians have developed resentment and indifference to the real poor. But the fact that the government has assumed the function of caring for the poor does not negate our responsibility. Welfare for the poor is biblical and necessary.

The Purpose of Welfare

"For the poor will never cease to be in the land; therefore I command you, saying, 'You shall freely open your hand to your brother, to your needy and poor in your land'" (Deuteronomy 15:11). God's Word says that there will always be needs in the world around us. The purpose is twofold: one, to test our commitment to obedience (Matthew 25:40); and two, to create an attitude of interdependence (2 Corinthians 8:14). We are admonished to meet the needs of the widows and orphans because they are unable to meet their own needs. But does welfare stop with the elderly widows and orphans? Unfortunately, in most of Christianity, it doesn't even include them. Simply because Satan has misused welfare for his purpose does not make welfare wrong.

It is impossible to read the epistles of James and John without recognizing the requirement to help others in need. John uses the lack of concern for the needs of others as evidence of lack of love (1 John 3:17-18). Therefore, we know that the true purpose of *welfare* (meeting the needs of others) is to demonstrate God's love through us. An outside observer would have to conclude that there is little evidence of God's love in America. That is exactly the conclusion many unsaved come to. The church is more interested in buildings, programs, and promotions than in caring.

Effects of Welfare

It is interesting to see the contrasting objectives of biblical welfare and government welfare. Sharing with others in need out of God's love should produce three results: one, a sense of fellowship and belonging (2 Corinthians 9:13); two, a stronger family unit (1 Timothy 5:8); and three, a high standard for work, which prohibits laziness (2 Thessalonians 3:9-10).

Unfortunately, the effects of social or government welfare are almost the opposite. Why is that? It is because the motivation is not love but pity or, even worse, guilt. When society tries to make up for previous wrongs by providing government welfare, the results will be permanent dependence and poverty. With the best of intentions, our welfare system traps people at the lowest economic level through indiscriminate giving. To qualify for support, most recipients must show only that they are not working, not that they cannot work.

Additionally, most welfare recipients resent the system and ultimately the society that supports them. Why? Because of the degrading method in which the funds are distributed and the stigma attached to "taking someone else's money." Government welfare recipients must adopt an attitude of "you owe it to me" to justify receiving the money even if they have legitimate needs. After only one generation, a welfare mentality and permanent dependence develops. The temptation of "free" money attracts more and more recipients until finally there are fewer givers than takers.

Biblical Absolutes

Christians are given clear and absolute direction about welfare in God's Word. Fortunately, the standards for welfare are also given. Indiscriminate welfare traps the recipients by making them dependent. Biblical welfare meets needs and always looks toward restoring the individual back to a position of productivity.

Qualifications for Welfare

Those who qualify for welfare are:

1. *The poor.* In Scripture, being poor literally meant being unable to meet even the most basic needs. Those who were poor—not lazy—were worthy of support (Deuteronomy 15:7-11; 2 Samuel 12:1-5; Proverbs 19:17).

2. *The diligent.* There are many people who are lazy by nature. They do not qualify for support and, in fact, require a good swift kick for motivation. Supporting such people is just as unscriptural as not supporting those with

legitimate needs. "A worker's appetite works for him, for his hunger urges him on" (Proverbs 16:26; see also 19:15; 20:4; 24:33; 2 Thessalonians 3:10).

3. *The widows.* A qualified widow is defined as a woman sixty years or older whose only husband has died (1 Timothy 5:3–10). In the first century it was acknowledged that families took care of their own widows. In our generation, the qualification could well be extended to those who cannot get help from their own families—divorcees included.

4. *The orphans.* It would seem evident that children who are parentless are dependent on others for help. All children belong to God's family. If Christians fulfilled their function, every child would have parents. Even if we can't adopt them all, we most assuredly can help care for their needs, both material and emotional.

5. *Those with immediate needs.* Long-term needs require welfare; immediate needs require benevolence. In James 2:15–16, we are admonished to help those in need. They do not have to qualify as "poor" or "widows" but only as "lacking of the daily food." Such temporary needs can easily be the result of illness, imprisonment, and unemployment. Benevolence means giving to the obvious needs of another.

6. *Those with legitimate needs.* Many Christians ask what constitutes a "legitimate need" in another's life. "For this is not for the ease of others and for your affliction, but by way of equality" (2 Corinthians 8:13). Reason would indicate that a need is relative to the society and times. A Cambodian's needs probably do not include an automobile. But for many, a car is necessary for earning a livelihood. Since there are no absolutes on this issue, it would seem that God allows individual discernment. However, the need for food, shelter, and clothing to survive are absolutes, and, unfortunately, there are many people in our world who are dying for the lack of these things.

Christian Responsibility

The truth is that Christians are doing a miserable job of caring for the physical needs of the poor. If we can't meet the needs of those around us, we won't meet the needs of those in other countries. Few churches today have any organized program for helping the poor of their own fellowship or community. Some have a benevolence fund to help meet some emergencies but nothing to meet continuing needs. Obviously, vision and leadership come from the top down. If the church doesn't practice the "body" concept of Christianity, it is a certainty that it will never reach the unsaved community.

At present, the governments of the world supply nearly 95 percent of all the care to the aged, ill, and impoverished, and the evidence shows they are using it as a tool to spread atheism. Is it any wonder that the unsaved are rejecting Christianity? Obviously, there are exceptions, and many Christian organizations do a great job of meeting the physical and spiritual needs of others, but they are few in comparison. It is not a question of ability or direction. Christians in North America have the resources to do at least ten times what we are presently doing for the poor, with little or no alteration of life-styles. Many Christians are going to be very ashamed to face the Lord and explain why they hoarded money for indulgences while others went hungry. "And he said, 'This is what I will do: I will tear down my barns and build larger ones, and there I will store all my grain and my goods.'". . . "But God said to him, 'You fool! This very night your soul is required of you; and now who will own what you have prepared?'" (Luke 12:18,20).

What Can We Do?

Welfare was transferred from the church because the church neglected it. It can be recovered, and the church can become a leader in caring about personal needs. That is not an option from God—it is an imperative. "He who gives to the poor will never want, but he who shuts his eyes will have many curses" (Proverbs 28:27).

Committed Christians should encourage their church leaders to establish a body life ministry. A portion of every church's budget should be designated for needs in the fellowship and in the community. There should also be an outreach to starving people in other countries. If your denomination doesn't have a care program, then support a good, independent ministry that feeds the hungry. Each church should have a resource committee set up to counsel families in need and to determine who does and does not qualify for help.

There should be such an atmosphere of sharing and caring that members would feel as free to share a financial burden as they would a physical burden. Ultimately, within the Christian community there should be health and child care centers, vocational training centers, and employment agencies so that when faced with needs from within the Christian community or the secular community, we could respond without relying on government help.

20
Fleecing the Flock

THERE ARE FEW things that really rile me as a Christian. But one thing that does is Christians who "fleece" other Christians. That can be done in a variety of subtle ways, from selling get-rich-quick schemes to selling soap. Fleecing is probably a pretty accurate analogy, because when you fleece sheep you don't really want to hurt them, you just shear them of a little extra wool. Most groups that fleece God's sheep simply want to sell them a product, not rob them. The products may even be good ones, although usually they are high priced. It is because they are higher priced that a personal marketing system is attractive. If most people were evaluating the products on a purely competitive basis, they would usually find a better deal.

Almost without exception, the real clincher in a "Christian" marketing scheme is the idea that you can sell to your friends and "help" them as well. After you've accepted that, objectivity disappears, and the plan or product becomes incidental to the profit motive.

One of the best marketing method within Christian circles is assumed credibility. That is when the sales group assumes someone else's credibility. Allow me to use a personal example. One thing I realized from the earliest stages when organizing Christian Financial Concepts was that a lot of wrong had been done to many Christians under the guise of "Christian finances." Many groups that had sprung up claiming to teach and counsel on biblical principles of finances were really sales companies in disguise. Many taught good concepts, but their intent was to sell a product or service, and the teaching was usually a gimmick to gather a group. As a result, many pastors were justifiably cautious about any financial "ministry."

From the beginning, CFC determined to operate as a ministry and sell no products or services, nor endorse any other group's product or services for a fee. Many times when funds were short it was truly tempting to compromise. As the ministry grew, we got offers from dozens of sales groups that would virtually underwrite the ministry if we would just send them people who needed products. I believed then, as now, that to do so would be to use God's Word for gain and would be deceptive. "But those who want to get rich fall

into temptation and a snare and many foolish and harmful desires which plunge
men into ruin and destruction" (1 Timothy 6:9).

Because of that stand, we earned the trust of those we taught and counseled and have been able to cross denominational and doctrinal boundaries
to share God's principles. Most pastors who know of the ministry know that
they can trust what we teach and say even though we may not always agree
on exact interpretations.

Quite often over the last few years, various groups have sprung up teaching biblical finances in the local church and selling a product as well. Many
have implied that CFC endorses them, and lately one group even said that we
asked them to call on a pastor (we did not). In many cases one of our staff
may use a product or service offered by a group. If that group assumes blan-
ket endorsement, that is deceptive and wrong. Very few groups can meet our
standards for recommendation, and we never accept a fee or commission. Any
staff member who endorses a group without our approval is subject to dis-
missal. That is not to tout CFC; we have made errors and will again, I'm sure.
But I want to demonstrate that when a sales group wants to assume someone
else's credibility, watch out; it is usually because they can't assume their own.

There is an old secular cliché that says, "If you walk like a duck, and talk
like a duck, and stay in the presence of ducks, maybe people will think you're
a duck." In Christianity, that would seem to hold true. If a nonbeliever knows
the words and hangs out in church a lot, quite often he will go undetected.
By the same principle, if a business hires mostly Christians, has them tell
everybody they're in a ministry, and uses mostly Christian terms, then others
will think they are a "ministry." Please don't misunderstand this. Any business can and should be used to minister. Business is an excellent tool through
which to share Christ. But a business sells a product and hopes to make a
profit. A ministry serves a function that cannot be done at a profit. For instance,
you cannot provide counsel to families in financial trouble profitably.

One of the keys to detecting a business being disguised as a ministry is to
see how the funds are generated. If it's through the sale of products and services (including Christian products and services), it is a business and should
be evaluated with a very critical eye. If a group uses "buzz words" to gain an
entry, beware.

"I would like to come by and share our *ministry*." This is a common buzz
word. If the business offers a legitimate product or service, then it ought to
stand on its own merit. It should not require a spiritual endorsement to get in
the door. My concern would be if someone would mislead about one part of
the business, what else might he mislead about?

"*Pastor,* we have something that will help your people." When a group
orients its sales pitch to pastors, be on guard. If it's a product for pastors or a
program for the local church, then pastors are the group to call on. But if it's
a product, diet plan, insurance, wills, trusts, gold mines, and so on, and it is

directed toward pastors, then be aware that the group is trying to ride in on his credibility.

Unfortunately, since many pastors are not well paid, they also fall into the finder's fee trap. Often the group will offer the pastor a fee for anyone he recommends who buys the products. There are many pastors who have lost their personal credibility by endorsing a company to their people. Integrity is won over a long time and can be lost all too quickly.

"You can *help* other Christians." Without a doubt this is the real clincher in fleecing the flock. If a company can convince its sales people that the end results of their efforts is to help others, then the methods can be justified. It's the old "the end justifies the means" syndrome. In other words, you're not really hurting them by deceiving them; after all, it's for their own good. The real test of motives is whether or not the salesman is willing to forgo all profit to "help" others. I personally know many honest, ethical Christian salespeople who refuse to profit when dealing with pastors or Christians encountered through their church. It's not that selling to Christian contacts is necessarily wrong. It's just that they believe the temptation to compromise is too strong. "For where jealousy and selfish ambition exist, there is disorder and every evil thing" (James 3:16). With certainty, God knows what our needs are, including our business needs. He will provide those who need the products without having to use the Christian community.

Matthew 21:12 describes the event when Christ ran the moneychangers out of the Temple. Why did He do that when obviously they were meeting a need of the people coming to the Temple to worship? The law gave the Jews the right to sell an animal designated for sacrifice if they had a long journey, then use the money to buy another animal for sacrifice. The moneychangers served this need and most of the people seemed satisfied. So why get so upset when both sides benefited? Because Christ knew that the motive of the moneychangers was to "fleece the flock." They bought low and sold high with the endorsement of the Temple priests and religious leaders. If the people wanted their sacrifices blessed, they had to use "blessed" animals.

Obviously, it didn't start out that way. It probably started with a money-changer who showed a priest how he could *help* a lot of people and make a little profit for himself. Later it became how he could make a lot of profit and help the people a little. Why do you suppose this event was reported in the Scriptures? One reason may well be that Jesus wanted His disciples to understand exactly how He felt about "fleecing the flock."

If we, as Christians, are to do business with each other, we must follow fundamental biblical principles to avoid the "fleecing" trap.

1. *Don't develop a sales program exclusively for the church.* Obviously, Christian teaching materials are created for a Christian market, but other products are not. Most programs aimed almost exclusively at the Christian market are really secular products with some Christian terms sprinkled in.

Recently, a Christian called to ask for an opinion about a ministry (for profit company) that wanted to sell him a "Christian" will and trust. Since we function under secular law in our country, I was interested to see what a Christian will and trust was.

It turned out to be a fairly standard will and trust with several Christian words sprinkled throughout. It seemed to be a fairly good document with a pretty good testimony, at about twice the price of a standard will and trust. Its real benefit was that the client could get his money back if four friends would sign up, and he could make a profit if more than four signed up. "And in their greed they will exploit you with false words; their judgment from long ago is not idle, and their destruction is not asleep" (2 Peter 2:3).

2. *Don't practice deception.* If you have a product to sell that you honestly believe will benefit other Christians, let it be known. But don't promote it as a "ministry" or as a spiritual "happening." Let your yes be yes and your no be no. In other words, let people know what the company is and what the product is. If there is a referral or finder's fee paid to another person for a lead, let that be known, too. If you're afraid of losing a sale because of total honesty, then the program is dishonest.

21
Church Borrowing

CHURCH BORROWING IS an emotional and controversial topic. It is difficult to teach on the subject directly because it is primarily an attitude rather than an absolute. However, anything taken to excess is destructive, and most certainly that is true of debt.

Debt defined. For the sake of simplicity, we will define church debt as any borrowing by a church that carries with it a contingent liability. That means that the lender *expects* the money to be repaid—no matter what. That would include building loans and bonds. A debt would be defined scripturally as "surety." Definition: "to deposit a pledge, either in money, goods, or part payment as security for a bargain."

Normal use. It is no more abnormal for a church to finance a building program today than for a business to do so. Approximately 90 percent of all church building programs carry with them indebtedness ranging from one to twenty years.

The use of debt to build or expand the outreach of a church is so common a practice today that to even challenge the idea can create an air of animosity. However, just because a practice is normal does not mean it is scriptural or best. It should be noted that most churches repay their indebtedness according to contract. So the discussion is not whether a church can repay; it is whether or not churches should borrow, even if they can repay.

Scriptural Guidelines

Borrowing is not prohibited in Scripture. It is *discouraged*. There are no positive references to borrowing, and, in fact, there are explicit warnings to avoid it. "The rich rules over the poor, and the borrower becomes the lender's slave" (Proverbs 22:7). Thus the Word indicates that an unnecessary authority is created by borrowing. The question is often asked, "If borrowing is allowable for individuals, why shouldn't churches also be able to borrow?" The answer is twofold. One, churches *can* borrow. The evidence is abundant around us. Second, just because they can doesn't mean they *should*. The church as an entity comes under a more stringent judgment from God's Word because of its visible position. "Let not many of you become teachers, my brethren, knowing that as such we shall incure a stricter judgment" (James 3:1). I would infer this condition to mean the visible church as well.

The church as a physical entity exists for just one purpose: to glorify God. It stands as the visible image of God's best, not subject to worldly compromise. It seems contradictory to profess the belief that God can heal the sick, feed the poor, and even transform the very heart of a corrupt man, but He can't supply the funds in advance with which to do these things. "And my God shall supply all your needs according to His riches in glory in Christ Jesus" (Philippians 4:19). Money is no different from any other promise that God gives us, except that it is physical, visible, and measurable. Many of the other promises are subject to feelings and interpretations, but money is a rare absolute; you either have it or you don't.

The argument that if individual Christians can borrow money, so should the church is not valid. In the first place, much of the borrowing that individual Christians do is, in itself, unscriptural because it is done in excess. That can be witnessed in the current level of divorce and bankruptcy, both of which are primarily motivated by the excessive use of credit. It is clear that the standards for leaders in the church are more stringent than for the individual members (1 Timothy 3:1–2). If that is so, then it would seem obvious that the standards of the church organization must be higher than that of its individual members.

Scriptural Precedent

In doing a survey of this subject, I tried to be as objective as possible, knowing that I rarely observe the good side of credit. Few families or churches share with us the great successes they have made using credit, but many share their failures. However, the mere fact that others have misused credit does not necessarily make it wrong. Only Scripture has the guidelines we are to follow—not opinion, no matter how normal it may seem.

After reviewing the references to borrowing in Scripture, I came to several conclusions:

1. Borrowing is always presented in the negative (Proverbs 17:18).
2. God never once made a promise to anyone and fulfilled it through a loan (Luke 6:38).
3. God promised His people that if they would obey His commandment, they would not have to borrow (Deuteronomy 28:12).
4. God had worship structures built at least three times in the Bible, and no credit was used. "Then the Lord spoke to Moses, saying, 'Tell the

sons of Israel to raise a contribution for Me; from every man whose heart moves him you shall raise My contribution'" (Exodus 25:1-2). "O Lord God, all this abundance that we have provided to build Thee a house for Thy holy name, it is from Thy hand, and all is Thine" (1 Chronicles 29:16; 1 Kings 6; 2 Kings 12).

It might be said that these aren't valid examples because borrowing was not a normal practice during those times. If not, then Solomon wasted a great many parables dealing with the dangers of too much credit.

In the New Testament, there are no direct references to church buildings or their funding. It would seem very out of character that the leaders of the first-century church who risked their very lives to deliver God's Word would have condoned or even permitted their churches to borrow. The basic attitudes reflected in Acts 4 and 2 Corinthians 8 would indicate a commitment to giving whatever was needed.

Why Not Borrow?

"If a church borrows money to do God's work and it is repaid on time, then what's the harm?" This question is logical and is frequently asked. There is no single answer but rather a series of them.

1. Each church leader and member must search God's Word with an open mind and heart and determine if God does or does not desire churches to be funded with debt. If it is determined that to borrow is a compromise to God's will, then to do so is to sin. "Therefore, to one who knows the right thing to do, and does not do it, to him it is sin" (James 4:17).

2. Borrowing denies God's people the opportunity to experience His overwhelming blessings in response to giving what is clearly within God's will (2 Corinthians 9:10). We are told in 1 John 3:22 that we can ask of God and expect to receive. Certainly, this would be true of the needs of the church. The experience of seeing God provide through His people is a witness to those within the church and to those looking at us.

3. A debt within the church restricts its ability to serve God. Quite often, controlling decisions are based on the need to meet debt payments rather than on God's redirection of funds to current needs.

4. Often, the ability to repay the debt is dependent on the ability of the pastor to preach. In many instances, lenders have required a signed contract from the pastor that he would not leave while the debt exists and would maintain an insurance policy to pay off the debt in the event of his death. "Come now, you who say, 'Today or tomorrow, we shall go to such and such a city, and spend a year there and engage in business and make a profit'" (James 4:13).

5. Huge sums of God's people's money go to meet interest payments. That money could otherwise be used to further God's kingdom rather than

Satan's. Many major denominations spend more on interest payments than on foreign missions.

Other Christian Ministries

There can certainly be no distinction between churches borrowing and other ministries borrowing. If an organization holds itself out to be an instrument of Jesus Christ, then it must be striving to meet God's standards. Certainly, there are no perfect ministries or churches, and try as we might, we will continue to fall below God's measure. Borrowing is not the only area of laxness; it just happens to be one of the most visible (and correctable).

Having faced the same choices in a ministry, I find the need to wait upon God's provision in advance to be confining. However, it is also tremendously freeing. If God can direct us by providing, then He can also direct by withholding. Many ministries have borrowed to do things God never intended they do. Others have borrowed to do God's will but have missed one of God's greatest areas of testimony. Very few nonbelievers could be convinced that there is anything supernatural or miraculous about a loan. Few would deny that there is something at least unique about a debt-free ministry.

Conclusion

I trust that this brief survey will not be viewed as any kind of indictment of churches or other ministries, because it is not. The purpose is to challenge church and ministry leaders, as well as their members, that God can and will provide through His people that which is *necessary* to do His will. One of our greatest assets is that God doesn't have a whole lot of talent with which to work down here. God will work with anyone willing to totally trust Him. Obviously, overnight changes are rarely possible, but God's people should always be aiming toward the "mark."

It is not a lack of funds that requires a church's borrowing. It is a lack of commitment on the part of God's people to give and trust. "So Moses issued a command, and a proclamation was circulated throughout the camp, saying, 'Let neither man nor woman any longer perform work for the contributions of the sanctuary.' Thus the people were restrained from bringing any more. For the material they had was sufficient and more than enough for all the work, to perform it" (Exodus 36:6–7).

22
The Church and Money

RECENTLY WHILE I was speaking at a conference, a man asked, "Why bother with teaching money in the church? God promises to supply what we need, doesn't He?" His question was actually more of a statement than a question. What he actually meant was that he didn't believe the church should be involved with teaching about money. One of his comments was, "It's best to leave the teaching on money to the experts." In actuality, it is *because* we have left the teaching to the "experts" that we have strayed so far from God's path.

Scripture does *not* support the premise that the church should stay out of the area of money. In fact, it teaches that wisdom comes from God (Proverbs 3:13; 3:19; 8:10–11). Thus, true wisdom in finances comes *only* by studying and teaching God's Word. Jesus says in Luke 16:10–12 that good stewardship of money is a prerequisite to being used by God for greater things. The way we handle finances is not so much a test as a reflection of what we *really* believe.

Do we Christians really believe that God owns everything? If we do, then we must manage according to *His* principles. We will be accountable for our stewardship and for the positive or negative witness it provides. Also, God's Word promises that slothfulness will result in loss, but diligence results in gain. "The soul of the sluggard craves and gets nothing, but the soul of the diligent is made fat" (Proverbs 13:4).

Thus, if God's church is to prosper materially and spiritually, its funds must be managed well. However, there must be a balance, because too much attention to money will divert the church and make it servant to materialism. "No servant can serve two masters; for either he will hate the one, and love the other, or else he will hold to one, and despise the other. You cannot serve God and mammon" (Luke 16:13).

The Church as an Example

The church in this case refers to the traditional institution, as opposed to the general Body of Christ. Any church should be the best possible example of good money management. Satan has been effective within the church, diverting God's people away from sound biblical principles.

Issues About Money

Budgeting. Should a church have an annual budget? One side says no, a budget removes the element of faith and brings the church down to a worldly level. However, quite often a church's creditors feel the absence of a budget puts the burden of faith on them. The other side of the budget issue is voiced by those who would operate the church just like a business, right down to eliminating the "nonproductive" benevolence program.

Both extremes are wrong biblically. A budget in itself does not reflect a lack of faith, but rather good planning (Luke 14:28-30). But it must not override the spiritual goals of God's church.

Savings account. One common question asked is, "Should our church maintain a savings account?" It's not the savings that really matters, but the purpose and attitude. There are many references to saving in God's Word (Proverbs 6:6; 21:20). In fact, a surplus should be normal to a church serving God; after all, God has promised to provide for every good work. But too often the money is hoarded rather than saved. It is not allocated to any needs, present or future, and represents a lack of trust, just as in the case of the rich fool in Luke 12:16-20.

Debt free. Perhaps no single issue about the church and money is more controversial than church debt. On one side it is argued that if borrowing is allowable for Christians, and it is within limits, then it must be allowable for the church too. And that would seem to be biblically correct; it is allowable. But does the church settle for the allowable, or the best? We know that God holds Christian teachers to a higher standard (James 3:1), and deacons and elders are held to a higher standard (1 Timothy 3). Since each of these is under the authority of the church, shouldn't we assume that the church is held to an even higher standard?

The church, as an institution, is to be a light of God's truth in a world of darkness. Our world is out of sync with God's Word on borrowing. The evidence is reflected in bankruptcy and divorce, and the sad truth is that the evangelical church has followed the lead of the secular world regarding debt.

Too often, building programs that should be a testimony of God's faithfulness and provision are more nearly a copy of the world's system called O.P.M. (other people's money). That is not to condemn or judge the leadership in churches that borrow. They are doing what they have been taught. But it's time we taught the truth: God can and *will* provide what He ordains by providing the surpluses to His people at the appointed time.

It's not a lack of money that necessitates church borrowing. It's lack of commitment to giving. Remember, the only source of true wisdom is God's Word, and you will not find a single instance of God manifesting Himself through a loan. "And my God shall supply all your needs according to His riches in glory in Christ Jesus" (Philippians 4:19).

Reveal needs. Many church leaders believe they should never let a material need be known to the congregation. Sometimes this is a deep conviction and is God's will. More often it is the reflection of a misguided notion that sharing needs openly is unspiritual. If that's true, then we would have to count the apostle Paul among the unspiritual. In 1 Corinthians 9:1-14 Paul voices his "right" to share in the material rewards of the church.

If the church never lets material needs be known, then the members will also be trapped in that same restraint. The way to determine if this is a conviction from the Lord is that the needs will be met without asking.

The common principle delivered in God's Word is expressed by Paul in 2 Corinthians 8:14, "At this present time your abundance being a supply for their want, that their abundance also may become a supply for your want, that there may be equality."

Caring Programs in the Church

Every church seeking to serve the Lord should have caring programs established to help its own needy, the needy in the community, and the needy in the world. The first step in any church is to teach God's people what His Word says about its own finances.

The surpluses that the church must have in order to minister to the needy are always available. Too often, Christians are consuming or wasting their funds. Every church needs a regular program for sharing the biblical principles of managing money in the home and practical courses on planning (budgeting, insurance, housing, and so on). Once God's people learn God's plan for their finances, the funds will be available to meet legitimate needs.

Statistics prove that in the average evangelical church, about 20 percent of the people tithe. In the churches we have surveyed where a consistent program of teaching God's principles of finances has been established, the percentage is over 80 percent. The average American family spends over $2,000 a year on interest payments alone. If they were shown how to live debt-free and offered that money to the church instead, a church of one hundred families would have an additional $200,000 a year available for other programs.

Benevolence. Every church should have a benevolence program to help those who have legitimate financial needs. But a benevolence program should not be a "give away" program. There are definite biblical guidelines for those whom we are to help. Members of any local church should be able to look to the fellowship they attend as an extension of God's provision. They should feel the freedom to stand up and share their financial needs as freely as they would physical or spiritual needs.

Too often a local church's benevolence program amounts to the pastor directing the secretary to write someone a check for food, gas, or rent. That is usually the worst thing they could do. Without any controls or follow-up, giving away money is like pouring gasoline on a fire. Also, the system doesn't help those who have long-term needs due to illness, layoff, age, and so on. Benevolence is not an *event,* it is a vital part of ministering within the body of believers and requires several coordinated ministries:

1. *Benevolence committee.* This committee is primarily made up of lay people who will meet and evaluate needs presented within the church. Often that requires emergency action by one or two members to evaluate needs that result from "drop-ins" at the church office or parsonage. A well-coordinated committee will free the pastor from the pressures of some emotional appeals. The most effective benevolence committees usually have members with varied spiritual temperaments.

2. *Resource ministry.* To meet the needs of families, resources must be accumulated in advance. That might include food and clothing for a church in the inner city, but it should not stop there. The church should have contact with businesses that can provide parttime or temporary work. One of the most effective ways to test the spirit of someone who can't find work is to help him find it.

Many times I have heard someone say, "He doesn't want to work or he would have found a job by now." What they don't grasp is that when a normally productive man is suddenly unemployed, especially late in life, it often results in depression that paralyzes him. He needs sound biblical counsel and a helping hand, but not a handout.

Other resources include the availability of legal or accounting advice, medical and dental care, and a number of well-trained financial counselors who will work with those in need. Accountability is an essential part of any good benevolence program.

No successful benevolence program will happen until God's people in the local church decide to get involved and make it happen. "Because of the proof given by this ministry they will glorify God for your obedience to your confession of the gospel of Christ, and for the liberality of your contribution to them and to all" (2 Corinthians 9:13).

23

Church Benevolence Programs

MANY CHURCHES ARE beginning to realize that they must give financial assistance to persons in their church and community. Benevolence funds and committees are being revamped or established with a genuine burden to "do good to all men, and especially to those who are of the household of faith" (Galatians 6:10). Because of the fact that virtually every congregation has experienced the abuse, misuse, or unwise management of such special funds, many churches have grown indifferent and overly protective in this area. In reality, the answer in this vital area is better planning, wiser management, and more realistic goals.

Our Lord told us, "By this all men will know that you are My disciples, if you have love for one another" (John 13:35).

There are many ways to show love apart from finances. However, it is impossible to deny that a great percentage of the needs within a typical church will be financial. The church is then confronted with a basic choice: Will they be "doers" of the Word or merely "hearers"? "If a brother or sister is without clothing and in need of daily food, and one of you says to them, 'Go in peace, be warmed and be filled,' and yet you do not give them what is necessary for their body, what use is that?" (James 2:15-16).

On the other hand, how does a benevolence committee genuinely and biblically determine who really deserves help? That is a vitally important question. It is just as damaging to give money to one who shouldn't receive it as to not give it at all.

There are some thoughts on practical ways to implement an effective benevolence program:

Screen applicants. That can be accomplished by thorough interviewing and the filling out of a questionnaire that provokes honest responses from the applicant. It is also important to have applicants submit a thorough budget and explain any anomalies in that budget.

The committee should be careful to be discerning, and yet still compassionate, of the real needs of the one seeking help.

Scripture tells us that clothing—and that might also allude to a roof over the head—and daily food are the key criteria in determining to whom the help should be given first. Certainly, then, our emphasis ought to be on meeting needs in these areas. How and when to help beyond basic food, clothing, and shelter needs can only be determined on an individual evaluation. The committee must realize that seeking wisdom through diligent prayer is an absolutely vital part of these evaluations.

With only rare exceptions, money should not be given. It is far better to provide the material items instead: for example, pay the rent, electricity, and purchase food. If the church is led of God to help, then it must face the issue of providing the long-term needs of some. That will include the widows (and divorcees who qualify), orphans, ill, and elderly.

The question always arises, "How much can we afford to give as a church?" On the other hand, Scripture says, "He who is gracious to a poor man lends to the Lord, and He will repay him for his good deed" (Proverbs 19:17).

If the one receiving the help is truly at a point of need, then a church must believe that they are literally lending to God. The money is simply a vehicle of God's love. God promises that as long as His people are faithful to give of the resources He has given them, those resources are limitless.

Creative Help

Many times the need for assistance may be temporary, particularly where young couples are concerned. For instance: consider a young couple that has recently committed their financial matters to God. In the past, they have not been as diligent in this area as they should have been, and they failed to either get medical insurance or save money to cover a pregnancy. The hospital refuses to admit them without a $1,000 deposit. They have no human source for this money. The church has established a "Hope Fund" for critical needs such as this. A committee evaluates the couple's budget and needs and makes a commitment to make the funds available. The check is drafted directly from Hope Fund to the hospital. The couple has committed to a monthly amount at no interest to pay the loan back to the fund. The benevolence committee will monitor the couple through a monthly review by a lay counselor. If, at that time, the monthly commitment needs adjusting, the committee will evaluate the new amount and encourage the family to be diligent in repayment.

The main objective of the Hope Fund is to have funds available for genuine needs. It is also a means of: (1) helping Christians keep a good testimony before the world; (2) encouraging Christians to be more diligent in personal budgeting; and (3) providing no-interest loans for genuine emergencies that would have otherwise ruined a family's budget and testimony.

Some would object to such a fund, claiming that we should either give money away or not make it available at all. We must remember the Scripture that tells us, "He who oppresses the poor reproaches his Maker, but he who is gracious to the needy honors Him" (Proverbs 14:31).

Part Three

INSURANCE
AND INVESTING

24

Avoiding "Get-Rich-Quick"

I T IS AMAZING how susceptible Christians are to get-rich-quick schemes and how logical they seem at first. A friend of mine once shared that he had invested several thousand dollars in a "fool proof" plan to buy surplus goods and resell them. The promoter promised a 10 percent per month return. He also presented the names of several people who had been "investing."

After risking a small amount of money for a couple of months and promptly receiving the promised return, my friend borrowed a large sum and invested it. The logic behind the loan was that he could borrow at 10 percent and earn over 100 percent a year. I'm sure you have already guessed the conclusion. The promoter had been bringing in more money to pay the interest to previous investors, and finally the circle got too big, and it collapsed, along with my friend's money.

Unfortunately, that is not a unique case. Every year, thousands of Christian families risk and lose money they cannot afford to lose seeking that "big deal." Can it be avoided? Most certainly, but not on the basis of human wisdom. There has never been a get-rich-quick scheme that didn't sound terrific on the surface. The promoters are a great deal better at disguising the bad deals than most people are at detecting them. Also, what may seem like a business deal to one person is get-rich-quick to another.

How then can a Christian avoid such schemes? The simple truth is that he cannot as long as he is emotionally caught up in his own desires and fails to yield control to God's wisdom. However, there is one source of wisdom that is not dependent on our attitude—God's Word. Our decisions can be aligned with God's by first considering His written principles. "Trust in the Lord with all your heart, and do not lean on your own understanding" (Proverbs 3:5). I have listed a few of the basic principles dealing with how to avoid get-rich-quick schemes.

1. *Stick with what you know.* "By wisdom a house is built, and by understanding it is established" (Proverbs 24:3). A great part of wisdom is recognizing our limitations. Seldom will anyone be duped into a get-rich-quick scheme in his area of expertise. It would be very difficult to convince a chicken

farmer that someone could get rich quick in the chicken business. Unfortunately, there have been many people who lost a great deal of money trying.

The vast majority of people who make money do so in the field in which they have the most training and experience. Those who lose it usually do so in an area they know little about.

2. *Don't risk borrowed money.* "A prudent man sees evil and hides himself, the naive proceed and pay the penalty" (Proverbs 27:12).

It's one thing to speculate with money you can afford to lose and quite another to lose money that literally belongs to another. The former is called speculation; the latter is surety. It doesn't necessarily mean that the investment should be paid in total, but it does mean that the down payment should not be borrowed.

However, the only time an investment should be financed (leveraged) is when there is adequate value to cover any liability or when payments can be made from a known source of funds and are not dependent on the sale of the investment. Otherwise, you are presuming on an uncertain event. "Do not boast about tomorrow, for you do not know what a day may bring forth" (Proverbs 27:1).

3. *Buy investments with utility.* "She considers a field and buys it; from her earnings she plants a vineyard . . . She makes linen garments and sells them, and supplies belts to the tradesmen" (Proverbs 31:16, 24). Utility simply means buying something of use to someone else.

Most get-rich-quick schemes deal with intangibles, or at least remote tangibles, such as oil wells, chicken farms, movies, motivational programs, and so on.

4. *Don't make quick decisions.* "The plans of the diligent lead surely to advantage, but everyone who is hasty comes surely to poverty" (Proverbs 21:5). The very essence of a get-rich-quick scheme is emotionalism. The promoter urges the potential buyer to act quickly before the opportunity is missed. The exact technique will vary, depending on the need. It may include pressure to become a "success," to avoid income taxes, or to "make it" for retirement. Above all else, a get-rich-quick scheme depends on convincing the prospect to buy without thinking about it too long. Once the money has changed hands, the promoter knows it's too late to back out.

The final ploy in closing is to develop an attitude of covetousness by hinting that another prospect is waiting to snap up the deal. What is the best way to avoid this trap? "Rest in the Lord and wait patiently for Him; do not fret because of him who prospers in his way, because of the man who carries out wicked schemes" (Psalm 37:7).

5. *Seek good counsel.* "The way of a fool is right in his own eyes, but a wise man is he who listens to counsel" (Proverbs 12:15).

It is amazing how quickly someone who is not emotionally involved with a get-rich-quick scheme can spot its flaws. Good, objective Christian counsel should be a prerequisite to any major financial decision. That counsel is most objective when it comes from someone who has no profit motive involved.

One of the best sources of counsel is a Christian spouse. It is astounding how many times I have observed that a wife comes to the right conclusion using the wrong facts. Most women are generally more conservative than men and can provide a balance. "House and wealth are an inheritance from fathers, but a prudent wife is from the Lord" (Proverbs 19:14).

Summary

A get-rich-quick scheme is usually one that offers an excessive gain for the apparent risk. It usually involves an area about which you know little or nothing, requires a quick decision, and was recommended by a friend.

Satan will often provide one good deal before presenting the real loser. He knows that a Christian who is defeated in one area, particularly finances, will not be an effective witness.

To avoid these financial traps, you must establish your standards by God's Word: seek God's plan for your life, stick with what you know, seek good counsel, and wait on God's peace for acting. "It is the blessing of the Lord that makes rich, and He adds no sorrow to it" (Proverbs 10:22).

25

The Purpose of Investing

ONCE I WAS asked a very penetrating question by a close Christian friend: "Why should we help rich people get richer?" The obvious answer is that teaching Christians to invest wisely is as necessary as teaching them to budget. God has commissioned us to help Christians to be better stewards, and that includes using surplus resources properly. In a very practical way, it is obvious that those with a surplus are able to give more to God's work than are others. That doesn't mean that everyone who has a surplus *will* give more, but that he *can*. One function of any ministry of finances is to teach Christians how and why to multiply their resources for giving. To do this, those with a surplus must be able to invest wisely.

History of Investing

The first investment can be found in Genesis 3:23. Adam was cast out of the garden and told to cultivate the soil for his food. To do so he had to risk planting seeds that could have been eaten; thus, he became an *investor*. Farmers understand the principle of investing. Each year they are faced with a choice of eating all the seeds, selling all the seeds, or retaining some to replant It would be a very short-sighted farmer who would either eat or sell his entire harvest. He would still have some harvest the next season from the seed that fell during picking, but it would be pretty slim. A wise farmer not only holds back some seed for replanting, but he also sorts out the best seed to insure a greater harvest. By doing so, he exercises self-discipline to achieve greater prosperity.

Contrary to what many people believe, God is not against prosperity. The Scriptures give evidence that one of God's blessings to those who love and obey Him is prosperity (2 Chronicles 16:9; Psalm 37:4; Proverbs 8:21). God hates evil attitudes. These include greed, covetousness, and pride. Attitudes like these are not isolated to those who have a surplus. They are abundantly evident even among the very poor.

Justification for Investing

A rational reason for not investing a surplus is to give it away to further God's work and to help the needy. However, there is no evidence in the Bible that God's plan was to *always* give away any surplus. Just the opposite is true. Saving was a sign of wisdom, while a lack was the sign of slothfulness. "There is precious treasure and oil in the dwelling of the wise, but a foolish man swallows it up" (Proverbs 21:20). Obviously, there are exceptions, but they were, and are, individual directives, not biblical principles.

In Matthew 25:14–30, several references are given to investing various amounts. In our economy today, the largest amount mentioned, five talents, would be equal to approximately $1,784,000, and the smallest, one talent, would be $356,835. The very intent of this parable is to reflect on the attitudes and faithfulness of investors in the absence of their master. If investing is prohibited or even discouraged, why would Jesus use it as an example and reward the most diligent? The obvious answer is: investing is just another part of stewardship—not more important than giving but not less important either.

Prerequisites for Investing

The number-one prerequisite for investing is *attitude.* Why are you investing, and how will the surplus be used? If a Christian wants God to entrust greater riches to him, he must be found faithful in the smaller amount first (Luke 16:10–11). To protect against the infectious diseases of greed and pride, the best weapon is a specific plan for returning the excess to God's kingdom. I find that once a commitment has been made to a disciplined life-style, regardless of the available income, the danger of greed and self-indulgence is drastically reduced.

The term used throughout Paul's writings is *contentment.* "But godliness actually is a means of great gain, when accompanied by contentment" (1 Timothy 6:6). In a society oriented to "more" and the "best," it is difficult to reach the right balance. Even within Christianity, the examples of those who could handle a surplus are few. Therefore, a plan to dispose of the profits is as important as a plan to invest the surplus.

Legitimate Reasons for Investing

There are several legitimate reasons for a Christian to invest:

First, to further God's work. Some Christians have received a gift of giving (Romans 12:8). To them, the multiplication of material worth is an extension of their basic ministry within the Body of Christ. Even to those who do not have a gift of giving, investments are a way to preserve and multiply a surplus that has been provided for a later time. In Acts 4:34, the believers sold their assets and surrendered the proceeds to meet the needs of other believers. God blessed some with surplus to be used at a later date.

Second, family responsibility. We are admonished to provide for those within our own households (1 Timothy 5:8). That provision was never limited to the life span of a father. It extended to providing for his family even after his death. Not everyone can do so, but if those who are able meet their own needs, the church can concentrate on the needs of the poor. "If a man fathers a hundred children and lives many years, however many they be, but his soul is not satisfied with good things, and he does not even have a proper burial, then I say, 'Better the miscarriage than he'" (Ecclesiastes 6:3).

If parents believe that God wants their children to go to college, is it more spiritual to expect the government and banks to educate them than to store for the eventual need? The parable of the ant in Proverbs 6:6 says to "observe her ways and be wise." One of her ways is to plan ahead by storing. In a highly inflationary economy, even storing requires investing.

Illegitimate Reasons for Investing

There are also several unbiblical reasons to invest. Unfortunately, these represent the greater number of investors, Christian and non-Christian, because Satan has so thoroughly dominated our attitudes about money.

Greed. Greed is the desire to continually have more and demand only the best. "But those who want to get rich fall into temptation and a snare and many foolish and harmful desires which plunge men into ruin and destruction" (1 Timothy 6:9).

Envy. Envy is the desire to achieve based on observation of other people's success. "For I was envious of the arrogant, as I saw the prosperity of the wicked" (Psalm 73:3).

Pride. Pride is the desire to be elevated because of material achievements. "Instruct those who are rich in this present world not to be conceited or to fix their hope on the uncertainty of riches, but on God, who richly supplies us with all things to enjoy" (1 Timothy 6:17).

Ignorance. Ignorance is following the counsel of other misguided people because of a lack of discernment. "Leave the presence of a fool, or you will not discern words of knowledge" (Proverbs 14:7).

There are many wrong motives for investing. The result of any of these is anxiety, frustration, and eventually a deadening of spiritual values.

Thus, as our Lord says, "No servant can serve two masters; for either he will hate the one, and love the other, or else he will hold to one, and despise the other. You cannot serve God and mammon" (Luke 16:13).

Investing to Serve God Better

Once a Christian has accepted the purpose of investing (to serve God better), the crucial decision is how much to invest. Obviously, there is no absolute answer. It is an individual decision made by a Christian after much prayer. With earnest prayer the decision is difficult—without it, impossible. There are some initial choices to be made that will greatly simplify the decision about how much to invest:

1. Before investing, give to God's work until you know that all of the needs God has placed on your heart are satisfied. Don't be misled into thinking that there will then be no more needs in the world. There will always be needs, but God doesn't place *every* need on anyone's heart. Giving, like spiritual discernment, is a matter of growth and practice. I believe the key here is: when in doubt, give. It is better to be wrong and give too much than to ignore God's direction and give too little. The Spirit is never dampened by too sensitive a will, only by developing calluses. "Therefore openly before the churches show them the proof of your love and of our reason for boasting about you" (2 Corinthians 8:24).

2. Settle on a level of family needs that is God's plan for you. Too much spending on a family can rob surplus funds as surely as bad investments. Each Christian family must decide on the level God has planned for them and stick to it in spite of available surpluses. Remember that balance is essential. Too much is waste; too little is self-punishment. "And whatever we ask we receive from Him, because we keep His commandments and do the things that are pleasing in His sight" (1 John 3:22).

3. Have a plan for the use of your potential surplus. One interesting characteristic about humans is that we can rationalize nearly anything, including reinvesting God's portion or saving it for Him. Therefore, it is important to settle on a plan for distributing the profits from investments before they arrive. Decide what portion is to be reinvested. Clearly, the greatest danger is to continually reinvest the profits and rationalize it because of taxes, lack of discernable needs, or a need for surplus security.

Do your planning *before* the money becomes available. One good way to do that is to give away a large percentage of the investment *before* it appreciates. "Because of the proof given by this ministry they will glorify God for your obedience to your confession of the gospel of Christ, and for the liberality of your contribution to them and to all" (2 Corinthians 9:13).

26
Selecting Good Counsel

A COMMONLY ASKED question is, "How can I find good Christian counsel?" But perhaps even more fundamental would be the question, "How can I tell when I find good Christian counsel?"

It is very difficult to give objective counsel when the counselor is selling a particular product. There is nothing wrong with product sales, however. Virtually everyone is a product salesman of one sort or another. But good, objective counsel must be separated from the necessity to sell a product; otherwise, a lot of objectivity is lost.

For instance, it would be very difficult to obtain objective counsel about what car would best suit your family's needs from a salesman who earns his living selling Hondas. He is going to be biased by his sales training, experience, and mostly by his need to sell a Honda. A good salesman will match his product as closely to your need as possible but will seldom suggest that you look elsewhere.

The bias toward a particular product is only one limitation in finding good counsel. Another critical limitation is finding counselors with "like" minds and attitudes, namely Christians. What makes it even more difficult is that there are many counselors who profess to be Christians but who give worldly advice. There are also many Christians who profess to be counselors but who give very unwise advice.

With all this confusion, I can thoroughly understand the difficulty and frustration of locating good Christian counsel, especially in the areas involving money. However, I know beyond a doubt that such counsel is available to anyone willing to take the time and effort to seek it out.

Why Bother with Counsel?

There are many guidelines in God's Word for seeking and selecting good counsel. The purpose of counsel is to aid us in making our decisions, not to actually make them for us. Too often we want someone to tell us what to do. When you allow someone else to tell you what to do, with rare exception, you're going to get bad advice. Many times I've had someone share that an advisor told him to buy a particular investment that ended up losing money, while the advisor made money through that purchase. Sometimes the advice is both right and wrong, as in the recent instance of a Christian couple who bought into a whiskey-aging partnership—the investment was great (about 25–30 percent growth per year) but not for Christians. Under a very strong conviction about being both stewards and witnesses, they ended up selling out at a sizable loss. The other investors will probably end up making a sizable profit over the next ten years. The investment advice was accurate; the counsel was entirely wrong.

Principles for Selecting Counselors

Principle 1: Christian counsel. Select your counselors on the basis of a common value system. For the Christian, that means those who acknowledge Jesus Christ as their Savior and Lord. "How blessed is the man who does not walk in the counsel of the wicked, nor stand in the path of sinners, nor sit in the seat of scoffers" (Psalm 1:1). In no way does that imply that non-Christians can't give good advice. Some of them give better advice than many Christians. But the standards by which decisions are made in our society today are quite often incompatible with God's standards.

Principle 2: Wise counsel. "He who walks with wise men will be wise, but the companion of fools will suffer harm" (Proverbs 13:20). The mere fact that someone is a Christian does not qualify him as an expert in every area of life. Too often Christians invest absolute confidence in the advice of someone solely on the basis of his salvation. The evidence that Christians can and do give bad counsel is all too evident today. The process of salvation does not eliminate attitudes of ego, pride, and greed in most of us. They are active by virtue of our self-will.

Additionally, many "Christian" counselors suffer from acute lack of common sense and wisdom. Wisdom comes from God, and in James 1:5 we are told, "But if any of you lacks wisdom, let him ask of God, who gives to all men generously." Therefore, both counselor and counselee must be in regular communication with God.

Most Christians have found that the majority of decisions they face can be answered on the basis of God's written Word, and that the wisdom they lack is the wisdom to understand (and accept) what God has already told them. Therefore, a counselor must be knowledgeable in his area of expertise and regularly in God's Word.

Principle 3: Multiple counselors. "Without consultation, plans are frustrated, but with many counselors they succeed" (Proverbs 15:22). No one can be expert enough in all areas of finance for anyone to depend upon his counsel exclusively. Any financial counselor who would steer clients away from other qualified sources of advice qualifies as foolish. "He who walks with wise men will be wise, but the companion of fools will suffer harm" (Proverbs 13:20).

The areas of taxes, securities, stocks, bonds, and real estate are so complex today that only with a variety of good counselors can you really get good advice. What inhibits most financial counselors from suggesting other advisors is the fear of losing a client or of a client's finding out that he has had bad advice. Counselors who are good at what they do and who seek the very best for their clients have no fear of losing them.

Principle 4: Weigh all counsel. "The naive believes everything, but the prudent man considers his steps" (Proverbs 14:15).

The purpose of counsel is to offer suggestions, alternatives, and options—not to make your decision. Even the best counsel in the world lacks an essential ingredient necessary to making decisions—God's plan for your life. Paul was given accurate, godly counsel not to return to Jerusalem in Acts 21. Paul listened and weighed that counsel against what God had impressed upon him to do and refused to be swayed from God's path for him.

Sometimes people call to ask what I think about some financial advice they have received. Often without offering any counsel at all, I ask them how they feel about the suggestions, and they will respond, "I really don't have a peace about doing it." Their decision was already made if they were willing to listen to their conscience. The investment may be great, but it's not for them. What is financial bondage? The absence of financial freedom. Anything that robs us of God's peace is contrary to God's plan for us.

How to Weigh Counsel

I have found that there are many people who know a great deal more about their area of expertise than I do. Those people I use as resources. But I have found that a lot more people know practically nothing about the areas in which they give advice. Those people I try to avoid. The problem is that it's sometimes difficult initially to tell the difference between the two groups. Later, when the good advice works, or the bad advice fails, it's a lot easier to see what they did or didn't know.

Test their counsel. When I'm evaluating someone's counsel in an area with which I am unfamiliar, I will pick a subject about which we should both be knowledgeable and test him. If I find his answers to be fundamentally wrong in an area I do understand, then I avoid his counsel in areas I don't understand.

Compare to God's Word. In Proverbs 3:5, we are told to "trust in the Lord with all your heart." Therefore, any counsel that runs contrary to God's Word should be counted as worthless. Recently, a friend was advised by his attorney to divorce his wife during a pending car accident lawsuit so that if she lost, she could file bankruptcy without endangering his assets. They could remarry later, he said, and everything would be all right. My advice was to divorce himself from ungodly counsel.

Test counselor's value system. Proverbs 13:5 says that "a righteous man hates falsehood." A consistent observation is that a man who will deceive someone else on your behalf will eventually deceive you as well, given the right set of circumstances. Just because someone calls himself a Christian does not mean that he holds to God's value system. Test the value system to see where his heart is.

Track record. Proverbs 21:5 says, "The plans of the diligent lead surely to advantage." A good test of a counselor's expertise is his past performance. If every financial advisor were graded on the basis of promises versus performance, many would grade rather low. Any time you choose to invest time and money with someone who has less than five years verifiable track record, you should assume that you're his on-the-job training.

References. Few people ask for multiple references from a financial counselor, and even fewer verify those references. A friend once asked me to check out an investment salesman for him from his own list of references. The very first reference spent ten minutes telling me what a poor job the man had done for him and ended up saying that he didn't even answer the salesman's calls anymore. Two more calls verified that this fellow never expected anyone to actually call a listed reference. Most people who list references try to list only the best; so, I assumed these were his best clients. Remember what Proverbs 21:29 says: "A wicked man shows a bold face." Most so-called "advisers" count on a good front to satisfy most clients.

How to Locate Good Counsel

The best method for locating good, Christian counsel is from other Christians who have been helped. Quite often, if you'll just ask others at your church, someone will recommend a good resource. You can also call several of the sound pastors in your area. They will almost always know of the quality people in their communities. Lastly, there are several Christian professional associations, such as the Christian Legal Society, the Christian Medical Association, and the Fellowship of Companies for Christ. Obviously, not everyone involved with these associations is either Christian or expert, but it's a good starting point. Without a doubt, the expert Christian counsel we need is available if we seek it diligently.

27
Insurance—Is It Scriptural?

Two QUESTIONS ARE often asked: "Is insurance scriptural?" and, "Does owning insurance reflect a lack of faith?" The answer is both yes and no. Insurance is not specifically defined in Scripture; however, the principle of future provision is. Owning insurance does not necessarily reflect a lack of faith in God, though it is increasingly being used for that purpose. However, just as damaging are the secondary effects that insurance is having on our society: those of greed, slothfulness, waste, and fear.

Some have developed an insurance ethic that often rationalizes cheating where insurance companies are concerned. Many committed Christians are willing to use insurance funds to do things they would never consider doing with their own money.

Recently, a Christian physician and I were discussing the issue when he related an all too common event. A Christian patient of his was in need of some tests to diagnose a problem. The doctor suggested that she receive the tests as a hospital outpatient because the costs would be substantially less. "Oh, no," she said, "my insurance only pays if I'm admitted to a hospital for at least two days, and I want the best." Certainly, this Christian lady would never consider willfully cheating somebody—but didn't she? "And if you have not been faithful in the use of that which is another's, who will give you that which is your own?" (Luke 16:12).

A counselee some time ago shared with me one of what he called God's "answers" to prayer. His car had been severely damaged in an airport parking lot while he was away on a trip, and, unfortunately, the "banger" didn't leave a note for the "bangee." He didn't carry collision insurance that would cover the damage because of the cost; so, he drove the car as it was for several weeks. Then one day he was hit from the rear in a multiple-car collision. Although the actual damage from that collision was slight, in getting an estimate for damages, he "neglected" to mention the previous damage done at the airport. Consequently, his car was entirely repaired by the liability insurance of the car that struck him from the rear. "What an answer from the Lord!" he exclaimed.

Unfortunately, this "answer" conflicted with God's Word. "The perverse in heart are an abomination to the Lord, but the blameless in their walk are His delight" (Proverbs 11:20).

I simply asked him to review a few passages of Scripture that dealt with this area, pray about it, ask God's direction, and then do what he felt God would have him do. He ended up repaying the insurance company for his share.

Current Attitudes

Why is it that even committed Christians are tempted to cheat and rationalize it? Several factors are involved: One is that insurance companies are seemingly wealthy and impersonal. Inwardly, many people feel that to be wealthy, they must be dishonest and therefore are "fair game." Also, since they don't actually know anyone at the insurance company, it's not like cheating a person. Another reason is that we have developed a protection attitude in our society so prevalent that most Christians don't consider whether the insurance they pay for is really necessary.

Biblical Perspective

A Christian must believe that *all* resources belong to God. Therefore, the resources that are in the control of an insurance company are still God's. As such, we will be held accountable for how they are spent on us just as certainly as if the funds came out of our savings account. "The righteousness of the upright will deliver them, but the treacherous will be caught by their own greed" (Proverbs 11:6).

Provision

God's Word teaches provision, not protection. Insurance can be used to provide where a potential loss would be excessive. That is especially true when another's loss must be considered, as in automobile liability coverage. "A prudent man sees evil and hides himself, the naive proceed and pay the penalty" (Proverbs 27:12).

That point was brought home clearly to me as I sought to insure our ministry buildings. A group of Christians had purchased our property and had given it to us to develop a counseling center. Even minimal insurance coverage turned out to be several thousand dollars a year. After seeking God's will, the answer became very clear. Certainly, if God was able to provide buildings initially, He could also replace them if necessary. So the erstwhile insurance money went to buy teaching materials. "And call upon Me in the day of trouble; I shall rescue you, and you will honor Me" (Psalm 50:15).

God does not want us to be foolish; He wants us to be responsible. Too often insurance is used to shift our responsibilities to someone else. Between the government welfare programs and the growth of insurance plans for virtually everything, the Christian community has been duped into believing that they don't *need* each other. That is a lie from the deceiver to suit his purpose. But when God decides "enough is enough," we will again discover the reality of Psalm 73:25. "Whom have I in heaven but Thee? And besides Thee, I desire nothing on earth." Prior to Christ's return, we will again be molded into a working body, and no amount of insurance will be able to buffer us from needing each other. The community plan described in Acts 4:34 will be our "insurance" plan. That does not mean that the use of insurance is unscriptural, but that the misuse of it is.

Net Effect of an Insurance Ethic

Unfortunately, one of the bad side effects of relying so heavily upon insurance to buffer every little problem is that we also buffer God's guidance. There is no evidence in Scripture that God promises or desires to buffer His people from every difficulty or inconvenience. In fact, conversely, evidence exists that these are specifically allowed to redirect us or allow us to "test" our faith (Romans 5:3; 2 Corinthians 8:2; Philippians 3:7; James 1:3). Thus, there is a transfer of trust from God to insurance if it is used in excess.

The apparently easy access to insurance company funds promotes an attitude of slothfulness both financially and spiritually. Financially, because there is less incentive to save and anticipate problems; spiritually, because there is less need to pray about future needs, of others as well as our own. Those who have access to employer-paid, low deductible insurance plans have a tendency to forget that not everyone in their community has the same opportunity. Legitimate needs within Christian families go wanting because others aren't aware that not everyone can afford the high cost of insurance.

The net effects from the misuse of insurance are to raise both the cost of insurance and the services that feed off of it. Much of the increased cost of credit is passed on to consumers (including those who pay cash); the increased cost of insurance abusers is passed on to the diligent. Obviously, that discourages conservatism and encourages even more abuses by others. The tendency is to say, 'I want to get my fair share, too."

Individual Responsibility

An overwhelmingly simple principle stands out in God's Word: individual responsibility. It really doesn't matter what others are doing. God holds each of us individually responsible for our actions. "But let each one examine his own work, and then he will have reason for boasting in regard to himself alone, and not in regard to another" (Galatians 6:4).

Each Christian must examine every area of daily life frequently to determine if it is up to God's standards. The best quick test is whether or not there is a peace about the actions.

Health. Health insurance provides a good benefit by making good health care available to most families. Unfortunately, adequate health care is now *dependent* upon insurance coverage. It costs more to stay one day in a hospital in Idaho than at a fancy hotel in New York City. That doesn't mean that everyone should give up health insurance, but that, as Christians, we must use it as we would our own money. Never sign a bill without thoroughly reviewing it. Require documentation for every expenditure. Ask for a reasonable estimate before committing to any health care plan or hospital stay. If you are an employer, check into higher deductible plans that may cost less but provide better catastrophe care. Give incentives to employees who do not abuse the insurance plan.

Life. The purpose of any life insurance plan is to provide for those who cannot provide for themselves. Many Christians have too little, while others have too much. It always baffles me to counsel a Christian who has purchased an enormous amount of life insurance to protect an estate that is probably far too large anyway. "When there is a man who has labored with wisdom, knowledge and skill, then he gives his legacy to one who has not labored with them. This too is vanity and a great evil" (Ecclesiastes 2:21).

On the other end of the spectrum are those who have the ability to provide for their families if they died unexpectedly but apparently don't think they need to. Both examples reflect disobedience to God's principles. "If a man fathers a hundred children and lives many years, however many they be, but his soul is not satisfied with good things, and he does not even have a proper burial, then I say, 'Better the miscarriage then he'" (Ecclesiastes 6:3).

Other insurance. To decide what is the correct balance, a simple test can be used. Can you provide for an unexpected loss yourself? If so, then to pay out money for insurance is a waste of God's resources. Great emotional appeals can be made for protecting everything from the dishwasher to possible termites. At what point should we say enough? That point has been reached when a Christian looks around and finds that trusting God no longer seems necessary for future material needs (Philippians 4:19).

Part Four

BORROWING
AND LENDING

28
Surety—What Is It?

SURETY MUST BE one of the least taught and least understood principles in God's Word. It's hard to understand why when you consider the number of references to surety in the book of Proverbs. Any time there is that much teaching on a single subject and it's still being violated, then you must conclude that Satan is at work to deceive us. The fact that so many people can violate a basic principle about money and get away with it for a long time does not negate the principle. It merely means that the cycle has not run its full course yet. I trust that Christians will decide to change—not because they have to, but because God's Word says to. One certainty is, just wait, eventually the economy will confirm the wisdom of God's Word.

In a literal sense, surety means to deposit a pledge in either money, goods, or part payment for a greater obligation. Surety means taking on an obligation to pay later without a "certain" way to pay. "A man lacking in sense pledges, and becomes surety in the presence of his neighbor" (Proverbs 17:18).

Why Is Surety Wrong?

Obviously, surety is not a biblical law—it is a principle. A principle is a biblical guide to keep you on God's path and out of the world's traps. You don't get punished for violating a principle unknowingly; you suffer the consequences. The consequences of violating the principle of surety is that you presume upon the future. In other words, when you sign surety for a debt, you pledge your future. If you have omniscient insights into the future, then there is really no danger. But, since only God has omniscient insight, when you sign surety, you presume upon God's will. "Come now, you who say, 'Today or tomorrow, we shall go to such and such a city, and spend a year there and engage in business and make a profit.' Yet you do not know what your life will be like tomorrow. You are just a vapor that appears for a little while and then vanishes away" (James 4:13–14.)

Why So Much Violation?

If surety is such an obvious biblical principle, why is there so much violation today? I would venture to say that over 95 percent of the Christians in America have, or will have in the future, violated the principle of surety. Why? Because surety is a modern day mechanism to "get rich quick." It allows us to buy things we really can't afford to own and allows us to speculate on the future. The fact that so many have speculated and have got away with it—even prospered—has dulled us to the fact that a get-rich-quick attitude eventually catches up with us.

"The plans of the diligent lead surely to advantage, but everyone who is hasty comes surely to poverty" (Proverbs 21:5). Nowhere is this seen more often than in the purchase of homes and cars. These industries are built on surety. They require an ever-expanding source of credit, and, with rare exception, the borrower pledges to pay regardless of any outside circumstances.

Co-signing. "He who is surety for a stranger will surely suffer for it, but he who hates going surety is safe" (Proverbs 11:15). Because co-signing is the most widely known form of surety, one would be led to believe that no Christian would sign for the debts of another. That simply is not the case. Many Christians sign for the debts of another. Why? Sometimes it's actually to avoid their scriptural obligation to give. It's easier to sign and allow someone to borrow than to give to their needs. Most of the time, however, Christians co-sign either out of ignorance of what God's Word teaches or out of misguided conviction and guilt. They feel guilty about what they have materially and co-sign for a friend. What happens, then, is if the borrower cannot repay and the co-signer has to pay, a friendship is lost.

Usually, the borrower feels guilt, then, and will avoid the co-signer. Remember, the definition of a distant friend is a close friend who owes you money and can't repay.

Practically speaking, when you co-sign a note for someone else, you allow him to borrow beyond his ability to repay. Why do you suppose that a banker requires a co-signer? Usually because the person borrowing is a high risk and lacks the ability to repay under certain circumstances. Remember this: God's people are to be counted among the wise, and the Word says that a man lacking in sense pledges.

Buy Now, Pay Later

If surety is taking on an obligation to pay without a certain way to pay it, then virtually every home mortgage is surety. Some states have laws that prohibit mortgage lenders from collecting a deficiency on a home mortgage, but most do not. The only thing that has kept most lenders from suing a defaulting home buyer is that inflation was driving up prices and there were few actual losses. However, many home buyers in states where prices have dropped during the last few years have been sued for defaults. It is quite possible that economic circumstances in the future could place many others in jeopardy. They will find that assets they thought were debt-free are actually pledged as surety against their home loan or another mortgage loan.

A few years back, I saw a vivid example of the problems brought about by surety through a Christian doctor's circumstances. He and his partner initially came to discuss an apartment complex they were considering buying. It seems that they could buy this complex, with an appraised value of over $4 million, for less than $2 million. It required that they put about $100,000 down and personally sign notes for the rest. My counsel from God's Word was, "Don't do it—no matter how good the deal looks." Well, they didn't like that advice, so they shopped around until they located some counsel they liked better and they "bought" the complex (against their wives' advice, too). Less than a year later, it was discovered that the buildings had been insulated with a hazardous substance, and the health department condemned the entire complex. In the meantime, the original lender, a foreign company, had sold their note to another lender, who threatened to sue to protect his interests. Ultimately, the complex was demolished and the property resold. Their final debt ended up at about $1 million, upon which they are now making payments.

There are no sure things economically, and God's Word anticipates that: "Know well the condition of your flocks, and pay attention to your herds; for riches are not forever, nor does a crown endure to all generations" (Proverbs 27:23-24).

Appreciating vs. Depreciating

Often I have heard someone say, "I know you're not supposed to borrow for depreciating items such as cars and clothes, but it's OK to borrow for appreciating assets because they're always worth more than you owe." There are two basic flaws in that logic: First, if anyone can pick out assets that can only appreciate, let me know, and we'll get every Christian to buy some. Second, God's Word doesn't say that it's bad to sign surety for a depreciating item but acceptable for an appreciating item. It says that if you sign surety, eventually you'll suffer. "He who is surety for a stranger will surely suffer for it (Proverbs 11:15a). Again, the simple truth is that no one can guarantee appreciation, and the time at which an asset might have to be sold may be the worst time, not the best. Avoid surety on appreciating or depreciating items.

Existing Surety

The question is often asked when discussing surety, "What if I am already signed as surety?" You can only do what you can do. Fortunately, God doesn't expect more out of us than we are capable of doing. If you can get out of surety, you should. But if you cannot, then work at reducing the liability and paying off the debts early. If you can't avoid surety in your business right now, then start planning toward a time when you can. If you never decide to be debt free, then most probably you never will be.

Hundreds and perhaps thousands of Christians now operate major businesses totally debt free as a result of deciding to do so on the basis of God's Word. Most of them would have never believed it was possible. One automobile dealer who had to borrow well over $1 million in 1973 now operates totally on a cash basis. He now makes more money than he ever has before and is practically unaffected by fluctuating interest rates. The same could be said about home builders, restaurant owners, and Christians in virtually every area of the economy.

How to Avoid Surety

"Do not boast about tomorrow, for you do not know what a day may bring forth" (Proverbs 27:1).

Let me repeat—surety is a principle—not a law. It is an observation that pledging for debt leads to financial ruin. While not pledging does not guarantee financial success, it does eliminate any "contingent liability," meaning a future obligation to pay when you might not be able to.

Does that mean that a Christian should never borrow? No, God's Word does not prohibit borrowing—although it doesn't encourage it either. But scriptural borrowing would be limited to contracts where the means to pay is certain. That means that the lender agrees to accept pledged collateral in total payment of the outstanding debt at any time.

For instance, if you wanted to purchase a piece of land for $10,000 but could only put up $1,000, you would finance the remaining $9,000 with the land pledged as total security. Therefore, if ever you couldn't continue to pay the note, the land would be surrendered and the debt canceled. There would be no contingent liability because you always have a certain way to pay. Would it be ethical to give the collateral in lieu of payment? Certainly, if that's what your agreement stated. There will be many opportunities to buy where the property will not stand for the debt. You must be willing to walk away from them even if they are good deals. As Christians, if we are to seek God's best, that means avoiding surety.

29
Borrowing:
A Biblical Perspective

W HEN YOU REVIEW the history of borrowing and lending, it is clear that we are living in a unique period of time in regard to credit. Prior to this century, a lender had almost absolute authority over a borrower. If a loan wasn't repaid exactly according to schedule, the borrower forfeited everything he owned to the lender. If the debt wasn't satisfied, the borrower was thrown into prison and became a bond-servant until every penny of the debt was repaid.

Today, almost the opposite extreme exists. The borrower has a legal method to avoid repayment of almost any indebtedness, regardless of how frivolously the money was spent. Eventually, the borrower will discover that the lender's authority has not been overruled, since it is established by God; it has merely been temporarily diverted. Ultimately, it will be the lenders who will come out on top.

I recently did a survey of several seminar groups to determine if they thought borrowing was scripturally forbidden. Over 70 percent responded that they believed the Bible prohibited borrowing. Perhaps it would be a lot easier if God's Word did prohibit a Christian from borrowing, but it does not. There is not a verse directing God's people *not* to borrow money (not even Romans 13:8). However, no Scripture *encourages* borrowing either. Borrowing is always discussed in the Bible as a negative rather than a positive principle. It would seem to be a consequence of disobeying God's statutes or rules of economics. "He shall lend to you, but you shall not lend to him. . . So all these curses shall come on you and pursue you and overtake you until you are destroyed, because you would not obey the Lord your God" (Deuteronomy 28:44–45).

God's Minimum

The absolute minimum that God's Word establishes for any borrower is found in Psalm 37:21: "The wicked borrows and does not pay back, but the righteous is gracious and gives."

If we don't want to be counted among the wicked, we must repay any debt we owe. Knowing that should cause any Christian to avoid unnecessary borrowing for any reason. It really doesn't matter if the "circumstances" are beyond our control. If we make a debt, we're stuck with it. "If therefore you are presenting your offering at the altar, and there remember that your brother has something against you, leave your offering there before the altar, and go your way; first be reconciled to your brother, and then come and present your offering" (Matthew 5:23–24).

God's Promises

Unfortunately, we live mostly by sight rather than by faith. Those who are overwhelmed by debts will require faith that God knows their needs and will provide them. I have seen God provide for those who, by faith, trusted Him even to the point of losing every material possession they had. In many instances, God's provision came from a totally unexpected source and only after the commitment had been made.

I recall a Christian real estate developer who had lost every asset during an economic downturn. His three "Christian" partners all filed bankruptcy, and he was left with the total debt of slightly more than $600,000. After seeking counsel, he and his wife determined that they could not file voluntary bankruptcy, and in accordance with Matthew 5:40, they surrendered every possession they had except their clothes. They literally begged their creditors (mostly banks) not to force them into bankruptcy and promised to pay what they could above their basic living expenses. Over the next two years, they were able to pay about $20,000 on the debt, which didn't even cover 20 percent of the interest. However, they did have many opportunities to share their testimony and were able to counsel dozens of families who were having financial and spiritual difficulties. Their two children, who were in college when the crisis hit, dropped out for a year to help with the finances and then went back to school on working scholarships.

In the third year, the economy recovered rapidly, and the properties that secured the debts began to sell. Some sold at modest profits and reduced the indebtedness to about $400,000. The last and biggest property sold for more than $400,000 above the total outstanding loans, and the bank returned the surplus to them, even though they had no legal obligations to do so. In less than three years, God had provided a means to pay off all the debts and a great surplus besides. The man's ex-partners approached him about their "share" of the profits. His response was correct: "If you don't share in the losses, you don't share in the profits."

The Only Biblical Way to Borrow

Perhaps the most abused and least understood financial principle in God's Word is "surety." Surety is assuming an obligation to pay an indebtedness without a "sure" way to pay it. Surety means that we presume upon the future. If everything goes as we expect, we'll be able to pay the loans back. But if things go wrong, as they often do, we may be left in debt. A common example of surety is an automobile loan. When you borrow to buy a car, the car is pledged as collateral. But since the outstanding loan often exceeds the sale value of the car, the borrower must also personally endorse the note. If the payments cannot be met and the car is repossessed and sold, the borrower is liable for any deficiency. Since there is no *certain* way to pay the debt, surety results. Only if the collateral totally secures the loan can you avoid surety.

If Christians would observe this one caution associated with borrowing, the most they could lose is the security they had pledged against a loan. "Do not be among those who give pledges, among those who become sureties for debts. If you have nothing with which to pay, why should he take your bed from under you?" (Proverbs 22:26–27).

After sharing that principle in a seminar, many times a Christian in the audience will respond, "Why, if I did that, I'd hardly ever be able to borrow money." To this I would have to respond, "Right!"

Present Day Application

Most of us were born into a debt-dominated society. Those under thirty cannot remember a time without home mortgages, automobile loans, and credit cards. However, just because these things are normal to our time, it does not make them normal to God's plan. It is important to remember that credit is not the problem; it's the *misuse* of credit. The misuse of credit can be traced back to some basic biblical root problems:

1. *Get-rich-quick.* Much debt exists because it seems faster and simpler to borrow than to save. Most of our economic cycles can be traced directly to the availability, or the lack of availability, of credit. "The plans of the diligent lead surely to advantage, but everyone who is hasty comes surely to poverty" (Proverbs 21:5).

2. *Lack of trust.* Continual borrowing, regardless of the apparent worldly logic, is an evidence of a lack of faith in God. Many Christians either don't understand God's promises or don't believe them. God says that He knows our needs and will provide them in His time according to His plan. Borrowing is not a sin, but dependence on credit is an indication that a Christian has not yielded all rights to God. "For all these things the Gentiles eagerly seek; for your heavenly Father knows that you need all these things. But seek first His kingdom and His righteousness; and all these things shall be added to you" (Matthew 6:32–33).

3. *Ignorance.* According to God's Word, ignorance is the absence of wisdom; wisdom comes from the mouth of God, and, therefore, God's Word is the cure for ignorance (Proverbs 1:32; 2:6; 3:4–6). Worldly wisdom says to multiply your goods and wealth by borrowing excessively. God's Word says

that it is better to have a dry crust of bread and peace than a feast with strife (Proverbs 17:1). The vast majority of divorced couples say debts were the number one cause of strife in the family. Many families are having debt-funded "feasts," but great strife as well. According to the Research Institute of America, the average American family pays one-fourth of their spendable income on debt.

"Necessary" Borrowing

In our society, it is nearly impossible for a young couple to buy a home without borrowing. However, with home loans has come a lifetime-debt mentality that causes couples to think in terms of what they must pay per month instead of what the total cost is. Unfortunately, most couples today don't ever plan toward a debt-free home. Worse, they don't even recognize the *need* for it. I have often heard someone say, "It's all right to borrow as long as the item appreciates." That's good common sense, but not a good biblical principle. First, God's Word doesn't state what borrowed money should be used for. Second, nothing appreciates forever, not even houses. Houses appreciate artificially because of the availability of cheap credit.

Business Borrowing

Most businesses are run on credit today. In fact, so widespread is the use of borrowed capital that many businessmen (including Christians) believe you cannot operate on a cash basis. That is not true—it is a dupe of Satan. Obviously, the debt-free can't sink as quickly. One long-range goal of every Christian businessman should be to become debt free. God never promises quick growth—He promises a solid foundation. "He is like a man building a house, who dug deep and laid a foundation upon the rock; and when a flood rose, the torrent burst against that house and could not shake it, because it had been well built" (Luke 6:48).

30
Lending to Others

THERE'S AN OLD saying that the definition of a distant friend is a close friend who owes you money.

That's not always true, but it has enough truth in it to cause us to evaluate lending as a biblical principle. Let's first evaluate lending from a human viewpoint.

Why would anyone want to lend another person money? There are several logical reasons:

1. *To make a profit.* When you place money in a savings account, you have *loaned* the bank money. Obviously, you would like your money back, plus interest. The interest represents a profit on the loan you made.

2. *Because they have a need.* You may know someone who is short of funds for a business or a personal need, and you want to help but don't feel you can give the money.

3. *Because they asked you.* Many Christians lend money to someone because they were asked and are too timid to say no. That is typically true where close friends or family are involved.

The History of Lending

There is no record of a society that operated for any period of time without borrowing and lending. Our society is a very rare instance where the laws favor the borrowers over the lenders. So lending is *not* a new principle. It is historically as old as man's written records and was common to Moses, Solomon, and Paul. Solomon's words in Proverbs 22:7 become much clearer in light of this: "The rich rules over the poor, and the borrower becomes the lender's slave."

Biblical Principle

It would be much simpler if God's Word merely said to be neither a borrower nor a lender. God doesn't say that anyone *has* to be a lender, but He also doesn't say you cannot be a lender. If you're a Christian in the lending business, this is a vital biblical issue. For if God's Word prohibited lending, the prohibition would, of necessity, carry over to working for a lender. Many Christians who work in banking have asked if they should be involved in a lending business. There may be reasons God would not want an individual to be involved in lending because of the morals or ethics of the day, but not because lending itself is unscriptural.

It is interesting that lending is one of the blessings promised by God for being obedient to His ways. Deuteronomy 28:12 says, "The Lord will open for you His good storehouse, the heavens, to give rain to your land in its season and to bless all the work of your hand; and you shall lend to many nations, but you shall not borrow."

Thus, God promises a surplus that can be loaned, at interest, to enhance His people's prosperity. There are many principles about collecting that must also be observed if we are in service to God, but clearly lending is not prohibited scripturally.

Lending at Interest

There is little Scripture dealing with the specifics of lending and charging interest, but what there is would seem to be very clear—don't charge interest to your "brothers." "You shall not charge interest to your countrymen: interest on money, food, or anything that may be loaned at interest" (Deuteronomy 23:19).

A loan can be made to anyone, but loans to those within God's family are to be a demonstration that God can provide without charging interest to one another. I personally believe this admonition relates to basic needs (food, shelter, clothing) and not to investment loans, but that is my opinion.

In regard to lending to others, God's Word says, "You may charge interest to a foreigner, but to your countrymen you shall not charge interest, so that the Lord your God may bless you in all that you undertake in the land which you are about to enter to possess" (Deuteronomy 23:20).

Thus we *can* charge interest on loans to nonbelievers. That doesn't mean that we *have* to charge interest. God may well convict someone to extend a loan at no interest as a testimony and a door-opener to be able to share the message of Christ.

Lending vs. Giving

It should be clear by now that lending is not unbiblical—even lending at interest, under most circumstances. But there are conditions under which God would have us give rather than lend. That is particularly true where basic necessities are involved. However, the difficulty is deciding what constitutes a necessity. Is a house a necessity? What about a car or a college education?

Needs vary by the society in which we live. A car may be a need for me but an extravagant luxury for an African. We may believe we're suffering by the lack of a comfortable home, and someone in Lebanon feels blessed by finding a rundown apartment that still has electricity.

The principle of lending without any consideration for whether or not the money can be repaid is shown in Luke 6:34: "And if you lend to those from whom you expect to receive, what credit is that to you? Even sinners lend to sinners, in order to receive back the same amount."

The obvious meaning is to give to those who have needs and would logically never have the ability to repay or reciprocate.

Collecting

God's principles of lending and collecting do not require a Christian to sit passively by if someone refuses to pay what is due. However, neither does it allow us to use the devices of the world to collect. There are boundaries within which we are to operate that are much narrower than those of the world. It is certain that if a Christian is involved in lending to any extent, especially in business, he will be tested in the area of collecting. "Then summoning him, his lord said to him, 'You wicked slave, I forgave you all that debt because you entreated me. Should you not also have had mercy on your fellow slave, even as I had mercy on you?'" (Matthew 18:32-33).

Boundaries

Collecting from Christians. Christians are clearly admonished in Paul's letter to the Corinthians *never* to take another Christian before the secular court for *any* reason. That would certainly apply to the collection of debts. "Does any one of you, when he has a case against his neighbor, dare to go to law before the unrighteous, and not before the saints?" (1 Corinthians 6:1).

We are told that it is better to be defrauded than to lose our witness by suing one another (1 Corinthians 6:7). According to Matthew 18:15-17, we are to confront the sin publicly, even before the church if necessary. Recently, a ministry was formed to provide Christians with an organized method to settle disputes. The group is called The Christian Conciliation Service. Using objective, non-biased lay-volunteers, they will act as a Christian court to settle disputes between believers.

Collecting from non-Christians. Many Christians assume that since Paul said not to sue other Christians, then it must be OK to sue non-Christians to collect debts. Just because there is a direct reference not to sue a Christian, that does not mean we *should* sue non-Christians. There are no direct references to not suing your mother or father, either, but several other Scriptures would clearly indicate that we should not.

To understand the principle of suing non-Christians to collect personal debts, it is necessary to look at our broad purpose. Our purpose as Christians is to represent our Lord Jesus Christ. We are told in Romans 10:9 to "believe" in our hearts. That means to "live in accordance with." In other words, we are to let our lives demonstrate what our mouths say. In Luke 6:30–31 the Lord says, "Give to everyone who asks of you, and whoever takes away what is yours, do not demand it back. And just as you want people to treat you, treat them in the same way."

That does not absolutely state that a Christian should never sue to collect a debt. But it certainly does imply that God desires a much higher standard of behavior from believers than is expected of others. Everything we do must be measured against eternal values and not short-term profit or loss. "Giving no cause for offense in anything, in order that the ministry be not discredited" (2 Corinthians 6:3).

Business Loans

Perhaps one of the most difficult areas associated with lending is that of business loans. Usually, that is where credit is extended for services or products. Obviously, the lender has incurred some out-of-pocket expenses for time, utilities, and products, and when the loan is not repaid as agreed upon, an additional hardship is experienced. It is easy to understand that the lender, Christian or not, would feel resentful. Therefore, a special caution must be added here to not strike out in vengeance, but to deal in love with those who don't pay. There are several alternatives to suing or to using a collection agency.

Contact the individual directly. Many people who feel they can't pay a bill will avoid the creditor out of embarrassment. Many times a well worded letter or phone call stating your willingness to work out a reasonable repayment plan will help to restore the relationship. "A gentle answer turns away wrath, but a harsh word stirs up anger" (Proverbs 15:1).

Sometimes harsher means are necessary. I recall a Christian newspaper publisher who was having great difficulty collecting on accounts from Christians in his church. He had tried everything including a request to go before the church, but the pastor refused to let him do that. Finally, in frustration, he published a "special" church edition of his newspaper listing the names of the Christians who owed for previous advertising but would not pay. He pledged that the money would go to a missionary program to remove all hint of personal motives and distributed the papers within the church. His collection went up to almost 90 percent within a week. *Note:* Be sure you consult an attorney before attempting any similar action.

31
Collecting Debts

COLLECTING IS ACTUALLY the other side of borrowing, because for every borrower there must be a lender. In our generation, most Christians have been either a borrower or a lender or both. What are a Christian's alternatives in collecting loans he has made? Recently, a Christian asked me about God's principles of collecting debts and about lending money to others who ultimately will end up in debt. Should a Christian extend credit to another person, knowing the many admonitions in God's Word against excessive borrowing?

Extending Credits

There are virtually no Scripture references prohibiting the extension of credit; indeed, the burden of prudence is placed on the borrower, except in the case of interest. For the lender, the Scriptures describe the methods of collection and whether or not interest should be charged. "You may charge interest to a foreigner, but to your countryman you shall not charge interest, so that the Lord your God may bless you in all that you undertake in the land which you are about to enter to possess" (Deuteronomy 23:20). "When you make your neighbor a loan of any sort, you shall not enter his house to take his pledge" (Deuteronomy 24:10).

The implication throughout most of the Scripture dealing with lending is that a loan could be made to anyone, but interest could not be charged to brothers.

On closer scrutiny, I believe that admonition applies specifically to loans made for basic needs or personal income and not to investment-type loans.

Certainly, no one has to make investments, and loans made in this regard would not be to the widows, orphans, or needy described as needing assistance. However, just because a Christian is not prohibited from doing something does not necessarily mean that it is the best or could not be prohibited for an individual. Let me use myself as an example. Although lending is acceptable spiritually, I believe that God has directed me to give, not lend, to others. Accepting this as God's plan for my life would greatly influence any type of investments or businesses in which I might be involved. That is important for every believer to keep in mind. The principles are there for general direction, but they in no way detail God's unique plan for each of us.

Understanding the scriptural guidelines for debt collecting should certainly make a Christian more cautious about extending credit, specifically for a Christian engaged in supplying basic needs, such as housing, food, and medical or dental care. The charging of interest is prohibited, and under some circumstances collection would be prohibited as well. I have counseled many doctors, dentists, and attorneys not to extend credit to their patients. Individuals who can't save and pay very possibly won't pay later, either. It would be far better to know in advance that someone couldn't afford to pay and treat him as a ministry than to carry him as a delinquent account and cause unnecessary financial pressures in his family.

Those who cannot pay should be screened by a Christian financial counselor to assess their financial position and have the fees adjusted accordingly. Those who can pay should do so, or an exchange of some kind should be made. I know of a doctor who offers reduced-fee clients the opportunity to paint, clean, and repair in exchange for his services. Another has set up a child-care clinic as a ministry and asks non-fee clients to work as volunteers to help others who cannot afford proper child care. The guiding principle here is that free care should be the professional's option, not the patient's. And by allowing the needy to work rather than adding another debt to their load, he becomes a friend rather than an involuntary authority.

Collecting

Supposing a Christian is owed a legitimate debt, what are the limits on collection?

1. *Collecting from Christians.* One counselor told me that he classified anyone who didn't pay as non-Christian, thereby removing the restriction against lawsuits. Unfortunately, it's not that clear-cut. Many Christians, through ignorance or otherwise, find they have borrowed more than they can repay, just as non-Christians do. It would seem abundantly clear from Paul's exhortation in 1 Corinthians 6 that Christians aren't to sue each other in the world's courts, even at the risk of being wronged and defrauded (1 Corinthians 6:7). We are to demonstrate to the unsaved world that God's people love and honor each other regardless of the personal cost. God never promised that it would be simple or painless to be a follower. "More than that, I count all things to be loss in view of the surpassing value of knowing Christ Jesus my Lord, for whom I have suffered the loss of all things, and count them but rubbish in order that I may gain Christ" (Philippians 3:8).

If a Christian creditor has been wronged by a nonpaying brother who will not submit to a plan of authority as outlined in Matthew 18:15-17, the first step is not collection of the debt, but rather discipline in the faith to correct the sin. Failure to pay a debt or to go before a Christian review group is not a sin—it is the outside reflection of an inner problem with authority. Once a Christian has exhausted scriptural remedies, if the debt remains unpaid, it should be forgiven and forgotten. "But if you bite and devour one another, take care lest you be consumed by one another" (Galatians 5:15).

2. *Collecting from nonbelievers.* It would be simple to take the position that, since Paul limited his discussion on not suing to believers in 1 Corinthians 6, it must be all right to sue nonbelievers. Such an assumption would be too broad. Paul stated that suing a brother would bring shame to the Body, but he did not imply that suing nonbelievers would be acceptable. "Giving no cause for offense in anything, in order that the ministry be not discredited" (2 Corinthians 6:3).

3. *Using collection agencies.* Is the use of a collection agency the same as suing? Not necessarily. However, for a Christian, the collection service becomes an extension of his own witness. It is important to consider what kind of witness a typical collection agency presents. Since in the collection process a partnership is formed, it would seem clear that only other believers should be used to pursue an obligation owed to a Christian. The certainty is that whatever image the collection service presents will be reflected back to the creditor. Just selling the collection accounts does not relieve that obligation on the part of a Christian creditor. I believe clearly that a Christian must first determine the need of those in debt before resorting to any formal collection process. "But whoever has the world's goods, and beholds his brother in need and closes his heart against him, how does the love of God abide in him?" (1 John 3:17).

4. *Collecting from a corporation.* A corporation, whether an insurance company, supplier, or contractor, is an entity, as opposed to an individual. It is literally a legal entity existing only under the law. When formed, the individuals associated with a corporation purposely relinquish their rights to the public law. In fact, for many corporations, there is no recourse or communication to them except through the channels of the law. When an insurance company signs a contract to pay for damages incurred to their client, they clearly state that in the event of an impasse on damage claims, they will use the court as the arbitrator. As far as I can determine, the Scripture is silent on this particular issue, leaving the decision to go before the law or not to the individual. Each Christian must test his motives and be willing to abandon any action if God so directs. "Let your character be free from the love of money, being content with what you have; for He Himself has said, 'I will never desert you, nor will I ever forsake you'" (Hebrews 13:5).

Best Position

With the emphasis on "rights" in our country, it is common and accepted to force payment from anyone who owes, even if it requires the harassment of suing. A Christian must always keep in mind his primary purpose for being here: to lead others to the Lord. Continually God's Word stresses mercy and forgiveness in every aspect of our lives. Because of God's mercy to us, He forgave our debt. In the same manner, God requires us to forgive the debts of others, some of which will be financial. "And be kind to one another, tenderhearted, forgiving each other, just as God in Christ also has forgiven you" (Ephesians 4:32).

Since that is the position given in Scripture, it should be the norm for God's people. Once a Christian realizes that, he should plan to make the extension of credit uncommon rather than a common event.

Knowing that God may well call upon us to forgive a debt, particularly one of necessity, means that a lender should know the spiritual character of the borrower thoroughly. Then the burden for repayment is shifted to the borrower, and collection becomes a matter of a gentle reminder. What a witness it would be to the unsaved if collecting debts between Christians would be as simple as a handshake.

However, until more Christians adhere to the principles of repayment, it is up to the lender to be very prudent and not extend credit to those who cannot reasonably repay it. It would be far better to turn down someone who could not pay than to have to spread the costs of a bad debt over those who do pay. Let the choice be yours, not theirs. "A prudent man sees evil and hides himself, the naive proceed and pay the penalty" (Proverbs 27:12.) The burden of repayment clearly rests upon the borrower.

God may well bring someone who cannot or will not pay debts to you for help and counsel. If you operate on a cash-only basis, those people can be identified and dealt with as a ministry. Otherwise, they will be just one more bad debt. For a business that has bad accounts receivable, each debt must be evaluated on a cash-by-cash basis. The scriptural principle of collection must be considered before extending credit to any business or individual.

Part Five

BUSINESS

32
Bankruptcy—Is It Scriptural?

BANKRUPTCY IS A subject that is very personal to the several hundred thousand people who use it each year. About half of the personal bankruptcies are taken by young couples who have charged and borrowed far beyond their abilities to pay. They see bankruptcy as their only release from the financial bondage that threatens their marriages and sometimes their health.

In a recent counseling session, a couple revealed that they owed $6,000 in credit card bills, $11,000 for a previous consolidation loan, and $15,000 for a family loan to buy a home. "Obviously," the husband said, "another consolidation loan won't help. The only thing that will help us is a fresh start." A friend in their church had offered to lend them the money to file for bankruptcy. They came for counsel because of a wise pastor who knew that bankruptcy would be just another "quick fix." A review of their financial history convinced me, and them, that history would repeat itself if they didn't change their past habits.

It's amazing that the average family filing for bankruptcy only owes about $4,000. The problem is that it's usually composed of many small bills, and most of them are delinquent. They may have the capacity to pay their creditors, but that would require at least two years of financial sacrifice. We are a generation of "quick-fix" addicts, and the idea of absolutes has been taught for a long time, even inside Christianity.

Bankruptcy Is a Spiritual Indicator

God's Word teaches that the way we handle our money is the clearest reflection of our spiritual value system. Excessive debts, even bankruptcies, are not our problems—they are the external indicators of internal spiritual problems. Literally, they are a person's attitudes being reflected in actions. That is not to indict those who are in debt or who file for bankruptcy, but only to reflect what Christ said: "He who is faithful in a very little thing is faithful also in much; and he who is unrighteous in a very little thing is unrighteous also in much. If therefore you have not been faithful in the use of unrighteous mammon, who will entrust the true riches to you?" (Luke 16:10-11).

I recently received a call from a pastor who was considering filing for bankruptcy because of a very heavy debt burden. He was fearful of his creditors obtaining judgments or even garnishments against him. "It's not fair that they can attach my salary," he said. "I won't be able to feed my family." I asked if they had tricked him into borrowing their money. They had not. Then I asked him to put himself in the place of the lender. If that lender were in his congregation, would he respond to a salvation message delivered by a pastor who had bankrupted to avoid paying a debt? Second, I asked him to consider what Christ would do if He were in his position. After all, isn't that what we're instructed to do as Christ's followers? We are to do nothing that would be solely for our own benefit. "Do not merely look out for your own personal interest, but also for the interest of others" (Philippians 2:4). Also, we are to be imitators of Christ. "Therefore be imitators of God, as beloved children" (Ephesians 5:1).

This pastor stood up to his burden, asked for the forgiveness of his creditors, and cut up all of his credit cards. He confessed his error before his church and found several kindred spirits in the congregation. There was some wagging of tongues, to be sure, but in great part there was healing and understanding.

Repayment Is a Vow

I believe a principle that has been greatly overlooked in our generation is that of making a vow. A vow is literally a promise. When someone borrows money, he makes a promise to repay according to the agreed-upon conditions of the loan. Once an agreement is reached, repayment is not an option. It's an absolute as far as God is concerned. The rights all fall to the lender, and the borrower literally becomes the lender's servant. "The rich rules over the poor, and the borrower becomes the lender's slave" (Proverbs 22:7).

As representatives of Jesus Christ before the world, Christians are admonished to think ahead and consider the consequences of their actions. That's why Scripture teaches so many principles dealing with borrowing and lending, and especially the misuse of credit. But once a Christian borrows, he's made a *vow* to repay. "When you make a vow to God, do not be late in paying it, for He takes no delight in fools. Pay what you vow! It is better that you should not vow than that you should vow and not pay" (Ecclesiastes 5:4-5).

Is Bankruptcy Allowable?

A counselee once asked, "Would God direct someone to go bankrupt?" My answer was, "I don't see how, since that would refute His own Word." God's Word says a wicked man borrows but does not repay (Psalm 37:21). God desires that we be righteous, not wicked.

"But would God forgive me if I go bankrupt?" he asked. God says He will forgive *any* sin, past, present, and future, if we confess that it is wrong. Bankruptcy is a legal remedy, *not* a scriptural remedy. It's understandable that under the pressures of excessive debts a Christian would yield to a quick-fix, but it doesn't make bankruptcy any more scriptural.

The Year of Remission and/or Jubilee

One counselee told me that bankruptcy was a biblical principle based upon the year of remission discussed in Deuteronomy 15:1-2. According to God's Word, there was to be a release of debtors every seventh year. However, this was a direction between God's children and was always an option of the lender, not the borrower.

The year of Jubilee, as discussed in Leviticus 25:10, was literally the seventh year of remission. Again, the same principle was involved. It was the responsibility and option of the lender, not the borrower, to release debts.

What If You Have No Alternative?

I was working with a young couple who had accumulated nearly $40,000 in business debts before they closed their doors. They were being hounded by creditors on every side. They had sold their home, one car, and virtually every worldly asset to reduce the debt from about $60,000. They didn't want to go bankrupt and tried to negotiate any kind of repayment with their creditors but to no avail. Creditor after creditor filed judgments against them. The bottom line was that virtually every creditor told them to file bankruptcy and get it over with—all at one time. They told the husband they wouldn't work with them because he had no assets and that they would rather write off the debts through bankruptcy.

My counsel was that he was not responsible for what the creditors did or didn't do. He was responsible before God for his actions. I recommended that he respond literally according to Proverbs 6:2-3. He should humble himself before his creditors and ask them to work with him. They, unfortunately, refused and forced him into involuntary bankruptcy. Once they filed bankruptcy against him, he was legally, but not scripturally, released from the debts. He has diligently worked ever since to pay off the debts, one at a time, and will continue to do so with God's help.

What About Involuntary Bankruptcy?

An involuntary bankruptcy can be initiated by several creditors who wish to attach all available assets and force an individual or corporation to liquidate. A good biblical case can be made for the position that since the creditors initiated the action, they have settled any and all claims. But in our society, this action is often necessary to pre-empt a debtor from liquidating all assets and spending the money. For a Christian, the obligation to repay according to the original terms still exists. "Do not withhold good from those to whom it is due, when it is in your power to do it" (Proverbs 3:27).

Chapter 13 Bankruptcy

According to the federal bankruptcy code, an individual can elect to come under a court administrated repayment plan, commonly called a Chapter 13. The court determines how much of the indebtedness an individual can pay and then directs the creditors to operate within that plan. I can find no biblical reason prohibiting a Christian from using such remedy, provided that once the court-appointed percentage was repaid, the remaining portion was also repaid. That would also be true of a Chapter 11 reorganization for corporations.

The key element in any decision involving a legitimate loan made to a Christian by another person is that our actions honor the Lord. In a society that is obsessed by desires for quick riches and then quick outs to the havoc that they reap, God has no "easy-in, easy-out" principles. We serve a holy and righteous God who desires that all men come to the saving knowledge of Jesus Christ. If any willful action on our part impedes that process in the life of another, it displeases Him. Just try to share your faith with a creditor involved in a bankruptcy, and the true loss will be evident. "A good name is to be more desired than great riches, favor is better than silver and gold" (Proverbs 22:1).

33
What Is a Christian Business?

O BVIOUSLY, THERE IS no such thing as a "Christian business." A business is a legal entity, such as a corporation, partnership, or proprietorship and, as such, has no spirit or soul. It may, however, reflect the values of the principal owners or managers. It is the reflection of these values that determines whether or not a business is labeled Christian or non-Christian.

A business is a tool to be used by God in demonstrating the truth of the gospel. In James 1:22 we are told to be "doers" of the Word. A business is the perfect environment for doing Christ's truth.

Applying God's Rules

One of the best ways to determine whether a business is being used to serve God is to look at the policies governing the day-to-day actions. If a Christian is truly committed to Jesus Christ and to serving His purposes, then the business will be run according to His principles and precepts. Obviously, that means that a Christian must first understand God's rules. Anyone attempting to follow God's plan for business will discover a startling difference between what the world says is normal and what God says is normal. Therefore, the committed Christian must accept that he is merely a manager of God's business. If God's Word says to do something a particular way, the committed Christian *will* do it. If the Word says not to do something, then he *will not* do it. Without a doubt, such decisions can potentially cost something economically. But the right decisions will also yield something even greater—God's wisdom and peace.

An additional reward that God promises those who follow Him is prosperity. After all, what kind of witness would we be if we failed every time we followed God's rules? Indeed, the opposite is true. God wrote the rules of business economics, and through the ages, those who followed God's path have prospered while bringing countless lost souls into God's eternal family. "For its profit is better than the profit of silver, and its gain than fine gold. She is more precious then jewels; and nothing you desire compares with her" (Proverbs 3:14-15).

What Is the Purpose of Business?

If a Christian business is to be used to serve God, it has but one overriding purpose—to glorify Him. Acknowledging that will make decisions much simpler. Each decision, hiring, firing, paying, promoting, and so on, must be made in harmony with God's written Word. Obviously, God's Spirit leads us day-by-day, but always within the boundaries of what He has chosen to commit to the written Word.

Balance in Business

The purpose of a Christian's business is to glorify God. The day-by-day functions are the things we do to accomplish that purpose. No one function is more or less important, and each must be done with excellence. For instance, if the business aspects are neglected for the sake of evangelism, quite often the business will fail. If the ministry functions are neglected to generate profits, the business loses its witness in the world.

That can certainly be observed in our society today. Often the term "Christian" in conjunction with a business brings to mind an image of a Bible-toting evangelist who doesn't pay his bills and tells the creditors he's just "trusting the Lord" for their money. On the other hand, there are many Christian-run businesses that are extremely profitable and are operated honestly and ethically, but few people even know the owner is a Christian. In his business life, he's a secret service Christian. Obviously, these extremes do not constitute every Christian-run business but too few present a balanced image of good business based on biblical principles.

The Functions of a Business

There are five basic business functions that together constitute the activities of a Christian *business.*

Function 1: Evangelism. There is no tool more effective for evangelism than a business dedicated to the Lord. Not only can employees be won by a dedicated owner or manager, but, similarly, so can suppliers, creditors, and customers. The key here is the *walk,* not the talk.

Function 2: Discipleship. Evangelism is sharing Christ's message of salvation with the lost. Discipleship is training Christians to grow stronger in their faith. In a business, that effort should be directed by the owner or manager to those immediately under his authority. It is they who will then be able to disciple the others under their authority. "And the things which you have heard from me in the presence of many witnesses, these entrust to faithful men, who will be able to teach others also" (2 Timothy 2:2).

"That's well and good," you say, "but what if my managers aren't saved?" If they aren't saved, then you simply back up to function 1. An excellent program for evangelism is the Christian Businessmen's Committee (CBMC) lifestyle evangelism. It is ideally suited for developing a witness with managers.

Function 3: To fund God's work. A business is the best tool for funding God's work ever created. A properly run business can generate excess capital to meet needs, share the gospel, and still continue its operations day-by-day. There are many creative ways to use such funds to further God's work. Obviously, giving to your church and to ministries is good and necessary to do God's work, but there are many ministries available within the business itself. For instance, several Christian businessmen have hired fulltime counselors who work with employees who have personal problems. Often, when one business is too small to afford a counselor, several businesses have combined to use a common counselor. Also, many businessmen have funds available for needy employees. Others provide cassette tape lending libraries and books as internal ministries to employees.

Function 4: Provide for needs. A business must provide for the needs of the employees, creditors, customers, and owners. That is done by paying salaries, paying for supplies and equipment in a timely fashion, and providing a quality product at a fair price. In our modern business environment, the principle seems to be to meet the owner's needs, wants, and desires first, then pay the employees what is necessary to keep them off his back. Many creditors are paid late, or not at all, and the customers are viewed as a necessary evil.

If a Christian business owner accepts meeting needs as a normal part of God's plan, his business will play an effective role in evangelism and discipleship. When employees know that those in authority put the needs of others ahead of their own, they will respond.

Function 5: To generate profits. Any business must be able to make a profit if it is to continue operations. Sometimes Christians seem to believe that God will bless them supernaturally, while they ignore every pretense of good management. If you believe that, you haven't studied God's Word very thoroughly. God's Word directs us to think and plan. "The mind of man plans his way, but the Lord directs his steps" (Proverbs 16:9).

I have counseled enough Christians in business to know that many claim to operate by faith, when, instead, they are being slothful. God's Word does not teach us to sit on our hands, waiting for Him to reveal His perfect will. We are to be active. In other words, we are not to be observers of God's plan, but participants in it. "The soul of the sluggard craves and gets nothing, but the soul of the diligent is made fat" (Proverbs 13:4).

Keys to Generate a Profit

The keys to generating a profit according to the principles in God's Word are not complicated. Many businessmen have followed them during their lifetimes and have been leaders in their industry. Some, like J. C. Penney, R. G. LeTourneau, Stanley Tamm, and Walt Meloon, became known, not only for their astute business acumen, but also for their Christian witness.

Acknowledge and obey God's eternal wisdom in operating your business. In other words, seek God's counsel first. "Trust in the Lord with all your heart, and do not lean on your own understanding. In all your ways acknowledge Him, and He will make your paths straight" (Proverbs 3:5-6) .

Too often, we seek God's wisdom but then violate the most basic principles taught in His Word. Remember what Christ taught in Matthew 21:31. Those who do what their Father says will inherit the kingdom of God.

Seek godly counsel in major decisions. Psalm 1:1 tells us, "How blessed is the man who does not walk in the counsel of the wicked," and Proverbs 15:22 says, "Without consultation, plans are frustrated, but with many counselors they succeed." Outside of God, a man's primary counselor is his wife. Proverbs 31:11 says, "The heart of her husband trusts in her, and he will have no lack of gain." That is a resource that few men utilize.

Often, drifting is the result of a lack of accountability. Too many Christian business owners are not really accountable to anyone. An accountability group of three or more godly men who know God's Word will provide the counsel God directs us to seek.

34
The Purpose of a Business

IT IS ENLIGHTENING to reflect on what the Bible has to say about business. Many Christians say they have a Christian business, but what does that mean?

Obviously, the actual business entity is neither Christian nor non-Christian. A Christian business, therefore, is one that is controlled by a Christian. The more control this Christian has, the more the business can reflect his or her spiritual values.

It is interesting to see how many Christians would like for God to make them a success so that they can be a witness for the Lord and how few really are witnesses once God does. Clearly, a Christian in business can be used by the Lord, but only if the correct priorities have been pre-established. One key to being useful to the Lord is making decisions on the basis of God's Word and not on circumstances, feelings, or what is acceptable to society.

The Purpose of a Christian's Business

The purpose of any Christian, in business or otherwise, is to glorify God, not just to make a profit. "Whatever you do, do your work heartily, as for the Lord rather than for men" (Colossians 3:23).

As in any other area of service, it is important to establish a priority system. We can quickly become so involved with the urgent things of this world that we neglect the important things. Early in a business career, the urgent thing is to make payroll. Later it becomes urgent to make a greater profit or build a bigger company.

Therefore, it is important always to strive for balance in business. That is true in a spiritual sense just as in a material sense. For example, sales are important to any business, but if a manufacturing company applies 100 percent of its labor force to sales, the imbalance will be readily apparent. One of the priorities of a business should be to lead others to the Lord. But if all other functions are ignored in pursuit of evangelism, the work will be short lived.

Therefore, the priorities really mean "What are my goals, and can my goals be balanced to achieve the overall objective of serving God while meeting material needs?"

Goal 1: Salvation. Compared to eternity, the profile of a business is rather trivial and a lifetime of work rather insignificant. If used wisely, though, a business can change the lives of countless lost people. When the primary thrust of a businessman's outreach is to insure that others within his sphere of influence hear the promises of Jesus Christ, a whole new perspective takes place. There is an old cliché that seems applicable here: "If it doesn't work in your life, don't export it." Nothing speaks louder than a phony, and nothing will turn others off more than a businessman who lives carnally and talks spiritually. However, if we wait until we're perfect, we'll never share Christ's claims. God expects application, not perfection.

There is no group more accessible to a businessman than his employees. It never ceases to amaze me that a businessman will spend thousands of dollars to travel around the world to speak to lost people about Christ, when there are many unsaved in his own business who have never heard the truth clearly from him. Often it is the fear of rejection that makes us first seek out those we don't know.

Once the message has been taken to the employees in an inoffensive manner, then it should be presented to others, such as suppliers, peers, and customers. Sharing Christ with others through the business environment should not be done under compulsion, nor should witnessing be used as a club. God prepares the hearts of men through the Holy Spirit and then provides the opportunity to share in a meaningful way.

A forced sharing is what we do for God; fruitful sharing is what God does through us. It is important to keep in mind that in the daily routine of operating a business "as unto the Lord," God will provide these opportunities to share. It is not necessary to sacrifice good business practices, and consequently the business, in order to serve the Lord. Satan would have us believe that serving the Lord requires abandoning good common sense. Indeed, serving the Lord provides good common sense. "Then you will discern the fear of the Lord, and discover the knowledge of God. For the Lord gives wisdom; from His mouth come knowledge and understanding" (Proverbs 2:5–6).

Goal 2: Use of funds. The first use of funds is to honor the Lord. Proverbs 3:9 says, "Honor the Lord from your wealth, and from the first of all your produce."

We can look at the Scriptures on sharing from any perspective, and they still say the same thing: God wants the first part of our increase. That is not a requirement; it is a promise. It is God's promise that by our honoring Him materially before the world, He will in turn honor us. Literally, we acknowledge His lordship. If Christ is Lord, then He is owner as well; our money is His to preserve or disburse as He sees fit. We only manage it for Him until He returns. Therefore, the firstfruits from any business should be surrendered in the name of the Lord. Where, how, and how much? That is a subject for a later principle.

The second use of funds from a business is to meet the needs of its employees.

In Deuteronomy 17:15-20 God establishes the standards for his leaders. One is to live moderately. Those who do not observe this simple rule often lose sensitivity for others who have less, and many become callous and corrupt. Any Christian businessman intent on serving the Lord must keep in mind Christ's example to this world. "But Jesus called them to Himself, and said, 'You know that the rulers of the Gentiles lord it over them, and their great men exercise authority over them. It is not so among you, but whoever wishes to become great among you shall be your servant, and whoever wishes to be first among you shall be your slave'" (Matthew 20:25-27).

To men, authority and position mean power and wealth. To God, they mean responsibility. A Christian businessman who seeks to serve the Lord will also belong to those faithful employees who helped to build the business.

The third use of funds is to pay suppliers and creditors on time. There is no poorer witness than a businessman who is consistently delinquent on accounts. It is the responsibility of every Christian businessman to budget wisely and live on surplus funds, not accounts payable. Many businesses operate on the principle of "I'll pay when and if it's convenient." They ride their creditors to the limit, believing that it is easier to owe someone else than to cut back during tough times. "Do not withhold good from those to whom it is due, when it is in your power to do it. Do not say to your neighbor, 'Go, and come back, and tomorrow I will give it,' when you have it with you" (Proverbs 3:27-28).

Goal 3: Discipleship. Once the goals for witnessing and the use of money have been determined, the next goal is to disciple those who have been won to the Lord. Obviously, for spiritual growth new Christians must be directed into a sound, Bible teaching church. But to help them become witnesses in the business environment requires some specialized training. The same principles that have become a part of your life should be ingrained within them. "And the things which you have heard from me in the presence of many witnesses, these entrust to faithful men, who will be able to teach others also" (2 Timothy 2:2).

It is difficult to share Christ in a meaningful way in any relationship. That difficulty is amplified even more for the salesman in someone else's office. That does not mean we should abandon witnessing, only that our sensitivity to the leading of the Holy Spirit is vital. Many times young, exuberant, and ill-trained Christians leave a trail of disaster behind them. Instead of picking the ripe fruit they mow down everything in their path. Obviously, the other danger is that a new believer will be timid to the point of becoming a "secret service" Christian.

A sound discipleship program is a good beginning. The teaching can be accomplished through written materials, audio, or video, but an essential element to the program's success will be the extent of personal follow-up and accountability. Every new disciple should ideally spend several months in a study plan where he meets regularly with one other person to discuss victories and defeats.

Does all of this sound difficult and time consuming? No doubt about it; God's way does not equate success with large numbers. The first step is to start with one or two who are truly seeking God's best. Once they are trained, they can help train others. In our society of instant potatoes and Minute Rice, God still prepares Christians the old-fashioned way—over time.

The Principle of Success

I would trust that by this point your image of a successful Christian businessman, owner or otherwise, has changed somewhat. While it's true that one essential element of a Christian business is a profit, it is not the most important element. There are many unsaved and uncaring men and women who have developed profitable businesses without the slightest regard for God. No, to qualify for God's round table requires much higher standards than just net profits. Consider these questions:

1. When people think of you, do they focus on your business success first or your visible image as a disciple for Jesus Christ?
2. Do your employees and close business contacts know and respect your unwavering stand for the Lord and His principles?
3. Does your family receive a fair share of your time and view the business as a ministry as well?
4. Are the bills paid on time and debts kept within the ability of your business to pay?
5. Does the Lord's work receive the best (firstfruits) from the business?
6. Does the business produce a good product or service at a fair price from the customer's perspective?
7. Does the business generate a reasonable profit to continue operating?

"For to a person who is good in His sight He has given wisdom and knowledge and joy, while to the sinner He has given the task of gathering and collecting so that He may give to one who is good in God's sight. This too is vanity and striving after wind" (Ecclesiastes 2:26).

35

Unequally Yoked

A S ALWAYS, A study of a particular principle from God's Word must begin with two pertinent questions: What does God's Word say about the subject and why?

In 2 Corinthians 6:14 Paul writes, "Do not be bound together with unbelievers; for what partnership have righteousness and lawlessness, or what fellowship has light with darkness?" Clearly, the "what" is specific in that believers are admonished not to be yoked to nonbelievers. But then other questions arise. What is a yoke, and how far does the principle extend? Does it cover only marriages or extend also to business relationships?

These questions can only be answered by knowing the answer to our second primary question: Why? I trust that you will discover, as I did, that the reason such an instruction is given to Christians is clear. We are to operate with a value system so different from the non-believing world that on a day-by-day basis we will be in conflict with the norm. Our purpose in life is to glorify God in every decision and every action. A non-Christian could not and would not accept decisions made from that perspective. However, before I get ahead of myself and discuss the "why," let's look at the "what" from God's Word.

What Is a Yoke?

Two distinct types of yokes are presented in the Scriptures. One is a collar used on slaves to show their total subjugation. The second, which is of concern here, is a harness used to link two working animals together. In 2 Corinthians 6:14, when Paul says, "Do not be yoked together with unbelievers" (NIV*), the yoke referred to is a farm implement.

The yoke was a common everyday device used to couple oxen together for plowing or hauling. The oxen were matched as closely as possible so the burden would be distributed equally. The two animals had to be trained to

New International Version.

work together, even walking stride for stride so that the heavy wooden bar would not rub the skin off of their backs as they worked.

Once connected by the yoke, the oxen were no longer two who could choose to go their own way; rather, they became one working unit. It was extremely critical that the yoked animals be closely matched in size, strength, and temperament. If one animal was larger, the weight of the yoke rested upon the smaller and fatigued it rapidly. If one was much stronger, he pulled the bulk of the attached load and would also fatigue more quickly. And even with two physically matched animals, if one would not yield to the task (and kicked against the traces), then the obedient animal suffered some whiplashes as the owner disciplined the wayward one. The yoke bound them together for the purpose of accomplishing a task, and without mutual compromise it could not be done.

Hence, the analogy of a yoke to a marriage is an accurate one. A marriage should be two people pulling in common bond toward compatible goals and sharing the load equally.

Why Avoid a Yoke?

People with opposite goals and values will not be compatible. When they are linked together either in marriage or business, their differing values will ultimately create conflicts. Christians are admonished not to be yoked together with unbelievers because the very purpose of our lives will be sidetracked.

When decisions must be made that involve spiritual principles, the unbeliever cannot be expected to be motivated by God's Spirit. Even elementary decisions, such as giving to the Lord, become sources of friction in an unequally yoked relationship.

A Financial Yoke

It is necessary to take the broad principle of a yoke and narrow down its applicability to the area of finances. But first we must look at what does not constitute a yoked relationship.

Employee/employer. When two or more people are related in a work situation by employee-employer agreement, they are not yoked. There is an authority relationship, but they are not bound together by either verbal or written agreement (Titus 3:1; Ephesians 6:5; Colossians 3:22; etc.). They are not expected to carry the same load, and either party is free to terminate the relationship according to the predetermined agreement.

Stock ownership. Normally, stock ownership would not create a yoke. The stockholder is not bound to the company, except to the limit of his financial risk. Actually, there is an authority relationship, but the authority rests in the hands of the stockholder. There is no attempt to create a binding, equal relationship.

However, each relationship must be reviewed individually. If the intent is to create an equal, binding relationship between two or more people, then a yoke exists.

Other than a marriage, there is no better defined yoke between two or more people than a partnership. The intent of a partnership is to create a binding business relationship where all parties are equal in responsibility, authority, and liability. Indeed, the law deals with partnerships in this manner. If one partner commits to a business decision, all partners are bound by it.

All of the partners' assets, both business and personal, are jointly and individually pledged. Partnerships are difficult under the best of circumstances but can become completely untenable if all the partners do not have compatible financial and spiritual goals. Indeed, a Christian may find himself in a situation where God chooses to discipline one partner through finances, and thus all other partners are equally affected.

It is not necessary to attempt to define every type of contractual relationship dealing with business. The intent is the important determination. If the intent is to create an equal and binding relationship, then a yoke is created.

Intent

There is no absolute method of predetermining what creates a yoke and what does not. Marriages and partnerships fit the description of yokes nearly perfectly, so in those cases we are admonished not to be bound to unbelievers.

The admonition for Christians not to be yoked to unbelievers should not imply that nonbelievers are less honest people. The principle is given because the believer and nonbeliever are not working toward the same ultimate goals. Literally, the believer must be willing to pay any price to serve God, while the unbeliever will not be willing to do so. Thus, their attitudes are incompatible, and ultimately, they will clash. "And whatever you do in word or deed, do all in the name of the Lord Jesus, giving thanks through Him to God the Father" (Colossians 3:17).

When a believer and a nonbeliever can maintain a partnership without conflict over the spiritual goals of the company, it is normally because the believer has compromised God's principles (Romans 12:2).

Not All Things Are Profitable

Just because we can have partnerships with other believers does not mean that we should. Paul said, "All things are lawful for me, but not all thing are profitable" (2 Corinthians 6:12*a*). Stretching that principle a little, we can say, "Any two Christians can be partners, but not all should be."

There are different levels of maturity, commitment, and human compatibility. Choosing a business partner should be done with the same caution with which you would choose a spouse.

Existing Partnerships

If you are already in an unequally yoked business situation, observe the principles taught by Paul in 1 Corinthians 7. If you have the opportunity to be released from the partnership, you should arrange to be. But if you don't have the opportunity, make your partner's salvation your number-one item of prayer. A general observation I would add is that through the consistently godly life-style of a Christian partner, an unsaved partner will often decide either to join God's family or to sever the partnership.

36
Keeping a Vow

WHILE I WAS teaching at a conference for professional athletes, an interesting question was asked about a pending players' walkout in the National Football League. The question was, "As Christians, what should our response be toward the strike?"

In order to get the problem in perspective, it is necessary to understand a little background information. Each player signs a contract with an NFL team for his services. Once drafted by a team, he has no option to negotiate with another team—he is stuck with either striking an agreement with the team that drafts him or sitting out a year if they won't trade him. Once signed with a team, he must play for them. The team, however, can drop him at any time up to the regular season with little or no compensation. Basically, he is bound to the team, but the team is not bound to him. Salaries are negotiated individually, and older, higher-paid athletes are often replaced by younger, lower-paid athletes.

That particular year, the players' association (an involuntary association set up to negotiate with the team owners on general compensation items, such as retirement benefits and uniform salaries) had asked for a percentage of total profits to be shared with players. To support that demand they had asked the players to participate in a walkout if necessary. Thus, the question was asked: "What do we, as Christians, do?"

Making a Vow

It is clear in God's Word that a vow of any kind is not to be taken lightly. Once someone has given his word, it becomes a binding contract to be fulfilled. Thus, before agreeing to any terms, it is assumed that an individual has carefully considered the consequences.

For the current generation, that concept is rarely taught and seldom applied. A vow is deemed something made under one set of circumstances that may be broken under another. Thus, a vow to pay a creditor is ignored when the usefulness of the product wears out. Indeed, all creditors can be avoided by a perfectly legal arrangement called bankruptcy, if necessary. When a couple gets married, they exchange vows or promises to each other. They promise to love each other and forsake all others no matter what. That will hold true, even if the other partner becomes a drunk, a thief, disabled, ugly, or old. Today, though, the common attitude is, "If it doesn't work out, I can always get out," and usually that's what happens. The original conditions that made the promises seem legitimate change, and one partner begins to think he got a bum deal. Usually it happens because, being older and wiser, he believes he could have negotiated a better "deal."

Legal Loopholes

The more prevalent this attitude becomes, the trickier the contracts or vows become. Everyone tries to leave loopholes so that if he changes his mind, he can always get out. Then the vows become clouded with attorneys and legal jargon, and a simple contract becomes the meeting ground for adversaries.

God's Promises

The reason most Christians are not able to claim God's promises is because they are not willing to meet His prerequisites. First John 3:21-22 explains that God will answer our prayers when we do the things that are pleasing in His sight and keep His commandments. Few scriptural principles are clearer than that of keeping our vows—literally keeping our word both to God and to others. "It is better that you should not vow than that you should vow and not pay" (Ecclesiastes 5:5).

A Survey of Vows

First, it's important to note that God never promised us fairness in this life. Many times we will be bound to a higher standard than those with whom we deal. Quite often as a result, we will come out second best in a two-man contest. In Psalm 73, Asaph confessed that he envied the arrogant until, as noted in verses 17-18, he "came into the sanctuary of God; then I perceived their end. Surely Thou dost set them in slippery places; Thou dost cast them down to destruction."

A promise that should govern our daily lives is found in Psalm 101:7. "He who practices deceit shall not dwell within my house; he who speaks falsehood shall not maintain his position before me."

Honesty

A Christian's usefulness to God is directly proportional to his honesty. When we give our word and then go back on it, we have made our "yes" "no" and our "no" "yes." "He who walks in his uprightness fears the Lord, but he who is crooked in his ways despises Him" (Proverbs 14:2).

Honesty goes beyond not telling an outright lie; it must include being reliable to fulfill promises made. God's Word calls that "loyalty." Loyalty on a Christian's part is not ultimately to another person. Indeed, few people are really deserving of our uncompromising loyalty. Our loyalty is to God and His Word. In being loyal, we become instruments for God to show others His loyalty. It would really be a tough life for us if God changed His mind whenever the "deal" wasn't right. Our only hope rests in the fact that God is loyal to His promises, regardless of how bad His end of the deal is. "Many a man proclaims his own loyalty, but who can find a trustworthy man? A righteous man who walks in his integrity—How blessed are his sons after him" (Proverbs 20:6-7).

Pride

The opposite of humility is pride. Pride is perhaps the major sin in Christendom today. Pride—the desire to be first—leads to greed—a craving for more. When someone backs down on a vow that has been made in good faith, it is usually either because of pride or because of greed. The real problem lies in the fact that when someone dishonors an agreement just to gain a little better deal, he is the real loser, because more money won't help replace what's been lost: integrity. "Everyone who is proud in heart is an abomination to the Lord; assuredly, he will not be unpunished" (Proverbs 16:5).

Trust

Many times Christians read through the Bible without grasping the fact that the truths presented are life's handbook. God's Word says that everyone will be accountable for his words and actions on the Day of Judgment. Jesus Christ said that our real motives are shown by our decisions about money. Many compromising Christians are going to be saddened to learn that their treasures were just wood, hay, and stubble. When it really counted, they couldn't be trusted in a small thing, so God never used them in larger things. "No one can serve two masters; for either he will hate the one and love the other, or he will hold to one and despise the other. You cannot serve God and mammon" (Matthew 6:24).

Rights/Responsibilities

We are so conscious of our rights today that I believe our rights will ultimately cost us our freedom. In the area of contracts, many people believe it's their right to strike a better deal later if the circumstances change. What about our responsibilities? The word means to be accountable for our actions. Christ said His followers must be willing to surrender their rights and become His stand-ins. It is inconceivable to think that our Lord would have made an agreement with someone and then change His mind and try to negotiate a better deal. As a carpenter, I rather imagine Jesus delivered His products at the agreed-upon price, regardless of what His costs were or what the market was doing.

In Matthew 20, Jesus gives us just such an example of being satisfied with a bargain once struck. Various workers were hired during the day at an agreed-upon sum, which happened to be exactly the same amount. At the end of the day, those who had worked all day for the same wages as those who had worked only one hour were grumbling at the landowner because they felt they had been cheated. The landowner's response was, "Friend, I am doing you no wrong; did you not agree with me for a denarius?" (v. 13).

The issue wasn't whether or not the wage was sufficient—it was just that someone else got a better deal, and that wasn't "right."

What We Deserve

The one certain rule of contract law is that once a contract is made, one party can't arbitrarily decide to modify or cancel it. As Christians, we can be truly thankful that God's contract with us is binding and firm. Otherwise, He might give us what we deserve. However, God says that if we wish to be forgiven, we must forgive others. If we wish to exercise God's promise to call upon Him in our day of trial, we must pay our vows. "Offer to God a sacrifice of thanksgiving, and pay your vows to the Most High; and call upon Me in the day of trouble; I shall rescue you, and you will honor Me" (Psalm 50:14-15).

Authority

Once a Christian has agreed to submit to an authority as in the case of a professional athlete by contract, he is admonished to give honor to that authority, even if the authority doesn't deserve it. Clearly, the apostle Paul did not condone or approve of slavery, but in Ephesians 6:5, he admonishes Christian slaves to be obedient to their masters, and not to give eyeservice, but to do their work sincerely, as unto Christ. When a Christian honors his authority, God promises his rewards will come from the Lord. "Knowing that whatever good thing each one does, this he will receive back from the Lord, whether slave or free" (Ephesians 6:8).

In conclusion, James puts it into proper perspective: "But prove your-selves doers of the word, and not merely hearers who delude themselves" (James 1:22) and, "Therefore, to one who knows the right thing to do, and does not do it, to him it is sin" (James 4:17).

Each believer will have to decide before the Lord what vows he has made and in each case be willing to fulfill them—regardless!

37
Financial Honesty

RECENTLY A BUSINESSMAN asked me, "Do you think it's possible to be totally honest in our business society?" Since that particular individual was a very committed Christian, I had no doubt that his question was an honest one.

He went on to explain that he didn't purposely cheat anyone, but even when negotiating a sale, the common practice was for the seller to begin at a price higher than desired, knowing that the buyer always started with a price lower than he knew was acceptable. As I considered his question, I realized what he had asked must be a conscious thought on the heart of many sincere Christians: "Can you truly be honest and, if so, at what cost?"

Money Is an Indicator

The Lord says in Luke 10:10*a*, "He who is faithful in a very little thing is faithful also in much." The small thing to which the Lord is referring is money. Naturally, this also includes the pursuit of money.

God has placed us in a physical world and expects us to live in it. Why is that? God could miraculously provide for us on a day-by-day basis if He chose to do so. Why then has He determined to leave us in a materialistic society, subject to the same problems and temptations as those who totally reject His ways? After all, the one who truly seeks to follow God's will will surely suffer at the hands of those who live only to please themselves.

The answer becomes clear in the light of God's Word. In Philippians 2:15, Paul tells us to hold ourselves above this wicked generation so that we can prove ourselves blameless. Thus we become "lights" in a world of darkness. We are placed in this society by God so that He can reveal Himself through us. For this to happen, we must avoid the devices of the accuser and hold to standards of the Lord.

Satan works through guile and selfishness and labels them "shrewdness" and "ingenuity." God calls guile "deceit" and selfishness "greed." "He who winks his eyes does so to devise perverse things" (Proverbs 16:30*a*). "For where jealousy and selfish ambition exist, there is disorder and every evil thing" (James 3:16).

Why the Dishonest Prosper

There is little doubt that in the short run a deceitful person will seem to prosper. But it doesn't take long for others to recognize his dishonesty, so he must continually seek out new prospects. Sometimes the deceitful person may gain materially as a result of his craftiness. We must remember that Satan does have limited authority over this earth and can indeed provide riches. The problem with his supply is that it is always accompanied by fear, anxiety, anger, greed, and resentment.

Every Christian must accept God's Word as the standard for doing business. Only the Lord's provision brings with it peace and contentment (Proverbs 10:22; Proverbs 3:4-6). It is also within God's power to grant material blessings to those who truly follow His directions. "Riches and honor are with me, enduring wealth and righteousness" (Proverbs 8:18). But many times God elects to store those riches for distribution in eternity, in which case the rewards are multiplied a thousandfold (Matthew 6:20).

The biggest loss associated with following the worldly path is the loss of God's full blessings. Many Christians fail to experience God's blessing because they conform to the image of the world (Romans 12:2). God declares that if we do not respond correctly in such a trivial thing as money, we will not be entrusted with any greater possessions. "If therefore you have not been faithful in the use of unrighteous mammon, who will entrust the true riches to you?" (Luke 16:11).

Material Witness

It becomes clear that God has placed us in this materialistic world not only to witness to the unsaved, but also for the purpose of examining our relationship to Him. There can be no clearer reflection of the true value system of a Christian than the way he handles his money and the way others are treated where a profit or loss is concerned.

Can a Christian be honest in our society? He *must* be to experience the fullness of God's power and love. There will be times when it will seem that others take advantage of that honesty. The Lord knew that would happen. "If anyone wishes to come after Me, let him deny himself, and take up his cross daily, and follow Me" (Luke 9:23). There is often a price to be paid for following in the path of Christ, but there is also a great reward as a result of doing so.

The Lord told us that a house built upon sand would fall when the storms come, while one built upon the rock would survive. We are in the midst of a materialistic storm today, and every Christian must decide whether to build upon the solid rock of God's Word or the shifting sands of society. The decision to do business by the world's normal standards—guile and deception—is a decision to deny Christ. "No servant can serve two masters; for either he will hate the one, and love the other, or else he will hold to one, and despise the other. You cannot serve God and mammon" (Luke 16:13).

Obedience to God

The principle passed down to us throughout the Scripture is: we don't serve God because of what He can do for us; we serve Him because He is God. Job understood this principle when he told his friends, "Though He slay me, I will hope in him" (Job 13:15).

Nebuchadnezzar, about to cast Shadrach, Meshach, and Abednego into the furnace because they did not worship the idol he chose, mocked God by saying, "What god is there who can deliver you out of my hands?"

They responded, "If it be so, our God whom we serve is able to deliver us from the furnace of blazing fire; and He will deliver us out of your hand, O king. But even if He does not, let it be known to you, O king, that we are not going to serve your gods or worship the golden image that you have set up" (Daniel 3:15b, 17-18).

Each Christian must come to the position where God's approval is more important than the world's riches. Then, and only then, will the full measure of God's peace and power be experienced. "But prove yourselves doers of the word, and not merely hearers who delude themselves" (James 1:22).

38
Retirement—Is It Scriptural?

THE FLOW OF our modern society has changed the way we live. One of the most far-reaching changes is our attitude about retirement. Retirement, to most, means that period of time in our latter years when we can stop work and start enjoying life.

Future Attitudes

We like the idea of retirement. After all, we worked hard to get where we are, and we "deserve" to enjoy it. Unfortunately, though many are geared to look forward to retirement, most do not have the means to do so. Therefore, at ages sixty-five to seventy, they are forced to retire and become wards of the state. We see them on the rolls of welfare and Social Security. They require the help of their own children, who are unable or unwilling to help because they are strapped financially by indulgent life-styles.

Benefits of Retirement

Obviously, not all retirement is wrong any more than all borrowing is wrong. It is a matter of degree. The problem is that we seem to do everything to excess today. In some professions, such as athletics, age is a critical factor, and retirement is inevitable. In other professions everyday stress eventually burns a person out. But there are other instances in which retirement is encouraged to attract workers, such as in government-related jobs. Retirement provides at least some benefits to society: (1) it makes room for younger, more aggressive people to be able to progress; (2) the shift to a lesser income at retirement necessitates a moderate life-style. Those who don't moderate their life-styles end up back at work; and (3) the goal of retirement creates savings that can be used to help build and create jobs for others.

Liabilities of Retirement

The biggest liability associated with retirement today is the mass notion that everyone should be made to retire. The truth is that the majority of those over sixty-five cannot afford to retire, and we cannot afford for them to retire. But since the idea of retirement has been sold to Americans over the last forty years, we now accept it as normal. It is not normal, either biblically or historically. There are some who can retire and a few who should retire, but most people (particularly Christians) should not consider traditional retirement.

Retirement for Christians should mean freeing time to devote to serving others more fully without the necessity of getting paid for it. If Christian retirees have this motivation in mind while locking forward to "retirement," then the Lord really will find us doing His work when He returns.

A second liability is the diversion of funds needed for God's work into retirement plans. Many of those funds will never be used because they far exceed the reasonable amount the retiree will need. Others won't be used because they will be lost or dissipated by inflation long before retirement. The only funds that should ever be allocated for retirement are those left after giving what God has directed and meeting family needs.

Biblical Guidelines

Since the Bible is our guide for day-by-day living, it is always necessary to verify what we're doing against that guide. Retirement, as we know it, is found only in one place in God's Word. Numbers 8:25 refers to the retirement of the Levites from the tent of meeting. The Levites were directed not to own land or accumulate riches but to receive their living from the tithes and offerings of God's people. As a reward for their service and obedience, they were retired at age fifty.

Other than that single event the people were not directed to retire. That does not mean they could not retire, but that it was not normal. The normal system of retirement that we see throughout God's Word is a sabbatical. The first sabbatical given was a day of rest each week called the Sabbath. Additionally, the Jew was required to let his land lie idle every seventh year.

Wouldn't it be great to take retirement through sabbaticals? That would mean we would work six years and take the seventh off. That year could be utilized for continued education, missions work, new technology training, or simply to enjoy our families while we are still young. "Six years you shall sow your field, and six years you shall prune your vineyard and gather in its crop, but during the seventh year the land shall have a sabbath rest, a sabbath to the Lord; you shall not sow your field nor prune your vineyard" (Leviticus 25:3-4).

Balance Between Too Little and Too Much

As stated many times before, one of the key principles in God's Word is balance. We seem to be a society of extremes. We borrow, spend, and work excessively during our early years—and then we want to quit altogether. For the vast majority of people, retirement is literally an impossible dream. They spend everything they make on a current basis and will actually save very little toward retirement. Even worse, a majority of sixty-five-year-olds will still owe on their homes for ten years or more. They are still in debt at retirement age and find it impossible to reduce their income needs substantially. For them, retirement will mean near poverty and dependency on the government. It is difficult to imagine that they are following God's direction.

For that group, their imbalance reflects a total lack of planning for the future. Granted, we shouldn't just stop working, but Christians should be wise enough to realize that, as we get older, our ability to maintain our income declines. Savings laid aside and invested wisely at an early age can be used to supplement income needed at an older age.

On the other side are those Christians who have planned too well for retirement. They have enough stored for at least three lifetimes already, and they continue to store even more. They have diverted funds that could be used to feed starving people and to change lives for eternity into a retirement account simply because it is a good "tax shelter." "And he said, 'This is what I will do; I will tear down my barns and build larger ones, and there I will store all my grain and my goods. And I will say to my soul, "Soul, you have many goods laid up for many years to come; take your ease, eat, drink and be merry."' But God said to him, 'You fool! This very night your soul is required of you; and now who will own what you have prepared?'" (Luke 12:18-20).

How Much is Enough?

Every Christian needs to realistically face some planning questions.

1. *Why should I retire?* You may be forced to retire because of your chosen vocation (such as an airline pilot). It may be company policy to retire at sixty-two or sixty-five. But it may also be that the decision is totally under your control, and you shouldn't retire. "For by me your days will be multiplied, and years of life will be added to you" (Proverbs 9:11).

2. *What will I do?* You should have a clear-cut picture of your life post-work. How will you spend your time, and how will you keep involved with God's work? Without a doubt, in our society we isolate the elderly from the young. In doing so we subvert God's plan for sharing learned wisdom. Make your plans to include involvement with younger families who need the benefit of your acquired wisdom. "A gray head is a crown of glory; it is found in the way of righteousness" (Proverbs 16:31).

3. *What if my retirement plan fails?* It really grieves me to see so many of God's people depending on an economic system that is so clearly operating outside of God's rules. It no longer seems to be a question of what we will do *if* the economy fails, but *when.* Most Christians are tied up in intangible assets, which could be gone in a financial crisis. Perhaps the best retirement plan of all is a service skill that others need. "A prudent man sees evil and hides himself, the naive proceed and pay the penalty" (Proverbs 27:12).

4. *What if I can't retire?* Many Christians simply need to give up the American concept of retirement and acclimate themselves to earning a living for the rest of their lives. That is probably true for the majority of Christians. Therefore, if you fit into this category, you need to plan your career by stages. The first stage would be to work until a given age (fifty to fifty-five) with the goal of being totally debt-free, including on your home. Once your children are grown, you need to seek retraining in a skill area that requires less physical strength—programming, accounting, art, or woodworking. These skills will successfully carry you throughout your lifetime.

Obviously, any plan such as this requires both husband and wife. If the husband is the primary wage earner, then enough life insurance must be maintained to adequately provide for the wife. "By wisdom a house is built, and by understanding it is established; and by knowledge the rooms are filled with all precious and pleasant riches" (Proverbs 24:3–4).

How to Use Your Retirement Plan

Many retirement plans are so restrictive that you have little or no control over the use of the funds. That would include IRAs, company retirement, and Social Security. However, many plans allow a reasonable amount of self-direction. That is particularly true of "vested" retirement plans, such as Keogh and private pension plans. As much as possible, these funds should be invested in economic growth areas, such as land, houses, and businesses.

39

Business Ethics

Perhaps NOTHING REFLECTS the decline of our society more than the state of current business ethics. It is not at all uncommon to read about major companies paying bribes to government officials or providing large kickbacks to company purchasing agents.

On a smaller scale, many sales companies offer incentives to buyers from other businesses in the form of coupons for merchandise, vacations, cash, or Christmas gifts. These are available on a voluntary basis in spite of the fact that nearly every company has established rules against their purchasing agents accepting such items. "A wicked man receives a bribe from the bosom to pervert the ways of justice" (Proverbs 17:23).

The Cost of Compromise

There is a price to be paid for every compromise, especially to God's Word. That price is the loss of peace from God. Compromise at any level results in further compromise until finally the conscience is seared, and right and wrong are no longer distinguishable. "And just as they did not see fit to acknowledge God any longer, God gave them over to a depraved mind, to do those things which are not proper" (Romans 1:28). An employee who will pad his expense account and rationalize it will eventually pad his income and rationalize that as well. "Bread obtained by falsehood is sweet to a man, but afterward his mouth will be filled with gravel" (Proverbs 20:17).

Fortunately, nobody is worthy before God. Our greatest advantage is the fact that God doesn't have much talent to work with down here. He will restore anyone who will acknowledge his sin and return to His way. If God commanded us to forgive each other seven times a day (Luke 17:4), how much more will He forgive us? "If we confess our sins, He is faithful and righteous to forgive us our sins and to cleanse us from all unrighteousness" (1 John 1:9).

Becoming a Light

In our society, most people are looking for guidance and unwavering commitment to principles. Unfortunately, when these can't be found, many people fall dupe to the humanist's argument that "values are established by society." The end result of this lie can be seen in the abuses of our day—drugs used to escape reality, sexual immorality, a high rate of divorce—and ultimately in the collapse of society itself. Why do people turn to enslavement through a form of government like Communism? It is because it offers an uncompromising set of principles that seem to represent stability.

In reality, only Christ assures both stability and love. It is the responsibility of every believer to adhere uncompromisingly to the set of values presented in God's Word. These values encompass the business as well as the personal life. A Christian must decide either to follow Christ or to follow Satan; there is no middle road. A business will be dedicated to the furtherance of either God's kingdom or Satan's. If the primary purpose of a Christian in business is to be a success and make money, then God's way is *not* for him. Christ promised that following His way would cost something. "And He was saying to them all, 'If anyone wishes to come after Me, let him deny himself, and take up his cross daily, and follow Me'" (Luke 9:23).

Certainly taking a stand for Christ won't always be admired, because it will cause a great deal of discomfort to those who know of Him but don't serve Him. Christ Himself said He came not to bring peace but division (Matthew 10:34). That is not a division based on pride, position, or anger, but on principle. The liars and the thieves will cheat those who obey godly principles, and it is quite possible that the ways of the wicked will cause them to prosper. A Christian must remember that all that is seen is not all that there is. "The wicked earns deceptive wages, but he who sows righteousness gets a true reward" (Proverbs 11:18).

Business Goals

The number-one goal of a Christian businessman must be to share Christ with others. The business is merely a tool to reach people who may never be reached otherwise. The method will vary according to the business and number of employees. One businessman may choose to call the employees in and give them his testimony. Another may use outside speakers in a weekly devotional.

The next step should be a plan for regular fellowship through a company devotional time that employees are invited, but not pressured, to attend. The important principle is to take a stand and present Christ's message to the lost and the wandering (Colossians 1:28). Once a plan has been implemented for sharing with employees, the next step is to share the message with suppliers and customers. Obviously a direct approach is not always possible, so other methods, such as written materials, may be utilized.

In addition to the spiritual goals established, a company should have some straightforward business goals. If the owners' goals are merely to make a lot of money, build a lot of buildings, and leave it all to their children, how are they different from those of non-Christians?

1. *Pay a fair wage.* Many Christian employers are guilty of paying some employees less than a livable wage. To hire someone at such a low wage is in direct violation of the principle of fairness. "You shall not oppress a hired servant who is poor and needy, whether he is one of your countrymen or one of your aliens who is in your land in your towns" (Deuteronomy 24:14).

To pay less than is reasonably needed to live places the employee in a position of not being able to provide for his family. If a job will not support a livable wage for a man with a family, then do not hire those who have families, for doing so will result in short-term, disgruntled employees.

2. *Build a good product.* "A good name is to be more desired than great riches, favor is better than silver and gold" (Proverbs 22:1). A company is known by the quality of its products or service. What a great witness it would be if every time a customer encountered a Christian-run company what was remembered was the quality.

3. *Make a fair profit.* It is an interesting observation that the primary thing that holds prices in line even for Christian-run companies is competition. Given a situation where little or no competition exists, most Christian businessmen will escalate prices until buyer demand drops off. Such pricing sounds like good business, but is it scriptural? "Better is a little with righteousness than great income with injustice" (Proverbs 16:8). Should a Christian in business, whether offering a factory product or a doctor's services, charge what the traffic will bear? Wouldn't it be a testimony to the Lord and His people if Christians established prices and fees on the basis of what is fair both for them and their customers?

4. *Be a godly leader.* "Where there is no guidance, the people fall, but in abundance of counselors there is victory" (Proverbs 11:14). Above all else, a Christian employer should be a godly leader. That means a life free from sin and corruption. Too often Christians are guilty of hypocrisy by taking a stand outside the business environment but not living it inside the company.

Purpose of Business

Does that mean, then, that Christians are supposed to be losers and never be successful? Obviously not, but priorities must be established outside of what the world calls success. Christ warned us that a man could gain the entire world and forfeit his soul in the pursuit of it. The purpose of a Christian in business is the same as any other Christian—to glorify God and lead others to Christ.

A business is nothing more than a tool to accomplish God's work. Making money and acquiring success are by-products of putting God first (Matthew 6:33). Both employees and employers need to take a stand based on God's Word and become lights to their unsaved counterparts. Will such a stand cost business? Almost beyond a doubt, it will initially. For some employees it may well cost them their jobs, if those jobs include bribes and other types of deceit. However, God's Word promises that He owns everything and that He delights in helping those who completely sell out to Him. "For the eyes of the Lord move to and fro throughout the earth that He may strongly support those whose heart is completely His" (2 Chronicles 16:9).

Cost of Commitment

It is not necessary to speak of Christ with everyone you meet in order to serve the Lord. Obviously there are situations in which sharing is not possible or productive. However, being a "silent witness" is a rationalization for being no witness at all. If Christ is first in someone's life, he will share Him with others. Good wisdom will determine the method; the Holy Spirit will provide the opportunity. For employees who are restricted by employer rules, it may mean using dinners or other opportunities outside of business hours. For employers it means using every available opportunity to glorify Christ in words and in actions, both to employees and to customers.

I recall a story that a Christian businessman told me about one of his key employees. That employee had secretly been praying for God to touch him and heal him of a desire for other women. The employee suffered a divorce and an emotional breakdown that led him from one counselor to another and ultimately to an attempt at suicide. One day, after nearly three years of depression, he came in elated to announce that he had found Christ as his Savior and had turned his life over to Him. The president congratulated him and shared that he also was a Christian and had been praying for him. To this, he exclaimed, "Why didn't you tell me where you got your strength and peace? I just thought it was because you owned the company."

40
Paying a Fair Wage

I ONCE ASKED a group of Christian employers, "How much should a Christian employer pay employees?" The answer ranged from minimum wage, as a legal requirement, to a large bonus for special employees. But not a single answer was confirmed on the basis of our source of truth—God's Word. Those Christian employers weren't just the run-of-the-mill Christians, either. They were mostly dedicated men and women seeking to do God's will as well as they knew it.

The difficulty is that in our generation, and in many previous generations, we have been conformed to the image of our world. In fact, in most instances we are indistinguishable in our daily activities. Our words may be different, but our faith is not always reflected through our works. I find that many Christian employers take an identical approach toward employee wages as do most non-Christian employers.

Business Cycles

Anyone who has read much business history recognizes that management attitudes go in cycles. When business is depressed and jobs are few, the managers and owners call the shots, and labor really can't do much about it. During those times wages are often cut, benefits are cut, and most new employees are recruited at reduced wages. Then the cycle reverses, business gets very good, trained labor is in short supply, and wages are forced up by organized labor unions.

Prior to the twentieth century, the cycles affected only a relatively few industries. Today, with our mass media, they develop quickly and in virtually every area of business. What we have developed is a traditional adversary relationship between owners and workers, where each tries to exploit the other whenever possible.

The Principles of Fair Pay

I believe the overwhelming principle about paying employees according to God's Word is fairness, but *not* fairness according to the world's standards. God is not concerned about what others think is fair, but what He thinks is fair. If you were to review all the passages dealing with paying employees and boil them down to a simple principle, I believe you would be left with two options regarding pay. You must either pay someone what he needs to live on or only hire those who can live on what you're able to pay. Once someone is in the employment of a Christian, we are obligated to meet his basic needs to the limit of our ability to do so. "You shall not oppress a hired servant who is poor and needy, whether he is one of your countrymen or one of your aliens who is in your land in your towns" (Deuteronomy 24:14).

Quite obviously, then, each employee's need level must be determined. Arriving at an actual dollar amount is difficult, but I have found some fundamental steps helpful. First, survey your employees to determine if they feel that they are making enough to live on. Then, have an experienced, qualified financial counselor work with them to develop a minimum family budget. Review that budget yourself, and simply put yourself in the employee's position to see if you could live on it.

What Can You Pay?

Obviously, some businesses do so poorly that paying adequate salaries is not always possible. But if that situation continues over an extended period of time, there has to be a doubt about the wisdom of continuing the operation. If God can direct by supplying, He can also direct by withholding. Perhaps the most obvious examples of this are some Christian organizations, most notable in recent years, Christian schools. Many of them pay so poorly (and seldom) that almost no one but the administration can live above the poverty level. If God has truly directed this effort, then adequate salaries should be the norm.

More often than not, the failure of most businesses to pay adequate salaries at the lowest levels is really one of choice rather than necessity. If you look at the assets of the company, the salaries of management, and particularly the indulgences of the owners, most often there is more than enough for the lowest paid employees to be paid fairly. Secular business philosophy teaches that "to the victor belong the spoils." That translates into a trait the Bible calls selfishness. "He who shuts his ear to the cry of the poor will also cry himself and not be answered" (Proverbs 21:13).

It is important for a Christian employer to review every attitude in the light of God's Word to determine if it meets God's minimum. It would be very difficult to stand before a group of employees and testify that you are a Christian and want to operate your business by Christian principles while many of them know that they can't meet even the basic needs of their families. Of course, you are not responsible if their financial problems are caused by their own indulgences.

Whose Needs Come First?

A commonly practiced but seldom expressed principle of management today is to do what you have to do to keep the employees pacified. In other words, respond according to the pressure they can exert. Thus, most wage negotiations become battles between adversaries. That has never been part of God's direction for meeting needs and building businesses. And that is exactly why we are now studying Japanese management to figure out why they are more productive. Their success isn't really very difficult to under-stand—they simply built a management system around a biblical principle known as caring. "Do nothing from selfishness or empty conceit, but with humility of mind let each of you regard one another as more important than himself; do not merely look out for your own personal interests, but also for the interests of others" (Philippians 2:3-4).

Since the Japanese don't have business management schools to teach that principle, it must be applied at the root level, face to face. They don't allow a "we against them" attitude in management. Instead, each employee shares in the financial success of the company.

If Christianity simply practiced what God's Word teaches on this subject, the world would be studying our management techniques, because we would have contented employees sharing in the most profitable businesses in the world. Instead, we are virtually nonidentifiable from the world.

Scriptural Warning

God's Word offers some sober counsel to believers who fit into the worldly mold of indulging while others in their care suffer. Deuteronomy 17 describes the kind of leader God desires for His people. The same character-istics would apply to a leader today. "Moreover, he shall not multiply horses for himself. . . . Neither shall he multiply wives for himself, lest his heart turn away; nor shall he greatly increase silver and gold for himself" (Deuteronomy 17:16-17).

James amplifies this and describes those who would act selfishly in the blunt language of a prophet. "Come now, you rich, weep and howl for your miseries which are coming upon you" (James 5:1). "Behold, the pay of the laborers who mowed your fields, and which has been withheld by you, cries out against you; and the outcry of those who did the harvesting has reached the ears of the Lord of Sabaoth. You have lived luxuriously on the earth and led a life of wanton pleasure; you have fattened your hearts in a day of slaugh-ter" (James 5:4-5).

Balance

God's Word does not suggest that a Christian employer has to pay the highest wages around and certainly not to the detriment of his business. What is required is that at least minimum needs are met and that we are not cheating our workers of their fair wages. No employer will lose by following God's principles for paying people. What you lose in current cash you make up for in long term stability. However, too much of a good principle can often backfire. If you pay everyone the maximum amount possible and don't lay aside any surplus funds, then economic cycles will play havoc with the business.

Every phase of a Christian's business must mesh together, and a part of that is anticipating difficulties. We live in a physical world and are subject to natural forces as well. It does not mean God can't or won't intercede on our behalf—He can and often does. But when you set out in a leaky boat, you may get wet. "There is precious treasure and oil in the dwelling of the wise, but a foolish man swallows it up" (Proverbs 21:20). Remember that the better the business does, the better everyone does.

Sowing and Reaping

"Do not be deceived, God is not mocked; for whatever a man sows, this he will also reap" (Galatians 6:7).

The principle of sowing and reaping is usually directly applicable to dealing with other people, and since employees are other people, it applies to them as well. When an employer is able to exercise total control because of prevailing economic circumstances, there is an opportunity to demonstrate with actions what words can never do. Literally, you are sowing attitudes into the lives of others. They will often take root, grow, and return to you. So, if you sow love and caring, you reap the same. If you sow indifference and contempt, you'll reap that also.

Let Us Be Doers

Ouite often, Christian business leaders fall short in the "doing" end of God's Word. I have observed that one reason many Christian business owners travel to give their personal testimony is that they have a rather cool reception at home. Obviously, you can't please everyone. Whatever you pay, there will be those who don't think it's enough or who will resent the fact that someone else makes more. But the principle is very clear—you don't have to please them. Just please God, and you'll do fine.

41

To Sue or Not to Sue

THE QUESTION OF lawsuits comes up frequently in our business seminars, particularly during a recession time when a lot of people don't pay their bills. A study of this principle turns out to be a study on rights and motives.

Does a Christian have a right to sue another person? Obviously, lawsuits are a common matter today. The reasons range from emotional distress caused by a neighbor's barking dog to legitimate losses caused by faulty products or personal injuries suffered in an accident. Many lawsuits are simply blatant fraud for the purpose of personal profit. Certainly for Christians, those kinds of lawsuits must be regarded the same as stealing.

But what about the right to justifiable legal remedy? How should a believer respond when cheated by another individual or corporation? Does it make a difference whether or not the offender is a Christian? What if a Christian is sued? Is countersuit a justifiable defense? Obviously, these are questions that can only be answered in the light of God's Word.

What Is a Lawsuit?

The purpose of a lawsuit is to provide someone who has suffered a loss at the hands of another party a legal means to recover the property or other damages from the offender. In practicality, it is one person's accusing another of an offense and requesting that a judge or jury make a decision about guilt or innocence and compensation.

Suing is certainly not a new concept. It is apparent from Paul's writing in 1 Corinthians 6 that lawsuits were commonplace in the first century. Unfortunately, suing today has become a first, rather than a last, recourse. As Christians, we must be able to discern what our rights are scripturally.

Personal Loss

Many lawsuits are initiated because of personal loss suffered due to the negligence or deceit of another. A common example is defective merchandise. Most department stores have a return policy that helps avoid such conflicts, but what about those that do not? Do you have the right, as a Christian, to pursue such matters into the secular courts?

Since a corporation is a legal entity established to protect the owners, I can find no scriptural basis for not bringing suit against one for legitimate losses. A corporation is a court-established entity that has no humanity and thus may be compelled by law to accept its legal responsibilities. In the case of an insurance company, that is particularly evident. The purpose of an insurance company is to provide financial remedy for losses. Recourse for inequitable settlement rests in the law. In reality, the company has contractually bound itself to compensating a liability of a client.

That certainly does not imply that God cannot or will not change the actions of corporate officers—only that a corporation has no personal rights in scriptural terms. That is not to say that a Christian should sue a corporation. God may well convict someone to give up the right to sue for several reasons, not the least of which is to have a witness in the lives of the principals involved. Also, God wants us to learn the principle of giving up our rights, and this may be an exercise in yielding a right. The guideline in regard to a suit against a corporation has to be twofold: motive and personal conviction. We must be certain about both; and if we have any doubt, we should stop.

Personal Lawsuits

What are our rights and options when we have a legitimate case against another individual for a loss? First, let's address the best defined situation—one Christian against another. The principle covering this situation is found in 1 Corinthians 6. We are directed to take our case before true believers when a brother is involved. "Does any one of you, when he has a case against his neighbor, dare to go to law before the saints?" (1 Corinthians 6:1).

The recourse provided when two Christians are involved is outlined in Matthew 18. The principle is simple: We are to take any offense directly to another believer. First, we are to see him alone, then with a witness, if necessary, and ultimately, we are to take him before the church. The purpose in every instance is for restoration in the faith, not collection. That procedure, if taken seriously, would certainly serve as a testimony to the unsaved. All too often, however, the witness is a negative one—first, because Christians ignore the admonition not to sue one another; and second, because the unsaved see our motives as self-centered. It is clearly a matter of giving up rights; something we would rather not do. "Actually, then, it is already a defeat for you, that you have lawsuits with one another. Why not rather be wronged? Why not rather be defrauded?" (1 Corinthians 6:7).

I would like to be able to tell you that by giving up this right to sue, God will intervene to recover the material assets lost, but no such promise is made in God's Word. God may choose to do so but He may also choose not to. "And someone in the crowd said to Him, 'Teacher, tell my brother to divide the family inheritance with me.' But He said to him, 'Man, who appointed Me a judge or arbiter over you?'" (Luke 12:13-14).

Suing Nonbelievers

Since the direct implication of 1 Corinthians 6 is of one believer's suing another, what about suing nonbelievers? There are no direct references to suing a nonbeliever, but there are some very revealing indirect references.

It is important to bear in mind that God's Word deals much more with our attitudes than with our actions. Many people have the right actions but the wrong attitudes. The Pharisees had many of the right actions but the wrong attitudes. When a Christian has the attitude toward others that God requires, most actions will change toward them. "Bearing with one another, and forgiving each other, whoever has a complaint against anyone; just as the Lord forgave you, so also should you" (Colossians 3:13).

Above all, God's Word teaches us to surrender our rights, even to the unbeliever. That means literally to put others first, even when they are wrong. "Whoever hits you on the cheek, offer him the other also; and whoever takes away your coat, do not withhold your shirt from him either. Give to everyone who asks of you, and whoever takes away what is yours, do not demand it back" (Luke 6:29-30).

That attitude can be very costly when you live in a society of opportunists. The result may be personal loss. A Christian friend recently told me of an instance where someone cancelled a contract with him and flatly told him, "I know you won't sue me because you're a Christian." Once you've taken a stand for the Lord, it may well cost you materially. Not every believer is willing or ready to live by God's highest standard. But when the decision is solely ours and the loss is solely ours, the question becomes, "Do we really believe it all belongs to God?" Most human counsel will run contrary to God's perfect will. The fairness of the situation is of primary importance to the Lord.

Allowable Defense?

A Christian asked about his scriptural right to defend himself when accused by someone else. His particular case involved a dispute over a real estate fee that the accuser said was due him. Everyone involved in the sale (broker, buyer, attorney) unanimously agreed that the claim was false. In fact, it was found that this individual had used the same ruse several times before. Many times the fee was paid just to avoid the inconvenience of a court battle. The question he asked was, "Can I and should I defend myself against an unjust claim?

I believe the answer can be found in Paul's defense against unjust claims throughout the book of Acts (16:37; 22:25; 25:11). Paul did not attack his accusers, nor did he attempt to extract any compensation from them. But he did vigorously defend himself against their claims, several times even reciting Roman law applicable to his case. As long as our motives are right and we are not seeking retribution, we can, and often should, defend the rightness of our actions. In this particular case, the claim was dropped the day the case was to go to court. It was clear that the accuser knew he would lose.

Recourse for a Crime

Although a believer is instructed not to sue another for personal loss, the same is not true for criminal action. By law a criminal act is committed against the whole of society. A Christian who has knowledge of a crime is obligated to report that crime and allow the law to respond. The only exception would be when the law is in conflict with God's Word. As Peter stated in Acts 5:29, "We must obey God rather than men." It may also be necessary to testify in court as a witness.

That does not relieve our responsibility to forgive the offender. Rather, it is our responsibility to obey the authority established by God. "Let every person be in subjection to the governing authorities. For there is no authority except from God, and those which exist are established by God" (Romans 13:1).

42

Work as unto the Lord

"WHATEVER YOU DO, do your work heartily, as for the Lord rather than for men; knowing that from the Lord you will receive the reward of inheritance. It is the Lord Christ whom you serve" (Colossians 3:23-24).

In addition to supplying our physical needs, work plays a very important role in our spiritual lives. It provides the opportunity to put into practice spiritual principles that would otherwise be mere academics. A Christian can study every passage in the Bible dealing with serving others and read every biography of those who were noted servants, such as George Mueller, and still not really understand the principle of surrendering rights.

On the job, however, the opportunity to yield our rights presents itself every day. The way we do our work provides the best exterior reflection of our commitment to serve the Lord in a real, physical way. It doesn't matter whether that work is in the home, on an assembly line, or in a corporate office. Our true Christian beliefs will be reflected more clearly there than in any other environment outside the immediate family relationships.

The chain of relationships from family to work is so intertwined that the apostle Paul listed them as a series in Colossians 3—first, husband-wife relationships (vv. 18-19); second, parent-children relationships (vv. 20-21); and third, authority-work relationships (vv. 22-23). Paul knew that unless a Christian had all of those managed properly, his life could not manifest joy, peace, or contentment. A great deal of teaching is available now on the first two areas—marriage and children. However, little has been written on an equally large area of difficulty—work.

Current Attitudes

For too many Christians, work is a necessary evil, while for others it is an area of "worship." Obviously, both are extremes and represent a spiritual imbalance. Many Christians view their jobs with drudgery. Literally, jobs are just a means to earn money so that they can enjoy themselves. They are dissatisfied with their vocation, disgruntled on the job, and resentful of others' success. A by-product of all this mental anxiety is quite often fatigue on the job and restlessness at home. To compensate, they fill their lives with endless outside activities. For nonbelievers, these are usually hunting, fishing, boating, skiing, and so on. For the Christian, they may be church activities and civic functions. None of these activities is bad in itself; in fact, they are quite good unless the activities are a substitute for the lack of fulfillment at work.

Somehow Christians have been duped into believing that work is a secular activity and therefore one shouldn't expect to feel spiritual about a job. That attitude destroys our greatest area of outreach and witness. Few Christians who view their work as a chore have much of a witness on or off the job.

Proverbs 22:29 says, "Do you see a man skilled in his work? He will stand before kings; he will not stand before obscure men."

Resentment

It is amazing how clearly spiritual problems are reflected on the job. I once taught at a company meeting, and afterward one of the employees cornered me to let me know how oppressed he was. It seemed that everyone else received bigger raises and better promotions, but he always did the most work. He went on and on until I told him I had to go. On the way out, the owner told me he believed the man could be a key employee, but he always had his feelings hurt about decisions even remotely affecting him, and he was resentful of anyone else's recognition. It was obvious that he had a spiritual problem that was being reflected in a physical way.

Such problems are not unique to industry alone. The leader of a large Christian organization once related that he had less trouble with employees when he was in business than he did in the ministry. He said, "I once naively thought that I could deal with Christian staff differently. On the contrary, in great part they see the other staff members as competitors, and if I do something extra for one, many of the others resent it." It would seem that we failed to teach Christians that the job is an extension of their walk with the Lord, not isolated from it.

Biblical Admonition

It is fortunate for all of us that God's Word is both simple and complete. No subject affecting our lives is left to our own imagination. Those who are resentful about the success of others, whose feelings are hurt because of the lack of recognition, or who use a job as their alter egos all suffer from the same spiritual malady—they are in service to men instead of God. Unfortunately, men will always fail; fortunately, God never will. If a Christian approaches a job with the attitude that some person must recognize him as the best, there will almost always be disappointment, because the first time the boss forgets to show appreciation, resentment creeps in.

Praise of Men

To get the praise of men is not difficult in business. Just do what they want, when they want it, and how they want it. The trick is guessing what, when, and how. One bad guess, and the praise is gone. It might require dropping a bomb on your coworkers from time to time, because if you're to get the praise of men, you certainly can't allow someone else to get it. "And He said to them, 'You are those who justify yourselves in the sight of men, but God knows your hearts; for that which is highly esteemed among men is detestable in the sight of God'" (Luke 16:15).

It is interesting to note that those workers whom bosses praise most highly are usually the ones who require the least praise. It takes a lot of energy to remember to praise someone for everything he does right. What a joy it is when a boss finds a quiet, efficient, self-starter who continually looks after the interest of other employees. Those qualities are so rare that the boss is torn between promoting that person and keeping him at the present job because it is so easy to get the work done.

I have found a common characteristic in Christians who don't rely on praise from men: they take literally the principle of work in Colossians 2:23–24. "Whatever you do, do your work heartily, as for the Lord rather than for men; knowing that from the Lord you will receive the reward of the inheritance. It is the Lord Christ whom you serve."

The key is that they look to the Lord for their rewards and in doing so find that His standards of conduct are so much higher than men's that they surpass any boss's expectations. It is not that they don't want continual praise from men, but that they don't need it.

How to Break the Trap

1. *Be honest.* The first step is to confess to God that any attitude of resentment, ego, pride, or desire for praise is unacceptable and needs to be corrected. First John 1:9 says, "If we confess our sins, He is faithful and righteous to forgive us our sins and to cleanse us from all unrighteousness."

2. *Admit openly.* The next step is to seek the forgiveness of those who may have been offended or hurt. Acknowledge this as a personal weakness and ask their help in detecting and correcting it in the future. Galatians 6:2–3 says, "Bear one another's burdens, and thus fulfill the law of Christ. For if anyone thinks he is something when he is nothing, he deceives himself."

A word of caution is necessary here. Do not expect everyone to appreciate or understand your actions. Remember that you serve Christ, not men. It is for your relationship to Him that you need to correct the problem. That is equally true of a housewife whose husband and children seemingly never "appreciate" her. Correct your attitudes and actions, and leave the results to God.

3. *Take correct action.* Satan's number-one weapon is defeat, but God's number-one promise is victory. When you find that the original problems have returned, never allow yourself to dwell on them. Confess them again, publicly if necessary. Many times a little ego deflation is necessary to make a commitment firm. That will also require that you forgive any offense that someone else commits against you.

Colossians 3:13 says, "Bearing with one another, and forgiving each other, whoever has a complaint against any one; just as the Lord forgave you, so also should you."

4. *Spiritual renewal.* Since the problems are spiritual, the solution must be spiritual also. The only source of spiritual renewal is the Holy Spirit. Examine your daily spiritual life honestly. Do you spend time regularly in prayer and the study of God's Word? Without regular spiritual food, even the most determined Christian will develop spiritual anemia. Group prayer, conferences, and church are not substitutes for a personal relationship with God. If Christ needed to withdraw and be alone with God, we must also.

Romans 12:2 says, "And do not be conformed to this world, but be transformed by the renewing of your mind, that you may prove what the will of God is, that which is good and acceptable and perfect."

43
Multi–Level Sales Programs

THE SUBJECT OF multi-level sales is an emotional subject to many. There have been good and bad effects on the lives of people who engage in this fastest growing area of consumer sales.

What Is a Multi-Level Sales Program?

In reality, every product is sold by a multi-level system. The manufacturer marks it up and sells it to a retailer who marks it up again and sells it to a customer. This is a delivery system that has proved very effective over the centuries.

The multi-level plan we will discuss is different in two ways: First, the products are usually sold through part-time sales people who sell primarily to personal acquaintances and friends; and second, there are several levels of distributors, each making a percentage on the sales of those under his authority. In most programs, distributors are encouraged to recruit others to sell for them, thus expanding their sales volume and income.

Many multi-level companies have grown from no sales to billions in less than a year. Usually the end price is higher than a similar product in a retail store because of the markups at the various levels of distribution. Consequently, the incentive to buy must be greater. That incentive is created in two ways: First, most sales are made by direct contact through referral—friends and family first. Second, the buyers of the product are recruited to sell it and thus make extra money themselves.

Assets and Liabilities

In counseling Christians involved with many of these multi-level sales programs, I have found both assets and liabilities within them. Before looking at the scriptural principles relating to them, it would be helpful to look at some assets and liabilities.

Part-time employment. Most of these plans provide the opportunity for part-time income without working at an office. Thus, most are oriented toward wives and mothers who can work out of their homes. That lowers their overhead costs and, in general, allows them to choose their own hours.

Small investment. A second asset is that most programs require very little capital investment to get started—usually under $50.

The liabilities are generally related to priorities rather than products. Quite often, what started out to be a part-time job ends up as an all-consuming passion to sell more products or recruit more prospects. After a while, everybody is viewed as a prospect, and every social activity as a sales platform. When a particular program is approaching its zenith in an area, Christians are stepping all over each other to recruit new salespeople and move to the next level in the company. A lot of otherwise well-meaning Christians have severely damaged their credibility and witness by becoming known as "Mr. and Mrs. Multi-level" in their community.

Why Get Involved?

There are many reasons why a Christian would be attracted to a multi-level program. Some are good and acceptable, while others are purely destructive. Perhaps the most destructive motive is the most common—get-rich-quick. Many multi-level plans (called pyramids) stage high-pitched emotional meetings that insinuate if you're content where you are financially, you're lazy and have failed God. Interestingly enough, almost all such promotions are aimed at the Christian community and receive an acceptance there. Why? Because many Christians are trusting and gullible with regard to anything having a spiritual ring to it.

Another reason many Christians get involved with these hyped-up programs is purely fad. Christ described us quite accurately as sheep, and a lot of people follow wherever somebody is leading. "The naive believes everything, but the prudent man considers his steps" (Proverbs 14:15).

Still others get involved with multi-level sales because of a need for money. My caution to these people is always to be patient in building a product sales organization. Be sure the product is not just a passing fad, and be sure it's meeting a genuine need for the ultimate user. "Prepare your work outside, and make it ready for yourself in the field; afterwards, then, build your house" (Proverbs 24:27).

Last, many Christians get involved in multi-level programs out of a genuine desire to help other people. Several Christians I know check out various companies and products to screen out the deceptive ones. They stock products from the best and then help others who need more income by putting them into business. The real test of their motives can be found in the fact that they themselves refuse to profit from their investment in other people. "The righteous is concerned for the rights of the poor, the wicked does not understand such concern" (Proverbs 29:7).

The True Test of Attitude

Before getting involved with any kind of public-oriented program, it's necessary for a Christian to test his motive. Then it's necessary to retest that motive periodically to be sure that simple greed has not taken control. Otherwise, everyone becomes a prospect. If most Christians would approach evangelism with the same zeal with which they approach product sales, we would saturate our communities with God's Word.

Anytime Christians look upon others as a source of revenue rather than service, they are caught in Satan's most common trap—greed. "Do nothing from selfishness or empty conceit, but with humility of mind let each of you regard one another as more important than himself" (Philippians 2:3). Many young Christians who were hungry for fellowship have been hurt immeasurably by other Christians who deceptively asked them over for an evening, only to attempt to recruit them to sell their product line.

Even more devastating are those who use the church environment to prospect. They have violated a God-given trust. A couple I was counseling related that they visited a church in their community and were asked twice that day by members of the church if they used a particular company's products. They responded that they didn't, and shortly thereafter received three visits from members of the church to sign them up. Be assured that they sought out another fellowship immediately. "A brother offended is harder to be won than a strong city" (Proverbs 18:19*a*).

Anything that we do, as Christians, must be approached with an attitude of service to others. That requires more than lip service, where a Christian rationalizes constant prospecting by saying that it's ultimately for *their* good.

God wants us to be unusually astute in the things of God and innocent in the guiles of the world. The only way to consistently test our motives is always to consider others first. Every new recruit that a Christian acquires should be thoroughly apprised of the benefits and liabilities of direct product sales. Also a Christian must adopt a nonaggressive sales attitude when there might be even the slightest motivation to prospect from a fellow believer. Since God really is the Creator of the universe, He knows what our needs and their needs are. If He can hang the stars in the sky, He can surely build an effective sales organization without any guile on our part. "For we are not like many, peddling the word of God, but as from sincerity, but as from God, we speak in Christ in the sight of God" (2 Corinthians 2:17).

Know God's Plan for You

Selling products door-to-door or friend-to-friend is not for most people. It requires two basic ingredients in order to be successful: first, service to God; and second, service to others. That's the same plan to be successful in any field. If someone is into multi-level sales just for money, ego, pride, or greed, then there will never be enough. "He who loves money will not be satisfied with money, nor he who loves abundance with its income. This too is vanity" (Ecclesiastes 5:10).

A Christian must know God's individual plan for his life. Most Christians don't know what God's plan for them is and consequently get led into many schemes that disrupt their lives.

Be Honest

In summary, I would say that the concept of multi-level direct sales is not wrong, but quite often its practices are. Anytime a Christian must trick another person into listening to a sales pitch while promising fellowship, it is wrong. Anytime a Christian is more interested in selling a product than in ministering to someone else's needs, that person is in service to money and not to God.

Each believer must test his own attitudes before the Lord. One Christian can be involved in a multi-sales program serving God and convincing others about Jesus Christ, while another is acting greedily and selfishly, storing up wrath for the day when even our attitudes will be revealed. "Set your mind on the things above, not on the things that are on earth. . . . Do not lie to one another, since you laid aside the old self with its evil practices" (Colossians 3:2, 9).

44
How to Identify Business Bondage

Financial bondage applies to more than just indebtedness. Certainly those who owe more than they can pay are in bondage. But those who have a large surplus and live in fear or pride are also in bondage. Literally, financial bondage is anything material that interferes with our relationship with God. Thus, the individual who has a surplus of $100,000 a year to invest, but spends all of his waking time worrying about how to multiply it and protect it, is in as much bondage scripturally as someone else who can't pay his credit card bills.

The key to whether or not someone lives in bondage is one's attitude. We are servants of the living God, and when material things bind us, we cannot fulfill our function. "So that you may walk in a manner worthy of the Lord, to please Him in all respects, bearing fruit in every good work and increasing in the knowledge of God" (Colossians 1:10).

All of this is to point out that just as financial bondage does not apply merely to debt, neither does business bondage apply only to failure. A Christian whose business involvement pre-empts God's greater plan for his life is in bondage. And it really doesn't matter that the efforts are materially successful or that large sums are given to God's work. God has never been impressed by our worldly successes. What He wants is our obedience to His will for our lives. "No one can serve two masters; for either he will hate the one and love the other, or he will hold to one and despise the other. You cannot serve God and mammon" (Matthew 6:24).

Symptom 1: Overcommitment to Work or Success

"It is vain for you to rise up early, to retire late, to eat the bread of painful labors; for He gives to His beloved even in his sleep" (Psalm 127:2).

Overcommitment is a term that cannot be defined in hours and minutes. One person can work ten hours and still maintain the correct priorities, whereas another may work ten hours on the job physically and another ten mentally even while at home. Overcommitment to business is usually a sign of fear, specifically the fear of failure. Most times a Christian will rationalize an overcommitment because "it's for my family." However, when put to a vote, most wives and children would decide otherwise.

Perhaps the most graphic consequence of that particular symptom is the swing toward liberalism in our young people. An overcommitted parent can supply things to his children but not direction and certainly not balance.

Symptom 2: An Air of Superiority

"Instruct those who are rich in this present world not to be conceited or to fix their hope on the uncertainty of riches, but on God, who richly supplies us with all things to enjoy" (1 Timothy 6:17).

Any of at least a hundred scriptural references could be used to demonstrate God's view of our human tendency to elevate people because of their worldly success. It is even worse when a Christian begins to adopt an air of superiority because of his stewardship over some of God's resources. There is no greater deterrent to a consistent walk with the Lord than false pride and self-elevation. Unfortunately, there is a very common tendency for those in management or ownership to assume these characteristics or symptoms.

Usually, an air of superiority begins with the internal attitude that says, "I started this business; I can do what I want to with it," or it can take a more directed course toward people, especially those who are hourly employees. A Christian executive who establishes a social barrier between himself and assembly workers or truck drivers will find that a spiritual barrier exists as well. But that means the Christian executive is in bondage—the bondage of phony superiority. Anyone who believes that God's message of salvation was primarily carried to or through the world by the educated and well-mannered needs to reread God's Book on evangelism. "For who regards you as superior? And what do you have that you did not receive? But if you did receive it, why do you boast as if you had not received it?" (1 Corinthians 4:7).

Those in positions of authority must exercise great caution to maintain the proper balance. Authority actually means responsibility according to God's Word. The single example of perfect leadership was Christ. He consistently told His followers that He came to serve, not to be served. By showing kindness and concern, He did not weaken His authority. He knew, as we should, that His authority and position were in God's kingdom. The leaders and followers of His day tried to convince Him to hold Himself above the poor. This He refused to do, and He condemned the practice. "But the greatest among you shall be your servant. And whoever exalts himself shall be humbled; and whoever humbles himself shall be exalted" (Matthew 23:11-12).

The question is often asked, "How can I maintain discipline if I get too close to my employees?" The answer is that if they know that you're applying God's principles fairly and consistently, then they will also know that administering justice along with compassion is a part of that plan. Justice without compassion is callousness, and compassion without justice is weakness. It should also be noted that you're not trying to make pets out of those under your authority. Nobody likes a condescending boss. What you should be striving to do is to treat all men equally.

The symptom of superiority is difficult to overcome. Those Christians I know who struggle to overcome it have discovered something in common. As soon as they begin to treat everyone they meet equally and fairly, some obnoxious employee immediately begins to see how much he can get away with. God's Word says not to look down at others, but it doesn't say that work rules can't be enforced. Some of those who resent authority must either be taught to respect that authority or be released.

Symptom vs. Problem

The symptom may be an air of superiority, but the real problem is either ego or pride. "Pride goes before destruction, and a haughty spirit before stumbling" (Proverbs 16:18). The way to deal with pride is to consciously put others first. Certainly it's difficult and without a doubt runs contrary to popular business management principles. But God wrote the book on business management, and if we really believe that everything belongs to Him, then we believe it is His plan we are to follow. Remember that the purpose of a Christian's business is to glorify God.

Symptom 3: Selfishness–Indulgence

"Come now, you rich, weep and howl for your miseries which are coming upon you. Your riches have rotted and your garments have become moth-eaten" (James 5:1-2).

A commercial for a luxury car once showed a late night scene in an office parking lot and a haggard looking executive walking up to his expensive car saying, "Sure I've had to sacrifice a lot, but I've earned the right to the best." What that commercial didn't show is that in real life often that executive is working on a second marriage, has rotten kids, and is desperately trying to indulge himself to prove that it has all been worth it. A thousand years from now it won't have made much of a positive impact on eternity, I imagine.

Far too often those who control a business adopt a "me first" attitude. They poorly pay many employees, establish their own retirement plans without thought to their employees' needs, and reap most of the available surplus for themselves. More often than not the owner will sell out a successful business, realizing a great profit and leaving the employees with little or nothing to show for the years of their lives they invested. Certainly they received their wages, but a Christian has to ask, "Does my responsibility end at payday?"

Symptom vs. Problem

The symptom may manifest itself through selfishness and indulgence, but the real problem is greed. We all have an inborn attitude of greed—always desiring more. Until it is brought under God's authority, we will not be good stewards. Consequently, we settle for trinkets now when God really desires to pour out His blessings upon us. "You ask and do not receive, because you ask with wrong motives, so that you may spend it on your pleasures" (James 4:3).

Symptom 4: Confusion–Disorganization

"The sluggard does not plow after the autumn, so he begs during the harvest and has nothing" (Proverbs 20:4). Almost in total contrast to the over-committed workaholic are those Christian businessmen who apply themselves at the minimal level. They're content to operate with sloppy records and poor work quality, and they exist in a mediocre society without a real Christian testimony.

Christians are instructed to be excellent in everything they do. "Whatever you do, do your work heartily, as for the Lord rather than for men" (Colossians 3:23). That is a part of our testimony before the unsaved.

God's way is not a cop-out; it is the best. It is astounding how mediocre society has become. We build defects into our equipment and appliances because of shoddy workmanship and wonder why we aren't competitive. As Christians, we should accept excellence as our minimum standard. The quality of our personal efforts should be so high that the unsaved around us are drawn to the Lord through our witness. Instead, few Christians really have such a testimony.

Without a doubt, excellence is an attitude that God commands of us. It would be very difficult to convince others that Christianity is the only way if the Christians they see are sloppy and in a state of confusion. Usually, these conditions result in frustration and anger for the Christian and for those around him.

Symptom vs. Problem

The symptom is disorganization, but the underlying problem is slothfulness, which is generally a by-product of a lack of commitment. In other words, it's an "I don't care" attitude. That is so uncharacteristic of a Christian that one would have to question God's leadership in the life of a slothful or lazy person. Anyone can have lapses of excellence caused by pressures, health, or overwork. But continual laziness is a sure sign of spiritual problems (1 Peter 4:11).

45

Too Busy to Serve

NOTHING INTERFERES MORE with our ability to serve God than our need to earn a living. An observer from 100 years ago would be awestruck by the improvement in our living standard and by the amount of leisure time our technology has provided. Few North Americans regularly work more than a fifty-hour week; most work forty-four hours or less. In addition, we now live an average of eighteen years longer than we did 100 years ago and have at least one-third more disposable income per family. When all of these factors are weighed together with the fact that in America alone there are perhaps 20 million Christians, it would seem clear that we ought to be getting out the message of Jesus Christ much better than we are.

The simple truth is that most Americans are too busy to serve God. We have grown complacent and comfortable in God's blessing and have forgotten the first commandment. In the meantime, immorality and cults have grown to alarming proportions because their advocates are more zealous in their support. Since God asks for obedience rather than demanding it, many Christians simply ignore the very reason for their existence: to glorify God. Without exception, God has a unique and meaningful plan for every believer, and it does not depend on age, income, or ability.

It is also clear that God calls each of us to fill his gap. Just as Esther did, every believer must decide either to be used by God or to be bypassed and another chosen instead. What a loss that we will allow temporary comforts and laziness to rob us of true riches both now and for all eternity! "Since all these things are to be destroyed in this way, what sort of people ought you to be in holy conduct and godliness" (2 Peter 3:11).

Time Out, Please

Most Christians would never "refuse" to do God's will; it's just that the timing is not right. When God calls us, He wants obedience first and worldly wisdom last. We have allowed the *urgent* things of this society in which we live to over-shadow the *important* things. That fact is neither new nor unique to our generation. In fact, Christ experienced it in His walk on earth and predicted it for us. He left a parable of God's calling men to follow Him. They were invited to a dinner, but most were far too busy to attend right then. They wanted to be part of what was happening but had a great many responsibilities. "And you will be blessed, since they do not have the means to repay you; for you will be repaid at the resurrection of the righteous" (Luke 14:14).

Consider the Cost

Service to Jesus Christ is demanding. It may actually mean that we will have to work as hard for God's kingdom as we do for earthly riches. Few salesmen consider it a great imposition on their time to tell about their product line. Being a success at anything requires dedication, training, and perseverance. It would be a very hungry company that trained its salesmen to expect perfect success on every call. Just one turndown and they would give up, considering themselves a failure. Instead, the key to successful salesmanship starts long before they ever see the first product. In fact, it starts at the job interview. A good sales manager knows that not everybody can be a good salesman, and many don't even want to be. Christ knew that not everybody will serve God, and most won't even want to.

Some would like to have a foot in both worlds. They are willing to be called Christians provided they can pick the times and places to serve. "But Jesus said to him, 'No one, after putting his hand to the plow and looking back, is fit for the kingdom of God'" (Luke 9:62).

These people are actually worse off in this life than they were before. They are content to know about God but are fruitless fakers who must generate false blessings. They are poorly nourished spiritually and quickly waste away until there is real doubt in their minds about their salvation. "And other seed fell on rocky soil, and as soon as it grew up, it withered away, because it had no moisture" (Luke 8:6). They truly fall prey to every wind of doctrine because they are too busy to grow firm roots.

Thorns of Life

"And the seed which fell among the thorns, these are the ones who have heard, and as they go on their way they are choked with worries and riches and pleasures of this life, and bring no fruit to maturity" (Luke 8:14).

In the parable of the sower, Christ defines the thorns as worries, riches, and pleasures of this world. At first glance, one could assume that committed service to God then would necessarily yield peace, but peace with poverty and blandness. Judging from the way Christians avoid total service to God, this would seem so.

However, Jesus Christ said that total service to God would yield peace and blessings within His will: "For all these things the nations of the world eagerly seek; but your Father knows that you need these things. But seek for His kingdom, and these things shall be added to you" (Luke 12:30-31).

Each of us has experienced the thorns of this world. Everything around us is moving at a frantic pace. A family can hardly get one car paid off before another is needed. Only twenty-five years ago our goal was a high school education to get a good job—now it's a college degree. Family life is degrading because it now takes both spouses working to hang on to the "good life."

Good Works

To a lesser degree, but just as misguided, are Christians who apply themselves to fruitless effort in the name of the Lord. They busy themselves to the point of exhaustion going to conferences and countless church activities and serving on many committees. However, they are rarely, if ever, quiet enough for the Lord to direct them. They are irritable and often envious of others. They are working *at* God's work but not *in* it. Even those who walked with the Lord suffered from this busy malady from time to time.

Once when Christ was visiting Martha's home, she complained to the Lord that she was stuck doing all the things while Mary was just sitting and listening to Jesus. Jesus told Martha, "You are worried and bothered about so many things; but only a few things are necessary, really only one, for Mary has chosen the good part, which shall not be taken away from her" (Luke 10:41b-42).

Many Christians have taken on a life of meaningless works to avoid the reality of serving God according to His will. The fruits of true service cannot be denied (Galatians 5:22-23), whereas the effects of human work cannot be hidden. I once heard someone ask how to determine if one's service was truly being blessed by the Lord. One response was, "Ask his pastor." Another was, "Ask his friends." But the best and by far the most enlightening was, "Ask his family."

Sowing and Reaping

Most Christians are familiar with the principle of sowing and reaping as it applies to giving—though few really believe it. That same principle applies to sharing time in the Lord's work. Just as God can multiply the fruits of our labor, He can also multiply the use of our time. Any good administrator knows that ten minutes spent in productive effort is more valuable than two hours spent in confusion and frustration. Therefore, one of the first things a busy, frustrated, overworked Christian needs to do is dedicate the best part of the day, week, month, and year to the Lord. To do so will mean reordering priorities at work and at home and establishing some sound goals (Luke 6:38).

Goal Setting

Personal. No other goals are going to be meaningful until the first and most important one is settled—one's relationship with God. In Psalm 51:10-13, David tells us of some prerequisites to teaching others God's way: assurance of salvation, a steadfast spirit, the Holy Spirit's control, and a clean heart. If any of these is missing, then utter frustration will result. If a Christian's first priority in life is God, then an understanding of God's way is mandatory. That means personal Bible study. It also means a personal prayer life dedicated to the needs of others as well as personal needs.

Family. Most families drift for lack of a rudder—the father's leadership. If a family's most important need is a godly father, then this need is far more important than all the material possessions a parent can provide.

Work. There is nothing wrong with being successful even when measured by worldly standards—unless one ends a failure by godly standards. The rate of divorce and bankruptcy among Christians is an undeniable indicator that Christians have been duped into accepting the world's yardstick as the first priority. Each Christian must ask, "Am I certain my priorities are in line with God's?" If not, then a change is in order—no matter what the cost in dollars and cents.

It is remarkable that usually those at the highest end of the material scale are the biggest violators of priorities (executives, doctors, attorneys, and so on). But equally guilty are many in full-time Christian service, with pastors leading the group. "It is vain for you to rise up early, to retire late, to eat the bread of painful labors; for He gives to His beloved even in his sleep" (Psalm 127:2).

Summary

We all, to a greater or lesser degree, suffer from being too busy to serve God. Some are so busy doing things for God that they fail to do the things of God. Some have already been called by God to go into full-time Christian service, but they weighed the call against the cost and decided they could serve God best where they were. Others clutter their lives with so much materialism that they never have time to listen to God. The urgent things crowd out the important things, and Christian service to others is shelved until "a better time."

We can all give thanks to those committed saints, from the apostles on down, who did not feel that fame and success in the eyes of men were as important as God's blessings. Without fear of contradiction, I can say that one day each of us will grade 100 percent of our success or failure on the basis of Christ's evaluation and none other. I trust that each of us will hear Him say, "Well done, My good and faithful servant."

Part Six

FAMILY

46
Husband-Wife Communications

Of ALL THE relationships described in God's Word, none depicts the partnership better than marriage. However, this partnership is not like a business or social partnership in which two people are merely working together toward a common goal. The relationship could be better described as a "yoke" (Greek, *zugos*) where two are tied to the same harness, pulling to accomplish a common task.

A marriage is more than that. At the end of a day, a yoke can be removed, as it was with oxen, and they need not be joined together again until the next work day. A marriage is much more like the partnership of the left and right hands of the same person. They are perfectly matched but totally opposite. God's Word says that two people become one. "For this cause a man shall leave his father and his mother, and shall cleave to his wife; and they shall become one flesh" (Genesis 2:24).

Understanding this can greatly enhance a marriage, because it virtually eliminates any idea that one person is subservient to another. They are merely different for the purpose of accomplishing various functions. One hand working alone will not accomplish half as much as two. Many tasks are impossible without two hands working together. It is truly enlightening to see how opposite couples really are. It would seem that opposites do attract. One will get up early, while the other stays in bed. One has a good sense of direction; the other gets lost. One is punctual; the other is always late. One usually talks; the other listens. There is an old cliché that is very true. "If husband and wife are identical, one of them is unnecessary."

Normal Situations

Unfortunately, in any relationship, a balance is hard to reach. Usually one personality will overwhelm the other, and a marriage will take on a one-sided tilt. More often than not, where finances are concerned, the husband makes all of the decisions, although in some families the wife takes on this responsibility.

The lack of training in such a fundamental and critical area of marriage is bad enough, but combined with little or no communication it can be disastrous. If a couple knows how to communicate, the natural balance will often keep them out of financial trouble. Most women have a decided fear of being in debt and will normally exercise restraint. If they find themselves in financial trouble, they will quickly seek help and do what is necessary to correct the situation. In general, that is not so with men. The majority of serious debts are the result of the husband's spending, and either his indifference, pride, or eternal optimism keeps him from seeking help initially.

It must be remembered that few families desire or plan financial problems. Most occur because of poor training, poor communications, and a childhood of conditioned desires. Too often, parents don't teach their children that their life-style was earned by many years of effort and usually started with several years of sacrifice. Equipped with a value system learned in a generally affluent home and a handful of credit cards, most young couples set out to duplicate or improve upon their parents' success. The result in the majority of marriages today is disaster.

Turning It Around

The first step in turnaround is to recognize that different is not inferior. God put different gifts and abilities in the marriage, and it takes two people working as one to succeed in the home. Since men are often guilty of excluding their wives from financial decisions, a concerted effort must be made to use her gifts and abilities as a counselor. Wives should remember that a counselor does not scream, cry, or throw temper tantrums. Honesty between partners is an absolute necessity. Almost anyone can handle a situation if he knows about it and is a part of the planning. It's the deceptions that later show up as crises that create distrust.

Get help. If the problems and the communication gap are very intense, most couples will need outside help to get on the right track. Seeking counsel for marriage or financial problems should be as normal as seeking medical counsel. God has established various gifts and abilities throughout His kingdom, and unless couples are free to use them, someone's ministry goes wanting. "Without consultation, plans are frustrated, but with many counselors they succeed" (Proverbs 15:22).

Many couples have been through the very same crises that others are now facing and have found God's solutions. Those couples must be willing to share their experiences so that others in the midst of problems will know to whom to turn for help. There will never be enough professional counselors to do the job. It is the function of the body of Christians to minister to others within the body as the need arises.

Set specific goals. In order to establish the right relationship about finances in the home, husband and wife together must establish specific goals. The first must obviously be to solve financial problems if there are any.

Any couple that has not done so previously should plan a weekend alone together where every aspect of the family's finances can be discussed and some specific goals agreed upon. Remember that any financial planning involves two people's seeking mutually compatible goals under the umbrella of God's plan for their lives. No one will ever understand God's plan better than those who are to live it. Two people operating as one with unity of mind will find God's plan. "I love those who love me; and those who diligently seek me will find me" (Proverbs 8:17).

Quite often a reasonable compromise will be necessary when establishing goals. One may be more committed to giving than the other; a home may be more important to one, while a bass boat seems like a basic necessity to the other. The first and most important aspect is to discern God's overall plan and then adjust as necessary to make it work. One method is for both spouses to find the answers they can agree upon first, write them down, and pray about them before moving on to more controversial areas. When an impasse is reached over any area, such as food, clothing, or education, each should list five positions from his best to worst. Then each should discard their first and last and find one of the other three they can agree upon.

Financial Responsibilities

Problems. If problems exist, the husband must assume the burden of direct control. He is to act as a buffer for his wife. That doesn't mean that the wife is not involved, but that he is the visible interface. One of the great causes of fear in most women, and ultimately strife in the marriage, is creditor pressure. The wife's responsibility becomes one of assisting and implementing the necessary financial controls, not frantically worrying about them. Quite often, the husband is concerned that his wife cannot make the adjustments to reduce spending. Usually, I have found the opposite to be true. If a husband will provide the direction and submit to the same controls, his wife will adjust as necessary. Communication and planning are the keys to success. It's a matter of determining where you are financially, having a plan that is fair to both, and talking about it calmly. "With all humility and gentleness, with patience, showing forbearance to one another in love" (Ephesians 4:2).

Bookkeeping. Assuming that there are no major financial problems, the task of recordkeeping should fall to the one better equipped to do it. Due to many factors, not the least of which are time and patience, the wife is often a better bookkeeper. If that is so and both agree, then she should maintain the records once a workable budget has been agreed upon. They should review the budget and discuss any problems on a regular basis.

Children's discipline. It is difficult, if not impossible, to establish financial discipline in children unless both parents agree upon the goals and enforce the rules consistently. Parents cannot wait until a situation arises to see if they agree. They must meet it with a unified front. The decisions should be based on the long-term goals of what is best for the children, not what necessarily pleases them. If a rule is established that the children must earn at least one-half of all entertainment money, and Mom slips them money without Dad's knowing about it, then they learn a double lesson: slothfulness pays, and authority can be manipulated. Eventually, an employer will correct that notion for them rather rudely. "The hand of the diligent will rule, but the slack hand will be put to forced labor" (Proverbs 12:24).

Developing Long-Range Goals

Nowhere is it more important to cement the husband-wife financial partnership than in the area of establishing long-range goals. Long-range goals are objective and measurable and give a couple the opportunity to communicate in a critical area. An excellent way to find out the long-range objectives of your spouse is simply to ask. Most women are excluded from long-range financial planning by their husbands, which is ridiculous because most women are excellent money managers.

Many men would be very shocked to discover that their wives actually manage their money better than they do. It is far better to include the wife, make her a primary consultant, and educate her on what she must ultimately know about finances. A side effect is that she will probably help keep her husband out of a great many unwise get-rich-quick schemes.

Remember—neither spouse is always right or always wrong. Balance is the key, and God provides it through both. "The mind of man plans his way, but the Lord directs his steps" (Proverbs 16:9).

47
Should Wives Work?

Few subjects in Christianity are more controversial than that of working wives. Many Christians feel that it is wrong for married women to be employed full-time outside the home because of the effect it has on their families, especially the children. However, it would seem the alternatives are few for most low-to-middle income families today. What are the alternatives for Christian families?

Social Opinion

It is commonly accepted in our generation that the cost of maintaining and operating a home requires that both spouses work in most families. On the surface, that is true. It doesn't take much arithmetic to determine that the costs of new homes, cars, food, and clothing are beyond the income ability of the average family. Currently, the payments on the average new home would require nearly 70 percent of the average husband's pay. The logical conclusion, then, is that two incomes are needed. The fault with that logic is that it doesn't consider whether or not the average family needs the average home.

Pressures

More and more married women are beginning to accept the pressures of a job as normal. That is unfortunate because wives provide a good family balance for their husbands, who have a tendency to work too much and too long. If wives begin to adjust similarly, then ultimately the family will suffer.

Most men seek employment in their primary skill area, such as administration, mechanics, bookkeeping, and so on. However, that skill is rarely applied at home because the fatigue of the daily tasks necessitates a change to unwind. Since many women are the primary teachers, trainers, organizers, and planners in the home, these attributes may be lost to their families if they are fatigued by a daily work routine.

Current Social Situation

The violation of basic biblical principles will result in basic biblical consequences. There are many direct and indirect consequences of women being pushed into the role of wage earners; not the least of these would appear to be the increasing divorce rate. Financial problems are listed as the number one source of marital problems in divorces. If two incomes would relieve this condition, then we should see fewer divorces. Just the opposite is true.

Confused Loyalties

When wives shift their need for approval to their work, the problems are increased. There is often a mixed loyalty between the demands at work and at home. On one hand, a wife may sense a lack of closeness to her family as a result of the time spent away from home and the normal mental fatigue of work stress. On the other hand, she may recognize the need to dedicate even more time to the job in order to succeed.

Misplaced Priorities

Just as many Christian men abandon the important priorities—God and family—because they believe they must be a success "for their families," so many women now rationalize the same way. For example, in a counseling session the mother of two young children justified what she considered to be a perfectly logical position: "Certainly, I'm not able to be with my children as much as I would like, and I know that my husband really doesn't want me to work, but how could we ever buy a car or take a vacation if I didn't work?" In the future, many sixty-year-old women will look back as many sixty-year-old men now do and say, "I wish I had taken the time to be with my family when I had the chance."

Positive Balance

Because there are so many negative side effects of working wives, does that mean that it is scripturally wrong for wives to work? Not necessarily. Satan can use anything out of balance, and he usually does. The fact that many women choose to work outside the home is not the problem. The fact that so many women think they *have* to work to maintain the family's finances is the real problem. Wives do not have to work. The proof of that can be seen in the tens of thousands of wives who do not work but still get along very well.

For those women who are involuntary heads of households, we, as Christians, must stand guilty before God for failing our responsibility to provide them an option.

Biblical Priorities

1. *Desire.* Nowhere in God's Word is there an admonition for wives not to work outside the home. But the lack of a prohibition does not automatically confer acceptability. There are no admonitions against holding one's head in a bucket of water, but there are logical consequences that should be avoided. The first priority of a working wife is a desire to work on her part. When a wife is compelled to work by design or circumstance, resentment will often develop. "A joyful heart makes a cheerful face, but when the heart is sad, the spirit is broken" (Proverbs 15:13).

2. *Husband's approval.* Many working wives are able to gain a tacit approval by pressuring their husbands. Although many husbands do not actually agree with their wives' working, they relent under an emotional assault called nagging. "It is better to live in a desert land, than with a contentious and vexing woman" (Proverbs 21:19). This is not the approval that a wife seeks or requires, because it will eventually undermine the marriage relationship.

3. *Disciplined children.* The role of the mother as the teacher of her children is incontestable. The father usually provides the policy decisions, but it is the wife who establishes discipline and direction day by day. The success or failure of children as individuals will, in great part, depend on her success or failure as their guide. "She looks well to the ways of her household, and does not eat the bread of idleness. Her children rise up and bless her; her husband also, and he praises her" (Proverbs 31:27–28*a*).

In our society today, we have arbitrarily determined that a child is prepared for outside contact and discipline at six years of age. That may or may not be true, and all parents must make their own decisions about how long parental supervision is necessary. The certainty is that with the current attitude of laxness in society, *more* direct input from the mother is needed, not less. The greater the trend grows toward women's fulfilling their emotional needs outside the home, the more rebellious and undisciplined their children become.

4. *Confused authority.* The next consideration is less measurable but just as vital: can a Christian wife, who is also an employee, handle the responsibilities of having two direct authorities? God's Word establishes the husband as the head of the household (1 Corinthians 11:3; Ephesians 5:23). For the working wife, the loyalties between job and family may get confused, and she may be duped into a feeling of independence that is actually rebellion. "The wise woman builds her house, but the foolish tears it down with her own hands" (Proverbs 14:1). If a wife senses this happening, she would be well advised to forego some financial flexibility to preserve her family relationship. In other words: quit.

Financial Dangers

Need to work. There is rarely an actual need for a wife to work outside the home. It may seem so because of the standard of living the family has chosen or because of past habits, but more money made just means more money to spend. Some very specific goals should be established for the wife's income, or additional debt will result. At least once a year every working couple should re-evaluate their goals and objectives, particularly the purpose of the wife's income. A young couple would be well advised not to merge the wife's income into their budget. To do so invites future disaster in the event of children, illness, or the husband's job change. They should learn to live on the husband's income and use the wife's for one-time purchases, such as a car, furniture, down payment on a home—on a cash basis only.

Comfort and convenience. Even if the wife's income is used for extra comforts such as new cars, vacations, and private school, there must be a continual self-analysis to determine if these things have become necessities. "Let your character be free from the love of money, being content with what you have; for He Himself has said, 'I will never desert you, nor will I ever forsake you'" (Hebrews 13:5).

Husband's needs. Many women are duped by society into believing that they must establish a "separate but equal" relationship, and to do so they must be working. The effect has been to undermine the husband's position as the leader and protector of his family. Naturally, no woman wants to be a slave, nor does God's Word support any such attitude. God's Word describes the wife's role as that of equal spiritually and dependent materially (1 Peter 3:1–7). A husband's needs can best be met by a wife who trusts him totally and will yield her human rights to him (Proverbs 31:10–12). The husband, likewise, is commanded to love her, care for her needs, treat her as his own body, and accept the responsibility for the family (Ephesians 5:25;1 Timothy 5:8; Ephesians 5:28). To best meet the needs of her husband, a wife must become his helpmate—supporter and companion. If working does not interfere with that role, then great. But if it does, then the marriage priority comes first.

48
Financial Authority in the Home

THE LACK OF godly leadership in the home can be devastating to a family. Women are experiencing pressures as never before because they are carrying burdens God never intended they have. Why? Because many men are abandoning their leadership responsibilities. Regardless of what psychologists say, God has not made a woman to function well under stress, particularly financial stress. The result of husbands' subjecting their mates to such stress can be seen in every community counseling center.

I am frequently confronted with women who have assumed the responsibility of negotiating with creditors, keeping the bills paid, disciplining the children, and maintaining a home. More often than not, it is because their husbands will not accept the responsibility.

That is not to say all men are irresponsible. Fortunately, most are very responsible. However, with the current social trend towards "equality," more and more men are encouraged to ignore their God-ordained responsibilities in order to find peer approval.

Many woman who assume the leadership role in the home find they have destroyed their health, their peace, and their marriage. "The wise woman builds her house, but the foolish tears it down with her own hands" (Proverbs 14:1).

In a counseling session a young wife commented, "I have to control all the money in our home. My husband doesn't know how to handle it, so I took over."

There was little doubt that she dominated the family, including the finances, and even less doubt that she had reduced her husband's authority in the family to approximately that of a child, She justified her action on the basis that it was "necessary." However, the net result of her takeover was emotional and physical stress and nearly a total breakdown in marriage communications.

Almost the exact opposite situation had occurred earlier with another couple. The husband felt so strongly about his role as the authority in the home that he refused to allow his wife to participate in financial decisions. Since he continually made decisions without consulting her, she naturally felt he neither trusted nor respected her. Over their married years, she had withdrawn into a shell of quiet resentment.

Balance

Both situations reflect that God's plan for authority in the home is not an either/or situation. It is a joint effort with differing responsibilities.

In any relationship as intimate as marriage, there must be a sharing of responsibilities and abilities. God often uses opposites in a marriage to balance the extremes. If husband and wife are identical in nature, undoubtedly the decisions will be unbalanced. Thus, a spender is balanced by a saver. A sensitive, discerning wife is a great asset to any husband, providing that he's willing to listen to her. "A prudent wife is from the Lord" (Proverbs 19:14*b*).

The management of the household, hence the burden, rests on the husband. "He must be one who manages his own household well, keeping his children under control with all dignity (but if a man does not know how to manage his own household, how will he take care of the church of God?)" (1 Timothy 3:4-5).

The wife's responsibility is to support her husband by following his direction—as opposed to nagging and pushing. Sometimes she must be willing to suffer with him and to let him fail if necessary: "In the same way, you wives, be submissive to your own husbands so that even if any of them are disobedient to the word, they may be won without a word by the behavior of their wives" (1 Peter 3:1).

Shared Responsibilities

For a wife to be submissive does not mean to be silent. She must take an active role in financial planning. The best way to do that is for a couple to dedicate one full day a year to doing some planning together. The place to start is deciding how their income will be allocated.

1. *Yearly budget.* Together husband and wife should establish a budget for everything to be spent during the year. Every item on the budget should be discussed thoroughly and prayerfully. The primary consideration should be to develop a fair, but reasonable, plan for family spending. I would recommend *The Financial Planning Workbook* as an excellent guide.

2. *Windfall plan.* In addition to the budget, which controls normal income, a family should agree beforehand on the disposition of additional income (gifts, overtime, and so on). The plan should be fair and equal for all concerned. The spending of extra income often frustrates the wife because her wants are ignored. Remember that a marriage is a true partnership, and partners share in all things, both profits and losses.

Without a doubt, one of the greatest potential sources of conflict is a "his money, her money" attitude. This is true with earned income and windfall income, such as inheritance. The minute a husband or wife attempts to segregate finances, the message is clearly communicated: "I don't trust you." For a husband or wife to reserve assets from a previous marriage or inheritance is to allow Satan to drive a wedge between two who are supposed to be one.

3. *Long-range plan.* Few women are involved in long-range financial planning. However, it is a statistical fact that more women will live to fulfill long-range goals than men. It's also a fact that many women don't want the bother of discussing things like business goals, wills and trusts, or investments. As a result, these plans lack the balance that God built into the marriage partnership. Planning is not an option, because if you wait long enough, they will become short-range plans with no alternatives available. "For which one of you, when he wants to build a tower, does not first sit down and calculate the cost, to see if he has enough to complete it?" (Luke 14:28).

What It Means to Share

Assuming there are no unresolved financial problems and a budget has been established that is fair and reasonable, there remains the decision of who keeps the books. There is no doubt that many wives are better at keeping financial records than their husbands. They usually have more time, patience, and motivation. There is no scriptural reason that the wife should not be the family bookkeeper, assuming that to do so is not an effort to take over. In fact, it's important for the wife to understand how to manage finances. Many widows are forced to make important financial decisions with little or no experience, and the results are often disastrous.

There should be a regular time set aside each month for husband, wife, and children to review the current status of the budget and make any necessary adjustments. During these sessions, problems should be discussed and resolved jointly. Obviously, in families where the finances are tight and there are existing debts, the tendency is to argue over finances. Couples must assess this realistically and calmly and determine if they need counseling help. Sometimes in Christianity counseling is viewed as the last step and, therefore, has an emotional stigma. That is absolutely false. God's Word says that counsel is a sign of wisdom (Proverbs 12:15; 13:20; 14:15; 15:22).

Women as Heads of Households

There are instances in which a woman is forced to become the head of a household as a result of divorce, her husband's death, or other reasons. In these instances, she has no choice but to assume an authoritative position.

A woman in this position should realize that, within the Body of Christ, God has provided the leadership she needs. The local fellowship she attends should be used as a source for counsel in establishing financial plans. Two things are important in this respect: Christian widows must be willing to let their needs for financial counsel be known, and the local church must equip itself to do this counseling under the control and direction of the church leadership. That will effectively eliminate any "fleecing of the flock."

49

The Wife's Role in Business

I WOULD VENTURE to say that in most businesses today the wife's role is nearly zero. It may well be that in the early stages of developing a business she was involved, but as the business grew and prospered, that involvement was lessened or eliminated. Through the intervening years, most wives become involved with raising the children and maintaining the home, while the husband builds a business. In itself that is not wrong, provided that the wife stays actively involved in the decision making and direction of the business. Unfortunately few do, and later in life when she would like to be more active again, it's nearly impossible.

Correcting an Imbalance

When women are not included in the decision-making process, a real imbalance can occur in a business. If, as Christians, we believe that God provides helpmates with strengths that offset our weaknesses, then not to include them ultimately causes great imbalances. Of course, many men refuse to take counsel from their wives. That is usually a product of training and observation in their homes as youths; but it is also a by-product of something called *pride.* Most men, particularly those who control others, want to be independent, to be able to make the snap decisions that usually result in disaster. That is not to say that, merely by including his wife in routine business decisions, all errors are eliminated. But without hesitation I can say that most of the problems I have observed in Christian-owned businesses would have been lessened or avoided if the men had been willing to seek the counsel of their wives before making major decisions, particularly those involving large amounts of borrowing.

Why didn't they? Because they knew they would not be able to rationally convince their wives that such risks were appropriate. So, instead, they sought the counsel of men of like mind who assured them that they knew at least one other "gambler" who had done the same thing and had got away with it.

"House and wealth are an inheritance from fathers, but a prudent wife is from the Lord" (Proverbs 19:14).

It may sound like I'm coming down too hard on men in business, but I believe it cannot be stated too strongly: when a man and wife are joined in marriage, they are no longer two—they're one. "For this cause a man shall leave his father and his mother, and shall cleave to his wife; and they shall become one flesh" (Genesis 2:24). Therefore, each brings a necessary part of God's wisdom to every decision.

Exclusion of the Wife

What commonly happens in our generation is that, as the business either prospers or fails, the wife is the last to be consulted. In our past agrarian society both husband and wife were acutely aware of how they were doing financially. Usually, the man plowed and planted while his wife managed the home; but come harvest time everybody got involved. Consequently, she knew about as much as did her husband on a year-by-year basis. Today, many men build successful businesses only to find that they have little in common with their wives of many years and eventually divorce when the children are grown. All too often the catalyst is a younger woman in the office who seems to be all the things that the wife is not. Few Christian men would ever actively solicit such a volatile situation, but one-sided decisions often allow such situations to develop.

The other extreme is that news of a failing business is kept from the wife until the collapse is imminent. Obviously, most women realize when a business is in trouble but are usually not aware of the extent of the crisis. The result is often conflict and deep hurt when she realizes that even the office staff knows more about the difficulties than she does.

Helpmate

By observation it would appear that most couples practice only extremes in business involvement: total or none-at-all. That means that the wife is either immersed in the day-to-day operation of the business or is totally isolated from any meaningful input. It is not necessary to go to either extreme. A wife can become a vital factor in decision making without functioning as a part of the daily office routine, but only if she is knowledgeable and informed. In reality, the wives who are actively involved in the office constitute only about 10 percent or less of the total; the other 90 percent represent the norm today. They are to be helpmates.

In Proverbs 31, an excellent wife is described. Above all others, her husband respects her counsel because she "fears the Lord," and fear of the Lord is a sign of great wisdom. A wife should be her husband's primary counselor. She provides balance to his decisions that can be provided by no one else. A husband who never, or seldom, accepts this counsel has not honored his wife, and, according to 1 Peter 3:7, his prayers will be hindered.

That does not mean that a wife's counsel is always right and must be followed to the exclusion of all else. But it does mean that it should be considered and weighed as the highest priority.

In a recent counseling session a businessman asked if I felt it was all right for him to borrow against their home to expand the business. My response was to ask him if he had asked his wife how she felt about it. No further discussion on that particular issue was necessary. Inside, he knew it was a bad idea, and he also knew that his wife would say so. In discussing it, his wife did say she thought it was a bad idea, but she also said she would support whatever decision he made. He was shocked. He discovered at that point that he had a counselor who was willing to give advice, leave the results to God, and share the outcome. He decided not to borrow the money.

To the wives I would give this counsel: don't allow yourselves to be ignorant of your spouse's business. Don't demand though—ask. As a counselor, you must be willing to give advice, offer alternatives, and leave the results to God. If your advice is sound, you won't have to continually remind your husband about it; he'll know. "The wise woman builds her house, but the foolish tears it down with her own hands" (Proverbs 14:1).

Accountability

I believe one of the least taught principles in Christianity is accountability. That means being responsible for our actions. Many businessmen are not held accountable for their time, money, or attitudes today because they report to no one.

Throughout God's Word are directions that we hold each other accountable. "And if your brother sins, go and reprove him in private; if he listens to you, you have won your brother" (Matthew 18:15).

The more knowledgeable someone is of our routine the more accountable we become. That's why a great many businessmen do not want anyone to know too much about what they do, lest they become accountable according to God's standard. A Christian who is truly seeking to serve God will find that, next to the Lord, his wife provides the maximum accountability. After living in the same home with their husbands, most wives do not miss even a small thing. For instance, don't just ask your wife to sign the joint tax return each year; explain how that tax shelter is really questionable if the I. R. S. checks. See if she has a peace from the Lord about it, too.

If husbands can get to a point where they are willing to share every major decision with their wives, they will have made themselves accountable. Since we are all accountable before the Lord, this will save a lot of grief later.

Wives must be able to accept their responsibilities to give counsel and not decisions. If your feelings are easily hurt, you'll probably be excluded from most decisions by your husband just to avoid the grief. I have often found myself delaying asking my wife's advice when I know I've gone further than I should have into a decision, for fear I'll hurt her feelings. The more I find I can trust her reactions to be under God's control, the more liberty I feel to share a decision. Sometimes I sense that she is avoiding telling me how she feels because she knows it's not what I want to hear. I then remind her of Philippians 2—we must be of the "same mind" for God to bless us. If she shares what she believes is God's wisdom and I don't listen, than I am accountable. But if she agrees with a decision, believing it to be wrong, then she's accountable.

How to Get Started

First and foremost, don't get discouraged. You may be one of those fortunate couples who discuss everything, but if you fall in the other 90 percent category, it will require a re-education. Make a commitment to make Christ the center of your marriage. If you do, then making decisions together is a fundamental part of your marriage and business. Even if the wife doesn't want to be involved, she must be in order to reach God's balance. Remember this as an incentive: wives outlive their husbands more than 80 percent of the time. Ultimately, she will be the decision-maker.

Set aside a regular time to discuss current events in the business and any pending redirections or problems. If you find you can't discuss things rationally right now, then write them out. I have found with many couples, when emotions flare and old hurts are dredged up, that having the wife write out her counsel helps considerably. If a major decision is pending, schedule time together to discuss it. Don't get sidetracked by feelings and neglect God's promise that "where two or three have gathered together in My name, there I am in their midst" (Matthew 18:20).

To the husband I would say that the commitment to begin involving your wife is up to you. If you don't want to make that commitment, then be honest with God about not desiring His best in your life. To the wife I would say that to the degree you are able to put aside old hurts and let God be the enforcer of your "rights," this plan will work. Be a counselor and a comforter, not a fault-finder. "Nevertheless let each individual among you also love his own wife even as himself; and let the wife see to it that she respect her husband" (Ephesians 5:33).

50
Disciplining Children

ONE OF THE most neglected areas in most families has to be teaching children financial discipline. Even in families where Bible study and prayer is an established way of life, finances are rarely, if ever, discussed. Is it any wonder then that so many young couples suffer because of financial mismanagement? Where are our children to learn good financial principles if not from us? "Train up a child in the way he should go, even when he is old he will not depart from it" (Proverbs 22:6).

The financial pressure placed upon young adults is impossible to resist unless they have been armed with an unshakeable source of strength—God's Word. In most schools today, a consumer economics class consists primarily of teaching them how to make out credit applications. The logic is simple—since "everybody" is going to need credit, we should concentrate on the best methods to obtain it. Whatever happened to the old principle of "if you can't afford it, don't buy it"? Whose responsibility is it to teach children the rules of self-discipline? Obviously, it is the parents'.

Self-Discipline

The place to start is with the parents. It will do no good to teach financial discipline to children until the principles are active in the parents' lives. Kids have an instinct for detecting insincerity, and the old adage "Don't do what I do, do what I say" doesn't work.

A husband and wife who don't communicate about financial goals will not be able to convince their children that they have anything worthwhile to say, either. It is important that adults develop self-discipline and use it. If parents continually buy luxuries on impulse, the children will come to expect the same privileges.

Parents who have not learned the discipline of balancing a checkbook should not be surprised to find that their children are sloppy in other areas of their lives.

Parents must set examples for their children. Unfortunately, it seems that kids are much quicker at mimicking bad habits than good ones. Why? Because being slothful and undisciplined requires less effort. Children, like most others, will usually seek the path of least resistance. Therefore, the authority must establish a positive, balanced example.

Child Discipline

"The rod and reproof give wisdom, but a child who gets his own way brings shame to his mother" (Proverbs 29:15). If too much discipline is harmful, too little is disastrous. The evidence of too little financial discipline with children can be seen in the number of sixteen-year-olds driving new, high-powered cars and the millions of dollars wasted on rock concerts and trash movies. Every time I see a teenager whip out a credit card to buy gas, I wonder if he can really be expected to understand the principle of "owe no man."

Minimum Standards

The principle behind establishing minimum standards is honoring parents. Tasks should be assigned with age and ability in mind. A child who makes a mess and leaves it for another to clean up or who drops clothes where they are removed does not show honor to his mother. Left to grow and mature, that dishonor will come out later in verbal abuse and disregard for the parents' feelings. "A foolish son is grief to his father, and bitterness to her who bore him" (Proverbs 17:25).

The best rewards for these jobs are verbal praise and privileges. For younger children a visual chart with smiling faces or stars works well.

The punishment for noncompliance should be determined by the age of the child and the frequency of violation. Recently I shared that principle with the parents of a totally undisciplined teenager. The mother said, "It won't work because our son really doesn't have an interest in anything." That turned out not to be true. He had a great interest in his car and his girl friend. However, his parents used him to pick up and deliver their other children, and his girl friend was their best babysitter. They were not willing to sacrifice themselves to discipline him.

Discipline—Fairness—Rewards

If you make rules, enforce them. That is sometimes difficult for parents, but discipline must be firm to be effective. Don't do the task yourself to avoid a confrontation. Be sure you are not expecting more than the child is capable of achieving. If the guidelines established include punishment, and they are violated, then punish. Remember that the value system you are trying to establish develops in their early years and must last their entire lives.

A simple rule of thumb in being fair with children is to remember that God is to the parents as the parents are to the children. Don't ever establish a harsher set of disciplines upon your children than you would like God to put upon you. God does not expect us to be Spirit-controlled, mature Christians immediately upon salvation. To expect too much would only discourage us and drive us away from God. Apply the same loving patience with your children.

In addition to having rules and punishment, parents should develop a reward system. Just as God rewards us for our work and obedience, we should reward our children. To live in a home where everything is rules and punishment is not very conducive to spiritual growth. Parents who operate this way are actually selfish. They want everything their way, and children are considered an irritation rather than a blessing.

Children who are not old enough to work outside the home should have ways to earn extra money within the family. These jobs can range from actual work tasks, such as washing the car or mowing the lawn, to special projects, such as a Bible study or memorizing Scripture. The tasks should be oriented to the abilities of each child.

Where to Start

Decisions about developing financial discipline in children must be made by both husband and wife. Start with a conference on family goals. Set aside a weekend and place where you can be alone. Be willing to compromise on the areas where you disagree. It's the compromise that will balance the extremes. The next step is a family session where the children can input their ideas and objections. Show them your willingness to compromise without losing sight that your goal is to teach God's financial principles. Be sure the plan covers the following:

Savings. Savings should be tied to a future event or purchase, such as a bike or a summer trip. That allows the results of the savings to be seen and enjoyed.

Budget. From the earliest stage of a child's earned income he should be on a budget. In a very young child, the budget may just consist of a portion given to God and the rest rationed out for a week. By adolescence, the money is divided into normal categories, such as tithe, clothes, entertainment, college, and so on. By the teenage years, the budget should include a checking and savings account and the associated bookkeeping. By graduation, parents should have full confidence that their children can function in a paper-money society without borrowing to exist.

Tithe. Encourage, do not demand, tithing. Explain that giving is a blessing and a demonstration of surrender to God's authority. If possible, arrange for them to see the end use of the money they give. If possible, have the church give the money to a specific family or missionary and help them communicate with the recipient. Difficult? Yes. But rewarding? Yes—for a lifetime.

Borrowing. The vast majority of people will borrow money during their adult lives. Parents can teach their children the realities of debt by allowing them to borrow according to a rigid repayment plan with interest. The purpose is to demonstrate the realities of borrowing money. Remember that if you don't do this, eventually a creditor will. "The rich rules over the poor, and the borrower becomes the lender's slave" (Proverbs 22:7).

Desires. Balance the discipline with love. God says that if we delight ourselves in Him, He will provide our heart's desires. As your children delight in you—honor and obey—be willing to bless them accordingly. That will demonstrate that your discipline is truly an act of obedience to God's Word.

51

Financial Discipline in Children

THERE ARE FEW events more uplifting for parents than to see their children develop into mature, disciplined adults. Conversely, there is nothing more frustrating and defeating than to see a son or daughter with great potential suffer and fail because of a lack of self-discipline. Many parents suffer additional grief because, seemingly without warning, their children get caught up in drugs or sex. Most outward signs are but symptoms of inner problems, and if the symptoms are not recognized and corrected, the problems persist and become more severe. Some symptoms are detectable at an early age and can be used as measures of spiritual problems. One of these early signs or symptoms is finances.

God's Word tells us that the way someone handles finances is a clear indication of whether or not he can handle greater things (Luke 16:19–11). That principle applies not only to adults but to children as well. Long before greater problems arise, parents can detect weaknesses that need to be dealt with by observing how their children handle money. (Obviously, money is not the sole indicator but should be used in conjunction with other signs.)

Personality Traits

Each child is a unique individual and is capable of exercising a free will. No amount of parental guidance or threats will change that. The mold has been made by God; parents are used by God to fill in the cracks. Nearly all parents find that each child is uniquely different about everything. One will be frugal, disciplined, and willing to accept directions about sharing, saving, and budgeting. Generally, these same characteristics will be found in other areas, such as school and work habits. Another child will spend nearly every penny available, borrow when possible, and defy all attempts at financial discipline. That attitude will also be observable in other areas, such as sloppiness, poor study habits, and disrespect.

Discipline vs. Desires

Scripture teaches that the relationship between God and parent is the same as between parents and children (Luke 11:11–13). God promises us the desires of our hearts (Psalms 37:4). But before we can achieve those desires, we must make His way our way (Psalm 37:5; Proverbs 3:6; Matthew 6:33). Just giving with no controls is not beneficial. You must be certain that their hearts are committed to God's way. Giving them the desires of *their* hearts will simply spoil them and develop greedy attitudes. A parent must help a child recognize that special gifts are rewards for correct attitudes (Proverbs 3:9–10; 8:21). Many parents give out of guilt or in hope that somehow they can bribe a child into being better. To do so does *not* help. It reinforces bad internal attitudes.

Short-Term Peace/Long-Term Prosperity

Often parents yield to the weaknesses of an undisciplined child to obtain some short-term peace. A disciplined child of any age expects very little and rarely demands anything, but an undisciplined child *forcefully* demands more and is rarely satisfied. Why? Possessions have little lasting value, and more is always required to satisfy. A parent must accept the responsibility of withholding in the short run in order for discipline to be ingrained in the long run. "The rod and reproof give wisdom, but a child who gets his own way brings shame to his mother" (Proverbs 29:15).

Visible Signs of Problems

Most young children like to spend their available money. A few are self-disciplined and save for future needs with little or no encouragement. When you have one of these, just praise the Lord and help him to reach a good balance between hoarding and spending. A large number of children will spend if allowed or will save if required. Parents who establish early, routine discipline will achieve good results with these children if they are consistent. At the other end of the spectrum are those children who must spend everything they have quickly and often foolishly. Any attempt at control is usually met by resentment and, where allowed, blatant disobedience. These are outward, visible symptoms of much greater spiritual problems. A parent of such a child would be well advised to pay careful attention to other indicators of rebellion and insecurity.

These attitudes are correctable by parents if handled at an early age. However, it may well require a sacrifice. The biggest sacrifice will probably be short-range peace. A rebellious or simply strong-willed child is actually testing his boundaries. If the boundaries are movable, the child will push them back; if not, he will adjust to them.

Contrary to popular opinion, discipline does not retard a child's potential; it expands it. "Whoever loves discipline loves knowledge, but he who hates reproof is stupid" (Proverbs 12:1).

Short-Term Financial Goals

It is necessary for parents to establish some short-term goals for their children to help them see the purpose and logic of saving money. Initially, these goals should be very short-range, such as saving to buy a book, record, or game. Later the goals should be extended to cover things such as trips, vacations, and bicycles. It is also important to instill written goals. That means keeping a savings ledger and a written prayer goal. "There is precious treasure and oil in the dwelling of the wise, but a foolish man swallows it up" (Proverbs 21:20).

Your goals and standards for handling money must be both fair and consistent. Both husband and wife should agree and be willing to live by the same standards they set for their children. Parents who never live on a budget will find it very difficult to teach their children to do so. A parent who continually borrows for cars, clothes, and vacations will have a difficult time convincing a son not to finance a car because it might preclude his going to college.

Allowances

In addition to having rules and punishment, parents should develop a reward system. Just as God rewards us for our work and obedience, we should reward our children. One method to do that is through an allowance. However, the traditional allowance is not scriptural, because it is usually given without any restrictions or controls. An allowance should be given only as a reward for completing assigned tasks.

Giving

Giving should be established as an early discipline. Obviously, most young children won't fully understand why they are giving. But if a parent can help them see the *result* of their gifts, they will come to understand. An early habit of giving does not insure a commitment to the Lord, but an early habit of not giving usually instills a later attitude of not giving. "Train up a child in the way he should go, even when he is old he will not depart from it" (Proverbs 22:6).

Parental Loans

Should a parent lend money to a child? I believe so. After all, eventually someone else will, and credit is not the problem; the misuse of credit is. If you lend money, do so only for specific projects, preferably those that will generate income, such as buying a lawn mower, materials for car washing, and a bicycle for a paper route. The contract to repay should be in writing, and interest should be charged and collected. The purpose is to establish a discipline and repayment under the same conditions as a creditor would operate. If he doesn't pay, repossess the bicycle. "How blessed is the man who finds wisdom, and the man who gains understanding" (Proverbs 3:13).

However, if you won't actually enforce the terms of your agreement, it would be better not to lend. Otherwise, you may be instilling an attitude of indifference toward debts. Remember in enforcing your rules that debt is the number-one symptom that most often leads to divorce. If you love your children, you must teach them that all borrowing is potentially disastrous and should be used sparingly and wisely.

Vocational Goals

No one is in a better position to give direction on vocational goals than you, as a parent. You will live with that child from birth through adulthood and should know his interests, desires, and personality. Therefore, it is important that, as basic abilities and desires become apparent, some vocational direction be suggested. It may not be possible to select the exact vocation, but it is possible to eliminate the wrong vocations. For instance, a parent will recognize whether or not a child is mechanically inclined, is outgoing, has a strong desire to serve, and so on. Early goal setting in this area will go a long way toward eliminating insecurities and frustration later in life. "A plan in the heart of a man is like deep water, but a man of understanding draws it out" (Proverbs 20:5).

Summary

The way anyone handles money is a visible indication of an inner spiritual condition. An observant parent can use this indicator to discern the inner needs of a child. At best, being a Christian parent is a learned rather than a taught skill, but by detecting character flaws early and applying consistent, loving, godly discipline, many deeper problems can be avoided. Use your child's attitudes toward money as a reliable indicator of later character. Fill in the mold according to God's plan rather than the world's. "And, fathers, do not provoke your children to anger; but bring them up in the discipline and instruction of the Lord" (Ephesians 6:4).

52
Symptoms of Financial Problems

WITHOUT QUESTION, FAMILY financial problems seem to increase dramatically during an economic slump. Why do families experience more problems during economic down-turns? The truth is they *don't*. They suffer more symptoms. The symptom may be unpaid bills, and the consequence may be that their lights are turned off or their car is repossessed. But with rare exception, the problems that precipitated that began years earlier, perhaps even in childhood.

Many of the symptoms we see so abundantly today—business failures, massive bankruptcies, divorce, and two-job families—stem back to the same basic problem of ignoring God's Word and His warnings. "Now it shall be, if you will diligently obey the Lord your God, being careful to do all His commandments which I command you today, the Lord your God will set you high above all the nations of the earth" (Deuteronomy 28:1).

God's instructions are neither complicated nor harsh. In fact, they are designed to free us, not bind us to a set of rigid dos and don'ts. The difficulty is that most American families have been duped into a life of "get rich quick" that includes the way we buy homes, cars, clothes, and food. God's principles in the area of finances have been largely ignored for the last forty years, and now we are reaping what has been sown.

I read an article in a business magazine that vividly brought this into focus. It seems that the largest mail order seed company in the country decided to go out of business, despite the fact that sales were higher than ever. Unfortunately, so were nonpayments by their mail order sales force. For nearly fifty years, the company had been supplying seeds to children who would sell them door-to-door, mostly in rural communities, to raise money. In recent years, the nonpayment rate to the company had risen steadily, until in 1981, it reached 70 percent. The average age of these delinquent salesmen was ten years! The final straw came when the company attempted to contact the parents, hoping they would help in collection, only to discover that the parents actually encouraged the kids.

The symptom described is nonpayment of a just debt, but the problem runs much deeper. It involves basic values that parents fail to instill in their children. It's an attitude that my rights come before others. The lack of integrity in the parents is reflected and amplified in the lives of their children.

It's unfortunate that later these parents probably won't understand why irresponsible children become irresponsible adults. "A righteous man who walks in his integrity—how blessed are his sons after him" (Proverbs 20:7).

Early Symptoms

The symptoms seen today in family counseling are distressingly predictable. It seems obvious that the same basic errors in early family training are being made throughout our society. Before looking at the problems and solutions, it's necessary to identify the symptoms. Most young couples today come from middle-class families with nice homes, two cars each, color television sets, and a variety of credit sources used to purchase them. Their parents don't operate on a budget, and consequently the children aren't trained to do so either. The parents use credit readily and usually make buying decisions based on monthly payments rather than the initial price of the item. In more affluent families, the children are often provided with credit cards to buy clothes for themselves and gas for their cars. Many of these families dissolve over debt-related problems, but usually the children are buffered from the circumstances and never make the connection.

Once married and on their own, a young couple attempts to duplicate in three years what may have taken their parents twenty years to accumulate. The results are predictable. Within three years they have a lot of assets, but they're all tied up in liabilities. Many, if not most, experience the following symptoms:

Symptom 1: They can't pay the monthly bills. Once the maximum limits have been reached on credit cards and other readily available credit sources, the pressures begin to build. Creditors begin to harass, and each month it gets worse. Finally, in desperation, a bill consolidation loan is made. That lowers the overall monthly payments and stretches the debt out for a longer period of time. A resolution is made to avoid the credit trap, and the pressure is eased. Within a year the small debts return (the consolidation loan eats up all the available surplus), and the situation is worse than before.

Symptom 2: More income is needed. That conclusion seems logical at the time because they have already tried a consolidation loan, and more credit can't be the answer. So, usually the wife goes to work. If there are small children, the result is a break-even situation or less. But where no children are involved, the end result is more money in and more money spent. Usually, within a year or less, the bills are larger rather than smaller, and the pressures are even greater, because now the extra income is necessary.

Symptom 3: Can't stand the pressure? Buy something new. Usually by this time the financed car and washing machine are breaking down, the house is beginning to need some repairs, and marital pressures are reaching a boiling point. The logical thing to do seems to be to buy a new car or take a vacation to "get away from it all." Unfortunately, it always gets worse later. Now desperation sets in, and loans are solicited from family and friends.

Many well-meaning Christians get involved with a bail-out program at this point, thinking they're helping without realizing they're only dealing with the symptoms rather than the problems. "A man of great anger shall bear the penalty, for if you rescue him, you will only have to do it again" (Proverbs 19:19).

Symptom 4: Divorce or bankruptcy. Once the financial pressures build, the marital pressures build as well. It's difficult to have much communication when all you ever talk about are problems. The wife may feel insecure, and the husband may get very defensive. For a few families, bankruptcy seems to be the solution, so they liquidate the debts and begin again. Since credit is easy to come by, they have no difficulty in borrowing again, particularly since they can't go bankrupt again for several years. Within a short period of time many of these couples face the same symptoms that promoted the bankruptcy.

Those who elect divorce find that the same symptoms appear in their next marriage. Fortunately, out of a feeling of panic, many seek immediate help. Many don't, however, and eventually find second and third marriages ruined by the lack of a sound spiritual and financial foundation.

It's bad enough that these symptoms occur over and over again in the non-Christian community. If we Christians were truly living by sound biblical principles, our lives would be lights to attract those who so desperately need help. In fact, nobody really *wants* to lose a marriage, to go bankrupt, or to commit suicide. People do so because they have lost all hope. But even a greater crisis is that the same symptoms are occurring within Christian families and at about the same ratio. This crisis can be traced back to not teaching or applying the basic biblical principles God has established for us. Some principles are so fundamental it would seem all Christians would understand them. But unfortunately, they don't.

Early Attitudes

1. *Borrowing.* "The wicked borrows and does not pay back, but the righteous is gracious and gives" (Psalm 37:21).

Scripture clearly indicates that borrowing is not normal to God's plan and was never intended to be used as a routine part of our financial planning. Logically, it should be limited to appreciating assets, but Scripture does not say to borrow only for appreciating assets. It says, "Repay what is owed." Children should be encouraged to save for needs, not borrow to get them. Parental examples of trusting God to provide without borrowing are woefully lacking today.

2. *Saving.* "There is precious treasure and oil in the dwelling of the wise, but a foolish man swallows it up" (Proverbs 21:20).

In our upside-down inflationary economy, spending and borrowing are promoted as logical, and saving is discouraged. But let me assure you that those who borrow and spend always look for a saver in time of crises. Children should be taught that it is sounder, biblically *and* financially, to save for future needs than to rely on creditors. It's a sad indictment of how far we have strayed from God's truth when the average sixty-five-year-old man today has accumulated less than $100 in free and clear assets.

3. *Hasty decisions.* "The plans of the diligent lead surely to advantage, but every one who is hasty comes surely to poverty" (Proverbs 21:5).

Patience and consistency, rather than quick decisions and instant success, are the ways to financial security. Children should clearly understand that a firm financial foundation is built by taking small steps over a long period of time. They should also remember that God's plan is not the same for everyone. Children are not promised automatic affluence just because their parents have it. One of the best disciplines a parent can teach a child is to allow him to work to reach a goal. Too often everything is given without effort, and that can easily develop into a lifetime habit.

4. *Budget.* "Poverty and shame will come to him who neglects discipline, but he who regards reproof will be honored" (Proverbs 13:18).

Every one of our children should learn to live on a reasonable budget themselves. There is no greater financial asset that parents can leave their children than the knowledge of how to establish and live on a balanced budget. Overspending should be so discouraged in Christian homes that children wouldn't even consider it a possibility in their own homes later. Remember, at best the tug of worldly ways will tempt them down the wrong paths. At worst, our lack of training will send them down those paths without a way back.

How to Help

Obviously many more principles needed to steer our families and friends down the right path to God's plan are found in God's Word. I would encourage every couple to start a study of God's financial principles and begin to implement them in their own lives.

Once you have applied God's principles in your own lives, begin a Bible study in your church or home, and share what you've learned with others. Help your church establish a regular teaching program on biblical finances and a counseling program to help families that have symptoms already. Every pastor's premarital counseling program should include a course on biblical principles of finance and a course on budgeting in which the couple actually establish their first year's budget.

53
Choosing the Right Vocation

A SURVEY IN *Business Week* magazine reported that only one out of six Americans is content with his job. That means nearly 83 percent are dissatisfied.

The most consistent complaint was a lack of fulfillment or long-term purpose. That is not surprising when you consider that the five most common factors expected by job seekers today are:

1. Long-term security
2. Advancement potential
3. Vacation and sick benefits
4. Pay (including automatic raises)
5. Limited authority over their work

The vast majority of Americans apparently believe a job should guarantee security against unseen perils. To accomplish that, they demand no-cut, no-layoff contracts, high-cost retirement plans, seniority rights, and new federal laws.

Certainly, many Christians also fall within this larger group of dissatisfied, fearful workers. Why? Because their value system has been altered by worldly standards to a great degree. Even within Christian schools and colleges, little or no attention is given to vocational planning on a spiritual rather than a material basis.

Well over half of the seniors in college have no specific vocation in mind. Why have they spent four years and thousands of dollars without actually finding a direction? Probably because they thought that somehow the system would settle that decision for them and also because parents consistently tell their children to "think of the future and get a good education." Unfortunately, the world says a success is someone with a good education, a secure position, and plenty of money. The Bible says a success is someone who serves God, is of service to other people, provides the needs of his family (spiritually, physically, and emotionally), and most of all is at peace. In other words, a success is someone with his priorities in order.

But just what are the priorities a Christian should consider in selecting a vocation, and how should Christian parents counsel their children?

God's Vocational Plan

Almost without exception, God's principles run contrary to prevailing worldly attitudes. For a Christian to accept non-Christian vocational goals is to invite future problems. "But those who want to get rich fall into temptation and a snare and many foolish and harmful desires which plunge men into ruin and destruction" (1 Timothy 6:9).

Most vocational principles are objective, such as those dealing with authority (Titus 3:1) or security (Hebrews 13:5), whereas others are subjective and require individual discernment by the Holy Spirit. Overwhelmingly such lifetime decisions fall into a scriptural priority system. Many alternatives can be eliminated because they conflict with these priorities. The remaining alternatives must be evaluated through prayer and Christian counsel.

God First

One of the overwhelming characteristics of those who discern God's will for their lives is that they continually seek to put God first. Most Christians experience doubts and anxieties when faced with major decisions. However, most major decisions are actually a series of minor decisions that converge into a change direction. Consistently putting God first eliminates most decisions before they become crises. "More than that, I count all things to be loss in view of the surpassing value of knowing Christ Jesus my Lord, for whom I have suffered the loss of all things, and count them but rubbish in order that I may gain Christ" (Philippians 3:8).

God has already endowed each Christian with unique abilities, desires, and gifts to accomplish His will through them. As a Christian seeks to truly serve God, the Holy Spirit will make known God's perfect vocation for him. "But when He, the Spirit of truth, comes, He will guide you into all the truth; for He will not speak on His own initiative, but whatever He hears, He will speak; and He will disclose to you what is to come" (John 16:13).

Unfortunately, most Christians do not sense that direction because of worldly pressures, or they sense it and then lose it by failing to act upon it. "And the one on whom seed was sown among the thorns, this is the man who hears the word, and the worry of the world, and the deceitfulness of riches choke the word, and it becomes unfruitful" (Matthew 13:22).

Quite often, putting God first in the area of vocation will necessitate choosing a vocation that has little or no retirement security or ego-building status. One example I often think of was a great college athlete who passed up a lucrative professional career to serve the Lord in a Mexican mission. Most of his friends and family urged him to go into the pros, but he knew what God called him to do.

Fulfillment

Regardless of the income, prestige, or security of a vocation, unless it truly merges with God's will, unrest will persist. Without exception, income is but a temporary satisfier. Most people who are trapped in a prestigious, well-paying job that does not meet their inner needs spend their lives envying the very people who are envying them. "There is one who pretends to be rich, but has nothing; another pretends to be poor, but has great wealth" (Proverbs 13:7).

Indicators

One of the best indicators of God's vocational direction is a spiritual gift (1 Corinthians 12). Our purpose on this earth is to serve God (Matthew 6:33). Thus, our vocation is simply an extension of our primary ministry. Many times we reverse the order and fail to recognize that the good salesman does not become a good teacher or exhorter; it is the other way around. Most often the helpful, kind secretary or housewife is the very one to whom people turn in time of distress. Why? Because she has a gift of mercy or help.

It is vital to seek discernment about God's plan and accept nothing less than the vocation that will complement and extend one's ministry.

Parents must play a vital role in vocational direction. That means teaching children to recognize and develop their gifts and talents and counseling them on God's value system. "Train up a child in the way he should go, even when he is old he will not depart from it" (Proverbs 22:6).

Purpose

So often, at the end of a lifetime, a successful man states: "If only I had known forty years ago what I know now, I would not have wasted my life pursuing wealth."

In fact, the world's wisest man put it this way: "Thus I considered all my activities which my hands had done and the labor which I had exerted, and behold all was vanity and striving after wind and there was no profit under the sun" (Ecclesiastes 2:11).

As Christians, we have the advantage of knowing a certain future. Thus, we have the responsibility to orient our lives accordingly.

There is nothing wrong with a successful career; in fact, God promises great blessings. "The reward of humility and the fear of the Lord are riches, honor and life" (Proverbs 22:4). However, attitude is the key ingredient in any vocational decision.

Is the decision made by worldly standards—security, ego, income—or is it made to please and serve God and thus serve other people? "He who loves money will not be satisfied with money, nor he who loves abundance with its income. This too is vanity" (Ecclesiastes 5:10).

As Christians, we have the advantage of being able to see life from God's perspective. We will spend eternity reaping the rewards of faithful service to God. Therefore, vocational planning for us and our children is based primarily on how we can best serve Him.

It is apparent that Solomon made nearly every human error possible concerning material things, and his assessment of vain pursuits could be summed up from Ecclesiastes 5:15: "As he has come naked from his mother's womb, so will he return as he came. He will take nothing from the fruit of his labor that he can carry in his hand."

Our Lord gives us some very sobering thoughts concerning how we invest our lives but none more convicting than in Matthew 16:26, "For what will a man be profited, if he gains the whole world, and forfeits his soul? Or what will a man give in exchange for his soul?"

54
Keeping Christ in Christmas

IT IRRITATES ME when I see Christ being taken out of Christmas. That is not limited to only non-Christians—even Christians have adjusted to the commercialism of the holiday season. Obviously not all of it is bad—in fact, the holiday season provides opportunities for families to reunite and also provides a pleasant break from our routines. I personally look forward to these days as an opportunity to visit with friends who are much too busy other times of the year to just stop and relax.

But we have become terribly imbalanced. We give a myriad of useless gifts at Christmas because it's expected of us, and we feel guilty if we don't. The commercialized world now makes a $100 toy seem perfectly normal. It's easy to observe the stress that our imbalanced society places on family members. Christian parents who cannot provide the latest indulgences to their children are often depressed and distraught. Obviously, no one person purposely makes them feel unworthy or insignificant, but the overwhelming emphasis we place on giving at Christmas certainly does.

So great is this social pressure that the closer we get toward Christmas Day, the more depressed and unworthy those who can't indulge feel. Unfortunately, the pressures don't end once Christmas is past, either. Those who can't afford to compete in their gift giving often dread congregating with their friends immediately after the holidays, because at "show and tell" time they don't have much to show. It is not a conscious act on the part of most people to openly display their pride. Rather, because we are in a competitive society we often determine a person's worth by his ability to buy things. "For you have died and your life is hidden with Christ in God" (Colossians 3:3).

Balance

One extreme is not balanced by going to the opposite extreme. The distortion of Christmas won't be corrected by eliminating all gift giving and observing Christmas as a "religious" holiday. The fact is we *do* live in this world, and our families *are* greatly influenced by others. What we need to do is swing back toward the middle and eliminate the need to compete with others. Then we will have the freedom to develop God's plan for our families without the pressure from the commercial world.

In order to do so, I believe that, as Christians, we must first believe that God's plan is different from the world's and is more, not less, fulfilling. It is a deception to think that, by adopting a more disciplined life-style, we are somehow denied the "good life." It's like saying that by avoiding drugs we deny our children the euphoria that would make them feel "good." But to decide that all drugs are evil and absolutely refuse to use them makes for a painful experience if you have to have a broken leg set. The key, as always in God's plan, is balance. That always comes from following God's wisdom.

Shift of Attitudes

Gift giving at Christmas is a relatively new idea. Until a couple of centuries ago, Christmas was reserved as a religious holiday on a noncommercial basis. Most of our forefathers would have believed that trading presents on the day set aside to observe Christ's birthday was near blasphemy. However, gift giving became a generally accepted practice and was used primarily to show appreciation to loved ones. Gifts were usually simple regardless of the means of the giver so as not to embarrass those who couldn't afford to give very much. For a long while in most countries gifts were exchanged on New Years's Day (not a bad idea today—think of the great buys you could get!). Christmas gifts were limited to food for the poor or special gifts to pastors and missionaries.

As with most things that start out right, somewhere along the way the direction shifted. By the early twentieth century, families were exchanging simple gifts, usually handmade, on Christmas Day. Certainly there was really nothing wrong with that, except that under the growing influence of secularism it was a golden opportunity for Satan to divert our attention from Christ to Santa Claus. By post-World War II, Santa was the dominant figure at Christmas, and December was the calendar month for retail sales of all kinds.

How did it happen? It would seem apparent that Christians aren't as wise in the things of the Lord as non-Cristians are in the things of the world. The secular world is always looking for ways to shift attention from God to material things, and we're naive enough to go along. By the time we realize that our whole direction has been diverted, as it has been at Christmas, we believe it's too late to change, so we give up. "For all that is in the world, the lust of the flesh and the lust of the eyes and the boastful pride of life, is not from the Father, but is from the world" (1 John 2:16).

What To Do?

By anyone's standard, the way Christmas is celebrated today is a gross commercialism of the most important birth in history. But we don't need to preach to the unsaved world to put Christ back into Christmas. They shouldn't; we should. One thing I learned a long time ago in counseling is not to try to overcorrect too quickly. Not only are past habits, such as overindulging at Christmas, difficult to change, but quite often others around us don't see things just the way we do. If you attempt to stamp out all Christmas gifts suddenly, you'll end up with a revolt on your hands. The correct way is to make some positive steps to establish a better balance.

Step 1: Stamp out Santa Claus. Christian parents should let their children know that Santa is a fraud. Santa's harmless you say? Not so, when parents knowingly deceive their children about an apparently omnipotent being who travels the world in the wink of an eye and disburses presents on the basis of good and bad. It may be a small matter, but it is a place to start.

Step 2: Husband and wife should pray together and agree on a reasonable amount of gift giving. Once you have reached a decision that you feel is God's plan for your family, don't get caught by Satan's condemnation as Christmas approaches. The pressure to buy when everyone else is buying will be difficult to resist unless you *absolutely* agree. And again, I repeat, don't overreact. Develop a balanced attitude that will accomplish your goals in the next few years.

One method that has proved successful to many families is to commit an equal amount spent on gifts to feeding the truly needy. In many areas of the world, an amount equal to most of our gift purchases would feed and clothe a family for several months. By giving to a specific family through a Christian organization, your children can see the purpose and value of your sacrifice and theirs. "And whoever in the name of a disciple gives to one of these little ones even a cup of cold water to drink, truly I say to you he shall not lose his reward" (Matthew 10:42).

Step 3: Stamp out credit. As bad as commercialized Christmas is, commercialized Christmas on credit cards is even worse. Many families literally indenture themselves to creditors for a whole year just to buy some useless junk at Christmas. As Christians, we need to decide if we *really* serve the God of the universe. If so, then He knows our needs and will meet them through His people, without indebtedness.

I know that some of the people reading this have some desperate needs. I also know that others sincerely want to help but don't know who has needs. The use of credit allows those who have needs to temporarily buffer themselves from God's real source. "As it is written, 'He who gathered much did not have too much, and he who gathered little had no lack'" (2 Corinthians 8:15). I believe Satan has used credit cards to cheat God's people out of blessings and to keep them in bondage.

Why Bother?

With all the other important issues to deal with, such as crime, abortions, and drugs, a logical question would be, "Why bother with such a minor issue as gifts at Christmas?" Because gift giving is one area totally under our control, and, like the Easter bunny, it is a leaven that Satan sprinkles in the church. The practice of giving gifts is *not* the problem, just as the use of credit is not the problem. It is the misuse of these things that entangles us and diverts attention from Jesus Christ to material things.

We have enlisted in God's army and now find we can't identify the real enemy. "No soldier in active service entangles himself in the affairs of everyday life, so that he may please the one who enlisted him as a soldier" (2 Timothy 2:4).

Our problem is that we keep trying to negotiate a compromise with an enemy who is totally dedicated to destroying us. It's time that, as Christians, we decide to draw a battle line again. When it comes to commercializing Christ's birth or resurrection, we need to establish a balance. "Instruct those who are rich in this present world not to be conceited or to fix their hope on the uncertainty of riches, but on God, who richly supplies us with all things to enjoy" (1 Timothy 6:17).

55
Setting Goals

ANYONE WHO HAS done much counseling will attest to the fact that those who are successful in any field are the goal setters. They have a desire to achieve that is coupled with discipline. That combination is essential to being successful in anything, including Christianity. Clearly, this is evident in reading about the apostles, particularly Paul. He established goals and stuck to them, refusing to get side-tracked into nonministry related areas.

For instance, I'm sure Paul felt that pastoral work was important because he established it in the churches he started. But he also knew that he wasn't called to be a pastor. He could have settled down to teach at one of the churches he established—without criticism. After all, he had paid his "dues" and run his race. But Paul knew he was an evangelist, called to carry God's Word to the unsaved. That single-mindedness on Paul's part is what we would describe today as having firm goals.

Few Set Goals Today

With the emphasis on mass media over the past thirty years has come a group-decision mentality. It seems that most people want to find out what others are doing and emulate it.

Today, the lack of goal setting is approaching a crisis level. Our problem is that we don't have to set goals. Our level of affluence allows us to drift along in the group with relative ease and comfort. Christ said that condition would ultimately be the greatest threat to Christianity.

First, it would be a threat because it would cause us to drift away from God's path. "For where your treasure is, there will your heart be also" (Matthew 6:21). And second, it would be a threat because, when comforts are in jeopardy, many will choose to follow those comforts rather than Christ. "Yet he has no firm root in himself, but is only temporary, and when affliction or persecution arises because of the word, immediately he falls away" (Matthew 13:21).

That danger is directly related to the lack of godly goals or what might be called singleness of purpose. Without singleness of purpose we drift and get caught up in following the crowd. It is a condition that James described as "double-minded." "For let not that man expect that he will receive anything from the Lord, being a double-minded man, unstable in all his ways" (James 1:7–8).

Dangerous Goals

There are many miserable people with well-thought-out goals. Unfortunately, their goals are selfish, materialistic plans that attempt to fill a need that can be filled only by a personal relationship with Jesus Christ. Being single-minded of purpose about the wrong things is still wrong. In setting goals a simple priority system will help to avoid these problems:

First, be certain that whatever goals you're setting are compatible with God's Word. Success goals to soothe our fears or feed our egos are doomed to failure. God promised to meet our needs and provide an abundance to give to others but not when we intend to hoard it or squander it. "You ask and do not receive, because you ask with wrong motives, so that you may spend it on your pleasures" (James 4:3).

Second, husband and wife must establish goals together. If you find that you cannot do so because of your relationship, that should be your first goal. When that relationship is not right, it's time to be honest and correct it. For those who are single, it's important to seek counsel from a mature believer who is as different from you as possible. As in a marriage, if both of you agreed about everything, one of you would be unnecessary.

Third, when establishing financial goals related to income, growth, or success, make a written commitment to give either most or everything above an established level into God's work. Literally, your goal would be to make more to give, not to spend more. When husband and wife are working together on these goals, a good balance will be established. Usually one is tempted to keep too much, while the other wants to give it all away.

Scriptural Case for Setting Goals

"The mind of man plans his way, but the Lord directs his steps" (Proverbs 16:9). God's Word says that we have been given both responsibility and authority on this earth. We are to plan our way, and God will provide the direction. Obviously, no one has a perfect insight into God's will for his life. It's a day-by-day process. But God promises us guidance to keep us on track if we're willing to listen. The prerequisite to receiving God's guidance is the willingness to accept it. "Commit your works to the Lord, and your plans will be established" (Proverbs 16:3).

Most Christians sincerely want God's guidance, but they aren't willing to pay the price to get it. God's way is not one of several available alternatives. It is the only way. We must decide to either follow or reject God's way. Christ told us that we cannot serve two masters (Matthew 6:24). Until we decide to accept God's will for our lives, He is not going to reveal it. Unfortunately, that's why so many people will never find God's will; they want to try it on for size first. By "faith" we must accept that God's plan for us is best regardless of where it leads us. "And without faith it is impossible to please Him, for he who comes to God must believe that He is, and that He is a rewarder of those who seek Him" (Hebrews 11:6).

Scriptural Goals

1. *Bible study.* Before any financial goals can be established, the proper spiritual goals should be developed. The best place to start is with a study of God's Word. The Bible is like God's road map for us. It will take us wherever we want to go if we just know how to read it. God promises the wisdom to understand His Word if we'll spend the time to study it. When I was a new Christian, my first pastor started me out on a simple plan called 9:59. It was nine minutes and fifty-nine seconds set aside to study the Bible daily. This is a plan anyone can achieve.

2. *Prayer.* If the Bible is God's road map, then prayer is God's headlights. It keeps us on the road and out of ditches. You get to know about God by studying His Word, but you get to know God through prayer. Even Christ Himself needed to withdraw and pray to God, and certainly we need to pray as much or more. The one common characteristic of dry Christians seems to be the lack of consistent prayer life. Set a goal to pray regularly and consistently, even if for only a few minutes a day.

3. *Church.* We are admonished not to forsake the assembling of ourselves together. "Not forsaking our own assembling together, as is the habit of some, but encouraging one another; and all the more, as you see the day drawing near" (Hebrews 10:25).

4. *Money.* Giving is the external evidence of an internal spiritual condition. But even more than that, giving is an objective, measurable commitment made to God. Few promises in God's Word are as clear as those related to giving. It is the principle of sowing and reaping found in 2 Corinthians 9:6. "Now this I say, he who sows sparingly shall also reap sparingly; and he who sows bountifully shall also reap bountifully."

Family Goals

1. *Marriage.* Once the previous goals have been made individually, they must become a part of your partnership with your spouse. If your spouse is not a Christian, then you have an excellent goal to establish in your personal prayer life. Don't give up praying for your spouse. One Christian lady I know

prayed for her husband twenty-two years before he accepted the Lord. It finally took the shock of three years in prison before he responded.

A minimum goal with which to start should be to read a few verses of Scripture together regularly and to pray for your family together.

2. *Children.* As Christian parents, we should teach our children God's principles. However, too much too soon will frustrate you and them. With very young children, study and prayer are relatively easy habits to develop in the family. Start with a good children's Bible guide, and pray for each other. With older children start where you can. Read a brief devotional at the breakfast or dinner table, and set aside a few minutes to pray together.

Financial Goals

Woven in among every other area of goal setting and planning is the financial area. Unless some realistic spiritual goals are established in this area, the others are doomed to failure. The one overriding goal in the financial area must be that our life-styles are glorifying to God.

A minimum goal should be for husband and wife to set aside one full day to do some goal planning. From the goal-planning day, some minimums should be established.

1. *Yearly budget.* Perhaps you can't determine precisely what the entire year's budget will be, but some basics can be started.

2. *Study God's plan.* A good place to begin a long-range goal-setting plan is by studying God's principles of finance.

56

The Issue of Inheritance

No GENERATION OF people has ever managed more material assets with less training to do so. In a single generation today, an individual can go from near poverty to an estate of millions of dollars. Unfortunately, the succeeding generation can just as quickly lose it all. We seem to be a people of extremes, and inheritance is no exception. One part of our society leaves enormous wealth to its generally untrained offspring, whereas another segment spends it all and leaves practically nothing.

I will delay discussing the latter group because that is really a discussion on current stewardship. It is sufficient to say that many Christians who spend all that they have without regard to their children are not good stewards. In fact, the legacy that many Christian parents leave today is one of debt. "If a man fathers a hundred children and lives many years, however many they be, but his soul is not satisfied with good things, and he does not even have a proper burial, then I say, 'Better the miscarriage than he'" (Ecclesiastes 6:3).

Most of us have the ability to create an estate today. It may be land, businesses, homes, or an insurance policy payable upon our death, but nevertheless it is an estate. The common strategy with most people, including Christians, is to keep as much as possible while we're alive and leave it to our heirs upon our death. Unfortunately, quite often the heirs are poorly trained to manage the assets.

I recall one man I was counseling who had accumulated a sizable estate. When I asked him what he planned to do with it all, he said, "I'll leave it to my children, I guess." I asked him why he didn't just give it to them right then, and he replied, "Why, they don't know how to handle money; they'd just lose it all." When asked if he thought they wouldn't lose it after he died, his response was, "Well, I'll be gone then, so who cares?" Well, God cares because being a good steward doesn't stop with death.

Poor stewardship also means leaving an untrained wife to take over the management of the finances. Unfortunately, that is most often the case, and the results are anxiety, frustration, and dependence on unwise counselors.

You would think that men would believe the statistics that tell us seven out of eight men die before their wives, but apparently they don't. Consequently, many women are forced into the role of estate manager with little or no knowledge in that area. To make matters worse, their husbands leave few guidelines for them to follow, and, in fact, in almost 70 percent of the cases they don't even leave a valid will. This leaves the asset distribution up to the state and its laws.

Further, the average man leaves about 20 percent of the minimum assets necessary to provide for his family. That includes total life insurance of about $20,000, or about the same average as in 1963. Why is this? Is it that the average American father doesn't care about his family? I don't think so. I believe it really boils down to two current flaws: ignorance and slothfulness—ignorance, because most of us haven't been taught good stewardship, which includes inheritance; and slothfulness, because many people know what they should do but procrastinate until it's too late.

Some Christians are superstitious without realizing it and avoid discussing death for fear that it will happen. This I can say with certainty—unless the Lord comes first, it will happen for each of us. Talking about death neither hastens nor delays it; it only makes it easier for those left behind. "The naive believes everything, but the prudent man considers his steps" (Proverbs 14:15).

Biblical Guidelines

God leaves no subject untouched in His Word, and fortunately that includes the area called inheritance. Even a brief survey of the Bible reveals that God provided for each generation through inheritance. In biblical times, the sons inherited their father's properties and thus provided for the rest of their family. "A good man leaves an inheritance to his children's children, and the wealth of the sinner is stored up for the righteous" (Proverbs 13:22).

What is not so obvious is that in most instances, the sons received their inheritance while their fathers were still living. Thus, a father was able to oversee their stewardship while they were learning.

The parable of the prodigal son in Luke 15 reflects that principle. The father divided his inheritance between his two sons and lived to see the younger one restored. It would be interesting to see what money management training most children would receive if their parents knew they would turn over all the estate to them and depend upon them for their support. Of course, since the average sixty-five-year-old man's financial worth is only about $100 today, it wouldn't take a lot of management. It's rather obvious that fifty years ago their parents failed to teach them basic stewardship. The Bible says save, but the government says don't bother. "House and wealth are an inheritance from fathers" (Proverbs 19:14a).

Godly Inheritance

Obviously the most important inheritance we can offer our children is a Christian influence that leads to salvation. It's a good thing that most Christian parents don't leave that inheritance training until after death. Neither should we leave good materials training until after death—it's too late then. I would challenge every Christian to develop a godly approach to inheritance beginning right now. Establish a few fundamental absolutes about your inheritance.

1. *Training for wife.* Insure that the wife understands how to handle money well. If a woman has never actually managed the money, the training starts with basic budgeting. The wife should actually manage the home finances for at least the next year. Then, if something happens to her husband, she will know that she can manage the money.

2. *Create wills/trusts.* Every living American should have the basic legal document for after-death asset distribution—a will. Without a will, the state in which you live will distribute your assets according to their laws of intestacy. Rarely, if ever, will this be according to your wishes. Husband and wife both need wills, and each should understand the other's will. First, pray about how you wish your estate to be distributed, including the Lord's work. Then, write it out as clearly as possible and have a competent attorney write your plan into your will.

Some families will need a "trust" to manage their assets in order to reduce estate costs and/or save taxes. There are many varieties of trusts, and, contrary to most opinions, their use is not limited only to large estates. Almost any good bookstore or library will have several easy-to-read books on the use of wills and trusts. Several large Christian ministries, such as Campus Crusade for Christ, Billy Graham Crusades, and Christian Broadcast Network offer free estate planning services for those who support their ministry. All of them will provide good quality materials upon request.

3. *Develop a plan.* In addition to the legal instruments necessary to distribute and manage your estate, you must have a plan. For instance, at what age do you want to begin your children's training? How much will you entrust to their management? Who will help advise them? Obviously, each family's plan will be somewhat different, but the one common factor for Christians should be an understanding of God's principles for managing money.

Age. There is really no best age to start teaching children good money management, but the younger, the better. For very young children (two to four), start their training by helping them to understand the value of money. That can be started by associating money with work. Pay them small sums for tasks around the home, and then help them decide whether to spend it or save it. As they get older, you should begin to expand their training, including a good study of God's principles.

Practice. Nothing helps more to reinforce principle than problems. As your children approach the teen years, you need to put them into real-life money situations. That includes letting them open checking and savings accounts and doing the monthly balancing.

Borrowing. The principle of borrowing can best be demonstrated by lending money to them at interest and requiring that they repay the loan—totally. Many young couples would have been better served if their parents had taught them about debt while they were living at home, rather than waiting for a creditor to do it.

Investing. The risk-reward system of our economy can be clearly demonstrated to young people by entrusting to them a sum of money (small at first) to be invested. It is interesting to see how real the economy and money become to a teenager who has his money at risk. Sometime back, I helped each of our sons get involved in an area of investing to demonstrate how free enterprise really works. For one, it was a car to fix up and resell; for another, it was repairing a small rental house; and for another, it was a small coin investment. The cost to me was relatively small, but the reward was helping to develop three free-market enthusiasts.

Giving. Teach your children to give to God's work out of their earnings, and you have made what I personally believe is the most essential step in molding them into good money managers. "Train up a child in the way he should go, and even when he is old he will not depart from it" (Proverbs 22:6).

Rarely will you find a generous giver who manages money poorly. God promises wisdom to those who trust Him; giving is an evidence of that trust.

Part Seven

MINISTRIES AND SCRIPTURAL HIGHLIGHTS

57
Christian Fund-Raising

FUND RAISING WOULD seem to be the national pastime of most non-profit organizations in America today. From the bulk of mail received by most Christian givers, there is little doubt that the competition for Christian support is acute. New organizations spring up every day, and as the number of organizations grows, the search for new funds grows more intense, as anyone who has donated money to one or more general appeal groups knows. Almost mystically, an unexpecting donor receives from scores of other organizations he never heard of. That is because many organizations either use a common fund-raising company or else they sell their donor lists to generate additional income.

Many well-meaning Christians get pressured into giving to groups they know little or nothing about because of emotional appeals or skilled manipulation.

Even many otherwise sound Christian ministries have turned to secular advertising and fund-raising companies to meet their growing demand for funds. Often they will pay up to 40 percent of all donations just to raise the money. Some promoters actually will be working on fund-raising campaigns for anti-Christian and Christian groups simultaneously. All of that is to say that each individual Christian must be responsible for how God's money is used, even in the most worthy of causes.

Who? What? How?

Before supporting any fund appeal, a Christian should ask some basic questions.

1. *Who is the group asking for the funds?* Get a list of references from the organization that can be easily verified through other well-known groups. It would be wise to drop a letter off to the Attorney General of the state of residence and also a letter to the head of a ministry or church nearby. Often the best method to do that is through your own pastor or church secretary.

2. *What are they going to use the funds for?* At least one good way to

determine this is to ask for a projected budget. The lack of a budget is one reason why many organizations continually send out "crisis appeal" letters.

3. *How do they raise funds, and how do they manage them?* It is wise to ask if a fund-raising group is involved and what percentage of the funds go to them. Also, how much of the ministry's budget is dedicated to fund raising? Obviously, some media ministries (radio and TV) would normally have a higher ratio. A good indication of financial management is the debt-income ratio and the change in overhead expenses from year to year.

Once a Christian has asked these questions, the burden of making the decision based on common sense is satisfied. However, the burden of exercising spiritual wisdom can be satisfied only by the application of God's Word.

Biblical Principles

There must be a balance in a Christian's attitude toward ministry support. Too often a Christian will read a spectacular biography of how God used a particular individual, and he will use that as an absolute rule against everyone else. Personal testimonies are exciting and rewarding and can be of great value in providing alternatives. However, they are *not* to be used as yardsticks, unless confirmed in God's Word. As an example: many Christians have read the story of George Mueller's life and how he trusted God for everything without asking. They then concluded that no Christian should ever let a material need be known. That is noble and admirable but not scriptural. Paul admonished the Corinthians because they felt that he didn't have the right to ask them for support (2 Corinthians 11:7-9). In Exodus 25:1-3, the Lord told Moses to tell the people of Israel to raise a contribution for the Tabernacle.

However, just because asking is acceptable doesn't mean that it's God's plan for everyone or that every letter sent to supporters should ask for more money. Again, balance is the key principle. Nowhere in Scripture is there any indication that God's people went begging. It would appear evident that many more needs were met by praying than by asking. It also seems clear that once God's people are made aware of their responsibilities to give and support God's work, the need to ask goes down dramatically (Exodus 36:5-6).

Which Group to Support

God does not intend for every Christian to give to every need. Attempting to do so will quickly result in frustration and, for most of us, poverty. Therefore, we must be able to sort out those we are to help from those we are not. That does not necessarily mean that the cause or the organization is not worthy—only that the need is meant for another to satisfy.

1. *God's work.* There are many worthy social organizations serving the needs of the poor, the sick, and the elderly. The vast majority make no pretense of going in the name of the Lord. That does not exclude them from

receiving the portion set apart for God. It is abundantly clear throughout the Bible that gifts dedicated to God were to be distributed in His name. Since God obviously did not need the material goods, they were redistributed to satisfy those who had needs (Exodus 34:19; Leviticus 1:2; 27:30; Deuteronomy 12:6; 14:28).

2. *Deserving.* Just because a group has an emotional presentation for a seemingly worthy Christian cause does not mean they automatically qualify for support. It is important to determine that the funds will actually be used for the purpose they were given.

Above all else be certain about the doctrinal stand of the ministry. Many committed believers have been shocked to discover that they were contributing to an organization that was anti-Christian.

3. *Personal benefit.* Those organizations that have met needs in your life should be high on the support list. Obviously, those who should be most supportive of a ministry are those who were ministered to by it. If that organization is not a highly visible one (does not advertise or regularly appeal), then the support of those they minister to is essential. "And let the one who is taught the word share all good things with him who teaches" (Galatians 6:6).

4. *Good stewards.* Just as in any other investment, a Christian should get the best benefit of his investment in God's work. Therefore, the organizations that manage their funds the best should be considered first. Obviously, the type of ministry each group is involved in must also be considered. A rural church and a national television ministry will have vastly different budgets and should not be evaluated by total expenditures. If you have a desire to support a particular type of ministry, then locate the most efficient and productive one available.

The leaders of any ministry should have a clear, concise plan for accomplishing God's work and a reasonable idea of costs and time. The lack of written goals and objectives if usually a sign of slothfulness. There are other signs to look for, such as a heavy debt burden, a bad credit history, unfinished projects, significant staff turnover, and soliciting support from the unsaved. "I passed by the field of the sluggard, and by the vineyard of the man lacking sense; and behold, it was completely overgrown with thistles" (Proverbs 24:30–31*a*; see also 1 Corinthians 9:14; Luke 16:13).

5. *God's leading.* The most important principle of all is to allow God to direct your giving. We are told to lean upon God's wisdom and not our own understanding (Proverbs 3:5), and that also applies to giving. Those people who have a problem in turning down anyone who asks must learn to wait and pray before giving. The others who have a problem sharing with anyone need to give more and wait less. "But whoever has the world's goods, and beholds his brother in need and closes his heart against him, how does the love of God abide in him?" (1 John 3:17).

An essential part of the balance system God has established is the husband and wife relationship. Almost without exception, one is prone to give too much and the other too little. Couples that can learn to communicate and accept each other's counsel will usually establish a reasonable balance.

Conclusion

It is impossible to lay down absolute guidelines for funding God's work, simply because God did not do so in His Word. However, there are some good guidelines available for both the askers and the givers. Any giver would be well advised to use biblical guidelines whenever possible to select those organizations that do or do not qualify. Then rely on God's inner direction to decide which groups to support. The biblical guidelines to be used are:

1. Adherence to sound biblical doctrine in the organization and ministry (Galatians 1:9)
2. Ministry in the name of the Lord Jesus Christ (Colossians 3:17)
3. Practice of good financial management within the organization (Luke 16:12)
4. Dependence on God's people for support (3 John 6–7)
5. Lives changed for Christ through the ministry (Galatians 5:22–23)

58

Give and It Will Be Given to You

"GIVE, AND IT will be given to you; good measure, pressed down, shaken together, running over, they will pour into your lap. For by your standard of measure it will be measured to you in return" (Luke 6:38).

Few Scripture verses are quoted more often Luke 6:38 regarding the principle of giving and receiving. When I first read this verse shortly after committing my life to Christ, I pondered it for many weeks. Did God really mean what that verse says? Do God's promises depend on our giving first? I read the previous and subsequent verses to see if perhaps it could be interpreted in another context. I then studied parallel and contrasting verses. After dedicating many hours of thoroughly enjoyable time to God's Word, I concluded that I really didn't understand the meaning of Luke 6:38. There were some seemingly obvious difficulties with the principle that receiving was a matter of giving first. What about those Christians I knew who gave but didn't receive much in return?

My first response was to assume the principle did not apply to all Christians. Perhaps it applied only to those with a gift of giving. I quickly eliminated the rationality of that. If Luke 6:38 applied to only a select few, Christ would not have delivered the message in Luke 6 to the masses. God may well select a few to receive and dispose of a large amount of His resources, but the principle described in Luke 6:38 is a promise to anyone who will apply it. I thought, *Perhaps the principle applies to spiritual, rather than material, rewards.* Indeed, further study confirmed that it does apply to spiritual rewards, as well as material. But there is no way to disassociate the material giving and receiving since in verses 30-35 Christ made direct reference to material things. The more I reviewed other Scripture dealing with the principle of giving and receiving, the more I realized there was no contradiction at all.

Observations

There were prerequisites that had to be met before even an understanding could be received. Once an understanding of God's promise is reached, then it is necessary to believe that promise. I determined to make a study of giving and receiving in the lives of Christians I knew, including myself, and match the result of my study to God's Word. Since all of God's principles are given as examples for living, an applied principle has to be verified in changed lives or else we either don't understand the principle or don't apply it. Before defining the scriptural principle, I would first like to share some observations of the study that started nine years ago and still continue.

1. Most Christians give far less than one-tenth of their incomes to work being done in the Lord's name.

2. Many Christians give at least a tenth of their incomes regularly but have not experienced what they assess as God's material or spiritual bounty.

3. Many Christians give at least a tenth of their incomes and can identify many instances of God's abundance, either materially, spiritually, or both.

4. A small percentage of Christians give far above a tenth of their incomes but cannot identify what they would describe as God's abundant return.

5. A very small percentage of Christians give far above a tenth of their incomes and can identify God's response, both generally and specifically.

Of course, there were other categories and instances in which Christians moved from one group to another. Many of these can be explained due to spiritual growth or withdrawal, which will obviously affect every area of our lives. A few can be classified as unique from a biblical perspective. That is most clear when a spiritually mature Christian gives in great abundance and outwardly appears to suffer materially. The apostle Paul would most assuredly identify with that group. God has a separate and unique plan for these people, and the depth of their commitment to Christ sets them apart in spiritual blessings.

I would like to make some observations about these groups without intending at all to be judgmental. I believe God has provided us with material indicators of spiritual condition. They are not for accusation; they are for admonition.

Don't Rob God

Those who give less than even a tenth of their increase have limited what God can do for them according to His own Word. "Will a man rob God? Yet you are robbing Me! But you say, 'How have we robbed Thee?' In tithes and offerings" (Malachi 3:8). Lest we somehow believe this principle applies only to the Old Covenant, Paul amplifies it for us in 2 Corinthians 9:6. "Now this I say, he who sows sparingly shall also reap sparingly; and he who sows bountifully shall also reap bountifully." The lack of giving is an external material indicator that spiritual changes need to be made.

Those who give more than a tenth but not necessarily sacrificially and experience God's abundance (according to God's plan for them) are meeting God's prerequisites for where they are right then.

Many of those who give what we consider a material abundance and do not experience any particular spiritual or material reply may actually give for self-motivated reasons. Many are trying to bribe God into blessing them. They are much like Simon in Acts 8, who upon observing the benefits of God's power tried to acquire it without meeting the spiritual prerequisites. They require and even demand God's blessing because of what they consider their sacrifice. They are not in subjection to God but are trying to exercise control over Him. Paul addressed that attitude also in Romans 11:34-35. "For who has known the mind of the Lord, or who became His counselor? Or who has first given to Him, that it might be paid back to him again?"

Believe God

The last group is made up of those who give, expecting but never demanding. And although God often returns far beyond their expectations both materially and spiritually, their giving is out of a desire to please God, not to profit from the relationship. The evidence of that can be found in the fact that usually their sacrificial giving came long before the response from God, and their ratios of giving far exceed their accumulation regardless of the supply.

A Christian friend in Atlanta exemplifies that principle clearly. I met him several years ago during a particularly difficult time in his life financially. He was totally committed to giving sacrificially into God's kingdom, had experienced great blessings, and in fact was noted in Christian circles as a giver. Then for an extended period of time the bounty was withdrawn, and for all intents and purposes he was broke. His Christian "Job's friends" quickly pointed out every character flaw he had and advised him to repent and get straight with God. After some soul searching, prayer, and fasting, he was where God wanted him to be, doing what God wanted him to do. Consequently, he and his wife decided to give more, not less.

Mark 11:24 says, "Therefore I say to you, all things for which you pray and ask, believe that you have received them, and they shall be granted to you."

He concluded that to believe, he had to act. So they began to give furniture and other things they had collected during the abundance to others who had greater needs. Now he is being used by God to supply enormous sums of money into His work. His love for giving is matched by a deep sensitivity to the needs of others, and there is never a doubt who gets the glory for the abundance to give.

Several times he and his wife have saved to build a new home, and each time they have given the money away to meet a need in God's work. Every time I see him he has an excitement to make more money so they can give more away. The only caution I have ever given this kind of giver is not to give away all of the "seed corn."

Sowing and Reaping

The spiritual principle behind Luke 6:38 is indeed giving and receiving, but it is not giving to receive. The prerequisites to receiving are found in Luke 6:27-37. A Christian who lives by these principles practices the surrendered life. Therefore, the giving is simply a material expression of the deeper spiritual obedience to Christ. Nearly every Christian desires to be obedient to God, and in many ways most are. However, Christ warned us that the greatest threat to our walk with God is the tug of our materialistic world. "And the one on whom seed was sown among the thorns, this was the man who hears the word, and the worry of the world and the deceitfulness of riches choke the word, and it becomes unfruitful" (Matthew 13:22).

59

Seek the Kingdom of God

"BUT SEEK FIRST His kingdom and His righteousness; and all these things shall be added to you" (Matthew 6:33).

The admonition to "seek first the kingdom of God" in Matthew 6:33 is given by the Lord as a contrast of worrying about material possessions. I believe there has never been a generation of Christians so caught up in worry about possessions as we are. We have a greater abundance available on a day by day basis than *any* previous generation. Most of us have machines that reduce the daily household labor required, our children are well-clothed and well-educated, and our life expectancy is more than God's promise of three score and ten. We have insurance plans, retirement plans, disability plans, and unemployment plans. Yet we are so caught up in making more money and buying bigger and better things that we have lost most of our thrust to reach the unsaved world. As I read through God's Word, it keeps asking the same fundamental question: "Are we seeking first the kingdom of God?"

What do You Stand For?

It would seem evident that if we are to spend an eternity in the presence of God and only seventy or so years on this earth, we should be more concerned about what we will receive then than what we are getting now. But when our priorities are reviewed it is apparent that most Christians live without real hope as Paul described it in Romans 8:24–25. We're willing to settle for what we can see, rather than what we cannot see. That is exactly the principle that Christ teaches in Matthew 6:19–33.

It's not the material things that cause the difficulties. God says that He will give us those things that the world cherishes so much. It is a matter of heart attitude. Are we more dedicated to accumulating material things than to serving God? Without a doubt the evidence of our lives shows that we are serving money—not God. "For where your treasure is, there will your heart be also" (Matthew 6:21).

The question is often asked, "What do Christians stand for?" The answer the world would give is, "Not much other than what we do." The sad part about it is that most people really want to know a personal God. They carve gods out of wood or rocks and worship idols, cows, demons, or whatever they can find. We have the only hope for a generation without hope, and yet we're spending the majority of our time pursuing vain things. Our energies are so depleted in accumulating bigger homes, businesses, cars, and retirement plans that we don't have much time to seek God's kingdom.

Only Two Choices

Christ says that we have only two choices as disciples: to follow God or to follow money. "No one can serve two masters; for either he will hate the one and love the other, or he will hold to one and despise the other. You cannot serve God and mammon" (Matthew 6:24).

The scriptural warning is clear, that we will be judged on the evidence of our material lives more than any other thing. The attraction of materialism is so great that Christ devoted two-thirds of His parables to warning His disciples about it. The writers of the epistles amplified that teaching as they observed the destructive force of materialism in the lives of believers. "For the love of money is a root of all sorts of evil, and some by longing for it have wandered away from the faith, and pierced themselves with many a pang" (1 Timothy 6:10). "Let your character be free from the love of money, being content with what you have; for He Himself has said, 'I will never desert you, nor will I ever forsake you'" (Hebrews 13:5).

Again, it's not material things that are the problem, it's materialism. The alarming thing about our generation of Christians is that we have found a way of scripturally rationalizing our excesses. Many Christians actually believe that we can attract the unsaved by having the best. Let me assure you that those who are seriously seeking God in their lives are not attracted by the luxuries of Christians. They are attracted by an uncompromising commitment to God. If that commitment also yields material blessings, it's just an added benefit.

Why Christians Stumble

It's unfortunate that the zeal and dedication seen in new believers often fade as they get back into the old rut. Within a few months, or at best a few years, most have learned the Christian language and fall back in step with the world. They talk a lot about God's blessings—usually material blessings—but seldom experience real joy and peace. Even worse, lives aren't changed through contact with them. Why? They have become too busy to listen to God's voice.

Too busy to serve. When the Lord entered Martha and Mary's home, Mary sat at His feet to listen as He taught. That distressed Martha, who was apparently trying to impress Him with her activities. When Martha asked Jesus to rebuke Mary, His reply would fit most of us today. "But the Lord answered and said to her, 'Martha, Martha, you are worried and bothered about so many things; but only a few things are necessary, really only one, for Mary has chosen the good part, which shall not be taken away from her'" (Luke 10:41–42).

Later Christ told His disciples a parable about being a part of the kingdom of God in Luke 14:16–26. Many will be called to serve in God's kingdom, but most will have excuses why they can't get involved.

At the conclusion of this parable we have one of the most convicting Scriptures of all Christ's teaching. "If anyone comes to Me, and does not hate his own father and mother and wife and children and brothers and sisters, yes, and even his own life, he cannot be My disciple" (Luke 14:26). Anyone who doubts the emphasis that God puts on placing His kingdom first should ponder that Scripture for a while.

Too many distractions. I find that the more things accumulate, the more distractions they cause. Two cars break down twice as often, two computers cause twice the errors, and so on. When most of us first began to work, our greatest concerns were a good job and a modest home. But as we make more, our expectations increase. Now we find ourselves distracted by buildings, cars, investments, and retirement plans for thirty years in the future. The very second that we cease to breathe, all of those concerns are going to be irrelevant. In counseling during the last few years, I have met several Christians who had learned they had terminal illnesses. Their perspective about the future and material things changed the instant they took on a short-range view of this world.

That is exactly what Christ is saying to us in Matthew 6:25: "For this reason I say to you, do not be anxious for your life, as to what you shall eat, or what you shall drink, nor for your body, as to what you shall put on. Is not life more than food, and the body than clothing?" Compared to eternity, we are all dying tomorrow. Don't be so distracted by the worries of this world.

Keys to the Kingdom

Over the last few years, I have read and reread Paul's letter to the Romans. It is obvious to me that somewhere between the seventh and tenth chapters, Paul describes a man (himself) who has found the keys to God's invisible kingdom. It becomes clear that what Paul is describing is a man who accepts God as the absolute authority in his life and is willing to surrender everything, if necessary, to serve Him—even to the point of death. Paul has learned, as he expressed in Philippians 1:21, that we live to serve Christ at any cost, even if death is what we must pay.

Several years ago I met a Chinese Christian who was saved as a member of the Red Brigade in Communist China. He was imprisoned, tortured, starved, and beaten in an effort to get him to renounce his faith. When he refused, his family was executed to "teach others a lesson." He said the thing that sustained him was an ever-deepening relationship with Christ and an unyielding commitment to serving God. When most of our commitments are weighed against his, it's easy to see why the keys to the kingdom elude us.

Perhaps God hasn't called us to the physical sacrifices that many Christian martyrs have suffered. But the admonition that Christ gives to all of us is absolutely clear. "Then Jesus said to His disciples, 'If anyone wishes to come after Me, let him deny himself, and take up his cross, and follow Me'" (Matthew 16:24).

Evidence of Our Commitment

It's always good to have some standard of measure to compare where we are to where God wants us to be. The evidence given in God's Word is clear and simple. All we have to do is eliminate our ego and pride and consistently put the needs of others before our own, and we'll know we're on the right track. Is it difficult? No, it is impossible. But in Romans 7:24-25 Paul gives us God's solution—let go and *trust* God.

Humility. Christ is to be the most exalted being in the eternal kingdom of God. Knowing this to be true, He assumed the lowliest, most humbling position possible during His life. He not only served others, but also assumed the position of a foot washer. In John 13:15 He says, "For I gave you an example that you also should do as I did to you." Perhaps to us this will mean giving up having the most and the best, and not just giving to someone else's need, but giving them the best.

"Self" denial. It is a contrast in human logic that by giving up something we can receive even more. But Christ taught this principle frequently; it's called sowing and reaping. We won't always reap the rewards immediately. In fact, I believe it is our choice whether to take what we want now or store it and receive it in God's eternal kingdom. When you compare the time to enjoy God's rewards to the time spent in this world, there is no contest.

"And He said to them, 'Truly I say to you, there is no one who has left house or wife or brothers or parents or children, for the sake of the kingdom of God, who shall not receive many times as much at this time and in the age to come, eternal life'" (Luke 18:29-30).

Love for others. Last as we conclude this survey, God's Word tells us that an evidence of our commitment to His way will be shown in our concern for others.

In Matthew 25, the Lord describes the gleaning of the righteous servants from the unrighteous. The righteous servants were those through whom the love of God showed itself by sharing. "And the King will answer and say to them, 'Truly I say to you, to the extent that you did it to one of these brothers of Mine, even the least of them, you did it to Me'" (Matthew 25:40).

As we start each day we have a choice: to follow God or to follow this world. If we decide to totally follow God's path, it *will* cost us. We will be buffeted by Satan as never before. We'll doubt our decision and the wisdom of it. But on the sole authority of God's Word we can clearly know that our priorities are in order. "I tell you that He will bring about justice for them speedily. However, when the Son of Man comes, will He find faith on the earth?" (Luke 18:8).

III

DEBT-FREE
LIVING

Contents

Introduction

NOTHING IN THE area of finances has so dominated or influenced the direction of our society during the last fifty years as debt. It's amazing when you consider that only a generation ago credit cards were unknown, car loans were a rarity, and mortgages were for G.I.s who were getting their starter homes. No one in our fathers' or grandfathers' generations would have believed that any banker would be so foolish as to lend a teenager money to go to college. Their counsel would have been (and was) to "Get a job."

Today it is not unusual for a young couple to owe nearly $100,000 within the first two years of marriage. A profile of a young couple's debt often reveals their financial training or lack of it—including a home mortgage of approximately $65,000, college loans (his and hers) of $20,000, and car loans (his and hers) of $13,000. Often the list extends even further to include consolidation loans, finance company loans, and parental loans. And why not? If it's good enough for the country, it's good enough for the family, right?

Christians would obviously say no, not necessarily. We're supposed to take our direction from God's Word, not from the world. So the logical decision would be to observe what the church is doing and use that as our guide. However, in doing so, we will find that the average American church is as deeply in debt as the average American business; and with about the same rate of delinquent payments and bankruptcies.

The only reliable source of wisdom is the Word of God itself. Only by going back to the true source of all wisdom can we possibly hope to find the right balance today. God's Word tells us that His plan for us is to be debt-free. And even better, that we would be lenders rather than borrowers. Read Deuteronomy 28:12, "The Lord will open for you His good storehouse, the heavens, to give rain to your land in its season and to bless all the work of your hand; and you shall lend to many nations, but you shall not borrow."

I hope to show that that is still God's plan and that it is entirely possible, even in this present generation. The blessings of becoming debt-free go far beyond the financial area. They extend to the spiritual and marital realms as well. No one who is financially bound can be spiritually free. The problems must certainly spill over into your prayer and study time. And the effects of financial bondage on a marriage relationship are measurable in the statistics of failed marriages. Approximately 50 percent of all first marriages fail, and finances are listed as the leading cause of divorce by a factor of four to one over any other cause, including infidelity.

If this were just another book on the problems associated with finances in a marriage, it would not be necessary. There are many good books available now that clearly define the problems and ways to avoid them. I have written at least two books that focus on the biblical principles of managing money in the home and ways to avoid the pitfalls of debt in a marriage. Thus I see no need for another book on those subjects. Instead, this book is oriented toward those who have already made the mistakes, and perhaps have even made previous attempts to correct the problems, but have failed. It is presented as a "how to" on getting out of debt.

I hope that if you're reading this book and aren't in debt yourself, you are doing so to help others who are in debt. If they are family members, especially grown children, I trust you will find this book a light in a world of darkness. I know of nothing more emotionally defeating for parents than to watch their children make financial mistakes repeatedly, while depending on their parents to bail them out of crisis after crisis. More money won't solve their problems. The old adage is "more money in, more money out." What is needed is a plan to help establish some financial discipline in their children's lives.

If you happen to be reading this book because a friend, a family member, or a counselor recommended it to you, I trust that you will reserve judgment until you have read enough to understand the concepts presented. It is not my purpose to condemn or accuse anyone. We all have weaknesses that cause difficulties in our lives. Yours may be in the area of finances, whereas mine may be another area. I don't pretend to have all the answers, but I believe that God's Word does, so I'll limit most of my counsel to those areas that can be dealt with from His Word.

One last thought: my intent is to provide you with specific "how to's" for solving debt problems. We will examine every option available, including consolidation, bankruptcy, and skipping out on the creditors. Some are biblical, some are legal, and others fit into neither category.

Part One

THREE COUPLES
SLIDE INTO DEBT

1

A National Policy of Growth Through Debt

IF YOU WERE born after 1950, you don't remember when home mortgages were rare and car loans were for twelve months or less. Prior to that time the local banker was considered the most conservative businessman in town. If someone was approved for a loan, it was generally accepted that he was good for the money. The only regular line of credit most people had was with the local butcher or grocer, and those loans were based on honesty and dependability.

The Great Depression made a lasting impact on millions of people who lost a lifetime of earnings in repossessed farms and mortgages. It also left a lasting impact on lenders, who found themselves in the position of having to repossess homes and farms that were virtually worthless to them. The Great Depression forced Americans to conserve again. Bankers began to make loans only with adequate collateral, and borrowers were extremely cautious because they realized the risks.

But after the Second World War, the government found itself with several million ex-G.I.s who needed homes, jobs, and education. With the impact of the Great Depression still fresh in their minds, commercial lenders such as banks and savings and loans were reluctant to extend credit to so many men who had virtually no credit history. So as a last resort, the government became the lender. Congress passed laws allowing the federal government to guarantee loans made to ex-servicemen, and the G.I. Bill was born. This law allowed commercial lenders to extend credit for education and housing to millions of wartime veterans, and it provided government guarantees to back those loans.

The impact on the economy was immediate and spectacular. Millions of Americans went off to college, and millions more borrowed money to build homes and start businesses. The great credit boom of the twentieth century was off and running. Never before in history had our government used tax-generated dollars to support private lending, but the American people supported the idea wholeheartedly and a new idea was born: consumer credit. Soon the government programs were expanded to provide government-backed loans to non-veterans through the Federal Housing Administration, the Federal Farm Loan Administration, the Small Business Administration, and so on.

With the stimulus of credit feeding the education, housing, and business sectors, prices went up—the natural outgrowth of the law of supply and demand. Credit allowed more people to compete for the available products and services, which in turn allowed prices to increase. Once the cycle began, others were forced to borrow to compete for those items, and private lenders stepped in to provide the loans. The boom of home loans in the fifties provided better housing to young couples at a much earlier age than they could have ever realized by saving to buy their homes.

But there was a price to be paid, and that price was inflation. Home prices began to creep up in the late fifties, as more and more families entered the market through a wide variety of mortgage options. But as prices climbed, many couples were forced out of the market because they could not afford the monthly payments. The bankers, still leaning to the conservative side, applied the 25 percent rule to housing loans, meaning that no more than 25 percent of the husband's total monthly income could be dedicated to home mortgage payments.

The impasse created by that policy led to a slowdown in buying, not only in the housing industry, but also in related industries such as appliances, carpeting, and real estate. A parallel predicament was evident in the automobile industry and in education, both of which had become heavily dependent on consumers' use of loans to buy their products and services. The answer came in the form of longer term loans. By extending the payment period, lenders enabled people with relatively low incomes to afford the monthly payments. Another boom was on.

By the mid-sixties the generation of bankers who had been through the Great Depression was retiring and turning operations over to younger, more aggressive people who had grown up with the debt-oriented mentality. The need to expand the credit base meant that even more loans had to be made available to more people for longer periods of time.

By the seventies virtually every segment of the economy was dependent on credit. Even consumer items such as food, clothing, medical care, and travel were dependent on credit through credit cards and small loans. Lenders extended long-term loans based on equity in assets. Thus consumers could borrow on the appreciated values of their homes, stocks, and businesses. But since the equity was dependent on the availability of loans to subsequent buyers, this created the need for even more lending. The economy was returning to the pre-Depression mentality of growth through debt.

In the seventies the government was no longer just the guarantor of loans. It was the stimulator of massive debt. The economy had become totally dependent on consumers' borrowing to keep it going. The traditional requirements for qualifying borrowers fell by the wayside as lenders sought wider markets for their loans. No longer was the rule in mortgage loans 25 percent of the husband's salary. Now it was 40 percent of both incomes. Car loans were extended to sixty months and often had balloon payments of up to 40 percent at the completion of the loan period.

By the eighties debt had become the engine that fueled the entire economy, and consumers were forced to borrow even the equity out of their homes in order to educate their children and purchase cars. Is it any wonder that in the midst of this steamroller of debt-financing the average family experienced financial problems? It is interesting that the increase in the American divorce rate can be tracked on a curve matching the growth of debt in the country. Does the increase in divorce cause the debt to increase, or is it the other way around? I believe that the increased incidence of divorce is a direct result of too much debt. Nearly 80 percent of divorced couples between the ages of twenty and thirty state that financial problems were the primary cause of their divorce.

What can a person do to break out of this cycle? How much credit can an individual or a family handle? These are the fundamental questions that will be addressed in this book.

My intent is twofold. First, I want to help those who are in debt develop a plan to manage their finances. Second, I want to convince anyone that he can become debt-free and stay that way, given the desire, discipline, and time.

I believe that we are headed for a massive economic recession (or depression), during which the present debt cycle will be reversed. Regardless of what anyone says to the contrary, we cannot continue to run our economy on borrowed money. Eventually the debt burden will become so excessive that even the interest payments cannot be made.

The government is rapidly approaching that point now. Each year it borrows the equivalent of the interest due, even during relatively good economic times.

Consumers and businesses owe nearly six trillion dollars in debt, much of it at floating or variable interest rates. Unfortunately, the rates tend to rise when the economy turns sour. Those who are caught in the debt cycle during any major recession quickly discover the meaning of Proverbs 22:7: "The rich rules over the poor, and the borrower becomes the lender's slave."

2

Sliding Toward a Crisis

P AUL AND JULIE were from middle-income families. They grew up in the suburban area of Chicago and had the normal amount of chores around the house. Julie's father was a realistic person who kept the household records and distributed the money. He gave Julie's mother a housing allowance to manage. He paid all the other bills and gave Julie a strict allowance. Julie was required to work for a portion of her clothing and entertainment money.

In Paul's family the distribution of tasks was different. His mother kept the checkbook and paid the bills. His father never got involved with family finances except when he wanted to buy something. Then he simply wrote a check for the amount he needed. That caused some terrible fights, since he never bothered to write down his checks. Paul could almost always go to his dad and get money when he needed it. When he did this, Paul's father usually told him not to tell his mother because she would have had a fit. Paul's father worked a great deal of overtime on his job and believed that the money was his to spend as he wished.

Paul held several part-time jobs while he was growing up but rarely stayed at any for longer than a few weeks. The money he made was his to spend as he desired. When he was in the twelfth grade, his father bought him a nice car (on time), and his mother blew up about it because she hadn't been consulted.

When Paul started college, he was encouraged to apply for student aid and government loans. By falsifying the credit reports, he was able to qualify for both. He completed two years of college while living at home but never really decided on a field of study. He took a summer job at a large auto assembly plant and received an offer to stay on permanently, which he accepted.

He and Julie dated for nearly a year after they met in college. When Paul took his permanent job, he asked Julie to marry him, with the understanding that she would complete her education in teaching—a field to which she was very strongly committed.

Neither Paul nor Julie received any detailed instructions from their parents about marriage. It was assumed that the pastor of Julie's church would provide the instruction they needed. Indeed, the pastor did require several hours of counseling on sex, communication, and spiritual values. Once he asked Paul if he would be able to support a family, to which Paul replied, "Yes sir, I'll be making six-fifty an hour at the plant. We'll have plenty of money."

Since that was more than the pastor was making himself (not counting housing or car allowances), he never pursued the subject further. So having completed what they thought were the requirements for marriage, Paul and Julie were married.

Julie reread the notice: "Dear Mr. and Mrs. Averal, Our records show that your VISA account is seriously overdue. We have made numerous attempts to contact you about this matter. This letter is to notify you that your account has been turned over to our Collections Department. You need to clear this account in total to avoid serious damage to your credit rating.

"Sincerely,

"Robert Bowers, Credit Manager"

I don't think I can stand much more of this, Julie thought. *I work hard all day long, and yet there never seems to be enough money anymore. I don't feel like I can ever go out and buy myself a new dress. And the nursery said they're going to increase Timmy's fees, too.* She remembered the embarrassing experience in bankruptcy court before the baby was born and the bad advice Mr. Moore had given them. After all that trouble their financial problems were no better. She groaned. *I wish I were dead*

Julie truly was at the end of her rope. She resented having to work and felt guilty about leaving her son with strangers every day. She felt trapped.

Meanwhile, Paul was trying to cope with feelings of inferiority and with overwhelming financial pressure. Unfortunately, his method of coping tended to amplify Julie's anxieties.

"Hey Paul, we're starting the new company bowling league. Are you interested in joining?"

"No, I guess not. I don't know where we'd get the money right now," Paul replied dejectedly.

"Ah, what's the matter, Paul? The wife won't let you have enough to go bowling? Man, I told my wife that I do what I want with my money, and if she doesn't like it, she can find herself another meal ticket."

Maybe that's what Julie is thinking about doing, Paul thought, as he punched out for the day. *It seems that all we ever do anymore is fight about money. I feel awful about our fight last night, but she acted like it's my fault that she has to work. That's so stupid. If she had taken her pills like she was supposed to, she wouldn't have gotten pregnant and we'd be doing fine. Women are supposed to know about those things. I can't help it if she can't go to college now.* But Paul knew his marriage was in serious trouble.

Paul made his way out to his car in the employee parking lot. His stomach felt twisted in knots. He thought about going to a doctor, but the company's insurance plan didn't pay for office visits, and he knew he and Julie didn't have the money.

Paul got into his car and turned the key. All he heard in response was a low growl and then a click.

"Oh nuts," he said as he looked around the nearly empty parking lot. "Now what am I going to do?"

Paul got out of his car and went back into the plant building. He saw one of the second shift maintenance crew and asked if he would help him jump start his car.

"Sure, I'll be glad to, Paul," he replied. "But you need to do something about that old clunker of yours. This is the third time in the last month it wouldn't take you home."

I wish I could do something about it, Paul thought as they headed out the door. *But we seem to get further behind every month. I had a better car when I was in high school than I do now.*

In a few minutes they had Paul's car started, and he headed home. "Boy, Julie's going to be mad again," Paul said out loud. "This is the second time I've been late this week." Then he thought, *It seems like she's always mad these days. I work as hard as I can, and she keeps nagging about how she always has to do without things. I wonder what she thinks I do?*

As Paul was driving by the Simmon's Auto Sales lot, he saw a sign that read, "Why put up with that old car? We'll put you in a new car for $118 a month, no previous credit necessary."

Paul thought, *I know we can't buy a new car, but it won't hurt to look. I spend more than that on this old pile of junk now, I'll bet.*

An hour later Paul was on his way home, driving a brand new Plymouth. He had signed the contracts, but the salesman had assured him that if there was a problem with the car he could trade it back in. Paul was excited to show it to Julie. He knew they could work the $132 a month into their budget. It cost more than the advertised price, but he knew Julie would want an automatic and air conditioning.

As he walked in the door, he could hear the baby screaming. Julie came out of the kitchen. "Paul, where have you been? I could use some help around here. Will you please go and see what's wrong with Timmy? I don't think I can stand his crying another minute." With that she turned back toward the kitchen.

Paul headed into the bedroom to pick up Timmy and snapped, "I don't know what's wrong with you. You're acting worse than a child." Julie did an abrupt about-face and followed him into Timmy's room.

"You're a good one to talk," she yelled with as much anger as she felt inside. "I feel like I've got to take care of two children instead of one. The bank sent me a note at work today about our VISA account. If we don't pay it, they're going to turn it over for collection. If my boss gets another garnishment, he'll probably fire me."

"Ah, that's stupid, Julie. They can't fire you for that. And the bill is not that far overdue anyway."

"So I'm stupid now, too, am I?" Julie shouted as she stormed out of the room. "If I'm that stupid, I guess you should have married somebody else." She slammed the door to their bedroom, and Paul heard the lock click shut.

Depression swept over him as he picked up their son and headed into the kitchen. He didn't know where to turn or what to do. *What would Julie say when she found out about the car?* he wondered. Paul knew she was seriously considering leaving him again. The last time he had been able to talk her into coming back. But he knew that Julie couldn't be talked into coming back if she left this time.

Carrying Timmy with him, Paul went outside and got into the new car. He eased it out of the driveway and drove back to Simmon's Auto Sales. He hoped he could get his old car back without Julie's discovering what he had done. And he, too, remembered their experience in bankruptcy court. It was supposed to have smoothed things out, but so far their financial condition had only got worse. He shuddered. How had things got so bad?

3

It Didn't Begin Yesterday

THE SEEDS OF financial collapse were planted early in Paul and Julie Averal's marriage. When they were married, she at twenty-one and he at twenty-two, neither one knew much about financial matters. Their financial plans were simple. They would delay having children for five years. Julie would use that time to finish college and get established in her teaching career. After that, they would begin a family. There was some thought that Paul might go back to college someday, but that was only a vague idea.

But after living in an apartment for five months, Paul decided that it didn't make any sense to keep throwing money away on rent. Some of the guys at work had told him he was losing all the tax breaks the government allowed home owners. "You're just paying the government's bills for welfare when you rent," another shift worker had said authoritatively. "Get yourself a house and start building some equity." Paul began to look for a home they could buy. He found one that was near their price range, but the bank wouldn't finance it on the basis of his income alone. So during the summer college break Julie took a job as receptionist for a local dentist. Based on their combined incomes, they signed to buy the home. Julie told Paul several times that she didn't think it was a good idea to buy a home, but he assured her that he would be getting raises to cover the additional costs. "Besides," he said, "with the tax breaks we'll get, it won't cost us any more than renting does."

They couldn't afford the down payment, so Paul's dad co-signed for a note at his credit union. Paul neglected to mention the loan on his mortgage application and also failed to mention that Julie's income was temporary. The monthly house payments required almost 60 percent of Paul's take-home pay. Almost immediately they were in financial trouble from the payments alone. With the insurance, taxes, and utilities added, Paul and Julie were on the road to debt without realizing it.

After the first month, Paul was unable to make the loan payment to his company's credit union. When it was sixty days delinquent, the credit union attached his salary and had the payments deducted automatically, as per their written agreement. Paul's father was sent written notice of collection proceedings against him for the two months in arrears. When he received the notice, he hit the roof and stormed over to Paul and Julie's to confront the issue.

By that point, Julie had gone back to school. She had had no knowledge of any financial problems. When she found out, she was devastated. Paul's dad demanded that they pay the past due bill. When Paul told him they could not, his dad suggested that Julie get a job.

"Paul, I can't see any way that we can keep this house," Julie said. "I would rather sell it than drop out of school."

"We won't have to sell the house," Paul replied emphatically. "I can get a loan on my car to catch up the payments. I'm due a raise pretty soon; then we'll have enough to make it."

"I don't know, Paul. What if the raise doesn't come through?" Julie asked.

"You don't need to worry, honey. I take care of the finances in this family. I know it will work out."

With that, Julie put the subject of finances out of her mind. But she couldn't shake the nagging feeling of impending disaster.

Paul negotiated a loan on his car for enough to catch up the credit union payment with some left over. He used that to buy a VCR, so they wouldn't have to go to the movies, he said. That would save a lot of money—he was sure.

When Paul received his next check with the loan payment taken out, he was shocked. His net pay for the first pay period of the month was just $175. He had already mailed the house payment anticipating his pay, and he realized that the check probably wouldn't clear. Sure enough, he received a note from the mortgage company that his check had been returned for insufficient funds. They demanded immediate payment or they would pursue legal action.

Not knowing what to do, Paul called a local loan company that advertised immediate second mortgage loans for home owners.

"Paul, I absolutely will not sign to get a second mortgage on this house," Julie screamed. "We can't pay the bills we have now! "

"There's nothing else we can do," Paul shouted back. "I have to pay the mortgage or they'll repossess the house."

"I don't care if they do," Julie said, beginning to cry. "I don't think I can take much more of this. I'm going home for a while. I just need to get away and think."

With that, Julie grabbed some clothes and called her mother to come after her. When Julie's dad came home that evening, he asked, "What's the problem, honey?"

"Oh, Daddy, we're in such a financial mess, and I can't get Paul to be honest with me. We seem to get into more trouble every month."

Julie's father was wise enough to call Paul and ask him to come over and talk. Paul explained the problem of the credit union payment being taken out of the first of the month's paycheck when he thought it would be taken out of the second check. He assured Julie's father that it was all a misunderstanding and that he would be able to make the adjustment the next month.

Rather than allow them to take out a second mortgage, Julie's dad decided to lend them the money himself. He just asked that Paul pay the loan back as soon as he could. Paul assured him that he would do so and that it would be no longer than two months.

Even a casual observer could see at this point that giving Paul and Julie more money was not the answer. But it's often much easier to see the truth in someone else's life than it is in your own. Certainly Paul wasn't trying to deceive anyone. He just didn't have enough information about the way finances worked to make an intelligent decision.

The loan from Julie's father didn't solve any problems. It merely delayed the inevitable. Within two months bills were backing up again. Creditors were calling day and night to pressure both Paul and Julie. But most often they wanted to reach Julie, because they knew that the wife would succumb to pressure more easily than the husband.

It was almost impossible for Julie to concentrate on her school work. For the first time in her life she began to let her grades slip. That put additional pressure on her, especially when her father called to chide her about her mid-term grades. "Julie, we're sacrificing to pay your college tuition and books, and we expect you to do your part," her father said. "If you don't keep your grades up, we'll stop helping. What's the matter with you? You're capable of doing better work."

Julie was shattered. She had always had the approval of her parents, and now they were putting pressure on her, too. An event that very evening became the final straw. She came home at about 6:00 P.M. from classes, almost on the verge of tears because of the earlier discussion with her father. She opened the door, flipped on the light switch and—nothing happened. She made her way to the dining room and tried that switch. Still nothing. In another five minutes she knew that their power had been turned off.

She grabbed a flashlight and began to look through the desk in their bedroom, where she found two delinquent notices warning that their lights would be turned off if the bill wasn't paid immediately. She also found similar notices from the gas and water companies. She sat there in the dark crying for nearly an hour until Paul came home.

When Paul came in he said, "Julie, what's the matter with the lights?"

"I'll tell you what's the matter. You haven't paid the bill for the last two months, and they turned our power off. That's what's the matter! And I found notices from the other utilities, too. Paul, what's the matter with you? Can't you even keep up with the utility bills?"

"I'm sorry, honey. I intended to pay them, but there wasn't enough money in the last paycheck. I'll try to get them caught up next paycheck."

"Oh, Paul, it's always the next paycheck with you. But we never seem to have enough money to catch up. I've decided to quit school and get a job. I just can't live like this anymore."

"I'm really sorry. But I think you're right. If you could just work for a while until we get caught up, it would really help. You should be able to go back next fall. I've got another raise coming that will help a lot then."

Julie quit school and took a job as a typist for a company in their city, making about $700 dollars a month net. She desperately wanted to tithe her income as she had done all of her unmarried life, but Paul said they couldn't afford to do so. He was supported in that decision by both sets of parents, who felt it would be better to pay off some of the debts first. That turned out to be a spiritual turning point in Julie's life. She had been taught that tithing was a way to keep bad things from happening. When she stopped tithing, she expected to have a disaster in her life. When it didn't happen, she began to doubt that there really was a God. If so, why didn't He punish her for not giving her tithe? Shortly after that, she stopped attending the church she had gone to all her life. Gradually, but steadily, she began to drift away from her relationship with God.

For several months things seemed to get better financially, and her relationship with Paul even improved. They had some extra money to go out periodically, and Julie was able to buy a used car so that she wouldn't be dependent on Paul to get back and forth to work.

Then Julie began to feel awful in the mornings. When she missed her period, she realized that she might be pregnant. She hadn't been disciplined about taking the birth control pills her doctor had prescribed.

A visit to a local health clinic confirmed her worst fears: she was pregnant. A general feeling of gloom came over her as she thought about Paul's reaction and the fact that not only would a baby curtail her education, but it would also greatly reduce her ability to work. She felt like she was in a box with no way out. She thought briefly about the prospect of an abortion but then put it out of her mind. Her strong Christian background would not allow her to do such a thing. But now she understood the terrible temptation that money pressures created for others who found themselves in the same situation.

"What do you mean, you're pregnant?" Paul shouted when Julie told him. "How could you be so stupid, Julie? All you had to do was take those pills, and you wouldn't have gotten pregnant."

"Do you think I got pregnant on purpose?" Julie screamed back. "I don't like this any more than you do, but there is nothing I can do about it now."

Paul stormed out of their bedroom. Julie collapsed on the bed in tears. She felt guilty about getting pregnant and anxious about the future.

"How will we ever be able to pay for a baby?" she wondered. "If I stop working, we won't even be able to pay the bills we have now."

The rest of that evening Julie stayed in the bedroom and Paul stayed downstairs. He began to feel guilty about his reaction to Julie and decided to apologize. But by the time he went upstairs she was asleep.

Julie tried to continue to work, but morning sickness forced her to miss more and more work. Finally her boss called her in to confront the issue.

"Julie, I know you've had a tough time with this pregnancy, but you've missed six days in the last two weeks. We need someone to do your work. Why don't you take a month's leave of absence and stay home? If you're doing better, then come back and see me, and we'll find something for you to do."

"Oh, Mrs. Moore, I can't afford to stay home," Julie replied through a rush of tears. "I have to work, or we can't keep up with our payments."

"Julie, I think that you and Paul ought to consider filing bankruptcy. You're not going to be able to work while you're so sick. And if you continue the way you're going, you will ruin your health and the baby's, too."

"Bankruptcy? I never thought about it," Julie said. "I thought bankruptcy was only for companies or people who owed millions of dollars."

"No, dear," Mrs. Moore replied. "My husband's firm handles personal bankruptcies all the time. It's certainly no sin to file for bankruptcy anymore. After all, those companies that lend to young couples ought to know better anyway. Here's one of his cards. Talk it over with Paul and give my husband a call if you would like to talk about it."

That evening Julie was quiet through dinner. Paul sensed something new was wrong, but he dreaded asking what it was. Their relationship had been so tense since Julie became pregnant that they rarely spoke to one another without getting into some kind of argument. Finally, he spoke up. "What's wrong now, Julie? You have barely said two words since I got home."

"I lost my job today," she replied matter-of-factly.

"You lost your job!" Paul bellowed as he came up out of the chair. "How did you lose your job?"

"Mrs. Moore said I was taking too much time off, and they needed someone who is more consistent."

"They can't do that. It's illegal," Paul shouted in fear, as much as anger.

"Yes, they can, Paul," Julie replied. "They're willing to give me another job when I can work again. But Mrs. Moore is right. If I keep up this pace, it may be detrimental to the baby's health."

"But what in the world will we do?" Paul said in despair as he sat back down. "We just bought your car, and we can barely make it even when you work."

"Mrs. Moore suggested that we file for bankruptcy protection," Julie replied. "She said her husband handles bankruptcies for couples like us all the time."

"I don't see how that's possible," Paul replied. "Most of our debts are credit cards and department store loans, outside of the house and cars. I don't think you can get out of those debts."

"She said we can," Julie replied, handing Paul the business card Mrs. Moore had given her.

Paul arranged a meeting with the attorney, Joe Moore. "Paul and Julie, I've reviewed your case, and I think I can help you," he said. "Most of your debts are relatively small bills owed to credit card companies and stores. And since you're really in this fix because of an unexpected pregnancy, I believe the judge will grant you a chapter thirteen."

"What's a chapter thirteen," Paul asked.

"It's an individual reorganization plan," the attorney replied. "It's set up for cases just like yours where a couple gets into debt over their heads through hardship. The court tells the creditors how much they will receive, based on a plan we submit. Once they receive what the judge allocates, you're cleared of any other liabilities you owe."

"And that's all there is to it?" Paul said in wonderment. "The judge tells them what we can pay, and they have to accept it?"

"That's about it," Mr. Moore replied. "I've seen it help dozens of couples just like you. After all, it's not your fault that Julie can't work anymore. And the letter you received from her company directing her to stay home for at least a month will really help sell this to the court."

"Mr. Moore, I don't feel completely at peace about this," Julie said. "What about the rest of the money we owe? Isn't it our responsibility to pay all of it?"

"Absolutely not. In the first place the creditors carry bad debt insurance to protect them against losses. And second, this law was written to protect young couples like you from abuse by ruthless collection agencies that try to get blood out of a turnip."

We certainly have been harassed by collection agencies, Julie said to herself. "Well, I guess if the law allows it, there is no problem. What do you think, Paul?"

"I think it's an answer to prayer. I don't know what we would have done with your losing your job and a baby on the way. Mr. Moore, go ahead with the chapter thirteen."

"There's just one more thing. My fee for filing the case will be four hundred fifty dollars, and you'll need to pay a fifty dollar fee to the court."

"Five hundred dollars?" Paul said in surprise. "We don't have five hundred dollars."

"Could you get it from your parents?" he asked.

"We've already borrowed from our parents," Julie said. "I don't think any of them would agree to lend us any more."

"That's too bad," the attorney replied. "I need the money up front before I can file the case. There is another alternative, however."

"What's that?" Paul replied.

"Why don't you charge your groceries and utilities on your credit cards for the next month? Then you'll have the money you need. When the bankruptcy takes effect, the charges will be lumped in with the other bills. In fact, it might even help our case because we'll be able to show the judge that your financial situation is getting worse."

"But is that honest?" Julie asked.

"Sure it is," Mr. Moore replied. "Besides, why do you think the credit card companies charge so much interest? They can afford to take a few losses. They're not hurting financially. If you don't believe that, just take a look at their buildings sometime."

"That's for sure," Paul agreed. "Besides, I don't see that we have any alternatives. This seems like an answer to our prayers. Now you'll be able to stay home until the baby's born. By then I'll be making overtime pay again, and you'll be able to go back to school."

"Sounds good," Mr. Moore replied. "I'm always glad to help kids like you. Maybe you'll come and visit our church sometime. In fact, I'd be glad to have you in my Sunday school class for young couples."

"Maybe we'll do that, Mr. Moore," Paul replied as they got up to leave. "Thanks for your help."

"Sure thing," he replied. "Remember, when the bills come in next month, just put them aside until after the court hearing. Just pay what you have to in order to keep the lights on. But don't put the cash in your checking account, or it will become a part of the assets. Just keep it in your home somewhere safe."

After they left Julie said, "Paul, I don't like the idea of using our credit cards when we know we're not going to pay the bills."

"Listen, Julie, Mr. Moore's a fine Christian man. He wouldn't tell us to do something illegal. Besides, what alternative do we have? With you pregnant, we can't pay any of the bills anyway. And as Mr. Moore said, the companies can afford the loss. That's why they carry insurance."

4

Things Come to a Head

"MR. AND MRS. Averal, I've decided to grant your petition for bankruptcy protection in accordance with chapter thirteen of the Federal Bankruptcy Code," Judge Brown said. "You need to understand the conditions of this action. Each month you must meet the minimum payments established in the budget plan you submitted. Failure to do so will constitute a breech of contract and may require this court to remove you from chapter thirteen protection. You will then have to file for personal dissolution under chapter seven of the Bankruptcy Code. Do you understand this clearly?"

"Yes sir, we do," replied Paul.

"Very well. But there is one further matter concerning your case that I need to address. There were several charges on your credit cards during the last month prior to filing your petition. Your creditors have requested that these accounts be set aside from this bankruptcy action on the grounds that they were made in contemplation of filing for bankruptcy protection. I have decided to grant their petition as the facts would seem to support that conclusion.

"I want to issue you both a stern warning that this court will not condone or allow such blatant attempts to deceive your creditors. The bankruptcy court is provided to give couples who have had personal financial setbacks beyond their control the chance to start over again. It is not to be used to defraud those who trusted you by extending credit to you.

"I hope you have learned from your bad experiences with the overuse of credit and that you will not repeat the same mistakes. You're young and can reestablish your lives and your credit if you discipline yourselves. The next time, this court will not deal with you so leniently. I set repayment at fifty percent and monthly payments at one hundred dollars a month. The court will review your petition in twelve months."

Julie sat in stunned silence. She didn't really hear what the judge said beyond the point where he chastened them for what he concluded to be an attempt to defraud the credit card companies. She realized that was exactly what they had attempted to do. She began to cry as the courtroom cleared.

"What's the matter, Julie?" Paul asked as he and the attorney approached her.

"Oh, Paul, I'm so ashamed of what we tried to do by charging all of our expenses last month while we hoarded our money. Those men from the credit card companies must think we're awful people."

"Don't worry about it, Julie," Joe Moore said. "Our plan worked, and now your total debt payments will be just one hundred dollars a month. And with that set aside at fifty percent, you should be totally clear in less than two years."

"I don't understand what set-aside is, Mr. Moore," Paul said.

"It means that you must repay the existing debts up to 50 percent of their current levels, but with no additional interest accumulation."

"You mean we don't have to repay the entire amount?" Paul asked in astonishment.

"No, the judge decided that based on the petition I made on your behalf it would be an undue burden on you to repay the entire amount."

"But I think we should repay the entire amount," Julie said. "After all, we did borrow the money in good faith. I don't think it would be honorable to repay only half."

"I appreciate your attitude, Julie, but you need to be realistic. You have a baby on the way, and you'll have additional expenses. Don't you think your first responsibility is to your baby?"

"Yes," Julie replied. "But—"

"I agree with Mr. Moore," replied Paul. "I think this is an answer from God."

"Of course," responded Joe Moore. "Even God provided a way to set aside debts so that His people wouldn't be caught up in debts they couldn't repay."

"He did?" Julie said in amazement.

"Sure. In the Old Testament God had a plan where every seven years all debts would be set aside. That's where our bankruptcy laws originated."

"I never heard anybody explain that before," Paul said. "So God allows for bankruptcy, too?"

"Absolutely," replied Joe Moore. "Otherwise I wouldn't be in this business."

"What's going to happen to the credit card bills we ran up last month?" Paul asked.

"The repayment plan will include those debts each month, but you'll have to repay one hundred percent of what's owed. It just means it will take you a little while longer to get out of debt, but it's no big deal. That's always a risk you run when you charge just before a bankruptcy hearing. But I knew the judge wouldn't throw your case out—not with Julie pregnant."

"You mean you knew the judge might not allow the recent charges to be set aside, Mr. Moore?" asked Julie in astonishment.

"Well, I knew it was a possibility. But in this business, nothing ventured, nothing gained. Besides, you're no worse off than you might have been otherwise."

"Only regarding our reputation—that's all," replied Julie as tears welled up in her eyes.

As they headed home Julie commented, "Paul, I don't think we did the right thing. I think we have cheated our creditors."

"I disagree," commented Paul. "It feels like a burden has been lifted off our shoulders. We have a chance to start fresh and get our lives back in order. Wait and see; things are going to work out OK from now on."

As the weeks passed, Julie began to believe that Paul was right. The pressures on their marriage eased as the financial strain from delinquent bills lessened. For several weeks Paul was able to work extra overtime as the plant increased its productivity. They used the extra income to buy baby supplies and the other items Julie would need. She was even able to return to work on a part-time basis, so they had more "free" money than during any previous time in their marriage.

The baby came, and Julie was totally occupied with learning to care for a new infant. Her mother helped until the baby was nearly a month old. Then she left Julie to return to her own home.

During the fifth week the baby began to cry more than usual, and Julie took him in for a general check-up. The doctor's diagnosis was colic, a non-life-threatening stomach condition common to many young babies. But as the weeks passed, the baby cried more frequently and eventually began to cry nearly every waking moment. Both Julie's and Paul's nerves began to wear thin.

Paul began to get lax about paying the household bills, and he began to pick up food in the evenings rather than cook at home. The baby took up so much of Julie's time that she was virtually unable to do anything else.

One evening on the way home Paul was involved in a minor automobile accident. He was ticketed and was required to appear in traffic court the next month. He didn't mention the incident to Julie and figured he could scrape together the fine, which he thought would be about $35.

Paul put the incident out of his mind and completely forgot about the court date. Late one evening after arriving home from work he answered the doorbell to find two policemen at his front door.

"Are you Paul Averal?" the older policeman asked.

"Yes, I am, officer," Paul answered. "What can I do for you?"

"Mr. Averal, I have a warrant for your arrest for failure to appear in court to answer charges on a traffic violation and for driving a vehicle without insurance," the officer said.

"Oh no!" Paul exclaimed. "I completely forgot about the ticket. But officer, there must be some mistake. I do have insurance on my car."

"Sir, I would suggest that you get a copy of your policy and come with us. We have a bench warrant for your arrest issued by Judge Simmons. You'll either have to pay the fines assessed or post bail to be released."

"How much are the fines?" Paul asked as Julie came to the door to see what was going on.

"The total is seven hundred fifty dollars, sir," the officer said.

"Seven hundred fifty dollars!" Paul exclaimed. "There must be some mistake. They can't be that much."

"Yes sir, they are," the officer said. "They include a traffic citation, a fine for failure to have liability insurance, and the court and summons charges."

"I know I have insurance," Paul said defiantly. "Wait here, and I'll get a copy of my policy."

Julie began to feel a familiar wave of depression come over her as she heard the conversation. She suspected that the officer was right and Paul was wrong. Her suspicions were confirmed when Paul returned in a few minutes.

"Officer, I found my policy, but it has lapsed. I'm afraid that I forgot to pay the premium. It must have been canceled without their telling me."

"I'm sorry, sir, but you will have to come with us to the station. Your wife can come and post the bail in the morning. Then you will need to see the judge about any details."

"How much will the bail be, officer?" Julie asked through her tears.

"It will be the amount of the fines and other charges, ma'am," the officer replied. "But you won't be able to post bail until nine tomorrow morning."

"You mean my husband will have to spend the night in jail?" she asked, almost in panic.

"Yes, ma'am," the officer replied. "But he'll be kept in the driver detention cell away from the other prisoners, so don't worry about him. He'll be fine."

With that, they led Paul out to the police car and placed him in the backseat. Julie rushed to the phone and called her father to tell him what had happened.

"Calm down, honey," her father said. "It'll be OK. We'll go down first thing in the morning and get Paul out. In the meantime, why don't you come over here and spend the night with us."

Julie willingly agreed. Her fear and depression were rising to a peak as she thought about the whole cycle of debt and money pressures starting all over again.

The next morning Julie's father put up the money for the bail, and Paul was released. On the way home Julie questioned him about their finances, and Paul confessed that several bills were delinquent.

"There just doesn't seem to be enough money each month," Paul said. "There was for a while, but it seems to evaporate. We just can't make it on my salary, Julie. You're going to have to go to work, especially now that this fine is hanging over our heads. The judge said that I won't be able to drive until the fines are paid and we show proof of insurance."

"But, Paul, we don't have anyone to keep the baby," Julie said as the tears began to flow. She felt like she was in a dark pit with the sides beginning to cave in.

"Maybe we can get your mom to keep him, at least for a while, until we can get some of the bills caught up," Paul said.

"I hate doing that," Julie screamed. "We're always asking someone to bail us out of our messes. I wish I had never met you, Paul."

Julie did go back to work and found that she actually enjoyed it. The baby was getting better, and being away from him during the day helped her to cope with the evenings. But soon her mother told her that she could no longer keep the baby. She had a life of her own to lead, and it wasn't fair that she had to raise a second family. Julie cried a lot over the decision, but in the end she knew her mother was right, so she started looking for someone to keep the baby. She was shocked at the cost of child care. She finally selected what she thought would be the best child care center, but it would cost her nearly $400 a month.

As the weeks passed, she and Paul continued to argue about money. Julie believed she was a slave to Paul's impulses. He often bought things he wanted—such as a new television or a CD player—but then there was no money for clothes or eating out. Finally, she decided that she would keep a portion of her paycheck for herself. Instead of bringing the check home as she had in the past, she would stop at the bank and deposit it, taking out the money she needed.

Paul was furious when she told him about it. "Julie, you can't do that," he shouted. "There won't be enough money to pay all the bills."

"Then they will have to go unpaid," Julie yelled back. "I'm not going to worry about it anymore. You never paid my dad back for your fines, and I'm going to start paying him back something every month. Paul, you're a totally irresponsible little boy. I'm sick and tired of working all day and never being able to spend any of my own money."

"Well, if it's your money, why don't you just keep it yourself, and I'll keep my money!" Paul shouted as he stormed out of the room.

"Then I'll do just that," Julie yelled back as he slammed the front door.

Julie spent the next two hours drawing up a budget dividing their respective expenses. She decided that she should pay for the baby's nursery costs, her transportation, and a fourth of the utilities.

The next day she left work a little early so that she could go to the bank and open a checking account in her name. That evening she informed Paul that she had decided to keep her money and pay her own bills. She handed him a copy of the division of expenses that she had drawn up.

Paul had a sinking feeling inside, as if something had died. And in truth he knew that something had: their marriage.

"Look Julie, I'm sorry for what I said last night. I didn't mean it really. I don't want us to have separate checking accounts and split the expenses."

"No, you just want to he able to spend what you want, when you want,"

Julie spat out. "Well, no more. You pay your part, and I'll pay my part from now on. And if you don't like it, I'll leave."

"Do you really mean that, Julie?" Paul asked with a hurt look on his face.

"I really do," she replied defiantly. "I don't know if I love you anymore, but I do know that I don't respect you. I've been on the giving end of our marriage from the first day. From now on I'm going to do what's best for me."

Paul felt as if someone had just hit him in the stomach with a sledgehammer. *Where did we go wrong?* Paul thought as Julie stormed out of the dining room. *How could I have been so stupid as to let our relationship slip into hatred? I don't know what to do now.* For the first time in a long time Paul fell to his knees and asked God to forgive him and help him to heal his marriage.

5

If I Don't Talk About It, It'll Go Away

PAUL AND JULIE Averal are not unique. Perhaps the exact circumstances are different in the lives of other couples, but the end result is the same in millions of marriages throughout America. Like Paul and Julie, most couples start out with the highest expectations for their marriages. Half end in divorce—the majority of those because of financial problems.

Unfortunately, few young couples know what they did to create their financial problems or what they need to do to solve them. But before discussing how to solve financial problems, I would like to present the story of another couple. Ron and Sue Hawkins were older than Paul and Julie when they got into financial trouble. But the problems they faced were equally devastating.

Ron and Sue Hawkins were Christians. Ron was a stockbroker and made an average annual salary of $50,000. He paid the major bills, such as the mortgage payments, car payments, and school bills. He gave Sue a household allowance for necessities, such as food, gas, clothes, and allowances.

Their marriage was a good one, except in the area of finances. Sue sensed that she was not a part of any major financial decisions in either their personal lives or the business where Ron was a participating partner. With their children in school most of the day, Sue would have liked to work part-time in Ron's office, as she did when he first started. However, the other members of the firm did not want their wives involved and established policies prohibiting the involvement of family members in the business.

Over the years, against Sue's counsel, Ron invested sizable amounts of borrowed money in various real estate ventures. He took on potential liabilities as a managing partner in several investments with others in the firm, again against Sue's vehement objections. Sue felt that she had been relegated to the position of a mere child in the family's financial matters, and she resented it greatly.

Then some of the investments in which Ron was involved generated financial problems, and a lawsuit initiated by a disgruntled investor threatened to totally destroy their financial worth.

"You know you brought this on yourself," Sue said as Ron read the summons delivered to their home.

"Please, not now, Sue," Ron pleaded, as he lowered his head into his hands. "I feel defeated by this whole thing. I had hoped you would understand."

"Sure, I understand. Your good friends have decided to let you hold the bag for the entire firm," Sue said with an accusing tone. "I told you not to do business with Al Groves. There was something about him I didn't like the first time I met him."

"Oh, spare me the sermon, Sue," he growled. "This has to be the nine hundred and ninety-ninth time you've said that. It's always, 'You never take my advice,' and, 'You never listen to me.' This is serious. Don't you realize how much trouble this can cause me?"

"Can cause *us*, Ron. How much trouble it can cause *us*. That's our main trouble now: you think you're in it alone when it comes to any financial decisions."

"I really don't know what you expect from me," Ron groaned. "I work hard, and I have tried my best to provide a good home for you and the kids."

"I don't care about material things, Ron," Sue replied in a softening tone. "I just want us to be one in our decisions. But you treat me like I'm an idiot when it comes to finances. You listen to everyone else's counsel but mine. Why?"

I just wish I could really be honest with her, Ron thought. *If I could just once share how I feel without her saying "I told you so," or rehashing the past. . . .*

"Ron, when will you finally admit that you don't really want my help?" Sue said as he started to leave the room. "But maybe this time you've gotten yourself in deep enough that you'll admit that you actually need it."

Over the next several weeks the financial situation got worse. The disgruntled investor continued to pursue the lawsuit against Ron and his company. And Ron continued to hide most of the facts from Sue, believing that he was sparing her the emotional trauma he was experiencing. But the crisis became both of theirs when Sue read in the local newspaper that all of their property and possessions were listed for possible auction by the district court, pending an upcoming assessment for fraud against Ron.

When Ron came home that evening, Sue was waiting for him. She began to vent the frustration she had been feeling for many years. Not that their marriage was all bad—in many ways they had a better marriage than most, and they had shared many pleasant times together. But Sue had always felt like an observer in their finances, instead of a partner.

She confronted him. "Ron, you told me that lawsuit would amount to nothing, and now I see we have a judgment against us! Is that what you call nothing?"

"I'm really sorry, Sue. I wanted to tell you, but I just didn't know how. The judge decided against us. We lost."

"Lost! I thought you told me there was no validity to the suit at all. How could you have lost?"

"I don't know," Ron said dejectedly. "They even offered to settle when the case began, but my attorney didn't want to because he felt the facts were so obviously in our favor."

"So exactly what does it mean that you lost?" Sue asked, as fear began to well up inside of her.

"It means that we must decide to go bankrupt, or they will take our home and everything else. But I don't want to go bankrupt. I know I've done a lot of foolish things, but the Lord has definitely gotten my attention. I'm just sorry that I didn't listen to you or let you be a part of the decisions."

"I have to be honest, Ron," Sue said with tears in her eyes. "I'm really scared too, but if this brings us closer together, I wouldn't have it any other way. I don't believe that we should go bankrupt. The Lord may not rescue us from the mess we're in financially, but if we don't give Him the chance, we'll always wonder what He would have done."

"But, honey, it may well mean that we'll end up totally broke after ten years of marriage."

"Ron, I don't care about that. You and I were closer when we had nothing than we are now. I told the Lord a long time ago I would willingly trade everything I have for the oneness that is promised in His Word. I guess He's trying to find out if I really meant *everything*," Sue said as she walked over to Ron and put her arms around him.

6

If Only the Baby Had Been Well

JACK AND MARY Thompson were each graduates of Bible colleges. They each took a teaching position with the same Christian school in the South after they graduated from college. They met while on staff there, fell in love, and got married.

Jack and Mary both came from Christian homes, but were from very different economic backgrounds. Mary's father was a successful dentist, and although he was not wealthy by any means, he made a very comfortable living. Mary was not indulged as a child, and she was expected to work to help pay her way from the teenage years on. Her college tuition was provided by her parents, but she was required to work summers to earn money for her books, clothes, and incidentals, which she did.

Jack came from a much more modest background. His mother and father were divorced when he was nine years old. His mother struggled financially after the divorce, and money was always in short supply in his home. He received a scholarship from his denomination to attend college, and worked long hours to pay his expenses while he was there.

Jack and Mary had been married two years when they had their first child. The school they worked for paid low salaries, and they had been unable to accumulate any significant savings. But they did have what seemed to be an adequate insurance plan, so they thought they would be all right financially. The baby would be born during their summer break, so Mary would be able to work right up to the time of the birth.

There were two things that they hadn't planned on. One was that Jack's salary alone was too low to meet their minimum needs, regardless of how much they scrimped. And two, that the baby would have major health problems. He was born with *spina bifida* and required constant attention. The initial hospital bill was more than $20,000, with their deductible portion being almost $8,000.

Within six months of the baby's birth they were in debt for nearly $12,000 and sinking further behind every month. When they attempted to pay any portion of the doctor or hospital bills, they fell behind on payments for their monthly living expenses. If they tried to keep up on their living expenses, they fell behind on their medical bills.

By the seventh month some of the accounts had been turned over to collection agencies, and Mary was getting frequent, often rude, calls at home. She was an emotional wreck, and her pediatrician—who was a friend from their church—suggested that Jack consider filing bankruptcy to relieve some of the financial pressure.

Coming home from the doctor's office Mary asked, "What did you think about what Doctor Reese said?"

"I don't know, Mary. I've always believed that you should pay your bills, but that seems to be impossible in our case. Every month we get further behind in our bills. What do you think?"

"I don't know the answer, either. But I do know I can't live under the kind of pressure I feel right now. We can't pay the doctor or hospital bills anyway, so I don't see what difference it would make if we file for bankruptcy. If we're ever able to pay, we can always start repaying the bills, can't we?"

"I guess so," Jack replied. "I don't feel at peace about it, but I honestly don't know of another alternative. I'll call Bill Johnson, an attorney in the men's group I meet with on Mondays, and ask if he handles cases like these. But we don't even have the money it takes to go bankrupt unless he'll agree to take his fee in installments."

7

Three Personal Traits That Lead to Debt

Hᴏᴡ ᴅɪᴅ ᴘᴀᴜʟ and Julie, Ron and Sue, and Jack and Mary get into debt? They did so through three avenues: ignorance, indulgence, and poor planning.

Ignorance

Paul and Julie represent the majority of young couples today, Christian and non-Christian alike. They enter marriage with little or no understanding of finances and quickly find themselves overwhelmed by the opportunities they encounter to spend more than they make. Since opposites do attract, usually one partner is an optimist, who generally looks toward the future to straighten out any errors in the present. The other is a worrier, who needs stability and security. The optimist doesn't purposely lie to his spouse. He convinces himself that things will change for the better. Paul was an optimist.

Julie, the worrier, became suspicious of Paul because of what appeared to be deceptions and financial irresponsibility. She was forced to drop out of school and give up her career plans, for which she blamed Paul. Then the additional pressure of an unexpected baby added to their financial problems, plus the fact that he was a screaming, colicky child. So Julie developed great hostility.

After counseling a multitude of young and old couples in circumstances nearly identical to Paul and Julie's, I think I can say with some degree of certainty that the financial situation in which they found themselves was indicative of their lack of training and knowledge. They were not stupid—just ignorant. As Proverbs 22:3 says, "The prudent sees the evil and hides himself, but the naive go on, and are punished for it."

Julie's rebellion could be the subject for an entire book. It was fed by unrealistic and unbiblical desires for self-fulfillment. Apparently she had been taught that her worth as a woman was dependent on attaining a college degree and developing a career outside the home. Neither of those goals is necessarily bad in itself, except where they conflict with God's greater plan for a woman—that of a wife and mother.

Paul, on the other hand, was living in a dream world all his own and angering his wife as he did so. He refused to take responsibility for his decisions and tried to blame their problems on Julie. If she went to work, their problems would be solved. If she had taken her pills, she wouldn't have gotten pregnant. God directed the husband to protect and comfort his wife, but Paul tried to shift the blame to her and sneak around behind her back with his personal indulgences.

A weak-willed man is often attracted to a strong-willed woman. If such a man doesn't take his responsibilities seriously, his wife will be forced to assume the role of authority in the home. Taken to the extreme, the husband and wife will usually end up right where Paul and Julie were—she'll be the boss and he'll be the wimp.

Indulgence

Indulgence, impulse buying, and get-rich-quick schemes all have the same root cause: greed. Most of us don't like to hear that because we're all prone to at least one of those problems. In reality, they are just different levels of the same basic problem. Ron suffered from a get-rich-quick mentality that manifested itself in his taking excessive investment risks. God brought a balancer into his life—his wife, Sue—but he excluded her from decisions involving money.

Ron indulged himself through his investments, just as another person might through the purchase of expensive cars, houses, or jewelry. Each of us has special indulgences that stem from an attitude of lust. Lust is not limited to the area of sex. In our society more people may lust after power and wealth than after sex.

Often we have the mistaken idea that more money will solve our financial problems. Ron—and others like him—is living proof that more money can easily result in bigger problems. Men who invest in high-risk deals that fail often transfer the blame to other people. Since the family is the most readily available scapegoat, they are the ones who usually receive the blame. "I was doing it to better provide for my family," the man says. Nonsense. He did it because it fed his ego and was a chance to get rich quickly.

Poor Planning

At first glance, it appears that Jack and Mary fell into financial difficulty through no fault of their own. And that is true to some extent. Who could have predicted the problems they had with their first child? Only God could have done so. Nor could most of us handle the expenses created by the medical treatment the child needed. But even without those extraordinary medical expenses, eventually Jack and Mary would have had financial problems anyway. Why? Because their break-even point was beyond Jack's income.

Without Mary's working, they simply couldn't make it. The child's medical expenses just made a bad situation impossible.

The symptom they faced was debt, but the real problem was poor planning. They had never been trained in finances and did not know how to establish a budget. Jack took a teaching position that did not have the potential to meet the most basic needs of his family, at least without Mary's income. So the expenses they faced because of the baby did not cause their financial difficulties—they merely amplified them.

Part Two

THREE COUPLES, AND A FOURTH, CLIMB OUT OF DEBT

8

The Bible Speaks on Debt and Borrowing

W E HAVE SEEN how three different couples got into debt. Now we need to examine how they got out of debt, because ultimately each of them did. Their marriages survived because the couples were willing to work together and to do the things required to put their financial affairs in order, no matter how difficult they were.

But before we do that, we need to discuss the principles the Bible gives concerning debt and borrowing, for much of the counsel on debt in this book is based on those principles.

Biblical Principles of Debt

Principle 1: The Debtor Is in Servitude
to the One Who Lends to Him

Debt is not a well-understood term today. Most people use the word *debt* to describe any borrowing, but although that is not entirely inaccurate, it is not precise enough.

Scripture goes beyond that definition to describe the conditions of indebtedness. Even if a debt is current (all payments up to date), the borrower is potentially in a position of servitude, according to Proverbs 22:7: "The rich rules over the poor, and the borrower becomes the lender's slave." But if the debt is delinquent, the lender is given an implied authority from God, according to the Bible. In the time of Christ that authority extended to imprisonment, slavery, and the confiscation of a borrower's total worldly possessions. Not once in Scripture is there even a hint that that was not the legitimate right of a lender. The only variable Scripture allows is that, if the lender and the borrower were both Jews, the borrower would be released from servitude at the end of seven years, unless he voluntarily elected to remain a slave. To say the least, borrowing was not a decision to be taken lightly.

The same basic rules applied in America even in the twentieth century. Almost any major city still has in its library records from a debtors' prison. I found several good examples from the turn of the century in Atlanta. One record read, "Abraham Johnston, white male, commended to debtors' prison for a period of six years, or until the debt is resolved, for failure to pay the agreed-upon sum of two hundred dollars for the purchase of a mule."

Another read, "Sara Wright is sentenced to debtors' prison for an indefinite period of time for habitual indebtedness." The sentence went on to describe her despicable crimes, such as charging food that she couldn't pay for at a merchant's store, charging dry goods at a department store, and signing for a loan with a local citizen without the ability to make restitution.

It is evident that our attitudes today about debt and those of our predecessors are somewhat different. The cause for the difference can be pinpointed as greed and indulgence. Not on the part of the borrowers—that came later. The initial greed was on the part of elected officials who desired to expand our economy by way of debt. To do so required a drastic alteration of the rules regarding borrowing and the consequences of failure to repay.

Few people today are willing to risk forfeiting their freedom and separation from their families to borrow money. The risk would simply be too great. So the laws were amended to make borrowing less risky and credit more available. And besides, who would tolerate the government's borrowing massive amounts of money that could not be repaid while friends and relatives languished in debtors' prisons for failure to repay their personal loans?

The old laws for delinquent debts seem harsh and unnecessarily cruel to us today, and perhaps they were. But the principles behind them were sound and just. The laws assumed that nobody was forced to borrow money—that people borrowed money voluntarily. The lender extended honor (money), and the borrower represented himself as trustworthy. Thus the punishment for defaulting on a debt was actually more severe than for theft because it was considered a breech of trust.

Principle 2: Borrowing Is Permitted in Scripture

Since I began teaching the biblical principles of handling money in 1973, many books have been written and seminars taught on the subject. Some well-intentioned teachers have taken the position that all borrowing is prohibited according to God's Word and that, consequently, Christians should not be involved in any borrowing or lending. Almost without exception, the biblical reference such teachers use to support their position is Romans 13:8: "Owe nothing to anyone except to love one another; for he who loves his neighbor has fulfilled the law."

I wish it were that simple, but it isn't. When I first came across Romans 13:8 in my study on finances I thought, "Aha! Here is the justification for telling Christians to get rid of all credit, especially Christians who have misused it." But then I found myself in a quandary. If God, through the apostle Paul, intended to tell His people that all borrowing was prohibited, why are there New Testament Scriptures instructing men to repay what they borrow? That would be like prohibiting theft and then giving detailed instructions in how to invest stolen money. Obviously, that is ridiculous, which is why in the Bible you don't find principles regarding the handling of stolen goods.

Of course, God may have decided that it was time for His people to become totally debt-free, and thus in the New Testament changed the rules that had previously held true concerning indebtedness. But only those two alternatives exist: either God changed the rules for His people and we had better get about the business of eliminating debt immediately, or Romans 13:8 does not mean that Christians should never borrow anything. So I did some evaluation of the passage in Romans. I'd like to share my conclusions, for I believe them to be accurate and confirmed by the preponderance of Scripture. You can read the same passages and make up your own mind. Just bear in mind that when I began my study I was looking for a justification of the teaching that all borrowing is unscriptural.

To understand Romans 13:8, it is necessary to go back to Romans 13:6, where Paul discusses the payment of taxes. Christians in Paul's day often took the position that they should not have to pay taxes to the government of Rome because it was a heathen government (sound familiar?). Paul admonished the believers that as Roman subjects they were to obey the laws regarding taxes. I'm sure that when he did this he was keeping in mind the Lord's discussion of taxes in Matthew 22:17–21 and that he believed that it was unscriptural for Christians to refuse to pay their taxes. In Romans 13:7 Paul expanded and restated his instructions concerning the payment of taxes: "Render to all what is due them: tax to whom tax is due; custom [another form of tax] to whom custom; fear to whom fear; honor [respect] to whom honor."

With the background of verses 6 and 7 in mind, Paul's directive to Christians to "owe no man" anything takes on a different significance than it might if it were read in isolation. Paul was summing up the legally-prescribed duty all men had to pay their taxes and respect government officials. He was not giving a new teaching on the subject of borrowing money but rather was re-confirming a previous admonition to obey the law. Thus we can say that although borrowing is not promoted scripturally, it is not prohibited, either.

Biblical Principles of Borrowing

Principles of borrowing appear in God's Word, although it needs to be remembered that these are principles, not laws. From time to time an overzealous teacher will present principles as if they were laws. They are not. A *principle* is an instruction from the Lord to help guide our decisions. A *law* is an absolute. Negative consequences may follow from ignoring a principle, but punishment is the likely consequence of ignoring a law God has given us.

An example from our society is driving and drinking. A good rule, or principle, to follow is never to drink. But the law says that if you drink and drive, you'll lose your license and perhaps go to jail.

The principle of borrowing given in Scripture is that it is better not to go surety on a loan. "A man lacking in sense pledges, and becomes surety in the presence of his neighbor" (Proverbs 17:18). Surety means that you have taken on an obligation to pay without a specific way to pay it.

The law of borrowing given in Scripture is that it is a sin to borrow and not repay. "The wicked borrows and does not pay back, but the righteous is gracious and gives" (Psalm 37:21). The assumption in the verse is that the wicked person can repay but will not, as opposed to an individual who wants to repay but cannot.

Principles are given to keep us clearly within God's path so that we can experience His blessings. To ignore them puts us in a constant state of jeopardy in which Satan can cause us to stumble at any time.

Principle 1: Debt Is Not Normal

Regardless of how it seems today, debt is not normal in any economy and should not be normal for God's people. We live in a debt-ridden society that is now virtually dependent on a constant expansion of credit to keep the economy going. That is a symptom of a society no longer willing to follow God's directions. We see this disobedience in abortion, homosexuality, pornography, and adultery. Why do we assume it is any different in the area of money? Yet Christians who would never think of actively participating in those other areas naively follow the world's path in the area of credit.

Listen to the promise God made His people: "Now it shall be, if you will diligently obey the Lord your God, being careful to do all His commandments which I command you today, the Lord your God will set you high above all the nations of the earth. . . . The Lord will open for you His good storehouse, the heavens, to give rain to your land in its season and to bless all the work of your hand; and *you shall lend to many nations, but you shall not borrow*" (Deuteronomy 28:1, 12; emphasis added).

Principle 2: Do Not Accumulate Long-term Debt

It's hard to believe that a typical American family accepts a thirty-year home mortgage as normal today, or that it is now possible to borrow on a home for nearly seventy years. That's correct—it is not a misprint—seventy years. The need to expand the borrowing base continually forces longer mortgage loans. Why? Because expansion through taking on debt causes prices to rise through inflation. As prices rise, mortgages lengthen.

Inflation is a reflection of the expansion of the money supply via borrowed money. For example, the average home in America sells for about $130,000 (mid-1989). Since the average income in America is only about $22,000 (by the most generous measure), those two averages just don't compute. Today it requires nearly 70 percent of the average family's total income to buy the average home, even with a thirty-year mortgage. But what is that average home really worth? To determine that, assume that homes could no longer be sold using long-term mortgages. How much would the average home sell for if it could be bought with cash only? Certainly not for $130,000. It would begin to sell at between $25,000 and $30,000. All of the additional cost is inflation created through the use of long-term debt.

The longest term of debt God's people took on in the Bible was about seven years. During the year of remission (the seventh year) the Jew was instructed to release his brother from any indebtedness. "At the end of every seven years you shall grant a remission of debts. And this is the manner of remission: every creditor shall release what he has loaned to his neighbor; he shall not exact it of his neighbor and his brother, because the Lord's remission has been proclaimed" (Deuteronomy 15:1–2). Thus the only debts that could exceed seven years were those made to non-Jews or from non-Jews.

How can new home loans be made for up to seventy years? It is done by creating a loan based on a thirty-year amortization schedule but using a seven-year loan period. Thus, the loan must be re-negotiated every seven years. Continuing that cycle to pay off the home makes the effective loan period approximately seventy years.

Principle 3: Avoid Surety

By now you understand that surety means accepting an obligation to pay without having a certain way to make that payment. The most recognizable form of surety is co-signing for the loan of another. But surety also can be any form of borrowing in which you sign an unconditional guarantee to pay.

The only way to avoid surety is to collateralize a loan with property that will cover the indebtedness, no matter what. Many home buyers think that because they buy an appreciating asset such as a home they are safe from surety, but that is not so. In most states a lender can sue to collect a deficit on a home mortgage in the event of a default. And remember that most defaults happen during a bad economy, when the prices of homes are most likely to drop.

Credit card purchases have become the most common form of surety in our generation. In this transaction one merchant sells you the material and another finances the purchase (except for in-store credit cards). In the event of a default, the return of the merchandise does not cancel the debt because the finance company has no interest in the merchandise.

Principle 4: The Borrower Has
an Absolute Commitment to Repay

In this generation situation ethics is widely accepted, so it is easy to rationalize not paying a debt, especially when the product or service is defective or when one's financial situation seems to be out of control, as with the third couple, Jack and Mary. Both the divorce rate in America and the number of bankruptcies attest to the fact that we are a situational society. The media present unrealistic expectations of what a marriage should be like, and the "me" generation expects individual rights to be totally upheld in a marriage. When those unrealistic expectations fail to materialize, about half of all spouses call it quits.

The same can be said of those who borrow money. The easy access to credit today leads many people to believe that paying their debts will be a snap. Unfortunately, many borrowers discover that it is possible for them to accumulate far more debt than they can repay and still maintain the life-style they want. As a result, they bail out. About 500,000 a year choose bankruptcy as a way to avoid repayment. Yet the average indebtedness for couples in bankruptcy is only about $5,000.

As the attorney for a couple in bankruptcy said, "Bankruptcy must be OK, or the government wouldn't allow it." That is true only if you assume that government in America today follows God's principles, which is hardly true from the Christian perspective.

Some Christian teachers draw a parallel between modern law on bankruptcy and the year of jubilee prescribed by God in Leviticus 25:10: "You shall thus consecrate the fiftieth year and proclaim a release through the land to all its inhabitants. It shall be a jubilee for you, and each of you shall return to his own property, and each of you shall return to his family."

I wish I could support the view that the year of jubilee and voluntary bankruptcy are comparable, but they aren't. Voluntary bankruptcy is an act by a borrower to avoid his or her creditors. The year of jubilee (as well as the year of remission) was a voluntary act by a lender to forgive indebtedness—a significant difference.

In some situations a voluntary bankruptcy is acceptable, but only in the context of trying to protect the creditors—never in the context of trying to avoid repayment. A Christian needs to accept the hard truth that God allows him no alternative to keeping his vows. That is why the Bible warns him often to be careful before making vows. "It is better that you should not vow than that you should vow and not pay" (Ecclesiastes 5:5).

9

Learn to Face Reality

HOW DID PAUL and Julie Averal get themselves out of debt? It took hard work and a commitment to follow scriptural principles concerning the handling of money.

Paul realized that he had placed his marriage in great jeopardy and that Julie was poised to leave at any time. She had left before over disputes concerning money, but had returned when Paul promised he would not repeat his mistakes. It was entirely likely that Julie would not return if she were to leave again.

Several times in the past Julie had asked Paul to call her pastor and set up an appointment for counseling. Paul had always refused, saying that he knew more about handling money than the average pastor. And he always had the promise of more income just around the corner that would solve their problems. But after Julie opened her own checking account, it was Paul who asked her if she would go to the pastor with him. She flatly refused.

No pastor is going to be able to help our marriage, Julie thought as she drove out of the driveway one morning not long after she had set up the new bank account in her name. *It really is finished. But why? Do I still love Paul?* she wondered. *I don't know. Our whole married life has been one continual struggle over finances.*

All day she thought about her options and silently prayed. As far as she was concerned, her marriage was finished—and she didn't know what she was going to do. She had purposely opened her own checking account so that she could accumulate some funds if, and when, she went out on her own. But she knew she didn't make enough money to pay for child care, a house, a car, and other expenses. She was shocked by her own thoughts. She had actually been planning to leave Paul. Then she realized that it was not a divorce she wanted. She wanted to be free of the pressures they had been facing since the day they got married. Paul was a good man, and she believed he loved her. It was just that he was so irresponsible in the area of finances.

That evening Julie found Paul already home and preparing supper in the kitchen. "Paul," she said in genuine astonishment, "why are you home so early? Is anything wrong at work?"

"No," Paul said without looking up. "I just realized that because of my stupidity I have lost something very precious to me. Julie, it's not more money I need. I need help. I called Pastor Rhimer today and explained what a mess I've made of our finances and our marriage. The pastor is willing to work with me on the marriage, but he recommended a financial counselor in the church to help with our finances."

"Paul, I think that's great," Julie said with enthusiasm.

"But the financial counselor won't meet unless we both go. I didn't know what to tell him," Paul said with tears in his eyes.

"Call and tell him we'll be glad to meet," Julie said as she gave Paul a big hug. "I just pray there is a way out of the mess we're in."

The next day Paul and Julie went to the counselor. Before he met with them, the counselor, Bob Woods, asked them each to complete a short personality test. A few minutes later he called them into his office.

"Come in," he said in a friendly tone. "Take a seat, and let's begin with prayer."

As Mr. Woods was asking the Lord to give them wisdom in their time together, Paul realized that it had been months since he had even felt the desire to pray or read the Bible, although both had been his habit for most of his life. The pressures they were under seemed to have stripped him of his ability to concentrate. He realized the same must have been true for Julie, only more so.

When he finished praying, Mr. Woods asked, "Paul, tell me what you think the problems are."

Paul was taken aback by the question. He had expected Mr. Woods to ask to see the multitude of records they had brought with them. "I honestly don't know," Paul answered. "I suppose it has to be my handling of the money. We never seem to have enough to pay all the bills. We still owe Julie's dad for most of the loan he made to reinstate our car insurance. We owe for two cars, a consolidation loan with the credit union, and our house."

"Thanks, Paul," Mr. Woods said. "Julie, what do you think the problem is?"

"Well, I guess it's much like Paul said, except that I believe the real problem—at least in our marriage—is that we don't discuss things. We argue, and I see it getting worse instead of better."

"Are you willing to make the changes necessary to cure the problems rather than just treat the symptoms?" Mr. Woods asked.

"I'm ready to do whatever I have to do," Paul said.

"I think I am, too," agreed Julie. "But is this going to be one of those lectures on wives obeying their husbands and being silent in the home?"

"I certainly don't think so," replied Mr. Woods. "Especially since I believe God put you two together to operate as a team. I generally find that the wife brings a needed perspective to the finances. But the specific problems must be dealt with first. Then we'll decide who should do what. I need to get an idea about where you are financially right now. So I'm going to ask you some questions, Paul. Feel free to speak up, Julie, if you think Paul has missed anything or you have some input."

With that, Mr. Woods took out one of his budget work sheets and started down the list of monthly expenses. Paul gave most of the answers, but when it came to regular expenses, such as those for clothes, food, laundry, and child care, he deferred to Julie's better memory.

When they had completed the list, Mr. Woods began to list their outstanding debts. Paul was noticeably hesitant once they had gone through the obvious debts, such as the house mortgage, credit union loan, car loans, and family loans.

"What's the problem, Paul?" Mr. Woods asked, sensing that Paul was holding back.

"I need to tell you something," Paul said hesitantly. "But I'm afraid Julie will really get upset if I do."

"Paul, I can't help you unless I know all the facts," Mr. Woods said. "If you owe something else that's not reflected in our records, you need to let me know about it."

"Well, about two months ago when Julie and I were having a lot of problems, I bought a new car," Paul confessed.

"You bought a new car!" Julie exclaimed. "How did you buy a new car? I've never seen it."

"Julie, give Paul a chance to explain," Mr. Woods said. "He is trying to be honest with you now."

"I bought the car from a local dealer with the understanding that I could return it if Julie wanted me to. When I got home, we had a big fight about our VISA account being turned over to a collection agency. When I tried to return the car I found that the dealer wanted six hundred fifty dollars to take it back."

"Paul, how could you do that without even asking me?" Julie said with anger in her voice.

"Wait a minute, Julie. Let Paul explain. What's done is done. Let's try to work this out," Mr. Woods said calmly.

"Julie, I know it was stupid and I should have asked you, but I just got carried away when I stopped to look at the cars. And I honestly thought I could return it. I didn't know they would charge a restocking fee."

"Where does the car loan stand now, Paul?" Mr. Woods asked.

"I signed a note for the $650 so they would take the car back. Now they're threatening to sue me if I don't pay up. But I don't know where the money will come from, Mr. Woods."

"OK, a six hundred fifty dollar note due and payable," Mr. Woods noted on his sheet. "Anything else?"

"One thing," Paul replied as he looked over at Julie and saw her grimace. "I owe five hundred dollars on our VISA for a car stereo I bought about a month ago."

"I thought you saved the money to buy that stereo from your overtime pay," Julie said.

"I did, but I also bought an equalizer and some new speakers, plus there was an installation fee. It all came to nearly five hundred dollars, and I didn't have the extra money so I charged the whole thing."

"What happened to the money you had for the stereo?" Mr. Woods asked.

"I kept it, planning to use that to pay the VISA bill," Paul replied. "But somehow it all was spent before the bill came."

"So now we owe another five hundred dollars on the VISA?" Julie shouted as the tears welled up in her eyes.

"Julie, please calm down," Mr. Woods said in a gentle voice. "We knew the situation was bad or you wouldn't have come here. But I appreciate Paul's honesty about the debts. I can't be of any help to you if I don't know the entire situation.

"As I see it, you have some pressing debts that have to be dealt with rather quickly. Paul, when you elected to file the chapter thirteen bankruptcy you made an agreement not to incur any additional debts until the three-year payment period expired. Now you have an additional fifteen hundred dollars in debt that the court doesn't know about. The first thing you need to do is deal with that situation. I assume you don't have any surplus funds that can be used to pay these bills, do you?"

"No sir," Paul replied. "Only what's in the checking account, which isn't much right now."

"You'll need that for normal living expenses," Mr. Woods said. "Do you have any surplus in your account, Julie?"

Julie sat silently for several moments before she spoke. "Yes, I do, Mr. Woods. But I don't want to use it to pay for Paul's indulgences."

"I can understand that," Mr. Woods said. "But if you're going to work out this situation and find a permanent solution, it will be because you do it together, working as one unit. If you're holding the money as a nest egg in case the marriage doesn't work out, it won't.

"Satan would like nothing better than to drive a wedge between you and Paul, and God can work in your marriage only if you make an irrevocable commitment to make it work. Just as God will not listen to a husband who ignores his wife's counsel, He also won't listen to a wife who rebels against her husband's authority."

"But Paul doesn't take the leadership in our home," Julie protested. "So am I supposed to turn over all the money to him knowing that it will be spent foolishly?"

"No," Mr. Woods replied. "The way to balance one extreme is not to go to another. God put you two together because you need the balance that each offers the other. You must work together as one. Now is your chance to decide whether you trust God or just say that you trust God.

"Anyone can help you manage the money and pay the bills. That's a matter of following a plan I'll outline for you. But the financial problems you have are really symptoms of greater problems that exist. So unless you deal with the root problems, the symptoms will always return. Since the problems are spiritual in nature, only God can cure them.

"The Lord told us that no one can serve both God and money. The same is true in a marriage relationship. No couple can keep their assets separated and be one. There are some risks when you totally surrender your rights, but there are also some big rewards.

"Julie, I can't tell you what to do. All I can do is offer you counsel based on what I believe God would have both you and Paul do. I want you each to take some time to think and pray about your decisions. Call me when you have made a decision, and we'll get back together.

"In the meantime, Paul, I want you to call the bankruptcy court's trustee, Mr. Helms, give him the facts, and let him know that we're working together. Mr. Helms and I have communicated many times, so if he has a question, tell him to call me. Also, I want you to contact the manager of the bank that holds the note on your car and tell him that we're working out a plan and will be in contact with him in the next two weeks. But you'll have to pay at least the minimum on the VISA bill, or your chapter thirteen plan will be in jeopardy."

During the next few days Julie hardly spoke to Paul. He tried to be as helpful as possible by doing things around the house and taking Timmy on walks in the evenings.

Julie found herself in a total state of confusion during the week. She had separated herself from Paul financially, if not physically. She considered what Mr. Woods had said about their problems being spiritual rather than financial. Inside she knew he was right. She had drifted so far from the Lord that she had begun to wonder if she really was a Christian. It was as if her faith had crumbled at the first real test she had ever faced.

Finally, she made the decision to cross the invisible line back into her marriage. She vowed to God that she would commit her resources to her marriage and work at becoming one with Paul. She also knew that she had to give up her personal goals of finishing college and having a career. She would work at her marriage and learn to be content as a secretary if that was God's will for her life.

Suddenly she felt free, as if a great burden had been lifted from her shoulders. She could hardly wait to get home to tell Paul about her decision.

She arrived home before Paul and was sorting through the mail when she came across an official-looking envelope from the Internal Revenue Service. Her stomach did such a flip that she thought she might throw up. She sank down in one of the dining room chairs. She just stared at the envelope for several minutes. She wasn't sure she even wanted to know what it said.

She suspected that Paul hadn't filed their taxes or that they were being audited.

Finally, she put the envelope down and slid out of the chair to her knees. Resting her elbows on the chair seat, she closed her eyes and began to pray. "Dear God, I know I'm living in fear and dread over our finances. I ask you to forgive my attitude and give me the peace that You promised. I know I have not been following Your path or living by Your plan, but I commit myself to You and to my husband, whatever the circumstances are."

She stood up and, picking up the envelope, started to open it. *No,* she thought, *I'll wait and let Paul open it. We'll face whatever it is together.* She dropped the letter on the table and began to fix their dinner.

Paul came home a few minutes later and walked over to where Julie was preparing dinner.

"Hi, honey, how did your day go?" Paul asked cheerfully.

"My day went great," Julie replied as she wiped her hands and hugged Paul's neck.

Paul was shocked by her sudden display of affection. It had been several months since she had even kissed him voluntarily. Their physical relationship had deteriorated to the point where Paul was afraid to show any affection, for fear she would totally reject him.

"Paul, I know I've been depressed and moody about our finances the last few months," Julie confessed.

"Don't worry about it, honey," Paul replied. "I've given you plenty of cause to be worried in the past. But I am committed to making a change. I want to be a good husband with God's help."

"Hush, Paul, and let me say what I want to say first. It doesn't matter about the problems anymore. We'll work them out together as long as you'll let me help. I have decided to close out my checking account and put the money into our joint account. I have about five hundred dollars in savings, and I want you to use it to pay off some of the debts."

"Honey, I can't do that," Paul protested. "That money is yours. It seems like somebody else always has to clean up my messes.

"No, you're wrong. The money is not mine," Julie said emphatically. "It's not really even ours. It belongs to God. We seem to have forgotten that somewhere along the way. I want the money in my account to be used for our expenses."

They just stood there several minutes holding each other. Then Julie said, "Paul, a letter came from the IRS today. I didn't want to open it, so I left it on the table."

"Oh no, what now?" Paul said as he picked up the envelope from the table. "I know we don't owe any money to the IRS, at least I certainly hope we don't."

Opening the envelope Paul let out a whoop. "Julie, we don't owe any money! This is a check for nearly nine hundred dollars."

"Why did they send us a check?" Julie asked as she began to relax her body from the shock she had expected.

"Let's see, the letter says that we overpaid our taxes because of an error in computation. Well, praise the Lord! At least my math errors worked in our favor this time. Honey, with this we'll be able to pay off the debts and still have some of your money left. Let's go out and celebrate tonight."

"No way," Julie responded. "That's the kind of thinking that got into this mess in the first place."

"Just kidding," Paul said with a big grin. "I would much rather stay home and celebrate with my family."

Two weeks later Paul and Julie were back in Mr. Woods's office. "Well, Paul and Julie, I'm really glad to see you back again," he began. "Obviously your presence here means you have decided to work together on your financial problems. I'll be honest with you. About half of the couples the pastor sends to me don't ever come back. They are looking for either a guaranteed miracle or some kind of quick fix. But if you didn't get into debt in three months, you won't get out of debt in three months. And as far as miracles go, I have seen God move in miraculous ways, but the more common approach is that He allows those who violate His principles to work their way out. Somehow the lessons seem to stick a lot better that way."

"Mr. Woods, we're not looking for a miracle or a quick fix," Paul said. "I know I created this mess by my own ignorance and childishness. I'm willing to do whatever is necessary to solve this once and for all."

"What about you, Julie?" Mr. Woods asked.

"I'm committed to the Lord, my husband, and whatever else it takes, Mr. Woods, in that order," Julie said confidently. "I have already closed my account and put the surplus in our joint account."

"Good for you. I believe Paul is going to be worthy of your trust, and I know God will honor your faith. Now let's get down to business."

"First, Mr. Woods, we would like to ask a couple of questions," Paul said.

"Certainly. What would you like to ask?"

"As you may have guessed, we haven't been attending a church regularly for the past year or so. But we made a commitment to join Pastor Rhimer's church last week. Julie feels very strongly that we should begin to tithe again. I want to also, but I can't figure out where the money would come from, even with the two new debts paid. Can we tithe even if it means we can't meet the obligations of the chapter thirteen."

"I commend your commitment to join a good church and to tithe the Lord's portion, but when you signed the court decree you pledged yourself to the plan you submitted. You can't legally break your commitment and remain under the plan.

"As I see it you have two choices. You can elect to come out from under the chapter thirteen plan and take your chances with the creditors. Or you can reduce your own living expenses to where you can tithe and still meet your obligations."

"How can we do that, Mr. Woods?" Paul asked. "There is no extra money available, except the small amount Julie was saving, but even that should go to buy some clothes for Timmy and her."

"I think we're jumping ahead a little here. Let me tell you what I think, and maybe some questions will be answered. First, your combined incomes are approximately twenty-four hundred dollars a month, is that right?"

"Yes," Paul replied. "That's pretty close."

"And your net take-home pay is about eighteen hundred dollars?"

"I don't really know," Paul replied.

"Yes it is," Julie chimed in.

"OK," Mr. Woods said. "I calculate your overall housing expense to be about a thousand dollars a month. That means it takes nearly 55 percent of your total spendable income just to maintain your home. That's at least 20 percent too high for your income. Even if you tithed, housing should never cost more than 40 percent of your spendable income after tithing."

"I was convinced all along that our home cost us too much," Julie said. "But I didn't know how to calculate what we could afford. The bank used 25 percent of our total incomes when we bought the house. But I was making more money then."

"Gross income doesn't mean a thing," Mr. Woods said. "It's what you have left over to spend that's important."

"Are you saying that we should sell our home and move to a cheaper one?" Paul asked.

"I'm not going to tell you to do anything," Mr. Woods replied. "I'm just going to point out some logical alternatives. Then you'll have to make your own choices. I know that usually the wife is attached to her home, and giving it up is a difficult decision."

"Not for me," Julie said quickly. "I have always viewed that house as an anchor around our necks. It was Paul who really wanted it in the first place."

"That's probably true," Paul said. "But the guys at work said it was stupid to pay rent when I could buy a home and get all the tax breaks."

"Usually that's pretty good logic, but not when you wreck your budget to buy. It would be better to rent and stay within your income than to buy and end up in debt," Mr. Woods said. "I believe you could potentially free up four hundred dollars a month by renting for a while."

"Four hundred dollars a month!" Paul exclaimed. "Why that's enough to pay our tithes and more. I guess I never realized the house was putting us into debt, Mr. Woods. I always thought of it as a good long-term investment."

"For most families it is, Paul. But only after they have settled into a lifestyle and found a home within their budget. Buying a home too quickly and one that is too expensive is the number one reason most young couples end up in financial trouble. And since about 50 percent end up in divorce, the home will eventually be sold anyway."

"But why doesn't someone tell young couples those things before they make the mistakes we made?" Julie asked.

"In our society people make money off the excesses of others, unfortunately. But in Proverbs 24:27 God does present the principle I'm talking about: "Prepare your work outside, and make it ready for yourself in the field; afterwards, then, build your house.""

"I never heard that before," Paul said in amazement. "I'll put the house up for sale today."

"Hold it just a minute, Paul," Mr. Woods said. "Don't do anything in haste. Pray about the decision first, and ask God to bring the right buyer for your home. You need to think about some other areas, too. I'm going to give you a workbook that will help you to plan each area of your budget. It's especially important that you allocate money for non-monthly expenses such as clothes, car maintenance, and annual insurance. Those are normally areas that create crises when they are due."

"That's certainly true in our case," Julie said.

"We want your budget to be totally realistic, or it will work only a short while. You're going to be tight on money for another year and a half, until your past debts are paid. But with some discipline you will be debt-free in less that two years.

"I have one additional recommendation for you. I believe Julie is far better equipped to maintain the records and pay the bills. The short personality test I gave you last time shows that she is a detail person, while you, Paul, are a generalist."

"I would agree with that," Paul said. "But I have always been taught that it is the man's responsibility to run the finances in his family."

"Paul, God gives each of us gifts and abilities to help us in our daily lives. It's clear that Julie is better suited to be the bookkeeper in your family. The two of you together need to work out a financial plan, and then she will pay the bills and maintain the records. God doesn't make mistakes; He provided the necessary talents in Julie that you lack, and vice versa. I suggest that you read Proverbs 31 together, because it describes a husband and wife working as a team. It's clear that each uses different and unique abilities to enhance the relationship.

"Our short-term goal will be to get your finances to the point where you're able to pay everyone what you owe them each month. That will mean Julie will need to continue to work, at least for a while. But our long-term goal will be to free you financially so that Julie does not have to work."

"But, Mr. Woods, we have tried that before. Every time I quit working we fell further and further behind," Julie said.

"That's because you started out with expenses larger than your income. I believe you'll find when you readjust your budget that you'll be able to get by on one income. Later, if you want to work, you should use your income for one-time purchases."

"What do you mean?" asked Paul.

"Save it up and buy a car, or save it for a down payment on a home. But don't commit yourselves to monthly expenses based on two incomes, especially at your age. If you do, something as normally exciting as a child can end up being the source of grief and conflict."

"That's for sure," Paul replied, looking at Julie.

"I want you both to go home with the plan I have given you and make the necessary adjustments in your budget. Remember that each and every category of spending must have some money allocated to it. To ignore areas like entertainment and recreation is unrealistic and will cause your budget to fail within a short period of time. Ignoring needs like clothing, auto repairs, and dental bills will make your budget look good but will also make it totally unrealistic."

"What about tithing, Mr. Woods?" Julie asked. "I always tithed before I was married, but we have been unable to for most of our marriage."

"Tithing is an important principle for a Christian because it demonstrates a commitment to God in the most visible area of our lives: the area of money. But God wants you to honor your word also. You have made an agreement with the court to pay your creditors according to the budget you submitted, so you must do so. One part of your long-term plan should be to reduce your monthly expenses so that you can give God His portion, too. But for now you'll have to stick to the plan you have. I believe God will honor the commitment of your heart. He doesn't care about the money nearly as much as He cares about your heart's attitude. Tithing will be a part of the next stage of financial planning for you and Paul once the expenses are reduced."

10

Develop and Carry Out a Plan for Paying Off Debts

I TRUST THAT by now you recognize the errors that Paul and Julie made in their finances. Their problem could be called "too much, too soon." It is a common malady for many young couples in our society. It has been said (and unfortunately is all too true) that a young couple today tries to accumulate in three years what took their parents thirty years to accumulate. The one thing couples need to learn very quickly is that individuals must be self-disciplined today. They cannot count on the lenders to force them to live within their means, as they once did.

Prior to the late sixties bankers were among the most conservative people in our society. Before anyone could borrow for consumables such as food or clothes, or even for non-consumables such as cars and houses, his financial status was thoroughly reviewed, and formulas were applied to insure his borrowing stayed within his means to repay. That is not true today. The increasing demand to make more loans has widened the parameters of acceptable loans. It is now assumed that the borrowers will discipline themselves to repay what they borrow. Unfortunately, many young couples have no idea how to calculate what they can or cannot afford to pay.

More than 60 percent of all first-time home loans require two salaries to make the payments. But since the vast majority of first-time home buyers are couples under thirty-five years old, the prospect of a baby's disrupting their cash flow is almost a certainty. So they have built-in potential financial problems from the outset. Combine that with the use of second mortgages to help make the down payments and loans for refrigerators, lawn mowers, and curtains, and you can see why so many young couples end up in financial trouble.

But the main purpose of this book is not to show how most people get into debt but rather to help you understand how to get out of debt. To do that, we need to follow Paul and Julie as they carried out the plan Mr. Woods worked out with them.

First, it's important to understand that by the time they went to Mr. Woods they were deeply in debt and had elected to file for a chapter 13 reorganization under the Federal Bankruptcy Code. Appendixes E, F, and G of this book contain a summary of chapters 7, 12, and 13 of the Federal Bankruptcy Code. The summary is taken from *Bankruptcy: Do It Yourself* and *Chapter 13: The Federal Plan to Repay Your Debts,* both by Janet Kosel (Nolo Press, 1987).

Table 10.1 is a summary of Paul and Julie's financial condition when Mr. Woods first saw them. The figures on the left reflect what an average family in their salary range would normally spend in a month on various household expenses. The figures on the right reflect what Paul and Julie had budgeted.

As you can see, Paul and Julie had a financial problem that could be solved only by creating more income or by spending less. Since more income wasn't an option for them, they had to spend less.

In reality, less spending is the answer for the vast majority of debt problems. Most of us would be able to spend almost unlimited amounts of money, given the chance. So more money coming in usually means more money going out. Remember that Paul had already tried a bill consolidation loan through

Table 10.1
Paul and Julie Averal's "As Is" Budget
Compared to a Recommended Spending Plan
for a Family with a Monthly Income of $1,800 Net

Average Spending		The Averal's "As Is" Budget	
Taxes	(taken out)	Taxes	(taken out)
Tithe	$180	Tithe	$ 0
Housing	567	Housing	1,080
Auto	230	Auto	280
Food	240	Food	200
Clothing	80	Clothing	0
Medical	80	Medical	0
Insurance	70	Insurance	0
Ent. & Recreation	95	Ent. & Recreation	25
Debt	80	Debt	250
Miscellaneous	90	Miscellaneous	25
Savings	80	Savings	0
Total	$1,792	Total	$1,860

his company's credit union. Usually that helps for a short while because the monthly payments are reduced through a lower interest, longer-term loan. But unless the conditions that caused the initial problems are changed, the end result will be even more debt. In Paul's case, he had to pay back not only the bill consolidation loan but also the credit card bills he had racked up a few months later, so he was actually worse off than he was before he got the bill consolidation loan.

A glance at the Averal's "as is" budget tells much of the story. Their budget could have handled the spending of 30 to 35 percent of their net pay for housing (about $490 per month), but they had committed themselves to payments that were nearly 60 percent of their income, or $840 per month. When utilities were added, their expenses for housing came to more than $1,000. They could not make it on such a budget, even from the beginning. They were running a deficit from the time they made the first mortgage payment until the home was sold.

Note also that they were overcommitted in the categories of transportation (cars) and outstanding debt. Those debts were the obvious result of the lack of money created each month by the high house payment. When necessities came up—such as clothes, insurance, or car repairs—Paul used credit to make up the difference. The overcommitment he made regarding the cars reflected a weakness in Paul toward cars. His weakness in this area is not unusual—in fact it is quite common in most young men. During the dating years in high school and college, they place such great importance on their automobiles that they become personal status symbols. That is a poor attitude when Mom and Dad are paying the bills and the young person is still single, but it is a disaster when the young man gets married and continues to cling to the same values.

When you look at the budget for clothing, entertainment, and medical/dental expenses, you will note that Paul and Julie allocated nothing on a regular monthly basis for those items. That does not mean they found a miraculous way to keep their clothes from wearing out or their teeth from developing cavities. It means they did not have money for those items and so left them out of their budget. When these expenses came due—as they were bound to—Paul and Julie had to rely on credit cards to make up the deficit. That is why so many couples say they use their credit cards only for necessities. Often that's true, except that other spending creates the need to use the cards for the necessities.

Mr. Woods gave Paul and Julie some suggestions to help them resolve both their immediate and their long-term problems.

1. Use the funds they already had on hand to pay the VISA bill and the outstanding balance on the car Paul had returned. Mr. Woods made direct contact with the owner of the car lot and told him what had happened with

Paul. The owner agreed to accept a reduced amount in total payment of the bill, which saved Paul $300.

2. Each month continue to meet the obligations established by the bankruptcy court. With Paul and Julie's combined incomes, they were able to pay at least the minimum amounts due.

3. Make a budget showing what they could afford to pay for housing, assuming that their bankruptcy debts were paid and they had only Paul's income. This showed how totally out of line their housing expenses were with their income. They decided to sell the home and find housing that would meet their needs.

4. Assign Julie the task of managing the books in their home. She would pay the bills each month, and she and Paul would review the budget together at least once a month.

5. Make a budget that they could live with, once the bankruptcy payments were completed, and assume in that budget that they would have only Paul's income to work with and that they would be repaying—in total—everyone to whom they owed money.

The budget shown in Table 10.2 is the Averals' "want to" budget. It shows where Paul and Julie wanted to be when the bankruptcy was cleared. Note the reduced amount for housing, which is a much more realistic figure for Paul's income. The new spending plan meant that Paul and Julie had to give up their home, and rent for a period of time. But that was a small sacrifice

Table 10.2
"Want to" Budget for Paul and Julie Averal
Based on an After Tax Income of $1,400 Per Month

Taxes	(Taken out)
Tithe	$150
Housing	450
Auto	200
Food	250
Clothing	50
Medical	50
Insurance	50
Ent. & Rec.	100
Debt	0
Miscellaneous	50
Savings	50
Total	$1,400

compared to the peace they had lost when they committed themselves to buying that home.

Also note that they committed the first portion of their income to God as a tithe. They prayed about repaying God's portion and, once the last creditor was repaid, used Julie's income for several months to repay their tithes. Mr. Woods told them that as far as he could tell, Scripture did not require or suggest a repayment of past tithes and offerings. After praying about what he said, they still committed themselves to repaying their tithes as a testimony that God truly was first in their marriage.

Paul and Julie had some questions about their situation that are common to couples in their situation. I thought it might be helpful to others to review those questions.

What effect will the chapter 13 bankruptcy have on our future credit?

According to the Fair Credit Reporting Act, any credit reporting agency can report that you filed for bankruptcy protection for up to ten years after the date of that action. Therefore, any potential lender inquiring about your credit history will receive that report.

Is there any way to clear our credit rating?

Not really. Too often in our society people act as if there are no consequences of a bankruptcy, but that is simply not true. The bankruptcy laws were originally created to help balance an unjust system that sent poor people to prison for bad debts. But too often today they are abused by people who don't want to repay money they have already spent. Consequently, legitimate creditors look upon those who use bankruptcy as deadbeats who don't want to pay their bills. The net effect is that those who go bankrupt are often refused credit from legitimate lenders later.

Is there any way we can prove that we are honest and reestablish a good credit rating?

Yes. Once the bankruptcy is cleared, you can continue to pay the entirety of the debts you owe. After a creditor is completely paid off, ask him to write you a letter of recommendation and send a copy to his local credit reporting agencies. Many agencies will include letters of recommendation in their official credit reports. But you can also give the letters to a potential lender when you apply for a loan yourself.

The best recommendation I can give to anyone is this: pay back what you borrow and never borrow frivolously. Remember what Proverbs 22:1 says: "A good name is to be more desired than great riches. Favor is better than silver and gold." (A summary of the Fair Credit Reporting Act is given in Appendix B of this book.)

What would happen if Paul's union went on strike or if he lost his job for any reason?

You should notify the bankruptcy court trustee immediately. Usually they will work out a temporary moratorium with your creditors. However, if the situation lasts for any extended period of time, the bankruptcy judge may elect to dissolve your debts through a chapter 7 dissolution. In other words, your assets are sold and the creditors paid with the proceeds of the sale.

Anyone who is not under a court order such as a bankruptcy needs to stay in direct contact with his creditors and tell them the absolute truth. Most creditors will work with a debtor who has temporary financial problems, as long as he is trying to be fair and honest.

11

Don't Use Borrowed Money
for Speculative Ventures

MANY MEN CAN identify with Ron Hawkins. He was a good person who tried to better himself and his family. Because he came from a relatively poor background—too little money and too many children—he was pretty much left to fend for himself. When he finished high school he thought about going to college, but he wasn't a scholarship candidate, and his parents had no money to help him. So he went into the Air Force for two years on reserve status. He saved as much money as he could and then started at a junior college in his hometown. He lived on his own, as there wasn't room in his parents' home.

While he was in college, he worked nearly full-time in the evenings and on weekends. He wasn't a straight-A student, but he made fairly good grades. He was sure he could have done even better if he had had more time to study.

He and Sue met when he was at the state university completing his last two years of college. They were married during Ron's last year in school and actually lived better than Ron had by himself. Sue had a nice off-campus condominium her parents had bought when she went to college.

Sue's father was a very successful trial attorney. Her parents were committed churchgoers, though probably not Christians. The church Sue had attended most of her life was socially "correct," and—as she put it—"Most of the sermons were straight out of the *Wall Street Journal* or *U.S. News and World Report.*"

Sue's parents didn't consciously indulge her. They simply included her in an indulgent life-style that meant a new wardrobe each year, a new car every other year, and winter vacations in Colorado.

She knew other people didn't have as much as her parents, because she had several close friends who came from middle income families. But she also experienced strife in her own family because her mother and father fought constantly. Usually their arguments revolved around her father's commitment to his work and the fact that he was rarely around. In truth, many times Sue, her mother, and one of Sue's friends spent those holiday trips to Aspen or Vail without Sue's father. He rarely accompanied them. By the time Sue was a senior in high school, her parents were separated. The separation later became semi-permanent, although there was never a divorce.

In college Sue's life was inalterably changed through a campus ministry. She was asked to a meeting by a boy she was dating and agreed to go because she considered herself a Christian. At that meeting she came face to face with the reality that she was not a Christian and accepted Christ.

At a later meeting she met Ron. She fell in love with him and married him within the year. As is so often the case, although Sue was not the least bit embarrassed by Ron's humble background, Ron was. Visiting Sue's home was agony for Ron because it made him feel inadequate. Nothing Sue could say would convince Ron that all was not bliss in that beautiful home. His goal was set: eventually he would have the same kind of home.

I share this background to help you realize that when someone gets into debt from indulgence and greed it is often not the result of a conscious decision. It is the result of decisions clouded by good intentions and rationalizations. I believe the worst thing that can happen to anyone is to achieve his financial goals. Then he is able to surround himself with enough "things" to avoid facing the reality of how miserable he really is. If you don't believe that's true, look at the amount of alcohol and drugs consumed by the "up and outers."

After college, Ron took a job with a major stock brokerage firm. He had a good aptitude and personality, and he did quite well. But within a few years Sue feared she was seeing the same attitudes developing in Ron that she had seen in her father. Ron was consumed by business and had a drive to succeed that pushed everything and everyone else into the background.

Sue began to nag Ron about his lack of care for his family and his non-involvement in their lives. In reality, he spent about the same amount of time with his family that many young businessmen do—two to three minutes a day.

The more Sue nagged, the less Ron knew how to handle it, so he began to substitute time at the office for time with her. As his income grew, so did opportunities to take part in some of the investments his company brokered. He began to risk larger amounts of borrowed money, secured only by his signature. Sue didn't know about most of the loans, because the lenders for most of them did not require her signature. As with many fast-moving investment markets (this one was in commercial properties), the lenders were only too willing to lend large amounts of money with little or no collateral and secured only by the signatures of the principal parties involved.

Within a few years Ron's net worth had grown to more than $200,000, and with it grew his ability to borrow even more. He bought a new home in a wealthy neighborhood—in spite of Sue's objections.

Ron even made several attempts to spend more time at home, but each time another deal would develop, and he would spend weeks of sixteen-hour days putting it together. When she saw the volumes of forms that had to be filed with their tax statements each year, Sue asked Ron to sit down and discuss their finances. Ron said he would, but never took the time to do so. He knew that Sue wouldn't agree with much of what he was doing, so it was just easier to avoid telling her.

As time passed, Sue felt more and more excluded from what had become the focus of Ron's activities. All she knew about their finances was how much Ron gave her to run the household. He was extremely generous, and Sue usually got whatever she asked for.

Then suddenly the economy, which had been inflating the real estate ventures Ron was handling, cooled off. Interest rates rose precipitously, and with the interest rate increases, the real estate market that had grown as a result of borrowed money suddenly stopped cold.

Within one month, what had been a hot market cooled to the point where no banker was willing to lend any money on speculative ventures. In fact, bankers began to call some of the demand notes that had been issued to numerous investors, including Ron.

Almost overnight, Ron found himself with virtually no income, for land sales had all but stopped, and the banks were unwilling to extend the signature notes secured by his land investments. The bankers already knew what Ron was about to find out—the reality of Proverbs 22:7: "The rich rules over the poor, and the borrower becomes the lender's slave."

When Ron couldn't sell any of the properties the banks were holding as collateral on his notes, the bankers suggested that he assign an interest in his home as substitute collateral. To do this he needed Sue's agreement, since the home was in both their names. Ron approached Sue that evening after their kids had gone to bed. "Sue, I've got a problem and I need your help," Ron said timidly.

Sue felt her heart take a flip as her mind conjured up the worst circumstances imaginable. She had inwardly assumed that Ron might be seeing someone else, just as her father had done. Now she feared that he, too, wanted a separation—or worse.

"What kind of a problem, Ron?" she asked defiantly.

"Without a second mortgage on the house, the banks won't renew some of the notes I have on the land investments I've made." Inwardly Sue breathed a sigh of relief, but outwardly the tough shell she had assumed as a defense stayed intact as she answered in a biting tone, "And just how much do you owe on your great investments, Ron?"

Ron winced at her tone and at the emphasis she had placed on the words "your" and "Ron." "I don't know exactly," he lied.

"Well, give me an approximate figure. Or do you think I'm too dumb to be trusted with information like that?" Sue said with tears coming to her eyes in spite of herself.

"Honey, you know I don't think you're dumb," Ron said with his head down.

"Well, you must. You have never once told me what you're doing. I learn more at the Christmas party when your so-called partners are there than I do living in the same house with you."

Ron didn't know where to go with the conversation. They had often been at this point before. He had wanted to tell Sue what he was doing and why, but when she took such an offensive position he just backed off and buried himself in his work. But he couldn't do that now. If he didn't assign the collateral the banks would call his notes immediately, and he would lose everything. Worse than that, he would probably still owe several thousands of dollars after the properties were sold in this down market. He knew if he could hold on and ride out the bad times the land values would recover. But the house was the only thing of value he had to pledge.

"Listen, honey, I know you've been hurt by my actions in the past, but this is a real crisis. If I can't give the banks some additional collateral, they will call the notes on the properties and sell them at cut-rate prices," Ron said as honestly as he could.

"You still didn't answer my question, Ron. How much do you owe?"

As he started to speak, Ron flinched at what he knew would be a verbal assault from Sue. "I owe nearly $200,000," he said.

And to his utter amazement he heard Sue reply, "Well good, then we'll be totally broke when this thing is over, I suspect. I'll be glad to see it all gone."

"Why did you say that?" Ron asked in total puzzlement.

"Because I have prayed for a long time that something would happen to bring all this to a head. We aren't married; we're just two people living in the same house, sharing the same bed.

"You really don't understand, do you?" she continued, as Ron dropped his head again. "I don't care about the money, the house, or anything money can buy. I would be perfectly satisfied in a subdivision home with a husband who came home at five and spent time with his family. Ron, I panic when I think about the years after our kids leave and I'm left here by myself. My mother took up drinking because she couldn't stand it. I don't know what I would do."

Because of the emotional state he was in, Ron didn't hear what Sue was really trying to say. All he heard was his wife saying she wished she had married someone else. In an attitude of resignation he asked, "Will you sign the power of attorney on the house, Sue?"

"You didn't hear a word I said, did you?" she spat out. "Yes, I'll sign so you can get your loans renewed. I don't want to hurt you; I just want us to be one—and we're not. But I can tell you this, when the bottom falls out of your business, your so-called friends are going to leave you high and dry. Then what are you going to do, turn and run, too?"

"I have never run from anything in my life," Ron responded. "I believe the investments I have made are sound, and I'll stand by the people who have invested with me, no matter what."

"You may get a chance to find out what 'no matter what' is," Sue said. "I can remember my dad talking about clients suing their financial advisers during a bad time in the real estate market. Yours will, too."

"The people who invest with me know that I always try to do what's best for them," Ron said defensively. "I can't help what the government does about interest rates. They know that."

"Get into the real world, Ron," she said. "Those people won't care if you spend twenty hours a day working for them. What most of them care about is that you sold them an investment that lost money."

Ron pledged his home as collateral against the bank loans and was able to hold off the foreclosures for the time being. But several months passed, and the economic situation didn't get any better. In fact, it got considerably worse. Many of the biggest banks had hundreds of non-performing loans and began to experience financial problems themselves. Loan managers were fired or moved, and new management was brought in to deal with the crisis. All real estate loans that had not been paid on in more than three months were immediately called as due and payable—Ron's included.

It didn't matter what arrangements had been made in the past. The rule was, pay up in full or surrender the properties. In an effort to salvage some of the more valuable properties, Run approached some of his wealthiest clients, who stood to lose the most if the ventures failed. He asked them to put up the necessary capital to collateralize the notes on the land they were already invested in. In exchange, he would subordinate his position (take a lesser profit after they got their money when the land was sold). He also guaranteed their additional collateral with a third mortgage on his home—without telling Sue.

Unfortunately, the interest rates remained high, and the real estate market dropped even further as desperate bankers dumped large inventories of unsold land on the already depressed market. Land prices dropped more than 70 percent from the pre-recession high. Now haggard bankers called for additional collateral on any outstanding notes. The investors Ron had convinced to put up additional collateral were faced with either risking more of their assets or losing what they had already pledged. They opted to lose what they had pledged and sue Ron and his partners for negligence.

Faced with the collapsed real estate market and a pending lawsuit, Ron's three partners elected to file for personal bankruptcy protection. It was only then that Ron learned that all of their personal assets were held in their wives' names, and that other than the now defunct properties they had no assets to lose. The investors were left with nothing to attach except Ron.

Ron knew he had done nothing illegal or unethical in his dealings with his investors, and he was certain he would be vindicated if the case came to trial. He tried to settle with the disgruntled investors, but since they already had a third mortgage on his home, they decided to sue out of anger and vindictiveness over the losses they had suffered.

Ultimately, the case came to trial, and Ron waived his right to a trial by jury so the case would be heard and decided by a single judge. Because of a lack of funds, Ron had elected to use an inexperienced attorney who had little courtroom experience. The investors, on the other hand, used a highly qualified trial attorney. He depicted Ron as a scheming manipulator who talked the investors into risking money in ventures they could not possibly understand. The conclusion the judge reached: guilty as charged.

The decision broke Ron. Not only was he judged to be guilty of defrauding investors, but his license to sell securities was suspended for five years. He was penniless and without the means to earn a living.

12

Commit to Faithfully Repay Creditors

NEARLY A MONTH had passed since the trial in which Ron had been found guilty. Since he lacked any unattached assets, the judge had awarded the plaintiffs a summary judgment that allowed them to attach anything of value Ron owned now or in the future. The plaintiffs elected to force Ron into bankruptcy by notifying all of Ron's outstanding creditors that they intended to attach and sell any and all properties Ron owned, including his home. With that action imminent, several of the unsecured creditors filed suit for judgment. Ron's family problems also continued to grow.

"Ron, you told me this lawsuit would amount to nothing, and now I see we have a judgment against us," Sue said, shaking the paper that the sheriff had delivered that day. "Do you call this nothing?"

"I'm really sorry, Sue. I wanted to tell you, but I just didn't know how. The judge decided against us. We lost. But that's not the worst of it. Now the investors have decided to use the judgment to force a bankruptcy. They know that if they demand payment, I won't be able to pay. So they're demanding a forced sale of the house and everything else. Then the other creditors will be forced to do the same. We'll be wiped out. I wouldn't blame you if you decided to leave, too. Because I lost the lawsuit, the SEC is suspending my license for five years. I won't even have a way to earn a living."

"Ron, I don't care about this house or the investments. I told you that before. I just want to be a part of your life. I will stick by you because we promised God that our marriage is for better or worse. I love you, and we'll be able to see this thing through together," Sue said in a softening tone. The tears welled up in her eyes. "I know I haven't been a good wife. I thought you were going down the same path I saw my own father go down before he left my mother, and it frightened me."

"I'm really sorry, Sue," Ron said as he put his arms around her. "I didn't know that's what you were thinking. I thought I was doing all these deals for you and the kids. Now I realize that I was doing them to feed my own ego and insecurity. I feared being poor so much I was willing to throw away the most important assets God ever gave me. Maybe in the long run this disaster will be the best thing that ever happened to us."

"Ron, we've drifted so far from God's path with our lives, I want to rededicate our lives to serving Him as we promised to do in college."

"I totally agree," Ron said as he felt a burden lift from his shoulders. "You know it's funny, we're totally broke and facing bankruptcy, but I finally feel free. Maybe you have to hit bottom before you can begin to look up."

"Ron, I feel that we should use this as an opportunity to witness for the Lord. Why don't you go to each of the creditors and ask them not to force you into bankruptcy. Tell them that we intend to pay every dime of the money back if they will work with us."

"But how in the world will we ever do that?" Ron asked, looking at his wife with an air of appreciation. "We're dead broke, and I lost my license."

"Then it's really up to the Lord to do it, isn't it?" Sue asked.

"That's for sure," Ron replied. "You know, Sue, that's really exciting. If any of the creditors are crazy enough to go along with us, it can be a testimony to God's greatness. I'll tell them the truth. If they join in the bankruptcy, they won't get anything. The first and second mortgage will wipe out any money from the house, and the cars are leased. I'll start calling first thing tomorrow."

Ron went to each of the creditors, most of whom were banks holding deficiency agreements on the property loans, and asked them not to force him into bankruptcy. When he was asked how he would ever repay the money he owed, he responded, "I don't know, but if the Lord chooses to bless us, I'll repay every dime if you don't join in the bankruptcy action. In the meantime I'll get a job and pay you what I can each month."

Ron's biggest creditor was the largest bank in town. Based on the current value of the land they had foreclosed, the bank estimated Ron owed them over $200,000. Ron met with the bank president (a former client) and asked him not to join in the bankruptcy action.

"But Ron, I have a responsibility to our stockholders," was the banker's reply. "If you're hiding any assets and we don't join the lawsuit, I could be sued for negligence."

"Sir, I give you my word that what you see on the paper before you is everything I own in the world, and it isn't much," Ron said.

"But why don't you want me to join in the lawsuit, Ron? If this is all you own and our agreement is thrown into the bankruptcy too, you won't have to repay us either."

"Because I believe that God is going to show Himself strong through this," Ron replied with confidence. "My part is to ask my creditors to trust me and God, too. Those who join in the bankruptcy action have voluntarily changed the agreement, and it's no longer my responsibility to fulfill the original obligation. Therefore, I would assume God is not bound to help me repay the debt."

Ron then shared a Scripture passage he and Sue believed God had given to them the night they pledged to repay everyone who did not join the bankruptcy action. "Offer to God a sacrifice of thanksgiving, and pay your vows to the Most High; and call upon Me in the day of trouble. I shall rescue you, and you will honor Me" (Psalms 50:14–15).

"Well, Ron, that's about the strangest proposal I have ever heard in my years as a banker, but I have been a Christian about that long too, so I know God can do it if He desires. I will take this to my board of directors at our meeting this Thursday. I'll recommend we go along with you on this, but the final decision is up to the board."

"I understand, sir, and I sincerely appreciate your confidence in me," Ron said as he started to leave.

"Ron, I believe you're an honest man, and you always did a good job for me. You made errors in judgment on some of the land deals we funded, but who hasn't? You borrowed too much on speculation, but we loaned too much on the same projects. It could just as well have been me the investors of this bank sued, except that we have more money to ride out the downturn."

"Thank you, sir, that really does encourage me. I trust we'll both see some miracles."

Later that week Ron heard from the banker that the board had agreed to maintain their notes and not join the bankruptcy.

The bankruptcy proceeded rapidly, with all but three creditors joining in the proceeding. Ron and Sue did not contest the bankruptcy action and surrendered all of their personal assets voluntarily, including personal jewelry, even Sue's wedding rings. The bankruptcy judge instructed them that they had the right to maintain ownership of certain personal assets, such as the wedding rings, but they refused, saying they wanted the creditors to receive as much as possible.

Ultimately, the disgruntled investors who had brought the action received nothing for their trouble except bills from their attorneys.

In the meantime, Ron had been searching for a job that would allow him to provide for his family. He decided eventually that selling was the only thing he knew how to do, and he took a job on a commission basis in product sales with a national company. Within three months he had met the minimum quota set by the company and was earning an average annual income of about $30,000. He and Sue worked out a budget that would allow them to live on an income of $24,000 a year, with the rest going to pay the creditors they still owed from the land deals. In the case of the large bank, Ron and Sue were able to pay an average of $200 a month. Although the interest alone on their debt would have been over $1,500 a month, the bank president elected to forgo the interest charges so that they would not be losing ground each month.

Ron and Sue settled into a greatly modified life-style and committed themselves to getting to know each other better and discovering what the Lord had in store for them.

13

Two Common Errors That Lead to Debt

RON HAD VIOLATED two fundamental biblical principles that ultimately resulted in his financial disaster. The first was allowing a get-rich-quick mentality to control his decisions.

Allowing a Get-Rich-Quick Mentality to Govern Decisions

Symptoms of get-rich-quick are evident in many of the investment schemes in this country and around the world today. There are three distinguishing characteristics.

Risking Borrowed Money

If investments in get-rich-quick schemes were limited to available cash only, most people would be wary of losing it. But somehow it is easier to risk borrowed money because it seems almost free—at least until you have to pay it back. The same principle applies to buying consumer goods on credit. Credit card companies understand the mentality of leveraged purchases (purchases bought with borrowed money). People who use their credit cards for clothes, food, and vacations are prime candidates for overbuying. Credit card issuers can prove to a merchant statistically that those people will buy more and pay a higher price than those who buy only with cash.

There is no argument that through the use of leveraged (borrowed) money you can get rich a lot faster. But there is as well no argument that the majority of those who do so end up losing it all in the long run, for the mentality that prompted them to take the initial risk will prompt them to take ever bigger risks—and eventually they will get wiped out in a bad economy. As the proverb says, "The plans of the diligent lead surely to advantage, but everyone who is hasty comes surely to poverty" (Proverbs 21:5).

You don't have to look any further than the oil industry in America to verify that principle. Thousands of multi-millionaires were totally wiped out between 1983 and 1985, when the price of oil dropped precipitously. But it wasn't the price of oil that destroyed them. It was the fact that they had borrowed against everything they owned to expand their investments. When the bottom fell out of the market, as it always does eventually, they lost everything.

The same principle destroyed much of the fortune accumulated by a well-known oil tycoon. Two of his sons decided to corner the silver market and nearly succeeded in doing so. But when the price of silver began to fall, they were unable to cover the margin accounts they held in connection with the trading they did in silver. They had purchased silver contracts on credit but were forced to sell those contracts at drastically reduced prices. Then they were forced to sell other assets to repay the money borrowed on the silver contracts. Before the cycle ended, the majority of a multi-billion dollar estate had evaporated.

Getting Involved in Things You Don't Understand

The second element of the get-rich-quick mentality—taking financial risks in fields you know little or nothing about—is dangerous if there is any possibility of losing sizable amounts of money in the investment. It would be difficult to convince a chemist to invest large amounts of borrowed money in a scheme to turn lead into gold. A chemist understands the physics of the elements too well to be trapped by such a wild scheme (usually!). So the logical candidate for such a venture is a businessman who made his fortune in frozen pizzas. He knows pizzas well, but knows nothing at all about the molecular structure of lead and gold. Obviously you won't find every pizza baron investing in lead-to-gold conversion schemes, but you definitely won't find any chemists doing it.

But Christians are particularly vulnerable to being tricked by foolish schemes because they tend to trust anyone who calls himself a Christian, especially if he claims to have a special "revelation" from God. Beware of anyone who is selling something and says, "I was praying about this idea and God told me to call you." If that person really is a prophet of the Lord, ask him to give a couple of short-range prophecies that you can verify before you put your trust in him.

Several years ago a scheme came through Atlanta that was a classic example of the type of investment I'm talking about. I found out about it because I'm frequently called on to evaluate new get-rich-quick schemes making their way into Christianity, and some of the potential investors wanted my appraisal of the project. The scheme involved a revolutionary automobile engine that supposedly ran on a gas plasma. The engine was small and lightweight and could fit into a Volkswagen-sized car. It was claimed that the engine could generate over 200 horsepower (the equivalent of a large V-8 engine).

But best of all, it ran on water—ordinary faucet water. All you needed for a fuel supply was a jug of water. When you needed a refill you simply poured the water into the tank. Now let me ask you, who would not invest in this revolutionary idea? Automotive engineers and physicists? They just laughed at the idea.

I tried to get a look at one of the engines that supposedly was powering the Volkswagen and scheduled several appointments. But each time an emergency arose that kept the "inventor" from being able to show me the engine. Usually the emergency was related to "hit squads" the inventor claimed the automotive companies had hired to kill him and steal his invention.

Before the plasma engine scheme was shut down, several Christians had invested tens of thousands of dollars, much of it borrowed, in return for shares in a company that supposedly was going to be bigger than General Motors. As you can guess, those Christian investors are still waiting for their fortunes— and are still paying off their loans. It's interesting to note that some of those investors still insist that the idea is real and that the car companies are keeping it off the market. They have convinced themselves that the inventor is in hiding—which is why he disappeared so suddenly and why they have not heard anything from him.

The lesson to be learned is this: Stay with what you know best, and you'll lose a lot less money in the long run. Ron was particularly good at evaluating and selling registered securities, and he made a very good living doing that. It was when he ventured into land development that he got in over his head.

Making Hasty Decisions

Ron's decision to borrow excessive amounts of money for his investment projects was compounded by the fact that when things started to go sour he rushed into more borrowing and talked other investors into doing the same thing. Had he counseled them (and himself) to stop and pray about their decisions before acting, the judge probably would have ruled in his favor. One of the key elements of the prosecution's case was the fact that as an investment adviser Ron had the opportunity to put undue pressure on his clients to act hastily.

In the final analysis it was the charged nature of the adviser-investor relationship and the inherent conflict between Ron's interests and the interests of his clients that caused the judge to be so harsh with him. The judge's point was well taken. He wanted to make an example of Ron so that others in the position of trusted adviser would not take that responsibility lightly again.

Bear in mind what God's Word says about a get-rich-quick attitude. "A faithful man will abound with blessings, but he who makes haste to be rich will not go unpunished" (Proverbs 28:20).

I said that Ron had violated two basic biblical principles in his finances. The first was having a get-rich-quick attitude. The second was ignoring the primary adviser the Lord had provided, his wife, Sue.

Ignoring the Primary Adviser the Lord Has Provided

I don't think I can stress this principle too strongly. It is very dangerous for a husband or wife to ignore the primary adviser the Lord has given him, his spouse. In His infinite wisdom, God created humankind as male and female. He didn't have to. After all, He did create asexual creatures who have no need of a mate or a friend. But I suspect they lead rather dull lives.

When you live with someone in a relationship as close as husband and wife, there are bound to be problems. Since opposites tend to attract, you won't agree about everything. In fact, you may never totally agree about anything. But that's OK, as long as you know how to work it out together and reach a reasonable compromise.

Ron's background made him a candidate for excesses in the area of finances. Often it is not the person from a wealthy background who is obsessed by success, but rather the one from a modest or poor background. We all have the tendency to overcompensate for what we lacked as children.

I came out of a relatively poor background in a wealthy community, and I tend to store rather than spend. Fortunately, God blessed me with a wife who prefers to sit on furniture and grow flowers, or I would probably be sitting on orange crates and investing in antique cars. She helps to balance my extremes, as I balance hers.

These distinctives in personality types should not be ignored when a couple works out the decision-making function in their marriage. We Christians have stereotyped the roles of husband and wife based on what the apostle Paul taught about roles of leadership in the organized church. When we do that we ignore the totality of God's Word on the subject and fail to recognize psychological realities.

The Scriptures do not draw an exact parallel between home relationships and the church. Instead, when the totality of God's Word is considered, and not just isolated passages, it is evident that mutual decision-making is a more accurate description of the Bible's counsel on the matter. Genesis 2:24 indicates that the woman is to have the role of helpmate in a marriage. In 1 Peter 1:7 the husband is warned to treat his wife with grace and honor, lest his "prayers be hindered." When a husband avoids or ignores his wife's counsel on any matter, including finances, he should expect his prayers to be hindered. The same can be said for a wife who does not give her husband the respect that God has assigned him as the head of his family.

Thus the stereotype does not work when it tends to diminish the balance God builds into a marriage. Even when the husband is the dominant personality and the decision-maker, there is still the danger that he will tend to exclude his wife from financial decisions and investments and major purchases, such as cars or boats.

But the stereotype completely breaks down when the husband is not naturally a dominant person. Sometimes he is, but in a high percentage of the families I have counseled, the wife is the dominant personality and the decision-maker. Does that mean that God made an error in giving her a dominant personality and her husband a subdued personality? No. But it does mean that the wife in such a marriage must learn to listen to the counsel of her husband, just as dominant husbands must listen to their less dominant wives. If the wife hasn't learned to do this, she will be seen as pushy, domineering, or unsubmissive.

God created husband and wife to function as a single working unit, each with different but essential abilities. Certainly those abilities will overlap in many areas, and often that will lead to differences of opinions. But just as certainly, without the balance that each can bring to the marriage, great errors in judgment will be made.

It has been my observation that a dominant woman operating on her own initiative will accumulate debt through credit cards and store accounts, because she buys too many clothes or too much furniture. A dominant husband operating on his own initiative will accumulate debt through the purchase of boats, airplanes, and other investments. Men don't buy very often, but when they do, they buy big.

Facing a Chapter 7 Bankruptcy with Prudence and Honor

Though the consequences of a chapter 7 bankruptcy are very severe, a bankruptcy may indeed occur when a get-rich-quick scheme fails.

Ron and Sue experienced the total dissolution of their assets through a creditor-initiated bankruptcy action. In most instances such action by any three creditors is sufficient to force a bankruptcy. In Ron's case he elected to file bankruptcy rather than to allow the few demanding creditors to sell off his remaining assets to their benefit and the detriment of all the others.

A bankruptcy action will usually provide only a fraction of the total debt owed to creditors, but creditors are required to accept the liquidation proceeds as total settlement of their debt. Again, in Ron's case, he and Sue committed themselves to repaying everyone who agreed not to join the bankruptcy action. They felt that those creditors who elected to take the bankruptcy proceeds did so voluntarily and thus settled the debt. To be as fair as possible to the creditors who joined the bankruptcy, Ron and Sue retained no salable assets, even though bankruptcy action allows the debtor to keep a small amount of the home equity (if there is a home), one automobile, and a limited amount of cash. Unlike many others who file bankruptcy for their convenience, Ron placed all assets held in Sue's name into the asset pool as well. They withheld nothing from the creditors.

Bankruptcy is never an action to be taken lightly. The financial consequences and the damage to a reputation are long-lasting for anyone, but especially for a Christian. A creditor has a right to expect to recover the money he has loaned in good faith, and the Bible is clear in its admonition to pay one's vows (promises). I believe that Ron and Sue fulfilled this scriptural principle by going to each of the creditors and explaining why they decided to file for bankruptcy. They believed that the disgruntled investors would force them to sell off all their assets and that the unsecured creditors had a right to a share, if they so elected. However, when Ron and Sue approached the creditors, they also explained their total financial situation and indicated that the sale of all their assets would yield only a small fraction of the total debt. They then asked each creditor not to join the bankruptcy action on the promise (in writing) that they would repay all debts in total at a future date, if the Lord chose to provide the funds.

This action was taken against the counsel of their attorney, who recommended that they place all debts in the bankruptcy and clear them. He said they could choose to repay the deficiencies later, if and when they had the funds. Ron and Sue decided not to take his advice because they thought it should be the choice of the creditor to take what was available immediately or trust them to repay later.

Because of the loan defaults as a result of the bankruptcy, Ron also owed nearly $100,000 in taxes to the IRS. Under a rule called Forgiveness of Debt, most of the unrecovered loan balances were declared income and as such were subject to taxes, interest, and penalties. The IRS agreed to waive the penalties, but Ron (and Sue) still ended up owing nearly $100,000 in back taxes. Since a bankruptcy action cannot remove tax-related debt, those taxes still remained. But without the ability to pay even a small fraction of the debt and without assets, Ron could do nothing but allow the debt to continue accumulating interest.

A short while later they received another financial shock through a letter from the IRS agent assigned to their case. He noted that since they had sold their home, the gain on that sale would also be taxable if they did not purchase a home of equal or greater value within the next two years. "Just a note to remind you," he wrote.

Needless to say, Ron and Sue felt like the weight of the world had been dropped on them. One evening after Ron had come home from work, they were having a devotion with their children and came across the passage in Philippians where the apostle Paul wrote, "Be anxious for nothing, but in everything by prayer and supplication with thanksgiving let your requests be made known to God. . . . And my God shall supply all your needs according to His riches in glory in Christ Jesus" (Philippians 4:6, 19).

Ron and Sue stopped and looked at each other and began to smile. Then they began to laugh out loud. The kids thought Mom and Dad had lost their senses.

"Don't you see, kids," they said, "we have the perfect chance to believe God for this promise made through Paul while he was sitting in a Roman prison waiting to be executed? All we're risking is money. And God promised that money is the smallest thing we will ever be asked to trust Him for.

"We're going to make a budget based on God's providing a great abundance to this family. That way we'll have our own spending under control and won't be tempted to indulge or hoard what God has entrusted to us."

Soon the children were excited about planning what to do with God's surplus. First Ron and Sue explained about the debts that were still outstanding, especially the ones to the bank. "They had the most to lose," Ron told the children. "So they showed the most faith in us. We need to pay them back before we assume any of the money is ours to manage."

Ron also explained about the IRS debt and that it would need to be paid, to which all the kids booed and hissed. They had all seen and heard the callous way the agent assigned to their case had acted when he thought they were trying to hide some assets.

"No," Ron said. "We're instructed to honor those in authority and pray for them." He then read Romans 13:1, 6–7: "'Let every person be in subjection to the governing authorities. For there is no authority except from God, and those which exist are established by God. . . . For because of this you also pay taxes, for rulers are servants of God, devoting themselves to this very thing. Render to all what is due them: tax to whom tax is due; custom to whom custom; fear to whom fear; honor to whom honor.'

"Guys, you need to remember that the government didn't cause our problems. I did. We might object to paying the taxes because it is a lot of money, but we need to remember that it's a consequence of my actions, not theirs. If I had listened to what God's Word said about borrowing and taking risks, we wouldn't have a tax problem. It was greed that caused our problems, not the government."

From that evening on, they made a commitment to pray that the agent would come to know Jesus as his Savior.

"After all," Sue commented, "nothing else will matter a hundred years from now anyway."

"Yeah," their ten-year-old said. "And maybe he'll be nicer if he's a Christian, too." And the other two clapped and yelled.

Ron and Sue planned a budget based on Ron's present income and decided that they would be able to manage quite well when they didn't have the debt burden to pay each month. So as a family they began to pray that God would provide the funds to retire all the debts.

Two years passed as Ron and Sue continued to pay a few hundred dollars a year on debts that accumulated thousands of dollars in interest each year. Ron did well in selling real estate, and his income increased to nearly $35,000 a year. They increased the shares they paid to the bank, to the IRS, and the amount they gave to the Lord. Two of their children had been in a fairly expensive Christian school prior to the financial problems. After praying about it, Ron and Sue decided that the money for the school should be paid to creditors, so they decided to remove the kids from the private school and send them to a public school. Sue later said that Ron had more difficulty with that decision than with any other. It's one thing to take responsibility for your mistakes, and quite another to ask your children to suffer for them. They had attended the school all their lives, and all their friends were there. But in the final analysis Ron and Sue believed it came down to a matter of obeying what they felt God was saying to them: put everything on the altar.

When Sue told the principal, he was shocked.

"You can't do that, Sue," he said. "Your children have been here since the school started. You're a part of this family."

"We have made up our minds, John," Sue replied. "We don't believe it is our right to keep our children in a private school when we owe so much. Other Christians' children go to public schools and survive. We believe that the decision is from the Lord and that He will protect them. We love this school, and I would like to continue helping out as a teacher's aide and volunteering during the banquets. But our decision is made."

"How do the children feel about this?" the principal asked.

"Naturally, they're disappointed," Sue answered. "But they understand that we must do what we believe God is telling us."

They agreed that the children would remain in the school until the spring break, which was about two weeks away. In the meantime, Sue went to the local public schools and made the necessary arrangements to have the children's records transferred. Later that week Sue received a call from the principal.

"Sue, I wanted to let you know that we had a meeting of the school board last night and that they voted to provide scholarships for your children."

"That's wonderful news, John! The children will be thrilled to hear it. Please tell the members of the committee how much we appreciate it and that we will repay the funds when the Lord provides."

"No, Sue," the principal replied. "I told them that you and Ron would take it as an obligation to repay. This is a gift from us to you. Several members of the board have already paid the tuition and book money themselves. We're just practicing what 2 Corinthians 8:14-15 tells us to do."

That evening Ron and Sue told their children the good news.

"Kids, I think this is God's way of saying thank you for your obedience to what we asked you to do," Ron said with tears in his eyes. The older two children clapped and yelled about what they viewed as a miracle on their behalf.

A few months later Ron was in his office when he got a call from the president of the bank.

"Ron, could we have lunch tomorrow? I'd like to talk to you about your outstanding loans."

"Certainly," Ron replied, feeling that old queasy feeling in the pit of his stomach. He imagined all kinds of things. Perhaps the bank had decided to sue him for collection. But that didn't make any sense. He still didn't have any assets to sell. They were living in a rented house and driving a six-year-old car. And they had been making regular monthly payments, even if they were pitifully small.

That evening Ron, Sue, and the kids all prayed for God's will in their lives, whatever that might be. Ron was able to go to sleep with the confidence that only trust in God could explain.

The next day at lunch Mr. Cross, the bank president, said, "Ron, I want to thank you for living up to my confidence in you. I have to tell you that I had a dickens of a time convincing the other members of the board to go along with your plan. Some thought you were pulling a fast one on us. And others thought it would be better to get the whole thing over with and write off the bad debts. But your commitment and dependability to make a payment each month has been the subject of praise at nearly every board meeting for the last two years."

"Thank you, Mr. Cross. But I don't think I deserve any praise for doing what is my responsibility anyway," Ron replied honestly.

"Perhaps not, Ron, but I'll tell you this: not one other major debtor to the bank has repaid any of the bad syndication loans. Most of them went bankrupt and put all their assets in someone else's name. Doing what is right is not the norm today.

"We recently had a contact on the land you surrendered on your loans. Two days ago we sold the land, thus clearing your notes totally."

"That's great, Mr. Cross. I know you didn't have to do that, and I sincerely appreciate it."

"But that's not all, Ron," he continued. "Our board has agreed to do something that I have never heard of a bank doing before. They have agreed to return all of the proceeds above the actual loan amounts to you. I have a check in the amount of three hundred eighty thousand dollars made out to you."

Ron was utterly taken aback.

"Mr. Cross, I really don't know what to say except that this truly is the last thing I expected."

"That makes two of us, Ron. Banks and bankers normally aren't very benevolent toward delinquent debtors, but we all recognize something different in your life. Thank you for being a good witness for God. I can tell you that more than a few people who call themselves Christians have been negative witnesses regarding their financial responsibilities."

Ron could hardly wait to get home and tell Sue the great news. When he burst through the door she met him saying, "I already know, honey. It's truly an answer from the Lord."

"How in the world could you know about it?" Ron asked. "I just found out an hour ago."

"News like this travels faster than AT&T in the Christian community," Sue replied. "I have had two calls already this morning. One from a friend of a friend at the bank, and the second from one of your ex-partners."

"Which one?" Ron asked cautiously.

"Bob," Sue replied with a hint of irritation in her voice. "He said he had heard that one of the partnership's investments had sold and wondered what his share would be. He asked that you call him when you came in. Are you planning to divide the proceeds with them, Ron?"

"Absolutely not!" Ron said emphatically. "They weren't willing to share in the losses, so they don't have any right to the profits. I know exactly where the first part of this money is going: to the Lord's work. Then we'll pay off the IRS debt and decide where the Lord would want us to put the rest of it."

"Remember our plan, Ron," Sue said jestingly. "God wants us to be debt-free. Does that mean owning a home?"

"Absolutely," Ron replied. "If I calculate properly, we should be able to pay the taxes on the profits and come out with about $80,000. That won't buy the house we had before, but we didn't need it anyway."

To conclude this particular couple's story, the bank to which Ron had been making the payments hired him to manage the foreclosed properties the bank had on its rolls. He did such a good job in that capacity that he was promoted to asset manager of the holding company's properties. Ron and Sue's children are still in the Christian school, and the couple has helped several other families attend the school through scholarships.

14

Learn to Live
Within a Financial Plan

THE FINANCIAL TROUBLES of the third couple discussed in this book, John and Mary Thompson, look at first as though they were the result of circumstances the couple could not control. Surely no one could have forseen the medical problems their son would have or that the bills for his care would be so high. An argument could be made that the expenses they had with him would have wrecked anyone's budget.

But the fact is that Jack and Mary Thompson's financial troubles were the result of poor planning. Though they were intelligent and committed people, they had never been taught the basics of finances. They had never measured Jack's income against normal monthly expenses and they had made no provision for any emergency spending they might someday have to make. The only way the couple made it financially was to use Mary's income to balance the budget.

This basic fact was not obvious to Jack and Mary, and as a consequence the steps they took as they began to slip into debt were ones that made a bad situation worse.

Shortly after the baby was born, Jack and Mary's church took up a collection to help them with the additional hospital expenses. However, the extent of the medical bills was far beyond the means of the small church, and soon the bills were accumulating again. After meeting with the doctor, Jack talked with the hospital administrator. He recommended that the couple consider filing for bankruptcy. Two other Christians, as well, counseled Jack to file for bankruptcy to relieve some of the financial pressure.

In the meantime, the couple found that they were unable to meet their mortgage payments and the payments on a small debt on some furniture they had purchased. But since they had no real budget, they naturally assumed their financial problems were the result of the baby's medical expenses.

They soon began to develop an "I don't care" mentality about their finances. They assumed the situation was hopeless. Though they continued to pray about their needs, they adopted the attitude of many Christians: they prayed and assumed God wouldn't answer.

They began to use their credit cards to fill the gaps in their budget. Jack bought his gas on credit and ate out on credit, while Mary bought baby supplies and food on credit. Without realizing it, they had adopted an attitude of despair and a philosophy that bankruptcy was inevitable. As is common, they were holding a pity party at their creditors' expense. With no visible means to repay, they were running up bills and living beyond their means. Although Jack would never have robbed a bank, he was in effect doing the same thing—stealing from his creditors.

Seven months after the baby was born the couple was beginning to reap the seeds they had sown. Creditors were calling daily because nearly all their bills were delinquent. Two credit card companies had filed judgments against them—which Jack had ignored because he felt there was nothing that could be done anyway. When Jack's pay was garnisheed, he was called into the school administrator's office.

"Jack, I just received a notice of attachment from the court," Mr. Mills said solemnly. "I have to comply with the request and withhold twenty percent of your net pay. Do you have financial problems?"

"Yes sir," Jack responded a little defiantly. "It's the medical bills for the baby."

"We know the bills must be a problem for you and Mary, and we're working on something that might help. But the garnishment is the result of a judgment from a VISA bill. Is that related to the medical expenses?"

"No, not directly," Jack said, looking down at the floor as he spoke. "We've had to use our credit cards for normal expenses during the last few months. But it all started because of the baby's problems."

Then Mr. Mills began to realize that Jack had allowed the problems with the baby to distort his thinking. He said, "Jack, I believe you have more financial problems than just the medical bills from the baby. I know we don't pay our teachers nearly what the public school systems do, and it's tough to make it on one salary. But you took the job knowing that, and now I suspect that even without the baby you would be in over your head. I want you to go to a financial counselor and get a clear picture of where you are financially. There is a potentially embarrassing situation developing through this whole thing."

"How so, Mr. Mills?" Jack asked. "Will I lose my job over the garnishment?"

"No, Jack," Mr. Mills responded. "We have neither the right nor the authority to dismiss you for that reason. But with Mary not working, you would have a difficult time making ends meet even if all your finances were in perfect order. We do have some teachers supporting families on one salary, but they must be very careful and live on a strict budget. With this garnishment I know your budget won't make it. Do you have other debts besides the VISA?"

"Well, yes, we do," Jack responded uncomfortably.

"More than one thousand dollars worth?"

"Well, yes, I guess so. But we have decided to file for bankruptcy anyway. The medical bills would make it impossible to live on my salary no matter what," Jack said with an air of finality.

"No one could argue with that," Mr. Mills said as he recognized Jack's defensiveness. "Jack, as Christians, and more so as teachers, you and I have a responsibility to demonstrate the attributes of Jesus to those around us. In the eyes of our generation, nothing is as visible as the way we handle our finances."

"I agree," Jack said, interrupting. "But God had to know our baby would need a lot of attention that would cost a great deal of money. Who's to say this is not His plan?"

"I would. And I would say that even if our roles were reversed and it was my son with the health problems. I believe you have allowed your circumstances to overrule your first commitment—to the Lord."

"That's easy for you to say, Mr. Mills, because it isn't your son, and you make more money than I do," Jack said defiantly.

"That's very true. But I would hope that our faith is not built on what someone else does or doesn't have, or on what they would or wouldn't do in similar circumstances. You see, there will always be someone else who is better off than either of us and someone who has more money than both of us."

Again Jack said, "That's easy enough to say when it's not your finances. But I don't see anyone paying our bills for us."

"Perhaps that is not entirely true, Jack."

"What do you mean?"

"Several members of the school board and the faculty have put money in a trust fund for the medical bills you and Mary have incurred. We realize that you can't meet all your expenses. We have been paying something on the bills for the last two months now. Didn't you notice that the hospital and doctors had stopped sending you notices?"

Jack stopped cold. No, he hadn't noticed. He had been so caught up in his problems that he had taken an antagonistic stance in relation to most of the creditors and had ignored all of the notices they had been sending. Mary had commented several times that they should try to contact the major creditors and let them know that they were having some severe financial problems. Jack had shrugged it off saying, "We can't pay them anyway. So what difference does it make?"

"Another thing," Mr. Mills continued. "One of the school board members applied to a foundation that specializes in cases like yours. Notice just came in today that a grant has been approved that will pay all the medical bills and the cost of care that Johnny will need over the next several years."

Jack was taken aback for the second time that day. "I don't know what to say, Mr. Mills."

"You don't need to say anything. We did what we did because we care. But now I fear that you have positioned yourself so that just paying the medical bills won't solve the problems anymore. You and Mary need to pray about what to do. But let me encourage you to seek good counsel and not listen to the counsel of those who look for the easy way out all the time."

Reality began to set in.

Jack was excited about going home and telling Mary the good news about the medical bills being taken care of by the foundation. But as he drove home, a feeling of depression came over him. He realized that they would still owe hundreds of dollars on credit cards that they had used during the last few months. He began to accept the fact that they would be paying for their ignorance and lack of self-discipline, perhaps for years.

Mary wasn't home when Jack arrived, so he decided to review some of the bills that had been sent during the last few weeks. Most of them were still in his desk drawer unopened. He opened the envelopes and began to sort the bills by date and amount. An hour passed as he sorted bills from oil company cards, department store cards, and three major credit cards. When he totaled what he had found, he was shocked. *Surely this must be some kind of mistake,* Jack told himself. *We can't possibly owe that much.*

Yet when he retotaled the stack, the figure came out the same: $6,764.34. Almost $7,000! And he knew that he still hadn't found all the bills. He had been so sure they only owed a few hundred dollars that even $1,000 would have been a shock. But $7,000. It seemed impossible.

When Mary arrived home, she knew immediately that something was wrong. Jack was still sitting at the desk looking at the stack of bills in front of him. "What's the problem, Jack?" she asked, not really wanting to know.

"I received word from Mr. Mills today that members of the school board have been paying on our medical bills. That's why we haven't been getting notices from the doctors or the hospital," he said.

"That's great," Mary responded enthusiastically. "But what's the problem?"

"That's not all, Mary," Jack continued in a somber mood. "Mr. Mills also said that a foundation has accepted all of Timmy's medical expenses from this point on. We won't have to pay anything except living expenses."

Mary was overwhelmed by the news. "Why, that's wonderful! The Lord has met every need we have."

"Not quite," Jack said "I just totaled up the credit card debts. We owe nearly $7,000, and I know that's not all of it."

"That's impossible," Mary nearly shouted.

"Unfortunately, it's not. We also have a judgment against my wages, as of today. I feel so stupid, Mary. I've been living as if there were no tomorrow and no God. I guess I just assumed that we would have to go bankrupt, so I didn't care how much debt we ran up. God has been faithful to fulfill His end, but I failed to hold up my end."

"What is our alternative now?" Mary asked as she moved to put Johnny in his crib.

"I believe we have but one. God stopped us from filing bankruptcy by removing any excuse we might have had. The debts we owe are a result of our own decisions, and I can't blame anyone but myself. I don't see how we can do anything but commit to paying all of our debts."

"But how will we be able to do that on your salary alone?" Mary asked.

"I don't think we can. I'll just have to tell Mr. Mills that I need to start looking for a new job. In the meantime I'll go to each of the creditors and ask for a reduced payment until I can generate more income. But we can't do much about the garnishment. That will come out of each paycheck until the bill is paid in full. It won't leave us a lot to live on, but we'll have to learn to do it.

"I want to cut up the credit cards, too. As long as we have them, we'll be tempted to use them. And I think we need to go back to driving one car. Maybe we can sell my car for enough money to clear the VISA and the garnishment."

"But, Jack, my car has nearly one hundred thousand miles on it. Can we get by with a car that old?"

"We'll have to, Mary. It's going to be tough for a while, but as I said, we'll just have to do it."

Jack left the Christian school for a job as a teacher and coach at a public school. He and Mary went to see the counselor Mr. Mills had suggested and worked out a plan with the creditors that allowed them some transition time. It was nearly two years before they began to see daylight in their finances, but in three years they were totally debt-free.

They began teaching a course on finances in their church and are still teaching it. Before any young couple can get married in their church, they must sit through a six-hour course on how to manage money God's way and then demonstrate that they can live on a budget. Jack's desire is to one day be the head of a Christian school where he can influence other young Christians before they make the mistakes he did.

15

Accept Responsibililty for Your Life

IN THIS CHAPTER I would like to look at another couple, Bill and Pam. They were both in their early twenties and in college. They were both Christians, although from different ends of the spectrum philosophically. Bill came from a more traditional background. I note this difference in their church backgrounds only because of the influence that the teaching they received in their churches had on their decisions.

Both came out of middle-class homes with parents who were Christians. They both attended public schools most of their lives but went to Christian high schools. Neither had ever attended a course on personal finances. Although they had both worked at a variety of summer jobs for several years, neither had more than a general idea of how to balance a checkbook.

They met at a rally held by a Christian group on campus and kept steady company thereafter. Both Pam and Bill were attending college on a variety of loans and grants available to them. By their senior year their loans totaled nearly $8,000 apiece. Bill knew he would be expected to repay his loans after graduation because his dad had made that clear from the beginning. Since he felt he had little choice, he continued to accumulate school loans.

Pam and her parents never discussed the repayment of the loans she was receiving. She assumed that her dad would pay them as he had all of her bills, but she never really gave it much thought. But then in the early part of her senior year Pam's father died of a sudden heart attack. Her mother was devastated by her loss and went into a prolonged state of depression. Pam dropped out of school for one quarter and then returned to finish her degree. In the past, her father had always given her money for the incidentals she needed just before she left for school. Since her father was gone, Pam approached her mother.

"Mom, I'll need some money for books and dorm fees," she said.

"Dad always handled the finances, honey. I don't know what you need. Why don't you take my credit card and get whatever is necessary. We'll work it out when you come home next time. Maybe Daddy's insurance will be settled by that time, and I'll know what we have."

Pam's mom then handed her two credit cards, one for buying gas for her car and the other for general expenses. Although Pam had never owned a card of her own, she had often used her mother's to fill up the family car or run errands for her mom. The cards had only her mother's initials and last name on them. Because Pam had the same initials as her mother, the merchants never questioned her signature.

Back at school Pam called home regularly to see how her mom was doing. She was still in a state of semi-shock and was virtually unaware that Pam called her almost every day. When the first month's phone bill came for Pam's dorm phone, it was nearly $200. She paid it with the card her mother had given her.

Pam needed some clothes for school and normally would have called and asked her dad for some money. Usually he sent her a check for a hundred dollars or so and she would buy a pair of jeans and a blouse or two. Since she knew her mother was in no shape to answer questions, she decided to use the card this time. By the time she finished the shopping trip she had charged over $500 worth of new clothes and had also charged a watch for Bill for another $120.

She and Bill had begun talking seriously about their plans after graduation. They knew they would get married, but beyond that had no definite plans for what they would do. Bill was earning a degree in music, and Pam's degree in elementary education required her to intern for at least three months. Then her employment would depend on finding an opening in the school system near the college. Bill wanted to go on to graduate school and gain his Master's degree so that he could teach music at the college level.

During the next three months, Pam fell into a routine of using her mother's credit card periodically to take Bill out to eat and buy him gifts. Then her car broke down, and she had the brakes fixed, again using the card. Without realizing it she began to develop a habit of small indulgences, using her mother's card to pay for them. None were particularly significant by themselves, but when totaled, they began to add up. The bills came to her mother's home where she put them on her desk and left them unopened. She couldn't cope with the details of daily life yet.

Suddenly Pam saw school coming to an end and was faced with entering the work force for the first time. She began to feel a little panicked herself. She thought more and more about getting married. She feared that if they waited until summer, something might happen to keep them from getting married. That thought really panicked her. She had lost her father; she couldn't stand the thought of possibly losing Bill, too.

One evening she said to Bill, "Why don't we go ahead and get married? I know mom is in no shape to take on a wedding, and I'm not sure she could emotionally handle seeing me get married anyway."

"But how will we make it financially?" Bill asked. "Neither of us has a job, and you still have your student teaching to complete."

"We already have my apartment," Pam replied. "And without your dorm fee our expenses would actually be less, wouldn't they?"

"Well, I guess so," he replied as he thought about the idea. "But I don't know if my dad would continue to pay my bills if I got married."

"We should be able to qualify for some grants if we're married," Pam responded enthusiastically. "And besides, we'll have your student loans while you're in grad school."

The more Bill thought about the idea, the more he liked it, too. Graduation was only two months away, and then Pam would be finished. They had planned to get married that next summer anyway, so what difference would three or four months make?

Besides, he thought. *Pam's right. Her mother is certainly in no shape to go through a wedding.* "I think it's a great idea," he said as he put his arms around her. "When would you like to get married?"

"What about right now?" she said.

"Right now?" Bill echoed as he looked at his watch. "But it's nearly eleven o'clock, and we have classes tomorrow. Besides, we have to wait at least three days for the blood tests."

"We could miss Friday's classes," she argued, a little hurt that Bill was hesitating. "And we can always drive to another state where there is no waiting period."

"But Pam, the nearest state is Virginia, and that's nearly two hundred miles. I don't even have gas money right now."

"I've got my credit cards," she responded eagerly. "It wouldn't cost that much, and we could stop over in Memphis on the way back and see my dad's sister. She's been wanting me to come and visit. It would be like a little honeymoon."

Bill had a nagging feeling inside about doing something this serious on impulse. He wondered what his mom would say when she found out. But seeing Pam so excited and knowing that they did love each other, he could come up with no logical arguments that would satisfy her. So he said, "OK, Pam, we'll get married. You pack some things, and I'll call my mom and let her know."

Pam panicked inside as Bill mentioned calling his mom. "Please don't tell anyone right now," she pleaded. "They'll just try to talk us out of it. I want this to be our surprise. We'll tell them after graduation, OK?"

Bill agreed reluctantly, but he knew his mom would be hurt when she found out. Pam said, "Let's just go like we are. We don't need any extra clothes. We'll only be gone two days at the most, and we can buy something if we really need it."

By this time Bill was totally into the idea as well, so he replied, "This is really crazy, but if that's what you want, honey, we'll do it. At least we'll have something to tell our grandchildren. But let's agree on one thing. No children until we're both out of school and settled into our jobs, OK?"

Pam agreed and grabbed Bill around the waist. "We're going to be so happy, Bill. I just know it."

Bill and Pam took off for Virginia. Four hours later they stopped to eat a very late dinner. While they were eating, they mentioned to the waitress that they were driving to Virginia to get married the next day.

"Do you have your license yet?" she asked.

"No," Bill replied. "We understand we don't have to wait in Virginia."

"Well, I don't know who told you that, honey," she said in a deep Southern drawl. "But it simply ain't true. You gotta wait at least two days."

"We can't wait," Pam said in alarm. "We have to be back in school Monday morning."

"Well, I'd suggest you go to New Jersey then," the waitress said authoritatively. "You don't have to wait at all up there. That's where we got married a few years back."

"We can't drive all the way to New Jersey," Bill argued. "It would take ten or twelve more hours."

"But we can't just turn around and go back home," Pam complained. "We've already come this far. Let's go on, please."

Bill was in no mood to discuss anything objectively, and when he saw the hurt on Pam's face, he surrendered. "OK," he said. "If you're willing, I am too. But let's get going. We'll just make it back in time."

Pam had literally jumped out of her seat and was headed toward the door when Bill asked, "Do you have any cash, Pam? I'm a little short to pay the bill."

Pam dug into her purse and found about three dollars in change. She asked the waitress, "Can I pay for the meal with my credit card?"

"Sorry, honey," the waitress replied, "the boss won't let us take credit cards. He says they cost him too much."

So Bill paid the check with what they could scrape together, and they headed toward New Jersey. Several hours later they entered New Jersey and encountered their first toll bridge. In the meantime their periodic stops had exhausted their small cash reserve. The toll gate attendant told them that they would either have to pay the toll or turn around and go back.

"Can we pay the toll with a credit card?" Pam asked.

"No, you can't, miss," he answered "Look, kids, the toll is only a dollar ten. Are you telling me you don't even have that much on you?"

Looking a little sheepish Bill replied, "I'm afraid not. You see, we were planning to get married in Virginia, but when we found out we had to wait two days, we decided to drive up here instead. We have to be back in school Monday."

"Well, good luck. But I don't think you're getting off to a good start this way. Exactly how much do you have?"

"About fifty-six cents," Pam said in a whisper.

"Tell you what I'll do," the attendant said in a stern voice. "Give me what you have, and I'll put in the difference. You're holding up traffic."

"Oh, thank you, sir," was Pam's reply.

"Just one thing," the man said. "How are you planning to get back across?"

Bill was suddenly struck by the same thought. "How are we going to get back across with no money?"

"I have an aunt who lives just a few miles further," Pam volunteered. "We'll go see her. I'm sure she will help."

With a sinking feeling inside, Bill drove across the bridge and into New Jersey. He realized that what they were doing didn't make any sense, but he didn't know what else to do. Pam was totally committed to the idea of marriage. He was, too, but he had some reservations about the timing.

They drove to Pam's aunt's home. She was speechless when Pam called her to say they were only a couple of miles away. But she asked them to come over and began to prepare some lunch.

When Pam and Bill rang the doorbell, she opened it to find two worn out and totally rumpled young people. "Pam, come in," she said. "Who is your young man, and what in the world brings you here?"

"This is Bill, Aunt Maye," she said. "We're getting married and just dropped by to see you."

"Getting married?" Pam's aunt said with surprise. "Does your mom know about this?"

"No, ma'am. She's really been depressed since Daddy's death, and we thought it would be better to elope and not put her through the stress of a wedding."

"Well, I can't argue that she's in no shape for any more emotional trauma," her aunt said. "But I don't know that running away to get married is the right answer, either. Do your parents know, Bill?"

"No, ma'am," he replied shyly. "But we are of legal age, and my folks know we plan to get married in the summer."

"Then why all the rush?" she asked.

Pam jumped in, "We just believe that's what God wants us to do, Aunt Maye. But we have a little problem and wondered if you could help."

"What kind of problem, dear?"

"We've had to drive further than we planned and run out of cash. I wondered if you would mind cashing a small check for me?"

"I don't want your check, dear. I'll be glad to give you some money as a wedding present. But I certainly wish you would think about this some more."

"We have already thought about it, and we know this is what we want to do," Pam said emphatically. Bill started to answer but changed his mind. Then Pam's aunt said something that set them both back.

"But I don't understand why you drove all the way up here. New Jersey has a three-day waiting period before you can get married."

"That can't be," Pam said almost in hysteria. "The waitress said she got married here herself without a wait."

"That must have been some time ago then," her aunt said. "I'll call and check for you, but I'm sure that's right."

A brief call to the local Justice of the Peace confirmed her statement. "He says the closest place to get married with no wait is Virginia."

"That's impossible," Bill moaned. "We were just there and someone told us they had a waiting period, too."

Another long distance call to the sheriff's department in Lynch County, Virginia, confirmed that they could get married without a wait if they were of legal age.

"I suspect the waitress thought you kids were not old enough to get married without permission," the aunt said. "And she probably had someone pull some strings for her here. I'm afraid you'll just have to wait until you get back to Virginia."

They decided to sleep a few hours before they headed back, and in the interim Pam's aunt washed and dried their well-worn clothes. Four hours later they were back on the road, headed toward Virginia, where they finally were married by a Justice of the Peace. By that time they were totally broke and running out of time before classes started.

"That'll be ten dollars," the Justice said. "And ten more for the license."

"Will you take a credit card?" Pam asked meekly.

"Sorry, honey, cash only." the Justice responded rather brusquely.

"But we don't have any cash," Pam pleaded. "Will you take a check?"

"I normally take cash only. It's Saturday night and nobody can cash your check until Monday. You kids don't have any money at all?" he asked, looking at Bill.

"No, sir," Bill replied.

"Well, I guess I'll have to take a check then," he said irritably. "But I'll need some collateral. I've been stiffed by too many of you college kids already."

"What kind of collateral?" Pam asked nervously. She knew that if they didn't get a license they weren't legally married.

"I'll take that Seiko you're wearing," he told Bill, pointing at his watch.

"But that's brand new," Pam protested. "And it was a gift from me."

"Well, take it or leave it," the Justice said gruffly. "Otherwise you can wait until Monday and cash your check at the bank."

"No, we can't wait," Bill said as he removed the watch. "Can we get it back after the check clears?"

"Why sure, kids. You just drop me a note, and I'll send it right along," he said with a chuckle.

A month later Pam's mother called her. "Pam, I've been looking through some of the bills from my bank, and I see that the credit card is overdrawn. I called our banker, and he said he had let it overdraft because he knew about

Daddy's death and figured I was waiting on the insurance payment. But Pam, I haven't used that card much at all, and it has more than four thousand dollars charged on it."

"Four thousand dollars! Mother, that's impossible," Pam explained. "I've used it for school expenses and some clothes, but I certainly didn't charge four thousand dollars!"

"And the Gulf card has nearly eight hundred on it too, Pam. Have you used it? There are charges on here from Virginia, Washington, New Jersey, and who knows where else. Did you drive up to New Jersey recently?"

Pam sat quietly for a few seconds. She was overwhelmed by the news from her mother. She had put the trip and the charges completely out of her mind during the last month. Being married was everything to her, and she and Bill had been very happy. But now she knew she had to tell her mother that they were married. "Mom, Bill and I got married a month ago. That's where the gas charges came from. But don't worry, we'll pay you back."

Pam's mother had already put two and two together and suspected something like that. She replied, "That was your choice, honey, but I wish you had at least let me know before you got married. Bill's mother is going to be very upset. But you'll have to work that out for yourselves. You know your dad and I always said that when you got married you would have to manage your own household. So I'm sending all the bills to you. You'll have to take care of them."

"But Mom," she pleaded, "we don't have the money to pay all the bills right now. I'm student teaching, and Bill is getting ready for his finals next month."

"I'm sorry, Pam, but you should have considered that before you got married and ran up those bills." With that, she hung up the phone.

Pam looked around the small room that served as their living area. There sat the television and stereo she had charged on the credit card before she and Bill were married, and she realized that she may well have charged $4,000—and more. She had been using the card since they got married and was frightened as she realized that they may well have charged another several hundred dollars. Graduation was still five weeks away, and they had no visible means of support. She decided not to tell Bill anything about what her mother had said until after graduation. He needed to concentrate on graduating, and she knew he would worry himself sick about the bills. He already looked haggard from concern over what he would tell his parents.

For nearly two weeks Pam tried diligently not to use the credit card for anything. Her mother had sent her the bills, and after looking through them she knew they were her charges. Then one evening while Bill was in a class she got a call from Bill's mother.

"Pam, is Bill home?" she asked. Without thinking Pam replied, "No, he's still in class."

There was a long pause on the other end of the line. Pam tried to think of something to say, but decided that this was as good a time as any for Bill's mother to find out.

"Are you and Bill living together?" Bill's mother asked with a measured calmness.

"Well, Mrs. Yates, we got married about a month ago." Pam replied. "I'm sorry we didn't tell you, but we just didn't know how."

"We knew something was wrong when the school wrote and told us Bill had moved out of the dorm," she said sternly. "I do think you both owed us enough respect to tell us yourselves. But if you're married, you're married. So let's make the best of it. Please tell Bill to call me when he comes in. We would like for you both to come down for a day as soon as you can."

"We will, I promise," Pam replied. "And we're very happy, Mrs. Yates. We do love each other, and we didn't do this to hurt anyone."

"Pam, you're a member of our family now, and we love you too. But you both need to learn that being honest up front is the only way the Lord wants us to live. I'm disappointed that you didn't trust us enough to believe we would allow you to make your own decisions. You can't start a relationship with an attitude of distrust. Please remember that in your marriage, too."

When they hung up Pam sat still for several minutes. What Bill's mother had said hit her in a sensitive spot. She knew they had been deceitful to their parents, and she knew she had been deceiving Bill. It had gone on so long now she was wondering how he would react when he finally knew the whole truth. When Bill came home, she told him about his mother's call. He looked like he was going to be sick for a minute. Then he said, "I don't blame her for being hurt and angry. I know I have been lying to them since we got married. I'd better call her and at least let her know I'm sorry."

"I'm sorry, Bill," Pam said honestly. "I suppose I'm the one at fault. You wanted to call her, and I talked you out of it. I was afraid she would convince you not to get married."

"No, Pam, I'm the one at fault. I know I'm supposed to be the leader in our home. If I had had the courage, I would have been honest with my parents up front. I just hope this doesn't affect our relationship with them from now on."

After a brief conversation with his mother and his father, Bill hung up the phone. "Well, they're both hurt," he said. "But they both want you to know they're glad to have you as a member of our family, and they will make the best of the situation. My dad said that we'll have to come up with the money for grad school ourselves. He believes we should stand on our own two feet. I guess that means I'll have to put it off for a while, at least until we can save a little money."

"What about graduation expenses and the school loans?" Pam asked apprehensively. She had intended to tell Bill about the other debts, but now she wondered if she should.

"He said he'll continue to pay until I graduate, and they're going to give us a five hundred dollar wedding gift to help us get started. The school loans are mine to pay, but I knew that from the beginning."

Pam decided she would wait to tell Bill about the debts until he had a chance to recover from the shock of telling his parents. The opportunity didn't come up again before graduation, and with the $500 from Bill's parents they were able to get by for the next month.

Bill found a job selling records in a music store. Although it didn't pay much, he figured he could find something better after the summer break when all the other students went back to school.

One evening Bill answered the doorbell, and there stood Pam's mother. "Mrs. Carlisle, come in. What are you doing over here?" he asked.

"Bill, I need to talk with you and Pam about something urgent. Is she here?"

"Yes, she is," he replied. At that moment Pam came around the door from the bedroom saying, "Who's at the door, Bill?" When she saw her mother, she paled to the point of looking ashen.

"Mother, what are you doing here?" she asked in a hollow voice.

"Pam, you know very well what I'm doing here," her mother answered. "It's about these." With that, she thrust a handful of credit card receipts in front of her. "You told me you were going to take care of these, and now I have received notice that the bank is filing suit against me."

"What are those?" Bill asked as Pam made her way back to the living room couch, nearly collapsing.

"They're bills run up on my credit cards," Pam's mother said in an accusing tone. "Didn't Pam tell you I called her about them nearly two months ago?"

Bill looked over at Pam. One glance told him the answer. "No, she didn't," he said. "But if they're our bills, I give you my word we'll pay every one of them, Mrs. Carlisle."

"Well, I hope you will," she replied as she headed for the door again. "I want you both to know how disappointed I am that you started out this way. It's partly my fault, too. Apparently we didn't teach Pam some things she needed to know, especially about handling money. We never had very much ourselves and always lived on what little we had. I guess we just assumed our daughter would know how to do the same." With that she walked over to Pam, who was crying softly, and hugged her.

"I love you, honey, but you need to grow up. When you take on the rights of an adult, you also take on the responsibilities. I can't pay these bills, but I wouldn't even if I could. You need to accept the consequences of your actions. And you need to be totally honest with your husband," she said in a solemn tone.

After Pam's mother left, Bill sat down to talk with her about the bills. "How much do we really owe, Pam?" he asked with as much control as possible.

"I don't know," she replied. "I haven't added up all the bills yet. I'm sorry for not telling you before. I didn't want to bother you during your finals, and then I was afraid to tell you."

"Pam, you don't need to be afraid to tell me anything. But we do need to figure out exactly how much we owe and how we're going to pay."

After two hours of poring over the bills that had come in and estimating those which had not been sent yet, Bill came up with a figure of nearly $5,000 between the gas card and the bank card.

"What are we going to do?" she asked Bill.

"I don't know right now," he answered. "But grad school is out for the fall. And I'm going to need to look for a better job, or we'll be going further in the hole each month."

"I can get a job, too," Pam offered. "I complete my internship in a little more than a week. But school doesn't start again for nearly three months, so I won't know about a teaching job for a month or more."

"Pam, we're both going to have to make some sacrifices to pay these debts," Bill said. "I've really been foolish not to see that we were living over our heads. I guess I didn't want to know. I'm going to Pastor Riggs tomorrow to see if he knows anyone who can help us work out a plan."

The next day Bill stopped by to see his pastor and told him the overview of what had happened. "Unfortunately, Bill, what has happened to you and Pam is not unusual today. Too much credit is put in the hands of young people who have little or no idea how to control their use of it. I'm sure Pam was as shocked as her mother to find out how much she had spent."

"There's no question about that, Reverend Riggs," Bill responded. "But I need to know what we can do about it. We'll pay back everything in time, but right now it looks kind of hopeless."

"It's never hopeless if you're willing to admit your mistakes and correct them," Pastor Riggs commented. "I want you to call one of our elders who heads up our financial counseling program. He'll work out a time to meet with you and Pam."

Bill immediately called Chris Wilson, the elder Pastor Riggs referred him to. "I'll be glad to see you and Pam this evening, Bill. I'll meet you at the church office at seven o'clock, if that's OK with you."

"That will be fine, Mr. Wilson," Bill responded. "And thank you for taking the time."

"Don't mention it. That's my area of ministry to our fellowship. See you tonight at seven."

At 7:00 Bill and Pam were waiting outside the church office. Chris Wilson arrived, and Bill recognized him from a meeting he had attended more than a year ago, where Mr. Wilson had spoken on the need to be good managers of the material things God has provided. *I sure wish I had listened better*, Bill said to himself.

Bill and Pam described the events of the past several months that had brought them to the point where they were. Chris Wilson made several notes as they discussed the particular events.

"As I see it," he said, "you have several symptoms and two basic problems."

"What do you mean, Mr. Wilson?" Pam asked. "What's the difference?"

"The problems created the symptoms," he responded. "For instance, you now owe nearly five thousand dollars in consumer debt. But that's a symptom of a much deeper problem, I believe. If your parents just gave you the money to pay the bills, I believe they would be doing you a disservice, because it's likely that you would repeat the same mistakes again."

"Not me," Pam said emphatically.

"I know that's what you think right now, Pam," he said. "And probably you wouldn't repeat the exact same mistakes. But indulgence comes in many forms, and future mistakes can create much more severe consequences. I've seen people making more than one hundred thousand dollars a year get deeply into debt because their impulses grew even faster than their salaries.

"I think I can help you get out from under the circumstances if you're willing to sacrifice for a while. But unless you recognize the problems and solve them, you'll be back again."

"What do you think the problems are, Mr. Wilson?" Bill asked.

"As I see it, Bill, your problem stems from a lack of self-confidence. But it shows itself in the fact that you haven't accepted your role as the head of your family."

"What do you mean, Mr. Wilson?"

"First you allowed yourself to be led into a quick elopement; and because you didn't want to hurt Pam's feelings, you weren't honest with her. No sound relationship can ever be built on a foundation of fear. Remember what the Bible teaches us—that perfect love casts out all fear."

"But I don't want to dictate to Pam," Bill argued. But even as he said it, he knew somewhere deep inside that what Mr. Wilson had said was right. He did fear losing Pam, and that was his prime motivation the weekend they eloped. He had seen the foolishness of what they were doing even from the beginning, but he didn't have the courage to tell her no.

"I don't mean that you should dictate to your wife, Bill. She is to be your partner. But you must accept that God's plan for the husband is that he be the head of his family and lead them, not follow his wife on a leash. That hasn't happened with you yet, but it will if you allow it. Pam has the stronger personality and will tend to set the pace."

"But, Mr. Wilson, I don't want to lead Bill around," Pam protested. "I want to be a good wife and a helpmate."

"And I believe you do, Pam, or I wouldn't have brought this up so bluntly on our first visit. But you need to realize that you have a more dominant personality and that you must learn to control it."

"Is that the second problem then?" she asked meekly.

"No, the second problem you need to deal with is your indulgent attitude," Mr. Wilson said bluntly.

"What!" Pam said as she came out of her chair. "I don't think I have an indulgent attitude. I've never wasted money before this."

"But Pam, you never had the opportunity before," Mr. Wilson said as she sat back down. "From what you said, I suspect that your dad ran your home and doled out the money he wanted you to have. And he was probably pretty cautious with his money, wasn't he?"

"Well, yes," Pam agreed. "I never thought about having an indulgent attitude."

"Some of the spending was ignorance about credit cards. But when the totals come to five thousand dollars, it usually goes far beyond just simple ignorance," Mr. Wilson said. "Some people have such an indulgent attitude that they cannot pass by anything they don't already have. It's almost an obsession. Often it's not even for themselves. They will even buy gifts for other people using their credit cards."

Pam thought about the watch she had bought Bill. She had bought him another one two weeks after they returned home. Bill had protested, but she'd convinced him to keep it.

Mr. Wilson continued, "We all like to buy things. And we can all indulge, given the opportunity and the resources. But some people are what I would call shop-a-holics. They feel best when they're buying something, even if they know they can't afford it."

Pam realized that much of what the counselor was saying did apply to her. She never had splurged very much, but she hadn't had the opportunity until she had her mother's credit card. Then it became a need that she had to satisfy. She had felt the same way about getting married that weekend. She didn't think she was going to lose Bill, but she wasn't willing to take the chance.

"Does that mean I should never handle the money again?" Pam asked dejectedly.

"Not at all. It just means that you need to realize that Bill is in your life to offset your imbalances, just as you are to offset his. When you recognize what those imbalances are and learn to communicate about them openly, you'll be further along than 90 percent of the couples today. I'll give you some homework to do together to help you better understand God's plan for your marriage and your finances.

"In the meantime we need to deal with the immediate problem—these debts. I notice in your list of assets that you own two cars. Is that right?"

"Yes, sir," Bill said. "Pam's and mine."

"How much do you think they're worth, Bill?"

"I would say mine is worth between fifteen hundred dollars and sixteen hundred dollars at best, and Pam's is worth one thousand dollars," Bill replied.

"And I see that you have a stereo and television. Anything else of any substantial value, like an insurance policy or stocks?"

"No, sir," Bill replied again, "just the normal junk furniture that most college students accumulate over the years."

"Bill, I do have a small insurance policy that Daddy bought for me when I was a little girl," Pam said.

"Do you know if it has any cash value, Pam?" Mr. Wilson asked.

"I think so. I had forgotten that I even had it until you mentioned the insurance. Daddy said it would pay either a lump sum or provide enough for burial, but I don't know how much."

"OK, what we have to work with, then, is the potential sale of one car, a stereo, TV, and some cash in an insurance policy."

"But Mr. Wilson, we need both of our cars if we're both going to work," Pam argued. "Bill works in one direction, and I work in another."

"I know it won't be easy, but it is possible. You both need to be totally realistic about your situation, and since we don't have a lot of leeway in time, I'm going to lay it out for you. I hope this doesn't frighten you off, but you need to face reality.

"First, the bank has already started action against Pam's mother. In less than two weeks there will be a court hearing, and I feel sure the judge will grant the petition to attach her property unless we can work out another arrangement in the meantime.

"Second, even without the debts, you're living beyond your means right now. You can't afford a second car. It takes extra insurance, maintenance, and gas.

"Third, I assume that the stereo and TV were bought with the credit card, so you need to sell them and return the money to the bank. Obviously you won't get back what you paid, but that's the way it is usually.

"Even after you do these things, your budget won't balance while you're paying off the remaining debts unless you both work. That means you have another choice to make. Pam, you will have to find a job as soon as possible, and Bill, you'll have to find another job with a more stable income."

"We already decided to do that," Bill offered. "And I realize that I won't be able to go to grad school in the fall."

"Not necessarily," Mr. Wilson said. "If you could live with one set of parents and go to school closer to home, it might be possible to at least start evening classes."

"I don't know about that," Bill said. "I think both of our parents are peeved at us right now."

"Do you really blame them?" Mr. Wilson said. "So far you have gotten married on an impulse, failed to tell the people who love you the most, charged five thousand dollars on someone else's credit card, and have a bank in your hometown ready to sue your mother."

"I guess when you look at it that way, we do look a little juvenile, don't we?" Pam said.

"To say the least," Mr. Wilson agreed. "Now it's time to start doing things God's way."

"What do you mean?" Bill asked.

"Principle number one is to sell whatever you don't actually need to live on and give the money to your creditors. Proverbs 3:27–28 says, 'Do not withhold good from those to whom it is due, when it is in your power to do it. Do not say to your neighbor, "Go, and come back, and tomorrow I will give it," when you have it with you.'

"Principle number two is to go to your creditors and ask their forgiveness. Then work out a repayment plan with them. As our Lord says in Matthew 5:25, 'Make friends quickly with your opponent at law while you are with him on the way, in order that your opponent may not deliver you to the judge, and the judge to the officer, and you be thrown into prison.'

"And the last principle you need to apply is to think and plan before you act. As the Lord said in Luke 14:28–29, 'For which one of you, when he wants to build a tower, does not first sit down and calculate the cost, to see if he has enough to complete it? Otherwise, when he has laid a foundation, and is not able to finish, all who observe it begin to ridicule him.' From this point on, you both need to vow that you won't make impetuous decisions and that you will pray about every decision and discuss it thoroughly.

"Pam, you have been blessed with an ability to lead and direct. Those qualities will be very beneficial both in your career and in your role as a homemaker. But you must be willing to listen and follow Bill's direction. God promises to guide your decisions, but only if you operate as a team with Bill at the head.

"Now I'd like for you both to contact the bank and the credit manager for the oil company and work out a repayment plan. Tell them you're in the process of selling some assets and will pay them that money up front. Feel free to tell them you're working with me. They can call me for verification. And one more thing. I will do everything I can to help you get out of this situation, but you must agree to develop a budget together and stick to it diligently during this process. If not, I would be better off to spend my time with those who are willing to listen."

"Mr. Wilson, I promise we'll stick to the plan. I want to get out of this mess and get our lives back on track," Bill said.

"And how about you, Pam?" Mr. Wilson asked.

"I want to get out of this mess, naturally," Pam responded. "But I am really afraid that what you said about my being an impulse spender is true. What if I can't control myself and do this again?"

"Pam, spending is not like alcoholism or drug addiction, although it can be if you don't exercise self-control. You need to establish some guidelines for yourself that include relying on Bill to balance your extremes. Once you make a budget, don't violate it. That doesn't mean you can't ever spend any money or that you won't need some free money for your own use. Everybody does. But limit yourself to what you can afford, and don't rely on credit cards to fill in the gaps. Credit makes it too easy to splurge and is too difficult to pay back. If you stick to your repayment plan, you'll be out of debt in a short while, perhaps even in a few months. But if you don't, you may well find yourselves as one of those unfortunate statistics of divorce. Nearly half of all new marriages fail, many of them Christian. And the vast majority claim that financial problems caused their marital problems."

"I can believe that," Bill said. "I don't know what we would have done if it weren't for you, Mr. Wilson. I really was beginning to feel the pressure."

"I haven't done anything but help you realize that there is an answer to your problems. Now it's up to you to work out the details and stick to them. I'll give you some materials that will help you understand the basic principles from God's Word. These must be your guide if you want to make good decisions in the future. You need to learn how to keep a checkbook accurately and keep up with your monthly budget. We'll work that out together over the next few weeks."

Bill and Pam called the vice-president of the bank in charge of credit card accounts and asked for a meeting the next day. They told him exactly what had happened and asked if there were a way they could work out a repayment plan. He agreed to converting the credit card debt into a personal loan collateralized by both of their cars. The next month Bill's car was sold, and they were able to pay the $1,800 they received toward the loan amount.

Pam sold the stereo and television and got another $1,200 to pay on the loan. Within a few weeks they had the loan amount down to less than $2,000. They worked out a repayment plan with the oil company with the help of Mr. Wilson, so they could pay the minimum amount until the bank loan was repaid. The cash from the insurance policy reduced the loan by another $500.

Bill took a job with a national delivery service that paid nearly twice what he had been making. Pam took a job in telephone sales and found that she really enjoyed the work. Between the two of them, they were able to pay off the bank loan in five months, although it meant a lot of scrimping and early mornings as Bill would drop Pam off at her job and then drive across town to his. But in three months Bill's employer allowed him to drive the company delivery van home in the evenings. That not only provided them a second vehicle, nearly cost-free, but also lowered their gas bill considerably.

Once the bank loan was totally paid off, Bill approached the loan officer about borrowing enough to eliminate the other credit card debt, which carried a 21 percent interest rate. The banker agreed, based on their recent track record, and they substituted a 12 percent loan for the higher one.

In the fall, Pam accepted a teaching position with a private school, and they began to settle into a reasonably normal routine. Over the course of three months they counseled with Mr. Wilson once a week. During that time they learned how to balance and maintain their checking account and how to develop a realistic budget. In the fourth month Mr. Wilson called Bill to ask if he and Pam would be willing to meet and counsel another young couple the pastor had sent to him. Bill asked Pam, who wholeheartedly agreed, and they began their first one-on-one counseling to help another couple.

Bill ultimately finished his Master's work and went on to get a Ph.D. in music. He now heads a department at the university where he and Pam attended school. They lived with Pam's mother for about a year and a half, during which time they helped her to get started on a budget. During that time she also trained for her new career in nursing, which she could afford to do only because of their financial assistance for nearly four years. Bill and Pam's financial recovery was possible only because they faced their problems honestly and worked through them together.

16

Three Major Expenses That Lead to Debt

AS OUR LOOK at four couples has demonstrated, a common thread in most of their experiences was the lack of thorough planning. Sometimes this flaw is amplified by ignorance or indulgence, but without some kind of financial plan (budget), most couples won't realize they have a problem until it overwhelms them.

Many couples think they live on a budget because they write down their checks and even balance their checking accounts. That is not a budget. A budget balances income and expenses and reports on the status of those each month. I'm not going to discuss the subject of budgeting here, because I have done so in several previous books, including a thorough plan outlined in *The Financial Planning Workbook* (Chicago: Moody, 1982). Instead, I am going to discuss some of the more common ways couples get into debt.

The Purchase of a Home

Nearly every young couple in America dreams of owning their own home. I use the term "owning" loosely here because what that means to most couples is to be paying a mortgage. So the common definition of owning is "as opposed to renting." Many couples try to buy a home too soon or pay too much and end up in financial trouble. Unfortunately, quite often they don't realize that owning the home created their financial troubles because it took too large a portion of their spendable income. Just as with Paul and Julie, the first couple discussed in this book, they find themselves sinking further behind every month.

The percentage of an average family's budget that should be spent on a house payment is no more than 25 percent of net spendable income (after tithes and taxes). Add to the mortgage payments the cost of utilities, insurance, maintenance, and incidentals, and the percentage climbs to around 35 or 36 percent. Unfortunately many couples commit more than 60 percent of their budget to housing. There is virtually no way to handle that kind of cost. If they plan out their spending as a whole for the year, the strain would be apparent. But because they usually look only at one month, they don't see it. The monthly budget couples typically work out informally lacks allocations for clothes, car repairs, and medical expenses. So it is unrealistic.

If you can afford to purchase a home within your budget, that makes sense. But if you wreck your budget just to get into a home, that makes no sense at all. The compulsion Americans have for buying large, expensive homes is just a reflection of poor stewardship in general. Most couples would be far better off saving for a down payment of at least 20 percent and buying a smaller, less expensive home initially. Certainly the purchase of a home for a young couple should never be determined on the basis of their combined incomes, for if one income fails (for example, if the wife becomes pregnant and she has to stay home with the child), the entire purchase will be in jeopardy. That violates the principle of good planning, according to Proverbs 22:3: "The prudent sees the evil and hides himself, but the naive go on, and are punished for it."

Too often Christians limit their faith in God only to the unseen things such as salvation and good health. But I happen to believe that God manifests Himself in material ways to those who trust Him. Let me make it very clear that I am not talking about a health and prosperity gospel. As Job said earlier, and the apostle Paul reiterated in Romans 11:34-35, "For who has known the mind of the Lord, or who became His counselor? Or who has first given to Him that it might be paid back to Him again?" I believe the decision to help individuals with their finances is the Lord's. But I do believe God wants to support strongly those who love and trust Him, just as a parent does a loving and obedient child. After all, that is what the Lord told us in Matthew 7:11: "If you then, being evil, know how to give good gifts to your children, how much more shall your Father who is in heaven give what is good to those who ask Him!"

I recall a practical example of this principle in a couple I counseled. Andy and Bea did what most young couples do within the first five years of their marriage: they bought a home based on two incomes, and even then it stretched their budget. Bea got pregnant and was unable to work regularly, so they fell steadily behind on their bills. Within a few months she was juggling payments based on which creditor was threatening legal action. The stress on Bea threatened her pregnancy and made her even more miserable. The doctor feared she might lose the baby and ordered her to bed for complete rest. But the problems didn't ease—they intensified because of the greater financial drain.

Andy found himself resentful of the fact that Bea couldn't work, and often they would end the evening sleeping in separate rooms in their "dream house." Andy also found himself using his credit cards to buy gas and other basic necessities because he was so low on cash. As a result of a seminar they attended at their church, they recognized a need for help, and they called for an appointment.

The home they had bought consumed nearly 70 percent of Andy's take-home pay. It was obvious that it was totally beyond their financial ability. When I pointed this out, Bea became very defensive. She was not willing to discuss the prospect of selling the home, and Andy was extremely uncomfortable even talking about it. Bea had grown up as a pastor's kid, and when her father was killed in an automobile accident, her mother was put out of the manse within a month. They were left homeless and nearly destitute for several years. That experience had left such a mark on Bea that she almost had a paranoia about selling her home.

The couple left that day with the details of how to establish a budget that would allocate something for every category of spending. In addition, they were asked to determine how much they could free up to begin repaying some of the existing debt.

When they returned in two weeks the answer was clear. When the house payment had been made, there was nothing left over to pay bills. In fact, the true monthly deficit was close to $300. They had tried to discuss the issue of the home as I had suggested, but it always ended with Bea crying, so Andy avoided the subject entirely. They were both committed Christians and wanted to do what was right but were stymied by something as material as a house.

I asked Bea if she really believed she could trust God. She said she did, but it was clear she had great difficulty with the idea of giving up her home. She was intelligent and realized that the home was beyond their means at that time—but as with any other paranoia, if it made sense it wouldn't have been a paranoia. I was convinced that neither I nor anyone else was going to talk her into voluntarily selling her home. She dug in her heels like an agoraphobic being dragged onto an elevator. Although selling their home might be the best thing for her, she couldn't see it that way at all.

The one thing Bea did agree with was the fact that the house was too expensive for their budget and that month by month the situation would get worse if they didn't do something. At that point the decision had to be Bea's. Either she would trust God in the matter of her home or she wouldn't.

A few weeks later she called back tearfully to report that their financial situation had deteriorated. Andy had made a commitment not to use the credit cards and actually had cut them up. Shortly after he did so the car broke down. Having no money for repairs, he decided to park the car and hitch rides to and from work. Their Sunday school class heard about this from a friend and took up a donation to get the car repaired. In fact, they even raised a small surplus of funds, and the class asked Andy to use it to take Bea out for an evening.

That made a great impact on Bea. Until that time she had been thinking that God only worked through supernatural miracles. She had prayed for everything from a total restoration of their car to asking God for someone to give them a new one. But she never even considered the simple alternative that those with a surplus might give a little to help get their old one running again. She also realized that even though she hated to see Andy struggling to find rides to and from work, she still had regarded the house discussion as off limits. The house had become her idol.

When they came in for the next session, Bea had already put the house up for sale and had a tentative offer from someone in their church. I don't think she was jubilant about the decision, but she was resolved. She was determined that nothing would make her take her eyes off the Lord again. I don't think I could have talked her out of selling the home if I had tried, which I didn't.

Several weeks later their home sold, and the equity from the sale cleared all the bills. They moved into a duplex, which they shared with an elderly couple. They became good friends with the couple and over the next few months were able to lead them to the Lord. Bea decided that was obviously why the Lord had moved them out of their home—to meet that greater need. But she was able to learn a lesson that most Christians miss because they never really surrender the material areas of their lives to the Lord.

Almost one year after they had sold their home, a member of their church called them. He was moving to Europe for several years and wanted to keep the home he lived in, since it had been in his family for several generations; but he didn't want to leave it vacant. The company he worked for was willing to pay all of his costs, so he didn't have a financial need to rent it. In fact, he was willing to pay the costs of a house-sitter.

He asked Andy and Bea if they would be willing to live in his house for five years—all expenses paid and a salary of $200 a month. They jumped at the chance and solved their housing problems in a single stroke.

They could have stayed in their home until they were evicted or until Bea went back to work after the baby was born. Then they probably could have limped along until the next crisis hit. Instead they chose to trust God and discover what was His plan for their lives. I truly believe that one of our greatest assets today is that God doesn't have to have a lot of talent to work with. He'll work with anyone who's available and willing to trust Him.

Car Purchases

The second most common source of debt is the purchase of a new car. Quite often a couple who can't qualify to buy a home springs for a new car as a compromise. Unfortunately, it's not a good compromise because cars now sell for prices that houses sold for twenty years ago. This is the major debt trap for most singles who overspend.

Most young people are so prone to debt-buying today that they don't even ask the price of a car—just how much the monthly payments are. I believe the automotive industry understands this mentality very well. When they want to stimulate sales for a product that has been inflated out of proportion to most other consumer products, they advertise low interest rates as the biggest selling feature. Usually that is the deciding factor for a generation that has been raised on new cars and nice houses. To the young couple already in debt because of a home that is too expensive, a new car appears to be an answer to their used car problems. So they trade in the old car that costs $75 a month to keep running for a new car with $150 monthly payments. But it's not good economics, as they will discover in about two months (the first month is usually free).

This debt problem is actually harder to deal with than over-spending on a home. In most areas, homes can be re-sold at or above their original purchase price because the market for used housing is still stronger than for new housing.

But a family seeking to sell an almost new car to relieve debt is usually shocked to discover how little it's worth on the open market. If it is sold at auction, which is often the case when a car is repossessed, the sale price may be half of what an identical car sells for on a lot. Typically, when a car is repossessed for failure to make the payments, the car is sold at a loss, and the lien holder sues the borrower for the difference.

The same is true of a leased car. The lease contract to pay is just as binding as a purchase agreement. If the leasing company has to repossess a leased car, it rarely will attempt to re-lease it. The typical lessee wants a brand new car, not a used one. The leased car is auctioned off, and the lessee is sued for the deficiency.

I have sometimes been accused of being negative about new cars, and to some extent that is true. Over the years I have seen the bondage that buying new cars has placed on many couples. However, if someone has his finances under control and can save for the cost of a new car, it is his decision whether or not to buy one. One person may think a new car is a bad buy, while another may think it represents better value. But the one thing neither of them can disagree about is that when you borrow money to buy a new car, you are going to become surety for the loan.

For most of my adult life I never bought a new car, for two reasons: one, I didn't have the funds to pay for one, and two, I couldn't see the need for one with so many good used cars available. In 1979 I was driving a ten-year-old station wagon with well over 100,000 miles on it, and I knew that I would have to buy another car within a short time. Then one of my sons attempted to back my car up our very steep driveway during a minor ice storm. Backing up our driveway in good weather was a real trick, but it was impossible in bad weather. Like most teenagers, he was not to be stymied by a "small" obstacle such as an ice storm, so he kept trying until he burned out the reverse gear.

The next time I got into my car I discovered it whirred but wouldn't move in reverse. So we got several of the neighborhood kids out and pushed the car around in the driveway so that I could pull up the hill. For several weeks

I drove it anyway, while we all prayed about what kind of a car I should buy. It didn't seem logical to spend the money to repair the old wagon when it had so many miles on it.

We didn't really have enough money to buy a new car, but with my teaching schedule and frequent trips to the airport, I knew that we needed a very dependable car. During the next few weeks I discovered how many times you pull into a parking space that you have to back out of.

While we were praying about what to do, someone actually gave a car to the ministry. But it had a lot of miles on it too, so I figured I might as well keep the one I had and give that car to a really needy family. One of my children suggested that I give away the car with no reverse, which I vetoed.

I drove my "no-reverse" car for several more months because the Lord directed us to use the money we had saved for another purpose. Then, in December someone I had counseled several years earlier dropped by to ask if we had any particular need for a car.

"Why do you ask?" I said.

"Because I am convinced that the Lord wants me to give you one," he replied as he handed me the keys to a brand-new Oldsmobile, which I drove for the next six years.

Scheduled Disasters

Do you know how to schedule a financial disaster? It is simple. Fail to plan for predictable expenses that haven't come due yet. A common example of this is failing to plan for predictable automobile maintenance. I don't know about your cars, but mine have a regular cycle of problems. About every twenty-five to thirty thousand miles they need tires, brakes, belts, spark plugs, and so on. Once I recognize that, the smart thing to do is to anticipate those expenses and budget for them.

Failure to plan this way is a major reason many people end up in debt. When the expenses occur, they must be paid, so the only alternative available is often a credit card.

Why do reasonably intelligent people fail to anticipate known expenses? Because when they try to work them into their spending plan (a budget), they don't fit. So they simply ignore those expenses until a crisis arrives. To do otherwise would require adjustments in the other areas of spending, such as housing, cars, and vacations. This is the head-in-the-sand syndrome.

It is common to see this problem when one counsels engaged couples about their first year's budget. When I ask if they have developed a budget, usually they respond, "Yes, we have, and everything worked out fine."

But when I review their budget with them, it reveals that they have made no provision for clothes, visits to the doctor, car repairs, or vacations. I *might* be convinced that they have a car that doesn't break down, and bodies that don't get sick, or even teeth that don't get cavities, but I absolutely refuse to believe they won't go to Disney World the first year they're married. And since they aren't nudists, I assume they will need to replace their clothes eventually.

I recall a couple who thought they had figured out a way to beat the system. They had financial problems that resulted from all of the above symptoms. In other words, they had a home that was too expensive, two new cars, school loans, and a variety of consumer debt items from department stores. There was absolutely no way their income could ever stretch far enough to manage their expenses, so they charged nearly everything each month except their utilities (the utility company wouldn't accept credit cards). They had been able to do that for nearly three years without being delinquent on a single bill.

Their method was to charge on one card until the limit was reached and then pay that card off with two or three others. Being a good credit customer, they had no trouble getting their credit limit raised on the first card so they could charge more, and on they went for the better part of three years. Ultimately, the whole house of credit came tumbling down because it became too large to manage. When their credit binge ended, they owed nearly $23,000 in credit card debts. They were advised to go bankrupt and were considering doing so until they received notice that two of the credit card issuers were considering filing fraud charges against them. The potential consequences of that forced them to face reality and make a commitment to repay the loans. As far as I know, they are still paying $500 in monthly payments—eight years later.

Part Three

OVERVIEW OF CREDIT, DEBT, AND BORROWING

17

Understanding Credit

SINCE WE'RE DISCUSSING the subject of debt in this book, we also need to discuss credit. Credit and debt are not synonymous terms, although they are used interchangeably in our society. Credit can best be defined as the establishment of a mutual trust relationship between a lender and a borrower, which can be the loan of something other than money. For instance, if I lend my lawn mower to a neighbor in exchange for the use of his garden tiller, we have a credit relationship. I have extended credit (the use of my lawn mower), and he is indebted to me until I use his tiller. This is called a barter exchange and is commonly done in business.

Debt, as defined previously, is a condition that exists when a loan commitment is not met, or inadequate collateral is pledged to unconditionally satisfy a loan agreement. Borrowing is not the only way to get into debt. A court decree in a lawsuit, for instance, can result in debt. But for the purpose of this book, we'll limit our discussion to credit related debt.

There are two important issues in the topic of credit: how to get it and how to lose it.

How to Establish Credit

Many young people get into trouble with credit because they are desperate to establish credit and because it is easy for them to qualify for more credit than they can manage.

The very best way to establish credit initially is to borrow against an acceptable asset. For example, if you have saved $1,000 and want to borrow the same amount, almost any bank will lend you $1,000 using the savings as collateral. Usually the lender will charge from 1 to 2 percent more for the loan than the prevailing savings rate. So in essence, it costs about 2 percent interest to establish a good credit history. For a one-year loan of $1,000, the net cost would be approximately $20.

Then, by using the bank as a credit reference, almost anyone can qualify for a major credit card, although the credit limit would normally be the minimum amount. I don't mean to imply that everyone should get a credit card, or that everyone will be able to manage one properly. But credit is relatively simple to establish if you have already acquired the discipline of saving.

It has been my experience that if someone who has never had credit wishes to acquire a credit card and tries enough places, somebody will issue him one. The difficulty with this method is that once the first company issues a card and the person uses it wisely, other companies will soon follow suit, and he will be swamped with credit card applications. The temptation of too much credit is often overwhelming for a young person (or couple), and he can quickly find himself over his head in debt.

I would offer the following advice to anyone using credit cards for the first time or who has ever got into trouble through the misuse of credit cards. It is good advice, and it will save you many problems.

1. *Never use a credit card to buy anything that is not in your budget for the month (which means, in turn, that you will need a budget).* It is tempting to use a credit card when you are on vacation and run out of your allocated vacation funds, or when you need clothes but don't have the money to take advantage of the great sale in progress, or when you need tires for the car but don't have the money saved, or when you're out of work and need food, utilities, and rent. But when you use a credit card as a buffer in place of trusting God, you may fall into a trap that will take you a long time to dig yourself out of.

2. *Pay the entire credit card bill each month.* I have heard many people say they never misused their credit cards because they paid them completely each month. I have since discovered that using credit cards—or any credit— wisely is not just a matter of being able to pay them off on time. Credit cards are the number one tool for impulse buying in our society. And impulse buying is generally the prerequisite for indulgent buying. Simply put, consumers will buy things they don't need and pay more for them, using credit.

I often use a credit card when traveling, and I always pay it off each month. At one time I assumed that because I never paid any interest on credit card purchases, I was using my card wisely. I decided to challenge my own use of credit, so I stopped using the credit card for a month.

Almost immediately I began to notice that I was less prone to accept a motel's summary of the bill when I paid in cash. The most frequent overcharge was for calls that I had placed but never completed. Also I found that I had gotten lax about verifying restaurant bills because I had been using credit cards. I discovered once again that credit is less personal than cash in your pocket, and people tend to use it more carelessly.

If you don't pay the credit card charges every month, you will pay a usurious rate of interest. Scripture defines usury as any interest rate in excess of 12 percent (the hundredth part). Certainly the interest on credit cards is far in excess of that, and paying that interest represents poor stewardship. In addition, by accumulating credit card charges you run the risk of *debt*.

3. *The first month you find yourself unable to pay the total charges, destroy the cards.* The problem is not the use of credit. It is the misuse of credit.

Credit to Avoid

There are some sources of credit that are simply bad deals, even by today's standards. In the constant drive to create more ways for couples to borrow money, many lenders have stepped over the borderline of common sense, in my opinion. But it is the responsibility of the borrower to avoid the use of credit that encourages poor stewardship. Following are a few examples of credit sources to avoid.

Bank Overdrafts

Most banks today offer what is called overdraft protection. Thus when a customer writes a check in excess of what he or she has in the bank, the check will be honored (paid by the bank).

Sounds like a good deal, doesn't it? After all, if you write a check beyond your balance, you don't want it to "bounce," do you? There would be penalties for the returned check and charges from the merchant as well. So why not take the overdraft protection?

I have counseled many couples who did take the overdraft protection and got deeply in debt as a result of it. The people who regularly overdraft are those who don't know their checkbook balances. Obviously there are those who are dishonest and purposely overdraft, but they are a minority and usually can't get overdraft protection anyway.

The overdraft protection is an enticement for couples to avoid balancing their checking accounts. Several people I have counseled were startled to find out that overdraft protection wasn't a benevolent act on the part of the bank. The overdrafts (and penalties) were charged to their credit account at 18 to 21 percent interest. Often those accounts accumulate interest from the date of transfer, not after the normal thirty days common to credit card accounts.

Finance Company Loans

I don't want to impugn the integrity of all finance companies, because there are many honest and ethical companies in business. But in general, local finance companies, especially those not regulated by federal laws, use high pressure tactics in their operation and charge very high interest. For instance, in many states finance companies that limit their loans to $600 or less can charge interest rates that go as high as 40 percent per year!

Finance companies specialize in lending to those who can't qualify for loans through normal channels such as banks, credit unions, or savings and loans. They also specialize in high pressure tactics to collect their money if necessary. If you are being pursued by one of these companies, you need to read the section on the Fair Debt Collection Act in Appendix C.

Home Equity Loans

Some people might wonder why I place home equity loans in this section about credit to avoid. After all, home equity loans are one of the few loans still available where the interest can be deducted from one's income taxes.

In general these loans have several features that make them hazardous to an individual's long-term financial health. First, they encourage someone to borrow against the equity in his home when in truth he should be working to pay the remaining mortgage off. Second, the interest rates are usually floating, meaning that they can be adjusted as the prevailing interest rates change. That puts the borrower in a position in which it is nearly impossible to control future costs. Third, most of these loans (to date) are demand notes, meaning they can be called for total payment at any time. This places the debtor in the position of constant jeopardy with the lender. During a bad economy the lender is likely to call the note to renegotiate the terms or sell the collateral (your home).

The IRS

If there is one source of credit you should diligently avoid, it is the IRS— or to put it another way, don't live on money that you owe to the IRS. I have counseled many couples who attempted to do this, especially couples who were self-employed. They found that the IRS will attach every asset to collect their money and will force a sale at drastically reduced prices if necessary.

The Consumer Credit Protection Act of 1968

Remember that if you have borrowed money from someone, he does have a right to collect what is due. But he doesn't have a right (legally) to harass you in the process. In the past, a creditor could do virtually anything he wanted—short of physical violence—in order to collect a debt, including late night calls, calls at work, and threats of legal action. But since Congress passed the Consumer Credit Protection Act of 1968, consumers have been given legal protection from such actions. A more detailed description of the act is provided in Appendix D, but I would like to summarize the pertinent points every borrower needs to understand.

Who is controlled by this act? All persons who regularly collect debts, such as attorneys, professional collection agencies, and office personnel. The key term here is "regularly." If someone only collects debts on an irregular basis, he is not covered. For example, you may owe a debt to your dentist, so he will call you to collect his money. But he doesn't perform that function on a routine basis, so he is not covered by the Consumer Credit Act.

When can a collector contact you? At any time during a normal daily routine, for instance between 8:00 A.M. and 6:00 P.M. A creditor may not contact a debtor at inconvenient or unusual times, such as late evening or early morning hours.

Can a collector call your place of work? Not if you have notified him that your employer disapproves of that practice.

Can a collector call other people about your debt? A collector may call other people in order to find your current address, but he may not contact them more than once if you have an attorney. Notify him that he can contact only your attorney. Under no circumstances may a collector discuss your debt with another person other than your designated attorney or agent.

How can you stop a collector from harassing you? By writing a letter to the collector and stating that he may not contact you again, except in regard to specific legal action taken in your case. (Obviously this should be done only in extreme cases. If a creditor has no means of communication other than legal action, he will probably take immediate legal action.)

What if you don't believe you owe the money? If you believe that you don't owe the money, you need to write the collector within thirty days after you are contacted for collection, stating that you don't owe the money. If you do that, the debt collector may not contact you again without sending written proof of the debt.

A debt collector is prohibited from:

1. Giving false information to frighten you.
2. Using an alias. He must give the company name and his name if you request it.
3. Using official-looking paper or forms that give the impression of being from a government agency.
4. Using profane or abusive language or threatening any bodily harm.
5. Advertising your debt, publishing a list of people who refuse to pay him, or otherwise embarrassing you.
6. Implying or stating that legal action is being taken when it is not.
7. Giving false information to a credit reporting agency to pressure you into paying a disputed bill.
8. Depositing a postdated check before the date on the check.

What are the penalties for a collector who violates the law? If you sue the collection agency and win, the penalties are court and attorney's fees, plus damages of up to $500,000, or 1 percent of the agency's net worth, whichever is lower.

Where should you report a violation? The State Attorney General's office or the office of the Federal Trade Commission (FTC) in Washington, D.C. (The FTC will provide information about how to pursue investigation of a violation.)

What can you do about disputed debts? Fortunately, most companies are honest merchants who are not seeking to collect more than what is legitimately owed them. From time to time a dispute will arise between a debtor and creditor over a bill. Usually that can be worked out by contacting the creditor directly and stating the discrepancy. It has been my experience that in most cases the company will adjust the bill immediately, if you have good records showing your objection to be valid. However, in cases where no settlement can be reached and you believe you have a valid argument against paying the bill, the small claims court in your district provides a means of settling the dispute amiably and inexpensively.

The cost of filing a case in small claims court in most states is about $50. Usually the amount of the disputed bill will govern whether the small claims court will hear the case. Generally most small claims are limited to $1,000 or less. You can choose to have an attorney represent you, although many disputes in small claims court are handled informally without attorneys.

Door-to-Door Sales

The Consumer Credit Protection Act provides that any merchandise sold door-to-door may be returned within seventy-two hours for a full refund. That holds true for door-to-door sales of encyclopedias, cosmetics, magazines, and so forth. You need to have proof that the merchandise was returned properly and in the same condition as delivered. Generally that means a post office receipt and a copy of the letter stating that you desire to return the merchandise. The purchaser is responsible for the return postage.

Unsolicited Merchandise

Items that are delivered to your home or business in your name but which you did not order may be kept without payment. The merchant must show proof of purchase in order to collect. Otherwise the unsolicited merchandise is yours to keep without cost.

Defective Merchandise

If you have made an honest attempt to get the merchant to repair or replace a defective item, you may legitimately stop payment on a check issued to pay for the item or stop further payments until the dispute is resolved (usually in small claims court). This does not apply to out-of-state purchases or most credit card purchases (other than with the merchant's card).

Lost or Stolen Credit Cards

You should notify the credit card company immediately when you realize that your card is missing. You are not responsible for any unauthorized charges on your card once notification is given. In any case you are never responsible for more than $50 worth of unauthorized charges on a lost or stolen credit card.

Unsolicited Credit Cards

It is illegal for card issuers to send you a credit card unless you request it. However, they may send a replacement card for one that is about to expire, and you are bound by the same rules as you were for the original card.

Electronic Funds Transfer Errors

In this modern electronic age we are faced with a new set of potential problems. One of the most common is outside teller and fund transfer errors. What are your rights when your account is billed for fund transfers that you didn't make?

A copy of the receipt or withdrawal slip printed by the bank's machine is proof of your claim. For transactions without such proof the bank has forty-five working days to complete an investigation and show proof of the transaction. However, if the institution hasn't completed its investigation within ten working days your account must be credited the disputed amount pending the outcome of their investigation. At the conclusion of the investigation the bank must show proof of its case. If you disagree, the discrepancy is resolved in the small claims court.

Loss or Stolen EFT Card

If you lose your electronic funds transfer (EFT) card, commonly called an outside teller card, and notify the bank within two days, your liability is limited to $50 in unauthorized transfers. If, however, you fail to notify them within two working days, your liability is $500, up to sixty days. Beyond sixty days your liability is virtually unlimited. Therefore it is vital that you balance all bank statements in a timely fashion each month and notify the bank (in writing) of any discrepancies.

Electronic funds theft is not an unusual event in our generation. I have counseled several couples who had bank errors in fund transfers. I also know several who had their cards stolen and money illegally transferred from their accounts.

The most common method of this type of theft today occurs when someone leaves his card in the outside teller and another person finds it. In many big cities there are thieves who hang around outside tellers waiting to snatch a neglected EFT card. They also use sophisticated surveillance equipment to spot the "secret code" often necessary to complete a fund transfer.

For more detailed information regarding your rights in Electronic Funds Transfers you can write the Federal Reserve System in Washington, D.C. 20551 and request information on the Electronic Funds Transfer Act.

How to Determine the "Real" Interest Rate

In conclusion to this discussion on credit, it is vital that you understand how to determine the true interest rate someone is quoting to you. Prior to 1980 that was almost impossible for most consumers. Lenders would advertise a low interest rate, but often it was based on a method of calculation that actually yielded a higher return than indicated.

The Truth in Lending Act now requires that all interest be stated in Annualized Percentage Rate (APR). That establishes one standard for all interest charged, regardless of how it is calculated. Let me present an example. If you borrowed $100 for one year and at the end of twelve months repaid $110, you had an APR of 10 percent. But suppose you borrowed $100 and made monthly payments of $9.17. At the end of one year you will have repaid $110, but the Annualized Percentage Rate would have been higher. Why? Because you didn't actually have use of the entire $100 for the whole year. The APR rate was closer to 12 percent.

Additionally, the Truth in Lending Act requires that all finance charges be clearly shown before you sign an installment contract. Many times service fees, discount points, and insurance fees can substantially increase the cost of a loan.

A lender who fails to reveal all the costs risks penalties and forfeiture of all accumulated interest. If you believe you have been the victim of unfair lending, you need to contact the Attorney General's office of your state. A more complete discussion of the Truth in Lending Act can be found in Appendix D.

In the final analysis, the best protection you can have against the misuse of credit is to determine that you will control the use of credit and refuse to allow it to control you. As stated earlier, there is no substitute for personal discipline and self-control in the area of credit.

By now I trust that you understand that the misuse of credit—not credit itself—is the problem. The Bible does not teach that you can never borrow. It teaches that borrowing is hazardous if done unwisely. Every Christian should have a goal to be debt-free eventually. If you can't be debt-free right now, set a goal and work toward it.

18

Bill Consolidation Loans

WHEN ALLEN AND Gladis came into my office, they were obviously "stressed out." They were nervous about being there and embarrassed to tell me their story. Allen was an attorney with a local firm specializing in real estate syndications. Just four years out of law school, Allen appeared to be the epitome of success. He was rising fast in the law firm because of his quick mind and hard work. He and Gladis had just bought a home in *the* section of their city and were expecting their first child. Their situation looked good, when viewed from the outside.

Inside, however, it was a different matter. Allen had graduated from law school owing nearly $16,000 in school loans. The interest rate on the loans was far better than average, but the monthly payments were still $125 for ten years. Gladis had school loans also, but she owed only $7,000, with payments of $80 a month. The loan payments restricted their spending but were within Allen's income capacity.

Within the last two years Allen's salary and bonus had increased from $25,000 a year to nearly $34,000, and the future prospects looked even better. They felt they could afford a better home and had decided to take the plunge and buy in the area where other, older members of the firm lived. The new home cost $140,000 and carried payments of $1,150 a month after a down payment of $20,000. They lacked the funds for the total down payment, but Allen arranged an $18,000 advance on his bonus to close on the house. When they moved, Gladis purchased custom curtains, drapes, and wall decorations with Allen's encouragement. He said (and believed) that what they were doing was in the best interest of his career. Before they were finished decorating and paying for moving costs, their bills totaled nearly $11,000.

By that time Gladis was beginning to feel a little nervous about their spending, particularly since they didn't have the money to pay for all their expenses. Allen told her not to worry because the sale of their first home would net enough to pay back the advance and the improvements to the new home. Indeed, they did have a contract on their first home that would net them nearly

$29,000. Unfortunately, the contract had an "if" clause in it, which meant that the buyer was obligated only if he sold his home, too. So Allen and Gladis bought a new home along with all the trappings based on the contingent sale of their old home, which was dependent upon the sale of the buyer's home (a lot of if's!). It's obvious that no one had ever explained to them the principle taught in Proverbs 27:1: "Do not boast about tomorrow, for you do not know what a day may bring forth."

As you have probably guessed, the sale of the buyer's home fell through, so he backed out of the sale on Allen and Gladis's home. They were already in a new home with payments of more than $1,100 a month, with $11,000 in new bills—and they were continuing payments on their old home of $700 a month as well. To say the least, Gladis was uneasy about their situation. Each month they fell further behind, and still their house didn't sell. She begged Allen to drop the price, but he refused, stating that it was worth what they were asking.

Finally, after six months, they had an offer on the house, though it was for $5,000 less than the original contract. By that time Allen was ready to sell, as he faced a higher mountain of unpaid bills each month. They netted $18,000 after paying the delinquent bills. Virtually all of the remaining proceeds from the house went to repay the firm. In the meantime they had accumulated another $3,500 in debts from miscellaneous sources.

Allen finally realized that their monthly obligations were beyond his income. So he approached the bank that held his new mortgage and asked about consolidating all of their outstanding bills into one loan. By that point, he needed about $20,000 to consolidate everything. The banker was a client of Allen's firm and thought that he would be a good risk, but Allen lacked adequate collateral for a loan that size. After a great deal of negotiating, they found a way to make the loan by taking out a second mortgage on their home and assigning that year's bonus as additional collateral.

Since the monthly payments on a $20,000 loan for three years would have been beyond Allen's income range, the banker set the payments based on a ten-year payoff, but with a balloon note to be paid in seven years (the maximum time the bank would grant for a second mortgage). It was further agreed that at least $5,000 of each year's bonuses would be paid to the bank to reduce the note.

The first year everything went fine, or so it seemed. Allen earned a bonus of $15,000, bringing his earned income to nearly $40,000. He paid $5,000 on the note, put $5,000 in savings, and paid nearly $4,000 in taxes on the bonus. With the rest he and Gladis took a vacation to a ski resort that winter.

Allen kept the books at home so Gladis didn't really have a clear idea of how they were doing month by month. But she began to see late notices coming from the bank and several credit card companies. Finally she asked

Allen to sit down and tell her exactly where they were financially. He confessed that he didn't really know. "It just seems like there is never enough money to pay everything we owe," he said. He agreed with Gladis that they needed to do something about their budget. But then he got busy on a new project, and they never got around to it.

As the late notices became more frequent, Gladis began to complain to Allen that he had to get some help in handling their situation. He agreed but never took the time to search out the help he needed. Finally, one afternoon the whole situation came to a head when the banker called Allen at his office. "Allen, I need to see you right away. Can you come by my office this afternoon?" he asked.

"I'm really busy right now, Mr. Barnes," Allen replied as he looked over the contracts on his desk. He had been getting less and less productive as the pressures at home built. It seemed that Gladis was always mad about one thing or another anymore.

"Allen, I must see you right away," Gary Barnes insisted. "The loan committee has been reviewing your note with the bank and is recommending that we begin foreclosure on your home."

Allen felt a cold wave of fear come over him. "They can't do that, Mr. Barnes," Allen pleaded. "It would ruin me with the firm. We have very strict rules about maintaining a good image in the community."

"Come on over and let's discuss it, Allen. Maybe there is a way we can find a resolution."

Allen put down the phone, his hand shaking. He knew he had financial problems, but until that moment he hadn't realized how bad they were. He was three months behind on his first mortgage and four months behind on the second. He had been promising the bank that he would catch up on the payments when his mid-year bonus came. But that bonus had been just $4,000, and it had been used to cover draws from the firm for living expenses. Allen's manager had called him in to review his work for the past six months because his productivity had dropped off severely. He knew that the bank's repossessing his home might cost him his job, and he was only a year away from being made a full partner in the firm. His salary and bonuses would increase substantially then. He felt cold fear rising inside as he realized that not only might he not get a partnership, he might even be released from the firm.

Allen put down his work and checked out of the office, telling the receptionist he would be back in a hour or so. He entered the bank and asked if he could see Mr. Barnes, who was the vice-president of the loan department. In a short while he was directed to the banker's office.

"Allen, sit down, won't you?" Mr. Barnes said politely. He walked over and closed the door to his office. "You have some severe financial problems, don't you?" he asked.

"Well, we do have some temporary problems, Mr. Barnes," he replied. "But I'll be able to clear them up when the next bonus comes."

"Allen, you need to face reality," Mr. Barnes said as he opened the file on his desk. "I took the liberty of checking into your recent credit history. You're behind on everything, even your utility payments."

"It seems that there's not enough money to make it every month," Allen explained. "But I'll be a partner in the firm in a few months, and my income will increase substantially then. Can't you extend the second mortgage? I would only need a few thousand dollars more to make it until then."

"No, I absolutely will not. It's not more money you need, and another consolidation loan won't help. You're simply digging yourself a bigger pit. You're living beyond your means and using loans to make up the difference. And you'll just continue to do so, no matter how much you make. I did you a disservice by giving you the first consolidation loan on your house. You're worse off now than you were then."

Allen slumped down in his chair. He wanted to argue with the banker, but he knew that he was telling the truth. They were worse off now, and there seemed to be no end to the flood of money going out.

"What can I do?" Allen asked in a subdued tone. "If you foreclose on my home, I may lose my job."

"Allen, I found that one of the credit card issuers is planning legal action to collect their money. You may well be facing a judgment and garnishment if they do."

Allen almost fainted when he heard that news. *That will definitely cost me my job,* he thought. "Can you help me, Mr. Barnes?" he pleaded.

"Yes, I think so. But not by advancing you any more money. The committee wouldn't allow it even if I wanted to. I want you to go to a financial counselor who will help you to work out a plan. I know him well, and we'll work with you in whatever action he decides you should take."

Allen called me for a meeting, and I asked him to come in the next day with Gladis. The solution to Allen and Gladis's problems was difficult, but not complicated.

The first step was to get an accurate picture of where they stood financially. We listed every debt and found that they had nearly $3,000 in additional debt since the consolidation loan. Basically they were back on the same track they had been on before the loan, but with greater expenses each month because of the second mortgage.

They were also delinquent on almost every debt, including a MasterCard bill that had not been paid in five months. Their basic household expenses, together with minimum payments on their debt, took 120 percent of their income, including the average bonus Allen received.

Even before Allen took on the consolidation loan, their average monthly expenses consumed over 95 percent of their income—without such costs as clothes, medical, and dental bills. The consolidation loan allowed them to avoid the reality of a bad situation for a few more months. They were unable to give anything to their church, even though both Allen and Gladis had been tithing Christians since their youth. During the past several months, they had stopped going to church and rarely prayed together, even though that also had been their commitment since before they were married. As with most couples experiencing financial problems, they simply lacked the desire to seek the Lord together.

Allen made contact with the bank that issued the MasterCard, and they agreed to accept a minimum payment on the account for three months while we were working out a permanent resolution. We then contacted Mr. Barnes and arranged for the bank to accept a three-month moratorium (no payments) on the second mortgage, provided that the first mortgage was brought up to date during the following month.

The plan was simple and direct. Both Allen and Gladis realized they were in over their heads financially and that they had to reduce their expenses. There were only two areas that could be cut substantially: housing and autos. The house and one car had to be sold if they were ever to balance their budget. Both decisions were difficult for them to accept until all the figures were on the table and visible. Then the facts dictated the decisions. They could stay in their home until it was repossessed, or sell it voluntarily. They could drive one new car, or lose them both. These were tough facts but easy decisions.

They had only one asset that could be converted into immediate cash to pay the bank: a cash value insurance policy that Allen had owned for several years. It had nearly $3,000 in cash value, and they used it to bring the first mortgage to a current status.

They put the house up for sale and found a buyer almost immediately. They recovered enough from the sale to pay off the credit cards and all but $4,000 of the second mortgage. The bank willingly agreed to carry a note for that amount, which was paid off within the next year.

Allen and Gladis rented a nice apartment and worked hard to get their finances under control. They developed a realistic budget and began to give to their church each month. Later they began to teach a class in their church on the biblical principles of handling money and now have become recognized authorities on budgeting.

Allen became a partner in the law firm and now, ten years later, is the senior partner in the real estate department. He instituted a policy that all young attorneys joining the firm must attend a class on budgeting and agree to live on a budget for the first year. His feeling was that if he could get them to live on a budget for a year, they would live on one forever. He tells his story to every new attorney and proudly points out that he and Gladis bought back the home they had to sell and now own it debt-free.

Is a Consolidation Loan Always Wrong?

One of the most common questions asked in counseling is, "Should we consolidate?" So the logical question a Christian needs to ask is, "Is it wrong to consolidate?"

The answer is no, not necessarily. But there are some inherent problems that must be dealt with before a consolidation loan is advisable.

First, unless the problems that created the need for a consolidation loan are corrected, you may well find yourself worse off in the long run. For instance, if the debt was created by overspending on a monthly basis, the consolidation loan won't solve that problem. It will only delay the inevitable. Until the problem of overspending is solved, no consolidation loans should ever be considered. Otherwise a year or so later all the little bills will be back again, and when they are combined with the consolidation loan, the situation will be worse.

I recommend that no one consider a consolidation loan until he has been living for six months on a budget that controls his overspending. Once you know you have the overspending under control, it may make sense to substitute one large loan at a reduced interest rate for several smaller ones at higher rates.

Second, with a consolidation loan, there is always the tendency to stop worrying once the supposed solution has been found. Many people actually spend more the month after consolidating than they ever did before, often taking vacations or buying a new TV or VCR. Why? Because they think the pressure is off and they can relax. That is a false security created by the temporary removal of financial pressure. You need to resist that urge to splurge.

Third, all too often when someone consolidates he borrows more than what is needed to pay the outstanding bills. Then he buys things he has wanted for several months but wasn't able to afford. The purchases may actually be needed items such as a refrigerator, a washing machine, or a car.

What's wrong with that? Nothing, as long as the individual has disciplined himself and saved the money to buy those things. But for those who already have discipline problems, it's just one more way to splurge.

In our generation there are almost limitless temptations to spend. Thousands of people actually make their living thinking of new ways to lend money and collect interest. Perhaps the most common method of consolidating in the late eighties is through home equity loans. Since the '86 Tax Reform Act made home loans virtually the only interest deductible on income taxes, more and more people have turned to home equity loans for consolidating.

I personally believe home equity loans are one of the worst ideas ever pushed on the average family. It encourages them to put their homes in jeopardy and borrow to buy things that they can easily do without, such as new cars.

Sources of Consolidation Loans

There are several places a couple can obtain a consolidation loan.

Cash Value Insurance

An often overlooked source of funds for consolidating is the cash value in an insurance policy. That money can be borrowed at far less than market rates normally. Even if you don't have a cash value policy, perhaps a parent does and would be willing to lend it to you.

Pledged Collateral

Most banks will provide loans at 1 or 2 percent below the market rate, where in-bank deposits are used as collateral. Obviously, not many people needing consolidation loans have spare cash that can be used as collateral, but often family members do. This requires a high degree of trust on the part of the family member, because the collateral is at risk if the loan is not repaid. I do not recommend this option unless the borrowers are in a financial counseling program where someone is monitoring their finances at least monthly.

A collateralized loan is certainly better than a co-signed note, which is highly discouraged in Scripture. With pledged collateral someone might lose the asset, but with a co-sign they can potentially lose what they don't have.

Credit Unions

Many people have access to credit union loans at lower-than-market rates. As long as all the previously mentioned cautions are observed, a credit union loan is one of the better sources of consolidation.

Family Loans

Unless the family member (usually a parent) is able and willing to lose the money, I discourage this option, particularly when the parent is not a Christian and the child is. I have seen many parents discouraged and hurt because their children failed to meet their financial obligations. I believe Satan uses this as a stumbling block to a parent's salvation. Obviously if the parent is a Christian and is willing to absorb the loss (if necessary), there is nothing wrong with parental loans.

However, a word of caution to parents is in order here. If you continually bail your children out of their financial messes, you are doing them a great disservice. If you want to help, be sure you require your children to get the counsel they need first. Remember, more money is not the answer to most financial problems. More discipline is the answer.

Retirement Accounts

Normally money saved in a retirement account, such as an IRA, should be left there for that purpose. However, if no other source of funds is available, you can invade the retirement account and withdraw funds. Be aware that there will be income taxes due and a 10 percent surtax. But when compared to borrowing from a loan company, this may be a better deal.

In past years it was possible for individuals to borrow funds from their own private retirement accounts. This is no longer possible, and doing so may jeopardize the deferred tax status of a retirement account.

19

Dealing with Creditors

THE WAY SOMEONE deals with his creditors says a lot about his character and about Christianity. In Matthew 5:25 the Lord said, "Make friends quickly with your opponent at law while you are with him on the way, in order that your opponent may not deliver you to the judge, and the judge to the officer, and you be thrown into prison." That is merely a confirmation of the principle taught in Proverbs 22:7: "The rich rules over the poor, and the borrower becomes the lender's slave."

Many times I have seen Christians take up an offense against a creditor who is especially aggressive about wanting his money back. But though in our generation we have legally limited a lender's ability to collect his money, that does not negate his authority over the borrower.

The principle to remember is always to run toward your creditors, not away from them. When I am counseling, the most difficult problem to overcome is attempting to negotiate with a creditor who has been ignored for a long time. Put yourself in the position of a creditor. Wouldn't you want to know that someone was willing to pay but couldn't, rather than to be left totally in the dark?

Unfortunately, many people who can't pay everything don't pay anything. That is also an error. Pay what you can each month, even if it's only a partial payment. And don't make unrealistic promises in order to get a creditor off your back. You need to approach a promise to pay with the same degree of caution that you would the signing of a contract. When you give your word, you need to keep it. If you make a promise when you know that you won't be able to meet the terms, you have violated the principle of vows. Listen to what the judge said about vows in Ecclesiastes 5:4-5: "When you make a vow to God, do not be late in paying it, for He takes no delight in fools. Pay what you vow! It is better that you should not vow than that you should vow and not pay."

Have a Written Plan

I have found consistently that creditors respond best to a specific request that is backed by a detailed plan in writing.

Most creditors have been deceived so many times by people making desperate promises that they have become calloused. Almost anyone under the threat of a court summons or wage attachment will make the appropriate promises. Consequently most creditors have developed an immunity to tearful pleas from delinquent debtors. However, most will respond to a written plan backed by guaranteed action on the part of a debtor.

That's why a counselor is often necessary in dealing with belligerent creditors. A counselor generally represents an objective third party who will enforce the agreements.

Step 1: A Detailed Report

You need to state in detail exactly how much you owe and what the minimum monthly requirements are. In *The Financial Planning Workbook* (Chicago: Moody, 1982), helpful forms are provided. Table 19.1 reproduces one of those forms and shows a typical list of outstanding debts.

It's vital to be totally honest and as accurate as possible. That's why I always work with both the husband and the wife in developing a debtors' list. One partner will often overlook something that the other will recall. The obvious difficulty is that if one spouse is hiding something from the other, he or she will avoid recording it in the creditor listing. Since financial problems are usually accompanied by other problems, it is not unusual for one spouse

Table 19.1
List of Debts

TO WHOM OWED	CONTACT PHONE NO.	PAYOFF	PAYMENT REMAINING	MONTHLY PAYMENT	DATE

to try to continue the deception if he is afraid of the reaction the truth will evoke. If you are in debt, I encourage you to be honest with your spouse. There is no way one person alone can resolve a debt problem that affects two people.

If you're the offended party, try to control your reaction to any new revelation about your finances. Your response will often determine whether or not your spouse will be honest in the future.

If you are the offending party, you need to accept the risks involved with total honesty and lay all the finances out on the table (literally). Ultimately the truth will be revealed anyway, and the reaction will be worse the longer it is delayed. Lying and deception are sins, and God has never said there will be no consequence of sin. But He also promised that if we confess our sin, He is faithful to forgive us and cleanse us (1 John 1:9).

Step 2: A Budget

Once the creditor list is complete and accurate, the next step is to develop a budget that will tell you and the creditors how much you can pay them each month.

In Table 19.2 I have depicted a budget from a couple I counseled several years ago. The left side shows their budget based on their previous spending records. They had to reconstruct some of it from memory because a check written to a grocery store often contained money for other expenses. I recommend that if you also do that, change it. It's better to write a check only for the purchase amount. It's difficult to reconstruct the spending later, and it's too easy to spend the surplus for indulgences.

The amounts on the right represent the new budget submitted to the creditors. Notice that the amount allocated for debts doesn't match the previous monthly total calculated from the creditor's chart. The only thing that can be done is to ask the creditors to accept a lesser amount for a period of time. Before that request can be made, however, we need to know how long that period will be. Often that depends on whether or not there are assets that can be sold and how long it will take to sell them. Also the option of a consolidation loan must be considered if it will satisfy all the creditors.

Obviously, creditors are not going to agree to a plan providing them with no payments if there is no promise of an appreciable change in the future. But I have often seen creditors accept smaller payments for a period of time when there does appear to be a logical reason for the temporary reduction. If the reduced payments are within 75 percent of the actual payments, there is usually no difficulty in getting the creditors to accept a reduced payment plan indefinitely. Obviously that depends on the creditor. Some are restricted by company policies. In those cases it is often necessary to appeal to higher management. In almost all cases they will require a third party to negotiate on behalf of the debtor.

Table 19.2
Budget Analysis

GROSS PER YEAR $24,000   GROSS PER MONTH $2,000

NET SPENDABLE INCOME PER MONTH $1,550

MONTHLY PAYMENT CATEGORY	EXISTING BUDGET	NEW MONTHLY BUDGET
1. Tithe	$ 200	$ 200
2. Taxes	$ 250	$ 250
NET SPENDABLE INCOME (PER MONTH)	$1,550	$1,550
3. Housing	$ 625	$ 625
4. Food	$ 200	$ 175
5. Automobile(s)	$ 260	$ 140[a]
6. Insurance	$ 0	$ 125[b]
7. Debts	$ 180	$ 115[c]
8. Enter. & Recreation	$ 75	$ 50
9. Clothing	$ 25	$ 75
10. Savings	$ 25	$ 50[d]
11. Medical	$ 110	$ 85
12. Miscellaneous	$ 100	$ 110
TOTALS (Items 3 through 12)	$1,600	$1,550

[a] Sold second car
[b] Added life and health (major medical) insurance
[c] Paid off two loans with car proceeds
[d] Increased the emergency fund

Many companies have a working agreement with the national Consumers' Credit Counseling Agency, which is a nonprofit group of credit counseling agencies located in most major cities. They can usually negotiate reduced payment schedules as well as reduced interest fees.

The ministry of Christian Financial Concepts also has an association of volunteer financial counselors located in many cities in the U.S. Usually they are volunteers who work with creditors in the local area.

What Happens When a Creditor Won't Cooperate?

Most attempts to get out of debt sound great because you usually hear the success stories. But what happens when the creditors refuse to cooperate? The principle to remember is this: don't give up too soon. Often when the debts are delinquent, the original lender has already turned the account over to a collection agency. The collection agency is less prone to cooperate and more likely to sue. But unless the debt has actually been sold to a third party, the original lender can still control the proceedings.

Generally speaking, the local credit office of a national company has only limited ability to negotiate once a loan has been declared delinquent. So your best chance to reach an agreement is to request the name of the regional or district credit manager and try to work out a settlement with him. You must suggest a reasonable plan, and you will usually need a third party reference, such as a counselor.

However, there are times when the best efforts don't work. That is usually because the debtor has made frequent promises that were not kept or because he failed to respond to the many warnings the company sent out before pursuing legal action. The actions a creditor normally takes will fall into one of three areas.

Repossession

If you have borrowed for a specific asset such as a car, television, refrigerator, or furniture and the asset is security for the loan, a creditor has the right to repossess it according to the terms of your loan agreement.

With rare exception those agreements give the creditor the right to repossess without written notice if the account is delinquent. (Many states do require written notice.) Most people have heard stories of professional car repossessors who sneak into the debtor's yard and pirate away the car. Indeed that does happen, and if a repossess order has been rendered, it is legal in most states.

More common is for a delinquent debtor to receive written notice that a creditor is taking action in court. Normally there is a legal waiting period (usually one month) during which you have the right to present your side, if there is a dispute. However, if a debtor ignores the notification and does not appear in court, the judgment award is automatic, and the creditor can and will repossess the assets.

I have received many an urgent phone call from a frantic homeowner whose house was about to be taken by foreclosure. Often I find out the day before the foreclosure hearing. It's usually too late then, unless the entire delinquent amount can be offered the lender. If a judgment has already been handed down, it may require the entire mortgage balance. Unfortunately, the lenders usually would have worked out a reasonable plan to avoid having to repossess the home because of the expenses involved and the bad publicity that often accompanies such action. But once the legal process is started, it is difficult to abort.

Armed with a court order a creditor can indeed come into a debtor's home to repossess an asset. If the collector is refused entry, he can simply bring a sheriff's deputy with him the next trip and order the debtor to comply. Failure to comply with the court order can result in arrest and additional expenses.

Most loan contracts contain clauses that allow the creditor to collect all costs associated with legal action or repossessions. You need to read any contracts you sign very carefully because the costs of such actions can be significant.

Once the merchandise is recovered, the creditor may choose to sell it and apply the proceeds against the outstanding debt. The difference between the loan balance and the sale proceeds is called a deficiency, and the creditor has the right to bill the debtor for that amount plus all costs associated with the repossession and sale.

Garnishment

In states that allow it, a creditor can petition the court to attach the wages of a debtor once a legal judgment has been issued. This can be a great shock to the unsuspecting debtor, as well as a source of great embarrassment. Unfortunately, it usually occurs at a time when everything else is going downhill financially. I remember the first time I encountered a garnishment. A pastor asked me to meet with a young couple who were having severe financial difficulties. They had misused credit cards, department store loans, retail appliance loans, and so on. They were unable to meet all their obligations, and rather than face the creditors, they had taken the traditional ostrich approach. One of the creditors was a leasing company that specialized in rent-to-own contracts for furniture and appliances. Once their account was sixty days past due, the leasing company moved swiftly and received a judgment to repossess the furniture. They then re-sold the furniture for a ridiculously low price to the same company that had sold it originally and then sued the young couple for the deficiency, plus $400 in collection fees.

The couple were sent notices that the company was filing suit but chose to ignore the warnings and did not go to court. Consequently, the company got a garnishment order and attached both of their salaries. It was a shock when the young wife's boss called her into his office and showed her the garnishment. The garnishment required that the employer withhold up to 25 percent of her wages to pay the judgment. For a family already having severe financial difficulties, that was a major crisis. The husband found that his wages were similarly attached.

Usually there is nothing that can be done once the judgment is finalized, but I remember this particular case because it had a somewhat happy ending. After some checking around, I found that the leasing company had had several complaints filed against it for re-selling repossessed furniture to the original sales outlet at prices substantially below fair market value. I also learned that the retail store had several outstanding lawsuits against it for re-selling used furniture as new.

Through a local attorney, we petitioned the court and got a rehearing. The judge withdrew the judgment and directed the leasing company to get three appraisals on the furniture in question as well as verification that the furniture had not been previously owned by another lessee. The leasing company chose not to pursue the issue and dropped all collection proceedings against the couple. Thus the couple avoided the garnishment but needed the next four years to work out their other financial problems.

The judge later told me that he had known the leasing company was suspect and would not have issued the judgment except that the couple didn't appear for the hearing, so he had no other choice.

Bad Credit Report

In states where a creditor cannot garnish a debtor's wages and the debt is non-collateralized (such as a credit card loan) the creditor has one last recourse: a bad credit report. Of course creditors will pursue collection through notices and telephone calls. But in the final analysis they must rely on the integrity of the borrower.

The purpose of a credit report is to notify other potential lenders that someone has failed to meet the conditions of a previous contract. The system relies on the fact that in our society people will need additional credit and thus will want to protect their credit rating. For a Christian the responsibility goes even further because the requirement to repay a debt is one of personal honor and integrity.

The reporting of your credit history is controlled by the Fair Credit Reporting Act. Basically this act governs the way a credit report is handled and gives the debtor certain rights.

1. *The debtor has the right to know the name and address of the agency that prepared a report used to deny credit.* To obtain that information, it is necessary to make the request in writing to any creditor that has refused credit.

2. *Anyone refused credit has the right to review his file with the reporting agency.* He also has the right to obtain a copy of the file concerning his

case history. The request must be made within thirty days of notification that he has been turned down for credit.

3. *Someone who is refused credit has the right to challenge the information in the credit report if he believes that it is inaccurate.* If the dispute cannot be resolved, a letter containing the debtor's version of the dispute must be placed in the file and sent to prospective lenders.

4. *Negative information cannot be reported beyond seven years, with the exception of a bankruptcy, which can be reported for ten years.*

Because the Fair Credit Reporting Act forms the foundation for all cooperative credit reporting in this country, there are several other aspects of the Act with which all consumers should be familiar. Appendix B contains a fuller description of the Fair Credit Act.

I have dealt with most of the major creditors in our country at one time or the other on the behalf of couples I have counseled, and as a member of the Consumer Counseling Service Board. I have found that most creditors are willing to go to great lengths to help anyone in financial trouble who is trying to be honest and repay what is owed. But when a debtor lies and defaults on commitments that were made, he is likely to find himself faced with powerful and hostile adversaries. It is always best to be totally honest and not to make promises that cannot be kept just for the sake of temporary peace.

I have also found that few things make a better impression on a creditor than a well-thought-out budget plan, a list of all other creditors, and a credit card cut into several pieces as a testimony of your commitment.

20

Living with Bankruptcy

In 1978 THERE were about fifty thousand personal bankruptcies in our country. In 1988 there were nearly six hundred thousand personal bankruptcies in America, according to an article in the *USA Today* newspaper. Assuming the trend will continue, we can realistically expect to see one million bankruptcies a year by the year 2000. That statistic spells great difficulty for many smaller merchants and for the credit industry as a whole. But even more important, it reflects a decline in the responsibility index for the average American family, both Christian and non-Christian alike. Bankruptcies aren't limited to non-Christians. In fact, the percentage of Christians going bankrupt appears to be about the same as that of the population in general, although accurate statistics are not readily available. I do know that an informal survey in almost any local church reveals a percentage approximating the national average.

The Federal Bankruptcy Act deals with four types of bankruptcy. These bankruptcy options are identified by the chapter in which they are outlined in the Bankruptcy Act. Two deal with corporate bankruptcy, and two deal with personal bankruptcy. They are each discussed in more detail in Appendixes E, F, and G of this book. Anyone considering bankruptcy action would be well advised to read the information in the appendixes on bankruptcy and then contact an attorney who specializes in this area.

Chapter 11 bankruptcy. This section of the bankruptcy code details how a corporation may file for federal bankruptcy protection and continue to operate while it works out a plan to repay the creditors. Normally a corporation has three years to repay the creditors the amount that a liquidation of the assets would have provided. If it fails to do so, it faces the possibility of total dissolution under chapter 7 of the code.

When a company files for chapter 11 protection, the creditors have a right to petition the court to dissolve the company and distribute the available assets. If the judge agrees, the company is abolished and sold to satisfy the debts.

If the judge grants a chapter 11 reorganization to the company, he can require the creditors to accept reduced or deferred payments and set aside all interest charges if he feels it is in the best interest of the company's survival.

This option was designed to give struggling companies that might otherwise fail a chance to become profitable and thus viable. For a great testimony on use of this bankruptcy law, I recommend the book *Waters of the World* (Chicago: Moody, 1989), which deals with the history of the Correct Craft company in Florida and its owners, Walt and Ralph Meloon.

Chapter 7 bankruptcy. If the bankruptcy judge does not think a company can realistically become viable, he can dissolve the company under chapter 7 of the code. The company is carefully inventoried, and, under the supervision of a bankruptcy trustee appointed by the court, is dissolved and the assets sold to satisfy the creditors. In most instances the creditors receive only a percentage of the original outstanding debts. Since secured debts must be satisfied before non-secured creditors are paid, often the latter receive nothing at all.

This corporate dissolution does not affect the assets or liabilities of the principals in the corporation except to the extent of their ownership in the corporation. Debts that were personally endorsed by individuals are still collectable by the creditors, which is obviously why many creditors require the personal endorsement of a loan by the officers and board members of a corporation.

Chapter 13 bankruptcy. This action is the equivalent for individuals of a chapter 11 bankruptcy for a corporation. It is intended to allow an individual (or a couple) to operate under court protection from their creditors for up to three years. As with the corporate bankruptcy, the couple must be able to show that a reasonable percentage of their debts can be paid during that period.

There are very specific limits placed on the amount of debt allowed and on the amount of assets owned. The court usually requires a frequent accounting and review of the finances to insure that the conditions are being met.

A chapter 13 bankruptcy action can be reported by credit reporting agencies.

Chapter 12 bankruptcy. This is a special provision for farmers under the bankruptcy code. It allows farmers a greater asset-to-debt ratio because of the requirement for land and equipment to perform their function.

Is bankruptcy unscriptural? That is not a simple question to answer. God's Word clearly says that a believer should be responsible for his promises and repay what he owes. Does that mean that in the interim he should not take the legal remedy of court protection until he has the ability to repay? Often that is an individual decision. First and foremost, a Christian must be willing to accept the absolute requirement to repay what he owes.

The issue of motive must be addressed. Is the action being taken to protect the legitimate rights of the creditors? I believe that answer can be found in asking whether or not assets are purposely withheld from the creditors. For example, many times when someone files for corporate or personal bankruptcy protection, assets have been transferred to the spouse or to other family members, as in the case of Ron's partners. If a husband and wife are treated as one, according to God's Word, then their assets must also be treated as one.

In general, the bankruptcy laws are meant to protect the debtor, not the creditor. But if the intent is merely to protect the assets of the debtor, it is unscriptural. It is better to suffer the loss of all assets rather than lose one's integrity.

What about personal or corporate lawsuits?

In the present generation it is not impossible or unlikely to be sued for millions of dollars over an accident. Also, given the present climate in jury decisions, it is not uncommon to be assessed huge damage awards. Is it scripturally acceptable then to file for bankruptcy protection rather than be wiped out financially because of an accident lawsuit? Again, there are no easy answers to that question. A Christian who is faced with such a dilemma needs to pray about the situation when it happens and trust in God's guidance.

I personally have no difficulty with those who use the court to avoid an unreasonable judgment. But because I want to protect myself from the costs incurred by another person's injury at my expense, I also choose to carry a sizable liability insurance policy that covers any accident where I am at fault. Beyond that amount I would feel the damages are punitive rather than compensatory.

Can I avoid the IRS through a bankruptcy?

Many people are under the mistaken impression that going bankrupt avoids an obligation to the IRS. Let me assure you that that is not true. The Federal Bankruptcy Code excludes several categories of debt from the set-aside provisions of the law, including federal and state income tax liabilities. Also excluded are federally backed school loans, loans from some nonprofit institutions, and secured property loans.

I have worked with many people who have undergone bankruptcy. Some chose to do so voluntarily, and others had it forced upon them by creditor actions. In both cases they quickly realized that bankruptcy is a serious matter, and at best both sides lose. The creditors lose much of the money they are owed, and the debtors lose some of the respect they previously had. There is a stigma associated with any bankruptcy, and until the last of the creditors are repaid it will probably remain. You can turn an otherwise negative situation into a positive one by making a commitment to repay what is legitimately owed. You can only do what you can do. Once you have made the commitment, it is then up to God to provide the means to do so.

Perhaps the scriptural principle that best describes the use of bankruptcy to avoid paying back legitimate debts is found in the parable of the unrighteous steward in Luke 16:1-12. In that parable the Lord describes a steward (a manager of another's property) who was guilty of misappropriating his master's property. When the master discovered what he had done, he determined to dismiss his steward. In an effort to maintain some security for himself the manager negotiated with his master's clients and reduced the amounts they owed—apparently in hopes that they would pay him something later. When the master discovered that, he marveled at the ingenuity of the deceitful manager (verse 8).

Does the Lord also marvel at one who goes bankrupt to avoid paying his creditors while holding assets that could be sold? Each Christian has to decide that issue individually. But what a shame it would be to appear before the Lord one day and learn, as Esau did, that he had traded his inheritance for a meal. Luke 16:13 says, "No servant can serve two masters; for either he will hate the one, and love the other, or else he will hold to one, and despise the other. You cannot serve God and mammon."

21
Where to Find Help

THE TYPE OF help a person in debt needs usually depends on the severity of the problems he is facing. If the problem is the overuse of credit cards and the total debt is a few hundred dollars, usually the solution can be worked out by writing up a good plan, as I described previously. In that case what is needed is a commitment to avoid further debt and a budget to verify that commitment.

If a consolidation loan is needed to help bring the monthly payments in line with the income, the help of a good volunteer counselor is beneficial. The danger of going deeper into debt is increased by the additional loan unless some monitoring takes place. That's the primary role of the volunteer counselor: to be an objective observer and provide accountability.

As the problems intensify, the need for professional help arises. If the monthly payments exceed the available income and a reduced payment plan is required, then a counselor who will intercede is almost always a necessity. Often a well-trained volunteer counselor can help negotiate lesser payments or a moratorium on some payments until assets can be sold. But if a negotiated settlement cannot be reached, then additional help is required. This may be a professional credit counselor, an accountant, or an attorney.

Once the problems have reached the legal action stage, the need for outside counsel becomes mandatory. It is critical for a debtor to understand the rules of small claims courts or perhaps the bankruptcy court. That does not mean a debtor cannot handle any of those areas without professional help. With proper knowledge anyone can do so. I have seen many counselees plead their own cases in a small claims court action and several who were able to respond to a legal judgment notice properly. But they are the exceptions. Proverbs teaches us that a wise man seeks the counsel of others. "Without consultation, plans are frustrated, but with many counselors they succeed" (Proverbs 15:22). But another proverb tells us to weigh all counsel carefully. "The naive believes everything, but the prudent man considers his steps" (Proverbs 14:15).

Of great importance to a Christian is the admonition to avoid the direct counsel of the unsaved. That in no way implies that unsaved people can't give good financial counsel. However, their counsel is lacking the most essential element: God's Word. It has been my experience that most counsel from unsaved financial advisers is aimed at protecting the assets of their clients, and that is to be expected. But a Christian must focus on the rights of the other parties involved before his own. To do otherwise limits the ability of God to intercede on our behalf. Proverbs 3:5–6 says, "Trust in the Lord with all your heart, and do not lean on your own understanding. In all your ways acknowledge Him, and He will make your paths straight."

I believe the primary source of any counsel should be the local church. It's unfortunate that most churches aren't equipped to provide financial counseling for their people, though more are getting trained to do so every year. Usually there are Christian accountants, bankers, and business people within the church who have the ability to help individuals with basic budgeting problems. If you need help, tell your pastor and ask him to refer you to someone in the church who can help on a volunteer basis. In general I have found that most people are willing to help and are even flattered by such a request. Most important, your request may stimulate the church to begin providing this needed ministry on a regular basis.

Churches interested in starting a financial ministry can become a part of a volunteer network established by Christian Financial Concepts. The address is 601 Broad Street S.E., Gainesville, GA 30501.

What can you expect from a volunteer counselor? Too often those who ask for help expect too much too soon. Consequently, they become disillusioned when the counselor doesn't have a magical formula that will make them debt-free in three months. Or, they expect the counselor to tap the church treasury to bail them out of their troubles. In reality, fewer than 15 percent of the counseling cases I have seen (where the church was willing and able to assist them financially) actually needed direct financial support. With most of those, the financial help was temporary and only met basic needs. In most cases the answer for a couple in financial difficulties is personal discipline—not more money. There are obvious exceptions, such as families in which a major illness has occurred or elderly people who are living on fixed incomes that are lower than the poverty level. Those are needs that must be met by other believers and generally are not one-time needs.

If there are urgent needs such as pending foreclosures, judgments, or evictions, we obviously try to deal with those immediately. But I make clear to everyone I counsel that there are no guarantees. If a foreclosure or eviction is imminent, it may be that nothing can be done to forestall it. Usually an experienced counselor will have contacts to assist in finding temporary housing or transportation, but beyond that, his (or her) function is counseling—not funding.

From a counselor's perspective I can't emphasize strongly enough how many Christians expect unrealistic results from their advisers. Unfortunately, too many counselors foster those expectations by presenting themselves as authorities on a great variety of topics ranging from sex to finances. Those assurances do help develop strong ties to the counselor, but they are also self-defeating when the counselees discover the hard truth that there is no substitute for personal discipline.

I have been doing financial counseling for more than fifteen years, and sometimes I think I have seen every possible problem and solution. Then someone comes up with an idea no one else has tried. Often when I pray with someone at the beginning of a counseling session, I am not really praying for them—I am praying for myself. I realize that I don't know all the answers, but I know that God does. If I can remember to draw from His wisdom, the counselees are not affected by my good or bad days.

One point must be made clear: God will not give us a direction in opposition to that which He has already given in His Word. Thus the fundamental step is for an individual to understand what the Word of God says. Once he knows the rules for managing God's money, life becomes much easier for both the counselor and the counselee. If someone is not willing to follow the instructions given in God's manual, the best counselor in the world can't help him. A counselor may deal with the immediate symptoms, but they will pop up again in a different place if the root problem is not resolved.

In Appendix A, I have listed most of the Scriptures dealing with the subject of credit. The minimum any Christian should do is spend a few minutes a day looking at those Scriptures and studying them. If he does that a couple of times, he will begin to get the flavor of what God's Word has to say about credit. As I have said consistently, credit is not prohibited, but it must be used properly.

I have had several counselees whom I practically adopted. They became so dependent on my input that they literally refused to make a decision without talking to me first. Most counselors have experienced that at one time or another. At first I was flattered and allowed myself to be put in the position of becoming almost a substitute for the Holy Spirit in their lives (although that certainly was not my intent).

Then I discovered that they had become so paralyzed by their own mistakes that they no longer trusted their own judgment. Sometimes that is a predictable but temporary condition. For instance, someone who has suffered a trauma such as a divorce or death of a spouse may well need the support of an advisor. But beyond a few weeks (at the very most), that can become a crippling dependency. We all need others to counsel with and confide in, but God must be our permanent source of support.

I say this because I'm sure that some who read this book are depending too much on a particular advisor. A counselor is there to guide you and offer alternatives but not to become a stand-in father or mother. Seek the face of

God and His wisdom as your primary source of counsel, and you'll never be disappointed. If you find that one of your counselors is giving you advice contrary to God's Word, seek another counselor.

I recall a man who asked for counsel regarding a situation he faced. He was in business with another Christian who had diverted money from a trust account for his own use. The caller, Ben, was being sued by his clients for the replacement of the funds (which he was willing to do). But his ex-partner had filed for bankruptcy protection and refused to repay any portion of the money.

The sum came to nearly one million dollars, which put Ben in the position of having to mortgage virtually everything he owned to cover the loss. His company carried liability insurance to cover such losses, but in order to collect that he had to file a civil suit against his partner. That action would be independent of the criminal charges that would possibly be brought against him for the theft.

All who counseled Ben told him to file suit against his partner. It was clear that the partner had willfully pilfered the funds and had shifted numerous assets to his wife's name to avoid losing them in the bankruptcy. But Ben was virtually the only person who could prove it.

He told me that he and his wife were thoroughly confused by the situation. His question to me was, "Do you think I should file suit against him?"

I replied, "I think you should sue him for everything he's got. It's pretty clear that he is a crook and needs to be brought to justice."

He responded, "Well, that certainly is not the answer we expected. But if that's what you think, we'll do it."

"Wait," I said, before he could hang up. "Would you like to hear what God thinks?"

"Why certainly," he replied instantly. "That's why we called you."

"Oh, I just thought you wanted to know what I thought about it. God presents a unique concept here. He says that a Christian should not sue another Christian."

"I've heard that," he replied immediately. "I don't know exactly where it is, but a Christian friend told me it doesn't really apply in this case."

"Do you have a Bible handy?" I asked.

"Sure," he responded.

"Turn to 1 Corinthians 6," I directed him. Then I read the first seven verses. When I had finished, I asked if he had any questions.

"No, I don't think so. But would it be all right if I called you back again if I do later?"

"Absolutely. In fact I would like for you to call me after you've had a chance to talk with your advisers."

The next day I received another call from Ben.

"Larry, one of my advisers said you used the wrong translation and that 1 Corinthians 6 doesn't mean what you think it does."

"All right," I replied. "What translation did he suggest?"

"He said he prefers the King James Version."

"OK, do you have a copy of the King James Version there?"

"Yes, I do," he replied.

"Then turn to 1 Corinthians 6:1–7, and read it to me if you would." He did so, and then I asked, "Well, what does it say to you in the King James translation?"

"It seems to say the same thing as the other version," he replied.

He hung up the phone and set out to find his adviser again. The next day I received another call from Ben saying that still another translation was needed. At the conclusion of this call I asked him a question. "What do you think God's Word says about suing the other person?"

"That it would be better to be defrauded than sue another believer," he replied.

"What do you think about that?"

"I don't like it," he responded honestly.

"Neither do I," I told him just as honestly. "Because you could probably win the suit if the facts are as you represent them. Now the next question is, what are you going to do?"

"I'm going to do what God's Word says, in spite of how I feel," he replied very deliberately.

"Good for you. I believe God will bless your decision. But in all honesty I can't promise that it won't cost you the money he diverted. God never promised that every act of obedience would be rewarded by an offsetting gain in this lifetime."

"I accept that," he responded. "My wife and I had already made up our minds that we would replace the funds. But I do hate to see him get away scott-free."

"I assure you that he hasn't, and he won't. I recommend that you do what the Lord directed in Matthew 18:15–18: 'And if your brother sins, go and reprove him in private; if he listens to you, you have won your brother. But if he does not listen to you, take one or two more with you, so that by the mouth of two or three witnesses every fact may be confirmed. And if he refuses to listen to them, tell it to the church; and if he refuses to listen even to the church, let him be to you as a Gentile and a tax-gatherer. Truly I say to you, whatever you shall bind on earth shall be bound in heaven.' He needs to be confronted and brought before the church (the community of believers)."

Armed with that advice Ben set out to confront his ex-partner. First, he attempted to do so privately but was refused an appointment. Then he tried to go back with his attorney, but both of them were thrown out of the office. Finally he decided to take his case before the church and went to his ex-partner's church one Sunday morning.

When the pastor asked if anyone had a prayer request, Ben announced to the entire church that he wished to convene the board of elders to hear the case against the man, who happened to be a deacon in the church. It took thirty minutes for the furor to die down in the service. During the interim the pastor asked both men to meet in his office after the service.

A few days later I received another call.

"Larry, I followed your advice and now I have a defamation of character suit against me by my ex-partner and his pastor. My attorney says we should file suit against my partner so he'll be forced to drop his suit. What do you think? No—wait," he hurried to correct himself, "what do you think God thinks?"

I suggested that he turn to 1 Corinthians 6 to see if the instructions had changed since the last time we had talked.

"But now he's suing me," was the response from the other end.

"Oh, well, if the other verses say to sue a brother who sues you, then that certainly justifies any such action," I responded. "The general principle is to do unto others as they do unto you, right?"

He mumbled a little bit and then hung up the phone. He didn't call me again for several weeks. I later found that the case had come to trial, and he had refused to counter-sue. Therefore, his attorney had refused to represent him in the civil suit. I also received several very stern letters from his pastor and friends about the "dumb" counsel I had offered and the fact that if he lost, I might be liable for the damages.

When the case came to trial, Ben and his wife sat quietly while the other side presented their case, which included a videotape of the Sunday morning episode. They claimed that irreparable damage had been done to the ex-partner's reputation, and they asked damages of one million dollars.

After hearing the plaintiff the judge asked if the defense had counsel representing him, to which Ben replied, "No, sir, I will represent myself."

The judge gave him the normal lecture on self-representation. Ben explained to the judge that his attorney would not represent him because he refused to counter-sue.

The judge then asked if he had evidence that he would like to present in his defense. Ben offered documents detailing the misappropriation of the trust funds and showing that he had attempted numerous times to contact the ex-partner and work out a settlement. His final comment was, "Your Honor, I believe that I did not falsely accuse him of a breach of trust, and therefore I cannot be guilty of libel."

The judge reviewed the documents and letters prepared by several independent accountants and attorneys who had reviewed the case. He then asked the defendant, plaintiff, and counsel to meet him in his chambers. Once inside he told the plaintiff, "If this man would file charges against you, I would personally have the bailiff arrest you. You have apparently violated several laws and should be brought to justice. I suggest that you consider yourself lucky and get out of my courtroom. The next time I see you it will be to oversee your trial for fraud."

With that the judge dismissed the case and recommended that my friend file charges against his accuser, to which he replied, "I can't do that, Your Honor."

"Why in the world not?" he shouted as he rose out of his chair. "The man's dishonest."

"Do you happen to have a Bible handy, your Honor?" Ben asked.

The final chapter of this story was later written by two of the individuals who had been cheated out of their money. When they heard the outcome of the court case, they returned the funds Ben had sent them out of his own finances and filed suit against the real thief. They also filed criminal charges against the ex-partner, and he was later convicted and sentenced to five years in a federal prison.

The point of this account is to help you realize that unless your counselors understand the Word of God, it is very likely that you will take the wrong action, even if you have the right motives.

A good counselor will take an objective look at the total financial picture and then make recommendations that will resolve the problems permanently. The basic counseling steps are as follows:

1. *Determine the actual spending level at present.* Rarely does a couple (and never a single person) in debt know exactly how much it costs them to live each month. If they did, most would have already taken remedial action themselves. There are a variety of methods to determine how much they're presently spending. I personally begin by asking them by category how much they believe they spend each month (see Table 21.1).

Usually they have an estimated amount of spending, but rarely is it within 15 percent of the actual amount. I will add a fixed percentage for many incidental expenses such as clothing, car repairs, and vacations. Also, I know from experience that if they have never lived by a budget, their miscellaneous spending may be as much as 50 percent higher than they estimate.

2. *Have the counselees keep a record of every expenditure they have for the next month.* In rare instances the couple has been writing checks for every purchase and their spending record can be determined from their checkbook stubs, but only rarely. As you would expect, most couples in debt resist writing down every single purchase. I try to emphasize that this procedure is only necessary for one month—not for the rest of their lives. But it does require each of them to carry a pocket notebook for the next month and write down every penny they spend.

Once there is a clear picture of the actual monthly spending, the next step is to develop a budget that will provide for all of the regular household expenses to be paid, with some money left over to pay the creditors (hopefully). As was discussed previously, this may require some adjustments in the living expenses—particularly in the areas of housing and auto.

3. *Have the counselees maintain the budget each month.* There are no quick fixes for most people who experience financial problems. As our examination of the finances of several couples showed, each had different cir-

Table 21.1
Monthly Income & Expenses

Salary	$1,250		7. Debts		90
Interest			Credit Card	80	
Dividends			Loans & Notes	10	
Notes			Other		
Rents			8. Enter. & Recreation		53
			Eating Out	20	
TOTAL GROSS			Trips		
INCOME	1,250		Babysitters	8	
			Activities	10	
LESS:			Vacation		
			Other	15	
1. Tithe	125		9. Clothing		50
2. Tax	187		10. Savings		
NET SPENDABLE			11. Medical Expenses		30
INCOME	938		Doctor	10	
3. Housing	391		Dentist	15	
Mortgage			Drugs	5	
(rent)	260		Other		
Insurance			12. Miscellaneous		69
Taxes			Toiletry,		
Electricity	52		cosmetics	10	
Gas	28		Beauty, barber	15	
Water	6		Laundry,		
Sanitation	5		cleaning	15	
Telephone	20		Allowances		
Maintenance	20		Lunches	16	
Other			Subscriptions	3	
4. Food	230		Gifts (Incl.		
5. Automobile(s)	85		Christmas)	10	
Payments			Special		
Gas & Oil	40		Education		
Insurance	20		Cash		
License	3		Other		
Taxes	4		TOTAL EXPENSES		1,037
Maint./Repair/					
Replacement	18		INCOME VS. EXPENSE		
6. Insurance	39		Net Spendable Income		938
Life	29		Less Expenses		1,037
Medical	10				-99
Other					

cumstances and required unique solutions. But one common denominator was the need for accurate records and control over their spending.

In solving financial problems, accountability is a key ingredient which cannot be overemphasized. The value of consistent accountability has been proved through Alcoholics Anonymous, Weight Watchers, and Bible studies. The knowledge that someone will be checking to see if the bank book is balanced and the creditors paid helps to establish discipline.

Developing a support group in the community where you live can be a great asset to others who need help and accountability as well. I know of many groups that meet as often as once a week to discuss their common problems and try to come up with practical solutions. They also study what God's Word has to say about the subject of finances and hold each other accountable to apply those principles.

Appendix A
Credit Related Scriptures

Subject:	Scripture:	Comments:
Borrowing	Exodus 22:14	Restitution for borrowed property
	Exodus 22:15	No restitution for rented property
	Deuteronomy 28:43-45	Disobey God and become borrower
	Nehemiah 5:2-5	Jews borrowing from Jews
	Psalm 37:21	Wicked does not repay
	Proverbs 22:7	Borrower is lender's slave
	Isaiah 24:2	Borrower will be like lender
Lending	Exodus 22:25	Lend to brothers without interest
	Deuteronomy 15:6	Lend but not borrow
	Deuteronomy 28:12	Obey God and lend
	Psalm 37:26	Godly man lends
	Psalm 112:5	God blesses lender
	Isaiah 24:2	Buyer like seller
	Jeremiah 15:10	I have not lent
	Ezekiel 18:7	Restore pledge to borrower

Condensed from *A Topical Concordance on Finances*, by Larry Burkett (Christian Financial Concepts, 1989)

	Ezekiel 18:8	Does not lend at interest
	Ezekiel 18:12	Evil retains pledge
	Ezekiel 18:13	Lends at interest
	Ezekiel 18:16–17	Does not keep pledge
	Habakkuk 2:6–7	Woe to those who lend at interest
	Luke 6:34–35	Lend, expecting nothing
Interest	Deuteronomy 23:19	Do not charge interest to a brother
	Deuteronomy 23:20	May charge foreigner interest
	Psalm 15:5	Do not charge interest
	Proverbs 22:26–27	Don't sign pledges
	Proverbs 28:8	Wrong to lend at interest
	Ezekiel 18:7	Godly returns pledge
	Ezekiel 18:8	Godly does not charge interest
	Ezekiel 18:12	Wicked keeps pledge
	Ezekiel 18:13	Wicked charges interest
	Ezekiel 18:16–17	Godly does not charge interest
	Ezekiel 18:18	Ungodly extort from poor
Usury	Leviticus 25:35–37	Do not charge a brother usury
	Nehemiah 5:7–10	Charging a brother usury
	Proverbs 28:8	Usury will revert to God
Surety	Genesis 43:9	Surety for Benjamin
	Genesis 44:32	Surety for Benjamin
	Exodus 22:26	Return a pledge
	Deuteronomy 24:10–13	Do not keep poor man's pledge
	Job 22:6	Has taken a pledge from brothers
	Psalm 109:11	Seize all a debtor has

	Proverbs 6:1-3	Beg to be released from surety
	Proverbs 11:15	Surety for a stranger
	Proverbs 17:18	Ignorant becomes surety
	Proverbs 20:16	Ignorant pledges cloak as surety
	Proverbs 21:27	Sacrifice of wicked
	Proverbs 22:26-27	Do not become surety
	Proverbs 27:13	Take his garment
Paying Debts	Genesis 38:20	Judah paid harlot
	Deuteronomy 15:1-5	Seven-year remission of debts
	Deuteronomy 31:10	Year of remission of debts
	2 Kings 4:1	Widow's children for debts
	2 Kings 4:7	Elisha pays widow's debt
	Proverbs 3:27-28	Pay when debt is due
	Matthew 5:25-26	Make friends of lenders
	Luke 12:58-59	Make friends of lenders
	Romans 13:8	Do not be left owing
	Colossians 2:14	Cancel debts
	Philemon 18-19	Paul offers to pay debts

Appendix B
Your Rights Under the Fair Credit Reporting Act

If you have a charge account, a mortgage on your home, a life insurance policy, or if you have applied for a personal loan or a job, it is almost certain that somewhere there is a "file" that shows how promptly you pay your bills, whether you have been sued or arrested, if you have filed for bankruptcy, and so forth.

The companies that gather and sell such information to creditors, insurers, employers, and other businesses are called "Consumer Reporting Agencies," and the legal term for the Report is a "Consumer Report."

The Fair Credit Reporting Act became law on April 25, 1971. This act was passed by Congress to protect consumers against the circulation of inaccurate or obsolete information and to ensure that Consumer Reporting Agencies adopted fair and equitable procedures for obtaining, maintaining, and giving out information about consumers.

Under this law you can take steps to protect yourself if you have been denied credit, insurance, or employment, or if you believe you have had difficulties because of an inaccurate or an unfair Consumer Report.

Your Rights Under the Fair Credit Reporting Act

You have the right:

1. To be told the name and address of the Consumer Reporting Agency responsible for preparing a Consumer Report that was used to deny you credit, insurance, or employment; or to increase the cost of credit or insurance.
2. To be told by a Consumer Reporting Agency the nature, substance, and sources (except investigative-type sources) of the information (except medical) collected about you.
3. To take anyone of your choice with you when you visit the Consumer Reporting Agency to check on your file.

SOURCE: Used by permission of the Office of Consumer Affairs, FDIC.

4. To obtain free of charge all information to which you are entitled within thirty (30) days after receipt of a notification that you have been denied credit. Otherwise, the Consumer Reporting Agency is permitted to charge a reasonable fee for the information.
5. To be told who has received a Consumer Report on you within the preceding six months, or within the preceding two years if the report was furnished for employment purposes.
6. To have incomplete or incorrect information reinvestigated unless the Consumer Reporting Agency has reasonable grounds to believe that the dispute is frivolous or irrelevant. If the information is investigated and found to be inaccurate, or if the information cannot be verified, you have the right to have such information removed from your file.
7. To have the Consumer Reporting Agency notify those you name (at no cost to you), who have previously received the incorrect or incomplete information, that this information has been deleted from your file.
8. If a dispute between you and the Reporting Agency about information in your file cannot be resolved, to have your version of such dispute placed in the file and included in future Consumer Reports.
9. To request that the Reporting Agency send your version of the dispute to certain businesses without charge, if your request is made within thirty (30) days of the adverse action.
10. To have a Consumer Report withheld from anyone who under the law does not have a legitimate business need for the information.
11. To sue a Reporting Agency for damages if the Agency willfully or negligently violates the law, and, if you are successful, to collect attorney's fees and court costs.
12. Not to have adverse information reported after seven years. One major exception is bankruptcy, which may be reported for ten years.
13. To be notified by a business that it is seeking information about you that would constitute an Investigative Consumer Report.
14. To request from the business that ordered an Investigative Consumer Report more information about the nature and scope of the investigation.
15. To discover the nature and substance (but not the sources) of the information that was collected for an Investigative Consumer Report.

What the Fair Credit Reporting Act Does Not Do

The Fair Credit Reporting Act does not:

1. Require the Consumer Reporting Agency to provide you with a copy of your file, although some agencies will voluntarily give you a copy.

2. Compel anyone to do business with an individual consumer.
3. Apply when you request commercial (as distinguished from consumer) credit or business insurance.
4. Authorize any Federal Agency to intervene on behalf of an individual consumer.
5. Require a Consumer Reporting Agency to add new accounts to your file; however, some may do so for a fee.

How to Deal With Consumer Reporting Agencies

If you want to know what information a Consumer Reporting Agency has collected about you, either arrange for a personal interview at the agency's office during normal business hours or call in advance for an interview by telephone. Some agencies will voluntarily make disclosure by mail.

The Consumer Reporting Agencies in your community can be located by consulting the "Yellow Pages" of your telephone book under such headings as "Credit" or "Credit Rating or Reporting Agencies."

The Federal Agency that supervises Consumer Reporting Agencies is the Federal Trade Commission (FTC). Questions or complaints concerning Consumer Reporting Agencies should be directed to the Federal Trade Commission, Division of Credit Practices, Washington, D.C. 20580.

Appendix C
The Fair Debt Collection Act

IF YOU USE credit cards, owe money on a loan, or are paying off a home mortgage, you are a "debtor." Most Americans are.

The Fair Debt Collection Practices Act was passed by Congress in 1977 to prohibit certain methods of debt collection. Of course, the law does not erase any legitimate debt you owe.

The following questions and answers may help you understand your rights under the Debt Collection Act.

What debts are covered?

Personal, family, and household debts are covered under the Act. This includes money owed for the purchase of a car, for medical care, or for charge accounts.

Who is a debt collector?

A debt collector is any person (other than the creditor) who regularly collects debts owed to others. Under a 1986 amendment to the Fair Debt Collection Practices Act, this includes attorneys who collect debts on a regular basis. The Act does not apply to attorneys who only handle debt collection matters a few times a year.

How may a debt collector contact you?

A debt collector may contact you in person, by mail, telephone, or telegram. However, a debt collector may not contact you at inconvenient or unusual times or places, such as before 8:00 A.M. or after 9:00 P.M., unless you agree. A debt collector may not contact you at work if the debt collector has reason to know that your employer disapproves.

Can you stop a debt collector from contacting you?

You may stop a debt collector from contacting you by writing a letter to the collection agency telling them to stop. Once the agency receives your

Adapted from materials supplied by the Federal Trade Commission.

letter, they may not contact you again except to say there will be no further contact or to notify you that some specific action will be taken.

May a debt collector contact any other person concerning your debt?

If you have an attorney, the collector may not contact anyone but the attorney. If you do not have an attorney, a debt collector may contact other people, but only to find out where you live or work. In most cases, the collector is not allowed to tell anyone other than you or your attorney that you owe money. Collectors are usually prohibited from contacting any person more than once.

What is the debt collector required to tell you about the debt?

Within five days after you are first contacted, the debt collector must send you a written notice telling you the amount of money you owe; the name of the creditor to whom you owe the money; and what to do if you believe you do not owe the money.

What if you believe you do not owe the money?

The debt collector may not contact you if, within thirty (30) days after you are first contacted, you sent the collector a letter saying you do not owe the money. However, a debt collector can begin collection activities again if you are sent proof of the debt, such as a copy of the bill.

What types of debt collection practices are prohibited?

Harassment. Debt collectors may not harass, oppress, or abuse any person. For example, debt collectors may not:

- use threats of violence or harm to the person, property, or reputation;
- publish a list of consumers who refuse to pay their debts (except to a credit bureau);
- use obscene or profane language;
- repeatedly use the telephone to annoy someone;
- telephone people without identifying themselves;
- advertise your debt.

False statements. Debt collectors may not use any false statements when collecting a debt. For example, debt collectors may not:

- falsely imply that they are attorneys or government representatives;
- falsely imply that you have committed a crime;
- falsely represent that they operate or work for a credit bureau;
- misrepresent the amount of the debt;
- indicate that papers being sent are legal forms when they are not.

Also, debt collectors may not say that:

- you will be arrested if you do not pay your debt or that they will seize, garnish, attach, or sell your property or wages, unless the collection agency or the creditor intends to do so, and it is legal;
- actions will be taken against you that legally may not be taken.

Debt collectors may not:

- give false credit information about you to anyone;
- send you anything that looks like an official document from a court or government agency when it is not;
- use a false name.

Unfair practices. Debt collectors may not engage in unfair practices in attempting to collect a debt. For example, debt collectors may not:

- collect any amount greater than your debt, unless allowed by law;
- deposit a post-dated check before the date on the check;
- make you accept collect calls or pay for telegrams;
- take or threaten to take your property unless this can be done legally;
- contact you by postcard.

What control do you have over payment of debts?

If you owe several debts, any payment you make must be applied to the debt you choose. A debt collector may not apply a payment to any debt you believe you do not owe.

What can you do if you believe a debt collector broke the law?

You have the right to sue a debt collector in a state or federal court within one year from the date you believe the law was violated. If you win, you may recover money for the damage you suffered. Court costs and attorney's fees also can be recovered. A group of people may sue a debt collector and recover money for damages up to $500,000, or 1 percent of the collector's net worth, whichever is less.

Where can you report a debt collector?

Report any problems with a debt collector to your state Attorney General's office. Many states also have their own debt collection laws, and your Attorney General's office can help you determine your rights.

If you have a question about your rights under the Fair Debt Collection Practices Act, the Federal Trade Commission may be able to assist you.

Appendix D
The Consumer Credit Protection Act

THE CONSUMER CREDIT Protection Act of 1968—which launched Truth in Lending—was a landmark piece of legislation. For the first time, creditors were required to state the cost of borrowing in common language so that you, the customer, could figure out exactly what the charges for borrowing would be, compare costs, and shop for credit.

The Cost of Credit

The Finance Charge and the Annual Percentage Rate (APR)

Credit costs vary. By remembering two terms, you can compare credit prices from different sources. Under Truth in Lending, the creditor must tell you—in writing and before you sign any agreement—the finance charge and the annual percentage rate.

The finance charge. The finance charge is the total dollar amount you pay to use credit. It includes interest costs and sometimes other costs, such as service charges and some credit-related insurance premiums or appraisal fees.

For example, borrowing $100 for a year might cost you $10 in interest. If there were a service charge of $1, the finance charge would be $11.

The *annual percentage rate.* The annual percentage rate (APR) is the percentage cost (or relative cost) of credit on a yearly basis. This is your key to comparing cost, regardless of the amount of credit or how long you have to repay it.

All creditors—banks, stores, car dealers, credit card companies, finance companies must state the cost of their credit in terms of the finance charge and the APR. The law says these two pieces of information must be shown to you before you sign a credit contract. Federal law does not set interest rates or other credit charges. But it does require their disclosure so that you can compare credit costs.

Cost of Open-End Credit

Open-end credit includes credit cards, department store "charge plates," and check-overdraft accounts that allow you to write checks for more than your actual balance with the bank. Truth in Lending requires that open-end creditors let you know these two terms that will affect your costs:

First, creditors must tell you the method of calculation of the finance charge. Creditors use a number of different systems to calculate the balance on which they assess finance charges. Some creditors add finance charges after subtracting payments made during the billing period. This is called the adjusted balance method. Other creditors give you no credit for payments made during the billing period. This is called the previous balance method. Under a third method—the average daily balance method—creditors add your balance for each day in the billing period and then divide by the number of days in the billing period.

Second, creditors must tell you when finance charges begin on your credit account, so you know how much time you have to pay your bills before a finance charge is added. Some creditors, for example, give you a thirty-day "free ride" to pay your balance in full before imposing a finance charge.

Truth in Lending does not set the rates or tell the creditor how to make interest calculations. It only requires that the creditor tell you the method that will be used. You should ask for an explanation of any terms you don't understand.

Leasing Costs and Terms

Leasing gives you temporary use of property in return for periodic payments. For instance, you might consider leasing furniture for an apartment you'll use only for a year. The Truth in Leasing law requires leasing companies to give you the facts about the costs and terms of their contracts to help you decide whether leasing is a good idea.

The law applies to personal property leased to you for more than four months for personal, family, or household use—for example, long term rentals of cars, furniture, and appliances, but not daily car rentals or leases for apartments.

Before you agree to a lease, the leasing company must give you a written statement of costs, including the amount of any security deposit, the amount of your monthly payments, and the amount you must pay for license, registration, taxes, and maintenance.

The company must also give you a written statement about terms, including any insurance you need, any guarantees, information about who is responsible for servicing the property, any standards for its wear and tear, and whether or not you have an option to buy the property.

Costs of Settlement on a House

The Real Estate Settlement Procedures Act, like Truth in Lending, is a disclosure law. The Act, administered by the Department of Housing and Urban Development, requires the lender to give you, in advance, certain information about the costs you will pay when you actually get the deed to the property. This event is called settlement, and the law helps you shop for lower settlement costs.

Applying for Credit

The Equal Credit Opportunity Act assures that all credit applicants will be considered on the basis of their actual qualifications for credit and not turned away because of personal characteristics.

Different creditors may reach different conclusions based on the same set of facts. One may find you an acceptable risk, whereas another may deny you a loan.

Information the Creditor Can't Use

The Equal Credit Opportunity Act does not guarantee that you will get credit. You must still pass the creditor's tests of credit-worthiness. But the creditor must apply these tests fairly, impartially, and without discrimination against you on any of the following grounds: age, sex, marital status, race, color, religion, national origin, or because you exercise your rights under federal credit laws.

Discrimination Against Women

Both men and women are protected from discrimination based on sex or marital status. But many of the law's provisions were designed to stop particular abuses that generally made it difficult for women to get credit.

The general rule is that you may not be denied credit just because you are a woman or because you are married, single, widowed, divorced, or separated.

The law also says that creditors may not require you to reapply for credit just because you marry or become widowed or divorced. There must be some sign that your credit-worthiness has changed. For example, creditors may ask you to re-apply if you relied on your ex-husband's income to get credit in the first place.

If You are Turned Down

Under the Equal Credit Opportunity Act, you must be notified within thirty days after your application has been completed whether your loan has been approved or not. If credit is denied, this notice must be in writing, and it must explain the specific reasons for denying credit.

Credit Histories for Women

Under the Equal Credit Opportunity Act, creditors must consider the credit history of any account women have held jointly with their husbands. Creditors must also look at the record of any account held only in the husband's name if a woman can show it also reflects her own credit-worthiness. If the

record is unfavorable—for example, if an ex-husband was a bad credit risk—
she can try to show that the record does not reflect her own reputation.

Correcting Credit Mistakes

The Fair Credit Billing Act sets up a procedure for promptly correcting
billing mistakes, for refusing to make credit card payments on defective goods,
and for promptly crediting your payments.

Truth in Lending gives you three days to change your mind about certain
mortgage contracts; it also limits your risk on lost or stolen credit cards.

Billing Errors

The Fair Credit Billing Act requires creditors to correct errors promptly
and without damage to your credit rating.

The law defines a billing error as any charge:

- for something you didn't buy or for a purchase made by someone unauthorized to use your account;
- that is not properly identified on your bill or is for an amount different
from the actual purchase price or was entered on a date different from
the purchase date;
- for something that you did not accept on delivery or that was not delivered according to agreement.

Billing errors also include:

- errors in arithmetic;
- the failure to reflect a payment or other credit to your account;
- failure to mail the statement to your current address, provided you
notified the creditor of an address change at least twenty (20) days
before the end of the billing period;
- a questionable item, or an item for which you need additional
information.

If you think your bill is wrong, or want more information about it, follow
these steps:

1. Notify the creditor in writing within sixty (60) days after the bill was
mailed. Include in this letter:

   - your name and account number;
   - a statement of your belief that the bill contains an error and why you
   believe it is wrong;
   - the date and suspected amount of the error or the item you want
   explained.

2. Pay all parts of the bill that are not in dispute. Note that while you are waiting for an answer, you do not have to pay the amount in question (the "disputed amount") or any minimum payments or finance charges that apply to it.

   The creditor must acknowledge your letter within thirty days, unless the problem can be resolved within that time. Within two billing periods—but in no case longer than ninety (90) days—either your account must be corrected or you must be told why the creditor believes the bill is correct.

   If no error is found, the creditor must send you an explanation of the reasons for that determination and promptly send a statement of what you owe.

3. If you still are not satisfied, notify the creditor in writing within the time allowed to pay your bill.

Maintaining Your Credit Rating

A creditor may not threaten your credit rating while you are resolving a billing dispute.

Once you have written about a possible error, a creditor is prohibited from giving out information to other creditors or credit bureaus that would damage your credit reputation. And until your complaint is answered, the creditor also may not take any action to collect the disputed amount.

After the creditor has explained the bill, you may be reported as delinquent on the amount in the dispute, and the creditor may take action to collect, if you do not pay in the time allowed. Even so, you can still disagree in writing. When the matter is settled, the creditor must report the outcome to each person who has received information about the case. Remember that you may also place your own side of the story in your credit record.

Appendix E
Introduction to the Bankruptcy Act Section 1

THE TERM *BANKRUPTCY* comes from two Latin words meaning "bench" and "break." Its literal meaning is "broken bench." Under Roman law, after gathering together and dividing up the assets of a delinquent debtor, the creditors would break the debtor's workbench as a punishment to the debtor and a warning to other indebted tradesmen. Bankrupts were regarded as thieves who deserved severe penalty. The Romans deprived bankrupts of their civil rights, and many other societies stigmatized them by requiring that they dress in a particular identifying garb.

Revisions to the bankruptcy laws and changes in consumer attitudes toward bankruptcy have fostered a climate in which people regard bankruptcy as a more plausible remedy for financial problems than they once did.

A revised bankruptcy code, the Bankruptcy Act of 1978, was enacted in 1978 and took effect on October 1, 1979. The code consolidated some chapters of previous law pertaining to business reorganizations and sought to streamline the administration of the bankruptcy courts, but its most sweeping changes involved personal bankruptcy. This revision made bankruptcy a more attractive option to troubled debtors, especially because it increased the amount of assets that could be exempt from liquidation.

Most important, the code introduced federal asset exemptions ($7,500 of equity in a home and approximately $3,000 in other designated assets) that were considerably more generous than were most state exemptions. It also permitted each individual of a married couple to claim such exemptions, thus doubling the amount of exemptions available to married persons.

The new code also removed a provision of the old law which stated that creditors had to approve any plan for repayment. The court was given sole discretion to accept a plan offered by a petitioner. A plan was to be confirmed if the court found that it had been proposed in good faith, that the amount to be paid the creditor was not less than what would have been paid to him

Portions of this appendix are taken from *Bankruptcy: Do It Yourself, by* Janet Kosel (Nolo Press, 1987). Used by permission.

through liquidation, and that the debtor would be able to make the payments contemplated by the plan.

Filings for personal bankruptcy shot up in 1980 and 1981. This led to some revision of the bankruptcy code in 1984. Courts were required, for instance, to prohibit the discharge of debts that financed eve-of-bankruptcy spending sprees.

Several developments seem to have diminished the stigma once attached to bankruptcy. The simple fact that consumer credit is more widely used today has made bankruptcy less rare, and therefore has made the bankrupt individual a more common entity. In 1988 bankruptcies topped the 500,000 mark. Certainly, too, the many revisions in the law and regulations concerning debtor rights, from the Truth in Lending Act, to restrictions on collection tactics of creditors, to the Bankruptcy Reform Act of 1978 itself, have fostered the notion that bankruptcy is not necessarily a shameful process.

The trend toward two-earner families has added to the likelihood of bankruptcy. If people base the levels of their spending and borrowing on the total amount of their dual incomes, interruption of either income stream could jeopardize a family's financial stability.

In sum, the rise in bankruptcies since 1984 seems most readily attributable to a large rise in consumer debt, an expansion that has boosted the aggregate indebtedness of households to nearly 19 cents per dollar of disposable income. This represents nearly 300 percent more than the average family's budget can comfortably manage.

Chapter 11: Corporate Reorganization

Because this book deals with personal finances and because the issues involved in corporate reorganization under chapter 11 of the Bankruptcy Code are extremely complex, chapter 11 is not discussed here. Those considering corporate reorganization should seek expert legal advice.

Chapter 7: Personal Financial Dissolution

Overview of the Bankruptcy Procedure

In order to file for personal bankruptcy, you must first list all of your debts and all of your property. The bankruptcy court will provide sample forms.

You can stop paying on your debts the very day you take those forms, together with $90 in cash, to the bankruptcy clerk. You can also arrange for wage attachments and deductions from your paycheck for debts to your credit union to stop right away.

About a month after you file your bankruptcy papers, you must go to the courthouse for a meeting with the trustee. He or she is the person in charge of your bankruptcy. It is the trustee's job to see if you have any property (called non-exempt property) that under the law must be turned over to your creditors. At that meeting, the trustee will ask you questions in order to determine which items (if any) of your property he or she can take.

A couple of months after that meeting, you must go to a court hearing. If you have been honest and truthful with your creditors and the trustee, the bankruptcy judge will grant you a discharge—the formal forgiveness of all debt.

In all likelihood, you won't be able to get rid of all the debts. Why? Because the law divides all debt and property into various categories—and from a debtor's point of view, some categories are more favorable than others.

What are Debts?

A debt is simply the legal obligation you have to pay someone money. Debts take many different forms—rent, mortgage payments, taxes, bills, alimony, loans, installment payments, and court judgments are a few examples. But remember, this book deals only with personal debts. If you have any business obligations, you must see a lawyer to discuss the impact of bankruptcy on them.

Debts are divided into two categories—those that are dischargeable in bankruptcy and those that are non-dischargeable in bankruptcy. A *dischargeable debt* disappears after bankruptcy. You are legally free not to repay it. Most debts are dischargeable. Typical examples include credit card purchases, rent, and medical bills.

A *non-dischargeable debt* is not affected by bankruptcy. You must still repay it. Examples of the most important non-dischargeable debts include student loans, alimony, and taxes.

Debts are also divided into two other categories: unsecured and secured. A debt is *unsecured* if you never signed a written agreement pledging some of your property to the payment of that obligation. Most unsecured debts are dischargeable, so they disappear after bankruptcy. Typical examples include most credit card and charge account purchases, and personal loans from friends and relatives.

A *secured* debt is created when you make a written promise (usually in the form of a printed security agreement) that, if you do not pay, the creditor can take some particular item of your property—either the item you purchased or perhaps another item you pledged. Examples of merchandise where secured debts are common include motor vehicles, major appliances, expensive jewelry, and furniture. Most secured debts are dischargeable in bankruptcy. But in exchange for discharging a secured debt, you must either return the secured item to the creditor or, if you want to keep the item, pay for it. Often the lender will require that a new agreement be executed after the bankruptcy discharge.

Secured debts are divided into two types. In the first type, the secured creditor sold you the property or loaned you the money to buy it. If this is the case, you must be ready to lose the secured property—unless, of course, you want to pay for it. According to law, after bankruptcy you must pay the secured creditor either the amount of the debt or the present value of the property—whichever is less—in order to keep the property you pledged.

With the second type of secured debt, the secured creditor loaned you money and you pledged property that you already owned as security. Usually you can get this debt wiped out and are free to keep the property after bankruptcy—without paying any more for it.

What Is Property?

Everything you own is property, including things you can reach out and touch—a home, a car, furniture, and so forth.

After bankruptcy, you are entitled to keep only what is called exempt property. The federal and state governments have prepared lists of exempt property—things they think people need to get a fresh start. If an item is on the exempt list, you can keep it. Some examples of exempt property include equity in your home or car, work tools, furniture, appliances, and clothes. Many types of exempt property are exempt only up to a certain dollar amount.

Even though an item of your property is listed as exempt, you may still lose it by going bankrupt if you pledged it as part of a secured debt that had to do with the purchase of the property. If the secured debt had nothing to do with the original purchase or financing of pledged household property, you do not have to pay in order to keep it.

Some Question and Answers

People who are thinking about bankruptcy usually have a great many questions. Here are some of the common ones.

Will I lose my job if I go through bankruptcy?

Both private employers and governmental agencies are forbidden to fire you merely because of your bankruptcy. But there are some kinds of jobs that may be jeopardized by a declaration of bankruptcy—primarily work in which the employee must be bonded, like a jewelry clerk or a bank teller.

How long does bankruptcy take?

It usually takes only a couple of months from the day you file to the day you appear in court to be told that you have received your formal discharge from debt. But the most important date is the day you file. The court will notify your creditors so that collection efforts, repossessions, and wage garnishments will cease within a couple of days.

Will bankruptcy be listed on my credit record?

Yes. Credit agencies are allowed to keep a notation of your bankruptcy on file for ten years. They list the total amount of dischargeable debts and specify which debts have been discharged in bankruptcy. It is up to individual creditors to decide what to do with that information.

How about debts co-signed by friends or relatives— what happens to them?

Bankruptcy protects only you. If a friend or relative co-signed your loan, he or she will have to pay it, even though you do not. You will not legally be required to reimburse your co-signing friend or relative if this happens; whether you do so is a matter between you and your conscience.

Appendix F
Chapter 13: Personal Financial Reorganization Section 3

THE WHOLE IDEA of chapter 13 is simple: to permit an individual under court supervision and protection to develop and perform a plan to pay his or her debts in whole or in part over a three-year period. Basically, chapter 13 means learning to live within a budget.

Filing a chapter 13 repayment plan is a lot like taking out a debt consolidation loan. You wipe out all your obligations in exchange for weekly or monthly payments to an officer of the court. Chapter 13, however, is different from any consolidation loan because

- you pay no interest or finance charges on most debts;
- you get to determine the amount of your periodic payments;
- you decide how much of your debts you are able to repay.

Chapter 13 was conceived in the early years of the Great Depression. It was first enacted law in 1937. Major revisions were made in chapter 13 by Congress in 1978 because it had become apparent over the years that the old law did not provide adequate relief for consumer debtors.

An Overview of Chapter 13 Proceedings

In order to actually file a chapter 13 debt repayment plan, you must fill out the forms showing your monthly income, ordinary living expenses, and the amount left over to apply to your debts.

Filling out and filing these forms stops all creditor collection efforts. Once you have filed your papers, you can arrange to stop wage attachments as well as any automatic debt payment deductions. Under chapter 13, all payments to creditors will be made through a court appointed trustee following the terms of your repayment plan.

Condensed from *Chapter 13: The Federal Plan to Repay Your Debts,* by Janet Kosel (Nolo Press, 1987). Used by permission.

About a month after you file your forms, you must go to the courthouse for a meeting with the trustee. He (or she) will ask you questions about your plan, your debts, and your property. The trustee will want to make sure that you were being reasonable and responsible when you designed your budget and that your plan has a good chance of success. After your meeting with the trustee, you will also have a brief meeting with a bankruptcy judge. If the judge finds that your plan complies with the law, he or she will confirm it and it will immediately go into operation.

Most plans call for repayment of all—or almost all—of your debts over a three-year period. During that time, you will pay the trustee a certain amount each month, and the trustee will take care of all your bills and deal with your creditors. If you live up to your promise and make all payments under the plan, at the end of three years you will go back to court a second time for a discharge hearing. If you have kept your promise, the judge will formally forgive any remaining balance due on all debts covered by your plan—except taxes and family support obligations.

That's the general idea, but like almost everything else, chapter 13 repayment plans can get more complicated, especially when you start to fill in the general picture with the details. None of the rules pertaining to chapter 13 are very difficult, though some rules are a little hard to understand at first.

Some Questions and Answers

What's the difference between straight bankruptcy and a chapter 13 repayment plan?

Straight bankruptcy is a legal way to make most debts disappear with no legal requirement to repay them. People whose financial problems are not as severe usually select chapter 13; it provides a means for repaying debts over time under court supervision and protection.

Can I file a chapter 13 plan if I once filed for straight bankruptcy?

Yes. You can file for straight bankruptcy only once every six years, but you can file a chapter 13 plan anytime—regardless of prior bankruptcy or chapter 13 proceedings.

How much does a chapter 13 proceeding cost?

You must pay a $60 fee when you file your repayment plan with the court. The court will also charge a small fee to administer your plan, but this charge will be deducted automatically from your regular payments.

How long do I have to repay my debts under a chapter 13 plan?

Most repayment plans take three years.

Is there a limit on the amount of debts that can repaid under a chapter 13 plan?

Yes. You must owe less than $100,000 in unsecured debts and $300,000 in secured debts.

Do I have to pay 100 percent of my debts under a chapter 13 plan'?

No. It works like this. Deduct your ordinary living expenses from your monthly income. Whatever is left will be paid to your creditors over the term of your repayment plan. Bear in mind, though, that if you can't pay all—or almost all—of your debts over the three-year term of your plan, chapter 13 may not be possible.

What happens if my creditors won't agree to my repayment plan?

Filing a chapter 13 plan is your decision alone. If you are willing to make an honest effort, and your plan is approved by the bankruptcy court, your creditors won't have any say in the matter.

Will I lose my property if I don't pay all of my debts in full under the plan?

Probably not. Filing a chapter 13 plan is one way to keep all of your property, even though you are unable to pay all of your debts. One exception is a Purchase Money Secured Debt (an asset purchased with a loan).

What happens to debts co-signed by friends or relatives?

If a friend or relative co-signed your loan, they will have to pay whatever portion of the debt you do not pay under the chapter 13 plan. You are not legally required to reimburse them—it is a matter of conscience.

Should my spouse and I both file repayment plans?

If you are married, it is usually best for you and your spouse to file a chapter 13 plan together—especially if each of you has incurred debts.

Do I have to be working in order to file a chapter 13 repayment plan?

No—but you must have some stable and regular source of income such as wages, earnings from self-employment or investments, pensions, social security, or public benefits.

Will my employer know about my repayment plan?

He doesn't have to know. You can choose to make regular payments directly to the trustee yourself.

NOTE: Both private employers and governmental agencies are forbidden to fire you merely because you file a chapter 13 plan. Nevertheless, there are some kinds of jobs that may be jeopardized by filing a chapter 13 plan—primarily work in which the employee must be bonded, such as work as a jewelry clerk or bank teller. If you have any concerns about the effect of a chapter 13 on your job, be sure to consult with your employer before you file.

What will a chapter 13 repayment proceeding do to my credit rating?

Credit reporting agencies are allowed to keep a notation of your chapter 13 proceedings on file for ten years. They list the total amount of your debts and specify how much you actually paid under your repayment plan.

Do I need a lawyer in order to file a chapter 13 repayment plan?

No. Filing a chapter 13 plan is often easier than preparing your income tax return. If you can do that, you can probably handle your repayment plan yourself.

Appendix G
The Taxpayers' Bill of Rights

Free Information and Help

You have the right to information and help in complying with the tax laws. In addition to the basic instructions, the IRS makes available other information.

Taxpayer Publications

The IRS publishes more than one hundred free taxpayer information publications on various subjects. One of these, Publication 910, "Guide to Free Tax Services," is a catalog of the free services the government provides. You can order these publications and any tax forms or instructions you need by calling, toll-free, 1-800-424-FORM (3676).

Copies of Tax Returns

If you need a copy of your tax return for an earlier year, you can get one by filling out Form 4506, "Request for Copy of Tax Form," and paying a small fee.

However, you often only need certain information, such as the amount of your reported income, the number of your exemptions, and the tax shown on the return. You can get this information free from any IRS office.

If you have trouble clearing up any tax matter with the IRS through normal channels, you can get special help from their Problem Resolution Office.

Privacy and Confidentiality

You have the right to have your personal and financial information kept confidential. You also have the right to know why the IRS is asking you for information, exactly how any information you give will be used, and what might happen if you do not give the information.

Adapted from Publication 1 (8-88), Department of the Treasury, Internal Revenue Service. Used by permission.

Information Sharing

Under the law, the IRS may share your tax information with state tax agencies with which they have information exchange agreements, the Department of Justice and other federal agencies under strict legal guidelines, and certain foreign governments under tax treaty provisions.

Courtesy and Consideration

You are entitled to courteous and considerate treatment from IRS employees at all times. If you ever feel that you are not being treated with fairness, courtesy, and consideration by an IRS employee, you should tell the employee's supervisor.

Payment of Only the Required Tax

You have the right to plan your business and personal finances in such a way that you will pay the least tax that is due under the law. You are liable only for the correct amount of tax. The purpose of the IRS is to apply the law consistently and fairly to all taxpayers.

Fairness if Your Return Is Examined

Most taxpayers' returns are accepted as filed. But if your return is selected for examination, it does not suggest that you are dishonest. The examination may or may not result in more tax. Your case may be closed without a change. Or you may receive a refund.

Arranging the Examination

Many examinations are handled entirely by mail. For information on this, get Publication 1383,"The Correspondence Process" (Income Tax Accounts), available free by calling 1–800–424–FORM (3676). If notified that your examination is to be conducted through a face-to-face interview, or you request such an interview, you have the right to ask that the examination take place at a reasonable time and place that is convenient for both you and the IRS.

Representation

Throughout the examination, you may represent yourself, have someone else accompany you, or, with proper written authorization, have someone represent you in your absence.

Recordings

You may make a sound recording of the examination if you wish, provided you let the examiner know in advance so that he or she can do the same.

Repeat Examination

If your tax return was examined for the same items in either of the two previous years and resulted in no change to your tax liability, contact the IRS as soon as possible to see if they should discontinue the repeat examination.

Explanation of Changes

If the IRS proposes any changes to your return, they must explain the reasons for the changes. It is important that you understand the reasons for any proposed change.

Interest

You must pay interest on additional tax that you owe. The interest is figured from the due date of the return. But if an IRS error caused a delay in your case, and this was grossly unfair, you may be entitled to a reduction in the interest. Only delays caused by procedural or mechanical acts that do not involve the exercise of judgment or discretion qualify. If you think the IRS caused such a delay, discuss it with the examiner and file a claim.

Business Taxpayers

If you are in any individual business, the rights covered in this publication generally apply to you. If you are a member of a partnership or a shareholder in a small business corporation, special rules (which may be different from those described here) may apply to the examination of your partnership or corporation items. For partnerships see Publication 556, "Examination of Return, Appeal Rights, and Claims for Refund." For regular corporations see publication 542, "Tax Information on Corporations." For S corporations see Publication 589, "Tax Information on S Corporations."

An Appeal of the Examination Findings

If you do not agree with the examiner's report, you may meet with the examiner's supervisor to discuss your case further. If you still don't agree with the examiner's findings, you have the right to appeal them. IRS Publication 5, "Appeal Rights and Preparation of Protests for Unagreed Cases," explains your appeal rights in detail and describes how to appeal.

Appeals Office

You can appeal the findings of an examination within the IRS through the Appeals Office. Most differences can be settled through this appeals system. If the matter cannot be settled to your satisfaction in Appeals, you can take your case to court.

Appeals to the Courts

Depending on whether you first pay the disputed tax, you can take your case to the U.S. Tax Court, the U.S. Claims Court, or your U.S. District Court. These courts are entirely independent of the IRS. As always, you can represent yourself or have someone admitted to practice before the court represent you.

If you disagree that you owe additional tax, you can take your case to the Tax Court if you have not yet paid the tax. Ordinarily, you have ninety days from the time the IRS mails you a formal notice (called a "notice of deficiency") telling you that you owe additional tax to file a petition with the Tax Court.

If you have already paid the disputed tax in full and filed a claim for refund that was disallowed (or on which the IRS did not take action within six months), then you may take your case to the U.S. District Court or U.S. Claims Court.

Recovering Litigation Expenses

If the court agrees with you on most issues in your case and finds the IRS's position to be largely unjustified, you may be able to recover some of your litigation expenses. But to do this, you must have used up all the administrative remedies available to you within the IRS, including going through the Appeals system.

Fair Collection of Taxes

If the IRS tells you that you owe tax because of a math or clerical error on your return, you have the right to ask them to send you a formal notice (a "notice of deficiency") so that you can dispute the tax, as discussed earlier. You do not have to pay the additional tax when you ask for the formal notice, if you ask within sixty days of formal notification.

If the tax is correct, you will be given a specific period of time to pay the bill in full.

Payment Arrangements

You should make every effort to pay your bill in full. However, if you can't, you should pay as much as you can and contact the IRS right away. In order to make other payment arrangements with you, the IRS may ask you for a complete financial statement to determine how you can pay the amount due. You may qualify for an installment agreement based on your financial condition, or may arrange for your employer to deduct amounts from your pay.

Only after the IRS has tried to contact you and given you the chance to pay any tax due voluntarily can they take any enforcement action (such as recording a tax lien, or levying on or seizing property). Therefore, it is very important for you to respond right away to any attempts to contact you (by mail, telephone, or personal visit).

Property That Is Exempt from Levy

If the IRS seizes (levies on) your property, you have the legal right to keep

- a limited amount of personal belongings, clothing, furniture, and business or professional books and tools;
- unemployment, worker's compensation, and certain pension benefits;
- court-ordered child support payments;
- mail;
- an amount of wages, salary, and other income ($75 per week, plus $25 for each legal dependent).

If at any time during the collection process you do not agree with the collection employee, you can discuss your case with a supervisor.

Access to Your Private Premises

A court order is not generally needed for a collection employee to seize your property. However, you don't have to allow the employee access to your private premises, such as your home or the private areas of your business, if the employee does not have court authorization to be there.

Withheld Taxes

If the IRS believes that you were responsible for seeing that a corporation withheld taxes from its employees, and the taxes were not paid, the IRS may look to you to personally pay the unpaid taxes. If you feel that you don't owe this, you have the right to discuss the case with the collection employee's supervisor. Also, you generally have the same IRS appeal rights as other taxpayers. Because the Tax Court has no jurisdiction in this situation, you must pay at least part of the withheld taxes and file a claim for refund in order to take the matter to the U.S. District Court or U.S. Claims Court.